Audi A4
Owners Workshop Manual

Martynn Randall

Models covered

(4609 - 384)

Saloon and Estate (Avant) (model range code B6), including special/limited editions
Petrol: 1.8 litre (1781cc) turbo & 2.0 litre (1984cc) 4-cylinder, inc. FSI
Turbo-diesel: 1.9 litre (1896cc) 4-cylinder

Also covers major mechanical features of Cabriolet models
Does NOT cover models with 1.6 litre petrol engine, 6-cylinder or V8 petrol engines or 6-cylinder diesel engines
Does NOT cover Quattro or S4 models, or new Audi A4 range introduced January 2005

© Haynes Publishing 2007

ABCDE
FGHIJ
KLMNO
P

A book in the **Haynes Owners Workshop Manual Series**

Printed in the USA

Haynes Publishing
Sparkford, Yeovil, Somerset BA22 7JJ, England

ISBN **978 1 84425 609 9**

Haynes North America, Inc
861 Lawrence Drive, Newbury Park, California 91320, USA

British Library Cataloguing in Publication Data
A catalogue record for this book is available from the British Library.

Haynes Publishing Nordiska AB
Box 1504, 751 45 UPPSALA, Sverige

Contents

LIVING WITH YOUR AUDI A4

Safety first!	Page	0•5
Introduction	Page	0•6

Roadside repairs

Introduction	Page	0•7
If your car won't start	Page	0•7
Jump starting	Page	0•8
Wheel changing	Page	0•9
Identifying leaks	Page	0•10
Towing	Page	0•10

Weekly checks

Introduction	Page	0•11
Underbonnet check points	Page	0•11
Engine oil level	Page	0•12
Coolant level	Page	0•12
Brake (and clutch) fluid level	Page	0•13
Screen washer fluid level	Page	0•13
Tyre condition and pressure	Page	0•14
Wiper blades	Page	0•15
Battery	Page	0•15
Electrical systems	Page	0•16

Lubricants and fluids

	Page	0•17

Tyre pressures

	Page	0•17

MAINTENANCE

Routine Maintenance and Servicing

Petrol models	Page	1A•1
Servicing specifications	Page	1A•2
Maintenance schedule	Page	1A•3
Maintenance procedures	Page	1A•5
Diesel models	Page	1B•1
Servicing specifications	Page	1B•2
Maintenance schedule	Page	1B•3
Maintenance procedures	Page	1B•5

Contents

REPAIRS & OVERHAUL

Engine and Associated Systems

1.8 and 2.0 litre indirect injection petrol engine in-car repair procedures — Page 2A•1

2.0 litre direct injection petrol engine in-car repair procedures — Page 2B•1

Diesel engine in-car repair procedures — Page 2C•1

Engine removal and overhaul procedures — Page 2D•1

Cooling, heating and ventilation systems — Page 3•1

Fuel system – indirect petrol injection models — Page 4A•1

Fuel system – direct petrol injection (FSI) models — Page 4B•1

Fuel system – diesel models — Page 4C•1

Emission control and exhaust systems — Page 4D•1

Starting and charging systems — Page 5A•1

Ignition system – petrol engine models — Page 5B•1

Pre/post heating system – diesel engine models — Page 5C•1

Transmission

Clutch — Page 6•1

Manual gearbox — Page 7A•1

Automatic transmission — Page 7B•1

Multitronic transmission — Page 7C•1

Driveshafts — Page 8•1

Brakes and Suspension

Braking system — Page 9•1

Suspension and steering — Page 10•1

Body Equipment

Bodywork and fittings — Page 11•1

Body electrical systems — Page 12•1

Wiring Diagrams

Page 12•24

REFERENCE

Dimensions and weights — Page REF•1

Conversion factors — Page REF•2

Jacking and vehicle support — Page REF•3

Radio/CD/cassette unit anti-theft system - precaution — Page REF•3

General repair procedures — Page REF•4

Buying spare parts — Page REF•5

Vehicle identification — Page REF•5

Tools and working facilities — Page REF•6

MOT test checks — Page REF•8

Fault finding — Page REF•12

Glossary of technical terms — Page REF•20

Index

Page REF•24

Advanced driving

Many people see the words 'advanced driving' and believe that it won't interest them or that it is a style of driving beyond their own abilities. Nothing could be further from the truth. Advanced driving is straightforward safe, sensible driving - the sort of driving we should all do every time we get behind the wheel.

An average of 10 people are killed every day on UK roads and 870 more are injured, some seriously. Lives are ruined daily, usually because somebody did something stupid. Something like 95% of all accidents are due to human error, mostly driver failure. Sometimes we make genuine mistakes - everyone does. Sometimes we have lapses of concentration. Sometimes we deliberately take risks.

For many people, the process of 'learning to drive' doesn't go much further than learning how to pass the driving test because of a common belief that good drivers are made by 'experience'.

Learning to drive by 'experience' teaches three driving skills:

☐ Quick reactions. (Whoops, that was close!)
☐ Good handling skills. (Horn, swerve, brake, horn).
☐ Reliance on vehicle technology. (Great stuff this ABS, stop in no distance even in the wet...)

Drivers whose skills are 'experience based' generally have a lot of near misses and the odd accident. The results can be seen every day in our courts and our hospital casualty departments.

Advanced drivers have learnt to control the risks by controlling the position and speed of their vehicle. They avoid accidents and near misses, even if the drivers around them make mistakes.

The key skills of advanced driving are **concentration,** effective all-round **observation, anticipation** and **planning.** When **good vehicle handling** is added to

these skills, all driving situations can be approached and negotiated in a safe, methodical way, leaving nothing to chance.

Concentration means applying your mind to safe driving, completely excluding anything that's not relevant. Driving is usually the most dangerous activity that most of us undertake in our daily routines. It deserves our full attention.

Observation means not just looking, but seeing and seeking out the information found in the driving environment.

Anticipation means asking yourself what is happening, what you can reasonably expect to happen and what could happen unexpectedly. (One of the commonest words used in compiling accident reports is 'suddenly'.)

Planning is the link between seeing something and taking the appropriate action. For many drivers, planning is the missing link.

If you want to become a safer and more skilful driver and you want to enjoy your driving more, contact the Institute of Advanced Motorists at www.iam.org.uk, phone 0208 996 9600, or write to IAM House, 510 Chiswick High Road, London W4 5RG for an information pack.

Working on your car can be dangerous. This page shows just some of the potential risks and hazards, with the aim of creating a safety-conscious attitude.

General hazards

Scalding

• Don't remove the radiator or expansion tank cap while the engine is hot.
• Engine oil, automatic transmission fluid or power steering fluid may also be dangerously hot if the engine has recently been running.

Burning

• Beware of burns from the exhaust system and from any part of the engine. Brake discs and drums can also be extremely hot immediately after use.

Crushing

• When working under or near a raised vehicle, always supplement the jack with axle stands, or use drive-on ramps. *Never venture under a car which is only supported by a jack.*
• Take care if loosening or tightening high-torque nuts when the vehicle is on stands. Initial loosening and final tightening should be done with the wheels on the ground.

Fire

• Fuel is highly flammable; fuel vapour is explosive.
• Don't let fuel spill onto a hot engine.
• Do not smoke or allow naked lights (including pilot lights) anywhere near a vehicle being worked on. Also beware of creating sparks (electrically or by use of tools).
• Fuel vapour is heavier than air, so don't work on the fuel system with the vehicle over an inspection pit.
• Another cause of fire is an electrical overload or short-circuit. Take care when repairing or modifying the vehicle wiring.
• Keep a fire extinguisher handy, of a type suitable for use on fuel and electrical fires.

Electric shock

• Ignition HT voltage can be dangerous, especially to people with heart problems or a pacemaker. Don't work on or near the ignition system with the engine running or the ignition switched on.

• Mains voltage is also dangerous. Make sure that any mains-operated equipment is correctly earthed. Mains power points should be protected by a residual current device (RCD) circuit breaker.

Fume or gas intoxication

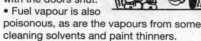

• Exhaust fumes are poisonous; they often contain carbon monoxide, which is rapidly fatal if inhaled. Never run the engine in a confined space such as a garage with the doors shut.
• Fuel vapour is also poisonous, as are the vapours from some cleaning solvents and paint thinners.

Poisonous or irritant substances

• Avoid skin contact with battery acid and with any fuel, fluid or lubricant, especially antifreeze, brake hydraulic fluid and Diesel fuel. Don't syphon them by mouth. If such a substance is swallowed or gets into the eyes, seek medical advice.
• Prolonged contact with used engine oil can cause skin cancer. Wear gloves or use a barrier cream if necessary. Change out of oil-soaked clothes and do not keep oily rags in your pocket.
• Air conditioning refrigerant forms a poisonous gas if exposed to a naked flame (including a cigarette). It can also cause skin burns on contact.

Asbestos

• Asbestos dust can cause cancer if inhaled or swallowed. Asbestos may be found in gaskets and in brake and clutch linings. When dealing with such components it is safest to assume that they contain asbestos.

Special hazards

Hydrofluoric acid

• This extremely corrosive acid is formed when certain types of synthetic rubber, found in some O-rings, oil seals, fuel hoses etc, are exposed to temperatures above 400ºC. The rubber changes into a charred or sticky substance containing the acid. *Once formed, the acid remains dangerous for years. If it gets onto the skin, it may be necessary to amputate the limb concerned.*
• When dealing with a vehicle which has suffered a fire, or with components salvaged from such a vehicle, wear protective gloves and discard them after use.

The battery

• Batteries contain sulphuric acid, which attacks clothing, eyes and skin. Take care when topping-up or carrying the battery.
• The hydrogen gas given off by the battery is highly explosive. Never cause a spark or allow a naked light nearby. Be careful when connecting and disconnecting battery chargers or jump leads.

Air bags

• Air bags can cause injury if they go off accidentally. Take care when removing the steering wheel and/or facia. Special storage instructions may apply.

Diesel injection equipment

• Diesel injection pumps supply fuel at very high pressure. Take care when working on the fuel injectors and fuel pipes.

⚠️ *Warning: Never expose the hands, face or any other part of the body to injector spray; the fuel can penetrate the skin with potentially fatal results.*

Remember...

DO

• Do use eye protection when using power tools, and when working under the vehicle.
• Do wear gloves or use barrier cream to protect your hands when necessary.
• Do get someone to check periodically that all is well when working alone on the vehicle.
• Do keep loose clothing and long hair well out of the way of moving mechanical parts.
• Do remove rings, wristwatch etc, before working on the vehicle – especially the electrical system.
• Do ensure that any lifting or jacking equipment has a safe working load rating adequate for the job.

DON'T

• Don't attempt to lift a heavy component which may be beyond your capability – get assistance.
• Don't rush to finish a job, or take unverified short cuts.
• Don't use ill-fitting tools which may slip and cause injury.
• Don't leave tools or parts lying around where someone can trip over them. Mop up oil and fuel spills at once.
• Don't allow children or pets to play in or near a vehicle being worked on.

The Audi A4 (B6) model was launched in January 2001, and is a further development of the existing A4 model. Available as a 4-door Saloon or 5-door Estate (Avant), with a choice of 1.8 litre turbocharged or 2.0 litre non-turbo 20V petrol engines, a new 2.0 litre 16V direct injection non-turbo FSI petrol engine, or turbocharged 1.9 litre direct injection diesel engines. The FSI petrol engine offers a high level of performance with industry leading standards of fuel consumption and emissions. The body shape has been developed to further reduce fuel consumption and emissions by having a Coefficient of drag (Cd) of 0.28, made possible by the fitment of underbody panels to smooth the flow of air under the vehicle. All models are equipped with light-weight aluminium independent front and rear suspension.

High standards of safety are achieved by the standard fitment of driver's airbag, passenger's airbag, side airbags, head airbags, and seat belt pretensioners. Safety levels are further enhanced by features such as: traction control, ABS, emergency brake assist, electronic stability program, and electronic differential lock. All models are fitted with an immobiliser, alarm, remote control central locking and air conditioning.

In November 2002 a Cabriolet version was launched. Although based on the Saloon model, the Cabriolet differs in the areas of bodywork, and interior trim. This manual does not cover all aspects of the Cabriolet model, but does cover major mechanical features, such as engines, transmissions, suspension, brakes, hood, fuel/exhaust/emission systems, etc.

For the home mechanic, the Audi A4 is a straightforward vehicle to maintain and most of the items requiring frequent attention are easily accessible.

Your Audi A4 manual

The aim of this Manual is to help you get the best value from your vehicle. It can do so in several ways. It can help you decide what work must be done (even should you choose to get it done by a garage). It will also provide information on routine maintenance and servicing, and give a logical course of action and diagnosis when random faults occur. However, it is hoped that you will use the manual by tackling the work yourself. On simpler jobs it may even be quicker than booking the car into a garage and going there twice, to leave and collect it. Perhaps most important, a lot of money can be saved by avoiding the costs a garage must charge to cover its labour and overheads.

The manual has drawings and descriptions to show the function of the various components so that their layout can be understood. Tasks are described and photographed in a clear step-by-step sequence. The illustrations are numbered by the Section number and paragraph number to which they relate – if there is more than one illustration per paragraph, the sequence is denoted alphabetically.

References to the 'left' or 'right' of the vehicle are in the sense of a person in the driver's seat, facing forwards.

Acknowledgements

Thanks are due to Draper Tools, who provided some of the workshop tools, and to all those people at Sparkford who helped in the production of this manual.

This manual is not a direct reproduction of the vehicle manufacturer's data, and its publication should not be taken as implying any technical approval by the vehicle manufacturers or importers.

We take great pride in the accuracy of information given in this manual, but vehicle manufacturers make alterations and design changes during the production run of a particular vehicle of which they do not inform us. No liability can be accepted by the authors or publishers for loss, damage or injury caused by any errors in, or omissions from, the information given.

Project vehicles

The main vehicle used in the preparation of this manual, and which appears in many of the photographic sequences, was an Audi A4 2.0 litre FSI Saloon.

The following pages are intended to help in dealing with common roadside emergencies and breakdowns. You will find more detailed fault finding information at the back of the manual, and repair information in the main chapters.

If your car won't start and the starter motor doesn't turn

☐ If it's a model with automatic/Multitronic transmission, make sure the selector is in P or N.

☐ Open the bonnet, remove the cover and make sure that the battery terminals are clean and tight.

☐ Switch on the headlights and try to start the engine. If the headlights go very dim when you're trying to start, the battery is probably flat. Get out of trouble by jump starting (see next page) using a friend's car.

If your car won't start even though the starter motor turns as normal

☐ Is there fuel in the tank?

☐ Is there moisture on electrical components under the bonnet? Switch off the ignition, then wipe off any obvious dampness with a dry cloth. Spray a water-repellent aerosol product (WD-40 or equivalent) on ignition and fuel system electrical connectors like those shown in the photos. Pay special attention to the ignition coil wiring connectors. (Note that diesel engines don't usually suffer from damp).

A Check the condition and security of the battery connections

B Check the fuel injection system airflow meter wiring is secure

C Check the ignition coils wiring is secure

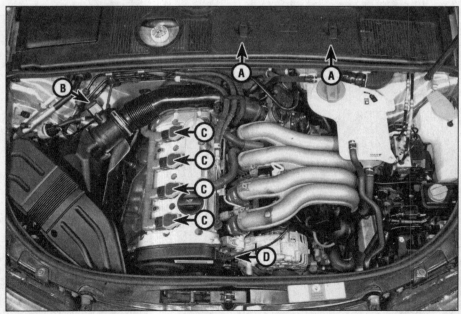

Check that electrical connections are secure (with the ignition switched off) and spray them with a water-dispersant spray like WD-40 if you suspect a problem due to damp

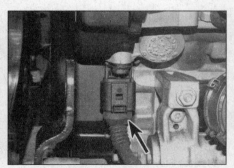

D Check the ignition system Hall sender wiring is secure

Jump starting

When jump-starting a car using a booster battery, observe the following precautions:

✔ Before connecting the booster battery, make sure that the ignition is switched off.

✔ Ensure that all electrical equipment (lights, heater, wipers, etc) is switched off.

✔ Take note of any special precautions printed on the battery case.

✔ Make sure that the booster battery is the same voltage as the discharged one in the vehicle.

✔ If the battery is being jump-started from the battery in another vehicle, the two vehicles MUST NOT TOUCH each other.

✔ Make sure that the transmission is in neutral (or PARK, in the case of automatic transmission).

 Jump starting will get you out of trouble, but you must correct whatever made the battery go flat in the first place. There are three possibilities:

1 The battery has been drained by repeated attempts to start, or by leaving the lights on.

2 The charging system is not working properly (alternator drivebelt slack or broken, alternator wiring fault or alternator itself faulty).

3 The battery itself is at fault (electrolyte low, or battery worn out).

1 Connect one end of the red jump lead to the positive (+) terminal of the flat battery

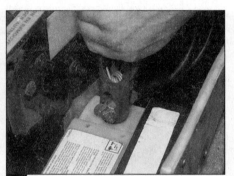

2 Connect the other end of the red lead to the positive (+) terminal of the booster battery.

3 Connect one end of the black jump lead to the negative (-) terminal of the booster battery

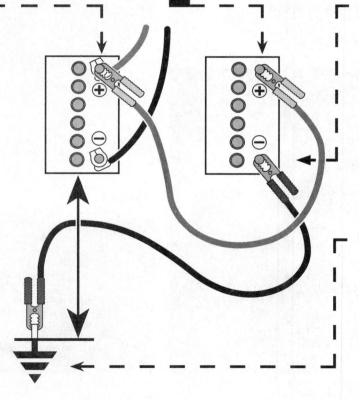

4 Connect the other end of the black jump lead to a bolt or bracket on the engine block, well away from the battery, on the vehicle to be started.

5 Make sure that the jump leads will not come into contact with the fan, drive-belts or other moving parts of the engine.

6 Start the engine using the booster battery and run it at idle speed. Switch on the lights, rear window demister and heater blower motor, then disconnect the jump leads in the reverse order of connection. Turn off the lights etc.

Wheel changing

⚠️ *Warning: Do not change a wheel in a situation where you risk being hit by other traffic. On busy roads, try to stop in a lay-by or a gateway. Be wary of passing traffic while changing the wheel – it is easy to become distracted by the job in hand.*

Preparation

- ☐ When a puncture occurs, stop as soon as it is safe to do so.
- ☐ Park on firm level ground, if possible, and well out of the way of other traffic.
- ☐ Use hazard warning lights if necessary and use the warning triangle supplied to alert other drivers of your presence.
- ☐ Apply the handbrake and engage first or reverse gear (or Park on models with automatic/Multitronic transmission).
- ☐ Chock the wheel diagonally opposite the one being removed – a couple of large stones will do for this.
- ☐ If the ground is soft, use a flat piece of wood to spread the load under the jack.

Changing the wheel

1 The spare wheel and tools are located under the floor in the luggage compartment.

2 Lift out the tools, then undo the retaining bolt and lift out the spare wheel.

3 Position the jack with the base directly under the jacking point. Turn the jack handle clockwise until the head of the jack fits snugly around the centre of the jacking point.

4 Before raising the vehicle, use the tweezers provided to remove the wheel bolt covers, and use the wheel bolt brace to slacken each of the wheel bolts half a turn. On models with alloy wheels, use the adapter provided to remove the locking wheel bolt.

5 Remove the wheel bolt nearest the top, and screw-in the mounting pin provided in the tool kit.

6 Turn the handle to raise the vehicle until the wheel is clear of the ground. If the tyre is flat make sure that the vehicle is raised sufficiently to allow the spare wheel to be fitted.

7 Lift the wheel from the vehicle. Place it beneath the sill as a precaution against the jack failing. Fit the spare wheel and tighten the bolts moderately with the wheel brace.

8 Lower the vehicle to the ground and tighten the wheel bolts in a diagonal sequence. Refit the wheel bolt cover where fitted.

Finally . . .

- ☐ Remove the wheel chocks.
- ☐ Stow the jack and tools in the correct locations in the car.
- ☐ Check the tyre pressure on the wheel just fitted. If it is low, or if you don't have a pressure gauge with you, drive slowly to the nearest garage and inflate the tyre to the correct pressure.
- ☐ Have the damaged tyre or wheel repaired as soon as possible.
- ☐ Have the wheel bolts tightened to the specified torque at the earliest opportunity.

Identifying leaks

Puddles on the garage floor or drive, or obvious wetness under the bonnet or underneath the car, suggest a leak that needs investigating. It can sometimes be difficult to decide where the leak is coming from, especially if the engine bay is very dirty already. Leaking oil or fluid can also be blown rearwards by the passage of air under the car, giving a false impression of where the problem lies.

 Warning: Most automotive oils and fluids are poisonous. Wash them off skin, and change out of contaminated clothing, without delay.

 HAYNES HiNT *The smell of a fluid leaking from the car may provide a clue to what's leaking. Some fluids are distinctively coloured. It may help to clean the car carefully and to park it over some clean paper overnight as an aid to locating the source of the leak.*
Remember that some leaks may only occur while the engine is running.

Sump oil

Engine oil may leak from the drain plug...

Oil from filter

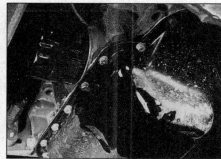

...or from the base of the oil filter.

Gearbox oil

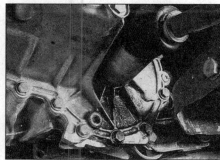

Gearbox oil can leak from the seals at the inboard ends of the driveshafts.

Antifreeze

Leaking antifreeze often leaves a crystalline deposit like this.

Brake fluid

A leak occurring at a wheel is almost certainly brake fluid.

Power steering fluid

Power steering fluid may leak from the pipe connectors on the steering rack.

Towing

When all else fails, you may find yourself having to get a tow home – or of course you may be helping somebody else. Long-distance recovery should only be done by a garage or breakdown service. For shorter distances, DIY towing using another car is easy enough, but observe the following points:

☐ Use a proper tow-rope – they are not expensive. The vehicle being towed must display an ON TOW sign in its rear window.
☐ Always turn the ignition key to the 'On' position when the vehicle is being towed, so that the steering lock is released, and the direction indicator and brake lights work.
☐ Towing eyes are provided front and rear **(see illustration)**.

☐ Lashing eyes are provided at the front and rear of the vehicle as a means of securing the vehicle onto a break-down truck.
☐ Audi state that the towing distance should not exceed 50 miles, and the towing speed should be limited to 30 mph.
☐ On automatic/Multitronic transmission models, if it is necessary to tow the vehicle on two wheels (suspended from a recovery vehicle), then it is essential that it is suspended at the front wheels, to prevent damage to the final drive assembly.
☐ Note that greater-than-usual pedal pressure will be required to operate the brakes, since the vacuum servo unit is only operational with the engine running, and because the power

steering will not be operational, greater-than-usual steering effort will be required.
☐ Only drive at moderate speeds and keep the distance towed to a minimum. Drive smoothly and allow plenty of time for slowing down at junctions.

Front towing eye

Introduction

There are some very simple checks which need only take a few minutes to carry out, but which could save you a lot of inconvenience and expense.

These *Weekly checks* require no great skill or special tools, and the small amount of time they take to perform could prove to be very well spent, for example:

☐ Keeping an eye on tyre condition and pressures, will not only help to stop them wearing out prematurely, but could also save your life.

☐ Many breakdowns are caused by electrical problems. Battery-related faults are particularly common, and a quick check on a regular basis will often prevent the majority of these.

☐ If your car develops a brake fluid leak, the first time you might know about it is when your brakes don't work properly. Checking the level regularly will give advance warning of this kind of problem.

☐ If the oil or coolant levels run low, the cost of repairing any engine damage will be far greater than fixing the leak, for example.

Underbonnet check points

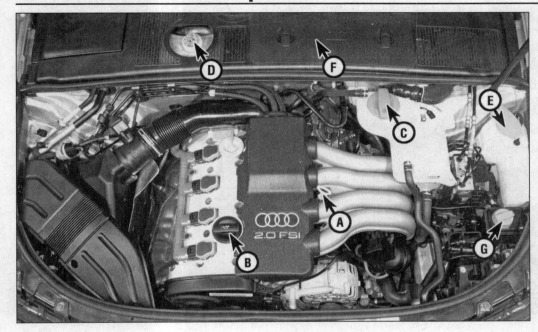

◄ 2.0 litre FSI petrol (other petrol models similar)

A *Engine oil level dipstick*

B *Engine oil filler cap*

C *Coolant expansion tank*

D *Brake fluid reservoir*

E *Screen washer fluid reservoir*

F *Battery (under cover)*

G *Power steering fluid reservoir*

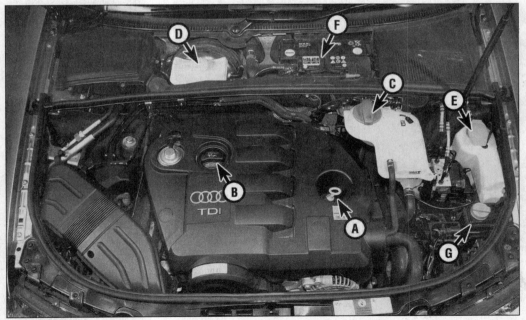

◄ 1.9 litre diesel

A *Engine oil level dipstick*

B *Engine oil filler cap*

C *Coolant expansion tank*

D *Brake fluid reservoir*

E *Screen washer fluid reservoir*

F *Battery*

G *Power steering fluid reservoir*

Engine oil level

Before you start
✔ Make sure that the car is on level ground.
✔ Check the oil level before the car is driven, or at least 5 minutes after the engine has been switched off.

HAYNES HINT *If the oil is checked immediately after driving the vehicle, some of the oil will remain in the upper engine components, resulting in an inaccurate reading on the dipstick.*

The correct oil
Modern engines place great demands on their oil. It is very important that the correct oil for your car is used (see *Lubricants and fluids*).

Car care
● If you have to add oil frequently, you should check whether you have any oil leaks. Place some clean paper under the car overnight, and check for stains in the morning. If there are no leaks, then the engine may be burning oil.
● Always maintain the level between the upper and lower dipstick marks (see photo 3). If the level is too low, severe engine damage may occur. Oil seal failure may result if the engine is overfilled by adding too much oil.

1 The dipstick is located on the left-hand side of the engine. It is brightly-coloured for ease of location. See *Underbonnet check points* for the exact location of the dipstick.

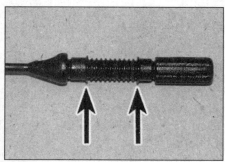
3 Note the oil level on the end of the dipstick, which should be between the upper and lower marks. Approximately 1.0 litre of oil will raise the level from the lower mark to the upper mark.

2 Withdraw the dipstick. Using a clean rag or paper towel, wipe all the oil from the dipstick. Insert the clean dipstick into the tube as far as it will go, then withdraw it again.

4 Oil is added through the filler cap on top of the engine. Rotate the cap through a quarter-turn anti-clockwise and withdraw it. Top-up the level. A funnel may help to reduce spillage. Add the oil slowly, checking the level on the dipstick often. Do not overfill.

Coolant level

Warning: Do not attempt to remove the expansion tank pressure cap when the engine is hot, as there is a very great risk of scalding. Do not leave open containers of coolant about, as it is poisonous.

Car Care
● With a sealed-type cooling system, adding coolant should not be necessary on a regular basis. If frequent topping-up is required, it is likely there is a leak. Check the radiator, all hoses and joint faces for signs of staining or wetness, and rectify as necessary.

● It is important that antifreeze is used in the cooling system all year round, not just during the winter months. Don't top up with water alone, as the antifreeze will become diluted.

1 The coolant level varies with the temperature of the engine. When the engine is cold, the coolant level should be on the MAX mark on the side of the expansion tank located in the left-hand rear corner of the engine compartment. When the engine is hot, the level will rise slightly.

2 If topping-up is necessary, wait until the engine is cold, then slowly unscrew the expansion tank filler cap anti-clockwise, to release any pressure in the system, and remove it.

3 Add a mixture of water and antifreeze through the expansion tank filler neck, until the coolant is up to the MAX level mark. Refit the cap, turning it clockwise as far as it will go until it is secure.

Brake (and clutch) fluid level

Note: *On models with a manual gearbox, the brakes and clutch share a fluid reservoir.*

Before you start

✔ Make sure that the car is on level ground.
✔ Cleanliness is of great importance when dealing with the braking system, so take care to clean around the reservoir cap before topping-up. Use only clean brake fluid.

Safety first!

● If the reservoir requires repeated topping-up, this is an indication of a fluid leak somewhere in the system, which should be investigated immediately.

● If a leak is suspected, the car should not be driven until the braking system has been checked. Never take any risks where brakes are concerned.

 Warning: Brake fluid can harm your eyes and damage painted surfaces, so use extreme caution when handling and pouring it. Do not use fluid which has been standing open for some time, as it absorbs moisture from the air, which can cause a dangerous loss of braking effectiveness.

1 The brake master cylinder and fluid reservoir are mounted on the vacuum servo unit in the engine compartment on the right-hand side of the bulkhead. The MAX and MIN level marks are indicated on the side of the reservoir and the fluid level should be maintained between these marks at all times. Pull off the rubber seal, and lift the plenum chamber cover slightly to view the reservoir.

2 If topping-up is necessary, wipe the area around the filler cap with a clean rag before removing the cap. It's a good idea to inspect the reservoir. The fluid should be changed if dirt is visible.

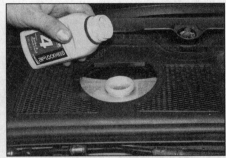

3 Carefully add fluid, avoiding spilling it on surrounding paintwork. Use only the specified hydraulic fluid; mixing different types of fluid can cause damage to the system and/or a loss of braking effectiveness. After filling to the correct level, refit the cap securely. Wipe off any spilt fluid.

Screen washer fluid level

● Screenwash additives not only keep the windscreen clean during bad weather, they also prevent the washer system freezing in cold weather – which is when you are likely to need it most. Don't top-up using plain water, as the screenwash will become diluted, and will freeze in cold weather.

Caution: On no account use engine coolant antifreeze in the screen washer system – this may damage the paintwork.

1 The reservoir for the windscreen and rear window (where applicable) washer systems is located in the front left-hand corner of the engine compartment. If topping-up is necessary, open the cap.

2 When topping-up the reservoir a screenwash additive should be added in the quantities recommended on the bottle.

Tyre condition and pressure

It is very important that tyres are in good condition, and at the correct pressure - having a tyre failure at any speed is highly dangerous. Tyre wear is influenced by driving style - harsh braking and acceleration, or fast cornering, will all produce more rapid tyre wear. As a general rule, the front tyres wear out faster than the rears. Interchanging the tyres from front to rear ("rotating" the tyres) may result in more even wear. However, if this is completely effective, you may have the expense of replacing all four tyres at once! Remove any nails or stones embedded in the tread before they penetrate the tyre to cause deflation. If removal of a nail does reveal that the tyre has been punctured, refit the nail so that its point of penetration is marked. Then immediately change the wheel, and have the tyre repaired by a tyre dealer.

Regularly check the tyres for damage in the form of cuts or bulges, especially in the sidewalls. Periodically remove the wheels, and clean any dirt or mud from the inside and outside surfaces. Examine the wheel rims for signs of rusting, corrosion or other damage. Light alloy wheels are easily damaged by "kerbing" whilst parking; steel wheels may also become dented or buckled. A new wheel is very often the only way to overcome severe damage.

New tyres should be balanced when they are fitted, but it may become necessary to re-balance them as they wear, or if the balance weights fitted to the wheel rim should fall off. Unbalanced tyres will wear more quickly, as will the steering and suspension components. Wheel imbalance is normally signified by vibration, particularly at a certain speed (typically around 50 mph). If this vibration is felt only through the steering, then it is likely that just the front wheels need balancing. If, however, the vibration is felt through the whole car, the rear wheels could be out of balance. Wheel balancing should be carried out by a tyre dealer or garage.

1 *Tread Depth - visual check*
The original tyres have tread wear safety bands (B), which will appear when the tread depth reaches approximately 1.6 mm. The band positions are indicated by a triangular mark on the tyre sidewall (A).

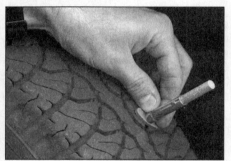

2 *Tread Depth - manual check*
Alternatively, tread wear can be monitored with a simple, inexpensive device known as a tread depth indicator gauge.

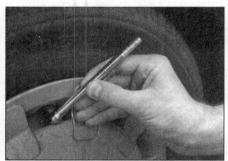

3 *Tyre Pressure Check*
Check the tyre pressures regularly with the tyres cold. Do not adjust the tyre pressures immediately after the vehicle has been used, or an inaccurate setting will result.

Tyre tread wear patterns

Shoulder Wear

Underinflation (wear on both sides)
Under-inflation will cause overheating of the tyre, because the tyre will flex too much, and the tread will not sit correctly on the road surface. This will cause a loss of grip and excessive wear, not to mention the danger of sudden tyre failure due to heat build-up.
Check and adjust pressures
Incorrect wheel camber (wear on one side)
Repair or renew suspension parts
Hard cornering
Reduce speed!

Centre Wear

Overinflation
Over-inflation will cause rapid wear of the centre part of the tyre tread, coupled with reduced grip, harsher ride, and the danger of shock damage occurring in the tyre casing.
Check and adjust pressures

If you sometimes have to inflate your car's tyres to the higher pressures specified for maximum load or sustained high speed, don't forget to reduce the pressures to normal afterwards.

Uneven Wear

Front tyres may wear unevenly as a result of wheel misalignment. Most tyre dealers and garages can check and adjust the wheel alignment (or "tracking") for a modest charge.
Incorrect camber or castor
Repair or renew suspension parts
Malfunctioning suspension
Repair or renew suspension parts
Unbalanced wheel
Balance tyres
Incorrect toe setting
Adjust front wheel alignment
Note: *The feathered edge of the tread which typifies toe wear is best checked by feel.*

Wiper blades

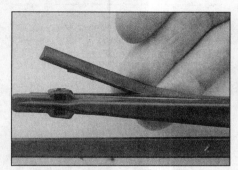

1 Check the condition of the wiper blades. If they are cracked or show any signs of deterioration, or if the glass swept area is smeared, renew them. For maximum clarity of vision, wiper blades should be renewed annually, as a matter of course.

2 To remove a wiper blade, pull the arm fully away from the glass until it locks. Depress the retaining catch and detach the blade from the arm. The rear wiper blade simply pulls from the arm.

3 When fitting the new blade, attach the retainers to the blade, then press the catch to lock the blade to the arm.

Battery

Caution: Before carrying out any work on the vehicle battery, read the precautions given in 'Safety first!' at the start of this manual.

✔ Make sure that the battery tray is in good condition, and that the clamp is tight. Corrosion on the tray, retaining clamp and the battery itself can be removed with a solution of water and baking soda. Thoroughly rinse all cleaned areas with water. Any metal parts damaged by corrosion should be covered with a zinc-based primer, then painted.

✔ Periodically (approximately every three months), check the charge condition of the battery as described in Chapter 5A. A 'magic eye' charge indicator is fitted to the standard battery – if the indicator is green in colour, the battery is fully-charged, however, if it is colourless, it should be recharged. If it is yellow in colour, the battery should be renewed.

✔ If the battery is flat, and you need to jump start your vehicle, see *Roadside Repairs*.

1 The battery is located on the rear left-hand side of the engine compartment under a cover. Slide the cover in the direction of the arrows to remove it. The exterior of the battery should be inspected periodically for damage such as a cracked case or cover.

2 Check the tightness of the battery cable clamps to ensure good electrical connections. You should not be able to move them. Also check each cable for cracks and frayed conductors.

HAYNES
HiNT

Battery corrosion can be kept to a minimum by applying a layer of petroleum jelly to the clamps and terminals after they are reconnected.

3 If corrosion (white, fluffy deposits) is evident, remove the cables from the battery terminals, clean them with a small wire brush, then refit them. Automotive stores sell a tool for cleaning the battery post . . .

4 . . . as well as the battery cable clamps.

Electrical systems

✔ Check all external lights and the horn. Refer to the appropriate Sections of Chapter 12 for details if any of the circuits are found to be inoperative.

✔ Visually check all accessible wiring connectors, harnesses and retaining clips for security, and for signs of chafing or damage.

 HAYNES HiNT *If you need to check your brake lights and indicators unaided, back up to a wall or garage door and operate the lights. The reflected light should show if they are working properly.*

1 If a single indicator light, brake light or headlight has failed, it is likely that a bulb has blown and will need to be renewed. Refer to Chapter 12 for details. If both brake lights have failed, it is possible that the stoplight switch operated by the brake pedal has failed. Refer to Chapter 9 for details.

2 If more than one indicator light or headlight has failed, it is likely that either a fuse has blown or that there is a fault in the circuit (see Chapter 12). The main fusebox is located behind a panel at the driver's end of the facia. To access the fusebox pull the panel from the end of the facia.

3 To renew a blown fuse, pull it out directly from the fusebox using the pliers provided (located on the inside of the facia end panel). Fit a new fuse of the same rating, available from car accessory shops. It is important that you find the reason that the fuse blew (see *Electrical fault finding* in Chapter 12).

Lubricants and fluids

Note: *The use of lubricants and fluids not to the Audi specifications may invalidate the warranty.*

Petrol engine
Standard (distance/time) service interval . . . . Multigrade engine oil viscosity 5W/30 to 15W/40, to specification ACEA A2 or A3 (VW 502.00)

LongLife (variable) service interval . . . . VW 504.00 LongLife oil, or better*

Diesel engine
Standard (distance/time) service interval . . . . Multigrade engine oil viscosity 5W/40 to 20W/50, to specification ACEA B3 or B4 (VW 505.00 or 505.01)

LongLife (variable) service interval . . . . VW 507.00 LongLife oil, or better**

Cooling system . . . . VW G12 Plus anti-freeze

Gearbox
Manual gearbox . . . . VW G 052 911 A1 SAE 75W 90 synthetic oil
Automatic transmission . . . . VW ATF
Multitronic transmission . . . . VW G 052 180 A2 CVT fluid

Final drive . . . . SAE 75W 90 synthetic oil

Braking system . . . . Hydraulic fluid to DOT 4

Power steering system . . . . VW Hydraulic fluid G002 000

Air conditioning system R134a

Cabriolet hood system . . . . VW Hydraulic fluid G004 000

* A maximum of 0.5 litres of standard VW 502.00 oil may be used for topping-up when LongLife oil is unobtainable
** A maximum of 0.5 litres of standard VW 505.00 or 505.01 oil may be used for topping-up when LongLife oil is unobtainable

Tyre pressures

The recommended tyre pressures are shown on a sticker attached to the base of the pillar in the driver's door aperture.

Chapter 1 Part A:
Routine maintenance and servicing – petrol models

Contents

	Section number		Section number
Air filter element renewal	24	Headlight beam adjustment	11
Airbag unit check	19	Hinge and lock lubrication	18
Antifreeze check	9	Hose and fluid leak check	7
Automatic/Multitronic transmission final drive oil level check	29	Introduction	1
Automatic/Multitronic transmission fluid renewal	28	Manual gearbox oil level check	13
Auxiliary drivebelt check and renewal	26	Pollen filter element renewal	12
Auxiliary drivebelt check	8	Power steering hydraulic fluid level check	27
Battery check	17	Regular maintenance	2
Brake (and clutch) fluid renewal	31	Resetting the service interval display	5
Brake hydraulic circuit check	10	Road test and exhaust emissions check	23
Brake pad check	4	Spark plug renewal	25
Coolant renewal	32	Steering and suspension check	16
Driveshaft gaiter check	15	Sunroof check and lubrication	22
Engine management self-diagnosis memory fault check	21	Timing belt check and renewal	30
Engine oil and filter renewal	3	Underbody protection check	14
Exhaust system check	6	Windscreen/tailgate/headlight washer system check	20

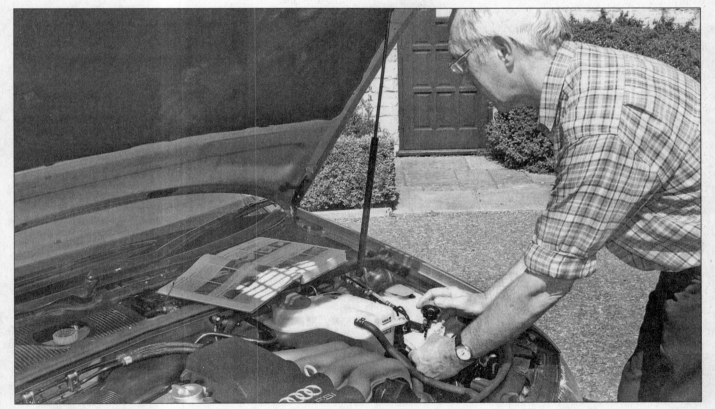

Degrees of difficulty

Easy, suitable for novice with little experience	**Fairly easy,** suitable for beginner with some experience 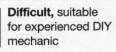	**Fairly difficult,** suitable for competent DIY mechanic	**Difficult,** suitable for experienced DIY mechanic 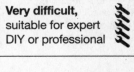	**Very difficult,** suitable for expert DIY or professional

Lubricants and fluids .... Refer to end of *Weekly checks* on page 0•17

Capacities

Engine oil (with filter)
1.8 litre engines .... 3.7 litres
2.0 litre engines .... 4.2 litres

Cooling system .... 7.0 litres approximately

Transmission
Manual gearbox:
   012/01W .... 2.25 litres
   01E/0A1/01X/0A9 .... 2.5 litres
Automatic transmission fluid:
   Initial filling .... 9.0 litres
   Fluid change .... 2.6 litres
   Final drive .... 0.75 litres
Multitronic transmission:
   Initial filling .... 7.5 litres (approximately)
   Fluid change .... 4.7 litres (approximately)
   Final drive .... 0.75 litres

Fuel tank .... 70 litres (approximately)

Washer reservoirs .... 4.8 litres (approximately)

Cooling system

Antifreeze mixture:
   40% antifreeze .... Protection down to -25°C
   50% antifreeze .... Protection down to -35°C

Air conditioning system

System capacity .... 500 grammes (approximately)

Ignition system

Spark plugs:
   1.8 litre engines .... NGK PFR6Q
       Audi 101000063AA

   2.0 litre engines:
     AWA .... NGK PZFR5N-11 TG
       Audi 101905620
     ALT .... NGK BKUR5ET-10
       Audi 101000033AG
Electrode gap .... 0.9 to 1.1 mm

Brakes

Front brake pad friction material minimum thickness .... 2.0 mm
Rear brake pad friction material minimum thickness .... 2.0 mm

Auxiliary drivebelt

Tension adjustment .... Automatically adjusted

Torque wrench settings

	Nm	lbf ft
Automatic transmission:		
Drain plug	40	30
Inspection plug	80	59
Final drive oil filler/level plug	25	18
Engine oil filter (FSI engines)	25	18
Manual gearbox filler/level plug:		
5-speed	25	18
6-speed	40	30
Multitronic transmission:		
Drain plug	24	18
Inspection plug	20	15
Final drive oil filler/level plug	20	15
Power steering pump mounting	25	18
Roadwheel bolts	120	89
Spark plugs	30	22
Sump drain plug	30	22

The maintenance intervals in this manual are provided with the assumption that you, not the dealer, will be carrying out the work. These are the minimum intervals recommended by us for vehicles driven daily. If you wish to keep your vehicle in peak condition at all times, you may wish to perform some of these procedures more often. We encourage frequent maintenance, since it enhances the efficiency, performance and resale value of your vehicle.

When the vehicle is new, it should be serviced by a dealer service department (or other workshop recognised by the vehicle manufacturer as providing the same standard of service) in order to preserve the warranty. The vehicle manufacturer may reject warranty claims if you are unable to prove that servicing has been carried out as and when specified, using only original equipment parts or parts certified to be of equivalent quality.

All models are equipped with a service interval display indicator in the instrument panel. Every time the engine is started the panel will illuminate for approximately 20 seconds with service information. With the standard non-variable display, the service intervals are in accordance with specific distances and time periods. With the LongLife display, the service interval is variable according to the number of starts, length of journeys, vehicle speeds, brake pad wear, bonnet opening frequency, fuel consumption, oil level and oil temperature, however the vehicle must be serviced at least every two years. At a distance of 2000 miles before the next service is due, 'Service in 2000 miles' will appear at the bottom of the speedometer, and this figure will reduce in steps of 100 as the vehicle is used. Once the service interval has been reached, the display will flash 'Service' or 'Service Now'. Note that if the variable (LongLife) service interval is being used, the engine must only be filled with the recommended LongLife engine oil (see Lubricants and fluids).

After completing a service, Audi technicians use a special instrument to reset the service display to the next service interval, and a print-out is put in the vehicle service record. The display can be reset by the owner as described in Section 5, but note that the procedure will automatically reset the display to the fixed non-variable interval. To have the display reset to the 'variable' (LongLife) interval, it is necessary to take the vehicle to an Audi dealer who will use a special instrument to encode the on-board computer.

Every 250 miles or weekly
☐ Refer to *Weekly checks*

OIL on display
☐ Renew the engine oil and filter (Section 3)
Note: *Frequent oil and filter changes are good for the engine. We recommend changing the oil at least once a year.*
☐ Check the front and rear brake pad thickness (Section 4)
☐ Reset the service interval display (Section 5)

01 on display
In addition to the items listed above, carry out the following:
☐ Check the condition of the exhaust system and its mountings (Section 6)
☐ Check all underbonnet components and hoses for fluid and oil leaks (Section 7)
☐ Check the condition of the auxiliary drivebelt (Section 8)
☐ Check the coolant antifreeze concentration (Section 9)
☐ Check the brake hydraulic circuit for leaks and damage (Section 10)
☐ Check the headlight beam adjustment (Section 11)
☐ Renew the pollen filter element (Section 12)
☐ Check the manual gearbox oil level (Section 13)
☐ Check the underbody protection for damage (Section 14)
☐ Check the condition of the driveshaft gaiters (Section 15)
☐ Check the steering and suspension components for condition and security (Section 16)
☐ Check the battery condition, security and electrolyte level (Section 17)
☐ Lubricate all hinges and locks (Section 18)
☐ Check the condition of the airbag unit(s) (Section 19)
☐ Check the operation of the windscreen/tailgate/headlight washer system(s) (as applicable) (Section 20)

01 on display (continued)
☐ Check the engine management self-diagnosis memory for faults (Section 21)
☐ Check the operation of the sunroof and lubricate the guide rails (Section 22)
☐ Carry out a road test and check exhaust emissions (Section 23)

Every 40 000 miles or 4 years, whichever comes first
Note: *Many dealers perform these tasks at every second 01 service.*
☐ Renew the air filter element (Section 24)
☐ Renew the spark plugs (Section 25)
☐ Check and renewal of the auxiliary drivebelt (Section 26)
☐ Check the power steering hydraulic fluid level (Section 27)
☐ Renew the automatic/Multitronic transmission fluid (Section 28)
☐ Check the automatic/Multitronic transmission final drive oil level (Section 29)
☐ Renew the timing belt (Section 30)
Note: *Audi specify timing belt inspection after the first 60 000 miles and then every 20 000 mile until the renewal interval of 120 000 miles, however, if the vehicle is used mainly for short journeys, we recommend that this shorter renewal interval is adhered to. The belt renewal interval is very much up to the individual owner but, bearing in mind that severe engine damage will result if the belt breaks in use, we recommend the shorter interval.*

Every 2 years
☐ Renew the brake (and clutch) fluid (Section 31)
☐ Renew the coolant (Section 32)*
* Note: *This work is not included in the Audi schedule and should not be required if the recommended Audi G12 Plus LongLife coolant antifreeze/inhibitor is used.*

Underbonnet view of a 2.0 litre FSI model

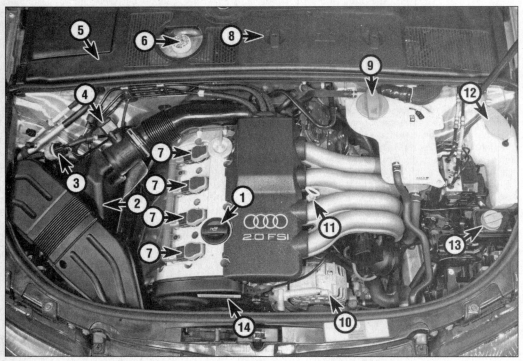

1 Engine oil filler cap
2 Air cleaner
3 Carbon canister solenoid valve
4 Airflow meter
5 Plenum chamber cover
6 Brake/clutch fluid reservoir
7 Ignition coils
8 Battery cover
9 Coolant expansion tank filler cap
10 Alternator
11 Engine oil level dipstick
12 Washer fluid reservoir
13 Power steering fluid reservoir
14 Engine code sticker

Front underbody view

1 Lower suspension arm – rear
2 Lower suspension arm – front
3 Engine oil drain plug
4 Auxiliary drivebelt
5 Exhaust pipe flexible section
6 Air conditioning receiver/drier
7 Anti-roll bar
8 Driveshaft
9 Air conditioning compressor
10 Engine oil temperature sensor
11 Brake caliper

Rear underbody view

1   Trapezium link
2   Handbrake cable
3   Fuel tank
4   Rear silencer
5   Subframe
6   Anti-roll bar
7   Shock absorber

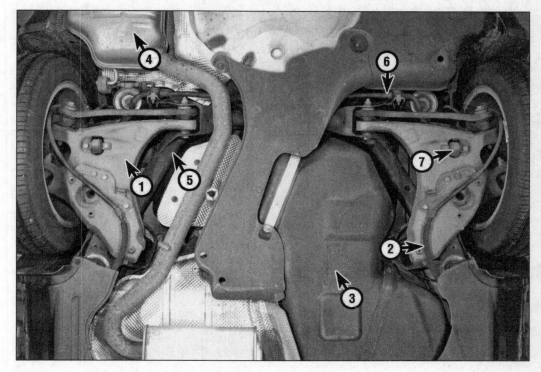

Maintenance procedures

1   Introduction

This Chapter is designed to help the home mechanic maintain his/her vehicle for safety, economy, long life and peak performance.

The Chapter contains a master maintenance schedule, followed by Sections dealing specifically with each task in the schedule. Visual checks, adjustments, component renewal and other helpful items are included. Refer to the accompanying illustrations of the engine compartment and the underside of the vehicle for the locations of the various components.

Servicing your vehicle will provide a planned maintenance programme, which should result in a long and reliable service life. This is a comprehensive plan, so maintaining some items but not others will not produce the same results.

As you service your vehicle, you will discover that many of the procedures can – and should – be grouped together, because of the particular procedure being performed, or because of the proximity of two otherwise unrelated components to one another. For example, if the vehicle is raised for any reason, the exhaust can be inspected at the same time as the suspension and steering components.

The first step in this maintenance programme is to prepare yourself before the actual work begins. Read through all the Sections relevant to the work to be carried out, then make a list and gather all the parts and tools required. If a problem is encountered, seek advice from a parts specialist, or a dealer service department.

2   Regular maintenance

1 If, from the time the vehicle is new, the routine maintenance schedule is followed closely, and frequent checks are made of fluid levels and high-wear items, as suggested throughout this manual, the engine will be kept in relatively good running condition, and the need for additional work will be minimised.

2 It is possible that there will be times when the engine is running poorly due to the lack of regular maintenance. This is even more likely if a used vehicle, which has not received regular and frequent maintenance checks, is purchased. In such cases, additional work may need to be carried out, outside of the regular maintenance intervals.

3 If engine wear is suspected, a compression test (refer to the relevant Part of Chapter 2) will provide valuable information regarding the overall performance of the main internal components. Such a test can be used as a basis to decide on the extent of the work to be carried out. If, for example, a compression test indicates serious internal engine wear, conventional maintenance as described in this Chapter will not greatly improve the performance of the engine, and may prove a waste of time and money, unless extensive overhaul work is carried out first.

4 The following series of operations are those most often required to improve the performance of a generally poor-running engine:

Primary operations

a) Clean, inspect and test the battery (See 'Weekly checks').
b) Check all the engine-related fluids (See 'Weekly checks').
c) Check the condition and tension of the auxiliary drivebelt (Section 8).
d) Renew the spark plugs (Section 25).
e) Check the condition of the air filter, and renew if necessary (Section 24).
f) Check the condition of all hoses, and check for fluid leaks (Section 7).

5 If the above operations do not prove fully effective, carry out the following secondary operations:

Secondary operations

All items listed under Primary operations, plus the following:

a) Check the charging system (see Chapter 5A).
b) Check the ignition system (see Chapter 5B).
c) Check the fuel system (see Chapter 4A).

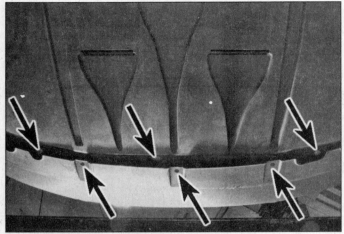

3.2a The front edge of the engine undershield is secured by 3 screws to the front bumper, and 3 screws to the lock carrier (arrowed)

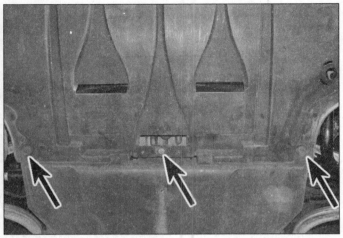

3.2b Engine undershield-to-transmission undershield fasteners (arrowed)

OIL on display

3 Engine oil and filter renewal

1 Frequent oil and filter changes are the most important maintenance procedures which can be undertaken by the DIY owner. As engine oil ages, it becomes diluted and contaminated, which leads to premature engine wear.

2 Before starting this procedure, gather all the necessary tools and materials. Also make sure that you have plenty of clean rags and newspapers handy, to mop-up any spills. Ideally, the engine oil should be warm, as it will drain better, and more built-up sludge will be removed with it. Take care, however, not to touch the exhaust or any other hot parts of the engine when working under the vehicle. To avoid any possibility of scalding, and to protect yourself from possible skin irritants and other harmful contaminants in used engine oils, it is advisable to wear gloves when carrying out this work. Access to the underside of the vehicle is possible if it can be raised on a lift, driven onto ramps, or jacked up and supported securely on axle stands (see *Jacking and vehicle support*). Whichever method is chosen, make sure that the vehicle remains level, or if it is at an angle, that the drain plug is at the lowest point. With the vehicle raised, undo the fasteners and remove the engine compartment undershield **(see illustrations)**.

3 Using a socket and wrench or a ring spanner, slacken the drain plug about half a turn. Position the draining container under the drain plug, then remove the plug completely **(see Haynes Hint)**. Recover the sealing ring from the drain plug **(see illustration)**.

4 Allow some time for the old oil to drain, noting that it may be necessary to reposition the container as the oil flow slows to a trickle.

5 After all the oil has drained, wipe off the drain plug with a clean rag, and fit a new sealing washer **(see illustration)**. Clean the area around the drain plug opening, and refit the plug. Tighten the plug to the specified torque.

6 If the filter is also to be renewed, move the container into position under the oil filter, which is located on the left-hand rear side of the cylinder block.

7 Using an oil filter removal tool if necessary, slacken the filter initially, then unscrew it by hand the rest of the way **(see illustrations)**. Empty the oil in the filter into the container.

8 Use a clean rag to remove all oil, dirt and sludge from the filter sealing area on the

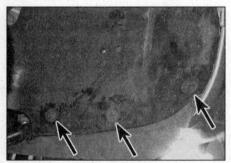

3.2c Engine undershield-to-wheel arch liner fasteners (arrowed)

3.3 The engine oil drain plug location on the sump (arrowed)

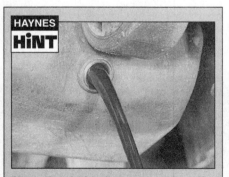

HAYNES HINT

Keep the drain plug pressed into the sump while unscrewing it by hand the last couple of turns. As the plug releases, move it away sharply so the stream of oil issuing from the sump runs into the container, not up your sleeve.

3.5 Position the new sealing washer on the plug, then tighten the plug to the specified torque

3.7a The oil filter (arrowed) is located on the left-hand side of the engine (viewed from under the vehicle

3.7b Unscrew the oil filter from the housing

3.9 Apply a little clean engine oil to the filter sealing ring

3.11a Remove the oil level dipstick . . .

3.11b . . . and unscrew the oil filler cap

engine. Check the old filter to make sure that the rubber sealing ring has not stuck to the engine. If it has, carefully remove it.

9 Apply a light coating of clean engine oil to the sealing ring on the new filter, then screw it into position on the engine **(see illustration)**. Tighten the filter firmly by hand only, except on FSI engines, where the specified torque should be observed.

10 Remove the old oil and all tools from under the car then refit the undershield and lower the car to the ground.

11 Remove the dipstick, then unscrew the oil filler cap from the cylinder head cover **(see illustrations)**. Fill the engine, using the correct grade and type of oil (see *Lubricants and fluids*). An oil can spout or funnel may help to reduce spillage. Pour in half the specified quantity of oil first, then wait a few minutes for the oil to settle in the sump. Continue adding oil a small quantity at a time until the level is up to the lower mark on the dipstick. Adding around 1.0 litre will bring the level up to the upper mark on the dipstick. Refit the filler cap.

12 Start the engine and run it at idle speed for a few minutes; check for leaks around the oil filter seal and the sump drain plug. Note that there may be a few seconds delay before the oil pressure warning light goes out when the engine is started, as the oil circulates through

the engine oil galleries and the new oil filter before the pressure builds-up.

Caution: On models with a turbocharger, leave the engine idling until the oil pressure light goes out. Increasing the engine speed with the warning light on may damage the turbocharger.

13 Switch off the engine, and wait a few minutes for the oil to settle in the sump once more. With the new oil circulated and the filter completely full, recheck the level on the dipstick, and add more oil as necessary.

14 Dispose of the used engine oil safely, with reference to *General repair procedures* in the *Reference* section of this manual.

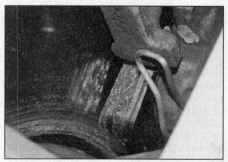

4.1 The outer brake pads can be observed through the holes in the wheels

4 Brake pad check

1 On some models, the outer brake pads can be checked without removing the wheels, by observing the brake pads through the holes in the wheels **(see illustration)**. If necessary, remove the wheel trim. The thickness of the pad lining must not be less than the dimension given in the Specifications.

2 If the outer pads are worn near their limits, it is worthwhile checking the inner pads as well. Apply the handbrake then jack up vehicle and support it securely on axle stands (see *Jacking and vehicle support*). Remove the roadwheels.

3 Use a steel rule to check the thickness of the brake pads (excluding the backing plate), and compare with the minimum thickness given in the Specifications **(see illustration)**.

4 For a comprehensive check, the brake pads should be removed and cleaned. The operation of the caliper can then also be checked, and the condition of the brake disc itself can be fully examined on both sides. Refer to Chapter 9.

5 If any pad's friction material is worn to the specified minimum thickness or less, *all four*

pads at the front or rear, as applicable, must be renewed as a set.

6 On completion of the check, refit the roadwheels and lower the vehicle to the ground. Tighten the roadwheel bolts to the specified torque.

5 Resetting the service interval display

1 After all necessary maintenance work has been completed, the service interval display must be reset. Audi technicians use a special dedicated instrument to do this, and a print-out is then put in the vehicle service record. It is possible for the owner to reset the display as described in the following paragraphs, but note that the procedure will automatically reset the display to a 10 000 mile interval. To continue with the 'variable' intervals which take into consideration the number of starts, length of journeys, vehicle speeds, brake pad wear, bonnet opening

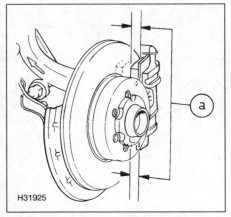

4.3 The thickness (a) of the brake pads friction material must not be less than the specified amount

frequency, fuel consumption, oil level and oil temperature, the display must be reset by an Audi dealership using the special dedicated instrument.

2 To reset the standard display manually,

5.2 Service indicator call up button (arrowed)

switch off the ignition, then press and hold down the service indicator call up button beneath the speedometer (see illustration). Switch on the ignition.

3 Release the button. The display will now show 'SERVICE IN ???? miles ???? days'. Now press and hold the trip reset button below the speedometer until the display is reset to 'SERVICE IN ---- miles ---- days'. Switch off the ignition.

01 on display

6 Exhaust system check

1 With the engine cold (at least an hour after the vehicle has been driven), check the complete exhaust system from the engine to the end of the tailpipe. The exhaust system is most easily checked with the vehicle raised on a hoist, or suitably supported on axle stands, so that the exhaust components are readily visible and accessible (see Jacking and vehicle support).

2 Check the exhaust pipes and connections for evidence of leaks, severe corrosion and damage. Make sure that all brackets and mountings are in good condition, and that all relevant nuts and bolts are tight. Leakage at any of the joints or in other parts of the system will usually show up as a black sooty stain in the vicinity of the leak.

6.3 Check the condition of the rubber mountings (arrowed)

3 Rattles and other noises can often be traced to the exhaust system, especially the brackets and mountings (see illustration). Try to move the pipes and silencers. If the components are able to come into contact with the body or suspension parts, secure the system with new mountings. Otherwise separate the joints (if possible) and twist the pipes as necessary to provide additional clearance.

7 Hose and fluid leak check

1 Visually inspect the engine joint faces, gaskets and seals for any signs of water or oil leaks. Pay particular attention to the areas around the camshaft cover, cylinder head, oil filter and sump joint faces. Bear in mind that, over a period of time, some very slight seepage from these areas is to be expected – what you are really looking for is any indication of a serious leak. Should a leak be found, renew the offending gasket or oil seal by referring to the appropriate Chapters in this manual.

2 Also check the security and condition of all the engine-related pipes and hoses. Ensure that all cable-ties or securing clips are in place and in good condition. Clips which are broken or missing can lead to chafing of the hoses, pipes or wiring, which could cause more serious problems in the future.

3 Carefully check the radiator hoses and heater hoses along their entire length. Renew any hose which is cracked, swollen or deteriorated. Cracks will show up better if

the hose is squeezed. Pay close attention to the hose clips that secure the hoses to the cooling system components. Hose clips can pinch and puncture hoses, resulting in cooling system leaks.

4 Inspect all the cooling system components (hoses, joint faces, etc) for leaks (see Haynes Hint). Where any problems of this nature are found on system components, renew the component or gasket with reference to Chapter 3.

5 Where applicable, inspect the automatic/Multitronic transmission fluid cooler hoses for leaks or deterioration.

6 With the vehicle raised, inspect the petrol tank and filler neck for punctures, cracks and other damage. The connection between the filler neck and tank is especially critical.

HAYNES HINT

A leak in the cooling system will usually show up as white- or antifreeze-coloured deposits in the area adjoining the leak.

8.3 Check the underside of the auxiliary drivebelt with a mirror

11.2 Headlamp aim adjuster screws (arrowed)

Sometimes a rubber filler neck or connecting hose will leak due to loose retaining clamps or deteriorated rubber.

7 Carefully check all rubber hoses and metal fuel lines leading away from the petrol tank. Check for loose connections, deteriorated hoses, crimped lines, and other damage. Pay particular attention to the vent pipes and hoses, which often loop up around the filler neck and can become blocked or crimped. Follow the lines to the front of the vehicle, carefully inspecting them all the way. Renew damaged sections as necessary.

8 From within the engine compartment, check the security of all fuel hose attachments and pipe unions, and inspect the fuel hoses and vacuum hoses for kinks, chafing and deterioration.

9 Where applicable, check the condition of the power steering fluid hoses and pipes.

8 Auxiliary drivebelt check

1 The main drivebelt drives the alternator, the power steering pump and the air conditioning compressor (where fitted).

2 For access to the drivebelt, apply the handbrake, then jack up the front of the vehicle and support it securely on axle stands (see *Jacking and vehicle support*). Remove the engine undershield, and where applicable remove the engine top cover as well.

3 Examine the auxiliary drivebelt along its entire length for damage and wear in the form of cuts and abrasions, fraying and cracking. The use of a mirror and possibly an electric torch will help, and the engine may be turned with a spanner on the crankshaft pulley in order to observe all areas of the belt (**see illustration**).

4 If a drivebelt requires renewal, refer to Chapter 2A or 2B for the removal, refitting and adjustment procedure.

9 Antifreeze check

1 The cooling system should be filled with the recommended G12 Plus antifreeze and corrosion protection fluid, which is designed to last the life of the vehicle. **Do not** mix this antifreeze with any other type apart from G11 or G12. **Note:** *If it is mixed with these other types, G12 Plus loses its 'filled for life' quality.* Over a period of time, the concentration of fluid may be reduced due to topping-up (this can be avoided by topping-up with the correct antifreeze mixture – see Specifications) or fluid loss. If loss of coolant has been evident, it is important to make the necessary repair before adding fresh fluid.

2 With the engine **cold**, carefully remove the cap from the expansion tank. If the engine is not completely cold, place a cloth rag over the cap before removing it, and remove it slowly to allow any pressure to escape.

3 Antifreeze checkers (Hydrometers) are available from car accessory shops. Draw some coolant from the expansion tank into the hydrometer and follow the manufacturer's instructions.

4 If the concentration is incorrect, it will be necessary to either withdraw some coolant and add antifreeze, or alternatively drain the old coolant and add fresh coolant of the correct concentration (see Section 32).

10 Brake hydraulic circuit check

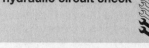

1 Check the entire brake hydraulic circuit for leaks and damage. Start by checking the master cylinder in the engine compartment. At the same time, check the vacuum servo unit and ABS units for signs of fluid leakage.

2 Raise the front and rear of the vehicle and support it on axle stands (see *Jacking and vehicle support*). Check the rigid hydraulic brake lines for corrosion and damage.

3 At the front of the vehicle, check that the flexible hydraulic hoses to the calipers are not twisted or chafing on any of the surrounding suspension components. Turn the steering on full lock to make this check. Also check that the hoses are not brittle or cracked.

4 Lower the vehicle to the ground after making the checks.

11 Headlight beam adjustment

Halogen headlamps

1 Accurate adjustment of the headlight beam is only possible using optical beam setting equipment, and this work should therefore be carried out by an Audi dealer or suitably-equipped workshop.

2 For reference, the headlights can be adjusted using the adjuster screws, accessible at the top of each light unit (**see illustration**).

3 Some models are equipped with an electrically-operated headlight beam adjustment system which is controlled through the switch in the facia. On these models, ensure that the switch is set to the basic 0 position before adjusting the headlight aim.

Gas discharge headlights

4 The headlamp range is controlled dynamically by an electronic control unit which monitors the ride height of the vehicle by sensors fitted to the front and rear suspension. Beam adjustment can only be carried out using Audi test equipment.

12.2a Pull up the rubber weatherstrip (arrowed) . . .

12.2b . . . then pull the plenum chamber cover (arrowed) forwards

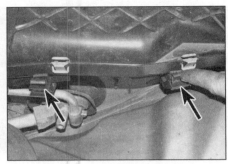

12.3a Release the retaining clips (arrowed) . . .

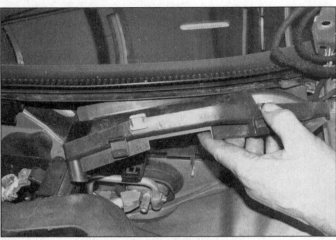

12.3b . . . then lift off the filter cover

12.4 The arrows on the side of the filter element point downwards

12 Pollen filter element renewal

1 The pollen filter is located on the bulkhead, in front of the windscreen – on RHD models it is on the left-hand side, and on LHD models it is on the right-hand side.
2 Pull up the rubber weatherstrip then pull the plastic lid from the plenum chamber forwards (see illustrations).
3 Unclip the battery vent tube from the filter

13.1 The gearbox oil filler/level plug may be a multi-splined security type, with a raised centre

cover, then release the two retaining tabs and lift the filter cover (see illustrations).
4 Lift out the pollen filter element (see illustration). Note the airflow arrows on the element. Remove the element from the frame.
5 Fit the frame to the new element and locate it in the plenum chamber cover, making sure that the airflow arrows are pointing downwards.
6 Close the plastic lid, however, make sure it is fitted correctly, otherwise water may enter the filter or heater assembly.

13 Manual gearbox oil level check

1 The oil filler/level plug is located on the left-hand side of the manual transmission, below the speedometer sender (where fitted), and on some models it may be concealed by a heat shield. The plug may be either of 17 mm Allen key type, or alternatively of multi-splined security type (see illustration).
2 Apply the handbrake, then jack up the front and rear of the vehicle and support it on axle stands (see Jacking and vehicle support). To ensure an accurate check, make sure that the vehicle is level.

3 Unscrew and remove the filler/level plug.
4 Using a length of wire bent 90°, measure how far the fluid level is below the bottom lip of the filler/level hole.

On 5-speed 012/01W/0A9 transmissions the level must be between 0 and 7 mm below the hole.

On 6-speed 01E/0A1 transmissions the level must be 4 ± 1 mm below the hole.

On 6-speed 01X transmissions the fluid must be level with the bottom of the hole.

5 If necessary, add the specified oil through the filler/level hole. If the level requires constant topping-up, check for leaks and repair.
6 Refit the plug and tighten to the specified torque, then lower the vehicle to the ground.

14 Underbody protection check

Raise and support the vehicle on axle stands (see Jacking and vehicle support). Using an electric torch or lead light, inspect the entire underside of the vehicle, paying particular attention to the wheel arches. Look for any damage to the flexible underbody coating, which may crack or flake off with age, leading to corrosion. Also check that the wheel arch liners are securely attached with any clips provided – if they come loose, dirt may get in behind the liners and defeat their purpose. If there is any damage to the underseal, or any corrosion, it should be repaired before the damage gets too serious.

15 Driveshaft gaiter check

1 With the vehicle raised and securely supported on stands, slowly rotate the roadwheel. Inspect the condition of the outer constant velocity (CV) joint rubber gaiters, squeezing the gaiters to open out the folds. Check for signs of cracking, splits or deterioration of the rubber, which may allow the grease to escape, and lead to water and grit entry into the joint. Also check the security and condition of the retaining clips. Repeat these checks on the inner joints **(see illustration)**. If any damage or deterioration is found, the gaiters should be renewed (see Chapter 8).

2 At the same time, check the general condition of the CV joints themselves by first holding the driveshaft and attempting to rotate the wheel. Repeat this check by holding the inner joint and attempting to rotate the driveshaft. Any appreciable movement indicates wear in the joints, wear in the driveshaft splines, or a loose driveshaft retaining nut.

16 Steering and suspension check

1 Raise the front and rear of the vehicle, and securely support it on axle stands (see *Jacking and vehicle support*).

2 Visually inspect the track rod end balljoint dust cover, the lower front suspension balljoint dust cover, and the steering rack-and-pinion gaiters for splits, chafing or deterioration. Any wear of these components will cause loss of lubricant, together with dirt and water entry, resulting in rapid deterioration of the balljoints or steering gear.

3 Check the power steering fluid hoses for chafing or deterioration, and the pipe and hose unions for fluid leaks. Also check for signs of fluid leakage under pressure from the steering gear rubber gaiters, which would indicate failed fluid seals within the steering gear.

4 Grasp the roadwheel at the 12 o'clock and 6 o'clock positions, and try to rock it **(see illustration)**. Very slight free play may be felt, but if the movement is appreciable, further investigation is necessary to determine the source. Continue rocking the wheel while an assistant depresses the footbrake. If the movement is now eliminated or significantly reduced, it is likely that the hub bearings are

at fault. If the free play is still evident with the footbrake depressed, then there is wear in the suspension joints or mountings.

5 Now grasp the wheel at the 9 o'clock and 3 o'clock positions, and try to rock it as before. Any movement felt now may again be caused by wear in the hub bearings or the steering track rod balljoints. If the inner or outer balljoint is worn, the visual movement will be obvious.

6 Using a large screwdriver or flat bar, check for wear in the suspension mounting bushes by levering between the relevant suspension component and its attachment point. Some movement is to be expected as the mountings are made of rubber, but excessive wear should be obvious. Also check the condition of any visible rubber bushes, looking for splits, cracks or contamination of the rubber.

7 With the car standing on its wheels, have an assistant turn the steering wheel back-and-forth about an eighth of a turn each way. There should be very little, if any, lost movement between the steering wheel and roadwheels. If this is not the case, closely observe the joints and mountings previously described, but in addition, check the steering column universal joints for wear, and the rack-and-pinion steering gear itself.

8 Check for any signs of fluid leakage around the front suspension struts and rear shock absorber. Should any fluid be noticed, the suspension strut or shock absorber is defective internally, and should be renewed. **Note:** *Suspension struts/shock absorbers should always be renewed in pairs on the same axle to ensure correct vehicle handling.*

9 The efficiency of the suspension strut/shock absorber may be checked by bouncing the vehicle at each corner. Generally speaking, the body will return to its normal position and stop after being depressed. If it rises and returns on a rebound, the suspension strut/shock absorber is probably suspect. Examine also the suspension strut/shock absorber upper and lower mountings for any signs of wear.

17 Battery check

1 The battery is located beneath a cover at the rear of the engine compartment. Slide the cover (where fitted) in the direction of the arrows on the handles, then remove the cover.

2 Check that both battery terminals and all the fuse holder connections are securely attached and are free from corrosion.

3 Check the battery casing for signs of damage or cracking and check the battery retaining clamp bolt is securely tightened. If the battery casing is damaged in any way the battery must be renewed (see Chapter 5A).

15.1 Check the condition of the driveshaft gaiters

4 If the vehicle is not fitted with a sealed-for-life maintenance-free battery, check the electrolyte level is between the MAX and MIN level markings on the battery casing. If topping-up is necessary, remove the battery (see Chapter 5A) from the vehicle then remove the cell caps/cover (as applicable). Using distilled water, top the electrolyte level of each cell up to the MAX level mark then securely refit the cell caps/cover. Ensure the battery has not been overfilled then refit the battery to the vehicle (see Chapter 5A).

5 On completion of the check, refit the cover.

18 Hinge and lock lubrication

1 Lubricate the hinges of the bonnet, boot, doors and tailgate with a light general-purpose oil. Similarly, lubricate all latches, locks and lock strikers. At the same time, check the security and operation of all the locks, adjusting them if necessary (see Chapter 11).

2 Lightly lubricate the bonnet release mechanism and cable with a suitable grease.

19 Airbag unit check

1 Inspect the exterior condition of the airbag(s) for signs of damage or deterioration. If an airbag shows signs of damage, it must be renewed (see Chapter 12). Note that it is

16.4 check for wear in the hub bearings by grasping the wheel and trying to rock it

not permissible to attach any stickers to the surface of the airbag, as this may affect the deployment of the unit.

20 Windscreen/tailgate/ headlight washer system check

1 Check that each of the washer jet nozzles are clear and that each nozzle provides a strong jet of washer fluid.

2 The tailgate jet should be aimed to spray at the centre of the screen, using a pin.

3 The inner windscreen washer nozzles should be aimed slightly above the centre of the screen, and the outer nozzles slightly below the centre of the screen and towards the outside. Use a pin to adjust the nozzle aim.

4 The aim of the headlight jets is set in the factory and there is no provision for adjustment.

5 Especially during the winter months, make sure that the washer fluid antifreeze concentration is sufficient.

21 Engine management self-diagnosis memory fault check

1 This work should be carried out by an Audi dealer or diagnostic specialist using special equipment. The diagnostic socket is located beneath the right-hand side of the facia on RHD models, and beneath the left-hand side on LHD models.

22 Sunroof check and lubrication

1 Check the operation of the sunroof, and leave it in the fully open position.

2 Wipe clean the guide rails on each side of the sunroof opening, then apply lubricant to them. Audi recommend lubricant spray G 052 778 A2.

23 Road test and exhaust emissions check

Instruments and electrical equipment

1 Check the operation of all instruments and electrical equipment.

2 Make sure that all instruments read correctly, and switch on all electrical equipment in turn, to check that it functions properly.

Steering and suspension

3 Check for any abnormalities in the steering, suspension, handling or road feel.

4 Drive the vehicle, and check that there are no unusual vibrations or noises which may indicate wear in the driveshafts, wheel bearings, etc.

5 Check that the steering feels positive, with no excessive sloppiness, or roughness, and check for any suspension noises when cornering and driving over bumps.

Drivetrain

6 Check the performance of the engine, clutch (where applicable), gearbox/transmission and driveshafts.

7 Listen for any unusual noises from the engine, clutch and gearbox/transmission.

8 Make sure that the engine runs smoothly when idling, and that there is no hesitation when accelerating.

9 Check that, where applicable, the clutch action is smooth and progressive, that the drive is taken up smoothly, and that the pedal travel is not excessive. Also listen for any noises when the clutch pedal is depressed.

10 On manual gearbox models, check that all gears can be engaged smoothly without noise, and that the gear lever action is smooth and not abnormally vague or notchy.

11 On automatic/Multitronic transmission models, make sure that all gearchanges occur smoothly, without snatching, and without an increase in engine speed between changes. Check that all the gear positions

can be selected with the vehicle at rest. If any problems are found, they should be referred to an Audi dealer.

12 Listen for a metallic clicking sound from the front of the vehicle, as the vehicle is driven slowly in a circle with the steering on full-lock. Carry out this check in both directions. If a clicking noise is heard, this indicates wear in a driveshaft joint, in which case renew the joint if necessary.

Braking system

13 Make sure that the vehicle does not pull to one side when braking, and that the wheels do not lock when braking hard.

14 Check that there is no vibration through the steering when braking.

15 Check that the handbrake operates correctly without excessive movement of the lever, and that it holds the vehicle stationary on a slope.

16 Test the operation of the brake servo unit as follows. With the engine off, depress the footbrake four or five times to exhaust the vacuum. Hold the brake pedal depressed, then start the engine. As the engine starts, there should be a noticeable 'give' in the brake pedal as vacuum builds-up. Allow the engine to run for at least two minutes, and then switch it off. If the brake pedal is depressed now, it should be possible to detect a hiss from the servo as the pedal is depressed. After about four or five applications, no further hissing should be heard, and the pedal should feel considerably harder.

17 Under controlled emergency braking, the pulsing of the ABS unit must be felt at the footbrake pedal.

Exhaust emissions check

18 Although not part of the manufacturer's maintenance schedule, this check will normally be carried out on a regular basis according to the country the vehicle is operated in. Currently in the UK, exhaust emissions testing is included as part of the annual MOT test after the vehicle is 3 years old. In Germany the test is made when the vehicle is 3 years old, then repeated every 2 years.

Every 40 000 miles or 4 years, whichever comes first

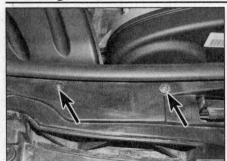

24.1a Undo the 2 screws (arrowed) securing the intake duct to the lock carrier

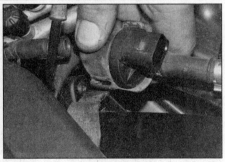

24.1b Pull the charcoal canister purge valve from the bracket on the intake duct . . .

24 Air filter element renewal

1 Undo the two bolts and remove the air intake duct from the lock carrier panel and the top of the air filter housing (see illustration). Unclip the charcoal canister purge valve from the intake duct (where applicable). On turbo models, unclip the wiring harness from the air cleaner body (see illustrations).

2 On non-FSI engines, release the clip and disconnect the charcoal canister valve pipe.

3 Undo the two bolts and lift off the air cleaner cover (see illustrations). On FSI engines, disconnect the airflow meter wiring plug as the cover is withdrawn.

4 On all engines, remove the air filter element, noting which way round it is fitted (see illustrations).

5 Wipe clean the main body. Use a vacuum cleaner to remove any debris, then fit the new air filter, making sure it is the correct way around.

6 The remainder of refitting is a reversal of removal.

25 Spark plug renewal

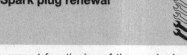

1 The correct functioning of the spark plugs is vital for the correct running and efficiency of the engine. It is essential that the plugs fitted are appropriate for the engine and if the engine is in good condition, the spark plugs should not need attention between scheduled renewal intervals. Spark plug cleaning is rarely necessary, and should not be attempted unless specialised equipment is available, as damage can easily be caused to the firing ends.

2 First remove the plastic cover from the top the engine.

3 Pull the wiring plug towards the coil, depress the retaining catch, and disconnect the wiring plugs from the ignition coils (see illustrations). On 2.0 litre engines, undo the two bolts securing the coil's harness to the cylinder head cover to give sufficient clearance when disconnecting the plugs.

4 Carefully pull each coil upwards from the cylinder head cover. Lever only on the underside of the thick rib at the top of the coils (see illustration). There is a special Audi tool available (T40039) for this task.

5 It is advisable to remove the dirt from the spark plug recesses using a clean brush, vacuum cleaner or compressed air before removing the plugs, to prevent dirt dropping into the cylinders.

6 Unscrew the plugs using a spark plug socket, suitable box spanner or a deep socket and extension bar (see illustration). Keep the socket aligned with the spark plug – if it is forcibly moved to one side, the ceramic insulator may be broken off. As each plug is removed, examine it as follows.

7 If the insulator nose of the spark plug is clean and white, with no deposits, this is indicative of a weak mixture or too hot a plug (a hot plug transfers heat away from the electrode slowly, a cold plug transfers heat away quickly).

8 If the tip and insulator nose are covered with hard black-looking deposits, then this is indicative that the mixture is too rich. Should the plug be black and oily, then it is likely that the engine is fairly worn, as well as the mixture being too rich.

9 If the insulator nose is covered with light tan

24.1c . . . and unclip the wiring harness

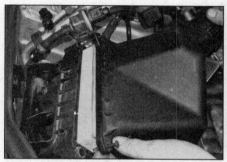

24.3b . . . and pull the cover from the housing

to greyish-brown deposits, then the mixture is correct and it is likely that the engine is in good condition.

10 The spark plug electrode gap is of considerable importance as, if it is too large or too small, the size of the spark and its

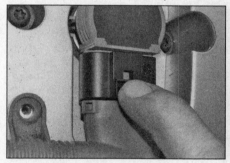

25.3a Push the connector towards the coil, depress the catch . . .

25.4 If the coils are difficult to move, lever under the thicker rib at the top of the coil

24.3a Undo the air cleaner cover screws (arrowed) . . .

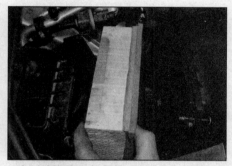

24.4 Lift the air filter element from the housing

efficiency will be seriously impaired. On engines fitted with multi-electrode spark plugs, it is recommended that the plugs are renewed rather attempting to adjust the gaps. With other spark plugs, the gap should be set to the value given by the manufacturer.

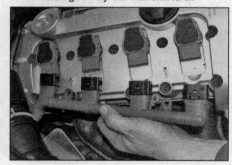

25.3b . . . and disconnect them

25.6 Unscrew the spark plugs using a spark plug socket

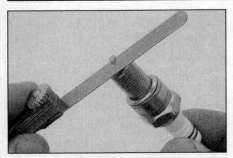

25.11a If single electrode plugs are being fitted, check the electrode gap using a feeler gauge . . .

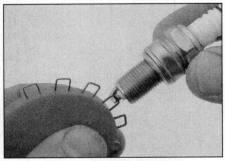

25.11b . . . or a wire gauge . . .

25.11c . . . and if necessary, adjust the gap by bending the electrode

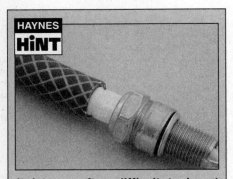

HAYNES HINT

It is very often difficult to insert spark plugs into their holes without cross-threading them. To avoid this possibility, fit a short length of rubber hose over the end of the spark plug. The flexible hose acts as a universal joint to help align the plug with the plug thread, the hose will slip on the spark plug, preventing thread damage to the aluminium cylinder head.

11 To set the gap, measure it with a feeler blade and then bend open, or closed, the outer plug electrode until the correct gap is achieved. The centre electrode should never be bent, as this may crack the insulator and cause plug failure, if nothing worse. If using feeler blades, the gap is correct when the appropriate-size blade is a firm sliding fit **(see illustrations)**.

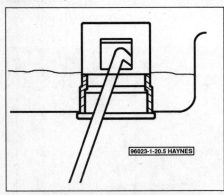

```
96023-1-20.5 HAYNES
```

28.5 The nozzle of the tool being used to add fluid must pass through the window in the deflector cap

12 Special spark plug electrode gap adjusting tools are available from most motor accessory shops, or from some spark plug manufacturers.
13 Before fitting the spark plugs, check that the threaded connector sleeves are tight, and that the plug exterior surfaces and threads are clean. It's often difficult to screw in new spark plugs without cross-threading them – this can be avoided using a piece of rubber hose **(see Haynes Hint)**.
14 Remove the rubber hose (if used), and tighten the plug to the specified torque using the spark plug socket and a torque wrench. Refit the remaining spark plugs in the same manner.
15 Refit the ignition coils, and reconnect their wiring plugs. Refit the coil's harness retaining bolts where applicable.
16 Refit the engine top cover.

26 Auxiliary drivebelt check and renewal

1 Refer to Section 8 for the checking procedure. If a drivebelt requires renewal, refer to Chapter 2A or 2B for the removal and refitting procedure.

27 Power steering hydraulic fluid level check

1 Refer to Chapter 10.

28 Automatic/Multitronic transmission fluid renewal

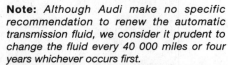

Note: *Although Audi make no specific recommendation to renew the automatic transmission fluid, we consider it prudent to change the fluid every 40 000 miles or four years whichever occurs first.*
1 Apply the handbrake, then jack up the front of the vehicle and support it on axle stands (see Jacking and vehicle support). Remove the transmission undershield (where fitted).
Note: *For an accurate fluid level check, Audi*

technicians use an electronic tester which is plugged into the transmission electronic system, and which determines that the temperature of the fluid is between 35 and 40°C. In view of this, it is recommended that the vehicle is taken to an Audi dealer to have the work done. The following procedure is given on the understanding that the level is checked by an Audi dealer on completion.
2 Note that the transmission must be refilled from below the vehicle, so make sure that the vehicle is supported in a level position.

Automatic transmission

3 Position a suitable container beneath the transmission. Wipe clean the pan, then unscrew the drain plug located on the right-hand side of the pan. Allow the fluid to drain into the container.
4 Fit a new seal on the drain plug and tighten to the specified torque.
5 Unscrew the inspection plug at the rear of the pan, and add fluid until it runs out of the hole **(see illustration)**.
6 With P selected, run the engine at idling speed until it reaches normal temperature. If necessary add more fluid until it runs out of the inspection hole.
7 Apply the footbrake pedal, then select each position with the selector lever, pausing for about 3 seconds in each position. Return the selector to position P.
8 At this stage, the Audi technician connects the tester to confirm that the fluid temperature is between 35 and 40°C. **Note:** *If the fluid level is checked when the temperature is too low, overfilling will occur. If the fluid level is checked when the temperature is too high, underfilling will occur.*
9 With the engine still running at idle speed, allow any excess fluid to run out of the overflow pipe.
10 Switch off the engine, then refit the inspection plug together with a new seal, and tighten to the specified torque.
11 Refit the engine/transmission undershield, and lower the vehicle to the ground.

Multitronic transmission

12 The refilling of this transmission requires specialist equipment, to overfill the casing and purge any air from the internals. Running the engine without purging the system could cause severe damage to the transmission. For this reason, we recommend entrusting this task to an Audi dealer or suitably-equipped repairer.

29 Automatic/Multitronic transmission final drive oil level check

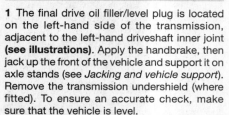

1 The final drive oil filler/level plug is located on the left-hand side of the transmission, adjacent to the left-hand driveshaft inner joint (see illustrations). Apply the handbrake, then jack up the front of the vehicle and support it on axle stands (see *Jacking and vehicle support*). Remove the transmission undershield (where fitted). To ensure an accurate check, make sure that the vehicle is level.
2 Unscrew and remove the filler/level plug. On automatic transmissions, the oil level must be up to the bottom lip of the filler hole, whilst on Multitronic transmissions, the oil must be 8.5 mm below the hole. If necessary, add the specified oil through the filler/level hole. If the level requires constant topping-up, check for leaks and repair.
3 Examine the sealing ring and renew if necessary, then refit the plug and tighten to the specified torque.
4 Refit the undershield and lower the vehicle to the ground.

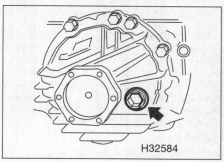

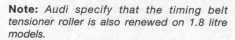

29.1a On automatic transmissions, the final drive filler/level plug is located on the left-hand side (arrowed)

30 Timing belt check and renewal

Note: *Audi specify that the timing belt tensioner roller is also renewed on 1.8 litre models.*

Inspection

1 Release the clips and remove the upper timing belt cover (refer to Chapter 2A or 2B).
2 Using a spanner or socket on the crankshaft pulley bolt, turn the engine slowly in a clockwise direction. **Do not** turn the engine on the camshaft bolt.

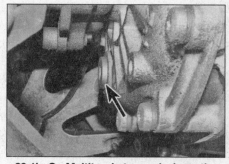

29.1b On Multitronic transmissions, the final drive filler/level plug is on the left-hand side (arrowed)

3 Check the complete length of the timing belt for signs of cracking, tooth separation, fraying, side glazing, and oil or grease contamination. Use a torch and mirror to check the underside of the belt.
4 If there is any evidence of wear or damage as described in the last paragraph, the timing belt **must** be renewed. A broken belt will cause major damage to the engine.
5 After making the check, refit the upper timing belt cover and remove the spanner/socket from the crankshaft pulley bolt.

Renewal

6 Refer to Chapter 2A or 2B for details.

Every 2 years

31 Brake (and clutch) fluid renewal

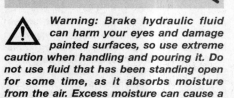

⚠ *Warning: Brake hydraulic fluid can harm your eyes and damage painted surfaces, so use extreme caution when handling and pouring it. Do not use fluid that has been standing open for some time, as it absorbs moisture from the air. Excess moisture can cause a dangerous loss of braking effectiveness.*

1 The procedure is similar to that for the bleeding of the hydraulic system as described in Chapter 9, except that the brake fluid reservoir should be emptied by syphoning, using a clean poultry baster or similar before starting, and allowance should be made for the old fluid to be expelled when bleeding a section of the circuit. Since the clutch hydraulic system on manual gearbox models also uses fluid from the brake system reservoir, it should also be bled at the same time by referring to Chapter 6, Section 2.
2 Working as described in Chapter 9, open the first bleed screw in the sequence, and pump the brake pedal gently until nearly all the old fluid has been emptied from the master cylinder reservoir.
3 Top-up to the MAX level with new fluid, and continue pumping until only the new fluid

remains in the reservoir, and new fluid can be seen emerging from the bleed screw. Tighten the screw, and top the reservoir level up to the MAX level line.
4 Work through all the remaining bleed screws in the sequence until new fluid can be seen at all of them. Be careful to keep the master cylinder reservoir topped-up to above the MIN level at all times, or air may enter the system and greatly increase the length of the task.
5 When the operation is complete, check that all bleed screws are securely tightened, and that their dust caps are refitted. Wash off all traces of spilt fluid, and recheck the master cylinder reservoir fluid level.
6 On models with a manual gearbox, once the brake fluid has been changed the clutch fluid should also be renewed. Referring to Chapter 6, bleed the clutch until new fluid is seen to be emerging from the slave cylinder bleed screw, keeping the master cylinder fluid level above the MIN level line at all times to prevent air entering the system. Once the new fluid emerges, securely tighten the bleed screw then disconnect and remove the bleeding equipment. Securely refit the dust cap then wash off all traces of spilt fluid.
7 On all models, ensure the master cylinder fluid level is correct (see *Weekly checks*) and thoroughly check the operation of the brakes and (where necessary) clutch before taking the car on the road.

32 Coolant renewal

Note: *This work is not included in the Audi schedule and should not be required if the recommended Audi G12 Plus LongLife coolant antifreeze/inhibitor is used. However, if standard antifreeze/inhibitor is used, the work should be carried out at the recommended interval.*

⚠ *Warning: Wait until the engine is cold before starting this procedure. Do not allow antifreeze to come in contact with your skin, or with the painted surfaces of the vehicle. Rinse off spills immediately with plenty of water. Never leave antifreeze lying around in an open container, or in a puddle in the driveway or on the garage floor. Children and pets are attracted by its sweet smell, but antifreeze can be fatal if ingested.*

Cooling system draining

1 With the engine completely cold, cover the expansion tank cap with a wad of rag, and slowly turn the cap anti-clockwise to relieve the pressure in the cooling system (a hissing sound will normally be heard). Wait until any pressure remaining in the system is released, then continue to turn the cap until it can be removed.

32.2 Slacken the drain plug in the lower left-hand radiator hose stub

2 Release the fasteners and remove the engine undershield. Some models are equipped with a drain plug in the radiator bottom hose, whilst on others, it's necessary to remove the hose-mounted temperature sensor. Position a suitable container beneath the radiator bottom hose, then pull out the retaining clip and ease the temperature sensor from the radiator hose, or undo the drain plug as applicable **(see illustration)**. Allow the coolant to drain into the container.

3 If the coolant has been drained for a reason other than renewal, then provided it is clean, it can be re-used, but this is not recommended.

4 Once all the coolant has drained, refit the sensor ensuring the retaining clip is properly seated, or tighten the drain plug as applicable.

Cooling system flushing

5 If coolant renewal has been neglected, or if the antifreeze mixture has become diluted, then in time, the cooling system may gradually lose efficiency, as the coolant passages become restricted due to rust, scale deposits, and other sediment. Flushing the system clean can restore the cooling system efficiency.

6 The radiator should be flushed independently of the engine, to avoid unnecessary contamination.

Radiator flushing

7 To flush the radiator, disconnect the top and bottom hoses and any other relevant hoses from the radiator, with reference to Chapter 3.

8 Insert a garden hose into the radiator top inlet. Direct a flow of clean water through the radiator, and continue flushing until clean

water emerges from the radiator bottom outlet.

9 If after a reasonable period, the water still does not run clear, the radiator can be flushed with a good proprietary cooling system cleaning agent. It is important that their manufacturer's instructions are followed carefully. If the contamination is particularly bad, insert the hose in the radiator bottom outlet, and reverse-flush the radiator.

Engine flushing

10 To flush the engine, remove the thermostat as described in Chapter 3, then temporarily refit the thermostat cover.

11 With the top and bottom hoses disconnected from the radiator, insert a garden hose into the radiator top hose. Direct a clean flow of water through the engine, and continue flushing until clean water emerges from the radiator bottom hose.

12 On completion of flushing, refit the thermostat and reconnect the hoses with reference to Chapter 3.

Cooling system filling

13 Before attempting to fill the cooling system, make sure that all hoses and clips are in good condition, and that the clips/connections are secure. Note that an antifreeze mixture must be used all year round, to prevent corrosion of the engine components (see following sub-Section).

14 Slacken the clip and withdraw the heater unit supply hose from its bulkhead stub **(see illustration)** until the bleed hole at the top of the hose is clear of the surface of the stub; do not disconnect the hose from the stub completely. Some models are also equipped with a bleed screw in the top coolant pipe **(see illustration)**.

15 Remove the securing screws and detach the expansion tank from the engine compartment. Raise it approximately 100 mm above the engine compartment and support it there on a block of wood or using a length of wire.

16 Remove the expansion tank filler cap, and fill the system by slowly pouring the coolant into the expansion tank to prevent airlocks from forming.

17 If the coolant is being renewed, begin by pouring in a couple of litres of water, followed

by the correct quantity of antifreeze, then top-up with more water.

18 Continue filling until coolant starts to run from the bleed hole in the heater hose. When this happens, refit the hose and tighten the clip securely.

19 Once the level in the expansion tank starts to rise, squeeze the radiator top and bottom hoses to help expel any trapped air in the system. Once all the air is expelled, top-up the coolant level to the MAX mark, refit the expansion tank cap, then refit the expansion tank to the bodywork.

20 Start the engine and run it at a fast idle for about three minutes. After this, allow the engine to idle normally until the bottom hose becomes hot.

21 Check for leaks, particularly around disturbed components. Check the coolant level in the expansion tank, and top-up if necessary. Note that the system must be cold before an accurate level is indicated in the expansion tank. If the expansion tank cap is removed while the engine is still warm, cover the cap with a thick cloth, and unscrew the cap slowly to gradually relieve the system pressure (a hissing sound will normally be heard). Wait until any pressure remaining in the system is released, then continue to turn the cap until it can be removed. Never remove the cap when the engine is still hot.

Antifreeze mixture

Caution: Audi specify the use of G12 Plus antifreeze (purple in colour). DO NOT mix this with any other type of antifreeze, as severe engine damage may result. If the coolant visible in the expansion tank is brown in colour, then the cooling system may have been topped-up with coolant containing the wrong type of antifreeze. If you are unsure of the type of antifreeze used, or if you suspect that mixing may have occurred, the best course of action is to drain, flush and refill the cooling system.

22 If the recommended Audi coolant is not being used, the antifreeze should always be renewed at the specified intervals. This is necessary not only to maintain the antifreeze properties, but also to prevent corrosion which would otherwise occur as the corrosion inhibitors become progressively less effective.

23 The quantity of coolant and levels of protection are indicated in the Specifications.

24 Before adding antifreeze, the cooling system should be completely drained, preferably flushed, and all hoses checked for condition and security.

25 After filling with antifreeze, a label should be attached to the expansion tank, stating the type and concentration of antifreeze used, and the date installed. Any subsequent topping-up should be made with the same type and concentration of antifreeze.

26 Do not use engine antifreeze in the windscreen/tailgate/headlight washer system, as it will cause damage to the vehicle paintwork.

32.14a Slide the hose forwards until the bleed hole (arrowed) is clear of the surface of the bulkhead stub

32.14b Some models are equipped with a bleed screw in the top coolant pipe (arrowed)

Chapter 1 Part B:
Routine maintenance and servicing – diesel models

Contents

Section number

Air filter element renewal 24
Airbag unit check 19
Antifreeze check.. 9
Automatic/Multitronic transmission final drive oil level check 29
Automatic/Multitronic transmission fluid renewal 28
Auxiliary drivebelt check and renewal 26
Auxiliary drivebelt check.................................... 8
Battery check 17
Brake (and clutch) fluid renewal 31
Brake hydraulic circuit check 10
Brake pad check 4
Coolant renewal 32
Driveshaft gaiter check..................................... 15
Engine management self-diagnosis memory fault check 21
Engine oil and filter renewal 3
Exhaust system check...................................... 6

Section number

Fuel filter renewal 25
Headlight beam adjustment 11
Hinge and lock lubrication 18
Hose and fluid leak check 7
Introduction 1
Manual gearbox oil level check 13
Pollen filter element renewal 12
Power steering hydraulic fluid level check 27
Regular maintenance 2
Resetting the service interval display......................... 5
Road test and exhaust emissions check 23
Steering and suspension check.............................. 16
Sunroof check and lubrication 22
Timing belt and tensioning roller renewal..................... 30
Underbody protection check 14
Windscreen/tailgate/headlight washer system check 20

Degrees of difficulty

| **Easy,** suitable for novice with little experience | | **Fairly easy,** suitable for beginner with some experience | 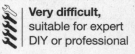 | **Fairly difficult,** suitable for competent DIY mechanic | | **Difficult,** suitable for experienced DIY mechanic | | **Very difficult,** suitable for expert DIY or professional | |

Lubricants and fluids................................. Refer to the end of *Weekly checks* on page 0•17

Capacities

Engine oil (including filter)
All models .... 4.5 litres

Cooling system
All models..................................... 6.0 litres

Transmission
Manual gearbox:
    012/01W.. 2.25 litres
    01E/0A1/01X/0A1............................... 2.5 litres
Automatic transmission fluid:
    Initial filling .... 9.0 litres
    Fluid change.................................. 2.6 litres
    Final drive.................................... 0.75 litres
Multitronic transmission:
    Initial filling .... 7.5 litres (approximately)
    Fluid change.................................. 4.7 litres (approximately)
    Final drive.................................... 0.75 litres

Fuel tank
All models..................................... 70 litres (approximately)

Washer reservoirs
All models..................................... 4.8 litres

Engine
Timing belt wear limit .... 22.0 mm wide

Cooling system
Antifreeze mixture:
    40% antifreeze .... Protection down to -25°C
    50% antifreeze .... Protection down to -35°C
Note: *Refer to antifreeze manufacturer for latest recommendations.*

Brakes
Front brake pad friction material minimum thickness .... 2.0 mm
Rear brake pad friction material minimum thickness............... 2.0 mm

Auxiliary drivebelt
Tension adjustment:
    Main drivebelt.. Automatically adjusted
    Air conditioning compressor drivebelt .... Apply a torque of 25 Nm to the hexagon on the tensioner body

Torque wrench settings

	Nm	lbf ft
Automatic transmission:		
Drain plug..	40	30
Inspection plug......................................	80	59
Final drive oil filler/level plug........................	25	18
Fuel filter top centre bolt (pre-01/2002 models).................	8	6
Manual transmission filler/level plug:		
5-speed	25	18
6-speed	40	30
Multitronic transmission:		
Drain plug...	24	18
Inspection plug......................................	20	15
Final drive oil filler/level plug........................	20	15
Oil filter cap	25	18
Power steering pump mounting...........................	25	18
Roadwheel bolts..	120	89
Sump drain plug.......................................	30	22

The maintenance intervals in this manual are provided with the assumption that you, not the dealer, will be carrying out the work. These are the minimum intervals recommended by us for vehicles driven daily. If you wish to keep your vehicle in peak condition at all times, you may wish to perform some of these procedures more often. We encourage frequent maintenance, since it enhances the efficiency, performance and resale value of your vehicle.

When the vehicle is new, it should be serviced by a dealer service department (or other workshop recognised by the vehicle manufacturer as providing the same standard of service) in order to preserve the warranty. The vehicle manufacturer may reject warranty claims if you are unable to prove that servicing has been carried out as and when specified, using only original equipment parts or parts certified to be of equivalent quality.

All models are equipped with a service interval display indicator in the instrument panel. Every time the engine is started the panel will illuminate for approximately 20 seconds with service information. With the standard non-variable display, the service intervals are in accordance with specific distances and time periods. With the LongLife display, the service interval is variable according to the number of starts, length of journeys, vehicle speeds, brake pad wear, bonnet opening frequency, fuel consumption, oil level and oil temperature, however the vehicle must be serviced at least every two years. At a distance of 2000 miles before the next service is due, 'Service in 2000 miles' will appear at the bottom of the speedometer, and this figure will reduce in steps of 100 units as the vehicle is used. Once the service interval has been reached, the display will flash 'Service' or 'Service Now'. Note that if the variable (LongLife) service interval is being used, the engine must only be filled with the recommended LongLife engine oil (see Lubricants and fluids).

After completing a service, Audi technicians use a special instrument to reset the service display to the next service interval, and a print-out is put in the vehicle service record. The display can be reset by the owner as described in Section 5, but note that for models using the 'LongLife' interval, the procedure will automatically reset the display to the fixed non-variable interval. To have the display reset to the 'variable' (LongLife) interval, it is necessary to take the vehicle to an Audi dealer or suitably-equipped specialist who will use a special instrument to encode the on-board computer.

Every 250 miles or weekly
- [ ] Refer to *Weekly checks*

OIL on display
- [ ] Renew the engine oil and filter (Section 3)

Note: *Frequent oil and filter changes are good for the engine. We recommend changing the oil at least once a year.*
- [ ] Check the front and rear brake pad thickness (Section 4)
- [ ] Reset the service interval display (Section 5)

01 on display
In addition to the items listed above, carry out the following:
- [ ] Check the condition of the exhaust system and its mountings (Section 6)
- [ ] Check all underbonnet components and hoses for fluid and oil leaks (Section 7)
- [ ] Check the condition of the auxiliary drivebelt (Section 8)
- [ ] Check the coolant antifreeze concentration (Section 9)
- [ ] Check the brake hydraulic circuit for leaks and damage (Section 10)
- [ ] Check the headlight beam adjustment (Section 11)
- [ ] Renew the pollen filter element (Section 12)
- [ ] Check the manual gearbox oil level (Section 13)
- [ ] Check the underbody protection for damage (Section 14)
- [ ] Check the condition of the driveshaft gaiters (Section 15)
- [ ] Check the steering and suspension components for condition and security (Section 16)
- [ ] Check the battery condition, security and electrolyte level (Section 17)
- [ ] Lubricate all hinges and locks (Section 18)
- [ ] Check the condition of the airbag unit(s) (Section 19)
- [ ] Check the operation of the windscreen/tailgate/headlight washer system(s) (as applicable) (Section 20)

01 on display (continued)
- [ ] Check the engine management self-diagnosis memory for faults (Section 21)
- [ ] Check the operation of the sunroof and lubricate the guide rails (Section 22)
- [ ] Carry out a road test and check exhaust emissions (Section 23)

Every 40 000 miles or 4 years, whichever comes first
Note: *Many dealers perform these tasks at every second 01 service.*
- [ ] Renew the air filter element (Section 24)
- [ ] Renew the fuel filter (Section 25)
- [ ] Check and renewal of the auxiliary drivebelt (Section 26)
- [ ] Check the power steering hydraulic fluid level (Section 27)
- [ ] Renew the automatic/Multitronic transmission fluid (Section 28)
- [ ] Check the automatic/Multitronic transmission final drive oil level (Section 29)

Every 60 000 miles
- [ ] Renew the timing belt and tensioning roller (Section 30)

Every 2 years
- [ ] Renew the brake (and clutch) fluid (Section 31)
- [ ] Renew the coolant* (Section 32)

* Note: *This work is not included in the Audi schedule and should not be required if the recommended Audi G12 Plus LongLife coolant antifreeze/inhibitor is used.*

Underbonnet view

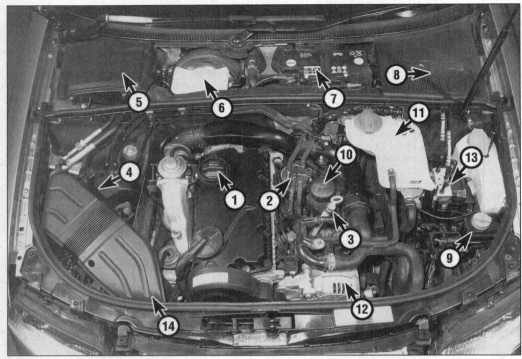

1   Engine oil filter cap
2   Fuel filter
3   Engine oil level dipstick
4   Air filter
5   ECM box
6   Brake/clutch fluid
     reservoir
7   Battery
8   Pollen filter
9   Power steering fluid
     reservoir
10   Oil filter
11   Coolant reservoir
12   Alternator
13   ABS modulator
14   Air intake ducting

Front underbody view

1   Exhaust front downpipe
2   Brake caliper
3   Guide link
4   Engine oil drain plug
5   Coolant drain tap
6   Anti-roll bar
7   Track control link
8   Driveshaft
9   Receiver/drier
10   Subframe
11   Intercooler
12   Air conditioning
     compressor
13   Auxiliary drivebelt

Rear underbody view

1   *Trapezium link*
2   *Handbrake cable*
3   *Fuel tank*
4   *Rear silencer*
5   *Subframe*
6   *Anti-roll bar*
7   *Shock absorber*
8   *Underbody cover trim*

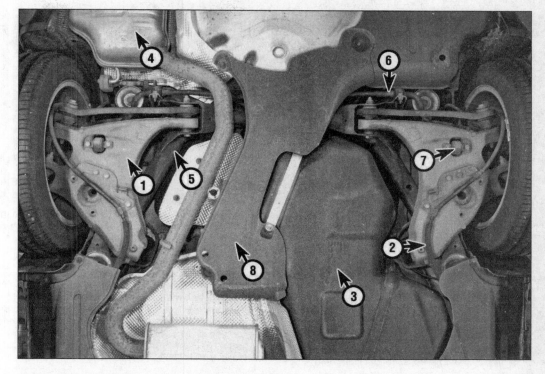

Maintenance procedures

1   Introduction

This Chapter is designed to help the home mechanic maintain his/her vehicle for safety, economy, long life and peak performance.

The Chapter contains a master maintenance schedule, followed by Sections dealing specifically with each task in the schedule. Visual checks, adjustments, component renewal and other helpful items are included. Refer to the accompanying illustrations of the engine compartment and the underside of the vehicle for the locations of the various components.

Servicing your vehicle will provide a planned maintenance programme, which should result in a long and reliable service life. This is a comprehensive plan, so maintaining some items but not others will not produce the same results.

As you service your vehicle, you will discover that many of the procedures can – and should – be grouped together, because of the particular procedure being performed, or because of the proximity of two otherwise unrelated components to one another. For example, if the vehicle is raised for any reason, the exhaust can be inspected at the same time as the suspension and steering components.

The first step in this maintenance programme is to prepare yourself before the actual work begins. Read through all the Sections relevant to the work to be carried out, then make a list and gather all the parts and tools required. If a problem is encountered, seek advice from a parts specialist, or a dealer service department.

2   Regular maintenance

1 If, from the time the vehicle is new, the routine maintenance schedule is followed closely, and frequent checks are made of fluid levels and high-wear items, as suggested throughout this manual, the engine will be kept in relatively good running condition, and the need for additional work will be minimised.

2 It is possible that there will be times when the engine is running poorly due to the lack of regular maintenance. This is even more likely if a used vehicle, which has not received regular and frequent maintenance checks, is purchased. In such cases, additional work may need to be carried out, outside of the regular maintenance intervals.

3 If engine wear is suspected, a compression test (refer to the relevant Part of Chapter 2C) will provide valuable information regarding the overall performance of the main internal components. Such a test can be used as a basis to decide on the extent of the work to be carried out. If, for example, a compression test indicates serious internal engine wear, conventional maintenance as described in this Chapter will not greatly improve the performance of the engine, and may prove a waste of time and money, unless extensive overhaul work is carried out first.

4 The following series of operations are those most often required to improve the performance of a generally poor-running engine:

Primary operations

a) *Clean, inspect and test the battery (See 'Weekly checks').*
b) *Check all the engine-related fluids (See 'Weekly checks').*
c) *Check the condition and tension of the auxiliary drivebelt (Section 8).*
d) *Check the condition of the air filter, and renew if necessary (Section 24).*
e) *Check the condition of all hoses, and check for fluid leaks (Section 7).*

5 If the above operations do not prove fully effective, carry out the following secondary operations:

Secondary operations

All items listed under *Primary operations*, plus the following:

a) *Check the charging system (see Chapter 5A).*
b) *Check the preheating system (see Chapter 5C).*
c) *Renew the fuel filter (Section 25) and check the fuel system (see Chapter 4C).*

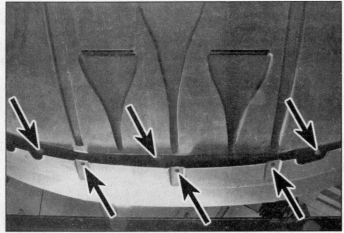

3.2a The front edge of the engine undershield is secured by 3 screws to the front bumper, and 3 screws to the lock carrier (arrowed)

3.2b Engine undershield-to-transmission undershield fasteners (arrowed)

OIL on display

3 Engine oil and filter renewal

1 Frequent oil and filter changes are the most important preventative maintenance procedures which can be undertaken by the DIY owner. As engine oil ages, it becomes diluted and contaminated, which leads to premature engine wear.

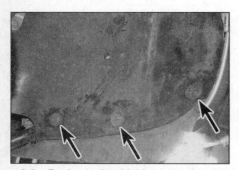

3.2c Engine undershield-to-wheel arch liner fasteners (arrowed)

3.3 If the special tool is not available, use a strap wrench to unscrew the oil filter cap

2 Before starting this procedure, gather all the necessary tools and materials. Also make sure that you have plenty of clean rags and newspapers handy, to mop-up any spills. Ideally, the engine oil should be warm, as it will drain better, and more built-up sludge will be removed with it. Take care, however, not to touch the exhaust or any other hot parts of the engine when working under the vehicle. To avoid any possibility of scalding, and to protect yourself from possible skin irritants and other harmful contaminants in used engine oils, it is advisable to wear gloves when carrying out this work. Access to the underside of the vehicle will be greatly improved if it can be raised on a lift, driven onto ramps, or jacked up and supported on axle stands (see *Jacking and vehicle support*). Whichever method is chosen, make sure that the vehicle remains level, or if it is at an angle, that the drain plug is at the lowest point. Undo the retaining fasteners and remove the engine undershield, then prise out the caps, undo the nuts and remove the engine top cover where applicable (**see illustrations**).

3 Slacken the oil filter housing cap (located

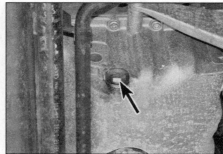

3.4 Engine oil sump drain plug (arrowed)

to the left of the cylinder head) to allow the oil within to drain into the sump. Although there is a special Audi tool to undo the cap, a strap wrench is a suitable alternative (**see illustration**). Place absorbent cloths around the filter housing to catch any spilt oil.

4 Working underneath the vehicle, slacken the sump drain plug about half a turn. Position the draining container under the drain plug, then remove the plug completely (**see illustration and Haynes Hint**). Recover the sealing ring from the drain plug.

5 Allow some time for the old oil to drain, noting that it may be necessary to reposition the container as the oil flow slows to a trickle.

6 After all the oil has drained, wipe off the drain plug with a clean rag, and fit a new sealing washer. Clean the area around the drain plug opening, and refit the plug. Tighten the plug securely.

7 Completely unscrew the oil filter

HAYNES HiNT

Keep the drain plug pressed into the sump while unscrewing it by hand the last couple of turns. As the plug releases, move it away sharply so the stream of oil issuing from the sump runs into the container, not up your sleeve.

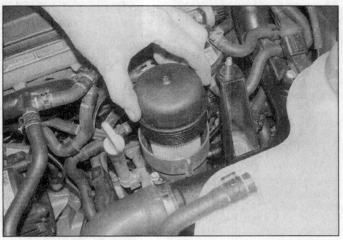

3.7a Completely unscrew the oil filter cap, and remove the filter element

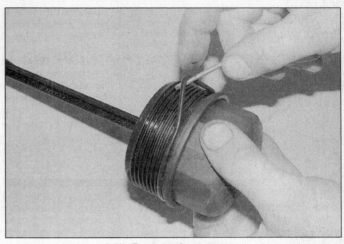

3.7b Remove the upper . . .

housing cap. Lift the filter element from the housing, and discard the two O-rings **(see illustrations)**.

8 Wipe clean the inside of the oil filter housing and cap. Insert the new filter element into the housing. Note that the filter element is marked TOP on one end **(see illustration)**.

9 Fit the new O-rings, screw the cap into the housing, and tighten it to the specified torque.

10 Remove the old oil and all tools from under the car then refit the undershield and lower the car to the ground. Also refit the engine top cover.

11 Remove the dipstick, then unscrew the oil filler cap from the cylinder head cover. Fill the engine, using the correct grade and type of oil (see *Lubricants and fluids*). An oil can spout or funnel may help to reduce spillage. Pour in half the specified quantity of oil first, then wait a few minutes for the oil to run to the sump (see *Weekly checks*). Continue adding oil a small quantity at a time until the level is up to the maximum mark on the dipstick. Refit the filler cap.

12 Start the engine and run it for a few minutes; check for leaks around the oil filter cap and the sump drain plug. Note that there may be a few seconds delay before the oil pressure warning light goes out when the engine is started, as the oil circulates through the engine oil galleries and the new oil filter (where fitted) before the pressure builds-up.

⚠️ **Warning: Do not increase the engine speed above idling while the oil pressure light is illuminated, as considerable damage can be caused to the turbocharger.**

13 Switch off the engine, and wait a few minutes for the oil to settle in the sump once more. With the new oil circulated and the filter completely full, recheck the level on the dipstick, and add more oil as necessary.

14 Dispose of the used engine oil safely, with reference to *General repair procedures* in the *Reference* chapter of this manual.

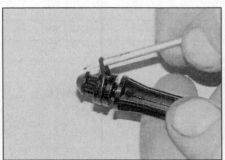
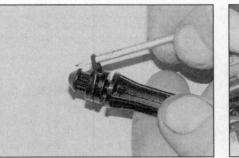

3.7c . . . and lower O-ring seals

4 Brake pad check

1 On some models, the outer brake pads can be checked without removing the wheels, by observing the brake pads through the holes in the wheels **(see illustration)**. If necessary, remove the wheel trim. The thickness of the pad lining must not be less than the dimension given in the Specifications.

2 If the outer pads are worn near their limits, it is worthwhile checking the inner pads as

4.1 The outer brake pads can be observed through the holes in the wheels

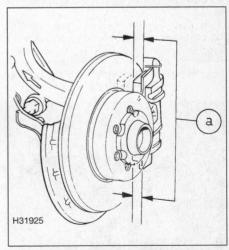

3.8 Fit the oil filter element with the end marked TOP uppermost

well. Apply the handbrake then jack up vehicle and support it on axle stands (see *Jacking and vehicle support*). Remove the roadwheels.

3 Use a steel rule to check the thickness of the brake pads (excluding the backing plate), and compare with the minimum thickness given in the Specifications **(see illustration)**.

H31925

4.3 The thickness (a) of the brake pads friction material must not be less than the specified amount

5.2 Service indicator call up button (arrowed)

4 For a comprehensive check, the brake pads should be removed and cleaned. The operation of the caliper can then also be checked, and the condition of the brake disc itself can be fully examined on both sides. Refer to Chapter 9.

5 If any pad's friction material is worn to the specified minimum thickness or less, *all four pads at the front or rear, as applicable, must be renewed as a set.*

6 On completion of the check, refit the road-wheels and lower the vehicle to the ground.

5 Resetting the service interval display

1 After all necessary maintenance work has been completed, the service interval display must be reset. Audi technicians use a special dedicated instrument to do this, and a print-out is then put in the vehicle service record. It is possible for the owner to reset the display as described in the following paragraphs, but note that the procedure will automatically reset the display to a 10 000 mile interval. To continue with the 'variable' intervals which take into consideration the number of starts, length of journeys, vehicle speeds, brake pad wear, bonnet opening frequency, fuel consumption, oil level and oil temperature, the display must be reset by an Audi dealership using the special dedicated instrument.

2 To reset the standard display manually, switch off the ignition, then press and hold down the service indicator call up button beneath the speedometer **(see illustration)**.

3 Release the button. The display will now show 'SERVICE IN ???? miles' or 'SERVICE!'. Now press and hold the trip reset button below the speedometer until the display is reset to 'SERVICE IN ---- km' or 'SERVICE!'. Switch off the ignition.

01 on display

6 Exhaust system check

1 With the engine cold (at least an hour after the vehicle has been driven), check the complete exhaust system from the engine to the end of the tailpipe. The exhaust system is most easily checked with the vehicle raised on a hoist, or suitably supported on axle stands, so that the exhaust components are readily visible and accessible (see *Jacking and vehicle support*).

2 Check the exhaust pipes and connections for evidence of leaks, severe corrosion and damage. Make sure that all brackets and mountings are in good condition, and that all relevant nuts and bolts are tight **(see illustration)**. Leakage at any of the joints or in other parts of the system will usually show up as a black sooty stain in the vicinity of the leak.

3 Rattles and other noises can often be traced to the exhaust system, especially the brackets and mountings. Try to move the pipes and silencers. If the components are able to come into contact with the body or suspension parts, secure the system with new

6.2 Check the condition of the exhaust rubber mountings

mountings. Otherwise separate the joints (if possible) and twist the pipes as necessary to provide additional clearance.

7 Hose and fluid leak check

1 Visually inspect the engine joint faces, gaskets and seals for any signs of water or oil leaks. Pay particular attention to the areas around the camshaft cover, cylinder head, oil filter and sump joint faces. Bear in mind that, over a period of time, some very slight seepage from these areas is to be expected – what you are really looking for is any indication of a serious leak. Should a leak be found, renew the offending gasket or oil seal by referring to the appropriate Chapters in this manual.

2 Also check the security and condition of all the engine-related pipes and hoses. Ensure that all cable-ties or securing clips are in place and in good condition. Clips which are broken or missing can lead to chafing of the hoses, pipes or wiring, which could cause more serious problems in the future.

3 Carefully check the radiator hoses and heater hoses along their entire length. Renew any hose which is cracked, swollen or deteriorated. Cracks will show up better if the hose is squeezed. Pay close attention to the hose clips that secure the hoses to the cooling system components. Hose clips can pinch and puncture hoses, resulting in cooling system leaks.

4 Inspect all the cooling system components (hoses, joint faces, etc) for leaks **(see Haynes Hint)**. Where any problems of this nature are found on system components, renew the component or gasket with reference to Chapter 3.

5 Where applicable, inspect the automatic transmission fluid cooler hoses for leaks or deterioration.

6 With the vehicle raised, inspect the petrol tank and filler neck for punctures, cracks and other damage. The connection between the filler neck and tank is especially critical. Sometimes a rubber filler neck or connecting hose will leak due to loose retaining clamps or deteriorated rubber.

7 Carefully check all rubber hoses and metal fuel lines leading away from the petrol tank. Check for loose connections, deteriorated hoses, crimped lines, and other damage. Pay particular attention to the vent pipes and hoses, which often loop up around the filler neck and can become blocked or crimped. Follow the lines to the front of the vehicle, carefully inspecting them all the way. Renew damaged sections as necessary.

8 From within the engine compartment, check the security of all fuel hose attachments and pipe unions, and inspect the fuel hoses and vacuum hoses for kinks, chafing and deterioration.

9 Where applicable, check the condition of the power steering fluid hoses and pipes.

HAYNES HINT

A leak in the cooling system will usually show up as white- or antifreeze-coloured deposits on the area adjoining the leak.

8.3 Check the underside of the auxiliary drivebelt with a mirror

11.2 Headlamp beam adjustment screws (arrowed)

8 Auxiliary drivebelt check

1 The main drivebelt drives the alternator, viscous coupling fan, and the power steering pump. Where air conditioning is fitted, a secondary drivebelt from the crankshaft pulley drives the air conditioning compressor.

2 For access to the drivebelts, apply the handbrake, then jack up the front of the vehicle and support it on axle stands (see *Jacking and vehicle support*). Remove the engine undershield, and remove the engine top cover as well **(see illustrations 3.2a, 3.2b, 3.2c, and 3.2d)**.

3 Examine the auxiliary drivebelts along their entire length for damage and wear in the form of cuts and abrasions, fraying and cracking. The use of a mirror and possibly an electric torch will help, and the engine may be turned with a spanner on the crankshaft pulley in order to observe all areas of the belt **(see illustration)**.

4 If a drivebelt requires renewal, refer to Chapter 2C for the removal, refitting and adjustment procedure.

9 Antifreeze check

1 The cooling system should be filled with the recommended G12 Plus antifreeze and corrosion protection fluid, which is designed to last the life of the vehicle. **Do not** mix this antifreeze with any other type apart from G11 or G12. **Note:** *If it is mixed with these other types, G12 Plus loses its 'filled for life' quality.* Over a period of time, the concentration of fluid may be reduced due to topping-up (this can be avoided

by topping-up with the correct antifreeze mixture – see Specifications) or fluid loss. If loss of coolant has been evident, it is important to make the necessary repair before adding fresh fluid.

2 With the engine **cold**, carefully remove the cap from the expansion tank. If the engine is not completely cold, place a cloth rag over the cap before removing it, and remove it slowly to allow any pressure to escape.

3 Antifreeze checkers (Hydrometers) are available from car accessory shops. Draw some coolant from the expansion tank into the hydrometer and follow the manufacturer's instructions.

4 If the concentration is incorrect, it will be necessary to either withdraw some coolant and add antifreeze, or alternatively drain the old coolant and add fresh coolant of the correct concentration (see Section 32).

10 Brake hydraulic circuit check

1 Check the entire brake hydraulic circuit for leaks and damage. Start by checking the master cylinder in the engine compartment. At the same time, check the vacuum servo unit and ABS units for signs of fluid leakage.

2 Raise the front and rear of the vehicle and support it securely on axle stands (see *Jacking and vehicle support*). Check the rigid hydraulic brake lines for corrosion and damage.

3 At the front of the vehicle, check that the flexible hydraulic hoses to the calipers are not twisted or chafing on any of the surrounding suspension components. Turn the steering on full lock to make this check. Also check that the hoses are not brittle or cracked.

4 Lower the vehicle to the ground after making the checks.

11 Headlight beam adjustment

Halogen headlamps

1 Accurate adjustment of the headlight beam is only possible using optical beam setting equipment, and this work should therefore be carried out by an Audi dealer or suitably-equipped workshop.

2 For reference, the headlights can be adjusted using the adjuster screws, accessible at the top of each light unit **(see illustration)**.

3 Some models are equipped with an electrically-operated headlight beam adjustment system which is controlled through the switch in the facia. On these models, ensure that the switch is set to the basic 0 position before adjusting the headlight aim.

Gas discharge headlights

4 The headlamp range is controlled dynamically by an electronic control unit which monitors the ride height of the vehicle by sensors fitted to the front and rear suspension. Beam adjustment can only be carried out using Audi test equipment.

12 Pollen filter element renewal

1 The pollen filter is located on the bulkhead, in front of the windscreen – on RHD models it is on the left-hand side, and on LHD models it is on the right-hand side.

2 Pull up the rubber weatherstrip then lift the plastic lid from the air inlet plenum chamber cover **(see illustrations)**.

3 Release the two retaining clips and lift the filter cover **(see illustrations)**.

12.2a Pull up the rubber weatherstrip (arrowed) . . .

12.2b . . . then pull the plenum chamber cover (arrowed) forwards

12.3a Release the retaining clips (arrowed) . . .

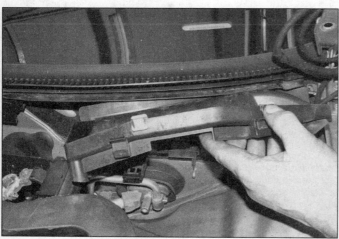

12.3b . . . then lift off the filter cover

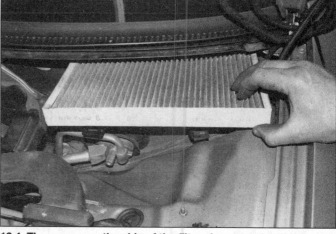

12.4 The arrows on the side of the filter element point downwards

4 Lift out the pollen filter element **(see illustration)**. Note the airflow arrows on the element. Remove the element from the frame.
5 Fit the frame to the new element and locate it in the plenum chamber cover, making sure that the airflow arrows are pointing downwards.
6 Close the plastic lid, however, make sure it is fitted correctly, otherwise water may enter the filter or heater assembly.

13 Manual gearbox oil level check

1 The oil filler/level plug is located on the left-hand side of the manual transmission, below the speedometer sender (where fitted), and on some models it may be concealed by a heat shield. The plug may be either of 17 mm Allen key type, or alternatively of multi-splined type **(see illustration)**.
2 Apply the handbrake, then jack up the front and rear of the vehicle and support it on axle stands (see *Jacking and vehicle support*). To ensure an accurate check, make sure that the vehicle is level.
3 Unscrew and remove the filler/level plug.
4 Using a length of wire bent 90°, measure how far the fluid level is below the bottom lip of the filler/level hole.

On 5-speed 012/01W/0A9 transmissions the level must be between 0 and 7 mm below the hole.
On 6-speed 01E/0A1 transmissions the level must be 4 ± 1 mm below the hole.
On 6-speed 01X transmissions the fluid must be level with the bottom of the hole.
5 If necessary, add the specified oil through the filler/level hole. If the level requires constant topping-up, check for leaks and repair.
6 Refit the plug and tighten to the specified torque, then lower the vehicle to the ground.

14 Underbody protection check

1 Raise and support the vehicle on axle stands (see *Jacking and vehicle support*). Using an electric torch or lead light, inspect the entire underside of the vehicle, paying particular attention to the wheel arches. Look for any damage to the flexible underbody coating, which may crack or flake off with age, leading to corrosion. Also check that the wheel arch liners are securely attached with any clips provided – if they come loose, dirt may get in behind the liners and defeat their purpose. If there is any damage to the underseal, or any

corrosion, it should be repaired before the damage gets too serious.

15 Driveshaft gaiter check

1 With the vehicle raised and securely supported on stands, slowly rotate the roadwheel. Inspect the condition of the outer constant velocity (CV) joint rubber gaiters, squeezing the gaiters to open out the folds. Check for signs of cracking, splits or deterioration of the rubber, which may

13.1 The gearbox oil filler/level plug may be a multi-splined security type, with a raised centre

allow the grease to escape, and lead to water and grit entry into the joint. Also check the security and condition of the retaining clips. Repeat these checks on the inner joints **(see illustration)**. If any damage or deterioration is found, the gaiters should be renewed (see Chapter 8).

2 At the same time, check the general condition of the CV joints themselves by first holding the driveshaft and attempting to rotate the wheel. Repeat this check by holding the inner joint and attempting to rotate the driveshaft. Any appreciable movement indicates wear in the joints, wear in the driveshaft splines, or a loose driveshaft retaining nut.

16 Steering and suspension check

1 Raise the front and rear of the vehicle, and securely support it on axle stands (see *Jacking and vehicle support*).

2 Visually inspect the track rod end balljoint dust cover, the lower front suspension balljoint dust cover, and the steering rack-and-pinion gaiters for splits, chafing or deterioration. Any wear of these components will cause loss of lubricant, together with dirt and water entry, resulting in rapid deterioration of the balljoints or steering gear.

3 Check the power steering fluid hoses for chafing or deterioration, and the pipe and hose unions for fluid leaks. Also check for signs of fluid leakage under pressure from the steering gear rubber gaiters, which would indicate failed fluid seals within the steering gear.

4 Grasp the roadwheel at the 12 o'clock and 6 o'clock positions, and try to rock it **(see illustration)**. Very slight free play may be felt, but if the movement is appreciable, further investigation is necessary to determine the source. Continue rocking the wheel while an assistant depresses the footbrake. If the movement is now eliminated or significantly reduced, it is likely that the hub bearings are at fault. If the free play is still evident with the footbrake depressed, then there is wear in the suspension joints or mountings.

5 Now grasp the wheel at the 9 o'clock and 3 o'clock positions, and try to rock it as before. Any movement felt now may again be caused by wear in the hub bearings or the steering track rod balljoints. If the inner or outer balljoint is worn, the visual movement will be obvious.

6 Using a large screwdriver or flat bar, check for wear in the suspension mounting bushes by levering between the relevant suspension component and its attachment point. Some movement is to be expected as the mountings are made of rubber, but excessive wear should be obvious. Also check the condition of any visible rubber bushes, looking for splits, cracks or contamination of the rubber.

7 With the car standing on its wheels, have

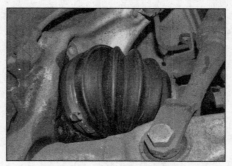

15.1 Check the condition of the rubber driveshaft gaiters

an assistant turn the steering wheel back-and-forth about an eighth of a turn each way. There should be very little, if any, lost movement between the steering wheel and roadwheels. If this is not the case, closely observe the joints and mountings previously described, but in addition, check the steering column universal joints for wear, and the rack-and-pinion steering gear itself.

8 Check for any signs of fluid leakage around the front suspension struts and rear shock absorber. Should any fluid be noticed, the suspension strut or shock absorber is defective internally, and should be renewed. **Note:** *Suspension struts/shock absorbers should always be renewed in pairs on the same axle to ensure correct vehicle handling.*

9 The efficiency of the suspension strut/shock absorber may be checked by bouncing the vehicle at each corner. Generally speaking, the body will return to its normal position and stop after being depressed. If it rises and returns on a rebound, the suspension strut/shock absorber is probably suspect. Examine also the suspension strut/shock absorber upper and lower mountings for any signs of wear.

17 Battery check

1 The battery is located beneath a cover (where fitted) at the rear of the engine compartment. Slide the cover in the direction of the arrows on the top of the cover and remove it.

16.4 Check for wear in the hub bearings by grasping the wheel and trying to rock it

2 Check that both battery terminals and all the fuse holder connections are securely attached and are free from corrosion.

3 Check the battery casing for signs of damage or cracking and check the battery retaining clamp bolt is securely tightened. If the battery casing is damaged in any way the battery must be renewed (see Chapter 5A).

4 If the vehicle is not fitted with a sealed-for-life maintenance-free battery, check the electrolyte level is between the MAX and MIN level markings on the battery casing. If topping-up is necessary, remove the battery (see Chapter 5A) from the vehicle then remove the cell caps/cover (as applicable). Using distilled water, top the electrolyte level of each cell up to the MAX level mark then securely refit the cell caps/cover. Ensure the battery has not been overfilled then refit the battery to the vehicle (see Chapter 5A).

5 On completion of the check, refit the cover.

18 Hinge and lock lubrication

1 Lubricate the hinges of the bonnet, doors and tailgate with a light general-purpose oil. Similarly, lubricate all latches, locks and lock strikers. At the same time, check the security and operation of all the locks, adjusting them if necessary (see Chapter 11).

2 Lightly lubricate the bonnet release mechanism and cable with a suitable grease.

19 Airbag unit check

1 Inspect the exterior condition of the airbag(s) for signs of damage or deterioration. If an airbag shows signs of damage, it must be renewed (see Chapter 12). Note that it is not permissible to attach any stickers to the surface of the airbag, as this may affect the deployment of the unit.

20 Windscreen/tailgate/ headlight washer system check

1 Check that each of the washer jet nozzles are clear and that each nozzle provides a strong jet of washer fluid.

2 The tailgate jet should be aimed to spray at the centre of the screen, using a pin.

3 The inner windscreen washer nozzles should be aimed slightly above the centre of the screen, and the outer nozzles slightly below the centre of the screen and towards the outside. Use a pin to adjust the nozzle aim.

4 The aim of the headlight jets is set in the factory and there is no provision for adjustment.

5 Especially during the winter months, make sure that the washer fluid antifreeze concentration is sufficient.

21 Engine management self-diagnosis memory fault check

1 This work should be carried out by an Audi dealer or diagnostic specialist using special equipment. The diagnostic socket is located beneath the right-hand side of the facia on RHD models, and beneath the left-hand side on LHD models.

22 Sunroof check and lubrication

1 Check the operation of the sunroof, and leave it in the fully open position.
2 Wipe clean the guide rails on each side of the sunroof opening, then apply lubricant to them. Audi recommend lubricant spray G 052 778 A2.

23 Road test and exhaust emissions check

Instruments and electrical equipment

1 Check the operation of all instruments and electrical equipment.
2 Make sure that all instruments read correctly, and switch on all electrical equipment in turn, to check that it functions properly.

Steering and suspension

3 Check for any abnormalities in the steering, suspension, handling or road feel.
4 Drive the vehicle, and check that there are no unusual vibrations or noises which may indicate wear in the driveshafts, wheel bearings, etc.
5 Check that the steering feels positive, with no excessive sloppiness, or roughness, and check for any suspension noises when cornering and driving over bumps.

Drivetrain

6 Check the performance of the engine, clutch (where applicable), gearbox/transmission and driveshafts.
7 Listen for any unusual noises from the engine, clutch and gearbox/transmission.
8 Make sure that the engine runs smoothly when idling, and that there is no hesitation when accelerating.
9 Check that, where applicable, the clutch action is smooth and progressive, that the drive is taken up smoothly, and that the pedal travel is not excessive. Also listen for any noises when the clutch pedal is depressed.
10 On manual gearbox models, check that all gears can be engaged smoothly without noise, and that the gear lever action is smooth and not abnormally vague or notchy.
11 On automatic transmission models, make sure that all gearchanges occur smoothly, without snatching, and without an increase in engine speed between changes. Check that all the gear positions can be selected with the vehicle at rest. If any problems are found, they should be referred to a Audi dealer.
12 Listen for a metallic clicking sound from the front of the vehicle, as the vehicle is driven slowly in a circle with the steering on full-lock. Carry out this check in both directions. If a clicking noise is heard, this indicates wear in a driveshaft joint, in which case renew the joint if necessary.

Braking system

13 Make sure that the vehicle does not pull to one side when braking, and that the wheels do not lock when braking hard.
14 Check that there is no vibration through the steering when braking.
15 Check that the handbrake operates correctly without excessive movement of the lever, and that it holds the vehicle stationary on a slope.
16 Test the operation of the brake servo unit as follows. With the engine off, depress the footbrake four or five times to exhaust the vacuum. Hold the brake pedal depressed, then start the engine. As the engine starts, there should be a noticeable 'give' in the brake pedal as vacuum builds-up. Allow the engine to run for at least two minutes, and then switch it off. If the brake pedal is depressed now, it should be possible to detect a hiss from the servo as the pedal is depressed. After about four or five applications, no further hissing should be heard, and the pedal should feel considerably harder.
17 Under controlled emergency braking, the pulsing of the ABS unit must be felt at the footbrake pedal.

Exhaust emissions check

18 Although not part of the manufacturer's maintenance schedule, this check will normally be carried out on a regular basis according to the country the vehicle is operated in. Currently in the UK, exhaust emissions testing is included as part of the annual MOT test after the vehicle is 3 years old. In Germany the test is made when the vehicle is 3 years old, then repeated every 2 years.

Every 40 000 miles or 4 years, whichever comes first

24 Air filter element renewal

1 Undo the two bolts and remove the air intake duct from the lock carrier panel, then pull the ducting from the top of the air cleaner cover (see illustration).
2 Undo the two bolts and lift off the air cleaner cover (see illustration).
3 Remove the air filter element, noting which way round it is fitted (see illustration).
4 Wipe clean the main body, then fit the new air filter, making sure it is the correct way round.
5 The remainder of refitting is a reversal of removal.

25 Fuel filter renewal

1 The fuel filter is located on the left-hand side of the engine. First prise out the caps, undo the nuts and remove the engine top cover. Place cloth rags around the area beneath the filter unit.

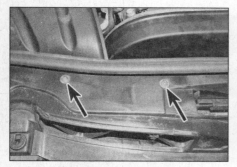

24.1 Undo the 2 screws securing the intake ducting to the lock carrier (arrowed)

24.2 Air filter cover screws (arrowed)

24.3 Note which way around the filter element is fitted

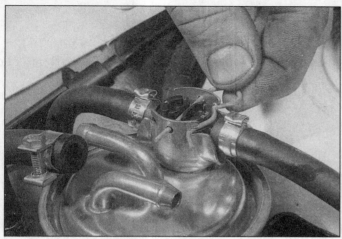

25.3a Release the clip . . .

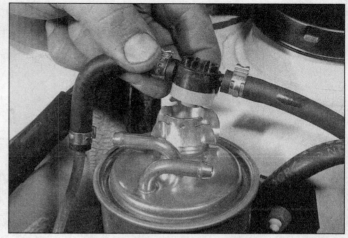

25.3b . . . and lift out the control valve, leaving the fuel hoses attached to it

25.5a Slacken the securing screw . . .

25.5b . . . and raise the filter out from the bracket

25.9 Reconnect the fuel supply and delivery hoses

2 Position a container underneath the filter unit and pad the surrounding area with rags to absorb any fuel that may be spilt.

3 At the top of the filter unit, release the clip and lift out the control valve, leaving the fuel hoses attached to it (see illustrations).

4 Slacken the hose clips and pull the fuel supply and delivery hoses from the ports on the top of the filter unit. If crimp-type clips are fitted, cut them off using snips, and use equivalent size worm-drive clips on refitting. Note the fitted position of each hose, to aid correct refitting later.

Caution: Be prepared for an amount of fuel loss. Do not allow diesel fuel to contact any of the coolant hoses.

5 Slacken the securing screw and raise the filter out of its retaining bracket (see illustrations).

6 Fit a new fuel filter into the retaining bracket and tighten the securing screw.

7 Fill the filter with clean diesel to aid restarting.

8 Refit the control valve to the top of the filter and insert the retaining clip. .

9 Reconnect the fuel supply and delivery hoses, using the notes made during removal – note the fuel flow arrow markings next to each port. Where crimp-type hoses were originally

fitted, use equivalent size worm-drive clips on refitting (see illustration).

10 Start and run the engine at idle, then check around the fuel filter for fuel leaks. Note: It may take a few seconds of cranking before the engine starts.

11 Raise the engine speed to about 2000 rpm several times, then allow the engine to idle again.

12 Remove the collecting container and rags, then refit the engine top cover.

26 Auxiliary drivebelt check and renewal

Check

1 See Section 8.

Renewal

2 Refer to Chapter 2C.

27 Power steering hydraulic fluid level check

1 Refer to Chapter 10.

28 Automatic/Multitronic transmission fluid renewal

Note: Although Audi make no specific recommendation to renew the automatic transmission fluid, we consider it prudent to change the fluid every 40 000 miles or four years whichever occurs first.

1 Apply the handbrake, then jack up the front of the vehicle and support it on axle stands (see Jacking and vehicle support). Remove the engine/transmission undershield. Note: For an accurate fluid level check, Audi technicians use an electronic tester which is plugged into the transmission electronic system, and which determines that the temperature of the fluid is between 35 and 40°C. In view of this, it is recommended that the vehicle is taken to an Audi dealer to have the work done. The following procedure is given on the understanding that the level is checked by an Audi dealer on completion.

2 Note that the transmission must be refilled from below the vehicle, so make sure that the vehicle is supported in a level position.

Automatic transmission

3 Position a suitable container beneath

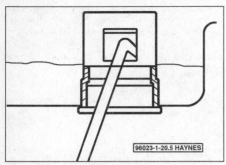

28.5 The nozzle of the tool being used to add fluid must pass through the window in the deflector cap

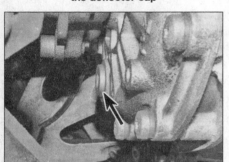

29.1b On Multitronic transmissions, the final drive filler/level plug is located on the left-hand side (arrowed)

the transmission. Wipe clean the pan, then unscrew the drain plug located on the right-hand side of the pan. Allow the fluid to drain into the container.

4 Fit a new seal on the drain plug and tighten to the specified torque.

5 Unscrew the inspection plug at the rear of

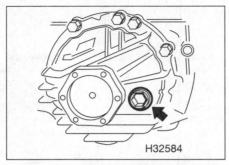

29.1a On automatic transmissions, the final drive filler/level plug is located on the left-hand side (arrowed)

the pan, and add fluid until it runs out of the hole **(see illustration)**.

6 With P selected, run the engine at idling speed until it reaches normal temperature. If necessary add more fluid until it runs out of the inspection hole.

7 Apply the footbrake pedal, then select each position with the selector lever, pausing for about 3 seconds in each position. Return the selector to position P.

8 At this stage, the Audi technician connects the tester to confirm that the fluid temperature is between 35 and 40°C. **Note:** *If the fluid level is checked when the temperature is too low, overfilling will occur. If the fluid level is checked when the temperature is too high, underfilling will occur.*

9 With the engine still running at idle speed, allow any excess fluid to run out of the overflow pipe.

10 Switch off the engine, then refit the inspection plug together with a new seal, and tighten to the specified torque.

11 Refit the engine/transmission undershield, and lower the vehicle to the ground.

Multitronic transmission

12 The refilling of this transmission requires specialist equipment, to overfill the casing and purge any air from the internals. Running the engine without purging the system could cause severe damage to the transmission. For this reason, we recommend entrusting this task to an Audi dealer or suitably-equipped repairer.

29 Automatic/Multitronic transmission final drive oil level check

1 The final drive oil filler/level plug is located on the left-hand side of the transmission, adjacent to the left-hand driveshaft inner joint **(see illustrations)**. Apply the handbrake, then jack up the front of the vehicle and support it on axle stands (see *Jacking and vehicle support*). Remove the transmission undershield. To ensure an accurate check, make sure that the vehicle is level.

2 Unscrew and remove the filler/level plug. On automatic transmissions, the oil level must be upto the bottom lip of the filler hole, whilst on Multitronic transmissions, the oil must be 8.5 mm below the hole. If necessary, add the specified oil through the filler/level hole. If the level requires constant topping-up, check for leaks and repair.

3 Examine the sealing ring and renew if necessary, then refit the plug and tighten to the specified torque.

4 Refit the undershield and lower the vehicle to the ground.

Every 60 000 miles

30 Timing belt and tensioning roller renewal

1 Refer to Chapter 2C for details of renewing the timing belt and tensioning roller.

Every 2 years

31 Brake (and clutch) fluid renewal

⚠️ *Warning: Brake hydraulic fluid can harm your eyes and damage painted surfaces, so use extreme caution when handling and pouring it. Do not use fluid that has been standing open for some time, as it absorbs moisture from the air. Excess moisture can cause a dangerous loss of braking effectiveness.*

1 The procedure is similar to that for the bleeding of the hydraulic system as described in Chapter 9, except that the brake fluid

reservoir should be emptied by syphoning, using a clean poultry baster or similar before starting, and allowance should be made for the old fluid to be expelled when bleeding a section of the circuit. Since the clutch hydraulic system on manual gearbox models also uses fluid from the brake system reservoir, it should also be bled at the same time by referring to Chapter 6, Section 2.

2 Working as described in Chapter 9, open the first bleed screw in the sequence, and pump the brake pedal gently until nearly all the old fluid has been emptied from the master cylinder reservoir.

3 Top-up to the MAX level with new fluid, and continue pumping until only the new fluid

remains in the reservoir, and new fluid can be seen emerging from the bleed screw. Tighten the screw, and top the reservoir level up to the MAX level line.

4 Work through all the remaining bleed screws in the sequence until new fluid can be seen at all of them. Be careful to keep the master cylinder reservoir topped-up to above the MIN level at all times, or air may enter the system and greatly increase the length of the task.

5 When the operation is complete, check that all bleed screws are securely tightened, and that their dust caps are refitted. Wash off all traces of spilt fluid, and recheck the master cylinder reservoir fluid level.

6 On models with a manual gearbox, once

the brake fluid has been changed the clutch fluid should also be renewed. Referring to Chapter 6, bleed the clutch until new fluid is seen to be emerging from the slave cylinder bleed screw, keeping the master cylinder fluid level above the MIN level line at all times to prevent air entering the system. Once the new fluid emerges, securely tighten the bleed screw then disconnect and remove the bleeding equipment. Securely refit the dust cap then wash off all traces of spilt fluid.

7 On all models, ensure the master cylinder fluid level is correct (see *Weekly checks*) and thoroughly check the operation of the brakes and (where necessary) clutch before taking the car on the road.

32 Coolant renewal

Note: *This work is not included in the Audi schedule and should not be required if the recommended Audi G12 Plus LongLife coolant antifreeze/inhibitor is used. However, if standard antifreeze/inhibitor is used, the work should be carried out at the recommended interval.*

⚠️ **Warning: Wait until the engine is cold before starting this procedure. Do not allow antifreeze to come in contact with your skin, or with the painted surfaces of the vehicle. Rinse off spills immediately with plenty of water. Never leave antifreeze lying around in an open container, or in a puddle in the driveway or on the garage floor. Children and pets are attracted by its sweet smell, but antifreeze can be fatal if ingested.**

Cooling system draining

1 With the engine completely cold, cover the expansion tank cap with a wad of rag, and slowly turn the cap anti-clockwise to relieve the pressure in the cooling system (a hissing sound will normally be heard). Wait until any pressure remaining in the system is released, then continue to turn the cap until it can be removed.

2 Release the fasteners and remove the engine undershield. Some models are equipped with a drain plug in the radiator bottom hose, whilst on others, it's necessary to remove the hose-mounted temperature sensor. Position a suitable container beneath the radiator bottom hose, then pull out the retaining clip and ease the temperature sensor from the radiator hose, or undo the drain tap as applicable **(see illustration)**. Allow the coolant to drain into the container.

3 If the coolant has been drained for a reason other than renewal, then provided it is clean, it can be re-used, but this is not recommended.

4 Once all the coolant has drained, refit the sensor ensuring the retaining clip is properly seated, or tighten the drain tap as applicable.

Cooling system flushing

5 If coolant renewal has been neglected, or if the antifreeze mixture has become diluted, then in time, the cooling system may gradually lose efficiency, as the coolant passages become restricted due to rust, scale deposits, and other sediment. Flushing the system clean can restore the cooling system efficiency.

6 The radiator should be flushed independently of the engine, to avoid unnecessary contamination.

Radiator flushing

7 To flush the radiator, disconnect the top and bottom hoses and any other relevant hoses from the radiator, with reference to Chapter 3.

8 Insert a garden hose into the radiator top inlet. Direct a flow of clean water through the radiator, and continue flushing until clean water emerges from the radiator bottom outlet.

9 If after a reasonable period, the water still does not run clear, the radiator can be flushed with a good proprietary cooling system cleaning agent. It is important that their manufacturer's instructions are followed carefully. If the contamination is particularly bad, insert the hose in the radiator bottom outlet, and reverse-flush the radiator.

Engine flushing

10 To flush the engine, remove the thermostat as described in Chapter 3, then temporarily refit the thermostat cover.

11 With the top and bottom hoses disconnected from the radiator, insert a garden hose into the radiator top hose. Direct a clean flow of water through the engine, and continue flushing until clean water emerges from the radiator bottom hose.

12 On completion of flushing, refit the thermostat and reconnect the hoses with reference to Chapter 3.

Cooling system filling

13 Before attempting to fill the cooling system, make sure that all hoses and clips are in good condition, and that the clips/connections are secure. Note that an antifreeze mixture must be used all year round, to prevent corrosion of the engine components (see following sub-Section).

14 Slacken the clip and withdraw the heater unit supply hose from its bulkhead stub (see Chapter 3) until the bleed hole at the top of the hose is clear of the surface of the stub; do not disconnect the hose from the stub completely **(see illustration)**.

15 Remove the securing screws and detach the expansion tank from the engine compartment. Raise it approximately 100 mm above the engine compartment and support it there on a block of wood or using a length of wire.

16 Remove the expansion tank filler cap, and fill the system by slowly pouring the coolant into the expansion tank to prevent airlocks from forming.

17 If the coolant is being renewed, begin by pouring in a couple of litres of water, followed

32.2 A coolant drain tap (arrowed) is located on the outlet at the base of the radiator. Turn the tap anti-clockwise to open it

32.14 Slide the heater hose forwards until the bleed hole (arrowed) is clear of the surface of the bulkhead stub

by the correct quantity of antifreeze, then top-up with more water.

18 Continue filling until coolant starts to run from the bleed hole in the heater hose. When this happens, refit the hose and tighten the clip securely.

19 Once the level in the expansion tank starts to rise, squeeze the radiator top and bottom hoses to help expel any trapped air in the system. Once all the air is expelled, top-up the coolant level to the MAX mark, refit the expansion tank cap, then refit the expansion tank to the bodywork.

20 Start the engine and run it at a fast idle for about three minutes. After this, allow the engine to idle normally until the bottom hose becomes hot.

21 Check for leaks, particularly around disturbed components. Check the coolant level in the expansion tank, and top-up if necessary. Note that the system must be cold before an accurate level is indicated in the expansion tank. If the expansion tank cap is removed while the engine is still warm, cover the cap with a thick cloth, and unscrew the cap slowly to gradually relieve the system pressure (a hissing sound will normally be heard). Wait until any pressure remaining in the system is released, then continue to turn the cap until it can be removed. Never remove the cap when the engine is still hot.

Antifreeze mixture

Caution: Audi specify the use of G12 Plus antifreeze (purple in colour). DO NOT mix this with any other type of antifreeze, as severe engine damage may result. If the coolant visible in the expansion tank is brown in colour, then the cooling system may have been topped-up with coolant containing the wrong type of antifreeze. If you are unsure of the type of antifreeze used, or if you suspect that mixing may have occurred, the best course of action is to drain, flush and refill the cooling system.

22 If the recommended Audi coolant is not being used, the antifreeze should always be renewed at the specified intervals. This is necessary not only to maintain the antifreeze properties, but also to prevent corrosion which would otherwise occur as the corrosion inhibitors become progressively less effective.

23 The quantity of coolant and levels of protection are indicated in the Specifications.

24 Before adding antifreeze, the cooling system should be completely drained, preferably flushed, and all hoses checked for condition and security.

25 After filling with antifreeze, a label should be attached to the expansion tank, stating the type and concentration of antifreeze used, and the date installed. Any subsequent topping-up should be made with the same type and concentration of antifreeze.

26 Do not use engine antifreeze in the windscreen/tailgate/headlight washer system, as it will cause damage to the vehicle paintwork.

Chapter 2 Part A:
1.8 and 2.0 litre indirect injection petrol engine in-car repair procedures

Contents

	Section number
Auxiliary drivebelts – removal and refitting	6
Camshaft cover – removal and refitting	7
Camshaft oil seals – renewal	8
Crankshaft oil seals – renewal	9
Cylinder compression test	3
Cylinder head – dismantling and overhaul	See Chapter 2D
Cylinder head – removal and refitting	10
Engine mountings – inspection and renewal	13
Engine oil and filter – renewal	See Chapter 1A
Engine oil level – check	See Weekly checks

	Section number
Engine valve timing marks – general information and usage	2
Flywheel/driveplate – removal, inspection and refitting	12
General information	1
Hydraulic tappets – operational check	11
Oil pump and pickup – removal, inspection and refitting	15
Sump – removal and refitting	14
Timing belt – removal, inspection and refitting	4
Timing belt tensioner and sprockets – removal, inspection and refitting	5

Degrees of difficulty

| Easy, suitable for novice with little experience | | Fairly easy, suitable for beginner with some experience | | Fairly difficult, suitable for competent DIY mechanic | | Difficult, suitable for experienced DIY mechanic | | Very difficult, suitable for expert DIY or professional | |

Specifications

General

Engine code*:
1781 cc:	
Bosch Motronic ME7.5:	
110 kW (143 bhp)	AVJ
125 kW (163 bhp)	AMB
Bosch Motronic ME7.1:	
120 kW (156 bhp)	BFB and BKB
140 kW (182 bhp)	BEX
1984 cc, Bosch Motronic ME7, 96 kW (125 bhp)	ALT
Bore:	
1.8 litre models	81.0 mm
2.0 litre models	82.5 mm
Stroke:	
1.8 litre models	86.4 mm
2.0 litre models	92.8 mm
Compression ratio:	
1.8 litre models	9.5 : 1
2.0 litre models	10.0 : 1
Compression pressures (wear limit):	
1.8 litre models	7.5 bar
2.0 litre models	7.0 bar
Maximum difference between cylinders	3.0 bar
Firing order	1 – 3 – 4 – 2
No 1 cylinder location	Timing belt end

* **Note:** See 'Vehicle identification' for the location of the code marking on the engine.

Lubrication system

Oil pump type	Inner and outer rotor type, chain-driven from crankshaft
Oil pressure (oil temperature 80°C):	
1.8 litre models:	
At 2000 rpm	1.3 bar minimum
At 3000 rpm	3.5 to 4.5 bar minimum
2.0 litre models:	
At idle speed	2.0 bar minimum
At 2000 rpm	2.7 to 1.5 bar minimum

Torque wrench settings

	Nm	lbf ft
Automatic camshaft adjuster bolt	10	7
Big-end bearing caps bolts*:		
Stage 1	30	22
Stage 2	Angle-tighten a further 90°	
Camshaft bearing cap:		
1.8 litre engines	10	7
2.0 litre engines	8	6
Camshaft cover	10	7
Camshaft position sensor:		
Rotor	25	18
Sensor housing	10	7
Camshaft sprocket bolt:		
Front sprockets	65	48
Rear sprocket (2.0 litre engines)*:		
Stage 1	80	59
Stage 2	Angle-tighten a further 90°	
Crankshaft front oil seal housing	15	11
Crankshaft pulley/vibration damper bolts*:		
Stage 1	10	7
Stage 2	Angle-tighten a further 90°	
Crankshaft rear oil seal housing	15	11
Crankshaft sprocket*		
Stage 1	90	66
Stage 2	Angle-tighten a further 90°	
Cylinder head bolts*:		
Stage 1	40	30
Stage 2	Angle-tighten a further 90°	
Stage 3	Angle-tighten a further 90°	
Damper unit (Multitronic transmission)	25	18
Driveplate mounting bolts*:		
Stage 1	60	44
Stage 2	Angle-tighten a further 90°	
Engine mounting to subframe	25	18
Engine-to-transmission bolts**:		
M10	45	33
M12	65	48
Flywheel mounting bolts*:		
22.5 mm long bolts:		
Stage 1	60	44
Stage 2	Angle-tighten a further 90°	
35.0 mm long bolts:		
Stage 1	60	44
Stage 2	Angle-tighten a further 180°	
43.0 mm long bolts:		
Stage 1	60	44
Stage 2	Angle-tighten a further 180°	
Intake manifold support bracket	23	17
Intake manifold	10	7
Main bearing cap bolts*:		
Stage 1	65	48
Stage 2	Angle-tighten a further 90°	
Oil jets	27	20
Oil pickup pipe	10	7
Oil pump cover bolts	10	7
Oil pump:		
1.8 litre engines	16	12
2.0 litre engines (with balancer shaft housing)*:		
Stage 1	15	11
Stage 2	Angle-tighten a further 15°	
Oil pump drive sprocket bolt	22	16
Sump:		
Sump to block (M7)	15	11
Sump to block (M10)	40	30
Sump to transmission	45	33
Timing belt cover bolts	10	7

Torque wrench settings (continued)

	Nm	lbf ft
Timing belt tensioner housing bolts:		
Idler pulley bolt	25	18
Housing bolt	15	11
Timing belt tensioner hub nut:		
Engine code ALT	27	20
Torque reaction support to sump	23	17
Turbocharger to exhaust manifold*	35	26

* *Do not re-use*

** *Audi insist that, on Multitronic models, the bolts are not re-used*

---

1 General information

Using this Chapter

Chapter 2 is divided into four Parts: A, B, C and D. Repair operations that can be carried out with the engine in the vehicle are described in Part A (indirect injection petrol engines), Part B (direct injection petrol engines) and Part C (diesel engines). Part B covers the removal of the engine/transmission as a unit, and describes the engine dismantling and overhaul procedures.

In Parts A, B and C, the assumption is made that the engine is installed in the vehicle, with all ancillaries connected. If the engine has been removed for overhaul, the preliminary dismantling information which precedes each operation may be ignored.

Access to the engine compartment can be improved by removing the bonnet as described in Chapter 11.

Engine description

The engines are water-cooled, double overhead camshaft, in-line four-cylinder units, with cast-iron or aluminium cylinder blocks and aluminium-alloy cylinder heads. All are mounted longitudinally at the front of the vehicle, with the transmission bolted to the rear of the engine.

The crankshaft is of five-bearing type, and thrustwashers are fitted to the centre main bearing to control crankshaft endfloat.

The timing belt drives the exhaust camshaft, and the intake camshaft is driven from the exhaust camshaft by chain at the rear of the camshafts. A hydraulic tensioner is fitted to the chain, to automatically vary the intake camshaft valve timing.

The valves are operated from the camshafts through hydraulic bucket type tappets, and the valve clearances are adjusted automatically.

The cylinder head carries the double camshafts. It also houses the intake and exhaust valves, which are closed by single coil springs, and which run in guides pressed into the cylinder head. The camshaft actuates the valves directly via hydraulic tappets, mounted in the cylinder head. The cylinder head contains integral oilways which supply and lubricate the tappets.

The engine coolant pump is driven by the toothed timing belt.

Lubricant is circulated under pressure by a pump, driven by a chain from the crankshaft. Oil is drawn from the sump through a strainer, and then forced through an externally-mounted, renewable screw-on filter. From there, it is distributed to the cylinder head, where it lubricates the camshaft journals and hydraulic tappets, and also to the crankcase, where it lubricates the main bearings, connecting rod big-ends, gudgeon pins and cylinder bores. An oil pressure switch is located on the oil filter housing, operating at 1.4 bars. On some engines, an oil cooler mounted above the oil filter is supplied with coolant from the cooling system to reduce the temperature of the oil before it re-enters the engine.

On 2.0 litre engines, a balancer shaft housing is fitted below the cylinder block. The two contra-rotating shafts are driven by the same chain that drives the oil pump. The shafts have integral weights fitted along their length, and as they spin, the forces created cancel out almost all of the vibration generated by the engine.

Repairs with engine in vehicle

The following operations can be performed without removing the engine:

a) Auxiliary drivebelts – removal and refitting.
b) Camshafts – removal and refitting*.
c) Camshaft oil seals – renewal.
d) Camshaft sprocket – removal and refitting.
e) Coolant pump – removal and refitting (refer to Chapter 3).
f) Crankshaft oil seals – renewal.
g) Crankshaft sprocket – removal and refitting.
h) Cylinder head – removal and refitting*.
i) Engine mountings – inspection and renewal.
j) Balancer shaft housing – renewal.
k) Oil pump and pickup assembly – removal and refitting.
l) Sump – removal and refitting.
m) Timing belt, sprockets and cover – removal, inspection and refitting.

* *Cylinder head dismantling procedures are detailed in Chapter 2D, with details of camshaft and hydraulic tappet removal.*
Note: *It is possible to remove the pistons and connecting rods (after removing the cylinder head and sump) without removing the engine. However, this is not recommended. Work of this nature is more easily and thoroughly completed with the engine on the bench, as described in Chapter 2D.*

2 Engine valve timing marks – general information and usage

General information

1 The crankshaft and camshaft sprockets are driven by the timing belt, and rotate in phase with each other. When the timing belt is removed during servicing or repair, it is possible for the shafts to rotate independently of each other, and the correct phasing is then lost.

2 The design of the engines covered in this Chapter is such that piston-to-valve contact will occur if the crankshaft is turned with the timing belt removed. For this reason, it is important that the correct phasing between the camshaft and crankshaft is preserved whilst the timing belt is off the engine. This is achieved by setting the engine in a reference condition (known as Top Dead Centre or TDC) before the timing belt is removed, and then preventing the shafts from rotating until the belt is refitted. Similarly, if the engine has been dismantled for overhaul, the engine can be set to TDC during reassembly to ensure that the correct shaft phasing is restored. **Note:** *The coolant pump is also driven by the timing belt, but the pump alignment is not critical.*

3 TDC is the highest position a piston reaches within its respective cylinder – in a four-stroke engine, each piston reaches TDC twice per cycle; once on the compression stroke, and once on the exhaust stroke. In general, TDC normally refers to No 1 cylinder on the compression stroke. Note that the cylinders are numbered one to four, starting from the timing belt end of the engine.

4 The crankshaft pulley has a marking which, when aligned with a reference marking on the

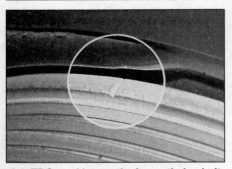

2.4 TDC marking on the lower timing belt cover and pulley

2.5 TDC markings on the camshaft sprocket and timing belt inner cover

timing belt cover, indicates that No 1 cylinder (and hence also No 4 cylinder) is at TDC (see illustration).

5 The exhaust camshaft sprocket is also equipped with a timing mark (see illustration) – when this is aligned with a mark on the small upper timing belt cover or camshaft cover, No 1 cylinder is at TDC compression.

Setting TDC on No 1 cylinder

6 Before starting work, make sure that the ignition is switched off.

7 Remove the engine top cover. On 2.0 litre engines, pull the cover upwards to release it from the fasteners. On 1.8 litre engines, undo the 3 fasteners (see illustrations 4.5a and 4.5b).

8 Remove all of the spark plugs as described in Chapter 1A.

9 Remove the timing belt upper, outer cover as describe in Section 4.

10 Turn the engine clockwise with a spanner on the crankshaft pulley until the timing mark on the outer circumference of the camshaft sprocket aligns with the mark on the timing belt cover. With this aligned, the timing mark on the crankshaft pulley should align with the mark on the lower timing belt cover.

3 Cylinder compression test

1 When engine performance is down, or if misfiring occurs which cannot be attributed to the ignition or fuel systems, a compression

test can provide diagnostic clues as to the engine's condition. If the test is performed regularly, it can give warning of trouble before any other symptoms become apparent.

2 The engine must be fully warmed-up to normal operating temperature, the battery must be fully-charged, and all the spark plugs must be removed (refer to Chapter 1A). The aid of an assistant will also be required. Remove the engine top cover. On 2.0 litre engines, pull the cover upwards to release it from the fasteners. On 1.8 litre engines, undo the 3 fasteners (see illustrations 4.5a and 4.5b).

3 Remove the spark plugs as described in Chapter 1A.

4 Disable the injectors by disconnecting the wiring from each of them.

5 Fit a compression tester to the No 1 cylinder spark plug hole – the type of tester which screws into the plug thread is preferable.

6 Have an assistant hold the throttle wide open. Crank the engine on the starter motor several seconds. After one or two revolutions, the compression pressure should build-up to a maximum figure, and then stabilise. Record the highest reading obtained.

7 Repeat the test on the remaining cylinders, recording the pressure in each. Keep the throttle wide open.

8 All cylinders should produce very similar pressures; a difference of more than 3 bars between any two cylinders indicates a fault. Note that the compression should build-up quickly in a healthy engine. Low compression on the first stroke, followed by gradually-

increasing pressure on successive strokes, indicates worn piston rings. A low compression reading on the first stroke, which does not build-up during successive strokes, indicates leaking valves or a blown head gasket (a cracked head could also be the cause).

9 Refer to the Specifications section of this Chapter, and compare the recorded compression figures with those stated by the manufacturer.

10 On completion of the test, refit the spark plugs, HT leads, injector wiring and top cover. Note that in some cases, disconnecting the wiring plugs from the coils and injectors, then cranking the engine, may cause fault codes to be stored by the engine management ECM – have these codes erased by means of a suitable diagnostic tool/fault code reader. See your Audi dealer or specialist.

4 Timing belt – removal, inspection and refitting

General information

1 The primary function of the toothed timing belt is to drive the camshafts. Should the belt slip or break in service, the valve timing will be disturbed and piston-to-valve contact will occur, resulting in serious engine damage. For this reason, it is important that the timing belt is tensioned correctly, and inspected regularly for signs of wear or deterioration.

Removal

2 Before starting work, disconnect the battery negative (earth) lead (see Chapter 5A).

3 Apply the handbrake, then jack up the front of the vehicle and support it on axle stands (see Jacking and vehicle support). Undo the fasteners and remove the engine undershield (see illustrations).

4 Access to the timing belt is achieved by moving the complete front panel (the lock carrier assembly) away from the front of the car as far as possible, but without disconnecting the radiator hoses or electrical wiring – this is known as the Service position – see Chapter 11.

5 Remove the plastic cover from the top of the engine. On 2.0 litre engines, pull the cover

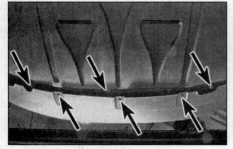

4.3a The front edge of the undershield is secured by 3 screws to the front bumper, and 3 screws to the lock carrier (arrowed)

4.3b Engine undershield-to-transmission undershield fasteners (arrowed)

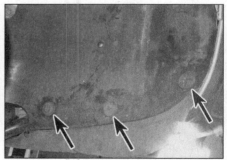

4.3c Engine undershield-to-wheel arch liner fasteners (arrowed)

4.5a Rotate the fasteners 90° anti-clockwise (arrowed) and lift of the plastic cover – 1.8 litre engines

4.5b Pull the plastic cover upwards from the mountings – 2.0 litre engines

4.6 Undo the 3 bolts and remove the auxiliary drivebelt tensioner

upwards to release it from the fasteners. On 1.8 litre engines, undo the 3 fasteners (see illustrations).

6 Remove the auxiliary drivebelt(s) with reference to Section 6. Also unbolt the tensioner from the front of the engine (see illustration).

7 Remove the top section of the timing belt cover. On 2.0 litre engines, the cover is retained by 2 screws, whilst on 1.8 litre engines, the cover is clipped in place (see illustrations). On 1.8 litre engines, unclip the pipes from the timing belt cover.

8 Rotate the crankshaft and align the timing marks as described in Section 2.

9 If the timing belt is to be refitted, mark its normal direction of travel with chalk or a marker pen.

10 While holding the crankshaft stationary with a socket on the centre pulley bolt, unscrew and remove the bolts securing the pulley to the sprocket. Withdraw the pulley (see illustrations). Discard the bolts, new ones must be fitted.

11 Unscrew the bolts and remove the timing belt lower and middle outer covers from the cylinder block (see illustration).

12 Insert an 8.0 mm Allen key into the tensioner hub and rotate the hub anti-clockwise to compress the piston in the hydraulic tensioner. Use only constant, moderate force or damage may result. Compress the tensioner piston until Audi locking plate T10008 can be inserted into the top of the tensioner housing to hold the piston in position. A home-made substitute

4.7a Release the clips (arrowed) and unclip the pipes from the timing belt upper cover – 1.8 litre engines

4.7b Undo the two screws (arrowed) and remove the timing belt upper cover – 2.0 litre engines

for T10008 can be fabricated from steel sheet (see illustrations).

13 With the piston locked in position, insert

Audi tool 3387 into the 2 holes in the tensioner hub arm, then slacken the hub retaining nut and rotate the tool clockwise to relieve the

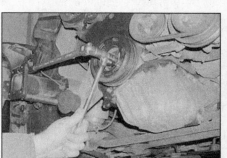

4.10a Undo the bolts . . .

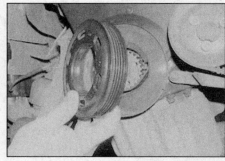

4.10b . . . and remove the pulley/vibration damper

4.11 Middle timing cover bolts (arrowed)

4.12a Insert an 8.0 mm Allen key into the hole (arrowed) and turn the pulley anti-clockwise gently

4.12b Insert the locking tool through the slot to lock the tensioner

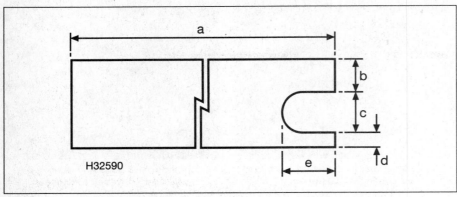

4.12c Home-made tensioner locking tool dimensions

A 52 mm   *B 4.5 mm*   *C 5.5 mm*   *D 2 mm*   *E 7 mm*

tension on the belt. In the absence of the special tool, a sturdy pair of right-angle circlip pliers will suffice.

14 Slip the timing belt off of the crankshaft, camshaft, and coolant pump sprockets, and remove it from the engine. **Do not** bend the timing belt sharply if it is to be re-used.

Inspection

15 Examine the belt for evidence of contamination by coolant or lubricant. If this is the case, find the source of the contamination before progressing any further. Check the belt for signs of wear or damage, particularly around the leading edges of the belt teeth. Renew the belt if its condition is in doubt; the cost of belt renewal is negligible compared with potential cost of the engine repairs, should the belt fail in service. The belt must be renewed if it has covered the mileage stated by the manufacturer (see Chapter 1A), however, even if it has covered less, it is recommended to renew it regardless of condition as a precautionary measure. **Note:** *If the timing belt is not going to be refitted for some time, it is a wise precaution to hang a warning label on the steering wheel, to remind yourself (and others) not to turn the engine.*

Refitting

16 Ensure that the timing mark on the camshaft and crankshaft sprockets are correctly aligned with the corresponding TDC reference marks on the timing belt cover; refer to Section 2 for details.

17 Temporarily refit the lower timing cover, then locate the pulley for the ribbed auxiliary drivebelt on the crankshaft sprocket, using two of the retaining screws – note that the pulley will only fit in one fitting position – with the hole in the pulley over the projection on the crankshaft sprocket. Make sure that the TDC marks are correctly aligned, then remove the pulley and timing cover.

18 Loop the timing belt under the crankshaft sprocket loosely, observing the direction of rotation markings if the old timing belt is being refitted.

19 Engage the timing belt teeth with the crankshaft sprocket, then manoeuvre it into position over the coolant pump and camshaft sprockets **(see illustration)**. Observe the direction of rotation markings on the belt.

20 Insert Audi tool 3387 (or circlip pliers) into the 2 holes in the tensioner hub arm, then rotate the tool anti-clockwise to compress the tensioner piston, and remove the locking tool (T10008 or home-made equivalent).

21 Turn the tensioner pulley hub clockwise with the tool until an 8.0 mm drill bit can be inserted between the top of the tensioner housing and the tensioning lever **(see illustration)**.

22 Hold the tool in this position, then tighten the tensioner pulley retaining nut securely.

23 Using a spanner or wrench and socket on the crankshaft pulley centre bolt, rotate the crankshaft through two complete revolutions. Reset the engine to TDC on No 1 cylinder with reference to Section 2, and check that the crankshaft pulley and camshaft sprocket timing marks are correctly aligned. Check the gap between the top of the tensioner housing and the tensioning lever – the gap must be between 6.0 and 10.0 mm. If the gap is incorrect, compress the tensioner piston and lock it in position as described in paragraph 12. Slacken the tensioner pulley retaining nut and tension the belt as described in paragraphs 20 to 22.

24 Refit the outer timing belt covers, then apply a little thread-locking compound and tighten the centre and lower cover retaining bolts to the specified torque.

25 Refit the crankshaft pulley/vibration damper using new bolts and tighten them to the specified torque.

26 Refit the auxiliary drivebelt tensioner and tighten the bolts. Refit the auxiliary drivebelt(s) with reference to Section 6.

27 Refit the lock carrier assembly using a reversal of the removal procedure.

28 Refit the engine undershield, then lower the vehicle to the ground.

29 Reconnect the battery negative (earth) lead (see Chapter 5A).

---

5 Timing belt tensioner and sprockets – removal, inspection and refitting

Removal

1 Remove the timing belt as described in Section 4.

Tensioner housing

2 Undo the 3 retaining bolts and remove the tensioner housing and idler pulley **(see illustration)**.

Tensioner pulley

3 Undo the pulley retaining nut and remove

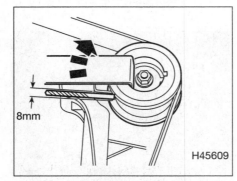

4.21 Turn the tensioner clockwise until a drill bit can be inserted between the top of the housing and the tensioner lever

4.19 Timing belt routing

1 *Camshaft sprocket*
2 *Tensioner pulley*
3 *Coolant pump sprocket*
4 *Crankshaft sprocket*
5 *Idler pulley*

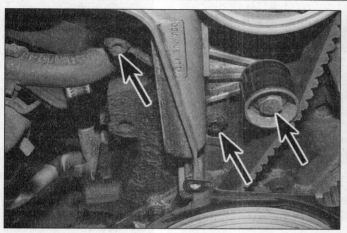

5.2 Undo the tensioner housing and idler pulley bolts (arrowed)

5.5 Use a home-made tool to counterhold the camshaft sprocket

the tensioner pulley. Note that the tensioner plate engages in a hole in the cylinder head.

Camshaft sprocket

4 Rotate the crankshaft 90° anti-clockwise to eliminate any possibility of accidental piston-to-valve contact.
5 Unscrew the camshaft sprocket bolt, while holding the sprocket stationary using a tool as shown. Remove the bolt, sprocket, and (where applicable) the key **(see illustration)**.

Crankshaft sprocket

6 Unscrew the crankshaft sprocket bolt, and remove the sprocket **(see illustrations)**. The bolt is very tight, and the crankshaft must be held stationary. On manual gearbox models, engage top gear and apply the footbrake pedal firmly. On automatic/Multitronic transmission models, unbolt the transmission front cover and use a wide-bladed screwdriver in the ring gear to hold the crankshaft stationary. Discard the bolt, a new one must be fitted.

Inspection

7 Clean all the sprockets and examine them for wear and damage. Spin the tensioner roller, and check that it runs smoothly.
8 Check the tensioner for signs of wear and/or damage and renew if necessary. It would be prudent to renew the tensioner pulley is there is any doubt as to its condition.

Refitting

Tensioner housing

9 Position the housing and tighten the retaining bolts to the specified torque.
10 Refit the timing belt as described in Section 4.

Tensioner pulley

11 Refitting is a reversal of removal.
12 Refit the timing belt as described in Section 4.

Camshaft sprocket

13 Locate the key on the camshaft then refit the sprocket and bolt. Tighten the bolt to the specified torque while holding the sprocket

5.6a Unscrew the bolt . . .

using the method employed on removal. Note the sprocket must be refitted with the narrow web and timing mark facing forwards.
14 Rotate the crankshaft 90° clockwise back to the TDC position.
15 Refit the timing belt as described in Section 4.

Crankshaft sprocket

16 Locate the sprocket on the crankshaft, then tighten the new bolt to the specified torque while holding the crankshaft stationary using the method employed on removal. **Note:** *Do not turn the crankshaft as the pistons may contact the valves.*
17 Refit the timing belt as described in Section 4.

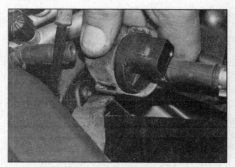

6.4 Detach the EVAP solenoid valve from the bracket

5.6b . . . and remove the crankshaft sprocket

6 Auxiliary drivebelt – removal and refitting

1 The poly-vee drivebelt drives the alternator, power steering pump and where fitted, the air conditioning compressor.
2 On all engines, the drivebelt tension is adjusted automatically.

Removal

3 Remove the plastic cover from the right-hand side of the engine (where fitted).
4 Detach EVAP canister solenoid valve from the bracket on the air intake duct **(see illustration)**.

6.5 Undo the intake duct screws (arrowed) at the bonnet slam panel

6.8a Using an open-ended spanner, rotate the tensioner clockwise

6.8b Insert a metal rod/drill bit/Allen key through the tensioner arm and body when the holes align

ducting on the right-hand side of the engine compartment.

3 Disconnect the EVAP canister solenoid valve **(see illustration 6.4)**.

4 Slacken the clamp and disconnect the crankcase breather hose from the cylinder head cover, then detach the secondary air injection pipe from the cover and heat shield **(see illustration)**.

5 Release the clips securing the timing belt upper cover to the cylinder head cover, then unscrew the nuts securing the camshaft cover to the cylinder head.

6 Lift the camshaft cover from the cylinder head and recover the gasket. Check the gasket for wear or damage – renew as necessary.

7 Remove the oil deflector from the camshaft cover.

Refitting

8 Clean the surfaces of the camshaft cover and cylinder head, then refit the oil deflector.

9 At the rear of the cylinder head apply suitable sealant to the two points where the hydraulic tensioner/camshaft adjuster contacts the cylinder head **(see illustration)**. Similarly, at the front of the cylinder head, apply the sealant to the two points where the camshaft double bearing cap contacts the cylinder head.

10 Carefully position the gasket, then refit the camshaft cover. Tighten the nuts progressively and evenly to the specified torque.

11 The remainder of refitting is a reversal of removal.

2.0 litre engines

Removal

12 Remove the engine top cover by pulling it upwards from its fasteners.

13 Pull up the plastic cover over the intake ducting on the right-hand side of the engine compartment (where fitted).

14 Detach the EVAP canister solenoid valve from the bracket on the air cleaner duct, then undo the 2 screws at the bonnet slam panel, and remove the intake ducting **(see illustration 6.5)**.

15 Undo the 2 screws and remove the timing belt upper cover **(see illustration 4.7b)**.

16 Release the clips, then disconnect the air outlet pipe from the air cleaner housing

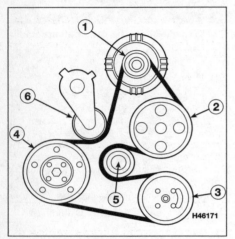

6.9 Auxiliary drivebelt routing

1 *Alternator*
2 *Power steering pump*
3 *Air conditioning compressor*
4 *Crankshaft*
5 *Idler pulley*
6 *Tensioner*

5 Undo the 2 bolts at the bonnet slam panel, and remove the intake duct **(see illustration)**.

6 If the drivebelt is to be re-used, mark it for clockwise direction to ensure it is refitted the same way round.

7 Although not essential, access to the drivebelt is best achieved by moving the complete front panel (the lock carrier assembly) away from the front of the car as far

as possible – this is known as placing it in the Service position – see Chapter 11.

8 To remove the drivebelt, the automatic tensioner must be released and held with a suitable pin or tool. Using an open-ended spanner on the top of the tensioner, move the tensioner clockwise until the pin holes are aligned then insert a metal rod, bolt or drill bit to hold the tensioner in its released position. Remove the drivebelt from the crankshaft, alternator, power steering pump and compressor pulleys **(see illustrations)**.

Refitting

9 Locate the drivebelt on the pulleys, then initially turn the tensioner clockwise and remove the retaining pin. Release the tensioner to tension the drivebelt, making sure that it is correctly located in all the pulley grooves **(see illustration)**.

10 The remainder of refitting is a reversal of removal.

---

7 Camshaft cover –
   removal and refitting

1.8 litre engines

Removal

1 Remove the ignition coils as described in Chapter 5B, disconnect the earth lead and move the wiring to one side **(see illustration)**.

2 Pull the up plastic cover over the air intake

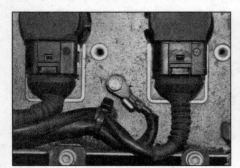

7.1 Disconnect the earth lead from the cylinder head cover

7.4 Disconnect the breather hose from the cylinder head cover (arrowed)

7.9 Apply sealant to the joints on the cylinder head

7.16a Air outlet pipe clip (arrowed)

7.16b Disconnect the breather pipe at the cylinder head cover

7.16c Squeeze together the sides of the collar (arrowed) to disconnect the breather pipe

and intake manifold/throttle housing (**see illustrations**). Disconnect the breather pipes, then remove the intake pipe. To disconnect the breather pipe on the underside of the air outlet pipe, squeeze together the sides of the collar on the connection (**see illustration**).

17 Remove the ignition coils as described in Chapter 5A, then undo the 2 bolts and move the wiring harness to one side (**see illustration**).

18 Disconnect the crankcase breather hose from the camshaft cover. Move the hose to one side.

19 Gradually and evenly, slacken and remove the camshaft cover bolts in the **reverse** of the sequence shown (**see illustration 7.22**)

20 Lift the camshaft cover from position. Recover the gasket, and check it for signs of wear or damage – renew as necessary.

Refitting

21 Clean the surfaces of the camshaft cover and cylinder head.

22 Position the gasket in the camshaft cover, then refit the cover and tighten the bolts gradually and evenly to the specified torque in the sequence shown (**see illustration**).

23 The remainder of refitting is a reversal of removal.

8 Camshaft oil seals – renewal

Exhaust camshaft

1 Remove the camshaft sprocket as described in Section 5.

2 Drill a small hole into the existing oil seal. Thread a self-tapping screw into the hole, and using a pair of pliers, pull on the head of the screw to extract the oil seal (**see illustrations 8.12a and 8.12b**). Take great care to avoid drilling through into the seal housing or camshaft sealing surface.

3 Clean out the seal housing and sealing surface of the camshaft by wiping it with a lint-free cloth. Remove any swarf or burrs that may cause the seal to leak.

4 Push the seal over the camshaft until it is positioned above its housing. Do not lubricate the seal lips prior to installation – the seal must be fitted dry.

5 Using a hammer and a socket of suitable diameter, drive the seal squarely into its housing (**see illustration 8.15**). Note: *Select a socket that bears only on the hard outer*

surface of the seal, not the inner lip which can easily be damaged.

6 Refit the camshaft sprocket with reference to Section 5.

Intake camshaft

7 Remove the auxiliary drivebelt as described in Section 6. Also unbolt the tensioner from the front of the engine.

8 Disconnect the wiring from the camshaft position sensor located on the front of the intake camshaft.

9 Unclip/unbolt and remove the upper timing cover.

10 Unscrew the retaining bolt and withdraw the camshaft position sensor assembly from the cylinder head.

11 Note the location of the sensor rotor and convex washer. Unscrew the central bolt and remove the washer and rotor. The rotor engages with the slot in the end of the intake camshaft.

12 Drill a small hole into the existing oil seal. Thread a self-tapping screw into the hole, and using a pair of pliers, pull on the head of the screw to extract the oil seal (**see illustrations**). Take great care to avoid drilling through into the seal housing or camshaft sealing surface.

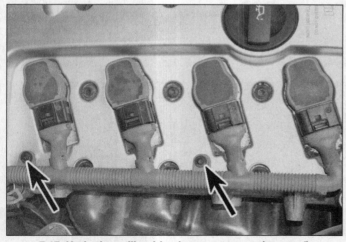

7.17 Undo the coil's wiring harness screws (arrowed)

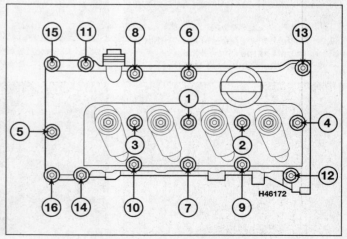

7.22 Camshaft cover bolts tightening sequence – 2.0 litre engines

H46172

8.12a Drill a small hole in the oil seal . . .

8.12b . . . the fit a self-tapping screw, and pull the seal from place

8.15 Use a socket that bears only on the hard, outer edge of the seal

13 Clean out the seal housing and sealing surface of the camshaft by wiping it with a lint-free cloth. Remove any swarf or burrs that may cause the seal to leak.

14 Push the seal over the camshaft until it is positioned above its housing. Do not lubricate the seal lips prior to installation – the seal must be fitted dry. To prevent damage to the sealing lips, wrap some adhesive tape around the end of the camshaft.

15 Using a hammer and a socket of suitable diameter, drive the seal squarely into its housing (see illustration). Note: *Select a socket that bears only on the hard outer surface of the seal, not the inner lip which can easily be damaged.*

16 Locate the sensor rotor on the end of the intake camshaft making sure that it engages the slot. Fit the convex washer and bolt, and tighten to the specified torque.

17 Locate the camshaft position sensor

assembly on the cylinder head, and retain with the bolt tightened to the specified torque.

18 Refit the upper timing cover, making sure that it engages the bottom cover correctly, and retain with the clips/bolts.

19 Reconnect the camshaft position sensor wiring.

20 Refit the tensioner to the front of the engine and tighten the bolts securely.

21 Refit the auxiliary drivebelt with reference to Section 6.

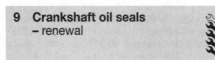

9 Crankshaft oil seals – renewal

Crankshaft front oil seal

1 Remove the timing belt and crankshaft sprocket, with reference to Section 5.

2 The seal may be renewed without removing the housing by drilling two small holes diagonally opposite each other, inserting self-tapping screws, and pulling on the heads of the screws with pliers (see illustrations). Alternatively, unbolt and remove the housing (including the relevant sump bolts), then lever out the oil seal on the bench (see illustration).

3 Use a guide sleeve (Audi tool T10053/1) over the end of the crankshaft, then slide the oil seal over the guide sleeve and into position, until it is flush with the housing. If the guide sleeve is not available, drive the new seal into the housing with a block of wood or a socket until flush, taking great care that the lip of the seal is not damaged by the edge of the crankshaft (see illustration). Make sure that the closed end of the seal is facing outwards – the seal must not be oiled prior to installation.

4 If the housing has been removed, prior to refitting, ensure the cylinder block, housing and sump mating faces are clean and free from debris. Apply a 2.0 mm bead of suitable sealant (available from Audi dealers and parts specialists) to the housing-to-block face, and a broad smear of sealant to the housing-to-sump face. Refit the housing, and tighten the bolts evenly in diagonal sequence to their specified torque. To prevent damage to the seal as it is being fitted, wrap some tape around the end of the crankshaft first (see illustrations).

5 Refit the timing belt and crankshaft sprocket, with reference to Section 5.

9.2a Drill 2 holes opposite each other in the hard part of the oil seal (take care not to mark the crankshaft surface) . . .

9.2b . . . insert a screw and pull the seal from place

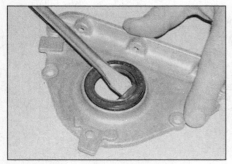

9.2c Use a screwdriver to lever out the crankshaft front oil seal from its housing

9.3 Use a socket to drive the oil seal squarely into the housing

9.4a Apply sealant to the front oil seal housing

Crankshaft rear oil seal

6 Remove the flywheel/driveplate, with reference to Section 12.

7 Unbolt and remove the housing (including the relevant sump bolts). Note that the housing locates on dowels, and is only available as an assembly complete with the seal.

8 Before fitting the new housing, ensure the sump and cylinder block mating faces are clean and free from debris.

9 New oil seals are provided with a fitting tool to prevent damage to the oil seal as it is being fitted. Locate the tool on the end of the crankshaft **(see illustration)**.

10 Apply a bead of suitable sealant (available from Audi dealers or parts specialists) to the housing mating faces.

11 Fit the housing and oil seal, and tighten the bolts evenly in diagonal sequence to the specified torque, then remove the tool **(see illustrations)**. Do not oil the seal lips prior to installation – the seal must be fitted dry.

12 Refit the flywheel/driveplate, with reference to Section 12.

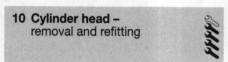

10 Cylinder head –
removal and refitting

Note: *Cylinder head dismantling and overhaul is covered in Chapter 2D.*

Removal

1 Before starting work, disconnect the battery negative (earth) lead (see Chapter 5A).

2 Apply the handbrake, then jack up the front of the vehicle and support it on axle stands (see *Jacking and vehicle support*).

3 Remove the camshaft cover as described in Section 7.

4 Remove the timing belt as described in Section 4.

5 Drain the cooling system as described in Chapter 1A.

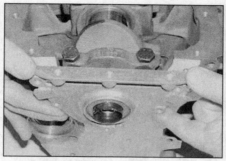

9.4b Wrap tape around the end of the crankshaft to prevent damage to the seal lips

9.11a With the seal/housing in place, remove the fitting guide

6 Remove the intake manifold as described in Chapter 4A.

1.8 litre engines

7 Slacken the clips, undo the bolts, and remove the coolant pipe from the left-hand side of the cylinder head **(see illustration)**.

8 Remove the air filter assembly as described in Chapter 4A.

9 Undo the bolts and remove the heat shield from the left-hand side of the cylinder head (where fitted).

10 Undo the 2 bolts securing the turbocharger

9.9 The new seal/housing is supplied with a fitting guide, which fits over the end of the crankshaft

9.11b Note how the adaptor plate engages with the seal housing

oil supply pipe to the cylinder head, then remove the 3 turbocharger-to-manifold bolts **(see illustration)**. Discard the turbocharger bolts, new ones must be fitted.

11 Disconnect the intake camshaft control valve wiring plug **(see illustration)**.

12 Disconnect the coolant temperature sensor wiring plug, also at the rear of the cylinder head.

13 Disconnect the vacuum hose from the secondary air injection valve **(see illustration 10.11)**.

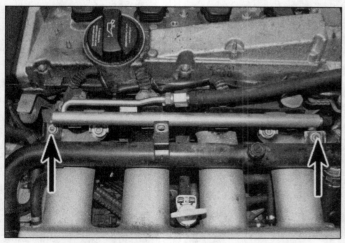

10.7 Coolant rail retaining bolts (arrowed)

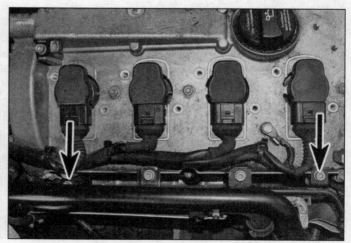

10.10 Turbocharger oil supply pipe bolts (arrowed)

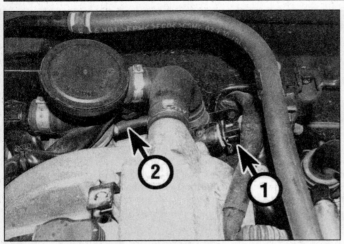

10.11 Intake camshaft wiring plug (1) and secondary air injection valve vacuum hose (2)

10.18 The coolant sensor is located at the rear of the cylinder head (arrowed)

14 Undo the 2 bolts and remove the coolant 'elbow' from the rear of the cylinder head.

15 Remove the bolt securing the oil pipe to the rear of the cylinder head.

16 Disconnect the heater hose from the rear of the cylinder head.

2.0 litre engines

17 Remove the catalytic converter and front exhaust pipe as described in Chapter 4A.

18 Note their fitted positions and harness routing, then disconnect the wiring plugs from the engine coolant temperature sensor and intake camshaft control valve – move the harness to one side **(see illustration)**.

10.21 Unscrew the cylinder head bolts

19 Release the clip and disconnect the coolant hose from the rear of the cylinder head.

All engines

20 Make a final check to ensure all electrical and coolant connections have been disconnected from the cylinder head.

21 Using a splined socket, unscrew the cylinder head bolts a turn at a time, in **reverse** order to the tightening sequence **(see illustration 10.30)** and remove them together with their washers **(see illustration)**. Discard the bolts – new ones must be fitted.

22 With all the bolts removed, lift the cylinder

10.22 Lift the cylinder head from the engine

head from the block together with the exhaust manifold **(see illustration)**. If it is stuck, tap it free with a wooden mallet. Do not insert a lever into the gasket joint.

23 Remove the cylinder head gasket from the block **(see illustration)**.

24 If required, remove the exhaust manifold from the cylinder head with reference to Chapter 4D.

Refitting

25 Thoroughly clean the contact faces of the cylinder head and block. Also clean any oil or coolant from the bolt holes in the block – if this precaution is not taken, not only will the tightening torque be incorrect but there is the possibility of damaging the block. The cylinder head bolts must be renewed whenever removed.

26 Refit the exhaust manifold to the cylinder head together with a new gasket with reference to Chapter 4D.

27 Ensure the camshaft and crankshaft TDC marks are still aligned as described in Section 2.

28 Locate a new gasket on the block, with the part number or words OBEN TOP facing upwards **(see illustration)**. Make sure that the location dowels are in position. Audi recommend that the gasket is removed from its packaging just prior to fitting it.

29 Carefully lower the head onto the block, making sure that it engages the location dowels correctly. Do not use any jointing compound on the cylinder head joint. Insert the new cylinder head bolts, together with their washers, and initially hand-tighten them.

30 Using the sequence shown **(see illustration)** tighten all the bolts to the Stage 1 torque given in the Specifications.

31 Angle-tighten the bolts in the same sequence to the Stage 2 angle given in the Specifications **(see illustration)**.

32 Angle-tighten the bolts in the same sequence to the Stage 3 angle given in the specifications.

10.23 Remove the cylinder head gasket

10.28 Cylinder head gasket markings

33 Refit the camshaft cover with reference to Section 7.

34 The remainder of refitting is a reversal of removal, noting the following points:

a) Tighten all fasteners to their specified torque where given.

b) Renew the coolant as described in Chapter 1A.

c) Ensure all wiring harnesses are routed as before, and secured with cable ties in their original positions.

d) After restarting, allow the engine to run until normal operating temperature is achieved and check for leaks.

11 Hydraulic tappets
– operational check

⚠️ **Warning: After fitting hydraulic tappets, wait a minimum of 30 minutes (or preferably, leave overnight) before starting the engine, to allow the tappets time to settle, otherwise the valve heads will strike the pistons.**

1 The hydraulic tappets are self-adjusting, and require no attention whilst in service.

2 If the hydraulic tappets become excessively noisy, their operation can be checked as described below.

3 Run the engine until it reaches its normal operating temperature. Switch off the engine, then refer to Section 7 and remove the camshaft cover.

4 Rotate the camshaft by turning the crankshaft with a socket and wrench, until the first cam lobe over No 1 cylinder is pointing upwards.

5 Using a non-metallic tool, press the tappet downwards then use a feeler blade to check the free travel. If this is more than 0.2 mm before the valve starts to open, the tappet should be renewed.

6 Hydraulic tappet removal and refitting is described as part of the cylinder head overhaul sequence – see Chapter 2D for details.

7 If hydraulic tappet noise occurs repeatedly when travelling short distances, renew the oil retention valve located in the rear of the oil filter mounting housing. It will be necessary to remove the oil filter, then unbolt the

housing from the cylinder block and recover the gasket. Use a suitable key to unscrew the valve, and tighten the new valve securely. Refit the housing together with a new gasket.

12 Flywheel/driveplate
– removal, inspection and refitting

Removal

1 On manual gearbox models, remove the gearbox (see Chapter 7A) and clutch (see Chapter 6).

2 On automatic transmission models, remove the automatic transmission as described in Chapter 7B.

3 On Multitronic transmission models, remove the transmission (Chapter 7C).

Manual transmission

4 These models are fitted with a dual-mass flywheel. Begin by making alignment marks between the flywheel and the crankshaft.

5 Rotate the outside of the dual-mass

flywheel so that the bolts align with the holes **(see illustration)**.

6 Unscrew the bolts and remove the flywheel. Use a locking tool to counterhold the flywheel **(see illustration)**. Discard the bolts, new ones must be fitted. **Note:** *In order not to damage the flywheel, do not allow the bolt heads to make contact with the flywheel secondary element during the unscrewing procedure.*

Multitronic transmission

7 Undo the screws and remove the damper unit from the flywheel **(see illustration)**.

8 Make alignment marks between the flywheel and crankshaft.

9 Unscrew the bolts and remove the flywheel. Use a locking tool to counterhold the flywheel. Discard the bolts, new ones must be fitted.

Automatic transmission

10 Make alignment marks between the driveplate and crankshaft.

11 Unscrew the bolts and remove the driveplate. Use a locking tool to counterhold the driveplate. Discard the bolts, new ones must be fitted.

12 Remove the shim from behind the driveplate.

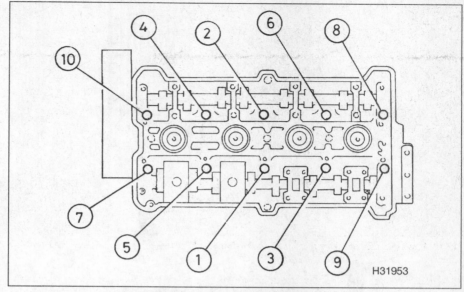

10.30 Cylinder head bolt tightening sequence

10.31 Angle-tighten the cylinder head bolts

12.5 Rotate the secondary element of the dual-mass flywheel so the bolt heads align with the holes

12.6 Use a locking tool (arrowed) to prevent the flywheel from rotating

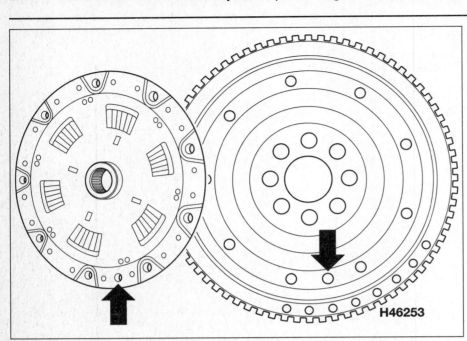

12.7 The locating pin on the flywheel must align with the corresponding hole in the Multitronic damper unit (arrowed)

Inspection

13 Check the flywheel/driveplate for wear and damage. Examine the starter ring gear for excessive wear to the teeth. If the driveplate or its ring gear are damaged, the complete driveplate must be renewed. The flywheel ring gear, however, may be renewed separately from the flywheel, but the work should be entrusted to an Audi dealer. If the clutch friction face is discoloured or scored excessively, it may be possible to regrind it, but this work should also be entrusted to an Audi dealer.

14 With the flywheel removed, check the spigot needle bearing in the end of the crankshaft for wear by turning it with a finger. If there is any evidence of excessive wear or if the bearing has been running dry, it must be renewed. To do this, use a bearing removal puller which engages the rear end of the bearing. Drive the new bearing into position until its outer end is 1.5 mm below the end of the crankshaft. **Note:** *A spigot needle bearing must not be fitted to the crankshaft on automatic or Multitronic transmission models.*

15 There should be no cracks in the drive surface of the flywheel. If cracks are evident, the flywheel may need renewing. The following are guidelines only, but should indicate whether professional inspection is necessary. A dual-mass flywheel should be checked as follows:

Warpage

Place a straight-edge across the face of the drive surface, and check by trying to insert a feeler gauge between the straight-edge and the drive surface (see illustration). The flywheel will normally warp like a bowl – ie, higher on the outer edge. If the warpage is more than 0.40 mm, the flywheel may need renewing.

Free rotational movement

This is the distance the drive surface of the flywheel can be turned independently of the flywheel primary element, using finger effort alone. Move the drive surface in one direction and make a mark where the locating pin aligns with the flywheel edge. Move the drive surface in the other direction (finger pressure only) and make another mark (see illustration). The total of free movement should not exceed 9.75 mm. If it's more, the flywheel may need renewing.

Total rotational movement

This is the total distance the drive surface can be turned independently of the flywheel primary element. Insert two bolts into the clutch pressure plate/damper unit mounting holes, and with the crankshaft/flywheel held stationary, use a lever/pry bar between the bolts and use some effort to move the drive surface fully in one direction – make a mark where the locating pin aligns with the flywheel edge. Now force the drive surface fully in the opposite direction, and make another mark. The total rotational movement should not exceed 43.60 mm. If it does, the flywheel may need renewing.

Lateral movement

The lateral movement (up and down) of the drive surface in relation to the primary element of the flywheel, should not exceed 1.67 mm. If it does, the flywheel may need renewing. This can be checked by pressing the drive surface down on one side into the flywheel (flywheel horizontal) and making an alignment mark between the drive surface and the inner edge of the primary element. Now press down on the opposite side of the drive surface, and make another mark above the original one. The difference between the two marks is the lateral movement (see illustration).

Refitting

16 Refitting is a reversal of removal, however on automatic transmission models temporarily refit the driveplate using the old bolts tightened to 30 Nm (22 lbf ft), and measure, through the torque converter mounting hole, the distance from the block to the torque converter *mounting face* on the driveplate. The correct distance is 18.9 to 20.5 mm. If necessary, remove the driveplate, and fit a spacer behind it to achieve the correct dimension. The raised pip on the outer shim must face the torque converter. Use new bolts when refitting the flywheel or driveplate, and coat the threads of the bolts with locking fluid before inserting them. Tighten them to the specified torque.

12.15a Flywheel warpage check – see text

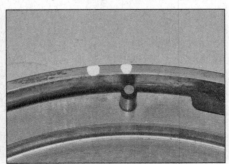

12.15b Flywheel free rotational movement check alignment marks – see text

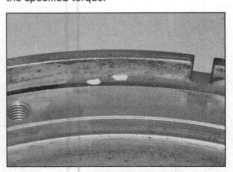

12.15c Flywheel lateral movement check marks – see text

13 Engine mountings
– inspection and renewal

Inspection

1 If improved access is required, raise the front of the car and support it securely on axle stands and remove the undershield where applicable.

2 Check the mounting rubbers to see if they are cracked, hardened or separated from the metal at any point; renew the mounting if any such damage or deterioration is evident.

3 Check that all the mounting's fasteners are securely tightened; use a torque wrench to check if possible.

4 Using a large screwdriver or a crowbar, check for wear in the mounting by carefully levering against it to check for free play. Where this is not possible, enlist the aid of an assistant to move the engine/transmission back-and-forth, or from side-to-side, while you watch the mounting. While some free play is to be expected even from new components, excessive wear should be obvious. If excessive free play is found, check first that the fasteners are correctly secured, then renew any worn components as described below.

Renewal

Front torque bracket

5 Apply the handbrake then jack up the front of the vehicle and support it on axle stands (see *Jacking and vehicle support*). Release the fasteners and remove the undershield.

6 Unscrew the bolts and remove the stop from the bracket on the front- right-hand corner of the engine **(see illustration)**.

7 If necessary, the stop-plate can be unbolted from the rear face of the lock carrier **(see illustration)**.

8 Fit the new rubber and bracket using a reversal of the removal procedure.

Right- or left-hand engine mounting

9 Apply the handbrake, then jack up the front of the vehicle and support it on axle stands (see *Jacking and vehicle support*).

10 Support the weight of the engine with a hoist. Alternatively, use a trolley jack and piece of wood beneath the sump.

11 Note their fitted positions, then unscrew the mounting nuts, then raise the engine and withdraw the mounting from the engine bracket and subframe **(see illustrations)**. Note that the mounting has an integral hydro action, to absorb movement of the engine and prevent engine noise transmission inside the car.

12 If necessary, unbolt the mounting bracket from the side of the cylinder block.

13 Fit the new mounting using a reversal of the removal procedure.

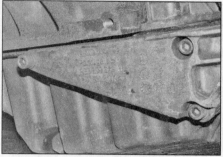

13.6 Undo the bolts and remove the stop bracket/torque arm from the engine

13.11a Note the position of the locating dowel (arrowed) – the mounting must be fitted with the dowel in its original position

13.7 Unbolt the stop-plate from the lock carrier

13.11b Undo the nut (arrowed) and detach the mounting from the bracket

14 Sump –
removal and refitting

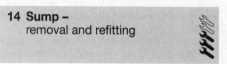

Removal

1 Apply the handbrake, then jack up the front of the vehicle and support it on axle stands (see *Jacking and vehicle support*).

2 Undo the fasteners and remove the engine undershield **(see illustrations 4.3a, 4.3b and 4.3c)**.

3 Position a container beneath the sump, then unscrew the drain plug and drain the engine oil. Clean the plug and if necessary renew the washer, then refit and tighten the plug after all the oil has drained. Remove the dipstick from the engine.

4 Remove the auxiliary drivebelt as described in Section 6.

5 On 1.8 litre engines, undo the 2 bolts and detach the oil return pipe from the sump **(see illustration)**.

6 Disconnect the oil temperature sensor wiring plug from the base of the sump.

7 Undo the bolt and detach the refrigerant pipe support bracket (where applicable) from the sump **(see illustration)**.

8 Disconnect the wiring plug, then undo the bolts and position the air conditioning compressor to one side (where applicable). Support the compressor by suspending it from the vehicle body with wire/string – there is no need to disconnect the refrigerant pipes, but ensure they are not damaged or kinked during the process.

9 Unbolt the torque arm bracket from the front of the engine.

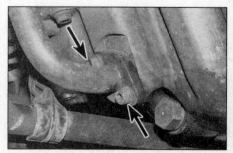

14.5 Undo the Allen screws (arrowed) securing the turbocharger oil return pipe to the sump

14.7 Detach the refrigerant pipe support bracket (arrowed) from the sump

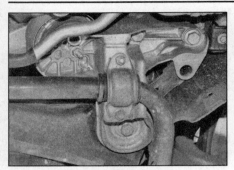

14.11 Undo the nuts and remove the anti-roll bar clamps each side

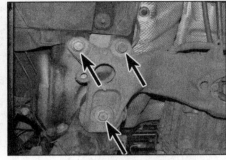

14.17a Front subframe rear mounting bolts (arrowed)

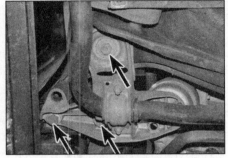

14.17b Front subframe front mounting bolts (arrowed)

14.18 Rotate the flywheel and align the cut-outs to access the rear sump bolts

14.21 Ensure the sump overhangs the engine block by 0.8 mm to allow for the adapter plate

10 On vehicles with gas discharge headlights, unclip the vehicle height sensor actuator rod from the front-left lower transverse link arm.

11 Undo the nuts and detach the inboard clamps from the front anti-roll bar **(see illustration)**.

12 Detach the starter motor cables from under the engine mounting by cutting the plastic cable ties.

13 Unscrew and remove the nuts from the bottom of each engine mounting.

14 Remove the engine top cover, then remove the crankcase breather hose and air intake duct from the rear of the engine.

15 On 2.0 litre engines, unbolt the intake manifold support bracket from the intake manifold and sump.

16 Connect a suitable hoist to the engine, then raise it as far as possible without damaging or stretching the coolant hoses and wiring.

17 Mark the fitted position of the subframe, then position a workshop trolley jack to take the weight, and undo the bolts and lower the front subframe **(see illustrations)**.

18 Unscrew and remove the sump bolts. Note that on manual transmission models, the two rear sump bolts are accessed through a cut-out in the flywheel – turn the flywheel as necessary to align the cut-out **(see illustration)**.

19 Remove the sump. If it is stuck, tap it gently with a mallet to free it.

Refitting

20 Thoroughly clean the contact faces of

the sump and block. It is recommended that a rotary wire brush is used to clean away the sealant.

Caution: Take care not to apply excessive amounts of sealant, in the hope of obtaining a better seal – if too much is applied, the excess may enter the sump and then block the oil pump strainer, causing oil starvation.

21 Apply a 2 to 3 mm bead of suitable silicone sealant to the sump mating surface. Run the bead of sealant around the inside of the bolt holes, and take particular care at the rear of the sump to keep the bead near the inner edge of the sump. The sump should be offered into position immediately, and the retaining bolts tightened hand-tight initially. If the engine is out of the car, make sure that the rear edge of the sump overhangs the rear edge of the cylinder block by 0.8 mm, so that

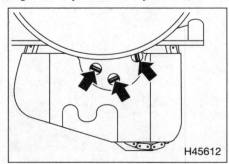

15.7 Release the cover locking clips with a screwdriver

it is flush when the intermediate (adapter) plate is fitted **(see illustration)**. Progressively tighten the sump bolts to the specified torque. Refer to the sealant manufacturer's advice on the length of time required for the sealant to set. Typically, it is advisable to wait at least 30 minutes before filling the engine with oil. If the car is to be left for some time with no oil in the sump, ensure that the battery remains disconnected, so that no attempt is made to start the engine.

22 The remaining refitting procedure is a reversal removal, but tighten the nuts and bolts to the specified torque where given in the Specifications. On completion, fill the engine with the correct quantity of oil as described in Chapter 1A.

15 Oil pump and pickup – removal, inspection and refitting

Removal

1 Remove the sump as described in Section 14.

1.8 litre engine

2 Undo the bolt and remove the baffle plate (where applicable).

3 Undo the retaining bolt, and pull the drive sprocket and chain from the oil pump shaft.

4 Unscrew and remove the oil pump mounting bolts, then withdraw the pump from the block. If necessary, press the subframe downwards to provide sufficient room to remove the oil pump.

5 Undo the bolts and remove the pump cover. Pull the inner and outer rotors from the housing.

2.0 litre engine

6 Undo the 2 bolts securing the oil pipe at the rear of the engine block.

7 Release the retaining clips, and remove the chain/sprocket cover from below the crankshaft sprocket **(see illustration)**.

8 Use a Torx bit to slacken the oil pump drive sprocket retaining bolt approximately 1 turn.

9 Using a screwdriver, push the drive chain tensioner blade to relieve the tension on the chain. Insert a 3 mm Allen key into the hole in the tensioner assembly to lock the blade in this position (see illustrations).

10 Remove the Torx bolt and pull the sprocket from the oil pump shaft. Disengage the sprocket from the chain.

11 Working from the outside-in, gradually and evenly slacken and remove the bolts securing the balance shaft housing and intermediate plate (see illustration). Remove the balancer shaft housing and plate from the engine block, noting that the housing locates on dowels. Discard the intermediate plate and the retaining bolts, new ones must be fitted.

12 Undo the retaining bolts and remove the drive chain tensioner from the balancer shaft housing.

13 Undo the 5 bolts and remove the oil pump cover. Note their fitted positions, then pull the inner and outer rotors from the pump (see illustration)

Inspection

14 Examine the drive chain for wear and damage. To remove the chain, the timing belt must first be removed (see Section 4), then the crankshaft front oil seal housing unbolted from the cylinder block.

15 On 2.0 litre engines, no attempt should be made to dismantle the balancer shaft's housing. No parts are available separately, and if faulty, the complete assembly must be renewed.

16 Clean the oil pump components and check them for wear and damage. Examine the inner and outer rotors for scoring or any signs of wear/damage. If evident, renew the oil pump.

17 If the components are re-usable, fit the outer, and inner rotors to the pump body. Refit the pump cover and tighten the retaining bolts to the specified torque.

Refitting

18 Prime the pump with oil by pouring oil into

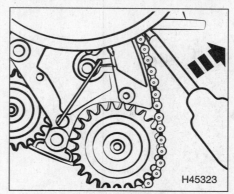

15.9a Press against the tensioner using a screwdriver – in the direction of the arrow . . .

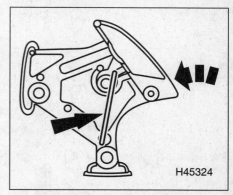

15.9b . . . then lock the tensioner in position with a 3 mm Allen key

the suction pipe aperture while turning the driveshaft.

1.8 litre engines

19 Clean the oil pump and block, then refit

the oil pump, insert the mounting bolts, and tighten them to the specified torque. Ensure the locating dowels are correctly fitted (see illustration).

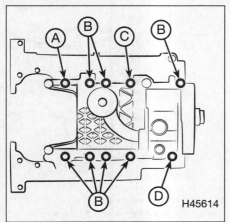

15.11 Balancer shaft assembly mounting bolt locations

A	M7 x 40	D	Bolt with
B	M7 x 55		sealing O-ring
C	M7 x 90		

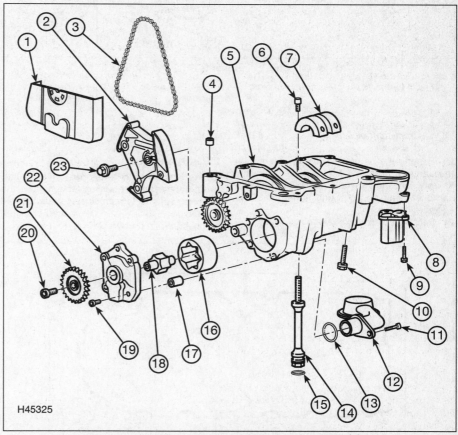

15.13 Layout of balancer shaft unit/oil pump – 2.0 litre engine

1 Chain protector cover	8 Oil return element with seal	16 Oil pump outer rotor
2 Chain tensioner	9 Bolt	17 Dowels
3 Chain	10 Bolt	18 Oil pump inner rotor
4 Dowels	11 Bolt	19 Bolt
5 Oil pump/balancer shaft	12 Oil strainer/suction pipe	20 Bolt
assembly	13 O-ring/seal	21 Oil pump drive sprocket
6 Bolt	14 Sealing bolt	22 Oil pump cover
7 Cover to prevent frothing	15 O-ring/seal	23 Bolt

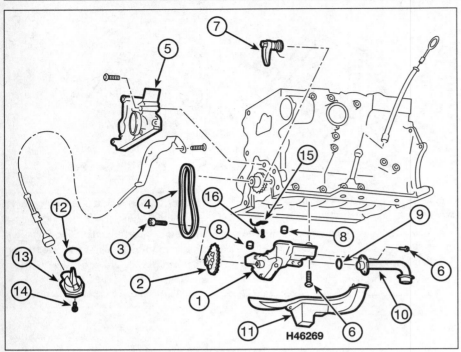

15.19 Oil pump components – 1.8 litre models

1 Oil pump	6 Bolt	12 Seal
2 Oil pump sprocket	7 Drive chain tensioner	13 Oil level/temperature
3 Bolt	8 Dowels	sensor
4 Oil pump drive chain	9 O-ring	14 Bolt
5 Crankshaft oil seal	10 Oil pick up pipe	15 Oil spray jet
housing	11 Oil baffle	16 Bolt

20 Engage the oil pump drive sprocket with the chain, noting that the sprocket will only fit only the shaft in one position. Refit the sprocket retaining bolts and tighten it to the specified torque.

21 Refit the sump with reference to Section 14.

2.0 litre engines

22 Refit the chain tensioner assembly to the balancer shaft housing, and tighten the retaining bolts to the specified torque. Ensure the tensioner blade is in the locked position, as described in paragraph 9.

23 Position the new intermediate plate over the locating dowels on the balancer shaft housing.

24 Apply a bead of suitable sealant, approximately 2.0 mm thick, to the intermediate plate mating surface (see illustration). Take great care not to apply the sealant too thickly, as any excess may find its way in the oil galleries.

25 Position the balancer shaft housing/intermediate plate on the base of the cylinder block, then insert the new bolts (ensure the new O-ring is fitted to the appropriate bolt). Working from the inside tighten the new bolts to the Stage one torque setting, then in the same order, tighten them to the Stage two setting.

26 Turn the crankshaft pulley clockwise until the TDC mark on the pulley aligns with the mark on the timing cover, then rotate the balancer shaft sprocket until the mark on the sprocket face is aligned with the locating hole. Insert Audi tool T10060, or a 5.0 mm drill bit into the hole to lock the sprocket in this position (see illustration).

27 Engage the drive chain with the balancer shaft sprocket, then fit the oil pump sprocket into the chain. Fit the sprocket on to the oil pump shaft, noting that the sprocket will only fit in one position – if necessary, rotate the oil pump shaft to enable the fitment of the sprocket.

28 Remove the balancer shaft sprocket locking tool (drill bit), and the Allen key locking the tensioner blade.

29 Refit the cover over the drive sprockets, and secure it with the retaining clips.

30 Refit the oil pipe to the housing, and tighten the bolts to the specified torque.

31 Refit the baffle plate (where applicable) followed by the sump with reference to Section 14.

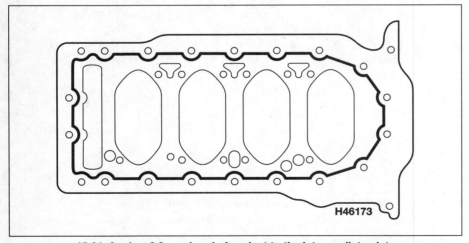

15.24 Apply a 2.0 mm bead of sealant to the intermediate plate

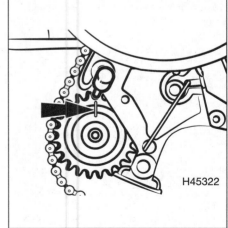

15.26 Align the timing mark (arrowed) insert the locking pin/drill bit

Chapter 2 Part B:
2.0 litre direct injection petrol engine in-car repair procedures

Contents

Section number

Auxiliary drivebelt – removal and refitting. 6
Camshaft cover – removal and refitting 7
Camshaft oil seals – renewal 8
Crankshaft oil seals – renewal 9
Crankshaft spigot bearing – renewal 16
Cylinder compression test 3
Cylinder head – dismantling and overhaul . . . . See Chapter 2D
Cylinder head – removal and refitting. 10
Engine mountings – inspection and renewal 13
Engine oil and filter – renewal. . . . . .See Chapter 1A
Engine oil level – check . . . . See Weekly checks

Section number

Engine valve timing marks – general information and usage. 2
Flywheel/driveplate – removal, inspection and refitting 12
General information 1
Hydraulic tappets – operational check. 11
Oil pump and balancer shaft housing – removal, inspection and
    refitting 15
Sump – removal and refitting 14
Timing belt – removal, inspection and refitting. 4
Timing belt tensioner and sprockets – removal, inspection and
    refitting 5

Degrees of difficulty

Easy, suitable for novice with little experience	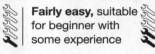	**Fairly easy,** suitable for beginner with some experience	**Fairly difficult,** suitable for competent DIY mechanic	**Difficult,** suitable for experienced DIY mechanic	**Very difficult,** suitable for expert DIY or professional	

Specifications

General

Engine code*:
  1984 cc, Bosch Motronic MED7.1, 110 kW (143 bhp) . . . . AWA
Bore . . . . 82.5 mm
Stroke. . . . . 92.8 mm
Compression ratio . . . . 11.5 : 1
Compression pressures (wear limit) . . . . 7.0 bar
  Maximum difference between cylinders. 3.0 bar
Firing order . . . . 1 – 3 – 4 – 2
No 1 cylinder location. . . . . Timing belt end
* Note: *See 'Vehicle identification' for the location of the code marking on the engine.*

Lubrication system

Oil pump type. . . . . Inner and outer rotor type, chain-driven from crankshaft
Oil pressure (oil temperature 80°C):
  At idle speed. . . . . 2.0 bar minimum
  At 2000 rpm . . . . 2.7 to 1.5 bar minimum

Torque wrench settings

	Nm	lbf ft
Ancillaries bracket to engine block	40	30
Auxiliary drivebelt idler pulley	25	18
Auxiliary drivebelt tensioner bolts	25	18
Balancer shaft/oil pump drive chain tensioner bolts	15	11
Balancer shaft housing bolts*:		
Stage 1	15	11
Stage 2	Angle-tighten a further 90°	
Big-end bearing caps bolts*:		
Stage 1	30	22
Stage 2	Angle-tighten a further 90°	
Camshaft adjuster-to-exhaust camshaft bolt	100	74
Camshaft adjuster chain tensioner	10	7
Camshaft adjuster rear cover	10	7
Camshaft bearing ladder*:		
Stage 1	8	6
Stage 2	Angle-tighten a further 90°	
Camshaft cover	10	7
Camshaft position sensor	10	7
Camshaft sprocket	65	48
Crankshaft front oil seal housing	15	11
Crankshaft pulley/vibration damper bolts*:		
Stage 1	10	7
Stage 2	Angle-tighten a further 90°	
Crankshaft rear oil seal housing	15	11
Crankshaft sprocket*:		
Stage 1	90	66
Stage 2	Angle-tighten a further 90°	
Cylinder head bolts*:		
Stage 1	40	30
Stage 2	Angle-tighten a further 90°	
Stage 3	Angle-tighten a further 90°	
Driveplate mounting bolts*:		
Stage 1	60	44
Stage 2	Angle-tighten a further 90°	
Engine mounting to subframe	25	18
Engine-to-transmission bolts:		
M10	45	33
M12	65	48
Flywheel mounting bolts*:		
Bolt length 22.5 mm:		
Stage 1	60	44
Stage 2	Angle-tighten a further 90°	
Bolt lengths 35.0 and 43.0 mm:		
Stage 1	60	44
Stage 2	Angle-tighten a further 180°	
Main bearing cap bolts*:		
Stage 1	65	48
Stage 2	Angle-tighten a further 90°	
Oil jets	27	20
Oil pump cover	10	7
Oil pump sprocket bolt*:		
Stage 1	20	15
Stage 2	Angle-tighten a further 90°	
Oil retention valve	8	6
Sump:		
Sump-to-block bolts:		
M10 bolts	40	30
All other bolts	15	11
Sump-to-transmission bolts	45	33
Timing belt cover bolts	10	7
Timing belt tensioner hub nut	23	17
Timing belt tensioner housing/roller (up to 04/2003):		
Upper bolt	20	15
Lower bolt (retains idler roller)	25	18
Roller pivot arm bolt	40	30
Timing belt tensioner mounting plate bolts	10	7

* Do not re-use

1 General information

Using this Chapter

Chapter 2 is divided into four Parts: A, B, C and D. Repair operations that can be carried out with the engine in the vehicle are described in Part A (indirect injection petrol engines), Part B (direct injection petrol engines) and Part C (diesel engines). Part D covers the removal of the engine/transmission as a unit, and describes the engine dismantling and overhaul procedures.

In Parts A, B and C, the assumption is made that the engine is installed in the vehicle, with all ancillaries connected. If the engine has been removed for overhaul, the preliminary dismantling information which precedes each operation may be ignored.

Access to the engine compartment can be improved by removing the bonnet as described in Chapter 11.

Engine description

The engines are water-cooled, double overhead camshaft, in-line four-cylinder direct-injection units, with aluminium cylinder blocks and cylinder heads. All are mounted longitudinally at the front of the vehicle, with the transmission bolted to the rear of the engine.

The crankshaft is of five-bearing type, and thrustwashers are fitted to the centre main bearing to control crankshaft endfloat.

The timing belt drives the exhaust camshaft, and the intake camshaft is driven from the exhaust camshaft by chain at the rear of the camshafts. A hydraulic tensioner is fitted to the chain, to automatically vary the intake camshaft valve timing.

The valves are operated from the camshafts through hydraulic bucket type tappets, and the valve clearances are adjusted automatically.

The cylinder head carries the double camshafts. It also houses the intake and exhaust valves, which are closed by single coil springs, and which run in guides pressed into the cylinder head. The camshaft actuates the valves directly via hydraulic tappets, mounted in the cylinder head. The cylinder head contains integral oilways which supply and lubricate the tappets.

The engine coolant pump is driven by the toothed timing belt.

Lubricant is circulated under pressure by a pump, driven by a chain from the crankshaft. Oil is drawn from the sump through a strainer, and then forced through an externally-mounted, renewable screw-on filter. From there, it is distributed to the cylinder head, where it lubricates the camshaft journals and hydraulic tappets, and also to the crankcase, where it lubricates the main bearings, connecting rod big-ends, gudgeon pins and cylinder bores. An oil pressure switch is

located on the oil filter housing, operating at 1.4 bars. An oil cooler mounted above the oil filter is supplied with coolant from the cooling system to reduce the temperature of the oil before it re-enters the engine.

A balancer shaft housing is fitted below the cylinder block. The two contra-rotating shafts are driven by the same chain that drives the oil pump. The shafts have integral weights fitted along their length, and as they spin, the forces created cancel out almost all of the vibration generated by the engine.

Repairs with engine in vehicle

The following operations can be performed without removing the engine:

a) Auxiliary drivebelt – removal and refitting.
b) Camshafts – removal and refitting*.
c) Camshaft oil seals – renewal.
d) Camshaft sprocket – removal and refitting.
e) Coolant pump – removal and refitting (refer to Chapter 3).
f) Crankshaft oil seals – renewal.
g) Crankshaft sprocket – removal and refitting.
h) Cylinder head – removal and refitting*.
i) Engine mountings – inspection and renewal.
j) Balancer shaft housing – renewal.
k) Oil pump and pickup assembly – removal and refitting.
l) Sump – removal and refitting.
m) Timing belt, sprockets and cover – removal, inspection and refitting.

* Cylinder head dismantling procedures are detailed in Chapter 2D, with details of camshaft and hydraulic tappet removal.

Note: *It is possible to remove the pistons and connecting rods (after removing the cylinder head and sump) without removing the engine. However, this is not recommended. Work of this nature is more easily and thoroughly completed with the engine on the bench, as described in Chapter 2D.*

2 Engine valve timing marks – general information and usage

General information

1 The crankshaft and camshaft sprockets are driven by the timing belt, and rotate in phase with each other. When the timing belt is removed during servicing or repair, it is possible for the shafts to rotate independently of each other, and the correct phasing is then lost.

2 The design of the engines covered in this Chapter is such that piston-to-valve contact will occur if the crankshaft is turned with the timing belt removed. For this reason, it is important that the correct phasing between the camshaft and crankshaft is preserved whilst the timing belt is off the engine. This is achieved by setting the engine in a reference condition (known as Top Dead Centre or TDC)

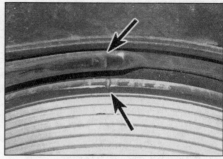

2.4 Crankshaft pulley and timing belt cover TDC markings (arrowed)

before the timing belt is removed, and then preventing the shafts from rotating until the belt is refitted. Similarly, if the engine has been dismantled for overhaul, the engine can be set to TDC during reassembly to ensure that the correct shaft phasing is restored. **Note:** *The coolant pump is also driven by the timing belt, but the pump alignment is not critical.*

3 TDC is the highest position a piston reaches within its respective cylinder – in a four-stroke engine, each piston reaches TDC twice per cycle; once on the compression stroke, and once on the exhaust stroke. In general, TDC normally refers to No 1 cylinder on the compression stroke. Note that the cylinders are numbered one to four, starting from the timing belt end of the engine.

4 The crankshaft pulley has a marking which, when aligned with a reference marking on the timing belt cover, indicates that No 1 cylinder (and hence also No 4 cylinder) is at TDC **(see illustration)**.

5 The exhaust camshaft sprocket is also equipped with a timing mark **(see illustration)** – when this is aligned with a mark on the small upper timing belt cover or camshaft cover, No 1 cylinder is at TDC compression.

Setting TDC on No 1 cylinder

6 Before starting work, make sure that the ignition is switched off.

7 Pull the engine top cover upwards from its fasteners.

8 Remove all of the spark plugs as described in Chapter 1A.

9 Remove the timing belt upper, outer cover as describe in Section 4.

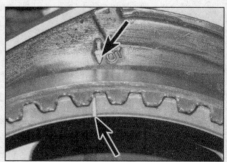

2.5 Camshaft sprocket and timing belt cover TDC markings (arrowed)

3.4 Disconnect the injector loom wiring plug (arrowed) – located beneath the intake manifold

10 Turn the engine clockwise with a spanner on the crankshaft pulley until the timing mark on the outer circumference of the camshaft sprocket aligns with the mark on the timing belt cover. With this aligned, the timing mark on the crankshaft pulley should align with the mark on the lower timing belt cover.

3 Cylinder compression test

1 When engine performance is down, or if misfiring occurs which cannot be attributed to the ignition or fuel systems, a compression test can provide diagnostic clues as to the engine's condition. If the test is performed regularly, it can give warning of trouble before any other symptoms become apparent.
2 The engine must be fully warmed-up to normal operating temperature, the battery must be fully-charged, and all the spark plugs must be removed (refer to Chapter 1A). The aid of an assistant will also be required. Pull the plastic cover on the top of the engine upwards from its fasteners.
3 Remove the spark plugs as described in Chapter 1A.
4 Disable the injectors by disconnecting the wiring plug under the intake manifold **(see illustration)**.
5 Fit a compression tester to the No 1 cylinder spark plug hole – the type of tester which screws into the plug thread is preferable.
6 Have an assistant hold the throttle wide open. Crank the engine on the starter motor several seconds. After one or two revolutions, the compression pressure should build-up to a maximum figure, and then stabilise. Record the highest reading obtained.
7 Repeat the test on the remaining cylinders, recording the pressure in each. Keep the throttle wide open.
8 All cylinders should produce very similar pressures; a difference of more than 3 bars between any two cylinders indicates a fault. Note that the compression should build-up quickly in a healthy engine. Low compression on the first stroke, followed by gradually-increasing pressure on successive strokes, indicates worn piston rings. A low compression reading on the first stroke, which does not build-up during successive strokes, indicates leaking valves or a blown head gasket (a cracked head could also be the cause).

9 Refer to the Specifications section of this Chapter, and compare the recorded compression figures with those stated by the manufacturer.
10 On completion of the test, refit the spark plugs, injector wiring plug and top cover. Note that in some cases, disconnecting the wiring plugs from the coils and injectors, then cranking the engine, may cause fault codes to be stored by the engine management ECM – have these codes erased by means of a suitable diagnostic tool/fault code reader. See your Audi dealer or specialist.

4 Timing belt – removal, inspection and refitting

General information

1 The primary function of the toothed timing belt is to drive the camshafts. Should the belt slip or break in service, the valve timing will be disturbed and piston-to-valve contact will occur, resulting in serious engine damage. For this reason, it is important that the timing belt is tensioned correctly, and inspected regularly for signs of wear or deterioration.

Removal

2 Before starting work, disconnect the battery negative (earth) lead (see Chapter 5A).
3 Apply the handbrake, then jack up the front of the vehicle and support it on axle stands (see *Jacking and vehicle support*). Undo the fasteners and remove the engine undershield **(see illustrations)**.
4 Access to the timing belt is achieved by moving the complete front panel (the lock carrier assembly) away from the front of the car as far as possible (in the Service position) as described in Chapter 11.
5 Pull the plastic cover on the top of the engine upwards to release it from the fasteners **(see illustration)**.
6 Remove the auxiliary drivebelt with reference to Section 6. Also unbolt the tensioner from the front of the engine **(see illustration)**.
7 On vehicles manufactured up to 05/2004, undo the 2 screws and remove the top section of the timing belt cover **(see illustration)**. On all vehicles after this date prise out the pin and

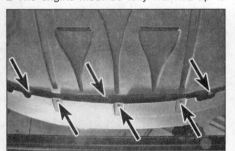

4.3a The front edge of the undershield is secured by 3 screws to the front bumper, and 3 screws to the lock carrier (arrowed)

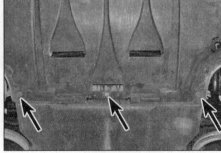

4.3b Engine undershield-to-transmission undershield fasteners (arrowed)

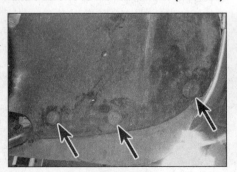

4.3c Engine undershield-to-wheel arch liner fasteners (arrowed)

4.5 Pull the engine top cover upwards from the fasteners

4.6 Undo the bolts and remove the belt tensioner (and engine lifting eye)

4.7 Undo the 2 screws (arrowed) and remove the timing belt upper cover

4.10a Undo the 4 Allen screws (arrowed) securing the pulley to the sprocket

remove the cap from the front section of the upper timing belt cover to observe the exhaust camshaft sprocket.

8 Rotate the crankshaft and align the timing marks as described in Section 2.

9 If the timing belt is to be refitted, mark its normal direction of travel with chalk or a marker pen.

10 While holding the crankshaft stationary with a socket on the centre pulley bolt, unscrew and remove the bolts securing the pulley to the sprocket. Withdraw the pulley **(see illustrations)**. Note that the bolts must not be re-used.

11 Unscrew the bolts and remove the timing belt covers from the cylinder block **(see illustration)**.

Engines up to 04/2003

12 Insert an 8.0 mm Allen key in the hole in the tensioner hub, and slowly turn the tensioner clockwise to compress the tensioner spring. Align the small holes in the top of the tensioner and the internal piston, and insert a 2.0 mm diameter twist drill to hold the tensioner spring compressed **(see illustration)**.

13 Undo the pivot bolt and remove the tensioning roller and washer.

Engines from 05/2003 to 05/2004

14 Insert Audi special tool T10020 into the holes in the tensioner hub arm, then slacken the tensioner nut and rotate the hub clockwise to relieve the tension **(see illustration)**. Temporarily tighten the nut to retain the tensioner in the released position. In the absence of the special tool, a sturdy pair of right-angle circlip pliers will suffice.

Engines from 06/2004

15 Slacken the nut in the centre of the tensioner pulley to relieve the tension in the belt.

4.10b Note the hole in the pulley (arrowed) locates over raised projection on the crankshaft sprocket

All engines

16 Slip the timing belt off of the crankshaft, camshaft, and coolant pump sprockets, and remove it from the engine. **Do not** bend the timing belt sharply if it is to be re-used.

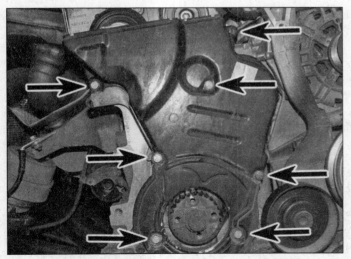

4.11 Undo the timing belt cover screws (arrowed)

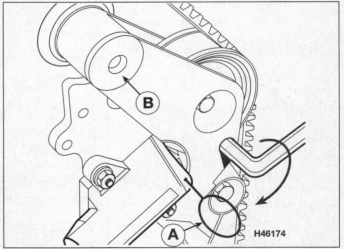

4.12 Rotate the tensioner clockwise, and insert a drill bit or locking (A) rod into the top of the tensioner and piston, then undo the pivot bolt (B)

4.14 Insert right-angle circlip pliers into the tensioner hub arm

4.19 Raised projection on the crankshaft sprocket (arrowed)

4.21 Refit the timing belt to the sprockets and pulleys

Inspection

17 Examine the belt for evidence of contamination by coolant or lubricant. If this is the case, find the source of the contamination before progressing any further. Check the belt for signs of wear or damage, particularly around the leading edges of the belt teeth. Renew the belt if its condition is in doubt; the cost of belt renewal is negligible compared with potential cost of the engine repairs, should the belt fail in service. The belt must be renewed if it has covered the mileage stated

by the manufacturer (see Chapter 1A), however, even if it has covered less, it is recommended to renew it regardless of condition as a precautionary measure. **Note:** *If the timing belt is not going to be refitted for some time, it is a wise precaution to hang a warning label on the steering wheel, to remind yourself (and others) not to turn the engine.*

Refitting

18 Ensure that the timing mark on the camshaft and crankshaft sprockets are correctly aligned with the corresponding TDC

reference marks on the timing belt cover; refer to Section 2 for details.
19 Temporarily refit the lower timing cover, then locate the pulley for the ribbed auxiliary drivebelt on the crankshaft sprocket, using two of the retaining screws – note that the pulley will only fit in one fitting position – with the hole in the pulley over the projection on the crankshaft sprocket **(see illustration)**. Make sure that the TDC marks are correctly aligned, then remove the pulley and timing cover.
20 Loop the timing belt under the crankshaft sprocket loosely, observing the direction of rotation markings if the old timing belt is being refitted.
21 Engage the timing belt teeth with the crankshaft sprocket, then manoeuvre it into position over the coolant pump and camshaft sprockets, tensioner pulley and finally the idler pulleys **(see illustration)**.

Engines up to 04/2003

22 Refit the tensioner roller and washer, then tighten the pivot bolt to the specified torque.
23 Using the 8.0 mm Allen key, turn the tensioner roller anti-clockwise then remove the drill bit and release the roller to tension the timing belt.

Engines from 05/2003 to 05/2004

24 Check the tensioner roller locating arm is correctly located in the backplate, then insert the Audi special tool T10020 (or circlip pliers) into the holes in the tensioner hub arm.
25 Slacken the retaining nut, and rotate the tensioner hub anti-clockwise until the notch in the hub is past the indicator (overtensioned), then slowly release the tension until the notch aligns with the indicator **(see illustration)**. Tighten the tensioner nut to the specified torque.

Engines from 06/2004

26 Slacken the tensioner centre nut, then insert an 8 mm Allen key into the tensioner arm in the centre of the pulley, and rotate the arm clockwise until the notch in the arm is past the indicator (overtensioned), then slowly release the tensioner until the notch is aligned with the indicator **(see illustration)**. Tighten the tensioner nut to the specified torque.

All engines

27 Using a spanner or wrench and socket on

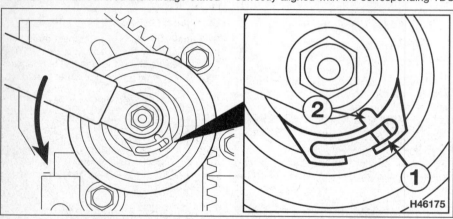

4.25 The notch (2) in the tensioner hub must align with the indicator (1) – from 05/2003 to 05/2004

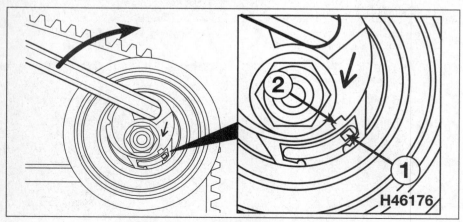

4.26 Align the notch (2) with the indicator (1) – from 06/2004

the crankshaft pulley centre bolt, rotate the crankshaft through two complete revolutions. Reset the engine to TDC on No 1 cylinder with reference to Section 2, and check that the crankshaft pulley and camshaft sprocket timing marks are correctly aligned. Recheck the timing belt tension and adjust it, if necessary.

28 Refit the lower section of the outer timing belt cover with thread-locking compound on the cover retaining bolts, then refit the pulley. Finally, insert and tighten the new pulley retaining bolts.

29 Refit the remaining timing belt covers, using a little locking compound on the retaining bolts.

30 Refit the auxiliary drivebelt tensioner and tighten the bolts. Refit the auxiliary drivebelt with reference to Section 6.

31 Refit the lock carrier assembly using a reversal of the removal procedure.

32 Refit the engine undershield, then lower the vehicle to the ground.

33 Reconnect the battery negative (earth) lead (see Chapter 5A).

5 Timing belt tensioner and sprockets – removal, inspection and refitting

Removal

1 Remove the timing belt as described in Section 4.

Tensioner/roller up to 04/2003

2 Undo the 2 bolts securing the tensioner housing to the cylinder block. Note that the lower bolt also secures the idler roller.

3 To remove the tensioner roller, undo the pivot bolt securing the rocker arm to the cylinder block. Remove the roller and recover the washer.

Tensioner/roller from 05/2003

4 Undo the tensioner hub nut and withdraw the assembly from position **(see illustration)**. Note that on engines from 06/2004, the tensioner hub locates in a recess in the cylinder head **(see illustration)**.

Camshaft sprocket

5 To prevent any accidental piston-to-valve contact, rotate the crankshaft 90° anti-clockwise.

6 Unscrew the camshaft sprocket bolt, while holding the sprocket stationary using a tool as shown. Remove the bolt, washer (where fitted), sprocket, and the key **(see illustrations)**. If necessary, use a 2-legged puller to remove the sprocket. If necessary, an Audi special puller (tool T40001) is available.

Crankshaft sprocket

7 To prevent any accidental piston-to-valve contact, rotate the crankshaft 90° anti-clockwise.

8 Unscrew and discard the crankshaft sprocket bolt, and remove the sprocket **(see**

5.4a Undo the tensioner retaining nut

illustrations). The bolt is very tight, and the crankshaft must be held stationary. On manual gearbox models, engage top gear and apply the footbrake pedal firmly. On automatic/Multitronic transmission models, remove the starter motor (Chapter 5A) and use a wide-bladed screwdriver in the ring gear to hold the crankshaft stationary.

Inspection

9 Clean all the sprockets and examine them for wear and damage. Spin the tensioner roller, and check that it runs smoothly.

10 Check the tensioner for signs of wear and/or damage and renew if necessary.

Refitting

Tensioner/roller

11 Refit the tensioner roller and spring assembly using a reversal of the removal procedure.

5.6a Use a home-made tool to counterhold the camshaft sprocket

5.8a Undo the crankshaft sprocket bolt. . .

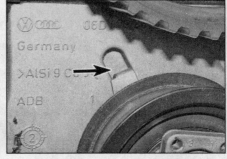

5.4b The tensioner hub locates in a recess in the cylinder head (arrowed)

12 Refit the timing belt as described in Section 4.

Camshaft sprocket

13 Locate the key on the camshaft then refit the sprocket and bolt. Tighten the bolt to the specified torque while holding the sprocket using the method employed on removal. Note the sprocket must be refitted with the narrow web facing forwards.

14 Carefully turn the crankshaft 90° clockwise, back to the TDC position.

15 Refit the timing belt as described in Section 4.

Crankshaft sprocket

16 Locate the sprocket on the crankshaft, then install the new bolt (do not oil the threads), and tighten the bolt to the specified torque while holding the crankshaft stationary using the method employed on removal. **Note:** *Do not allow the crankshaft to rotate.*

5.6b Recover the Woodruff key from the camshaft

5.8b . . . and remove the sprocket. Note the locating lug and slot (arrowed)

6.4 Disconnect the EVAP canister solenoid valve

6.5 Undo the 2 screws and remove the intake ducting from the lock carrier

17 Carefully turn the crankshaft 90° clockwise, back to the TDC position.
18 Refit the timing belt as described in Section 4.

6 Auxiliary drivebelt – removal and refitting

1 The poly-vee drivebelt drives the alternator, power steering pump and where fitted, the air conditioning compressor.
2 On all engines, the drivebelt tension is adjusted automatically.

Removal

3 Remove the plastic cover from the right-hand side of the engine (where fitted).
4 Disconnect the EVAP canister solenoid valve from behind the air intake duct (see illustration).
5 Undo the 2 bolts at the lock carrier, and remove the intake duct (see illustration).
6 If the drivebelt is to be re-used, mark it for clockwise direction to ensure it is refitted the same way round.
7 Although not essential, access to the drivebelt is best achieved by moving the complete front panel (the lock carrier assembly) away from the front of the car as far as possible, but without

disconnecting the radiator hoses or electrical wiring – in the Service position as described in Chapter 11. Audi technicians use special tools to hold the assembly, however support bars may be made out of threaded metal rod and screwed into the underbody channels.
8 To remove the drivebelt, the automatic tensioner must be released and held with a suitable pin or tool. Using an open-ended spanner on the top of the tensioner, move the tensioner clockwise until the pin holes are aligned then insert a metal rod, bolt or drill bit (approximately 5.5 mm diameter) to hold the tensioner in its released position. Remove the drivebelt from the crankshaft, alternator, power steering pump and compressor pulleys (see illustration).

Refitting

9 Locate the drivebelt on the pulleys, then

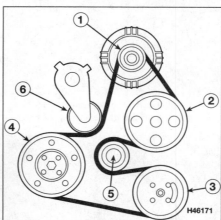

6.9 Auxiliary drivebelt routing

1 Alternator
2 Power steering pump
3 Air conditioning compressor
4 Crankshaft pulley
5 Idler pulley
6 Tensioner

initially turn the tensioner clockwise and remove the retaining pin. Release the tensioner to tension the drivebelt, making sure that it is correctly located in all the pulley grooves (see illustration).
10 The remainder of refitting is a reversal of removal.

7 Camshaft cover – removal and refitting

Removal

1 Remove the ignition coils as described in Chapter 5B.
2 Undo the 2 bolts securing the timing belt upper cover to the camshaft cover.
3 Release the clips and disconnect the air intake hose from the throttle body and air cleaner housing. Pull the hose upwards from the stud at the rear, then remove the hose from the engine compartment. Note its routing then release the wiring harness cable tie.
4 Disconnect the engine breather hose(s) from the camshaft cover (see illustration).
5 Working in the reverse of the sequence shown (see illustration 7.9), unscrew the bolts securing the camshaft cover to the cylinder head.

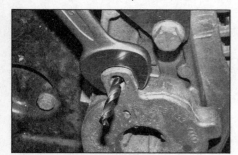

6.8 Rotate the tensioner clockwise with a spanner until a drill bit (or similar) can be inserted, locking the tensioner in position

7.4 Disconnect the breather hoses from the cover by squeezing together the sides of the collars

6 Lift the camshaft cover from the cylinder head and recover the gasket.

Refitting

7 Clean the surfaces of the camshaft cover and cylinder head.
8 Check the condition of the camshaft cover gasket and renew if necessary.
9 Carefully fit the gasket to the camshaft cover, ensuring the bolts locate correctly in the gasket, and position the assembly on the cylinder head. Tighten the bolts in sequence to the specified torque **(see illustration)**.
10 Reconnect the breather hose to the camshaft cover, and refit the air intake hose to the throttle body and air cleaner housing.
11 Apply a little thread-locking compound, then refit the timing belt cover bolts and tighten them to the specified torque.
12 Refit the ignition coils (Chapter 5A).

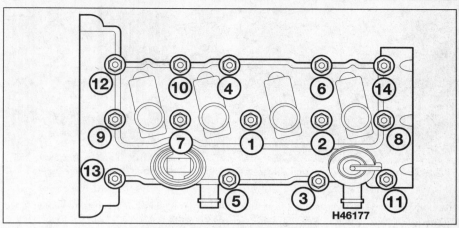

7.9 Camshaft cover bolt tightening sequence

8	Camshaft oil seals –
	renewal

Exhaust camshaft

1 Remove the camshaft sprocket as described in Section 5. Recover the key from the camshaft **(see illustration 5.6b)**.
2 Drill two small holes into the existing oil seal, diagonally opposite each other. Thread two self-tapping screws into the holes, and using two pairs of pliers, pull on the heads of the screws to extract the oil seal. Take great care to avoid drilling through into the seal housing or camshaft sealing surface.
3 Clean out the seal housing and sealing surface of the camshaft by wiping it with a lint-free cloth. Remove any swarf or burrs that may cause the seal to leak.
4 Carefully wrap adhesive tape around the end of the camshaft, to protect the seal lip from the edges of the shaft and keyway **(see illustration)**.
5 Do not lubricate the lip of the new oil seal – it must be fitted dry. Push the new seal over the end of the camshaft, ensuring the lip of the seal is not damaged by the sharp edges of the camshaft and keyway. Use a suitable tubular spacer (socket or similar) that bears only on the hard outer edge of the seal, and a hammer to gently and gradually/evenly push the seal

into place. Try to install the seal as squarely as possible **(see illustration)**.
6 Refit the camshaft sprocket with reference to Section 5.

Intake camshaft

7 Remove the upper section of the timing belt cover as described in Section 4.
8 Using a screwdriver or pry bar, pierce the centre of the rubber cap, and lever it from place **(see illustration)**.
9 Ensure the bore of the cylinder head/bearing ladder is clean, then drive the new cap into place, until it's flush with the casing **(see illustration)**. Note that the rubber cap should be fitted dry; no oil, grease or sealant is to be used.

8.4 Wrap tape around the end of the camshaft to protect the seal lips

8.8 Pierce the centre of the seal, and lever it from place

8.9 Drive the new seal into place until it's flush with the casing

10 Refit the timing belt cover as described in Section 4.

9	Crankshaft oil seals
	– renewal

Crankshaft front oil seal

1 Remove the timing belt and crankshaft sprocket, with reference to Section 5.
2 The seal may be renewed without removing the housing by drilling two small holes diagonally opposite each other, inserting self-tapping screws, and pulling on the heads of the screws with pliers **(see illustrations)**.

8.5 Install the seal so its outer edge is flush with the casing

9.2a Drill 2 holes opposite each other in the hard part of the oil seal (take care not to mark the crankshaft surface) . . .

9.2b . . . insert a screw and pull the seal from place

9.2c   Or remove the belt idler pulley . . .

Alternatively, remove the auxiliary belt idler pulley (where applicable) unbolt and remove the housing (including the relevant sump bolts) and remove the gasket then lever out the oil seal on the bench **(see illustrations)**.

3 If the seal housing is still in place, position the new seal over the end of the crankshaft, ensuring the closed side of the seal faces outwards. Ease the seal lip over the shoulder of the crankshaft to prevent any damage to the seal. Drive the new oil seal into place using a suitable tubular spacer that bears only on the hard outer edge of the seal, until it's flush with the housing.

4 If the housing has been removed, remove all traces of the sealant from the mating faces of the housing, cylinder block and sump. Use a socket (or similar) to drive the new seal into place (flush with the housing), then apply a thin bead (2.0 mm) of suitable sealant (available from Audi dealers/parts specialists) to the housing mating faces. Ensure the bead of sealant is routed 'inside' the bolts holes **(see illustrations)**. Do not apply too much sealant, as any excess may find its way into the oil system. Apply a bead of sealant to the joint between the sump and cylinder block. Refit the housing, easing the seal over the

end of the crankshaft, and tighten the bolts to the specified torque. Tighten the bolts securing the housing to the cylinder block first, followed by the sump bolts. **Note:** *The housing must be in position with the bolts tightened within 5 minutes of applying the sealant.*

5 Refit the timing belt and crankshaft sprocket, with reference to Section 5.

Crankshaft rear oil seal

6 Remove the flywheel/driveplate, with reference to Section 12.

7 Pull the adapter plate from the locating dowels on the rear of the cylinder block, and remove it from the engine.

8 Unbolt and remove the housing (including the relevant sump bolts). The seal is only available complete with the housing.

9 Carefully remove any gasket residue from the cylinder block and sump mating surfaces.

10 Apply a little sealant to the joint between the sump and cylinder block, then apply a thin layer of sealant to the base of the new housing. The new seal is supplied with a guide sleeve fitted to the centre of the seal. Position the housing and seal over the end of the crankshaft and gently, evenly, push it into position, and tighten the bolts evenly in

9.2d . . . undo the cover screws (arrowed) . . .

9.2e . . . and drive out the seal

9.4a Use a socket or tubular drift that bears only on the hard outer edge of the seal

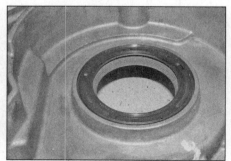

9.4b The seal must be flush with the housing

9.4c Apply the bead of sealant inboard of the mounting holes

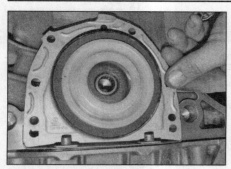

9.10a The new seal/housing is supplied with a fitting guide, which fits over the end of the crankshaft

9.10b With the seal/housing in place, remove the fitting guide

9.11 Note how the adapter plate engages with the seal housing

diagonal sequence to the specified torque, then remove the tool **(see illustrations)**.
11 Refit the adapter plate, locating it over the oil seal housing, and onto the 2 dowels at the back of the cylinder head **(see illustration)**.
12 Refit the flywheel/driveplate, with reference to Section 12.

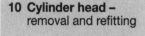

10 Cylinder head –
removal and refitting

Note: *Cylinder head dismantling and overhaul is covered in Chapter 2D.*

Removal

1 Before starting work, disconnect the battery negative (earth) lead (see Chapter 5A).
2 Apply the handbrake, then jack up the front of the vehicle and support it on axle stands (see *Jacking and vehicle support*).
3 Remove the engine top cover by pulling it upwards from its fasteners.
4 Remove the timing belt as described in Section 4.
5 Drain the cooling system as described in Chapter 1A.
6 Remove the camshaft cover as described in Section 7.
7 Remove the intake manifold and disconnect the fuel supply and return hoses as described in Chapter 4A **(see illustration)**. Plug/cover the openings to prevent fuel spillage/contamination.
8 Working at the rear of the engine, undo

the nut and detach the EGR connection pipe bracket from the large coolant pipe, then disconnect the coolant temperature sensor wiring plug, and remove the bolt securing the coolant pipe to the cylinder head.
9 Undo the bolts and move the electrical connector bracket to one side **(see illustration)**.
10 Release the clips and detach the various coolant hoses from the large coolant pipe, then undo the 2 nuts and pull the coolant pipe from the rear of the cylinder head.
11 Release the retaining clip, then undo the bolts and remove the crankcase oil separator from the intake side of the engine **(see illustration)**.
12 Note their fitted positions, then disconnect all electrical connectors from the cylinder head, including the injector loom connectors

10.7 Disconnect the fuel supply and return hoses (arrowed)

under the manifold, oil pressure switch plug and the electrically-controlled thermostat plug **(see illustration)**. Release the wiring harness from the small coolant pipe on the left-hand side of the engine.
13 Undo the retaining bolt, and pull the oil level dipstick guide tube upwards from the engine.
14 Undo the 3 Torx bolts and remove the vacuum pump rearwards from the cylinder head **(see illustration)**. Note the 2 earth connections on the upper mounting bolt.
15 Remove the timing belt tensioning roller as described in Section 5.
16 Undo the bolts and remove the tensioning roller mounting plate from the front of the engine **(see illustration)**.
17 Remove the start-up (forward-most) catalytic converter as described in Chapter 4D.

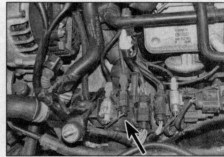

10.9 Undo the bolts/nuts and move the electrical connector bracket under the manifold to one side (arrowed)

10.11 Prise out the clip and remove the oil separator (arrowed)

10.12 Disconnect the various wiring plugs under the intake manifold

10.14 Vacuum pump Torx bolts (arrowed) – note the earth connection

10.16 Tensioner roller mounting plate bolts (arrowed)

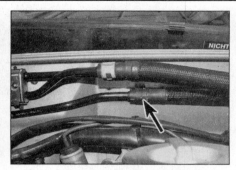

10.18 Disconnect the fuel pump return hose at the bulkhead (arrowed)

10.19 Use an M10 Ribe bit to unscrew the cylinder head bolts

10.25a Fit the new gasket with the part number facing upwards . . .

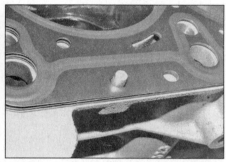

10.25b . . . and ensure the locating dowels are in place

18 Release the clip and disconnect the fuel pump return hose at the engine compartment bulkhead **(see illustration)**. Make a final check to ensure all relevant electrical connectors and coolant hoses have been disconnected. Plug or cover any openings to prevent fluid spillage and contamination.

19 Unscrew the M10 Ribe cylinder head bolts a turn at a time, in **reverse** order to the tightening sequence **(see illustration 10.28)** and remove them **(see illustration)**. Discard the bolts, new ones must be fitted.

20 With the help of an assistant, lift the cylinder head from the block together with the exhaust manifold. If it is stuck, tap it free with a wooden mallet. Do not insert a lever into the gasket joint.

21 Remove the cylinder head gasket from the block.

22 If required, remove the exhaust manifold from the cylinder head with reference to Chapter 4D.

Refitting

23 Thoroughly clean the contact faces of the cylinder head and block. Also clean any oil or coolant from the bolt holes in the block – if this precaution is not taken, not only will the tightening torque be incorrect but there is the possibility of damaging the block.

24 If removed, refit the exhaust manifold to the cylinder head together with a new gasket with reference to Chapter 4D.

25 Locate a new gasket on the block, with the part number facing upwards, and readable from the intake side of the engine **(see illustrations)**. Make sure that the location dowels are in position. Audi recommend that the gasket is removed from its packaging just prior to fitting it. Handle the gasket with great care – damage to the silicone or indented areas will lead to leaks.

26 At this point the crankshaft should still be set at TDC on cylinders 1 and 4. In order to prevent any accidental piston-to-valve contact, rotate the crankshaft a quarter of a turn anti-clockwise.

27 Carefully lower the head onto the block, making sure that it engages the location dowels correctly. Do not use any jointing compound on the cylinder head joint. Insert the new cylinder head bolts (the washers should still be in place on the cylinder head), and initially hand-tighten them.

28 Using the sequence shown **(see illustration)** tighten all the bolts to the Stage 1 torque given in the Specifications.

29 Angle-tighten the bolts in the same sequence to the Stage 2 and Stage 3 angles given in the Specifications **(see illustration)**.

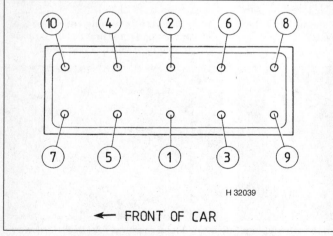

H 32039

← FRONT OF CAR

10.28 Cylinder head bolt tightening sequence

10.29 Angle-tighten the cylinder head bolts

30 Rotate the crankshaft a quarter of a turn clockwise, back to TDC on cylinders 1 and 4.
31 Refit the camshaft cover with reference to Section 7.
32 The remainder of refitting is a reversal of removal, noting the following points:
a) *Ensure all electrical connectors are securing reconnected, and the harnesses are correctly routed – renew any cable clips remove during dismantling.*
b) *Ensure all coolant hoses are reconnected, and all retaining clips are refitted in their original positions.*
c) *Apply a little thread-locking compound to the tensioner roller mounting plate bolts.*
d) *If any of the coolant hose clips appear weak or corroded – renew them.*
e) *Reconnect the battery as described in Chapter 5A.*
f) *On completion, refill the cooling system with new antifreeze mixture (see Chapter 1A).*
g) *If you suspect the engine oil has been contaminated with coolant, change the oil and filter as described in Chapter 1A.*

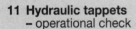

11 Hydraulic tappets
– operational check

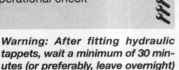

⚠️ *Warning: After fitting hydraulic tappets, wait a minimum of 30 minutes (or preferably, leave overnight) before starting the engine, to allow the tappets time to settle, otherwise the valve heads will strike the pistons.*

1 The hydraulic tappets are self-adjusting, and require no attention whilst in service.
2 If the hydraulic tappets become excessively noisy, their operation can be checked as described below.
3 Run the engine until it reaches its normal operating temperature. Switch off the engine, then refer to Section 7 and remove the camshaft cover.
4 Rotate the camshaft by turning the crankshaft with a socket and wrench, until the first cam lobe over No 1 cylinder is pointing upwards.
5 Using a non-metallic tool, press the tappet downwards then use a feeler blade to check the free travel. If this is more than 0.2 mm before the valve starts to open, the tappet should be renewed.
6 Hydraulic tappet removal and refitting is described as part of the cylinder head overhaul sequence – see Chapter 2D for details.
7 If hydraulic tappet noise occurs repeatedly when travelling short distances, renew the oil retention valve located in the rear of the oil filter mounting housing. It will be necessary to remove the oil filter, then unbolt the housing from the cylinder block and recover the gasket. Use a suitable key to unscrew the valve, and tighten the new valve to the specified torque. Refit the housing together with a new gasket.

12.5 Rotate the secondary element of the dual-mass flywheel so the bolt heads align with the holes

12 Flywheel/driveplate
– removal, inspection and refitting

Removal

1 On manual gearbox models, remove the gearbox (see Chapter 7A) and clutch (see Chapter 6).
2 On automatic transmission models, remove the automatic transmission as described in Chapter 7B.
3 On Multitronic transmission models, remove the transmission (Chapter 7C).

Manual transmission

4 These models are fitted with a dual-mass flywheel. Begin by making alignment marks between the flywheel and the crankshaft.
5 Rotate the outside of the dual-mass flywheel so that the bolts align with the holes **(see illustration)**.
6 Unscrew the bolts and remove the flywheel. Use a locking tool to counterhold the flywheel

12.6 Use a locking tool (arrowed) to prevent the flywheel from rotating

(see illustration). Discard the bolts, new ones must be fitted. **Note:** *In order not to damage the flywheel, do not allow the bolt heads to make contact with the flywheel second element during the unscrewing procedure.*

Multitronic transmission

7 Undo the screws and remove the damper unit from the flywheel **(see illustration)**.
8 Make alignment marks between the flywheel and crankshaft.
9 Unscrew the bolts and remove the flywheel. Use a locking tool to counterhold the flywheel. Discard the bolts, new ones must be fitted.

Automatic transmission

10 Make alignment marks between the driveplate and crankshaft.
11 Unscrew the bolts and remove the driveplate. Use a locking tool to counterhold the driveplate. Discard the bolts, new ones must be fitted.
12 Remove the shim from behind the driveplate.

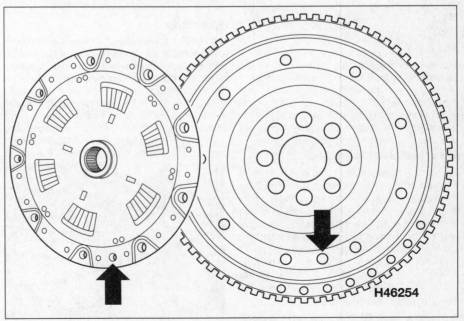

12.7 The locating pin on the flywheel must align with the corresponding hole in the Multitronic damper unit (arrowed)

12.15a Flywheel warpage check – see text

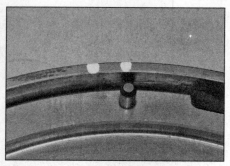

12.15b Flywheel free rotational movement check alignment marks – see text

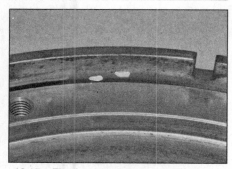

12.15c Flywheel lateral movement check marks – see text

Inspection

13 Check the flywheel/driveplate for wear and damage. Examine the starter ring gear for excessive wear to the teeth. If the driveplate or its ring gear are damaged, the complete driveplate must be renewed. The flywheel ring gear, however, may be renewed separately from the flywheel, but the work should be entrusted to an Audi dealer. If the clutch friction face is discoloured or scored excessively, it may be possible to regrind it, but this work should also be entrusted to an Audi dealer.

14 With the flywheel removed, check the spigot needle bearing in the end of the crankshaft for wear by turning it with a finger. If there is any evidence of excessive wear or if the bearing has been running dry, it must be renewed – see Section 16. **Note:** *A spigot needle bearing must not be fitted to the crankshaft on automatic/Multitronic transmission models.*

15 There should be no cracks in the drive surface of the flywheel. If cracks are evident, the flywheel may need renewing. The following are guidelines only, but should indicate whether professional inspection is necessary. The dual-mass flywheel should be checked as follows:

Warpage

Place a straight-edge across the face of the drive surface, and check by trying to insert a feeler gauge between the straight-edge and the drive surface (see illustration). The flywheel will normally warp like a bowl – ie, higher on the outer edge. If the warpage is more than 0.40 mm, the flywheel may need renewing.

Free rotational movement

This is the distance the drive surface of the flywheel can be turned independently of the flywheel primary element, using finger effort alone. Move the drive surface in one direction and make a mark where the locating pin aligns with the flywheel edge. Move the drive surface in the other direction (finger pressure only) and make another mark (see illustration). The total of free movement should not exceed 10.0 mm. If it's more, the flywheel may need renewing.

Total rotational movement

This is the total distance the drive surface can be turned independently of the flywheel primary element. Insert two bolts into the

clutch pressure plate/damper unit mounting holes, and with the crankshaft/flywheel held stationary, use a lever/pry bar between the bolts and use some effort to move the drive surface fully in one direction – make a mark where the locating pin aligns with the flywheel edge. Now force the drive surface fully in the opposite direction, and make another mark. The total rotational movement should not exceed 44.00 mm. If it does, have the flywheel professionally inspected.

Lateral movement

The lateral movement (up and down) of the drive surface in relation to the primary element of the flywheel, should not exceed 2.0 mm. If it does, the flywheel may need renewing. This can be checked by pressing the drive surface down on one side into the flywheel (flywheel horizontal) and making an alignment mark between the drive surface and the inner edge of the primary element. Now press down on the opposite side of the drive surface, and make another mark above the original one. The difference between the two marks is the lateral movement (see illustration).

Refitting

16 Refitting is a reversal of removal, however on automatic transmission models temporarily refit the driveplate using the old bolts tightened to 30 Nm (22 lbf ft), and measure, through the torque converter mounting hole, the distance from the block to the torque converter *mounting face* on the driveplate. The correct distance is 18.9 to 20.5 mm. If necessary, remove the driveplate, and fit a spacer behind it to achieve the correct dimension. The raised

13.6 Undo the bolts and remove the stop bracket/torque arm from the engine

pip on the outer shim must face the torque converter. Use new bolts when refitting the flywheel or driveplate. Tighten them to the specified torque.

13 Engine mountings – inspection and renewal

Inspection

1 If improved access is required, raise the front of the car and support it securely on axle stands and remove the undershield where applicable.

2 Check the mounting rubbers to see if they are cracked, hardened or separated from the metal at any point; renew the mounting if any such damage or deterioration is evident.

3 Check that all the mounting's fasteners are securely tightened; use a torque wrench to check if possible.

4 Using a large screwdriver or a crowbar, check for wear in the mounting by carefully levering against it to check for free play. Where this is not possible, enlist the aid of an assistant to move the engine/transmission back-and-forth, or from side-to-side, while you watch the mounting. While some free play is to be expected even from new components, excessive wear should be obvious. If excessive free play is found, check first that the fasteners are correctly secured, then renew any worn components as described below.

Renewal

Front torque bracket

5 Apply the handbrake then jack up the front of the vehicle and support it on axle stands (see *Jacking and vehicle support*). Release the fasteners and remove the undershield.

6 Unscrew the bolts and remove the stop from the bracket on the front right-hand corner of the engine (see illustration).

7 If necessary, the stop-plate can be unbolted from the rear face of the lock carrier (see illustration).

8 Fit the new rubber and bracket using a reversal of the removal procedure.

Right- or left-hand engine mounting

9 Apply the handbrake, then jack up the front

13.7 Unbolt the stop-plate from the lock carrier

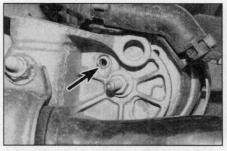

13.11a Note the position of the locating dowel (arrowed) – the mounting must be fitted with the dowel in its original position

13.11b Undo the nut (arrowed) and detach the mounting from the bracket

of the vehicle and support it on axle stands (see *Jacking and vehicle support*).

10 Support the weight of the engine with a hoist. Alternatively, use a trolley jack and piece of wood beneath the sump.

11 Note their fitted positions, then unscrew the mounting nuts, then raise the engine and withdraw the mounting from the engine bracket and subframe **(see illustrations)**. Note that the mounting has an integral hydro action, to absorb movement of the engine and prevent engine noise transmission inside the car.

12 If necessary, unbolt the mounting bracket from the side of the cylinder block.

13 Fit the new mounting using a reversal of the removal procedure.

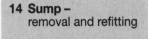

14 Sump –
removal and refitting

Note: *Audi insist that the intermediate plate between the oil pump/balancer shaft housing and the engine block must be renewed when the sump is removed. Oil pump/balancer shaft renewal is described in Section 15.*

Removal

1 Apply the handbrake, then jack up the front of the vehicle and support it on axle stands (see *Jacking and vehicle support*).

2 Release the fasteners, remove the engine undertray, then undo the bolts and detach the undertray bracket.

3 Position a container beneath the sump, then unscrew the drain plug and drain the engine

oil. Clean the plug and if necessary renew the washer, then refit and tighten the plug after all the oil has drained. Remove the dipstick from the engine.

4 Remove the auxiliary drivebelt as described in Section 6.

5 Disconnect the oil temperature sensor wiring plug from the base of the sump.

6 Undo the bolt and detach the refrigerant support pipe from the sump **(see illustration)**.

7 Disconnect the wiring plug, then undo the bolts and position the air conditioning compressor to one side (where applicable). Support the compressor by suspending it from the vehicle body with wire/string – there is no need to disconnect the refrigerant pipes, but ensure they are not damaged or kinked during the process.

8 Unbolt the stop bracket/torque arm bracket from the front of the engine.

9 On vehicles with gas discharge headlights, unclip the vehicle height sensor actuator rod from the front-left lower transverse link arm.

10 Undo the bolts and detach the inboard clamps from the front anti-roll bar.

11 Detach the starter motor cables from under the engine mounting by cutting the plastic cable ties and easing them from the plastic ducting.

12 Unscrew and remove the nuts from the bottom of each engine mounting.

13 Remove the engine top cover, then release the clips and remove the intake ducting from the air cleaner to the throttle body.

14 Connect a suitable hoist to the engine, then raise it as far as possible without damaging or stretching the coolant hoses and wiring.

15 Mark the fitted position of the subframe, then position a workshop trolley jack to take the weight, then undo the bolts and lower the front subframe.

16 Gradually unscrew and remove the sump bolts working in a diagonal pattern. Note that on manual transmission models, the two rear sump bolts are accessed through a cut-out in the flywheel – turn the flywheel as necessary to align the cut-out **(see illustration)**.

17 Remove the sump. If it is stuck, tap it gently with a mallet to free it.

Refitting

18 Thoroughly clean the contact faces of the sump. It is recommended that a rotary wire brush is used to clean away the sealant.

19 Refit the sump and tighten the retaining bolts hand-tight initially. If the engine is out of the car, make sure that the rear edge of the sump overhangs the rear edge of the cylinder block by 0.8 mm, so that it is flush when the adapter plate is fitted **(see illustration)**. Progressively tighten the sump bolts in a diagonal pattern to the specified torque. It is advisable to wait at least 30 minutes for the intermediate plate sealant to set before filling the engine with oil. If the car is to be left for some time with no oil in the sump, ensure that the battery remains disconnected, so that no attempt is made to start the engine.

20 The remaining refitting procedure is a reversal removal, but tighten the nuts and bolts to the specified torque where given in the Specifications. On completion, fill the engine with the correct quantity of oil as described in Chapter 1A.

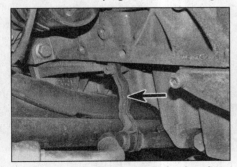

14.6 Detach the refrigerant pipe bracket (arrowed) from the sump

14.16 Rotate the flywheel and align the cut-outs to access the rear sump bolts

14.19 Ensure the sump overhangs the engine block by 0.8 mm to allow for the adapter plate

15.3 Oil pipe securing bolts (arrowed)

15.4a Use a screwdriver to release the 3 retaining clips . . .

15.4b . . . and pull the cover from the oil pump drive chain

15.5 Slacken the oil pump drive sprocket one turn

15.6 Compress the tensioner blade, then lock it in place with a 3.0 mm drill bit (arrowed)

15 Oil pump and balancer shaft housing – removal, inspection and refitting

Removal

1 Set the engine to TDC on No 1 cylinder as described in Section 2.

2 Remove the sump as described in Section 14.

3 Undo the 2 bolts securing the oil pipe at the rear of the engine block **(see illustration)**.

4 Using a small screwdriver, depress the tabs to release the retaining clips, and remove the chain/sprocket cover horizontally **(see illustrations)**.

5 Use a Torx bit to slacken the oil pump drive sprocket retaining bolt approximately 1 turn **(see illustration)**.

6 Using a screwdriver, push the drive chain tensioner blade to relieve the tension on the chain. Insert a 3 mm drill bit into the hole in the tensioner assembly to lock the blade in this position **(see illustration)**.

7 Remove the Torx bolt and pull the sprocket from the oil pump shaft. Disengage the sprockets from the chain.

8 Working from the outside-in, gradually and evenly slacken and remove the bolts securing the balancer shaft housing and intermediate plate. Note the fitted positions of the bolts

– some are longer than others. Remove the balancer shaft housing and plate from the engine block, noting that the housing locates on dowels. Discard the retaining bolts, new ones must be fitted. Audi insist that the intermediate plate is renewed.

9 Undo the retaining bolts and remove the drive chain tensioner from the balancer shaft housing **(see illustration)**.

10 If required, undo the 5 bolts and remove the oil pump cover. Pull the inner and outer rotors from the pump **(see illustration)**

Inspection

11 Examine the drive chain for wear and damage. To remove the chain, the timing belt must first be removed (see Section 4), then the crankshaft front oil seal housing unbolted from the cylinder block.

12 It is not advisable to dismantle the balancer shafts and housing. No separate parts are available. If faulty, the complete assembly must be renewed.

13 If the oil pump has been dismantled, clean the components and check them for wear and damage. Examine the inner and outer rotors for scoring or any signs of wear/damage. If evident, renew the oil pump.

14 If the oil pump components are re-usable, fit the outer, and inner rotors to the pump body, with the marks on the ends of the inner

15.9 Undo the tensioner retaining bolts (arrowed)

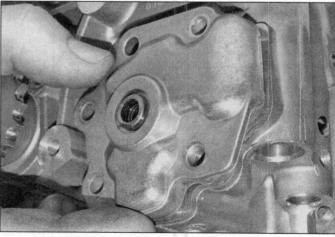

15.10 Undo the bolts and remove the oil pump cover

15.14a Fit the outer rotor with the mark facing outwards (arrowed) . . .

15.14b . . . then refit the inner rotor

rotor facing inwards and the one on the outer rotor facing outwards (see illustrations). Refit the pump cover and tighten the retaining bolts to the specified torque.

Refitting

15 Prime the pump with oil by pouring oil into the suction pipe aperture while turning the driveshaft.

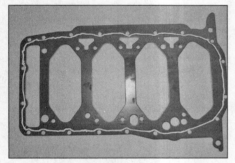

15.17 Apply a 2.0 mm bead of sealant to the intermediate plate

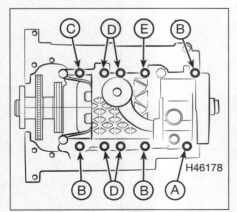

15.19 Balancer shaft housing bolts

A Screw plug with O-ring
B M7 x 55 mm
C M7 x 40 mm
D M7 x 70 mm
E M7 x 90 mm

16 Refit the chain tensioner assembly to the balancer shaft housing, and tighten the retaining bolts to the specified torque. Ensure the tensioner blade is in the locked position, as described in paragraph 6.

17 Apply a bead of suitable sealant, approximately 2.0 mm thick, to the cylinder block side of the intermediate plate (see illustration). Take great care not to apply the sealant too thickly, as any excess may find its way in the oil galleries.

18 Position the intermediate plate over the locating dowels on the cylinder block sealing surface. Feed the drive chain through the intermediate plate.

19 Position the balancer shaft housing on the base of the cylinder block/intermediate plate, then insert the new bolts (ensure the new O-ring is fitted to the appropriate bolt). Working from the inside tighten the new bolts to the Stage 1 torque setting, then in the same order, tighten them to the Stage 2 setting. Ensure the correct length bolt is fitted to the correct positions (see illustration).

20 Ensure the crankshaft pulley is still in the TDC, then rotate the balancer shaft sprocket until the mark on the sprocket face is aligned with the locating hole, Insert an 5.0 mm drill bit into the hole to lock the sprocket in this position (see illustration).

21 Engage the drive chain with the balancer

15.20 Align the mark on the sprocket face with the hole in the housing, and insert a 5.0 mm drill bit to lock it

shaft sprocket, then fit the oil pump sprocket into the chain. Fit the sprocket on to the oil pump shaft, noting that the sprocket will only fit in one position – if necessary, rotate the oil pump shaft to enable the fitment of the sprocket (see illustration). Fit the new sprocket retaining bolt and tighten it to the specified torque.

22 Remove the balancer shaft sprocket locking tool (drill bit), and the Allen key locking the tensioner blade.

23 Refit the cover over the drive sprockets, and secure it with the retaining clips.

24 Refit the oil pipe to the housing, and tighten the bolts securely.

25 Refit the sump with reference to Section 14.

16 Crankshaft spigot bearing – renewal

Note: The spigot bearing is only fitted to manual transmission models.

1 Remove the flywheel as described in Section 12.

2 Pack the gap behind the bearing with general purpose grease (see illustration).

3 Insert a round bar into the centre of the bearing. The bar should be of a diameter just less than the internal diameter of the bearing.

15.21 The flat on the shaft and sprocket hole ensure it will only fit in position

16.2 Pack the spigot bearing hole with grease

16.4 As the bar is driven into the hole, the bearing is forced from place

16.5a Drive the new bearing into the crankshaft . . .

16.5b . . . so the end of bearing is 1.5 mm from the end face of the crankshaft

4 Drive the bar into the bearing using a hammer. As the grease is compressed, it should force the bearing from the crankshaft **(see illustration)**.

5 Remove all traces of grease from the crankshaft, then position the new bearing in the crankshaft, and using a socket or tubular spacer that bears only on the outer edge of the bearing, drive the bearing into the crankshaft. Note that the seal in the bearing must face rearwards. The bearing is correctly fitted when the distance from the end of the bearing to the end of the crankshaft is 1.5 mm **(see illustrations)**.

6 Refit the flywheel as described in Section 12.

Chapter 2 Part C:
Diesel engine in-car repair procedures

Contents

Section number

Auxiliary drivebelt(s) – removal, refitting and tensioning 6
Camshaft cover – removal and refitting 7
Camshaft oil seal – renewal 9
Camshaft – removal and overhaul . . . . See Chapter 2D
Crankshaft oil seals – renewal 10
Cylinder compression and leakdown test 3
Cylinder head – dismantling and overhaul . . . . See Chapter 2D
Cylinder head – removal and refitting 11
Engine mountings – inspection and renewal 14
Engine oil and filter – renewal . . . . See Chapter 1B

Section number

Engine oil level – check . . . . See Weekly checks
Engine valve timing marks – locating TDC on No 1 cylinder 2
Flywheel/driveplate – removal, inspection and refitting 13
General information 1
Hydraulic tappets – operation check 12
Oil pump and pickup – removal, inspection and refitting 16
Pump injector rocker shaft assembly – removal and refitting 8
Sump – removal, inspection and refitting 15
Timing belt – removal, inspection and refitting 4
Timing belt tensioner and sprockets – removal and refitting 5

Degrees of difficulty

Easy, suitable for novice with little experience 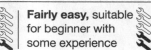	**Fairly easy,** suitable for beginner with some experience	**Fairly difficult,** suitable for competent DIY mechanic	**Difficult,** suitable for experienced DIY mechanic	**Very difficult,** suitable for expert DIY or professional

Specifications

General

Engine code*:
74 kW (96 bhp)	AVB
85 kW (111 bhp)	BKE and BRB
96 kW (125 bhp)	AVF and AWX
Bore	79.5 mm
Stroke	95.5 mm
Capacity	1896 cc
Compression ratio	19.0 : 1
Compression pressures (wear limit)	19.0 bar
Firing order	1 – 3 – 4 – 2
Cylinder No 1 location	Timing belt end

* Note: *See 'Vehicle identification' for the location of the code marking on the engine.*

Lubrication system

Oil pump type	Sump mounted, drive by chain from the timing end of the crankshaft

Normal operating oil pressure (oil temperature 80°C):
At idle speed	0.8 bar minimum
At 2000 rpm	2.0 bar minimum

Auxiliary drivebelt tension

Alternator/viscous fan/power steering pump/coolant pump	Automatically adjusted by tensioner
Air conditioning compressor	Apply 25 Nm (18 lbf ft) to tensioner body

Torque wrench settings

	Nm	lbf ft
Auxiliary drivebelt idle pulley bolt (06/2003-on)*:		
Stage 1	20	15
Stage 2	Angle-tighten a further 90°	
Auxiliary drivebelt tensioner	25	18
Big-end bearing caps bolts*:		
Stage 1	30	22
Stage 2	Angle-tighten a further 90°	
Brake vacuum exhauster clamp	20	15
Camshaft bearing cap*:		
Stage 1	8	6
Stage 2	Angle-tighten a further 90°	
Camshaft cover	10	7
Camshaft sprocket bolt:		
Sprocket to hub	25	18
Hub to camshaft	100	74
Camshaft position sensor bolt (use thread-locking compound)	10	7
Coolant outlet (rear of cylinder head)	9	7
Coolant pump	15	11
Cooling fan-to-viscous coupling bolts*	10	7
Crankshaft front oil seal housing	15	11
Crankshaft pulley/vibration damper to sprocket*:		
Stage 1	10	7
Stage 2	Angle-tighten a further 90°	
Crankshaft rear oil seal housing	15	11
Crankshaft sprocket bolt*:		
Stage 1	120	89
Stage 2	Angle-tighten a further 90°	
Cylinder head bolts*:		
Stage 1	40	30
Stage 2	60	44
Stage 3	Angle-tighten a further 90°	
Stage 4	Angle-tighten a further 90°	
Driveplate mounting bolts*:		
Stage 1	60	44
Stage 2	Angle-tighten a further 90°	
Engine front mounting buffer stop	30	22
Engine mounting to console	40	30
Engine mounting to support	25	18
Engine-to-transmission bolts**:		
M10	45	33
M12	65	48
Flywheel mounting bolts*:		
Bolt length 22.5 mm:		
Stage 1	60	44
Stage 2	Angle-tighten a further 90°	
Bolt lengths 35.0 and 43.0 mm:		
Stage 1	60	44
Stage 2	Angle-tighten a further 180°	
Glow plug:		
Metal glow plug	15	11
Ceramic glow plug	12	9
Main bearing cap bolts*:		
Stage 1	65	48
Stage 2	Angle-tighten a further 90°	
Oil drain plug	30	22
Oil filter cap:		
Top	25	18
Bottom	25	18
Oil filter housing to block*:		
Stage 1	15	11
Stage 2	Angle-tighten a further 90°	
Oil jets	25	18
Oil level/oil temperature sender	10	7
Oil pressure switch	20	15
Oil pump chain tensioner	15	11
Oil pump sprocket bolt*	25	18
Oil pump mounting bolt	15	11

Torque wrench settings (continued)

	Nm	lbf ft
Oil return pipe to cylinder block	30	22
Oil return pipe to turbocharger	15	11
Pump injector rocker shaft bolts*:		
Stage 1	20	15
Stage 2	Angle-tighten a further 90°	
Speed sender wheel to crankshaft*:		
Stage 1	10	7
Stage 2	Angle-tighten a further 90°	
Suction tube to oil pump	15	11
Sump:		
Stage 1: Tighten bolts 1 to 18 (M7) in diagonal sequence	5	4
Stage 2: Tighten sump-to-transmission bolts	45	33
Stage 3: Tighten M10 bolts	40	30
Stage 4: Tighten bolts 1 to 18 (M7) in diagonal sequence	15	11
Tandem pump:		
M6	9	7
M8	22	16
Timing belt small lower idler roller	20	15
Timing belt tensioner:		
Stage 1	20	15
Stage 2	Angle-tighten a further 45°	
Timing cover bolts (use thread-locking compound):		
M6	10	7
M8	25	18
Torque reaction bracket and stop	25	18
Viscous fan coupling pulley	45	33

*Do not re-use
** On vehicles with Multitronic transmission, Audi insist the bolts must be renewed

1 General information

Using this Chapter

Chapter 2 is divided into four Parts; A, B, C and D. Repair operations that can be carried out with the engine in the vehicle are described in Part A (indirect injection petrol engines), Part B (direct injection petrol engines) and Part C (diesel engines). Part D covers the removal of the engine/transmission as a unit, and describes the engine dismantling and overhaul procedures.

In Parts A, B and C, the assumption is made that the engine is installed in the vehicle, with all ancillaries connected. If the engine has been removed for overhaul, the preliminary dismantling information which precedes each operation may be ignored.

Access to the engine compartment can be improved by removing the bonnet as described in Chapter 11.

Engine description

The engines are water-cooled, single overhead camshaft, in-line four cylinder units with cast-iron cylinder blocks and aluminium-alloy cylinder heads. All are mounted longitudinally at the front of the vehicle, with the transmission bolted to the rear of the engine.

The cylinder head carries the camshaft, which is driven by a toothed timing belt. It also houses the intake and exhaust valves, which are closed by double coil springs, and which run in guides pressed into the cylinder head. The camshaft actuates the valves directly via hydraulic tappets, mounted in the cylinder head. On all engines covered by this manual, a rocker shaft and roller rocker assembly mounted in the camshaft upper bearing caps uses an additional set of camshaft lobes to pressurise the pump injectors – see Chapter 4C. The cylinder head contains integral oilways, which supply and lubricate the tappets.

The engines are of direct injection design. Unlike indirect injection engines where the cylinder head incorporates swirl chambers, the piston crowns are shaped to form combustion chambers.

The crankshaft is supported by five main bearings, and endfloat is controlled by thrustwashers fitted each side of the centre (No 3) main bearing. A tandem pump, incorporating a vacuum pump and a fuel pump, is fitted to the rear of the cylinder head, and driven by the camshaft. The coolant pump is driven by the timing belt.

Lubricant is circulated under pressure by a pump, chain-driven from the crankshaft. Oil is drawn from the sump through a strainer, and then forced through an externally-mounted, screw-on filter. From there, it is distributed to the cylinder head, where it lubricates the camshaft journals and hydraulic tappets, and also to the crankcase, where it lubricates the main bearings, connecting rod big- and small-ends, gudgeon pins and cylinder bores. Oil jets are fitted to the base of each cylinder – these spray oil onto the underside of the pistons, to improve cooling. An oil cooler, supplied with engine coolant and mounted on the oil filter housing, reduces the temperature of the oil before it re-enters the engine.

Repairs with engine in vehicle

The following operations can be performed without removing the engine:

a) Auxiliary drivebelt – removal and refitting.
b) Camshaft – removal and refitting*.
c) Camshaft oil seal – renewal.
d) Camshaft sprocket – removal and refitting.
e) Coolant pump – removal and refitting (refer to Chapter 3)
f) Crankshaft oil seals – renewal.
g) Crankshaft sprocket – removal and refitting.
h) Cylinder head – removal and refitting*.
i) Engine mountings – inspection and renewal.
j) Oil pump and pickup assembly – removal and refitting.
k) Pump injector rocker shaft assembly
l) Sump – removal and refitting.
m) Timing belt, sprockets and cover – removal, inspection and refitting.

* Cylinder head dismantling procedures are in Chapter 2D, and also contain details of camshaft and hydraulic tappet removal.

Note: It is possible to remove the pistons and connecting rods (after removing the cylinder head and sump) without removing the engine from the vehicle. However, this procedure is not recommended. Work of this nature is more easily and thoroughly completed with the engine on the bench – refer to Chapter 2D.

2.5a Prise up the plastic caps . . .

2.5b . . . and unscrew the cover retaining nuts

2 Engine valve timing marks – locating TDC on No 1 cylinder

General information

1 The crankshaft and camshaft sprockets are driven by the timing belt; the sprockets move in phase with each other to ensure correct valve timing.

2 The design of the engines covered in this Chapter is such that piston-to-valve contact will occur if the crankshaft is turned with the timing belt removed. For this reason, it is important that the correct phasing between the camshaft and crankshaft is preserved whilst the timing belt is off the engine. This is achieved by setting the engine in a reference condition (known as Top Dead Centre or TDC) before the timing belt is removed, and then preventing the shafts from rotating until the belt is refitted. Similarly, if the engine has been dismantled for overhaul, the engine can be set to TDC during reassembly to ensure that the correct shaft phasing is restored.

3 TDC is the highest position a piston reaches within its respective cylinder – in a four-stroke engine, each piston reaches TDC twice per cycle; once on the compression stroke, and once on the exhaust stroke. In general, TDC normally refers to No 1 cylinder on the compression stroke. Note that the cylinders are numbered one to four, starting from the timing belt end of the engine.

Setting TDC on No 1 cylinder

4 Access to the timing belt is achieved by moving the complete front panel (the lock carrier assembly) away from the front of the car as far as possible, but without disconnecting the radiator hoses or electrical wiring. Place the lock carrier in the Service position as described in Chapter 11.

5 Pull the engine oil level dipstick from place, then prise out the caps, undo the nuts and remove the cover from the top of the engine **(see illustrations)**.

6 Remove the auxiliary drivebelt(s) as described in Section 6. **Note:** *Audi special tool (T10050 or T10100) is required to lock the crankshaft sprocket in the TDC position.*

7 Remove the viscous fan unit with reference to Chapter 3. Briefly, it is removed by inserting an Allen key from behind, while holding the unit stationary using a scissor-type tool engaged with two of the holes in the pulley – if the Audi tool cannot be obtained, make up a similar tool out of two lengths of metal with bolts to engage the holes, or use a strap wrench around the pulley.

8 Unscrew the two retaining bolts and remove the auxiliary drivebelt tensioner assembly **(see illustration)**.

9 Release the retaining clips and remove the upper timing belt cover **(see illustration)**.

10 Undo the 2 retaining bolts, and remove the small timing belt cover from the right-hand side of the engine, then move the charge pressure control solenoid valve to one side

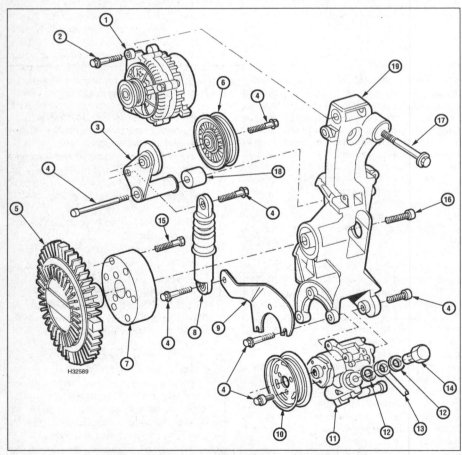

H32589

2.8 Auxiliary drivebelt tensioner assembly

1 Alternator	6 Pulley	11 Power steering	15 Bolt
2 Bolt	7 Pulley	pump	16 Bolt
3 Lever	8 Tensioner	12 Washer	17 Bolt
4 Bolt	9 Bracket	13 Pipe	18 Spacer
5 Viscous fan pulley	10 Pulley	14 Banjo bolt	19 Bracket

2.9 Unclip the timing belt upper cover

2.10a Undo the 2 Allen screws and remove the cover

– there's no need to disconnect the vacuum hoses **(see illustrations)**.

11 Remove the auxiliary drivebelt drive pulley from the crankshaft by prising out the centre cap and removing the four retaining bolts **(see illustration)**. Discard the bolts, new ones must be fitted.

12 Undo the 5 retaining bolts, and remove the centre and lower timing belt covers **(see illustration)**.

13 Using a spanner or socket on the crankshaft sprocket bolt, turn the crankshaft in the normal direction of rotation (clockwise) until the alignment mark on the face of the sprocket is as shown, and the arrow (marked 4Z) on the rear section of the timing belt upper cover aligns between the lugs on the camshaft hub sender wheel. In this position it should be possible to insert Audi tool T10050 (for engine codes AVB, AVF and AWX) or T10100 (for engine codes BKE and BRB) to lock the crank-

2.10b Move the charge pressure control solenoid valve to one side without disconnecting the hoses

shaft, and 6 mm diameter rod to lock the camshaft **(see illustrations)**. **Note:** *The mark on the crankshaft sprocket and the mark on the Audi tool T10050 must align, whilst at the same time the shaft of tool T10050 must engage in the drilling in the crankshaft front oil seal housing.*

14 The engine is now set to TDC on No 1 cylinder.

| 3 | Cylinder compression and leakdown test |

Compression test

Caution: This test applies only to engine codes AVB, AVF, AWX and BRB. Engines with code BKE are fitted with ceramic glow plugs, which Audi insist must not be removed to perform the compression test.

2.11 Prise out the auxiliary drivebelt pulley centre cap

Instead, the relative compression pressures can be measured by plugging in Audi test equipment into the diagnostic connector (see Chapter 4C) – consult an Audi dealer or specialist.
Note: *A compression tester specifically designed for diesel engines must be used for this test.*

1 When engine performance is down, or if misfiring occurs, a compression test can provide diagnostic clues as to the engine's condition. If the test is performed regularly, it can give warning of trouble before any other symptoms become apparent.

2 A compression tester specifically intended for diesel engines must be used, because of the higher pressures involved. The tester is connected to an adapter which screws into the glow plug hole. It is unlikely to be worthwhile buying such a tester for occasional use, but it may be possible to borrow or hire one – if not, have the test performed by a garage.

2.12 Timing belt centre cover retaining bolts (arrowed)

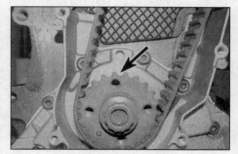

2.13a Position the crankshaft so that the mark on the sprocket is almost vertical (arrowed) . . .

2.13b . . . and the Audi special tool can be inserted . . .

2.13c . . . and the marks on the tool and sprocket align (arrowed)

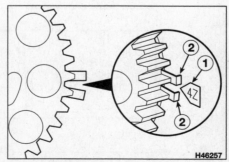

H46257

2.13d Align the 4Z mark (1) between the lugs on the camshaft sender wheel (2)

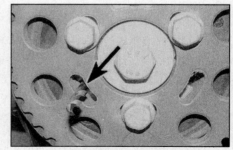

2.13e . . . and insert a 6 mm drill bit through the camshaft hub into the cylinder head to lock the camshaft (arrowed)

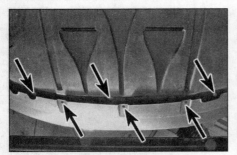

4.3a The front edge of the undershield is secured by 3 screws to the front bumper, and 3 screws to the lock carrier (arrowed)

3 Unless specific instructions to the contrary are supplied with the tester, observe the following points:

a) *The battery must be in a good state of charge, the air filter must be clean, and the engine should be at normal operating temperature.*

b) *All the glow plugs should be removed before starting the test.*

c) *Disconnect the injector solenoids by pulling apart the connector at the back of the cylinder head. As a result of the wiring being disconnected, faults will be stored in the ECU memory. These must be erased after the compression test.*

4 There is no need to hold the accelerator pedal down during the test, because the diesel engine air inlet is not throttled.

5 The manufacturers specify a wear limit for compression pressure – refer to the Specifications. Seek the advice of an Audi dealer or other diesel specialist if in doubt as to whether a particular pressure reading is acceptable.

6 The cause of poor compression is less easy to establish on a diesel engine than on a petrol one. The effect of introducing oil into the cylinders (wet testing) is not conclusive, because there is a risk that the oil will sit in the recess on the piston crown, instead of passing to the rings. However, the following can be used as a rough guide to diagnosis.

7 All cylinders should produce very similar pressures; a difference of more than 5.0 bars between any two cylinders indicates the existence of a fault. Note that the compression should build-up quickly in a healthy engine; low

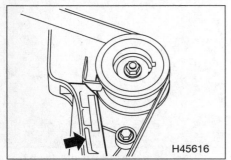

4.6 The hydraulic tensioner has a damper below it

H45616

4.3b Engine undershield-to-transmission undershield fasteners (arrowed)

compression on the first stroke, followed by gradually-increasing pressure on successive strokes, indicates worn piston rings. A low compression reading on the first stroke, which does not build-up during successive strokes, indicates leaking valves or a blown head gasket (a cracked head could also be the cause).

8 A low reading from two adjacent cylinders is almost certainly due to the head gasket having blown between them; the presence of coolant in the engine oil will confirm this.

Leakdown test

9 A leakdown test measures the rate at which compressed air fed into the cylinder is lost. It is an alternative to a compression test, and in many ways it is better, since the escaping air provides easy identification of where pressure loss is occurring (piston rings, valves or head gasket).

10 The equipment needed for leakdown testing is unlikely to be available to the home mechanic. If poor compression is suspected, have the test performed by a suitably-equipped garage.

| 4 | Timing belt –
removal, inspection
and refitting |
|---|---|

Removal

1 The primary function of the toothed timing belt is to drive the camshaft, but it also drives the coolant pump. Should the belt slip

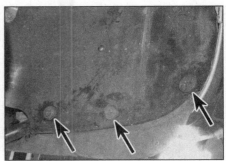

4.3c Engine undershield-to-wheel arch liner fasteners (arrowed)

or break in service, the valve timing will be disturbed and piston-to-valve contact may occur, resulting in serious engine damage. For this reason, it is important that the timing belt is tensioned correctly, and inspected regularly for signs of wear or deterioration.

2 Disconnect the battery (see Chapter 5A), then prise up the caps, undo the nuts and remove the engine top cover.

3 Apply the handbrake, then jack up the front of the vehicle and support it on axle stands (see *Jacking and vehicle support*). Undo the fasteners and remove the engine undershield **(see illustrations)**.

4 Set the engine to TDC on No 1 cylinder as described in Section 2. This procedure includes moving the complete front panel (lock carrier assembly) away from the front of the car, and removing the auxiliary drivebelt(s), viscous fan (where fitted) and timing belt covers.

5 Audi state that the camshaft sprocket **must** be reset each time the timing belt is removed – it is not acceptable to simply refit the belt to the sprocket without carrying out the resetting procedure. Hold the sprocket stationary using the tool shown in Section 5, and loosen the three bolts by half a turn – **do not** unscrew them completely.

6 At this stage, it is necessary to determine which tensioning system is fitted to the timing belt. The hydraulic tensioner is identified by having a damper below it **(see illustration)**, whereas the friction-type incorporates a friction mechanism inside the tensioning roller.

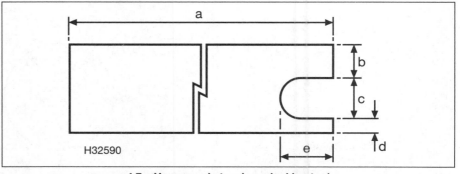

4.7a Home-made tensioner locking tool

A 52 mm   B 4.5 mm   C 5.5 mm   D 2 mm   E 7 mm

4.7b Insert the locking tool through the slot to lock the tensioner

Hydraulic tensioner

Note: *Audi technicians use special tool T10008 to lock the timing belt tensioner in the released position. It is possible to manufacture a home-made alternative – see below.*

7 Insert an Allen key fully into the tensioner hub, then slacken the tensioner nut, and rotate the Allen key anti-clockwise, until the locking plate (Audi tool T10008) can be inserted into the slot in the tensioner body. If this special tool is not available, an alternative can be manufactured **(see illustrations)**. Note that as the tensioner is hydraulically damped, it can only be compressed slowly using constant pressure.

8 Examine the timing belt for manufacturer's markings that indicate the direction of rotation. If none are present, make your own using typist's correction fluid or a dab of paint – do not cut or score the belt in any way.

Caution: If the belt appears to be in good condition and can be re-used, it is essential that it is refitted the same way around, otherwise accelerated wear will result, leading to failure.

9 Undo the bolt and remove the idler roller **(see illustration)**.

10 Slide the belt off the sprockets, taking care to avoid twisting or kinking it excessively if it is to be re-used.

Friction damper tensioner

11 Loosen the tensioner nut, then turn the tensioner hub anti-clockwise with circlip pliers until it can be locked by inserting a suitable drill bit or metal rod through the hole provided **(see illustration)**.

4.17 Position the camshaft sprocket clockwise so the securing bolts are at the ends of the elongated holes

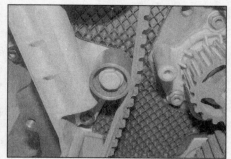

4.9 Unbolt the idler roller

12 Turn the tensioner hub clockwise onto the stop, and hand-tighten the nut.
13 Slide the belt off the sprockets, taking care to avoid twisting or kinking it excessively if it is to be re-used.

Inspection

14 Examine the belt for evidence of contamination by coolant or lubricant. If this is the case, find the source of the contamination before progressing any further. Check the belt for signs of wear or damage, particularly around the leading edges of the belt teeth. Renew the belt if its condition is in doubt; the cost of belt renewal is negligible compared with potential cost of the engine repairs, should the belt fail in service. The belt must be renewed if it has covered 40 000 miles, however if it has covered less it is prudent to renew it regardless of condition, as a precautionary measure.

15 If the timing belt is not going to be refitted for some time, it is a wise precaution to hang a warning label on the steering wheel, to remind yourself (and others) not to attempt to start the engine.

Refitting

16 Ensure that the crankshaft and camshaft are still set to TDC on No 1 cylinder, as described in Section 2.

Hydraulic tensioner

17 Turn the camshaft sprocket fully **clockwise** until the three bolts are against the ends of the elongated holes of the hub **(see illustration)**.
18 Loop the timing belt loosely over the

4.20 Refit the idler roller

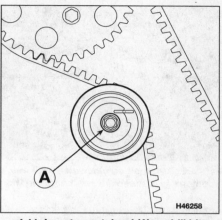

4.11 Insert a metal rod (A) or drill bit through the hole in the tensioner

camshaft sprocket. **Note:** *Observe any direction of rotation markings on the belt.*
19 Engage the timing belt with the tensioning roller, crankshaft sprocket, and coolant pump sprocket. Make sure that the belt teeth seat correctly on the sprockets. **Note:** *Slight adjustment to the position of the camshaft sprocket may be necessary to achieve this. Avoid bending the belt back on itself or twisting it excessively as you do this.*
20 Refit the idler roller and tighten the bolt to the specified torque **(see illustration)**.
21 Ensure that any slack in the belt is in the section of belt that passes over the tensioner roller.
22 Using a suitable tool (eg, circlip pliers) engaged with the two holes in the tensioner hub, turn the tensioner pulley anti-clockwise until the locking plate (T10008) is no longer under tension and can be removed. Turn the tensioner in a clockwise direction until gap of 4 mm exists between the tensioner backplate arm and the top edge of the tensioner housing **(see illustration)**.
23 With the tensioner held in this position, tighten the tensioner locknut to the specified torque and angle.
24 Tighten the camshaft sprocket bolts to the specified torque, remove the sprocket locking pin and the crankshaft locking tool.
25 Using a spanner or wrench and socket on the crankshaft pulley centre bolt, rotate the

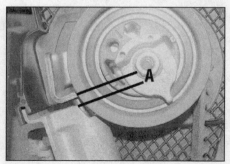

4.22 The gap between the top edge of the tensioner housing and the backplate arm (A) must be 4 mm

4.30 Turn the hub clockwise until the pointer is in the middle of the gap in the rear plate

crankshaft clockwise through two complete revolutions. Reset the engine to TDC on No 1 cylinder, with reference to Section 2 and check that the camshaft sprocket locking pin (3359 or 6 mm rod) can still be inserted, and that the correct gap still exists between the tensioner backplate arm and top edge of the tensioner housing. If the tensioner gap is incorrect, carry out the tensioning procedure again. If the camshaft sprocket locking pin cannot be inserted, slacken the retaining bolts, turn the hub until the pin fits, and tighten the sprocket retaining bolts to the specified torque and angle.

Friction damper tensioner

26 Turn the camshaft sprocket fully anti-clockwise until the three bolts are against the ends of the elongated holes of the hub.
27 Loop the timing belt loosely over the camshaft sprocket. **Note:** *Observe any direction of rotation markings on the belt.*
28 Engage the timing belt with the tensioning roller, crankshaft sprocket, and coolant pump

To make a camshaft sprocket holding tool, obtain two lengths of steel strip about 6 mm thick by 30 mm wide, one 600 mm long, the other 200 mm long (all dimensions are approximate). Bolt the two strips together to form a forked end, leaving the bolt slack so that the shorter strip can pivot freely. At the end of each 'prong' of the fork, secure a bolt with a nut and a locknut, to act as the fulcrums; these will engage with the cut-outs in the sprocket, and should protrude by about 30 mm.

sprocket. Make sure that the belt teeth seat correctly on the sprockets. **Note:** *Slight adjustment to the position of the camshaft sprocket may be necessary to achieve this. Avoid bending the belt back on itself or twisting it excessively as you do this.*
29 Remove the locking pin, then loosen the tensioner nut, but make sure that the arm on the rear plate remains engaged with the hole in the timing belt rear cover.
30 Using a suitable tool (eg, circlip pliers) engaged with the two holes in the tensioner hub, turn the tensioner hub clockwise until the pointer is in the middle of the window in the rear plate **(see illustration)**.
31 Hold the tensioner pulley in this position and tighten the nut to the specified torque and angle. **Note:** *When tightening the retaining nut, the pointer may move up to 5 mm (maximum) to the right of the slot in the rear plate. This is acceptable and must not be adjusted, because the new timing belt stretches slightly when first used.*
32 Tighten the camshaft sprocket bolts to the specified torque, remove the sprocket locking pin and the crankshaft locking tool.
33 Using a spanner or wrench and socket on the crankshaft pulley centre bolt, rotate the crankshaft clockwise through two complete revolutions. Reset the engine to TDC on No 1 cylinder, with reference to Section 2 and check that the camshaft and crankshaft sprocket locking pins can still be inserted. If not, carry out the tensioning procedure again.

All models

34 Refit the timing belt covers (using a little thread-locking compound), viscous fan (where fitted), auxiliary drivebelt(s) and lock carrier assembly using a reversal of the removal procedure.
35 Refit the engine top cover then reconnect the battery negative lead (see Chapter 5A).

5 Timing belt tensioner and sprockets – removal and refitting

1 Disconnect the battery (see Chapter 5A).
2 To gain access to the components detailed in this Section, first refer to Section 6 and remove the auxiliary drivebelts.

5.11 Hand-tighten the camshaft sprocket bolts at this stage

Timing belt tensioner

3 With reference to the relevant paragraphs of Sections 2 and 4, set the engine to TDC on No 1 cylinder, then remove the upper section of the timing belt outer cover.
4 Relieve the tension on the timing belt with reference to Section 4.
5 Undo the retaining nut fully, and remove the tensioner pulley.
6 To remove the tensioner damper housing on models with an hydraulic tensioner, remove the right-hand cover (where fitted), and the housing retaining bolts.
7 Refit the tensioner, and tension the timing belt as described in Section 4.
8 Refit the timing belt covers using a little thread-locking compound on the retaining bolts, in the reverse of the description in Section 2.

Camshaft sprocket

9 Refer to Section 2 and 4, set the engine to TDC on No 1 cylinder. Slacken the three bolts securing the camshaft sprocket to the hub **(see Tool Tip)**.
10 Remove the timing belt as described in Section 4. To eliminate any possibility of accidental piston-to-valve contact, turn the crankshaft 90° anti-clockwise. Unscrew the three retaining bolts and remove the camshaft sprocket.
11 Locate the sprocket on the camshaft hub, and hand-tighten the retaining bolts **(see illustration)**.
12 Turn the crankshaft clockwise 90° back to TDC. Refit and tension the timing belt as described in Section 4.

Camshaft hub

Note: *Audi technicians use special tool T10051 to counterhold the hub, however it is possible to fabricate a suitable alternative – see below.*
13 Remove the camshaft sprocket as described in paragraphs 9 and 10.
14 Engage special tool T10051 with the three locating holes in the face of the hub to prevent the hub from turning. If this tool is not available, fabricate a suitable alternative as described in the *Tool tip* associated with paragraph 9. Whilst holding the tool, undo the central hub retaining bolt about two turns **(see illustration)**.

5.14 Counterhold the camshaft hub and undo the central retaining bolt about two turns

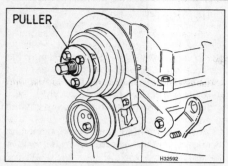

5.15 Attach a three-legged puller to the hub

5.16 The key in the hub taper must align with the keyway in the camshaft (arrowed)

5.23 Refit the crankshaft sprocket with a new retaining bolt

15 Leaving the central hub retaining bolt in place, attach Audi tool T10052 (or a similar three-legged puller) to the hub, and evenly tighten the puller until the hub is free of the camshaft taper **(see illustration)**.

16 Ensure that the camshaft taper and the hub centre is clean and dry, locate the hub on the taper, noting that the built-in key in the hub taper must align with the keyway in the camshaft taper **(see illustration)**.

17 Hold the hub in this position with tool T10051 (or similar home-made tool), and tighten the central bolt to the specified torque.

18 The remainder of refitting is a reversal of removal.

Crankshaft sprocket

19 Remove the timing belt as described in Section 4. If the timing belt is to be re-used, make sure it is marked for direction of rotation.

20 The crankshaft sprocket must be held stationary whilst its retaining bolt is slackened. If access to the Audi flywheel/driveplate locking tool is not available, lock the crankshaft in position by removing the starter motor, as described in Chapter 5A, to expose the ring gear. Get an assistant to insert a wide-bladed screwdriver between the ring gear teeth and the transmission bellhousing whilst the sprocket retaining bolt is slackened. Withdraw the bolt, and lift off the sprocket. Discard the sprocket retaining bolt, a new one must be fitted.

21 With the sprocket removed, examine the crankshaft oil seal for signs of leaking. If necessary, refer to Section 10 and renew it.

22 Wipe the sprocket and crankshaft mating surfaces clean.

23 Offer up the sprocket to the crankshaft, engaging the lug on the inside of the sprocket with the recess in the end of the crankshaft. Insert the new retaining bolt and tighten it to the specified Stage 1 torque while holding the crankshaft stationary as described for removal (do not lubricate the bolt). Then angle-tighten the bolt by the specified angle **(see illustration)**.

24 The remainder of refitting is a reversal of removal.

6 Auxiliary drivebelt(s) – removal, refitting and tensioning

Vehicles up to 05/2003

General information

1 One main auxiliary drivebelt is fitted to drive the alternator, viscous fan, and power steering pump. On models with air conditioning, a separate drivebelt drives the compressor. Both drivebelts are driven from pulleys mounted on the front of the crankshaft, and both drivebelts are of poly-vee type **(see illustration)**.

2 The main drivebelt tension is adjusted automatically by a spring-tensioned idler. Where fitted, the air conditioning compressor drivebelt is adjusted using a torque wrench on the idler.

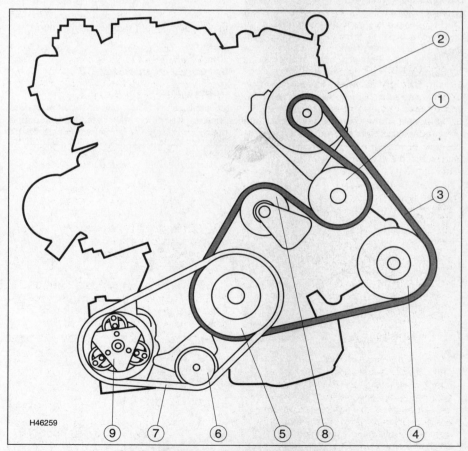

6.1 Auxiliary drivebelt routing – up to 05/2003

1 Viscous fan pulley
2 Alternator
3 Belt
4 Power steering pump
5 Crankshaft pulley
6 Tensioner
7 Air conditioning compressor drivebelt
8 Tensioner
9 Air conditioning compressor

Removal

3 To remove the drivebelts first apply the handbrake, then jack up the front of the vehicle and support it on axle stands (see *Jacking and vehicle support*). Remove the undershield from under the engine compartment, as described in Section 4.

4 If any drivebelt is to be re-used, mark it for clockwise direction to ensure it is refitted the same way round.

5 Access to the drivebelt is best achieved by moving the complete front panel (the lock carrier assembly) away from the front of the car as far as possible, but without disconnecting the radiator hoses or electrical wiring. To do this, first remove the front bumper as described in Chapter 11, then unscrew the three quick-release clips from the noise insulation panel and unbolt the air duct from between the lock carrier and the air cleaner. On the left-hand side of the radiator, release the wiring from the clips. Unscrew the bolts securing the lock carrier/bumper bar assembly to the underbody channels, then unscrew the upper side bolts – one at the top/front of each wing, and one alongside each headlamp. Unscrew the bolts securing the bumper guides beneath each headlamp, and unclip them from the front wings. With the help of an assistant, pull the complete assembly away from the front of the car as far as possible. Audi technicians use special tools to hold the assembly, however support bars may be made out of threaded metal rod and screwed into the underbody channels.

6 On models with air conditioning, loosen the pivot and tension bolts and move the tensioner roller upwards to release the tension on the drivebelt. Slip the drivebelt from the crankshaft, compressor and tensioner pulleys.

7 To remove the main drivebelt, first note how it is fitted to each pulley to ensure correct refitting. In particular note that the flat outer surface of the drivebelt is located on the viscous fan pulley. Use a 19 mm spanner on the hexagon cast into the tensioner pulley bracket, and push the tensioner pulley downwards (anti-clockwise).

Refitting

8 Locate the drivebelt on the alternator, viscous coupling fan, power steering pump, and crankshaft pulleys, making sure that each rib is correctly located in a groove. Turn the automatic tensioner anti-clockwise and locate the drivebelt on the pulley, then release the tensioner to tension the drivebelt.

9 On models with air conditioning, locate the drivebelt on the compressor and crankshaft pulleys, making sure that each rib is correctly located in a groove. Move the tensioner pulley downwards and engage the drivebelt with the pulley grooves. Tension the drivebelt by applying a torque of 25 Nm (18 lbf ft) to the hexagon on the tensioner body. Hold this torque then tighten the adjustment and pivot bolts.

10 Refit the lock carrier assembly into position.

Vehicles from 06/2003

General information

11 On these vehicles, one drivebelt is used to drive the alternator, power steering pump, and the air conditioning compressor (where fitted).

The poly-vee belt is driven from the crankshaft pulley/vibration damper **(see illustration)**.

Removal

12 To remove the drivebelts first apply the handbrake, then jack up the front of the vehicle and support it on axle stands (see *Jacking and vehicle support*). Remove the undershield from under the engine compartment as described in Section 4.

13 If the drivebelt is to be re-used, mark it for clockwise direction to ensure it is refitted the same way round.

14 Although not absolutely necessary, Access to the drivebelt is best achieved by moving the complete front panel (the lock carrier assembly) away from the front of the car as far as possible, but without disconnecting the radiator hoses or electrical wiring. To do this, first remove the front bumper as described in Chapter 11, then unscrew the three quick-release clips from the noise insulation panel and unbolt the air duct from between the lock carrier and the air cleaner. On the left-hand side of the radiator, release the wiring from the clips. Unscrew the bolts securing the lock carrier/bumper bar assembly to the underbody channels, then unscrew the upper side bolts – one at the top/front of each wing, and one alongside each headlamp. Unscrew the bolts securing the bumper guides beneath each headlamp, and unclip them from the front wings. With the help of an assistant, pull the complete assembly away from the front of the car as far as possible. Audi technicians use special tools to hold the assembly, however support bars may be made out of threaded metal rod and screwed into the underbody channels.

15 Use a spanner to rotate the tensioner centre bolt clockwise, and relieve the tension on the belt **(see illustration)**. Remove the belt from the pulleys.

Refitting

16 Locate the drivebelt on the alternator, power steering pump, crankshaft, air conditioning compressor (where applicable), and idler pulleys, making sure that each rib is correctly located in a groove. Rotate the automatic tensioner clockwise and locate the drivebelt on the pulley, then release the tensioner to tension the drivebelt.

17 The remainder of refitting is a reversal of removal.

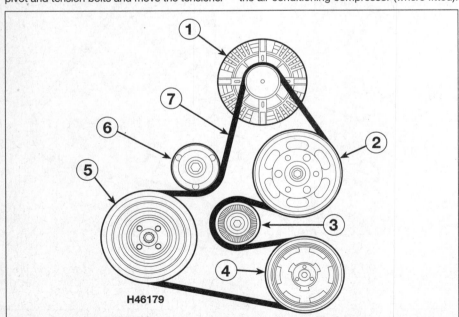

6.11 Auxiliary drivebelt routing – from 06/2003

1	Alternator	3	Idler	5	Crankshaft pulley
2	Power steering pump	4	Air conditioning compressor	6	Tensioner pulley
				7	Belt

6.15 Rotate the tensioner clockwise to relieve the tension on the belt

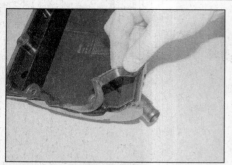

7.4 The camshaft cover gasket locates in a groove in the cover

7.6 Apply sealant to the points at the front and rear where the camshaft bearing cap contacts the cylinder head (arrowed)

8.2 Gradually and evenly slacken the rocker shaft retaining bolts, starting with the outer bolts first

7 Camshaft cover – removal and refitting

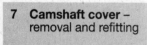

Removal

1 Pull out the engine oil level dipstick, then prise out the cover caps, undo the retaining nuts and remove the engine top cover, and disconnect the breather hose from the camshaft cover. Pull away the foam insulation around the camshaft cover.

2 Release the 2 retaining clips and remove the timing belt upper cover.

3 Working gradually and evenly in a diagonal pattern, unscrew the camshaft cover retaining bolts and lift the cover away. If it sticks, do not attempt to lever it off – instead free it by working around the cover and tapping it lightly with a soft-faced mallet.

4 Recover the camshaft cover gasket **(see illustration)**. Inspect the gasket carefully, and renew it if damage or deterioration is evident.

5 Clean the mating surfaces of the cylinder head and camshaft cover thoroughly, removing all traces of oil and old gasket – take care to avoid damaging the surfaces as you do this.

Refitting

6 Refit the camshaft cover by following the removal procedure in reverse, noting the following points:

  a) Apply suitable sealant to the points at the front and rear where the camshaft bearing cap contacts the cylinder head **(see illustration)**.

  b) Tighten the camshaft cover retaining bolts to the specified torque.

8 Pump injector rocker shaft assembly – removal and refitting

Removal

1 Remove the camshaft cover as described in Section 7. In order to ensure that the rocker arms are refitted to their original locations, use a marker pen or paint and number the arms 1 to 4, with No 1 nearest the timing belt end of

the engine. If the arms are not fitted to their original locations the injector basic clearance setting procedure must be carried out as described in Chapter 4C, Section 6.

2 Starting with the outer bolts first, carefully and evenly slacken the rocker shaft retaining bolts. Discard the rocker shaft bolts, new ones must be fitted **(see illustration)**.

Refitting

3 Carefully check the rocker shaft, rocker arms and camshaft bearing cap seating surface for any signs of excessive wear or damage.

4 Ensure that the shaft seating surface is clean and position the rocker shaft assembly in the camshaft bearing caps, making sure that, if re-using the original rocker arms, they are in their original locations.

5 Insert the new rocker shaft retaining bolts, and starting from the inner bolts, gradually and evenly tighten the bolts to the Stage 1 torque setting.

6 Again, starting with the inner retaining bolts, tighten the bolts to the Stage 2 angle as listed in this Chapter's Specifications.

7 Refit the camshaft cover as described in Section 7.

9 Camshaft oil seal – renewal

1 Refer to Section 5 and remove the camshaft sprocket, and the camshaft hub.

10.2 Remove the crankshaft front oil seal using self-tapping screws

2 Note the fitted position of the seal in the housing, and drill two small holes into the existing oil seal, diagonally opposite each other. Thread two self-tapping screws into the holes, and using two pairs of pliers, pull on the heads of the screws to extract the oil seal. Take great care to avoid drilling through into the seal housing or camshaft sealing surface.

3 Clean out the seal housing and sealing surface of the camshaft by wiping it with a lint-free cloth. Remove any swarf or burrs that may cause the seal to leak.

4 Do **not** lubricate the lip and outer edge of the new oil seal, and push it over the camshaft until it is positioned above its housing.

5 Using a hammer and a socket of suitable diameter, drive the seal squarely into its housing. **Note:** Select a socket that bears only on the hard outer surface of the seal, not the inner lip which can easily be damaged.

6 Refit the camshaft hub and sprocket as described in Section 5.

7 The remainder of refitting is a reversal of removal.

10 Crankshaft oil seals – renewal

Front oil seal

1 Remove the crankshaft sprocket with reference to Section 5.

2 Note the fitted location of the seal, drill two small holes into the existing oil seal, diagonally opposite each other. Thread two self-tapping screws into the holes and using two pairs of pliers, pull on the heads of the screws to extract the oil seal **(see illustration)**. Take great care to avoid drilling through into the seal housing or crankshaft sealing surface.

3 Clean out the seal housing and sealing surface of the crankshaft by wiping it with a lint-free cloth – avoid using solvents that may enter the crankcase and affect component lubrication. Remove any swarf or burrs that could cause the seal to leak.

4 Note that the new oil seal must **not** be oiled or greased, as it is manufactured of special material.

5 Using a hammer and a socket of suitable

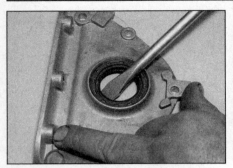

10.14 Prise the oil seal from the housing

10.16 Apply a bead of sealant to the front oil seal housing

10.18 Slide the oil seal and housing over the taped end of the crankshaft

diameter, drive the seal squarely into its housing. **Note:** *Select a socket that bears only on the hard outer surface of the seal, not the inner lip, which can easily be damaged.*
6 Refit the crankshaft sprocket with reference to Section 5.

Front oil seal housing gasket

7 Remove the crankshaft sprocket with reference to Section 5.
8 Unbolt the torque reaction bracket from the front of the engine.
9 On vehicles from 06/2003, undo the bolt and remove the auxiliary drivebelt idler pulley. Discard the bolt, a new one must be fitted.
10 Remove the sump as described in Section 15.
11 Progressively slacken and then remove the oil seal housing retaining bolts.
12 Lift the housing away from the cylinder block, together with the crankshaft oil seal, using a twisting motion to ease the seal along the shaft.
13 Thoroughly clean the housing and block surfaces.
14 If necessary, prise the old oil seal from the housing using a screwdriver **(see illustration)**.
15 Wipe the oil seal housing clean, and check it visually for signs of distortion or cracking. Lay the housing on a work surface, with the mating surface face down. If removed, press in a new oil seal, using a block of wood as a press to ensure that the seal enters the housing squarely.
16 Apply a 2 to 3 mm wide bead of suitable sealant (available from Audi dealers) to

the oil seal housing sealing surface **(see illustration)**.
17 Wrap the end of the crankshaft with tape to protect the oil seal as the housing is being refitted.
18 Ease the seal along the shaft using a twisting motion, until the housing is flush with the crankcase **(see illustration)**. **Note:** *The oil seal must **not** be oiled or greased.*
19 Insert the bolts and tighten them progressively to the specified torque.
20 On vehicles from 06/2003, refit the auxiliary drivebelt idler pulley, and tighten the new bolt to the specified torque.
21 Refer to Section 15 and refit the sump.
22 Refit the torque reaction bracket to the front of the engine and tighten the bolts.
23 Refit the crankshaft sprocket with reference to Section 5.

Rear oil seal and housing

Note: *The oil seal is integral with the housing and must be renewed as one complete assembly.*
24 Remove the transmission as described in the relevant Part of Chapter 7.
25 Refer to Section 13 of this Chapter and remove the flywheel (manual/Multitronic transmission) or driveplate (automatic transmission).
26 Remove the intermediate plate from the dowels on the cylinder block.
27 Remove the sump as described in Section 15.
28 Progressively slacken then remove the oil seal housing retaining bolts.
29 Lift the housing away from the cylinder

block, together with the crankshaft oil seal, using a twisting motion to ease the seal off the shaft.
30 Wipe clean the block before fitting the new oil seal and housing. Note that no gasket is fitted as the housing incorporates sealant on its mating surface.
31 A protective plastic guide is supplied with genuine Audi crankshaft oil seals; when fitted over the end of the crankshaft, the guide prevents damage to the inner lip of the oil seal as it is being fitted **(see illustration)**. Use adhesive tape wrapped around the end of the crankshaft if a guide is not available.
32 Offer up the seal and its housing to the end of the crankshaft. Carefully ease the seal along the shaft using a twisting motion, until the housing is flush with the crankcase **(see illustration)**. **Note:** *The oil seal must **not** be additionally oiled or greased.*
33 Insert the retaining bolts and tighten them progressively to the specified torque.
34 Refit the sump with reference to Section 15.
35 Refit the intermediate plate to the cylinder block, then insert and tighten the retaining bolts.
36 Refit the flywheel (manual/Multitronic transmission) or driveplate (automatic transmission) with reference to Section 13 of this Chapter.
37 Refit the transmission with reference to the relevant Part of Chapter 7.

11 Cylinder head – removal and refitting

Note: *Cylinder head dismantling and overhaul is covered in Chapter 2D.*
Note: *In order to remove the cylinder head on diesel engines fitted with unit injectors, it is necessary to unplug the central connector for the injectors – this may cause a fault code to be logged by the engine management ECU. This code can only be erased by an Audi dealer or suitably-equipped specialist.*

Removal

1 Disconnect the battery negative (earth) lead (see Chapter 5A).
2 Drain the engine oil with reference to Chapter 1B.

10.31 A protective cap is supplied with genuine Audi crankshaft oil seals

10.32 Locate the crankshaft rear oil seal housing over the protective plastic cap

3 Drain the cooling system with reference to Chapter 1B.

4 Prise out the cover caps, undo the retaining nuts and remove the engine top cover.

5 Remove the timing belt with reference to Section 4, and the camshaft sprocket and hub as described in Section 5.

6 Undo the two bolts securing the timing belt inner cover to the cylinder head **(see illustrations)**.

7 With reference to Section 5, remove the timing belt tensioner pulley.

8 Using a stud extractor or two nuts locked together, unscrew and remove the timing belt tensioner pulley mounting stud **(see illustration)**.

9 Unscrew the retaining bolts and remove the camshaft cover as described in Section 7.

10 Remove the bolt securing the camshaft position sensor to the cylinder head. There is no need to disconnect it at this stage **(see illustration)**.

11 Disconnect the charge air pipe from the intake manifold to the intercooler at the back of the engine and place to one side.

12 Remove the air cleaner housing as described in Chapter 4C.

13 Note their fitted positions, then disconnect the vacuum hoses/electrical connectors from the EGR valve, intake manifold changeover flap, and boost pressure control valve **(see illustration)**.

14 Release the clips and disconnect the coolant hose from the EGR cooler (where fitted).

Engine codes
AVB, AVF, AWX and BKE

15 Undo the nuts securing the turbocharger to the catalytic converter, then slacken the pipe sleeve nuts, and slide the front exhaust pipe and catalytic converter rearwards.

Engine code BRB

16 Remove the front exhaust pipe and particulate filter as described in Chapter 4D.

All engines

17 Lift the retaining clip and detach the intake hose from the turbocharger.

18 On vehicles with manual or Multitronic transmissions, undo the nuts/bolts and remove the turbocharger support brackets.

19 Undo the bolts/union and disconnect the oil return pipe from the turbocharger or cylinder block. Be prepared for oil spillage, and recover the gasket/seal.

20 Slacken the clamp bolt, pull the fuel filter upwards from its bracket and position it to one side. There is no need to disconnect the fuel hoses.

21 Remove the upper bolt securing the fuel filter bracket to the cylinder head. Slacken the three bolts securing the fuel filter bracket to the cylinder block, pull the top of the bracket away from the cylinder head, and disconnect cylinder No 4 glow plug. Disconnect the rest of the glow plugs – if necessary, refer to Chapter 5C.

22 Disconnect and remove the hoses

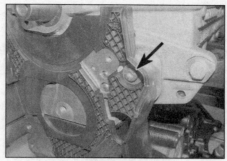

11.6a Undo the timing belt inner cover-to-cylinder head bolt (arrowed) . . .

11.6b . . . and the one on the right-and side

11.8 Using a stud extractor, or two nuts locked together, unscrew the tensioner mounting stud

11.10 Unscrew the bolt and remove the camshaft position sensor

connected to the upper coolant pipe **(see illustration)**.

23 Slacken and remove the bolt securing the upper metal coolant pipe to the cylinder head.

24 Disconnect the central connector for the unit injectors **(see illustration)**.

25 Undo the banjo bolt and disconnect the oil supply pipe from the oil filter housing.

26 Undo the two bolts securing the coolant junction to the rear of the cylinder head **(see illustration)**. There is no need to disconnect the pipes or wiring plugs at this stage.

11.13 Disconnect the vacuum pipes from the EGR valve and manifold flap actuator

11.22 Disconnect the various hoses from the coolant pipe on the top of the cylinder head

11.24 Rotate the collar anti-clockwise to disconnect the central connector for the unit injectors

11.26 Undo the two bolts (arrowed) and push the coolant outlet from the rear of the cylinder head

11.27 Undo the four tandem pump retaining bolts (arrowed)

11.34 Remove the heat shield from the exhaust manifold

11.38a Fit the new exhaust manifold gasket

11.38b Refit the exhaust manifold and tighten the retaining nuts

11.40a Fit the new intake manifold gasket to the cylinder head . . .

11.40b . . . then lift the intake manifold into position

27 Unscrew the four retaining bolts and pull the tandem pump away from the cylinder head without disconnecting the fuel or vacuum hoses **(see illustration)**.

28 On vehicles with engine code BRB, undo the bolts and remove the EGR pipe from the cooler to the intake manifold.

29 On all models, using a multi-splined tool, undo the cylinder head bolts, working from the outside-in, evenly and gradually. Check that nothing remains connected, and lift the cylinder head from the engine block. Seek assistance if possible, as it is a heavy assembly, especially as it is being removed complete with the manifolds. Discard the bolts, new ones must be fitted. **Note:** *It is essential that the cylinder head is not placed on a surface with the combustion chambers facing downwards, as the heater/glow plugs protrude below the gasket surface, and are easily damaged.*

30 Remove the gasket from the top of the block, noting the locating dowels. If the dowels are a loose fit, remove them and store them with the head for safe-keeping. Do not discard the gasket yet – it will be needed for identification purposes.

31 If the cylinder head is to be dismantled for overhaul, refer to Chapter 2D.

Manifold separation and reassembly

32 With the cylinder head on a workbench, if not done previously, remove the turbocharger with reference to Chapter 4C.

33 Remove the EGR valve (see Chapter 4D).

34 Where applicable, unscrew the nuts and

remove the small heat shield from the front of the exhaust manifold **(see illustration)**.

35 Progressively unscrew the mounting bolts and remove the intake manifold from the cylinder head. Remove the gasket and discard it.

36 If necessary, unbolt the oil supply pipe and bracket from the exhaust manifold.

37 Progressively unscrew the mounting nuts and remove the exhaust manifold from the cylinder head. Remove the gaskets and discard. Discard the self-locking mounting nuts and obtain new ones.

38 Ensure that the intake and exhaust manifold mating surfaces are completely clean. Refit the exhaust manifold, using new gaskets and nuts. Ensure that the gaskets are fitted the correct way around, otherwise they will obstruct the intake manifold gasket. Tighten the exhaust manifold retaining nuts to the specified torque (see Chapter 4D) **(see illustrations)**.

39 Where necessary, refit the oil supply pipe and bracket to the exhaust manifold and tighten the bolt.

40 Fit a new intake manifold gasket to the cylinder head, then lift the intake manifold into position. Insert the retaining bolts and tighten them to the specified torque (see Chapter 4C) **(see illustrations)**.

41 Refit the heat shield to the studs on the exhaust manifold, then fit and tighten the retaining nuts.

42 Refit the EGR valve with reference to Chapter 4D. Refit the turbocharger to the intake and exhaust manifolds with reference to Chapter 4C.

Preparation for refitting

43 The mating faces of the cylinder head and cylinder block must be perfectly clean before refitting the head. Use a hard plastic or wood scraper to remove all traces of gasket and carbon; also clean the piston crowns. Take particular care during the cleaning operations, as aluminium alloy is easily damaged. Also, make sure that the carbon is not allowed to enter the oil and water passages – this is particularly important for the lubrication system, as carbon could block the oil supply to the engine's components. Using adhesive tape and paper, seal the water, oil and bolt holes in the cylinder block/crankcase. Take great care not to damage the glow plugs – they are very delicate.

44 Check the mating surfaces of the cylinder block/crankcase and the cylinder head for nicks, deep scratches and other damage. If slight, they may be removed carefully with abrasive paper, but note that head machining will not be possible – refer to Chapter 2D.

45 If warpage of the cylinder head gasket surface is suspected, use a straight-edge to check it for distortion. Refer to Part D of this Chapter if necessary.

46 Clean out the cylinder head bolt drillings using a suitable tap. If a tap is not available, make a home-made substitute **(see Tool Tip opposite)**.

47 On the engines covered in this Chapter, it is possible for the piston crowns to strike the valve heads if the camshaft is rotated with the timing belt removed and the crankshaft set to TDC. For this reason, the camshaft must be

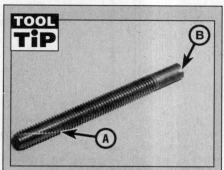

If a tap is not available, make a home-made substitute by cutting a slot (A) down the threads of one of the old cylinder head bolts. After use, the bolt head can be cut off, and the shank can then be used as an alignment dowel to assist cylinder head refitting. Cut a screwdriver slot (B) in the top of the bolt to allow it to by unscrewed.

11.48 The thickness of the cylinder head gasket can be identified by notches or holes – see Chapter 2D

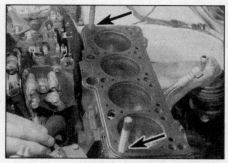

11.51 Two of the old head bolts (arrowed) can be used as cylinder head alignment guides

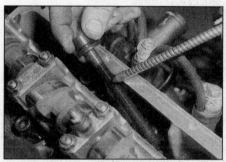

11.54 Oil the cylinder head bolt threads prior to fitting

locked at its TDC position using the locking bar engaged with the slot in the end of the camshaft while the cylinder head is being refitted. Turn the crankshaft to TDC on No 1 cylinder, and then anti-clockwise 90° so that all pistons are half-way up the cylinders.

Refitting

48 Examine the old cylinder head gasket for manufacturer's identification markings. These will either be in the form of notches or holes, and a part number, on the edge of the gasket **(see illustration)**. Unless new pistons have been fitted, the new cylinder head gasket must be the same type as the old one.

49 If new piston assemblies have been fitted as part of an engine overhaul, before

purchasing the new cylinder head gasket, refer to Chapter 2D and measure the piston projection. Purchase a new gasket according to the results of the measurement (see Chapter 2D Specifications).

50 Lay the new head gasket on the cylinder block, engaging it with the locating dowels. Ensure that the manufacturer's TOP and part number markings are facing upwards.

51 Cut the heads from two of the old cylinder head bolts. Cut a slot, big enough for a screwdriver blade, in the end of each bolt. These can be used as alignment guides to assist in cylinder head refitting **(see illustration)**.

52 With the help of an assistant, place the cylinder head and manifolds centrally on the cylinder block, ensuring that the locating dowels engage with the recesses in the cylinder head.

53 Unscrew the home-made alignment dowels using a screwdriver and remove them.

54 Oil the new bolt threads, then carefully enter each bolt (with washers) into its relevant

hole (*do not drop them in*) and screw in, by hand only, until finger-tight **(see illustration)**.

55 Working progressively and in sequence, tighten the cylinder head bolts to the Stage 1 torque setting, using a torque wrench and socket **(see illustrations)**. Repeat the exercise in the same sequence for the Stage 2 torque setting.

56 Once all the bolts have been tightened to their Stage 2 settings, working again in sequence, angle-tighten the bolts through the specified Stage 3 angle, using a socket and extension bar. It is recommended that an angle-measuring gauge is used during this stage of the tightening, to ensure accuracy. If a gauge is not available, use white paint to make alignment marks between the bolt head and cylinder head prior to tightening; the marks can then be used to check the bolt has been rotated through the correct angle during tightening. Repeat for the Stage 4 setting (see

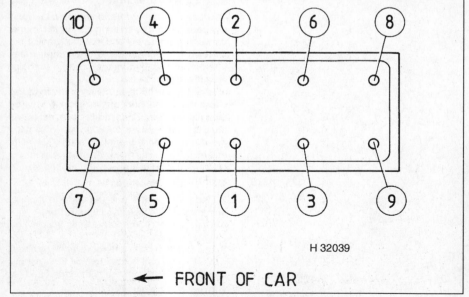

H 32039

← FRONT OF CAR

11.55a Cylinder head bolt tightening sequence

11.55b Tighten the cylinder head bolts using a torque wrench . . .

11.56 . . . then using an angle-tightening gauge

illustration). Note: *No further tightening of the cylinder head bolts is required after the engine has been started.*

57 Turn the crankshaft 90° clockwise (to TDC), and check that the TDC timing marks are still aligned with reference to Section 2.

58 The remainder of refitting is a reversal of the removal procedure, but on completion carry out the following:

13.5 Rotate the outside of the dual-mass flywheel to align the bolts with the holes

a) *Refill the cooling system with the correct quantity of new coolant with reference to Chapter 1B.*

b) *Refill the engine with the correct grade and quantity of oil with reference to Chapter 1B.*

59 Have the engine management ECU's fault memory interrogated and erased by an Audi dealer or suitably-equipped specialist.

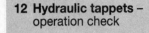
12 Hydraulic tappets – operation check

⚠ **Warning: After fitting hydraulic tappets, wait a minimum of 30 minutes (or preferably, leave overnight) before starting the engine, to allow the tappets time to settle, otherwise the valve heads will strike the pistons.**

1 The hydraulic tappets are self-adjusting, and require no attention whilst in service.

2 If the hydraulic tappets become excessively noisy, their operation can be checked as described below.

13.6 Use a locking tool (arrowed) to prevent the flywheel from rotating

3 Run the engine until it reaches its normal operating temperature, then increase the engine speed to approximately 2500 rpm for 2 minutes.

4 If irregular noisy tappets occur mainly when driving the car on short distances, but disappear after running the engine as described in paragraph 3, renew the oil retention valve located in the oil filter housing (see Chapter 2A, Section 11).

5 In the case of a regular noisy tappet, the faulty tappet must be renewed. To determine which one is faulty, switch off the engine, then refer to Section 7 and remove the camshaft cover.

6 Rotate the camshaft by turning the crankshaft with a socket and wrench, until the first cam lobe over No 1 cylinder is pointing upwards.

7 Using a non-metallic tool, press the tappet downwards then use a feeler blade to check the free travel. If this is more than 0.2 mm, the tappet should be renewed.

8 Hydraulic tappet removal and refitting is described as part of the cylinder head overhaul sequence – see Chapter 2D for details.

13 Flywheel/driveplate – removal, inspection and refitting

Removal

1 On manual gearbox models, remove the gearbox (see Chapter 7A) and clutch (see Chapter 6).

2 On automatic transmission models, remove the automatic transmission as described in Chapter 7B.

3 On Multitronic transmission models, remove the transmission (Chapter 7C).

Manual transmission

4 These models are fitted with a dual-mass flywheel. Begin by making alignment marks between the flywheel and the crankshaft.

5 Rotate the outside of the dual-mass flywheel so that the bolts align with the holes **(see illustration)**.

6 Unscrew the bolts and remove the flywheel. Use a locking tool to counterhold the flywheel **(see illustration)**. Discard the bolts, new ones must be fitted. **Note:** *In order not to damage the flywheel, do not allow the bolt heads to make contact with the flywheel secondary element during the unscrewing procedure.*

Multitronic transmission

7 Undo the screws and remove the damper unit from the flywheel **(see illustration)**.

8 Make alignment marks between the flywheel and crankshaft.

9 Unscrew the bolts and remove the flywheel. Use a locking tool to counterhold the flywheel. Discard the bolts, new ones must be fitted.

Automatic transmission

10 Make alignment marks between the driveplate and crankshaft.

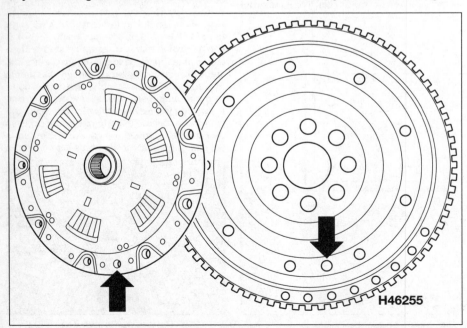

13.7 The hole in the damper unit aligns with the locating pin in the flywheel (arrowed)

11 Unscrew the bolts and remove the driveplate. Use a locking tool to counterhold the driveplate. Discard the bolts, new ones must be fitted.

12 Remove the shim from behind the drive-plate.

Inspection

13 Check the flywheel/driveplate for wear and damage. Examine the starter ring gear for excessive wear to the teeth. If the driveplate or its ring gear are damaged, the complete driveplate must be renewed. The flywheel ring gear, however, may be renewed separately from the flywheel, but the work should be entrusted to an Audi dealer. If the clutch friction face is discoloured or scored excessively, it may be possible to regrind it, but this work should also be entrusted to an Audi dealer.

14 With the flywheel removed, check the spigot needle bearing in the end of the crankshaft for wear by turning it with a finger. If there is any evidence of excessive wear or if the bearing has been running dry, it must be renewed. To do this, use a bearing removal puller which engages the rear end of the bearing. Drive the new bearing into position until its outer end is 1.5 mm below the end of the crankshaft. **Note:** *A spigot needle bearing must not be fitted to the crankshaft on automatic/Multitronic transmission models.*

15 Check the dual mass flywheel as described in Chapter 2B.

Refitting

16 Refitting is a reversal of removal, however on automatic transmission models temporarily refit the driveplate using the old bolts tightened to 30 Nm (22 lbf ft), and measure, through the torque converter mounting hole, the distance from the block to the torque converter *mounting face* on the driveplate. The correct distance is 18.9 to 20.5 mm **(see illustration)**. If necessary, remove the driveplate, and fit a spacer behind it to achieve the correct dimension. The raised pip on the outer shim must face the torque converter. Use new bolts when refitting the flywheel or driveplate, and coat the threads of the bolts with locking fluid before inserting them. Tighten them to the specified torque.

14 Engine mountings – inspection and renewal

Inspection

1 If improved access is required, raise the front of the car and support it securely on axle stands then remove the engine undershield.

2 Check the mounting rubbers to see if they are cracked, hardened or separated from the metal at any point; renew the mounting if any such damage or deterioration is evident.

3 Check that all the mounting's fasteners are

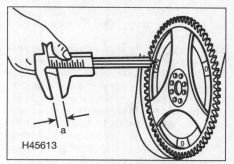

13.16 Check the torque converter fitting dimension

a = 18.9 to 20.5 mm

securely tightened; use a torque wrench to check if possible.

4 Using a large screwdriver or a crowbar, check for wear in the mounting by carefully levering against it to check for free play. Where this is not possible, enlist the aid of an assistant to move the engine/transmission back-and-forth, or from side-to-side, while you watch the mounting. While some free play is to be expected even from new components, excessive wear should be obvious. If excessive free play is found, check first that the fasteners are correctly secured, then renew any worn components as described below.

Renewal

Front torque arm

5 For improved access, apply the handbrake then jack up the front of the vehicle and support it on axle stands (see *Jacking and vehicle support*).

6 Where fitted, remove the engine undertray. Access is much improved if the lock carrier is placed in the Service Position (see Chapter 11).

7 Unscrew the bolts and remove the torque arm from the front of the engine **(see illustration)**.

8 Pull the rubber element from the front crossmember

9 Fit the rubber element and/or bump stop using a reversal of the removal procedure.

Right- or left-hand engine mounting

10 Apply the handbrake, then jack up the front of the vehicle and support it on axle stands (see *Jacking and vehicle support*).

14.7 Undo the bolts and detach the torque arm (arrowed) from the engine

11 Support the weight of the engine with a hoist.

12 Unscrew the upper mounting nut, then carefully raise the engine and unbolt the mounting from the bracket.

13 Fit the new mounting using a reversal of the removal procedure.

15 Sump – removal, inspection and refitting

Note: *The following procedure applies only to models with 5-speed manual gearbox or Multitronic gearbox. Models with a 6-speed manual gearbox must have the engine (Chapter 2D) and flywheel (Section 13) removed prior to sump removal. Once the engine and flywheel have been removed, proceed from paragraph 9.*

Removal

1 Apply the handbrake, then jack up the front of the vehicle and support it on axle stands (see *Jacking and vehicle support*). Also remove the undershield from under the engine and radiator.

2 Pull out the engine oil level dipstick, then prise out the cover caps, undo the retaining nuts and remove the engine top cover. Recover the insulation under the cover, and refit the dipstick.

Vehicles up to 05/2003

3 In order to remove the sump, it is necessary to move the complete front panel (the lock carrier assembly) away from the front of the car as far as possible (into the Service position – see Chapter 11).

Vehicles from 06/2003

4 Remove the auxiliary drivebelt as described in Section 6.

All vehicles

5 Undo the retaining bolt and move the coolant expansion tank to one side. Disconnect the level sensor wiring plug as the tank is moved. There is no need to disconnect the coolant hoses.

6 Release the clips and remove the air intake pipe from the intake manifold. Disconnect any wiring connectors as necessary **(see illustration)**.

15.6 Release the clip (arrowed) and disconnect the air intake pipe

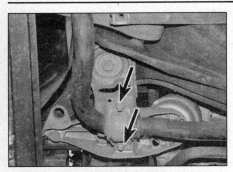

15.14 Undo the clamp nuts each side (arrowed) and lower the anti-roll bar

7 Support the weight of the engine using a suitable hoist.

8 Position a container beneath the sump, then unscrew the drain plug (refer to Chapter 1B) and drain the engine oil. Clean, refit, and tighten the plug after all the oil has drained. Remove the dipstick from the engine.

9 Detach the starter motor cables from under the engine mounting by cutting the plastic cable ties. Disconnect the engine oil level/ temperature sensor wiring plug from the underside of the sump.

10 On vehicles from 06/2003, disconnect the wiring plug from the left-hand side engine mounting.

11 On vehicles with air conditioning, undo the bolts and detach the refrigerant pipe brackets from the sump, then undo the mounting bolts and move the compressor to one side, without disconnecting the refrigerant pipes. Use string or wire to suspend the compressor from a suitable point on the vehicle body. Do not allow the pipes to be stretched, kinked or bent. Disconnect the wiring plug as the compressor is withdrawn.

12 Undo the bolts and remove the torque arm from the front of the engine (see illustration 14.7).

13 On models fitted with self-levelling suspension, unclip the actuator rod from the suspension transverse link.

14 On all models, undo the clamp nuts and lower the front anti-roll bar (see illustration).

15 Make sure the engine is adequately supported on the hoist. Support the left- and right-hand front subframe with a trolley jack and length of wood. In order to avoid having to perform the front wheel re-alignment check, only slacken the subframe front mounting bolts. In order to be sure of correct alignment, mark the position of the subframe in relation to the vehicle body to ensure correct refitting.

16 Mark the installation positions of the engine mountings on each side, then unscrew and remove the bottom nuts.

17 Undo the bolts and remove the brackets each side from below the engine mountings.

18 Undo the bolts securing the undertray mounting bracket.

19 Use the trolley jack to lower the front of the subframe, and the hoist to raise the engine slightly. Ensure the gearchange rod and exhaust to not become trapped.

20 Gradually and evenly, working in a diagonal sequence, unscrew and remove the sump bolts. Note that on manual transmission models, the two rear sump bolts are accessed through a cut-out in the flywheel – turn the flywheel as necessary to align the cut-out.

21 Remove the sump. If it is stuck, tap it gently with a rubber mallet to free it.

Refitting

22 Clean the contact surfaces of the sump and block. Evenly apply a 2 to 3 mm wide bead of silicone sealant to the sump (see illustration).

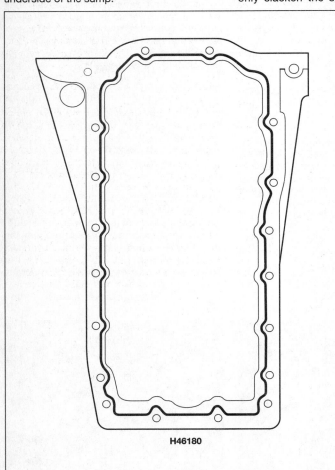

H46180

15.22a Apply sealant as shown by the black line

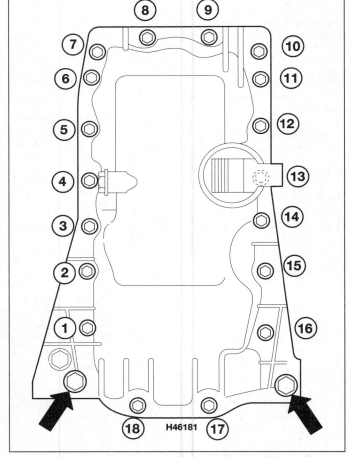

H46181

15.22b Sump bolt numbering – the arrows indicate the 10 mm diameter bolts

16.11a The oil pump sprocket will only fit in one position due to the flat machined on the oil pump shaft

16.11b Refit the oil pump drive chain tensioner

16.13 Refit the baffle plate using the remaining oil pump mounting bolt

Immediately install the sump, ensuring that the rear face of the sump is flush with the rear face of the cylinder block. **Note:** *If the sump is being fitted with the engine removed from the car and the transmission removed, make sure that the end face of the support bracket is flush with that of the intermediate plate. If the intermediate plate is removed, allow 0.8 mm for its thickness, and position the face of the bracket 0.8 mm protruding from the rear face of the cylinder block.* Tighten bolts 1 to 18 in a diagonal sequence to 5 Nm, then tighten the sump-to-gearbox bolts to 45 Nm. Now tighten the 10 mm diameter bolts to 40 Nm, and finally tighten bolts 1 to 18 to 15 Nm **(see illustration)**.

23 The remaining refitting procedure is a reversal removal, but tighten the nuts and bolts to the specified torque where given in the Specifications. On completion, fill the engine with the correct quantity of oil as described in Chapter 1B.

16 Oil pump and pickup
– removal, inspection and refitting

Removal

1 Remove the sump as described in Section 15.
2 Unscrew the bolt, release and remove the baffle plate from the bottom of the crankcase.
3 Slacken and remove the Torx screw

securing the drive sprocket to the oil pump. Insert a screwdriver through one of the holes in the sprocket and against the oil pump body to prevent the sprocket from turning whilst the Torx screw is undone. Discard the screw, a new one must be fitted.
4 Unscrew and remove the remaining two mounting bolts, and release the oil pump from the dowels in the crankcase. Unhook the oil pump drive sprocket from the chain and withdraw it from the engine. Note that the tensioner will attempt to tighten the chain, and it may be necessary to use a screwdriver to hold it in its tensioned position before releasing the oil pump sprocket from the chain.
5 Unscrew the flange bolts and remove the suction pipe from the oil pump. Recover the O-ring seal. Unscrew the bolts and remove the cover from the oil pump. Before removing the rotors, mark them to ensure they are refitted the original way round.
6 Examine the drive chain for wear and damage. To remove the chain, the timing belt must first be removed (see Section 4), then the crankshaft front oil seal housing unbolted from the cylinder block. With the housing removed, unbolt and remove the chain tensioner, then unhook the chain from the sprocket on the front of the crankshaft.

Inspection

7 Clean the pump thoroughly, and inspect the rotors for signs of damage or wear. A suitable puller will be required to remove the sprocket

from the front of the crankshaft, however note that it must be heated to 220°C for 15 minutes when refitting. Note that the broad collar of the sprocket faces the engine. Examine the pump rotors for signs of excessive wear and damage. If evident, renew the oil pump.

Refitting

8 Lubricate the rotors with fresh engine oil, then refit the cover to the oil pump and tighten the bolts securely. Prime the pump by pouring oil into the suction pipe aperture while turning the driveshaft.
9 If the drive chain, crankshaft sprocket and tensioner have been removed, delay refitting them until after the oil pump has been mounted on the cylinder block.
10 Locate the oil pump on the dowels, then insert and tighten the two mounting bolts to the specified torque.
11 Where applicable, refit the drive chain, crankshaft sprocket, tensioner and oil pump sprocket using a reversal of the removal procedure. Note that the oil pump sprocket will only fit in one position due to the flat machined on the oil pump shaft **(see illustrations)**.
12 Refit the crankshaft front oil seal housing and timing belt where applicable. Apply suitable sealant to the front oil seal housing before fitting it.
13 Refit the baffle plate using the remaining oil pump mounting bolt and tighten it to the specified torque, followed by the sump with reference to Section 15 **(see illustration)**.

Chapter 2 Part D:
Engine removal and overhaul procedures

Contents

	Section number
Crankshaft – refitting	12
Crankshaft – removal and inspection	8
Cylinder block/crankcase – cleaning and inspection	9
Cylinder head – dismantling, cleaning, inspection and reassembly	6
Engine – initial start-up after overhaul and reassembly	15
Engine – removal and refitting	4
Engine overhaul – general information	2
Engine overhaul – preliminary information	5

	Section number
Engine overhaul – reassembly sequence	11
Engine removal – preparation and precautions	3
General information	1
Main and big-end bearings – inspection and selection	10
Piston/connecting rod assemblies – refitting	14
Piston/connecting rod assemblies – removal and inspection	7
Pistons and piston rings – assembly	13

Degrees of difficulty

Easy, suitable for novice with little experience	**Fairly easy,** suitable for beginner with some experience	**Fairly difficult,** suitable for competent DIY mechanic	**Difficult,** suitable for experienced DIY mechanic	**Very difficult,** suitable for expert DIY or professional

Specifications

Engine codes*

Petrol engines

1781 cc:
Bosch Motronic ME7.5:	
110 kW (143 bhp)	AVJ
125 kW (163 bhp)	AMB
Bosch Motronic ME7.1:	
120 kW (156 bhp)	BFB and BKB
140 kW (182 bhp)	BEX
1984 cc, Bosch Motronic ME7, 96 kW (125 bhp)	ALT

1984 cc:
Bosch Motronic ME7, 96 kW (125 bhp)	ALT
Bosch Motronic MED7.1, 110 kW (143 bhp)	AWA

Diesel engines
74 kW (96 bhp)	AVB
85 kW (111 bhp)	BKE and BRB
96 kW (125 bhp)	AVF and AWX

* **Note:** See 'Vehicle identification' for the location of the code marking on the engine.

Cylinder head

Cylinder head gasket surface, maximum distortion	0.1 mm
Minimum cylinder head height:	
Petrol engines	139.20 mm
Diesel engines	Head resurfacing not possible
Cylinder head gasket selection (diesel engines):	
Piston projection 0.91 to 1.00 mm	1 hole/notch*
Piston projection 1.01 to 1.10 mm	2 holes/notches*
Piston projection 1.11 to 1.20 mm	3 holes/notches*

* *Disregard single and double oval holes.*

Valves

	Intake	Exhaust
Valve stem diameter:		
Petrol engines	5.96 ± 0.01 mm	5.95 ± 0.01 mm
Diesel engines	6.980 mm	6.956 mm
Maximum valve head deflection (end of stem flush with top of guide):		
Petrol engines	0.80 mm	0.80 mm
Diesel engines	1.3 mm	1.3 mm

Camshaft

Maximum endfloat:
  Petrol engines:
    Engine codes AWA . . . . 0.17 mm
    Engine codes AVJ, AMB, BEX, BFB, ALT, BKB . . . . 0.20 mm
  Diesel engines . . . . 0.15 mm
Maximum runout, all engines . . . . 0.01 mm

Pistons and piston rings

Piston diameter:
  Petrol engines:
    1.8 litre . . . . 80.950 mm nominal
    2.0 litre . . . . 82.465 mm nominal
  Diesel engines . . . . 79.720 mm nominal
Ring-to-groove clearance:
  Petrol engines:
    Compression rings . . . . 0.20 mm maximum
    Oil control ring . . . . 0.15 mm maximum
  Diesel engines:
    Compression rings . . . . 0.25 mm maximum
    Oil control ring . . . . 0.15 mm maximum
Piston ring end gap clearance (ring 15 mm from bottom of bore):
  Petrol engines:
    New:
      Compression rings . . . . 0.20 to 0.40 mm
      Oil scraper ring . . . . 0.25 to 0.50 mm
    Wear limit . . . . 0.8 mm
  Diesel engines:
    New:
      Compression rings . . . . 0.20 to 0.40 mm
      Oil scraper ring . . . . 0.25 to 0.50 mm
    Wear limit . . . . 1.0 mm

Cylinder block

Bore diameter:
  Petrol engines:
    1.8 litre . . . . 81.01 mm nominal
    2.0 litre . . . . 82.51 mm nominal
  Diesel engines . . . . 79.51 mm nominal

Crankshaft

Spigot needle bearing depth . . . . 1.5 mm

Endfloat:	**New**	**Wear limit**
Petrol engines.	0.07 to 0.23 mm	0.30 mm
Diesel engines	0.07 to 0.17 mm	0.37 mm

Main bearing journal diameter:
  Petrol engines. . . . . 54.00 mm nominal
  Diesel engines . . . . 54.00 mm nominal
Big-end bearing journal diameter:
  Petrol engines. . . . . 47.80 mm nominal
  Diesel engines:
    Engine code AVB . . . . 47.80 mm nominal
    Engine codes AVF, AWX, BKE, BRB. . . . . 50.90 mm nominal

Torque wrench settings

Refer to Chapters 2A, 2B or 2C.

---

1 General information

Included in this Part of Chapter 2 are details of removing the engine from the car and general overhaul procedures for the cylinder head, cylinder block and all other engine internal components.

The information given ranges from advice concerning preparation for an overhaul and the purchase of parts, to detailed step-by-step procedures covering removal, inspection, renovation and refitting of engine internal components.

After Section 5, all instructions are based on the assumption that the engine has been removed from the car. For information concerning in-car engine repair, as well as the removal and refitting of those external components necessary for full overhaul, refer to the relevant in-car repair procedure section (Chapters 2A, 2B or 2C) and to Section 5 of this Chapter. Ignore any preliminary dismantling operations described in the relevant in-car repair sections that are no longer relevant once the engine has been removed from the car.

Apart from torque wrench settings, which are given at the beginning of the relevant in-car repair procedure in Chapters 2A, 2B or 2C, all specifications relating to engine overhaul are at the beginning of this Part of Chapter 2.

2 Engine overhaul – general information

It is not always easy to determine when, or if, an engine should be completely overhauled, as a number of factors must be considered.

High mileage is not necessarily an indication that an overhaul is needed, while low mileage does not preclude the need for an overhaul. Frequency of servicing is probably the most important consideration. An engine which has had regular and frequent oil and filter changes, as well as other required maintenance, should give many thousands of miles of reliable service. Conversely, a neglected engine may require an overhaul very early in its life.

Excessive oil consumption is an indication that piston rings, valve seals and/or valve guides are in need of attention. Make sure that oil leaks are not responsible before deciding that the rings and/or guides are worn. Perform a compression test, as described in the relevant Part A, B or C of this Chapter, to determine the likely cause of the problem.

Check the oil pressure with a gauge fitted in place of the oil pressure switch, and compare it with that specified (see Chapter 2A, 2B or 2C). If it is extremely low, the main and big-end bearings, and/or the oil pump, are probably worn out.

Loss of power, rough running, knocking or metallic engine noises, excessive valve gear noise, and high fuel consumption may also point to the need for an overhaul, especially if they are all present at the same time. If a complete service does not remedy the situation, major mechanical work is the only solution.

An engine overhaul involves restoring all internal parts to the specification of a new engine. During an overhaul, the pistons and the piston rings are renewed. New main and big-end bearings are generally fitted; if necessary, the crankshaft may be renewed, to restore the journals. The valves are also serviced as well, since they are usually in less-than-perfect condition at this point. While the engine is being overhauled, other components, such as the starter and alternator, can be overhauled as well. The end result should be an as-new engine that will give many trouble-free miles. **Note:** *Critical cooling system components such as the hoses, thermostat and coolant pump should be renewed when an engine is overhauled. The radiator should be checked carefully, to ensure that it is not clogged or leaking. Also, it is a good idea to renew the oil pump whenever the engine is overhauled.*

Before beginning the engine overhaul, read through the entire procedure, to familiarise yourself with the scope and requirements of the job. Overhauling an engine is not difficult if you follow carefully all of the instructions, have the necessary tools and equipment, and pay close attention to all specifications. It can, however, be time-consuming. Plan on the

car being off the road for a minimum of two weeks, especially if parts must be taken to an engineering works for repair or reconditioning. Check on the availability of parts and make sure that any necessary special tools and equipment are obtained in advance. Most work can be done with typical hand tools, although a number of precision measuring tools are required for inspecting parts to determine if they must be renewed. Often the engineering works will handle the inspection of parts and offer advice concerning reconditioning and renewal. **Note:** *Always wait until the engine has been completely dismantled, and until all components (especially the cylinder block and the crankshaft) have been inspected, before deciding what service and repair operations must be performed by an engineering works. The condition of these components will be the major factor to consider when determining whether to overhaul the original engine, or to buy a reconditioned unit. Do not, therefore, purchase parts or have overhaul work done on other components until they have been thoroughly inspected. As a general rule, time is the primary cost of an overhaul, so it does not pay to fit worn or sub-standard parts.*

As a final note, to ensure maximum life and minimum trouble from a reconditioned engine, everything must be assembled with care, in a spotlessly-clean environment.

3 Engine removal – preparation and precautions

If you have decided that the engine must be removed for overhaul or major repair work, several preliminary steps should be taken.

Locating a suitable place to work is extremely important. Adequate work space, along with storage space for the vehicle, will be needed. If a workshop or garage is not available, at the very least a solid, level, clean work surface is required.

If possible, clear some shelving close to the work area and use it to store the engine components and ancillaries as they are removed and dismantled. In this manner, the components stand a better chance of staying clean and undamaged during the overhaul. Laying out components in groups together with their fixings bolts, screws, etc, will save time and avoid confusion when the engine is refitted.

Clean the engine compartment and engine before beginning the removal procedure; this will help visibility and help to keep tools clean.

The help of an assistant is essential; there are certain instances when one person cannot safely perform all of the operations required to remove the engine from the vehicle. Safety is of primary importance, considering the potential hazards involved in this kind of operation. A second person should always be in attendance to offer help in an emergency.

If this is the first time you have removed an engine, advice and aid from someone more experienced would also be beneficial.

Plan the operation ahead of time. Before starting work, obtain (or arrange for the hire of) all of the tools and equipment you will need. Access to the following items will allow the task of removing and refitting the engine to be completed safely and with relative ease: a heavy-duty trolley jack – rated in excess of the weight of the engine, complete sets of spanners and sockets as described in the back of this manual, wooden blocks, and plenty of rags and cleaning solvent for mopping-up spilled oil, coolant and fuel. A selection of different sized plastic storage bins will also prove useful for keeping dismantled components grouped together. If any of the equipment must be hired, make sure that you arrange for it in advance, and perform all of the operations possible without it beforehand; this may save you time and money.

Plan on the vehicle being out of use for quite a while, especially if you intend to carry out an engine overhaul. Read through the whole of this Section and work out a strategy based on your own experience and the tools, time and workspace available to you. Some of the overhaul processes may have to be carried out by a Audi dealer or an engineering works – these establishments often have busy schedules, so it would be prudent to consult them before removing or dismantling the engine, to get an idea of the amount of time required to carry out the work.

When removing the engine from the vehicle, be methodical about the disconnection of external components. Labelling cables and hoses as they are removed will greatly assist the refitting process.

Always be extremely careful when lifting the engine from the engine bay. Serious injury can result from careless actions. If help is required, it is better to wait until it is available rather than risk personal injury and/or damage to components by continuing alone. By planning ahead and taking your time, a job of this nature, although major, can be accomplished successfully and without incident.

On all models described in this manual, the engine is lifted from the engine compartment leaving the transmission in the car. Note that the engine should ideally be removed with the vehicle standing on all four roadwheels, but access to the exhaust system downpipe and lower bolts will be improved if the vehicle can be temporarily raised onto axle stands.

4 Engine – removal and refitting

Removal

1 Select a solid, level surface to park the vehicle on. Give yourself enough space to move around it easily.

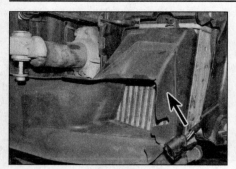

4.7 Unclip the intercooler air duct (arrowed) – turbo models only

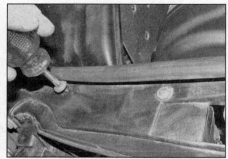

4.12 Undo the two screws securing the intake duct to the lock carrier

4.14 Disconnect the wiring plugs adjacent to the radiator top hose

2 Disconnect the battery negative (earth) lead (see Chapter 5A). On models with automatic or Multitronic transmissions, position the selector lever in position N.

3 Apply the handbrake, then jack up the front of the vehicle and support it on axle stands (see *Jacking and vehicle support*). Remove both front roadwheels.

4 Remove the retaining clips and screws, and remove engine compartment undershield, then undo the bolts and remove the undershield mounting bracket.

5 Where applicable, prise out the cover caps, undo the retaining bolts/nuts and remove the cover from the top of the engine.

6 Remove the front bumper with reference to Chapter 11.

7 On turbocharged engines, release the clips and remove the left- and right-hand intercooler air ducts **(see illustration)**.

8 With reference to the relevant Part of Chapter 1, carry out the following:
 a) *Drain the cooling system.*
 b) *Drain the engine oil.*

9 On turbocharged models, slacken the clamps and remove the intercooler hoses.

10 Clamp the hoses, then disconnect the power steering cooling hoses from the cooler. Be prepared for coolant spillage.

11 On models with automatic/Multitronic transmissions, position a suitable container beneath the engine, then loosen the union nuts and disconnect the transmission fluid pipes alongside the engine. Plug the pipe openings

to prevent entry of dust and dirt. Also unbolt the fluid pipe bracket from the engine.

12 Unbolt the air duct leading to the air cleaner from the lock carrier **(see illustration)**. Where fitted, remove the plastic cover over the power steering fluid reservoir.

13 Disconnect the radiator top hose from the engine, and the coolant hoses from the engine oil cooler (where applicable).

14 Disconnect the airbag crash sensor wiring plug from its location beneath the radiator top hose connection **(see illustration)**.

15 Disconnect the headlight wiring plugs on both sides.

16 Note their fitted locations, then disconnect the wiring plugs in front of the power steering fluid reservoir.

17 Disconnect the horn's wiring plugs.

18 Unbolt the rubber air shrouds each side of the radiator.

19 Unclip the ambient air temperature sensor from in front of the radiator/condenser (as applicable), then undo the bolts and remove the power steering cooling pipe.

20 On models with air conditioning, disconnect the high pressure sensor wiring plug from the left-hand side of the condenser, then undo the bolts and pivot the condenser downwards, without disconnecting the refrigerant pipes. Protect the condenser with card or cloth sheets to prevent damage to it when removing the engine.

Caution: Do not kink, stretch or bend the rigid metal refrigerant pipes.

21 Disconnect the bonnet release cable at the bonnet lock.

22 Detach the engine compartment rubber seal from the lock carrier and wings.

23 Unscrew the lock carrier mounting bolts – one at the front/top of each wing, and one at the side of each headlamp. Unscrew the three bolts securing each bumper guide below each headlamp, and unclip them from the front wings. Unscrew the bolts retaining the lock carrier/bumper bar to the underbody channels and, with the help of an assistant, withdraw the complete lock carrier from the front of the car and place it in a safe position **(see illustrations)**.

24 Remove the auxiliary drivebelt as described in the relevant part of Chapter 2.

25 At the base of the engine sump, disconnect the wiring plug from the oil temperature sensor.

26 On models with air conditioning, undo the bolt securing the refrigerant pipe bracket to the sump, then disconnect the compressor wiring plug, undo the bolts and detach the compressor from the engine without disconnecting the refrigerant pipes. Suspend the compressor using cable ties or wire from a suitable location on the left-hand side of the engine compartment.

Caution: Do not kink, stretch or bend the rigid metal refrigerant pipes.

27 Disconnect the earth lead at the engine compartment bulkhead, then disconnect the servo vacuum hose – also at the bulkhead

4.23a Undo the bolts at each end of the lock carrier (arrowed) . . .

4.23b . . . the one under each headlamp (arrowed) . . .

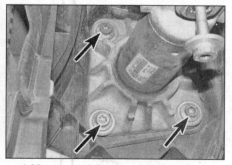

4.23c . . . and the 3 securing the lock carrier to the underbody channels each side (arrowed)

4.27 Disconnect the earth lead (arrowed) and the servo vacuum hose

4.30 Oxygen sensor wiring plugs (arrowed) – non-turbo models

4.33 Power steering pump supply and return hoses (arrowed) – engine code AWA

4.37a Disconnect the vacuum hoses from the EGR valve . . .

4.37b . . . and disconnect the wiring plug from the airflow meter

4.40 Undo the bolt (arrowed) and detach the EGR solenoid valve

(see illustration). Release the earth lead harness clip from the bulkhead.

28 On petrol engines, disconnect the charcoal canister hose from the connection at the rear of the cylinder head.

29 Release the clips, disconnect the hoses, then undo the bolt and remove the coolant expansion tank. Disconnect the level sensor wiring plug as the tank is removed.

Petrol models

30 Note their fitted positions and disconnect the oxygen sensor wiring plugs at the engine compartment bulkhead (turbo models) or rear of the intake manifold (non-turbo models) **(see illustration)**.

31 Depressurise the fuel system as described in Chapter 4A or 4B, then undo the union and disconnect the fuel supply and return pipes (where applicable). Plug the pipe openings to prevent dirt ingress.

32 Disconnect the secondary air injection pump wiring plug (where applicable), and the hose from the pump leading to the combination valve

33 On all models except engine code AWA, working through the holes in the power steering pump pulley, undo and remove the pump mounting bolts, then remove the mounting bolt at the rear of the pump. On models with engine code AWA, clamp the return hose, undo the banjo bolt, then disconnect the hydraulic hoses from the power steering pump **(see illustration)**.

34 Disconnect the air mass meter wiring plug, then remove the air cleaner housing (see Chapter 4a or 4B).

Diesel models

35 Disconnect the fuel supply and return lines from the filter cover on the left-hand side of the engine.

36 Release the clips, undo the bolt and remove the intake duct from the rear of the engine.

37 Note their fitted positions, and disconnect the vacuum hoses from the EGR valve, and the mass airflow meter wiring plug **(see illustration)**.

38 Undo the bolts securing the power steering pump pulley, then remove the power steering pump mounting bolts and move the pump to one side. Tie it to one side using string or wire.

39 Remove the air cleaner housing as described in Chapter 4C.

40 On models with engine codes AVB, AVF or AWX, undo the bolt securing the EGR valve

solenoid to the right-hand chassis member **(see illustration)**.

41 On models with engine code BRB, release the clip and disconnect the coolant hose from the EGR cooler. Be prepared for coolant spillage.

42 Note their fitted positions, and the harness routing, then disconnect the various electrical connectors at the engine compartment bulkhead.

All models

43 Pull up the rubber seal, then pull the windscreen scuttle trim panel forwards.

44 Remove the wiper arms as described in Chapter 12, then prise off the 3 clips (1 in the centre, 1 at each end) and pull the trim panel upwards from the base of the windscreen **(see illustrations)**.

45 Undo the Torx bolts and remove the cover from the electronics box in the plenum chamber.

4.44a Release the clip at each end (arrowed), and the one in the centre . . .

4.44b . . . the pull the trim at the base of the windscreen upwards from place

4.46 Release the ECM clip

4.47 Release the clips and detach the auxiliary relay carrier from the electronics box

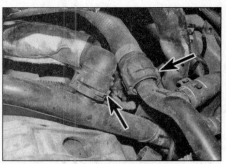

4.56 Prise out the clips (arrowed) and disconnect the heater hose quick-release couplings

46 Use a screwdriver to release the ECM retaining clip, then lift the ECM from place and disconnect the connectors under the ECM **(see illustration)**.

47 Release the clips and slide the relay carrier assembly upwards from the electronics box. Release the ECM wiring harness from the retaining clips and the engine compartment bulkhead, then lay the engine wiring harness, complete with ECM, over the engine **(see illustration)**.

48 On turbocharged petrol models, release the clips and remove the air intake hose between the turbocharger and air cleaner housing.

49 On non-turbocharged petrol models, release the clips and remove the intake hose between the air cleaner and the intake manifold.

50 On models with Multitronic transmission, undo the nut securing the ATF pipes bracket to the engine, and undo the bolt and disconnect the ATF pipes from the transmission. Be prepared for fluid spillage.

51 Disconnect the earth lead on the underside of the right-hand chassis member in the engine compartment.

52 Undo the bolts and remove the heat shield over the right-hand driveshaft.

53 Remove the front section of the exhaust pipe/catalytic converter as described in Chapter 4D.

54 Note their fitted positions, then disconnect the wiring plugs from the transmission.

55 Remove the starter motor with reference to Chapter 5A.

56 Prise out the retaining clips and disconnect the heater hoses at the quick release connections at the rear of the intake manifold **(see illustration)**.

57 Disconnect the wiring from the speedometer sender on the left-hand side of the transmission (1.8 litre models only).

58 Working underneath the vehicle, note the fitted positions of the locating sleeves, then undo the engine mounting bottom nuts each side. **Note:** *Different mounting holes are used for different engine versions.* Where applicable, disconnect the wiring plugs from the engine mountings.

59 On automatic transmission models,

unscrew and remove the three torque converter nuts accessible through the starter motor aperture. It will be necessary to turn the engine for access to each nut. To prevent the driveplate from turning while loosening the nuts, either counterhold the crankshaft pulley bolt, or place a screwdriver in the teeth of the starter ring gear.

60 Slacken the engine mounting top nuts several turns.

61 Attach a suitable hoist to the engine, and lift the engine and transmission slightly. Make sure that the engine is adequately supported.

62 Unscrew and remove the bolts securing the transmission to the rear of the engine, then lower the engine to its original position. At this stage leave one of the bolts loosely fitted. Unbolt and remove the engine torque mounting bracket.

63 Using a trolley jack and piece of wood, support the front of the transmission. Alternatively, a support bar for the transmission can be placed over the rear of the engine compartment.

64 Remove the last bolt, then check that all wiring and hoses have been disconnected, and lift the engine from the engine compartment. On automatic transmission models, make sure that the torque converter remains firmly in the transmission as the engine is being removed, and to prevent it falling out fit a metal bar across the bellhousing, secured with two bolts.

65 If they are loose, recover the location dowels from the rear of the cylinder block. Where necessary, remove the intermediate plate from the rear of the engine.

66 On manual transmission models, remove the clutch as described in Chapter 6.

Refitting

67 Refitting is a reversal of removal, but on manual or Multitronic transmission models first smear the splines of the input shaft with a little clutch assembly grease. On manual gearbox models, lightly grease the contact surface of the release bearing, but **do not** grease the guide sleeve for the release bearing. On automatic transmission models, check that the torque converter is fully entered on the input shaft by checking that the distance between the bellhousing mounting

flange and the torque converter is approximately 23.0 mm. If it is only 13.0 mm, the torque converter is not fully entered. Ensure that all engine and transmission mountings are fitted free of strain, and tighten all nuts and bolts to the specified torque. Refit, and where applicable adjust, all engine related components and systems with reference to the Chapters concerned. Ensure that the engine is filled with oil and that the cooling system is refilled as described in Chapter 1A or 1B before starting the engine.

5 Engine overhaul – preliminary information

It is much easier to dismantle and work on the engine if it is mounted on a portable engine stand. These stands can often be hired from a tool hire shop. Before the engine is mounted on a stand, the flywheel should be removed, so that the stand bolts can be tightened into the end of the cylinder block/crankcase. **Note:** *Do not measure cylinder bore dimensions with the engine mounted on this type of stand.*

If a stand is not available, it is possible to dismantle the engine with it blocked up on a sturdy workbench, or on the floor. Be very careful not to tip or drop the engine when working without a stand.

If you intend to obtain a reconditioned engine, all ancillaries must be removed first, to be transferred to the new engine (just as they will if you are doing a complete engine overhaul yourself). These components include the following:

Petrol engines

a) *Alternator (including mounting brackets) and starter motor (Chapter 5A).*
b) *The ignition system including HT components, sensors, and spark plugs (Chapters 1A and 5B).*
c) *The fuel injection system components (Chapter 4A or 4B).*
d) *All electrical switches, actuators and sensors, and the engine wiring harness (Chapters 4A, 4B and 5B).*
e) *Intake and exhaust manifolds (Chapters 4A, 4B and 4D).*

f) Engine oil dipstick and tube.
g) Engine mountings (Chapter 2A and 2B).
h) Flywheel/driveplate (Chapter 2).
i) Clutch components (Chapter 6).

Diesel engines

a) Alternator (including mounting brackets) and starter motor (Chapter 5A).
b) The glow plug/preheating system components (Chapter 5C).
c) All fuel system components, including all sensors and actuators (Chapter 4C).
d) The tandem pump (Chapter 4C).
e) All electrical switches, actuators and sensors, and the engine wiring harness (Chapters 4C and 5C).
f) Intake and exhaust manifolds, and turbocharger (Chapters 4C and 4D).
g) The engine oil level dipstick and its tube.
h) Engine mountings (Chapter 2C).
i) Flywheel/driveplate (Chapter 2C).
j) Clutch components (Chapter 6).

All engines

Note: When removing the external components from the engine, pay close attention to details that may be helpful or important during refitting. Note the fitted position of gaskets, seals, spacers, pins, washers, bolts, and other small components.

If you are obtaining a short engine (the engine cylinder block/crankcase, crankshaft, pistons and connecting rods, all fully assembled), then the cylinder head, sump, oil pump, timing belt (together with its tensioner and covers), auxiliary belt (together with its tensioner), coolant pump, thermostat housing, coolant outlet elbows, oil filter housing and where applicable oil cooler will also have to be removed.

If you are planning a full overhaul, the engine can be dismantled in the order given below:

a) Intake and exhaust manifolds (see the relevant part of Chapter 4).
b) Timing belt, sprockets and tensioner (see Chapter 2A, 2B or 2C).
c) Cylinder head (see Chapter 2A, 2B or 2C).

d) Flywheel/driveplate (see Chapter 2A, 2B or 2C).
e) Sump (see Chapter 2A, 2B or 2C).
f) Oil pump or balancer shaft assembly (see Chapter 2A, 2B or 2C).
g) Piston/connecting rod assemblies (see Section 7).
h) Crankshaft (see Section 8).

6 Cylinder head – dismantling, cleaning, inspection and reassembly

Note: New and reconditioned cylinder heads are available from Audi, and from engine specialists. Specialist tools are required for the dismantling and inspection procedures, and new components may not be readily available. It may, therefore, be more practical for the home mechanic to buy a reconditioned head, rather than to dismantle, inspect and recondition the original head.

Dismantling

1 Remove the cylinder head from the engine block as described in Part A, B or C of this Chapter. Also remove the camshaft sprocket as described in Part A, B or C of this Chapter.
2 On diesel models, remove the injectors and glow plugs (see Chapters 4C and 5C).
3 Where applicable, remove the rear coolant outlet elbow together with its gasket/O-ring.
4 It is important that groups of components are kept together when they are removed and, if still serviceable, refitted in the same groups. If they are refitted randomly, accelerated wear leading to early failure will occur. Stowing groups of components in plastic bags or storage bins will help to keep everything in the right order – label them according to their fitted location, eg, No 1 exhaust, No 2 intake, etc **(see illustration)**. Note that No 1 cylinder is nearest the timing belt end of the engine.

Engine codes
AVJ, AMB, BFB, BEX and BKB

5 Check that the manufacturer's orientation

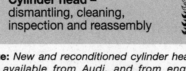

6.4 Keep groups of components together in labelled bags or boxes

markings are visible on camshaft bearing caps; if none can be found, make your own using a scriber or centre-punch.
6 At the front of the intake camshaft, unbolt the camshaft position sensor then unscrew the bolt from the camshaft and remove the tapered washer and rotor.
7 Check that the camshafts are still in the TDC position – the marks on the camshaft flanges must align with the corresponding marks on the No 1 camshaft bearing caps (at the rear of the cylinder head).
8 Clean the chain and the camshaft sprockets in line with the arrows on the top of the camshaft rear bearing caps, then mark the sprockets and chain in relation to each other. Note that the distance between the two marks must be 16 rollers on the chain, but also note that the mark on the exhaust camshaft is slightly offset towards the centre of the cylinder head.
9 The automatic camshaft adjuster must now be locked before removing it. Audi technicians use special tool 3366 to do this. Alternatively, it is possible to make up a similar tool using a threaded rod, nuts and a small metal plate to keep the adjuster compressed. As a safety precaution, use a plastic cable tie to keep the home-made tool in position **(see illustrations)**.
10 Progressively slacken the bolts from bearing caps 3 and 5 then 1 and 6 on both

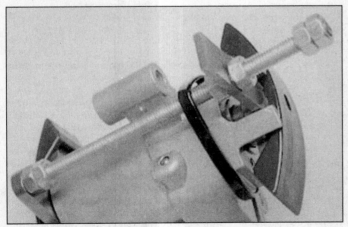

6.9a Home-made tool for holding the automatic adjuster in its compressed state

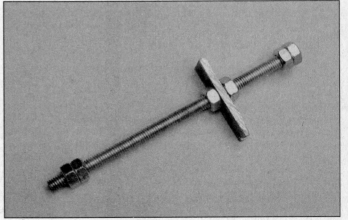

6.9b Home-made tool

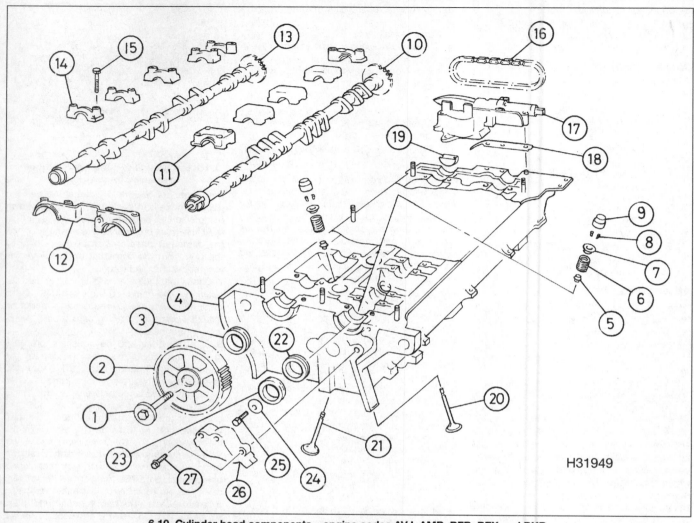

6.10 Cylinder head components – engine codes AVJ, AMB, BFB, BEX and BKB

1 Camshaft sprocket bolt
2 Camshaft sprocket
3 Oil seal
4 Cylinder head
5 Valve stem oil seal
6 Valve spring
7 Upper valve spring seat
8 Split collets
9 Hydraulic tappets
10 Intake camshaft
11 Bearing cap, intake camshaft
12 Front combined bearing cap
13 Exhaust camshaft
14 Bearing cap, exhaust camshaft
15 Camshaft bearing bolt
16 Drive chain
17 Automatic camshaft adjuster
18 Rubber seal
19 Half round rubber grommet
20 Exhaust valve
21 Intake valve
22 Oil seal
23 Hall sender ring
24 Tapered washer
25 Ring retaining bolt
26 Hall sender
27 Hall sender retaining bolt

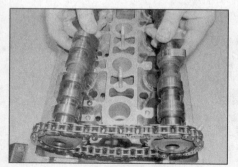

6.12 Lift the camshafts and chain from the cylinder head

6.13 Remove the camshaft adjuster

the intake and exhaust camshafts **(see illustration)**. **Note:** *The caps are numbered from the rear of the cylinder head, number 6 being the combined cap that straddles the front of both camshafts.*

11 Unscrew the automatic camshaft adjuster mounting bolts.

12 Progressively slacken the bolts from bearing caps 4 and 2 on both the intake and exhaust camshafts, then lift both camshafts from the cylinder head together with the automatic adjuster and chain **(see illustration)**.

13 Release the adjuster from the chain and remove the chain from the camshaft sprockets. Remove the oil seals from the front of each camshaft **(see illustration)**.

Engine code ALT

14 Check that the camshafts are still in the TDC position – the marks on the camshaft flanges must align with the corresponding marks on the rear of the camshaft bearing ladder.

15 Clean the chain and the camshaft sprockets in line with the arrows on the top of the camshaft bearing ladder, then mark the sprockets and chain in relation to each other. Note that the distance between the two marks must be 16 rollers on the chain, but also note that the mark on the exhaust camshaft is slightly offset towards the centre of the cylinder head.

16 The automatic camshaft adjuster must now be locked before removing it. Audi technicians use special tool T10092 to do this. Alternatively, it is possible to make up a similar tool using a threaded rod, nuts and a small metal plate to keep the adjuster compressed. As a safety precaution, use a plastic cable tie to keep the home-made tool in position **(see illustrations 6.9a and 6.9b)**.

17 Working from the outside-in, gradually and evenly slacken and remove the camshaft bearing ladder retaining bolts.

18 Use two M6 bolts to release the bearing ladder from the cylinder head **(see illustration)**.

19 Remove the bolts securing the hydraulic chain tensioner, then lift out the camshafts and disengage them from the chain.

20 Remove the seals from the camshafts.

Engine code AWA

21 Remove the high-pressure fuel pump as described in Chapter 4B, then undo the retaining bolts and remove the cover from the chain adjuster at the rear of the cylinder head.

22 Using Audi tool T10092 and an M5 nut, lock the tensioner in place, then undo the tensioner retaining Torx bolts. In the absence of the Audi tool, use a 5 mm bolt and locknut **(see illustration)**.

23 Paint alignment marks between the chain links, the adjuster, and the intake sprocket **(see illustration)**. Count the number of links between the alignment marks and make a note in case the chain needs to be renewed. In which case the alignment marks can be transferred to the new chain.

24 Working gradually and evenly, from the outside-in, slacken and remove the camshaft bearing ladder Torx bolts. Remove the bearing ladder.

25 Lift the camshafts from place along with the tensioner. Disengage the camshafts from the chain and discard the oil seal.

Diesel engines

Note: *It is possible to remove the camshaft with the cylinder head still fitted to the engine in the vehicle. However access is severely restricted.*

26 In order to ensure that the pump injector rocker arms are refitted to their original locations, use a marker pen or paint and number the arms 1 to 4, with No 1 nearest the timing belt end of the engine. If the arms are not fitted to their original locations the injector basic clearance setting procedure must be carried out as described in Chapter 4C. Starting with the outer bolts first, carefully and evenly slacken the rocker shaft retaining bolts. Discard the rocker shaft bolts, new ones must be fitted.

27 Slacken the nuts from bearing caps Nos 5, 1 and 3 first, then from bearing caps 2 and 4 **(see illustration overleaf)**. Slacken the nuts alternately and diagonally half a turn at a time until they can be removed, then remove the bearing caps. Keep the caps in order and note their fitted positions. **Note:** *The camshaft bearing caps are numbered 1 to 5 from the timing belt end.*

28 The camshaft rotates in shell bearings. As the camshaft bearing caps are removed, recover the shell bearing halves from the camshaft. Number the back of the bearings

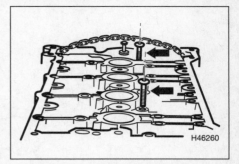

6.18 Use two M6 bolts (arrowed) to release the bearing ladder

with a felt pen to ensure that, if re-used, the bearings are fitted to their original locations. **Note:** *Fitted into the cylinder head, under each camshaft bearing cap, is a washer for each cylinder head bolt.*

29 Slide the oil seal from the front of the camshaft and discard it; a new one must be used on reassembly **(see illustration)**.

30 Carefully lift the camshaft from the cylinder head, keeping it level and supported at both ends as it is removed so that the journals and lobes are not damaged. Remove the oil seal from the front of the camshaft. Recover the lower shell bearing halves from the cylinder head, number the back of the shells with a felt pen to ensure that, if re-used, the bearings are fitted to their original locations.

All engines

31 Lift the rocker arms (where applicable) and hydraulic tappets from their bores and store them with the valve contact surface facing downwards, to prevent the oil from draining out **(see illustration)**. It is recommended that the tappets are kept immersed in oil for the period they are removed from the cylinder head. Make a note of the position of each tappet and rocker arm, as they must be fitted to the same valves on reassembly

6.22 Use an M5 bolt and nut to lock the tensioner in position

6.23 Paint alignment marks (arrowed) on the chain and sprockets to aid refitment

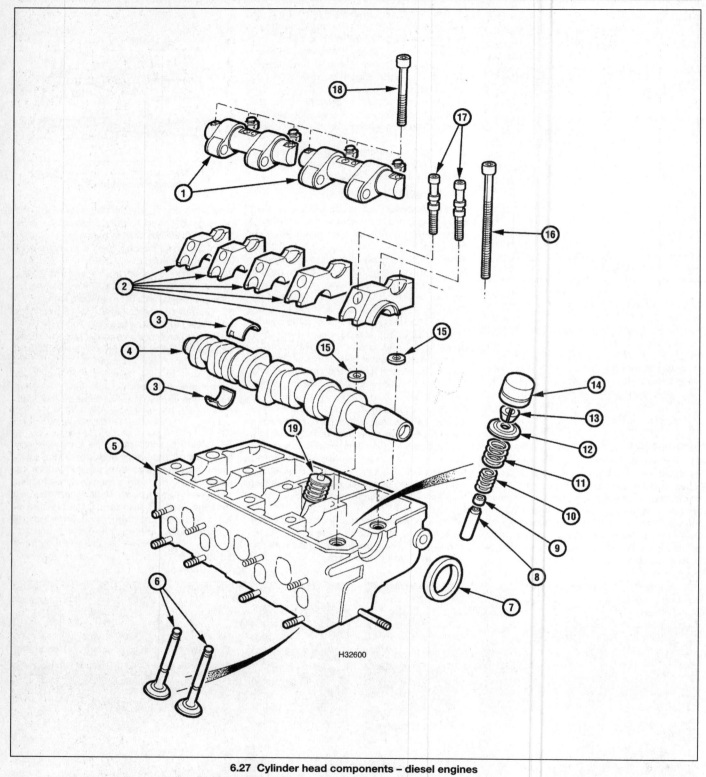

6.27 Cylinder head components – diesel engines

1 Injector rocker shaft assembly	5 Cylinder head	10 Inner spring	15 Washers
2 Bearing caps	6 Valves	11 Outer spring	16 Bolt
3 Bearing shells	7 Oil seal	12 Upper valve spring seat	17 Bolt
4 Camshaft	8 Guide	13 Collets	18 Bolt
	9 Oil seal	14 Hydraulic tappet	19 Unit injector

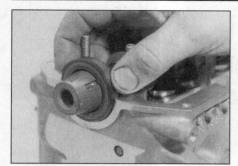

6.29 Remove the camshaft oil seal

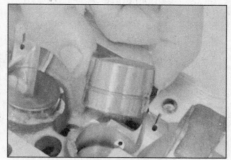

6.31 Lift the hydraulic tappets from their bores

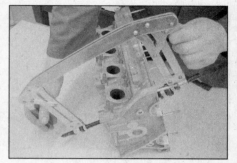

6.32a Compress the valve springs with a compressor tool

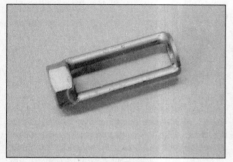

6.32b Home-made tool to access the intake valve springs on 20 valve engines

6.33a Remove the upper spring seat . . .

6.33b . . . and valve spring

– accelerated wear leading to early failure will result if they are interchanged.

32 Turn the cylinder head over, and rest it on one side. Using a valve spring compressor, compress each valve spring in turn, extracting the split collets when the upper valve spring seat has been pushed far enough down the valve stem to free them. If the spring seat sticks, tap the upper jaw of the compressor with a hammer to free it **(see illustration)**.
Note: *On 20 valve petrol engines, the access holes to the intake valves are considerably smaller in diameter than those to the exhaust valves, and the standard size valve spring compressor may be too large. If a tool cannot be obtained from an Audi dealer, a home-made tool will have to be fabricated out of a suitable nut, washer and metal bar welded together (see illustration).*
33 Release the valve spring compressor and remove the upper spring seat, and single valve

spring (petrol engines) or double valve springs (diesel engines) **(see illustrations)**.
34 Use a pair of pliers or a special removal tool to extract the valve stem oil seal, then on diesel engines remove the lower spring seat from the valve guide. Withdraw the valve itself from the head gasket side of the cylinder head. Repeat this process for the remaining valves **(see illustrations)**.

Cleaning

35 Using a suitable degreasing agent, remove all traces of oil deposits from the cylinder head, paying particular attention to the journal bearings, hydraulic tappet bores, valve guides and oilways. Scrape off any traces of old gasket from the mating surfaces, taking care not to score or gouge them. If using emery paper, do not use a grade of less than 100. Turn the head over and using a blunt blade, scrape any carbon deposits from

the combustion chambers and ports. Finally, wash the entire head casting with a suitable solvent to remove the remaining debris.
36 Clean the valve heads and stems using a fine wire brush. If the valve is heavily coked, scrape off the majority of the deposits with a blunt blade first, then use the wire brush.
37 Thoroughly clean the remainder of the components using solvent and allow them to dry completely. Discard the oil seals, as new ones must be fitted when the cylinder head is reassembled.

Inspection

Cylinder head

38 Examine the head casting closely to identify any damage or cracks that may have developed. Pay particular attention to the areas around the valve seats and spark plug holes. If cracking is discovered in this area, Audi state that the cylinder head may be re-

6.34a Use a removal tool . . .

6.34b . . . to remove the valve stem oil seals

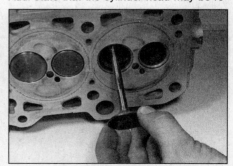

6.34c Remove the valves (typical)

6.41 Use a straight-edge and feeler gauges to measure the distortion of the cylinder head

6.46 Check the camshaft endfloat using a DTI gauge

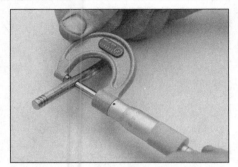

6.48 Measure the diameter of the valve stems with a micrometer

used, provided the cracks are no larger than 0.3 mm wide on petrol engines or 0.5 mm wide on diesel engines. More serious damage will mean the renewal of the cylinder head.

39 Moderately pitted and scorched valve seats can be repaired by grinding in the valves in during reassembly, as described later in this Section.

40 On all petrol engines, recutting is not allowed as this has an adverse effect on the hydraulic tappets. On diesel engines, badly worn or damaged valve seats may be restored by recutting, however this work should be entrusted to an engineering works. After recutting and lapping, the maximum permissible reworking dimension **must** not be exceeded – consult an Audi dealer or engine reconditioning specialist.

41 Measure any distortion of the gasket surfaces using a straight-edge and a set of feeler blades. Take one measurement longitudinally on both the intake and exhaust manifold mating surfaces. Take several measurements across the head gasket surface, to assess the level of distortion in all planes **(see illustration)**. Compare the measurements with the figures in the Specifications.

42 On petrol engines, if the head is distorted out of specification, it may be possible to have it machined by an engineering works.

43 Minimum cylinder head heights (measured between the cylinder head gasket surface and the cylinder head cover gasket surface) are listed in Specifications.

Camshaft

44 Visually inspect the camshaft for

evidence of wear on the surfaces of the lobes and journals. Normally their surfaces should be smooth and have a dull shine; look for scoring, erosion or pitting and areas that appear highly polished, indicating excessive wear. Accelerated wear will occur once the hardened exterior of the camshaft has been damaged, so always renew worn items. **Note:** *If these symptoms are visible on the tips of the camshaft lobes, check the corresponding tappet, as it will probably be worn as well.*

45 If the machined surfaces of the camshaft appear discoloured or blued, it is likely that it has been overheated at some point, probably due to inadequate lubrication. This may have distorted the shaft, so have it checked by an Audi dealer or engine reconditioning specialist.

46 To measure the camshaft endfloat, temporarily refit the camshaft to the cylinder head, then fit the first and last bearing caps (and shell bearings where applicable)/bearing ladder, and tighten the retaining nuts to the specified first stage torque setting. Anchor a DTI gauge to the timing belt end of the cylinder head and align the gauge probe with the camshaft axis. Push the camshaft to one end of the cylinder head as far as it will travel, then rest the DTI gauge probe on the end of the camshaft, and zero the gauge display. Push the camshaft as far as it will go to the other end of the cylinder head, and record the gauge reading. Verify the reading by pushing the camshaft back to its original position and checking that the gauge indicates zero again **(see illustration). Note:** *The hydraulic tappets*

must not be fitted whilst this measurement is being taken.

47 Check that the camshaft endfloat measurement is within the limit listed in the Specifications. Wear outside of this limit is unlikely to be confined to any one component, so renewal of the camshaft, cylinder head and bearing caps/ladder must be considered.

Valves and associated components

Note: *On all engines, the valve heads cannot be recut, although they may be ground in. On petrol engines, if new valves are to be fitted, the old valves must be disposed of carefully (do not dispose of them as normal scrap), as the valve stems are filled with sodium. Consult your local scrap or recycling centre for advice.*

48 Examine each valve closely for signs of wear. Inspect the valve stems for wear ridges, scoring or variations in diameter; measure their diameters at several points along their lengths with a micrometer **(see illustration)**.

49 The valve heads should not be cracked, badly pitted or charred. Note that light pitting of the valve head can be rectified by grinding in the valves during reassembly, as described later in this Section.

50 Check that the valve stem end face is free from excessive pitting or indentation; this would be caused by defective hydraulic tappets.

51 Insert each valve into its respective guide in the cylinder head and set up a DTI gauge against the edge of the valve head. With the valve end face flush with the top of the valve guide, measure the maximum side-to-side deflection of the valve in its guide **(see illustration)**.

52 If the measurement exceeds that given in the Specifications, the valve and valve guide should be renewed as a pair. **Note:** *Valve guides are an interference fit in the cylinder head and their removal requires access to a hydraulic press. For this reason, it would be wise to entrust the job to an engine reconditioning specialist.*

53 Using vernier calipers, measure the free length of each of the valve springs. As a manufacturer's figure is not quoted, the only way to check the length of the springs is by comparison with a new component. Note that valve springs are usually renewed during a major engine overhaul **(see illustration)**.

6.51 Measure the maximum deflection of the valve in its guide, using a DTI gauge

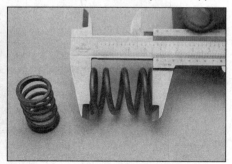

6.53 Measure the free length of each valve spring

6.54 Check the squareness of the valve springs

6.56 Grind in the valves with a reciprocating rotary motion

6.61 Fit the lower spring seat with the convex face facing the cylinder head (diesel engines)

54 Stand each spring on its end on a flat surface, against an engineer's square **(see illustration)**. Check the squareness of the spring visually, and renew it if it appears distorted.

Reassembly

55 To achieve a gas-tight seal between the valves and their seats, it will be necessary to grind in (or lap in) the valves. To complete this process you will need a quantity of fine/coarse grinding paste and a grinding tool – this can either be of the rubber sucker type, or the automatic type which is driven by a rotary power tool.

56 Smear a small quantity of *fine* grinding paste on the sealing face of the valve head. Turn the cylinder head over so that the combustion chambers are facing upwards and insert the valve into the correct guide. Attach the grinding tool to the valve head and using a backward/forward rotary action, grind the valve head into its seat. Periodically lift the valve and rotate it to redistribute the grinding paste **(see illustration)**.

57 Continue this process until the contact between valve and seat produces an unbroken, matt grey ring of uniform width, on both faces. Repeat the operation on the remaining valves.

58 If the valves and seats are so badly pitted that coarse grinding paste must be used, bear in mind that there is a maximum protrusion of the end of the valve stem from the valve guide; refer to an Audi dealer or engine reconditioning specialist. If this dimension is

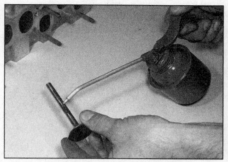

6.62a Lubricate the valve stem with clean engine oil before fitting it

outside the limit due to excessive grinding-in, the hydraulic tappets may not operate correctly.

59 Assuming the repair is feasible, work as described previously but use coarse grinding paste initially, to achieve a dull finish on the valve face and seat. Wash off the coarse paste with solvent and repeat the process using fine grinding paste to obtain the correct finish.

60 When all the valves have been ground in, remove all traces of grinding paste from the cylinder head and valves with solvent, and allow them to dry completely.

61 Turn the head on its side. On diesel engines, fit the first lower spring seat into place, with the convex side facing the cylinder head **(see illustration)**.

62 Working on one valve at a time, lubricate the valve stem with clean engine oil, and insert it into the guide. Fit one of the protective plastic sleeves supplied with the new valve

6.62b Fit the protective sleeve over the valve stem before fitting the stem seal

stem oil seals over the valve end face – this will protect the oil seal whilst it is being fitted **(see illustrations)**.

63 Dip a new valve stem seal in clean engine oil, and carefully push it over the valve and onto the top of the valve guide – take care not to damage the stem seal as it passes over the valve end face. Use a suitable long reach socket or special installer to press it firmly into position **(see illustrations)**. Remove the protective sleeve.

64 Locate the valve spring(s) over the valve stem **(see illustration)**. On diesel engines, ensure that the springs locate correctly on the lower seat.

65 Fit the upper seat over the top of the springs, then using a valve spring compressor, compress the springs until the upper seat is pushed beyond the collet grooves in the valve stem. Refit the split collet, using a dab of grease to hold the two halves in the grooves

6.63a Fit a new stem seal over the valve

6.63b Use a special installer or suitable long reach socket to fit the valve stem oil seals

6.64 Fit the valve spring(s)

6.65a Fit the upper seat over the top of the valve spring

6.65b Use grease to hold the two halves of the split collets in the groove

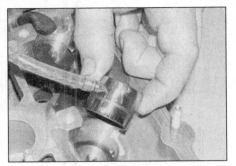

6.67a Fit the hydraulic tappets into the bores in the cylinder head

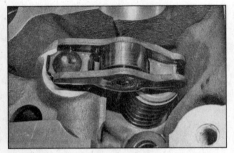

6.67b Ensure the rockers arms (where fitted) are correctly located on the valve stems and tappets – engine code AWA

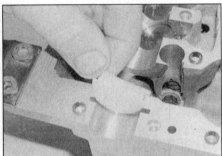

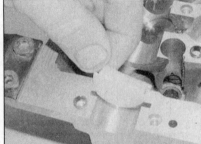

6.68a Fit the half-round seal

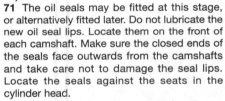

6.68b Apply sealant compound in the area shown

(see illustrations). Gradually release the spring compressor, checking that the collet remains correctly seated as the spring extends. When correctly seated, the upper seat should force the two halves of the collet together, and hold them securely in the grooves in the end of the valve.

66 Repeat this process for the remaining sets of valve components. To settle the components after installation, strike the end of each valve stem with a mallet, using a block of wood to protect the stem from damage. Check before progressing any further that the spilt collets remain firmly held in the end of the valve stem by the upper spring seat.

67 Smear some clean engine oil onto the sides of the hydraulic tappets/rocker arms, and fit them into position in their bores in the cylinder head. Push them down until they contact the valves, then lubricate the camshaft lobe contact surfaces (see illustrations).

Engine codes
AVJ, AMB, BFB, BEX and BKB

68 Locate the rubber/metal gasket for the automatic camshaft adjuster, together with the half-round seal on the rear of the cylinder head. If the gasket does not have any sealant compound already on it, smear a little in the area shown (see illustrations).

69 Lubricate the camshafts and cylinder head bearing journals with clean engine oil.

70 Engage the chain with the camshaft sprockets making sure that the distance between the marks on the sprockets is 16 rollers (see illustration). Locate the adjuster between the chain runs, then carefully lower the camshafts into position on the cylinder head. Support the ends of the shafts as they are fitted, to avoid damaging the lobes and journals. Alternatively, it is possible to fit the camshafts together with the chain in the cylinder head, then slightly raise the sprocket

ends of the camshafts in order to fit the adjuster.

71 The oil seals may be fitted at this stage, or alternatively fitted later. Do not lubricate the new oil seal lips. Locate them on the front of each camshaft. Make sure the closed ends of the seals face outwards from the camshafts and take care not to damage the seal lips. Locate the seals against the seats in the cylinder head.

72 Insert the automatic camshaft adjuster mounting bolts and tighten to the specified torque.

73 Oil the upper surfaces of the camshaft bearing journals, then fit Nos 2 and 4 bearing caps to both camshafts. Ensure that they are fitted the right way around and in the correct locations, then progressively tighten the retaining bolts to the specified torque. **Note:** *The bearing caps are numbered from the rear of the engine.*

74 Fit the No 1 bearing caps to each camshaft and progressively tighten the retaining bolts to the specified torque.

75 Remove the locking tool from the automatic camshaft adjuster.

76 Apply a thin film of sealant to the contact face of the combined front bearing cap, then fit the cap making sure that the oil seals locate against their seating (see illustration). Progressively tighten the retaining bolts to the specified torque.

77 Fit Nos 3 and 5 bearing caps and progressively tighten the retaining bolts to the specified torque.

78 Refit the camshaft sensor rotor and tapered washer to the front of the intake

6.70 Engage the chain with the sprockets – note the marks indicating the distance of 16 rollers

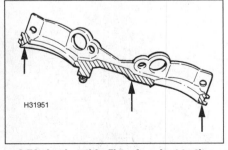

6.76 Apply a thin film of sealant to the contact face of the combined front bearing cap in the area shown

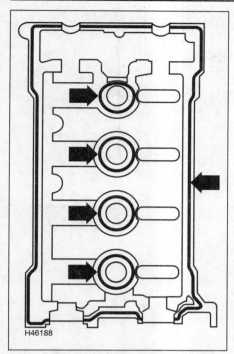

6.83 Camshaft bearing ladder sealant (arrowed) – engine code ALT

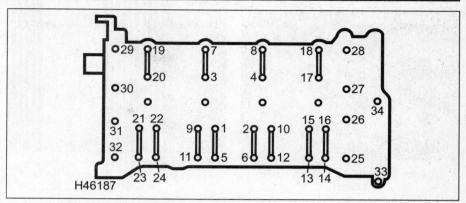

6.84 Tighten the bearing ladder bolts in the sequence/pattern shown

camshaft and tighten the bolt to the specified torque.

79 Refit the camshaft position sensor and tighten the retaining bolt.

Engine codes ALT

80 Lubricate the camshafts and cylinder head bearing journals with clean engine oil.

81 Engage the chain with the camshaft sprockets making sure that the distance between the marks on the sprockets is 16 rollers **(see illustration 6.70)**. Locate the adjuster between the chain runs, then carefully lower the camshafts into position on the cylinder head. Support the ends of the shafts as they are fitted, to avoid damaging the lobes and journals. Alternatively, it is possible to fit the camshafts together with the chain in the cylinder head, then slightly raise the sprocket ends of the camshafts in order to fit the adjuster.

82 Insert the automatic camshaft adjuster

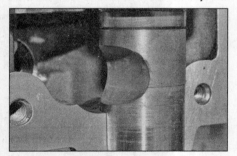

6.87 The cut-outs in the camshafts must face each other and the sides must be exactly vertical

mounting bolts and tighten to the specified torque.

83 Apply a 2.0 mm wide bead of suitable sealant to the underside of the bearing ladder as shown **(see illustration)**. Note: *The sealant will start to harden as soon as it makes contact with the cylinder head sealing surface – waste no time!*

84 Refit the bearing ladder to the cylinder head, then insert the retaining bolts. Gradually and evenly, tighten the bolts until the ladder makes contact with the cylinder head over the full surface, then tighten them in sequence to the specified torque **(see illustration)**. Note: *Do not attempt to fully-tighten the bolts until the bearing ladder makes contact with the cylinder head over the entire surface.*

85 Remove the automatic chain adjuster

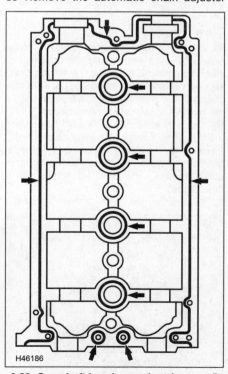

6.89 Camshaft bearing sealant (arrowed) – engine code AWA

locking bolt, and check the marks on the camshaft sprocket flanges align with the marks on the bearing ladder. If necessary, rotate the camshafts to achieve the alignment.

86 Remove the end cover behind the exhaust camshaft, and refit the intake camshaft control valve. Fit new camshaft seal(s) as described in Chapter 2A.

Engine code AWA

87 Refit the chain onto the camshaft sprockets, aligning the previously made marks, and position the tensioner in the chain. Ensure the cylinder head bolt cut-outs in the camshafts face each other **(see illustration)**. Note that the side surfaces of the cut-outs should be exactly vertical.

88 Lubricate the running surfaces of the cylinder head and camshafts with clean engine oil, then lay the camshafts in position in the cylinder head.

89 Apply a 2.0 mm wide bead of sealant (available from Audi dealers/parts specialists) to the grooves on the underside of the bearing ladder as shown **(see illustration)**. As the sealant starts to harden immediately, no time should be allowed to elapse before fitting the bearing ladder.

90 Refit the bearing ladder to the cylinder head, then fit the new bolts and working from the inside-out tighten the bolts in several stages until the bearing ladder make contact the with cylinder head over the complete area of the mating surface. Now tighten the bolts to the specified torque in sequence **(see illustration)**.

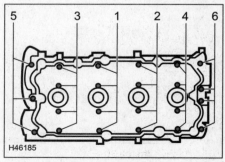

6.90 Tighten the pairs of bearing ladder bolts in the sequence shown

6.93 Fit the chain cover using a new gasket

6.95 Fit the camshaft shell bearing lower halves into the cylinder head into their original locations

6.96 Lower the camshaft into position

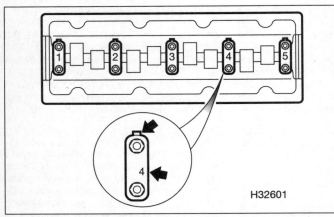

6.98a Fit the bearing caps with the lug (arrowed) on the intake side

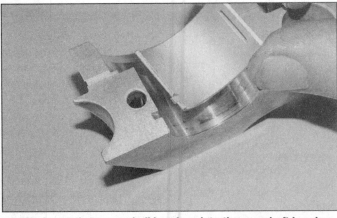

6.98b Insert the upper shell bearings into the camshaft bearing caps into their original locations

91 Fit Audi special tool T10252 over the camshafts to check the alignment. It may be necessary to rotate the camshafts slightly to fit the tool. In the absence of the tool, have an assistant hold the exhaust camshaft stationary, and rotate the intake camshaft so the chain free-play is equal on the top and lower run of the chain. The sides of the cut-outs in the camshafts must be vertical.

92 Remove the Audi tool (where applicable), then apply a little thread-locking compound and tighten the tensioner retaining bolts. Remove the bolt used to lock the tensioner.

93 Refit the camshaft adjuster rear cover with a new gasket, then apply a little thread-locking compound and tighten the retaining bolts to the specified torque (**see illustration**).

94 Fit new camshaft seal(s) as described in Chapter 2B.

Diesel engines

95 Fit the camshaft shell bearing lower halves into the cylinder head into their original locations, making sure that the locating lugs engage correctly with the corresponding cut-outs in the cylinder head. Once fitted, lubricate the bearing surfaces (**see illustration**).

96 Carefully lower the camshaft into position in the cylinder head making sure that the cam lobes for No 1 cylinder are pointing upwards. Support the ends of the shaft as it is fitted, to avoid damaging the lobes and journals (**see illustration**).

97 Locate the new seal on the front of the camshaft – do not oil the lip of the seal. Make sure the closed end of the seal faces outwards from the camshaft and take care not to damage the seal lip. Locate the seal against the seat in the cylinder head.

98 The bearing caps have their respective cylinder numbers stamped onto them, and have an elongated lug on one side. When correctly fitted, the numbers should be readable from the exhaust side of the cylinder head, and the lugs should face the intake side of the cylinder head. Oil the upper surfaces of the camshaft bearing journals, then insert the upper shell bearings into the camshaft bearing caps into their original locations, making sure that the locating lugs engage correctly with the corresponding cut-outs in the bearing caps. If the camshaft is being refitted with the cylinder head removed from the engine, position the cylinder head bolt washers in their locating holes in the cylinder head. Fit Nos 2 and 4 bearing caps. Ensure that they are fitted the right way around and in the correct locations, then progressively tighten the retaining bolts to the specified torque (**see illustrations**).

99 Smear the mating surfaces of bearing cap No 1 with sealant then fit caps 1, 3 and 5 over the camshaft and progressively tighten the nuts to the specified torque (**see illustration**).

All engines

100 Where applicable, refit the coolant sensor and oil pressure switch to the cylinder head.

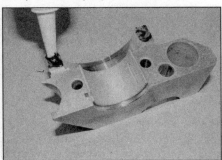

6.99 Smear the mating surfaces of cap No 1 with sealant

6.101 Fit the coolant elbow using a new O-ring or gasket

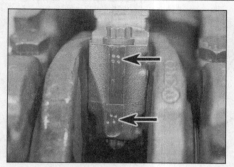

7.3 Mark the big-end caps and connecting rods with their numbers (arrowed)

7.4a Unscrew the big-end cap bolts . . .

7.4b . . . and remove the cap

101 Where applicable, refit the coolant outlet elbow together with a new gasket/O-ring **(see illustration).**

102 On diesel models, refit the injectors, pump injector rocker shaft and glow plugs (see Chapters 2C, 4C and 5C).

103 Refit the cylinder head with reference to Parts A, B or C of this Chapter. Also refit the camshaft sprocket as described in Part A, B or C of this Chapter.

7 Piston/connecting rod assemblies – removal and inspection

Removal

1 Refer to Part A, B or C of this Chapter (as applicable) and remove the cylinder head, flywheel, sump and baffle plate, oil pump and pickup tube or balancer shaft assembly.

2 Inspect the tops of the cylinder bores for ridges at the point where the pistons reach top dead centre. These must be removed otherwise the pistons may be damaged when they are pushed out of their bores. Use a scraper or ridge reamer to remove the ridges.

3 Rotate the crankshaft until piston No 1 is at bottom dead centre; piston No 4 will also be at bottom dead centre. Unless they are already identified, mark the big-end bearing caps and connecting rods with their respective piston numbers, using a centre-punch or a scribe **(see illustration)**. Note the orientation of the bearing caps in relation to the connecting rod; it may be difficult to see the manufacturer's

markings at this stage, so scribe alignment arrows on them both to ensure correct reassembly.

4 Unscrew the bearing cap bolts/nuts, half a turn at a time, until they can be removed and the cap withdrawn **(see illustrations)**. Recover the bottom shell bearing, and tape it to the cap for safe-keeping. Note that if the shell bearings are to be re-used, they must be refitted to the same connecting rod.

5 Drive the piston out of the top of the bore using a piece of wooden dowel or a hammer handle. As the piston and connecting rod emerge, recover the top shell bearing and tape it to the connecting rod for safe-keeping. On engines fitted with piston cooling jets at the bottom of the cylinders, take care not to allow the connecting rod to damage the jet as the piston is being removed.

6 Remove No 4 piston and connecting rod in the same manner, then turn the crankshaft

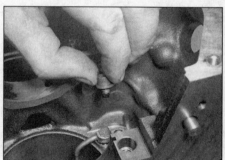

7.7a Remove the piston cooling jet retaining screws . . .

through half a turn and remove No 2 and 3 pistons and connecting rods. Remember to maintain the components in their cylinder groups whilst they are in a dismantled state.

7 If applicable, remove the retaining screws and withdraw the piston cooling jets from the bottom of the cylinder **(see illustrations)**.

Inspection

8 Insert a small flat-bladed screwdriver into the removal slot and prise the gudgeon pin circlips from each piston. Push out the gudgeon pin, and separate the piston and connecting rod **(see illustrations)**. Discard the circlips as new items must be fitted on reassembly. If the pin proves difficult to remove, heat the piston to 60°C with hot water – the resulting expansion will then allow the two components to be separated.

9 Before an inspection of the pistons can be carried out, the existing piston rings must be removed, using a removal/installation tool,

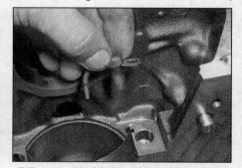

7.7b . . . and withdraw the jets from their mounting holes

7.7c Piston cooling jet and retaining screw

7.8a Insert a small screwdriver into the slot and prise out the circlips

7.8b Push out the gudgeon pin to separate the piston and connecting rod

7.9 Piston rings can be removed using an old feeler gauge

7.11 The piston crown on a diesel engine

7.17 Measure the piston ring-to-groove clearance using a feeler gauge

7.19a The piston crown is marked with an arrow which must point towards the timing belt end of the engine

or an old feeler blade if such a tool is not available. Always remove the upper piston rings first, expanding them to clear the piston crown. The rings are very brittle and will snap if they are stretched too much – sharp edges are produced when this happens, so protect your eyes and hands. Discard the rings on removal, as new items must be fitted when the engine is reassembled **(see illustration)**.

10 Use a section of old piston ring to scrape the carbon deposits out of the ring grooves, taking care not to score or gouge the edges of the groove.

11 Carefully scrape away all traces of carbon from the tops of the pistons **(see illustration)**. A hand-held wire brush (or a piece of fine emery cloth) can be used, once the majority of the deposits have been scraped away. Be careful not to remove any metal from the piston, as it is relatively soft. **Note:** *Make sure each piston is kept identified for position during cleaning.*

12 Once the deposits have been removed, clean the pistons and connecting rods with paraffin or a suitable solvent, and dry thoroughly. Make sure that the oil return holes in the ring grooves are clear.

13 Examine the pistons for signs of excessive wear or damage. Some normal wear will be apparent, in the form of a vertical 'grain' on the piston thrust surfaces and a slight looseness of the top compression ring in its groove. Abnormal wear should be carefully examined, to assess whether the component is still serviceable and what the cause of the wear might be.

14 Scuffing or scoring of the piston skirt may indicate that the engine has been overheating, through inadequate cooling or lubrication. Scorch marks on the skirt indicate that gas blow-by has occurred, perhaps caused by worn bores or piston rings. Burnt areas on the piston crown are usually an indication of pre-ignition, pinking or detonation. In extreme cases, the piston crown may be melted by operating under these conditions. Corrosion pit marks in the piston crown indicate that coolant has seeped into the combustion chamber. The faults causing these symptoms must be corrected before the engine is brought back into service, or the same damage will recur.

15 Check the pistons, connecting rods, gudgeon pins and bearing caps for cracks. Lay the connecting rods on a flat surface, and look along the length to see if it appears bent or twisted. If you have doubts about their condition, get them measured at an engineering workshop. Inspect the small-end bush bearing in the connecting rod for signs of wear or cracking.

16 Have the diameter of the pistons checked by an engine reconditioning specialist at the same time as the cylinder block is inspected.

17 Locate a new piston ring in the appropriate groove and measure the ring-to-groove clearance using a feeler blade **(see illustration)**. Note that the rings are of different widths, so use the correct ring for the groove. Compare the measurements with

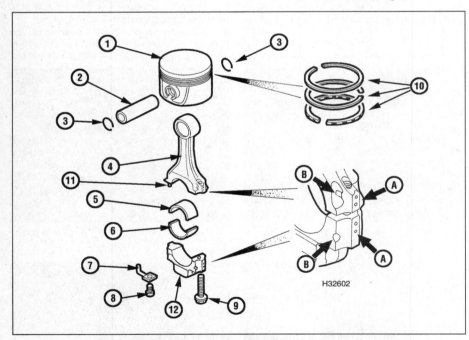

7.19b Piston assembly – petrol engines (typical)

1 Piston	5 Big-end shell	9 Big-end bearing cap
2 Gudgeon pin	6 Big-end shell	bolts
3 Circlip	7 Oil jet for piston cooling	10 Piston rings
4 Connecting	(where applicable)	11 Locating dowel
rod	8 Oil jet retaining screw	12 Big-end bearing cap

A Connecting rod/bearing cap identification marks
B Connecting rod/bearing cap orientation marks

those listed; if the clearances are outside of the tolerance band, then the piston must be renewed. Confirm this by checking the width of the piston ring with a micrometer.

18 Examine the small-end bearing and gudgeon pin for wear and damage. If excessive, the gudgeon pin will have to be renewed and a new bush fitted to the connecting rod. This work must be entrusted to an engine reconditioning specialist.

19 The orientation of the piston with respect to the connecting rod must be correct when the two are reassembled. The piston crown is marked with an arrow (which may be obscured by carbon deposits); this must point towards the timing belt end of the engine when the piston is installed. On diesel engines if the arrows are not visible, assemble the pistons to the connecting rods so that the combustion recess in the top of the piston is on the water pump side of the engine block. The connecting rod and its bearing cap both have recesses/lugs machined into them, close to their mating surfaces – these recesses/lugs must both face the same way as the arrow on the piston crown (ie, towards the timing belt end of the engine) when correctly installed **(see illustrations)**. Reassemble the two components to satisfy this requirement.

20 Lubricate the gudgeon pin and small-end bush with clean engine oil. Slide the pin into the piston, engaging the connecting rod small-end. Fit two new circlips to the piston at either end of the gudgeon pin. Repeat this operation for the remaining pistons.

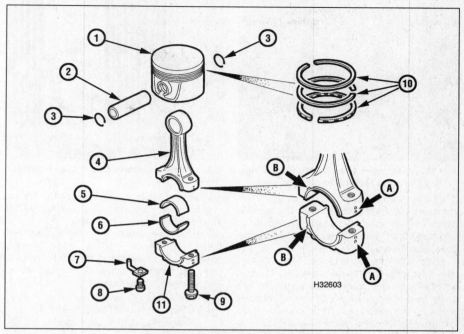

7.19c Piston assembly – diesel engines

1 Piston	5 Bearing shell	9 Big-end bearing cap bolts
2 Gudgeon pin	6 Bearing shell	
3 Circlips	7 Oil jet for piston cooling	10 Piston rings
4 Connecting rod	8 Oil jet retaining screw	11 Bearing cap

A Connecting rod/bearing cap identification marks
B Connecting rod/bearing cap orientation marks

8 Crankshaft – removal and inspection

Note: *The use of an engine stand is strongly recommended. If no work is to be done on the pistons and connecting rods, then removal of the cylinder head and pistons will not be necessary. Instead, the pistons need only be pushed far enough up the bores so that the connecting rods are positioned clear of the crankpins.*

Removal

1 With reference to Chapter 2A, 2B or 2C as applicable, carry out the following:

a) Remove the timing belt and crankshaft sprocket.
b) Remove the clutch components and flywheel or driveplate (as applicable).
c) Remove the sump, baffle plate **(see illustration)**, oil pump and pick-up tube or balancer shaft assembly.
d) Remove the front and rear crankshaft oil seals and housings.

2 Remove the pistons and connecting rods or disconnect them from the crankshaft as described in Section 7 (see Note above).

3 With the cylinder block upside-down on the bench, carry out a check of the crankshaft endfloat as follows. **Note:** *This can only be accomplished when the crankshaft is still installed in the cylinder block/crankcase, but*

is free to move. Set up a DTI gauge so that the probe is in line with the crankshaft axis and is in contact with a fixed point on the end of the crankshaft. Push the crankshaft along its axis to the end of its travel, and then zero the gauge. Push the crankshaft fully the other way, and record the endfloat indicated on the dial **(see illustration)**. Compare the result with the figure given in the Specifications and establish whether new thrustwashers are required.

4 If a dial gauge is not available, feeler blades can be used. First push the crankshaft fully towards the flywheel end of the engine, then use a feeler blade to measure the gap between cylinder No 3 crankpin web and the main bearing thrustwasher **(see illustration)**. Compare the results with the Specifications.

8.1 Remove the baffle plate (where applicable)

8.3 Measure the crankshaft endfloat using a DTI gauge . . .

8.4 . . . or feeler gauges

8.5 Manufacturer's identification markings on the main bearing caps (arrowed)

5 Observe the manufacturer's identification marks on the main bearing caps. The number indicates the cap position in the crankcase, as counted from the timing belt end of the engine **(see illustration)**.

6 Loosen the main bearing cap bolts half a turn at a time, until they can be removed. Using a soft-faced mallet, strike the caps lightly to free them from the crankcase. Recover the lower main bearing shells, using tape to attach them to the cap for safe-keeping. Mark them to aid identification, but do not score or scratch them in any way. Remove the thrustwashers from each side of the No 3 main bearing cap where applicable.

7 Carefully lift the crankshaft out, taking care not to dislodge the upper main bearing shells **(see illustration)**.

8 Extract the upper main bearing shells from the crankcase, and tape them to their respective bearing caps. Remove the two thrustwasher bearings from either side of No 3 bearing saddle (where applicable).

9 With the shell bearings removed, observe the recesses machined into the bearing caps and crankcase – these provide location for the lugs which protrude from the shell bearings and so prevent them from being fitted incorrectly.

Inspection

10 Wash the crankshaft in a suitable solvent and allow it to dry. Flush the oil holes thoroughly, to ensure they are not blocked.

11 Inspect the main bearing and crankpin journals carefully. If uneven wear, cracking, scoring or pitting are evident then the

9.6 Use a correct sized tap to clean the cylinder block threads

8.7 Lift the crankshaft from the crankcase

crankshaft should be reground by an engineering workshop, and refitted to the engine with undersize bearings.

12 Have the crankshaft measured and inspected by an engine reconditioning specialist. If the crankshaft is worn and can be reground, they will be able to carry out the work and supply suitable undersize bearing shells.

9 Cylinder block/crankcase – cleaning and inspection

Cleaning

1 Remove all external components as applicable including lifting eyes, mounting brackets, the coolant pump and housing, viscous fan idler, oil cooler and filter mounting housing and electrical switches/sensors from the block. For complete cleaning, the core plugs should ideally be removed. Drill a small hole in the plugs, then insert a self-tapping screw into the hole. Extract the plugs by pulling on the screw with a pair of grips, or by using a slide hammer.

2 Scrape all traces of gasket and sealant from the cylinder block/crankcase, taking care not to damage the sealing surfaces.

3 Remove all oil gallery plugs (where fitted). The plugs are usually very tight – they may have to be drilled out, and the holes retapped. Use new plugs when the engine is reassembled.

4 If the casting is extremely dirty, it should be steam-cleaned. After this, clean all oil holes and galleries one more time. Flush all internal passages with warm water until the water runs clear. Dry thoroughly, and apply a light film of oil to all mating surfaces and cylinder bores, to prevent rusting. If you have access to compressed air, use it to speed up the drying process, and to blow out all the oil holes and galleries.

 Warning: Wear eye protection when using compressed air.

5 If the castings are not very dirty, you can do an adequate cleaning job with hot, soapy water and a stiff brush. Take plenty of time, and do a thorough job. Regardless of the cleaning method used, be sure to clean all

oil holes and galleries very thoroughly, and to dry all components well. Protect the cylinder bores as described above, to prevent rusting.

6 All threaded holes must be clean, to ensure accurate torque readings during reassembly. To clean the threads, run the correct-size tap into each of the holes to remove rust, corrosion, thread sealant or sludge, and to restore damaged threads **(see illustration)**. If possible, use compressed air to clear the holes of debris produced by this operation. **Note:** *Take extra care to exclude all cleaning liquid from blind tapped holes, as the casting may be cracked by hydraulic action if a bolt is threaded into a hole containing liquid.*

7 Apply suitable sealant to the new oil gallery plugs, and insert them into the holes in the block. Tighten them securely. Similarly, apply sealant to the core plugs and tap them into the cylinder block using a close-fitting tube or socket.

8 If the engine is not going to be reassembled immediately, cover it with a large plastic bag to keep it clean; protect all mating surfaces and the cylinder bores as described above, to prevent rusting.

Inspection

9 Visually check the casting for cracks and corrosion. Look for stripped threads in the threaded holes. If there has been any history of internal water leakage, it may be worthwhile having an engine overhaul specialist check the cylinder block/crankcase with professional equipment. If defects are found, have them renewed or if possible, repaired.

10 Check the cylinder bores for scuffing or scoring. Any evidence of this kind of damage should be cross-checked with an inspection of the pistons (see Section 7 of this Chapter). If the damage is in its early stages, it may be possible to repair the block by reboring it. Seek the advice of an engineering workshop.

11 Have the cylinder bores measured and inspected by an engine reconditioning specialist. If the bores are worn/damaged, they will be able to carry out any remedial work (reboring) and supply suitable oversize pistons, etc.

12 Apply a light coating of engine oil to the mating surfaces and cylinder bores to prevent rust forming.

13 Refit all the components removed in paragraph 1.

10 Main and big-end bearings – inspection and selection

Inspection

1 Even though the main and big-end bearings should be renewed during the engine overhaul, the old bearings should be retained for close examination, as they may reveal valuable information about the condition of the engine **(see illustration)**.

2 Bearing failure can occur due to lack of

lubrication, the presence of dirt or other foreign particles, overloading the engine, or corrosion. Regardless of the cause of bearing failure, the cause must be corrected before the engine is reassembled, to prevent it from happening again.

3 When examining the bearing shells, remove them from the cylinder block/crankcase, the main bearing caps, the connecting rods and the connecting rod big-end bearing caps. Lay them out on a clean surface in the same general position as their location in the engine. This will enable you to match any bearing problems with the corresponding crankshaft journal. *Do not* touch any shell's internal bearing surface with your fingers while checking it, or the delicate surface may be scratched.

4 Dirt and other foreign matter gets into the engine in a variety of ways. It may be left in the engine during assembly, or it may pass through filters or the crankcase ventilation system. It may get into the oil, and from there into the bearings. Metal chips from machining operations and normal engine wear are often present. Abrasives are sometimes left in engine components after reconditioning, especially when parts are not thoroughly cleaned using the proper cleaning methods. Whatever the source, these foreign objects often end up embedded in the soft bearing material, and are easily recognised. Large particles will not embed in the bearing, but will score or gouge the bearing and journal. The best prevention for this cause of bearing failure is to clean all parts thoroughly, and keep everything spotlessly-clean during engine assembly. Frequent and regular engine oil and filter changes are also recommended.

5 Lack of lubrication (or lubrication breakdown) has a number of interrelated causes. Excessive heat (which thins the oil), overloading (which squeezes the oil from the bearing face) and oil leakage (from excessive bearing clearances, worn oil pump or high engine speeds) all contribute to lubrication breakdown. Blocked oil passages, which usually are the result of misaligned oil holes in a bearing shell, will also oil-starve a bearing, and destroy it. When lack of lubrication is the cause of bearing failure, the bearing material is wiped or extruded from the steel backing of the bearing. Temperatures may increase to the point where the steel backing turns blue from overheating.

6 Driving habits can have a definite effect on bearing life. Full-throttle, low-speed operation (labouring the engine) puts very high loads on bearings, tending to squeeze out the oil film. These loads cause the bearings to flex, which produces fine cracks in the bearing face (fatigue failure). Eventually, the bearing material will loosen in pieces, and tear away from the steel backing.

7 Short-distance driving leads to corrosion of bearings, because insufficient engine heat is produced to drive off the condensed water and corrosive gases. These products collect in the engine oil, forming acid and sludge. As the

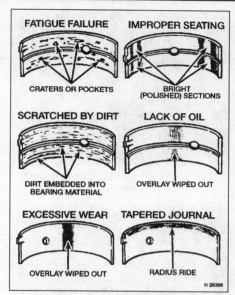

10.1 Typical bearing failures

oil is carried to the engine bearings, the acid attacks and corrodes the bearing material.

8 Incorrect bearing installation during engine assembly will lead to bearing failure as well. Tight-fitting bearings leave insufficient bearing running clearance, and will result in oil starvation. Dirt or foreign particles trapped behind a bearing shell result in high spots on the bearing, which lead to failure.

9 *Do not* touch any shell's internal bearing surface with your fingers during reassembly as there is a risk of scratching the delicate surface, or of depositing particles of dirt on it.

10 As mentioned at the beginning of this Section, the bearing shells should be renewed as a matter of course during engine overhaul. To do otherwise is false economy.

Bearing selection

11 Main and big-end bearings for the engines described in this Chapter are available in standard sizes and a range of undersizes to suit reground crankshafts. Refer to an engine reconditioning specialist for details.

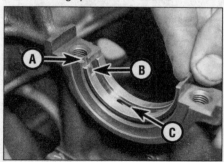

12.4 Upper main bearing shells correctly fitted

A *Recess in the bearing saddle*
B *Lug on the bearing shell*
C *Oil hole*

11 Engine overhaul – reassembly sequence

1 Before reassembly begins, ensure that all new parts have been obtained, and that all necessary tools are available. Read through the entire procedure to familiarise yourself with the work involved, and to ensure that all items necessary for reassembly of the engine are at hand. In addition to all normal tools and materials, thread-locking compound will be needed. A suitable tube of liquid sealant will also be required for the joint faces that are without gaskets. It is recommended that the manufacturer's own products are used, which are specially formulated for this purpose; the relevant product names are quoted in the text of each Section where they are required.

2 In order to save time and avoid problems, engine reassembly should ideally be carried out in the following order:

   a) *Crankshaft (see Section 12).*
   b) *Piston/connecting rod assemblies (see Sections 13 and 14).*
   c) *Oil pump or balancer shaft assembly (see Chapter 2A, 2B or 2C).*
   d) *Sump (see Chapter 2A, 2B or 2C).*
   e) *Flywheel/driveplate (see Chapter 2A, 2B or 2C).*
   f) *Cylinder head (see Chapter 2A, 2B or 2C).*
   g) *Timing belt tensioner, sprockets and timing belt (see Chapter 2A, 2B or 2C).*
   h) *Intake and exhaust manifolds (see the relevant part of Chapter 4).*
   i) *Engine external components and ancillaries (see list in Section 5 of this Chapter).*

3 At this stage, all engine components should be absolutely clean and dry, with all faults repaired. The components should be laid out (or in individual containers) on a completely clean work surface.

12 Crankshaft – refitting

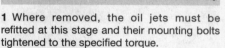

1 Where removed, the oil jets must be refitted at this stage and their mounting bolts tightened to the specified torque.

2 If new shells are being fitted, ensure that all traces of the protective grease are cleaned off using paraffin.

3 Clean the backs of the bearing shells, and the bearing locations in both the cylinder block/crankcase and the main bearing caps.

4 With the cylinder block positioned on a clean work surface, with the crankcase opening uppermost, press the bearing shells into their locations, ensuring that the tab on each shell engages in the notch in the cylinder block or bearing cap, and that the oil holes in the cylinder block and bearing shell are aligned **(see illustration)**. Note that the shells with the oil groove are fitted to the cylinder block, whilst the ones without the groove are fitted to

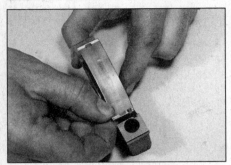

12.5 **Fit the new lower half main bearing shells into the main bearing caps**

12.8 **Lubricate the upper main bearing shells . . .**

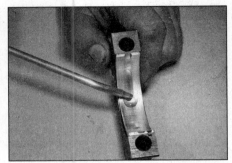

12.10a **. . . and lower main bearing shells with clean engine oil . . .**

12.10b **. . . then fit the thrustwashers each side of the bearing cap . . .**

12.10c **. . . and/or bearing saddle (see text)**

12.11a **Fit the No 3 main bearing cap**

the bearing caps. Take care not to touch any shell's bearing surface with your fingers.

5 Wipe off the rear surfaces of the new lower half main bearing shells and fit them to the main bearing caps, ensuring the locating lugs engage correctly **(see illustration)**.

12.11b **Fit the No 1 main bearing cap**

6 At this point, it is assumed that the crankshaft, cylinder block/crankcase and bearings have been cleaned, inspected and reconditioned or renewed.

7 Give the newly-fitted main bearing shells and the crankshaft journals a final clean

12.11c **No 1 main bearing cap – diesel engine**

with a cloth. Check that the oil holes in the crankshaft are free from dirt, as any left here will become embedded in the new bearings when the engine is first started.

8 Liberally coat the bearing shells in the crankcase with clean engine oil of the appropriate grade **(see illustration)**. On diesel engines, install the new thrustwashers each side of the No 3 bearing position in the cylinder block. Use a small quantity of grease to hold them in place. Ensure that they are seated correctly in the machined recesses, with the oil grooves facing outwards.

9 Lower the crankshaft into position so that No 1 cylinder crankpin is at BDC, ready for fitting No 1 piston.

10 Lubricate the lower bearing shells in the main bearing caps with clean engine oil, then fit the thrustwashers to each side of No 3 bearing cap. Use a small quantity of grease to hold them in place. Ensure that they are seated correctly in the machined recesses, with the oil grooves facing outwards **(see illustrations)**.

11 Fit the main bearing caps in the correct order and orientation – No 1 bearing cap must be at the timing belt end of the engine and the bearing shell locating recesses in the bearing saddles and caps must be adjacent to each other **(see illustrations)**. Insert the new bearing cap bolts and hand tighten them only.

12 Working from the centre bearing cap outwards, tighten the new retaining bolts to their specified torques and angles in the stages given **(see illustrations)**.

13 Check that the crankshaft rotates freely by turning it manually.

12.12a **Tighten the main bearing cap bolts to the specified torque . . .**

12.12b **. . . and angle**

14 Carry out a check of the crankshaft endfloat as described at the beginning of Section 8. If the thrust surfaces of the crankshaft have been checked and new thrustwashers have been fitted, then the endfloat should be within specification.

15 Refit the pistons and connecting rods or reconnect them to the crankshaft as described in Section 14.

16 With reference to Chapter 2A, 2B or 2C as applicable, carry out the following:

a) *Refit the crankshaft front and rear oil seal housings, together with new oil seals.*

b) *Refit the oil pump and pickup tube or balancer shaft assembly, baffle plate and sump.*

c) *Refit the flywheel and clutch or driveplate (as applicable).*

d) *Refit the crankshaft sprocket and timing belt.*

13 Pistons and piston rings – assembly

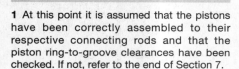

1 At this point it is assumed that the pistons have been correctly assembled to their respective connecting rods and that the piston ring-to-groove clearances have been checked. If not, refer to the end of Section 7.

2 Before the rings can be fitted to the pistons, the end gaps must be checked with the rings fitted into the cylinder bores.

3 Lay out the piston assemblies and the new ring sets on a clean work surface so that the components are kept together in their groups during and after end gap checking. Place the crankcase on the work surface on its side, allowing access to the top and bottom of the bores.

4 Take the No 1 piston top ring and insert it into the top of the bore. Using the No 1 piston, push the ring close to the bottom of the bore, at the lowest point of the piston travel. Ensure that it is perfectly square in the bore.

5 Use a set of feeler blades to measure the gap between the ends of the piston ring. The correct blade will just pass through the gap with a minimal amount of resistance **(see illustration)**. Compare this measurement with that listed in Specifications. Check that you

13.5 Check the piston ring end gap using feeler gauges

have the correct ring before deciding that a gap is incorrect. Repeat the operation for the remaining rings.

6 If new rings are being fitted, it is unlikely that the end gaps will be too small. If a measurement is found to be undersize, it must be corrected or there is the risk that the ends of the ring may contact each other during operation, possibly resulting in engine damage. This is achieved by gradually filing down the ends of the ring, using a file clamped in a vice. Fit the ring over the file such that both its ends contact opposite faces of the file. Move the ring along the file, removing small amounts of material at a time. Take great care as the rings are brittle and form sharp edges if they fracture. Remember to keep the rings and piston assemblies in the correct order.

7 When all the piston ring end gaps have been verified, they can be fitted to the pistons. Work from the lowest ring groove (oil control ring) upwards. Note that the oil control ring may comprise of two side rails separated by a expander ring, or a one-piece oil control ring with a internal expander spring. Note also that the two compression rings are different in cross-section, and so must be fitted in the correct groove and the right way up, using a piston ring fitting tool. Both of the compression rings may have marks stamped on one side to indicate the top facing surface. Ensure that these marks face up when the rings are fitted **(see illustration)**.

8 Distribute the end gaps around the piston, spaced at 120° intervals to the each other.

Note: *If the piston ring manufacturer supplies specific fitting instructions with the rings, follow these exclusively.*

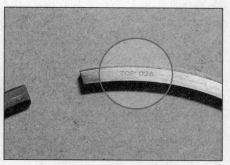

13.7 Piston ring top marking

14 Piston/connecting rod assemblies – refitting

Note: *At this point, it is assumed that the crankshaft has been fitted to the engine, as described in Section 12. A piston ring compressor tool will be required for this operation.*

1 Clean the backs of the bearing shells, and the bearing locations in both the connecting rods and the big-end bearing caps.

2 Press the bearing shells into their locations in the connecting rods and caps. On all engines, the shells are not positively located by lugs and recesses – simply ensure the shells are fitted squarely and centrally into place **(see illustration)**. On diesel engines, the upper bearing shell is more wear-resistant than the lower, and is identified by a black line on the bearing surface in the area of the bearing joint. On petrol engines, the upper bearing shell has an oil hole, which must align with the corresponding oil hole in the connecting rod. Take care not to touch any shell's bearing surface with your fingers.

3 Lubricate the cylinder bores, the pistons, piston rings and upper bearing shells with clean engine oil **(see illustrations)**. Lay out each piston/connecting rod assembly in order on a work surface. Where the bearing caps are secured with nuts, pad the threaded ends of the bolts with insulating tape to prevent them scratching the crankpins and bores when the pistons are refitted.

4 Start with piston/connecting rod assembly

14.2 Ensure the shells are fitted squarely into place

14.3a Lubricate the pistons . . .

14.3b . . . and the big-end upper bearing shells with clean engine oil

14.7 Use a hammer handle to tap the piston into its bore

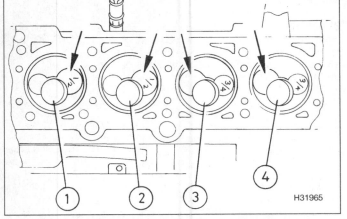

14.9 Piston orientation and coding on diesel engines

No 1. Make sure that the piston rings are still spaced as described in Section 13, then clamp them in position with a piston ring compressor.

5 Insert the piston/connecting rod assembly into the top of cylinder No 1. Lower the big-end in first, guiding it to protect the cylinder bores. Where oil jets are located at the bottoms of the bores, take particular care not to break them off when guiding the connecting rods onto the crankpins.

6 Ensure that the orientation of the piston in its cylinder is correct – the piston crown, connecting rods and big-end bearing caps have markings, which must point towards the timing belt end of the engine when the piston is installed in the bore – refer to Section 7 for details.

7 Using a block of wood or hammer handle against the piston crown, tap the assembly into the cylinder until the piston crown is flush with the top of the cylinder **(see illustration)**.

8 Ensure that the bearing shell is still correctly installed. Liberally lubricate the crankpin and both bearing shells with clean engine oil. Taking care not to mark the cylinder bores, tap the piston/connecting rod assembly down the bore and onto the crankpin. Fit the big-end bearing cap, tightening its new retaining bolts finger-tight at first. Note that the orientation of the bearing cap with respect to the connecting rod must be correct when the two components are reassembled. The

connecting rod and its corresponding bearing cap both have recesses/lugs machined into them – these recesses/lugs must both face in the same direction as the arrow on the piston crown (ie, towards the timing belt end of the engine) when correctly installed – refer to the illustrations in Section 7 for details. Some of these engines are fitted with 'fractured' split connecting rods. On these engines, the bearing caps are split from the connecting rod during the manufacturing process. The resultant mating surfaces are unique, and consequently will only fit properly to their original positions. Any attempt to fit them in an alternative position with ruin both connecting rod and bearing cap.

9 On diesel engines, the piston crowns are specially shaped to improve the engine's combustion characteristics. Because of this, pistons 1 and 2 are different to pistons 3 and 4. When correctly fitted, the larger intake valve chambers on pistons 1 and 2 must face the flywheel/driveplate end of the engine, and the larger intake valve chambers on the remaining pistons must face the timing belt end of the engine. New pistons have number markings on their crowns to indicate their type – 1/2 denotes piston 1 or 2, 3/4 indicates piston 3 or 4 **(see illustration)**.

10 Tighten the retaining bolts to the specified Stage 1 torque **(see illustration)**.

11 Angle-tighten the retaining bolts to the specified Stage 2 angle **(see illustration)**.

12 Refit the remaining three piston/connecting rod assemblies in the same way.

13 Rotate the crankshaft by hand. Check that it turns freely; some stiffness is to be expected if new parts have been fitted, but there should be no binding or tight spots.

Diesel engines

14 If new pistons are fitted or if a new short engine is installed, the projection of the piston crowns above the cylinder head at TDC must be measured, to determine the type of head gasket that should be fitted.

15 Turn the cylinder block over (so that the crankcase is facing downwards) and rest it on a stand or wooden blocks. Anchor a DTI gauge to the cylinder block, and zero it on the head gasket mating surface. Rest the gauge probe on No 1 piston crown and turn the crankshaft slowly by hand so that the piston reaches TDC. Measure and record the maximum projection at TDC **(see illustration)**.

16 Repeat the measurement for the remaining pistons and record.

17 If the measurements differ from piston-to-piston, take the highest figure and use this to determine the head gasket type that must be used – refer to the Specifications for details.

18 Note that if the original pistons have been

14.10 Tighten the big-end bearing cap bolts to the Stage 1 setting . . .

14.11 . . . and then angle-tighten them to the Stage 2 setting

14.15 Measure the piston projection using a DTI gauge

refitted, then a new head gasket of the same type as the original item must be fitted.

All engines

19 Refer to Part A, B or C of this Chapter (as applicable) and refit the oil pump and pickup or balancer shaft assembly, sump and baffle plate, flywheel and cylinder head.

15 Engine – initial start-up after overhaul and reassembly

1 Refit the remainder of the engine components in the order listed in Section 11 of this Chapter. Refit the engine to the vehicle as described in Section 4 of this Chapter. Double-check the engine oil and coolant levels and make a final check that everything has been reconnected. Make sure that there are no tools or rags left in the engine compartment.

Petrol models

2 Remove the spark plugs, referring to Chapter 1A for details.
3 The engine must be immobilised such that it can be turned over using the starter motor, without starting – disable the fuel pump by removing the fuel pump fuse from the fusebox with reference to the relevant Part of Chapter 4.

Caution: To prevent damage to the catalytic converter, it is important to disable the fuel system.
4 Turn the engine using the starter motor until the oil pressure warning lamp goes out. If the lamp fails to extinguish after several seconds of cranking, check the engine oil level and oil filter security. Assuming these are correct, check the security of the oil pressure switch cabling – do not progress any further until you are satisfied that oil is being pumped around the engine at sufficient pressure.
5 Refit the spark plugs, and the fuel pump fuse.

Diesel models

6 Disconnect the injector harness wiring plug at the rear of the cylinder head – refer to Chapter 4C for details.
7 Turn the engine using the starter motor until the oil pressure warning lamp goes out.
8 If the lamp fails to extinguish after several seconds of cranking, check the engine oil level and oil filter security. Assuming these are correct, check the security of the oil pressure switch cabling – do not progress any further until you are satisfied that oil is being pumped around the engine at sufficient pressure.
9 Reconnect the injector wiring plug. Note that disconnecting the injector harness may

result in fault codes being stored by the engine management ECM. Have these codes erased by an Audi dealer or suitably-equipped specialist.

All models

10 Start the engine, but be aware that as fuel system components have been disturbed, the cranking time may be a little longer than usual.
11 While the engine is idling, check for fuel, water and oil leaks. Don't be alarmed if there are some odd smells and the occasional plume of smoke as components heat up and burn off oil deposits.
12 Assuming all is well, keep the engine idling until hot water is felt circulating through the top hose.
13 After a few minutes, recheck the oil and coolant levels, and top-up as necessary.
14 There is no need to retighten the cylinder head bolts once the engine has been run following reassembly.
15 If new pistons, rings or crankshaft bearings have been fitted, the engine must be treated as new, and run-in for the first 600 miles. *Do not* operate the engine at full-throttle, or allow it to labour at low engine speeds in any gear. It is recommended that the engine oil and filter are changed at the end of this period.

Notes

Chapter 3
Cooling, heating and ventilation systems

Contents

Section number

Air conditioning compressor (auxiliary) drivebelt –
  renewal . . . . See Chapter 2A, 2B or 2C
Air conditioning system – general information and precautions 10
Air conditioning system components – removal and refitting 11
Antifreeze mixture. .See Chapter 1A or 1B
Coolant level check and top-up . . . . See *Weekly checks*
Coolant pump – removal and refitting 7
Cooling fan(s) – removal and refitting. 5

Section number

Cooling system – draining, flushing and refilling .See Chapter 1A or 1B
Cooling system hoses – disconnection and renewal 2
Engine coolant temperature sensor – testing, removal and refitting . 6
General information and precautions. 1
Heater/ventilation components – removal and refitting 9
Heating and ventilation system – general information 8
Radiator – removal, inspection and refitting. 3
Thermostat – removal, testing and refitting 4

Degrees of difficulty

Easy, suitable for novice with little experience	**Fairly easy,** suitable for beginner with some experience	**Fairly difficult,** suitable for competent DIY mechanic	**Difficult,** suitable for experienced DIY mechanic	**Very difficult,** suitable for expert DIY or professional

Specifications

Engine codes*

Petrol engines
1781 cc:
  Bosch Motronic ME7.5:
    110 kW (143 bhp) . . . . AVJ
    125 kW (163 bhp) . . . . AMB
  Bosch Motronic ME7.1:
    120 kW (156 bhp) . . . . BFB and BKB
    140 kW (182 bhp) . . . . BEX
  1984 cc, Bosch Motronic ME7, 96 kW (125 bhp). . . . . ALT
1984 cc:
  Bosch Motronic ME7, 96 kW (125 bhp) . . . . ALT
  Bosch Motronic MED7.1, 110 kW (143 bhp) . . . . AWA

Diesel engines
74 kW (96 bhp) . . . . AVB
85 kW (111 bhp) . . . . BKE and BRB
96 kW (125 bhp) . . . . AVF and AWX
* Note: *See 'Vehicle identification' for the location of the code marking on the engine.*

General
Maximum system pressure . . . . 1.4 to 1.6 bar

Thermostat
Opening temperature
  Petrol engines. . . . . 105 °C (approximately)
  Diesel engines . . . . 87 °C (approximately)

Torque wrench settings

	Nm	lbf ft
Air conditioning compressor	25	18
Alternator/power steering pump bracket:		
Bracket to cylinder block	30	22
Strut to cylinder block	25	18
Strut to bracket.	40	30
Coolant pump.	15	11
Thermostat-to-housing bolts:		
Petrol engines.	10	7
Diesel engines	15	11
Thermostat housing-to-cylinder block bolts	15	11
Viscous cooling fan coupling/drive pulley shaft bolt	45	33
Viscous cooling fan coupling-to-drive pulley bolts	10	7

1 General information and precautions

General information

The cooling system is of the pressurised type, with a coolant pump, an aluminium radiator, cooling fan(s), a thermostat, heater matrix, and all associated hoses and switches. The coolant pump is driven by the camshaft timing belt. Some models are fitted with a viscous-coupled primary cooling fan, which is driven by the auxiliary drivebelt, whilst others are fitted with an electrically-operated fan, and an auxiliary cooling fan which is also electrically-operated. The system functions as follows.

When the engine is cold, the coolant in the engine is pumped around the cylinder block and head passages, and through an engine oil cooler (where fitted). After cooling the cylinder bores, combustion surfaces and valve seats, the coolant passes through the heater, and is returned via the cylinder block to the coolant pump. The thermostat is initially closed, preventing the cold coolant from the radiator entering the engine. On petrol engines, the thermostat incorporates a heating element and is electronically-controlled and mapped by the engine management ECU. This system monitors engine load to determine the most efficient engine temperature.

When the coolant in the engine reaches a predetermined temperature, the thermostat opens. The cold coolant from the radiator is then allowed to enter the engine through the bottom hose and the hot coolant from the engine flows through the top hose to the radiator. As the coolant circulates through the radiator, it is cooled by the inrush of air when the car is in forward motion. The airflow is supplemented by the action of the cooling fan(s) when necessary. As the coolant reduces in temperature, it passes to the bottom of the radiator and the cycle is repeated.

On some models the operation of the primary cooling fan is controlled by a viscous coupling. The coupling is driven by the auxiliary drivebelt and transmits drive to the fan through a temperature-sensitive fluid coupling arrangement. At lower temperatures the fan blade is allowed to spin freely on the coupling. At a predetermined temperature (around 75°C), an internal valve in the coupling opens, which effectively locks-up the coupling, and transmits drive to the fan. Once the temperature drops again, the valve closes and the fan is allowed to spin freely again.

On other models, the primary cooling fan is electrically-powered, and is controlled by the engine management ECM, which receives data from the engine coolant temperature sensor. The operation of the electrically-operated auxiliary cooling fan is controlled by a thermostatic switch. At a predetermined coolant temperature, the switch/sensor actuates the fan. The switch then cuts the power supply to the fan when the coolant temperature has reduced sufficiently.

On models with an automatic/Multitronic transmission unit, a transmission fluid cooler is built into the radiator. The transmission unit is linked to the radiator by two pipes and the fluid is circulated around the cooler to keep its temperature stable under arduous operating conditions.

Precautions

⚠️ **Warning: Do not attempt to remove the expansion tank filler cap, or to disturb any part of the cooling system, while the engine is hot, as there is a high risk of scalding. If the expansion tank filler cap must be removed before the engine and radiator have fully cooled (even though this is not recommended), the pressure in the cooling system must first be relieved. Cover the cap with a thick layer of cloth to avoid scalding, and slowly unscrew the filler cap until a hissing sound is heard. When the hissing has stopped, indicating that the pressure has reduced, slowly unscrew the filler cap until it can be removed; if more hissing sounds are heard, wait until they have stopped before unscrewing the cap completely. At all times, keep well away from the filler cap opening, and protect your hands.**

⚠️ **Warning: Do not allow antifreeze to come into contact with your skin, or with the painted surfaces of the vehicle. Rinse off spills immediately, with plenty of water. Never leave antifreeze lying around in an open container, or in a puddle in the driveway or on the garage floor. Children and pets are attracted by its sweet smell, but antifreeze can be fatal if ingested.**

⚠️ **Warning: If the engine is hot, the electric cooling fan may start rotating even if the engine is not running. Be careful to keep your hands, hair, and any loose clothing well clear when working in the engine compartment.**

⚠️ **Warning: Refer to Section 10 for precautions to be observed when working on models equipped with air conditioning.**

2 Cooling system hoses – disconnection and renewal

Note: *Refer to the warnings given in Section 1 of this Chapter before proceeding. Hoses should only be disconnected once the engine has cooled sufficiently to avoid scalding.*

1 If the checks described in the relevant part of Chapter 1 reveal a faulty hose, it must be renewed as follows.

2 First drain the cooling system (see the relevant part of Chapter 1). If the coolant is not due for renewal, it may be re-used, providing it is collected in a clean container.

3 To disconnect a hose, release the retaining clips, then move them along the hose, clear of the relevant inlet/outlet **(see illustrations)**. Carefully work the hose free. The hoses can be removed with relative ease when new – on an older car, they may have stuck.

4 In order to disconnect the radiator inlet and outlet hoses, and the heater hoses fitted to some models, apply pressure to hold the hose on to the relevant union, pull out the spring clip and pull the hose from the union. Note that the radiator inlet and outlet unions are fragile; do not use excessive force when attempting to remove the hoses. If a hose proves to be difficult to remove, try to release it by rotating the hose ends before attempting to free it.

5 If a hose proves to be difficult to remove, try to release it by rotating its ends before attempting to free it. Gently prise the end of the hose with a blunt instrument (such as a flat-bladed screwdriver), but do not apply too much force, and take care not to damage the pipe stubs or hoses. Note in particular that the radiator inlet stub is fragile; do not use excessive force when attempting to remove the hose. If all else fails, cut the hose with a sharp knife, then slit it so that it can be peeled off in two pieces. Although this may prove expensive if the hose is otherwise undamaged, it is preferable to buying a new radiator. Check first, however, that a new hose is readily available.

6 When fitting a hose, first slide the clips onto the hose, then work the hose into position. On

2.3a On some hoses, prise up the retaining clip a little, and pull the hose from the connection . . .

2.3b . . . whilst on others, squeeze together the ends of the clip to release them (arrowed)

some hose connections alignment marks are provided on the hose and union; if marks are present, ensure they are correctly aligned.

7 Ensure the hose is correctly routed, then slide each clip back along the hose until it passes over the flared end of the relevant inlet/outlet, before tightening the clip securely. Prior to refitting a radiator inlet or outlet hose, renew the connection O-ring regardless of condition **(see illustration)**. The connections are a push-fit over the radiator unions.

8 Refill the cooling system with reference to the relevant part of Chapter 1.

9 Check thoroughly for leaks as soon as possible after disturbing any part of the cooling system.

3 Radiator – removal, inspection and refitting

Removal

1 Remove the front bumper as described in Chapter 11. On diesel models, place the lock carrier in the Service position as described in Chapter 11.

2 Undo the fasteners and remove the engine/radiator undershield. On diesel models, undo the nuts and remove the plastic cover from the top of the engine.

3 Drain the cooling system as described in the relevant part of Chapter 1.

4 Disconnect the radiator top and bottom coolant hoses (see Section 2), noting the correct fitted locations **(see illustration 2.3a)**. Note: *On some models, quick-release couplings are fitted to the hoses.*

5 Undo the retaining bolts and remove the air intake duct from the lock carrier **(see illustration)**.

6 On models with automatic/Multitronic transmission, wipe clean the area around the fluid pipe unions on the radiator. Slacken and remove the retaining bolts then carefully ease both pipes out from the radiator. Plug the pipe ends and cooler ports to minimise fluid loss and prevent the entry of dirt into the hydraulic system. Discard the sealing rings from the pipe end fittings, new ones must be used on refitting.

7 Disconnect the left- and right-hand horn wiring plugs.

8 Undo the bolts and remove the left- and right-hand air deflector panels from each side of the radiator **(see illustration)**.

9 Unclip and ambient temperature sensor from the bracket in front of the radiator **(see illustration)**.

10 Undo the bolts and move the hydraulic fluid cooling pipe to one side. There is no need to disconnect the fluid pipes.

11 On models equipped with air conditioning, slacken and remove the bolts securing the condenser, and any nuts/bolts securing the refrigerant pipe clips in position. Release the condenser from the radiator and support it to prevent excessive strain being placed on the

2.7 Renew the radiator hose connection O-rings

pipes. **Do not** disconnect the refrigerant pipes (see Section 10).

12 Press in the retaining clips, then prise up the radiator retaining pins, then pivot the radiator towards the front and lift it away from its lower mountings **(see illustration)**. On models with air conditioning, take great care to avoid damaging the condenser as the radiator is removed.

Inspection

13 If the radiator has been removed due to suspected blockage, reverse-flush it as described in the relevant part of Chapter 1. Clean dirt and debris from the radiator fins, using an airline (in which case, wear eye protection) or a soft brush. Be careful, as the fins are sharp, and easily damaged.

14 If necessary, a radiator specialist can perform a flow test on the radiator, to establish whether an internal blockage exists.

3.5 Undo the 2 screws (arrowed) and remove the intake ducting from the lock carrier

3.9 Unclip the ambient air temperature sensor

15 A leaking radiator must be referred to a specialist for permanent repair. Do not attempt to weld or solder a leaking radiator, as damage to the plastic components may result.

16 If the radiator is to be sent for repair or renewed, remove all hoses and switches (where fitted).

17 Inspect the condition of the radiator mounting rubbers, and renew them if necessary.

Refitting

18 Refitting is a reversal of removal, bearing in mind the following points.

 a) Ensure that the radiator is correctly engaged with its mounting rubbers and that the upper retaining pins are securely refitted.

 b) On models with automatic/Multitronic transmission, fit new sealing rings to the fluid pipe end fittings, lubricating them with fresh transmission fluid to ease installation. Ease both pipes fully into position before refitting the retaining bolts and tighten them securely.

 c) Make sure all coolant hoses are correctly reconnected and securely retained by their clips.

 d) Refill the cooling system with new antifreeze as described in the relevant part of Chapter 1.

 e) On models with automatic/Multitronic transmission, on completion check the transmission fluid level and, if necessary, top-up as described in the relevant part of Chapter 1.

3.8 Undo the screw (arrowed) and remove the rubber air deflector plates each side

3.12 Press in the clip and prise up the radiator retaining pins

4 Thermostat –
removal, testing and refitting

1 On petrol engines, the thermostat is fitted to a distribution housing on the left-hand side of the cylinder block, behind the coolant pump position. On diesel engines, the thermostat is fitted beneath an inlet elbow/cover on the left-hand side of the cylinder block.

Removal

2 Disconnect the battery negative lead (see Chapter 5A). Remove the plastic cover from the top of the engine.
3 Drain the cooling system as described in Chapter 1A or 1B.

Engines codes
AVJ, AMB, BEX, BKB and BFB

4 Remove the intake manifold support bracket from behind the alternator.
5 Release the clips and disconnect the

4.7 Prise out the clip (arrowed) and disconnect the coolant hose from the thermostat housing

coolant hoses from the bottom coolant pipe, and undo the 2 bolts and pull the coolant pipe from the thermostat housing.
6 Disconnect the wiring plug from the thermostat housing.
7 Release the clips and disconnect the coolant hoses from the thermostat housing (see **illustration**).

8 Undo the bolts and detach the thermostat housing from the cylinder block, then undo the bolts and detach the thermostat from the housing (see **illustration**). Discard the O-ring seal, a new one must be fitted.

Engine code ALT

9 Remove the intake manifold as described in Chapter 4a.
10 Undo the 2 bolts and remove the intake resonator from below the intake manifold (see **illustration**).
11 Release the clips and disconnect the hoses from the bottom coolant pipe, then undo the bolts and pull the pipe from the base of the thermostat housing.
12 Disconnect the wiring plug from the thermostat housing.
13 Release the clips and disconnect the coolant hoses from the thermostat housing (see **illustration 4.7**).
14 Undo the bolts and detach the thermostat housing from the cylinder block, then undo the bolts and detach the thermostat from the housing (see **illustration 4.8**). Discard the O-ring seal, a new one must be fitted.

Engine code AWA

15 Remove the intake manifold as described in Chapter 4B.
16 Remove the alternator as described in Chapter 5A.
17 Disconnect the breather hose from the cylinder head cover.
18 Release the crankcase breather oil separator clip from the oil filter housing, then undo the bolt and remove the separator (see **illustration**).

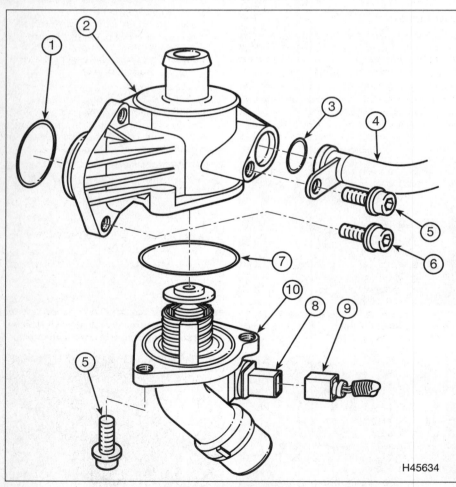

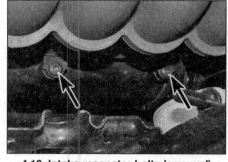

4.10 Intake resonator bolts (arrowed) – engine code ALT

4.18 Oil separator retaining clip (arrowed)

4.8 Thermostat and housing

1 O-ring	4 Coolant pipe	7 O-ring	9 Wiring plug
2 Distributor housing	5 Bolt	8 Heating element socket	10 Thermostat and housing
3 O-ring	6 Bolt		

H45634

4.19 Bottom coolant rail retaining bolts (arrowed)

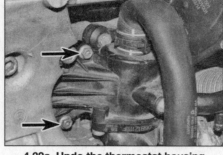

4.22a Undo the thermostat housing retaining bolts (arrowed)

4.22b Undo the thermostat Torx bolts

4.22c Renew the O-ring seal

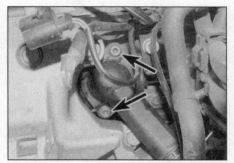

4.24 The thermostat cover is secured by 2 Allen screws (arrowed)

4.25 The thermostat rib aligns with the moulded interior of the cover – diesel engines only

19 Release the clips and disconnect the hoses from the bottom coolant pipe, then undo the bolts and pull the pipe from the base of the thermostat housing **(see illustration)**.
20 Disconnect the wiring plug from the thermostat housing.
21 Release the clips and disconnect the coolant hoses from the thermostat housing.
22 Undo the bolts and detach the thermostat housing from the cylinder block, then undo the bolts and detach the thermostat from the housing **(see illustrations)**. Discard the O-ring seal, a new one must be fitted.

Diesel engines

23 If necessary, to improve access, release the retaining clip and disconnect the coolant hose from the thermostat cover.
24 Unscrew the retaining screws and remove the thermostat housing cover and sealing ring from the engine **(see illustration)**. Discard the sealing ring; a new one must be used on refitting.
25 Remove the thermostat, noting which way around it is fitted **(see illustration)**.

Testing

Note: *If there is any question about the operation of the thermostat, it's best to renew it – they are not usually expensive items. Testing involves heating in, or over, an open pan of boiling water, which carries with it the risk of scalding. A thermostat which has seen more than five years' service may well be past its best already.*

Diesel engines

26 A rough test of the thermostat may be made by suspending it with a piece of string in a container full of water. Heat the water to bring it to the boil – the thermostat must be fully open by the time the water boils. If not, renew it.
27 If a thermometer is available, the precise opening temperature of the thermostat may be determined; compare with the figures given in the Specifications. The opening temperature should also be marked on the thermostat.
28 A thermostat which fails to close as the water cools must also be renewed.

Petrol engines

29 With the thermostat cold, the large valve plate on the end of the spring must seal completely on the housing.
30 Place the thermostat vertically in a container of boiling water, then connect a 12 volt supply to the terminals. A minimum lift of 7.0 mm must occur within 10 minutes.

⚠️ *Warning: Do not carry out the test with the thermostat out of water, otherwise it will be damaged.*

31 If the thermostat does not perform as indicated, it must be renewed.

Refitting

32 Refitting is a reversal of removal, noting the following points:
 a) *Use new sealing ring(s).*
 b) *On diesel engines, ensure that the curved brace of the thermostat body is positioned vertically.*
 c) *Tighten the housing retaining bolts to the specified torque setting.*
 d) *Refill the cooling system as described in Chapter 1A or 1B (as applicable)*
 e) *On completion reconnect the battery.*

5 Cooling fan(s) – removal and refitting

Note: *All petrol models are fitted with one, or two electrical cooling fans, whereas diesel models are fitted with an auxiliary drivebelt driven fan with a viscous coupling, and in some cases, an electric auxiliary cooling fan fitted alongside.*

Electric cooling fan removal

1 Place the lock carrier assembly in the Service position as described in Chapter 11.

Petrol models

2 Unclip the plastic cover from the power steering fluid reservoir, then disconnect the cooling fan and bonnet lock wiring plugs **(see illustration)**. Unclip the wiring loom from any retaining clips.

5.2 Disconnect the wiring plugs adjacent to the power steering reservoir (arrowed)

5.3 Undo the control module retaining bolt (arrowed)

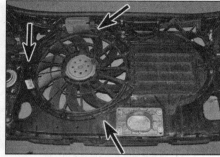

5.6 Undo the fan shroud bolts (arrowed)

5.7 Undo the Torx bolts and detach the motor from the shroud (arrowed)

3 Undo the bolt securing the fan control module to the lock carrier (see illustration).

Diesel models

4 On models with Multitronic transmission, undo the bolts and disconnect the ATF cooling pipes from the radiator. Be prepared for fluid spillage. Plug the holes to prevent dirt ingress.
5 Unplug the fan motor and bonnet lock wiring plugs, then remove the bolt securing the fan control unit to the radiator shroud. Move the wiring to one side.

All models

6 Slacken and remove the retaining bolts and remove the fan shroud assembly from the rear of the radiator (see illustration).

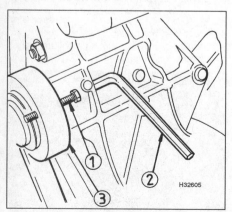

5.16 Viscous coupling drive pulley removal

1 5 x 60 mm bolt   *3 Drive pulley*
2 8 mm Allen key

5.15 Detach the fan blades from the coupling

7 Unclip the motor wiring from the rear of the shroud then undo the retaining Torx screw and pull the motor assembly away from the shroud (see illustration). If the motor is faulty, the complete unit along with the control module may have to be renewed – consult your Audi dealer or parts specialist.

Electric cooling fan refitting

8 Fit the motor assembly to the shroud and securely tighten its retaining nuts. Ensure the motor wiring is correctly routed and clipped securely in position.
9 Refit the shroud assembly to the radiator and securely tighten its retaining bolts.
10 Reconnect the wiring plugs and refit the lock carrier.

Viscous-coupled cooling fan

Testing

11 The operation of the viscous coupling cannot be easily checked by the home mechanic. The only check which can be performed is a visual one to check the coupling assembly for signs of fluid leakage and the fan blade for signs of damage. When the coupling is cold, the fan should spin freely on the coupling and when it is hot (temperature above approximately 75°C), the coupling should lock-up, causing the fan to rotate. If there is any doubt about the operation of the coupling, it should be renewed.

Removal

12 Place the lock carrier in the Service position as described in Chapter 11.
13 Pull the engine oil level dipstick from

place, then undo the nuts and remove the plastic cover from the top of the engine, Refit the dipstick.
14 Remove the auxiliary drivebelt as described in Chapter 2C. Note that the air conditioning compressor drivebelt (where fitted) can remain in place.
15 Undo the retaining bolts and separate the fan blades from the coupling, noting which way around the fan blades are fitted (see illustration).
16 Counterhold the drive pulley with a 5 x 60 mm bolt engaged with the small holes located around the pulley rim. Pass an 8 mm Allen key through the drive pulley mounting bracket, and engage it with the rear of the pulley shaft bolt. Slacken and withdraw the bolt and remove the drive pulley and viscous coupling from the engine (see illustration).
17 If required, the viscous coupling unit can be separated from the drive pulley by slackening and withdrawing the securing bolts.

Refitting

18 Refit the viscous coupling to the drive pulley (where removed) and tighten its retaining bolts to the specified torque.
19 Manoeuvre the drive pulley and coupling into position, then insert the shaft bolt and tighten it to the specified torque using a suitable 8 mm hex bit inserted through the rear of the drive pulley housing, whilst counter-holding the drive pulley with the 5 x 60 mm bolt, as during removal.
20 Refit the fan blade unit ensuring that it is mounted the correct way around.
21 Refit the auxiliary drivebelt as described in Chapter 2C.
22 Refit the plastic cover to the top of the engine.
23 Refit the lock carrier as described in Chapter 11.

6 Engine coolant temperature sensor – testing, removal and refitting

Testing

1 On all models, an engine coolant temperature sensor is located at the rear of the cylinder head, whilst on some engines, a second sensor is fitted to the radiator outlet pipe (see illustrations).
2 The sensor is a thermistor housed in a two-pin unit. A thermistor is an electronic component whose electrical resistance changes at a predetermined rate as the temperature changes. The fuel injection/ engine management electronic control module (ECM) supplies the sensor with a set voltage and then, by measuring the current flowing in the sensor circuit, it determines the engine's temperature. This information is then used, in conjunction with other inputs, to control the injector timing, the temperature gauge/ warning light, the idle speed, etc. It is also

6.1a Coolant temperature sensor
(arrowed) – diesel engines . . .

6.1b . . . petrol engines . . .

6.1c . . . some engines also have a sensor
on the radiator outlet (arrowed)

used to determine the glow plug preheating and post-heating times.

3 If the sensor circuit should fail to provide adequate information, the ECM's back-up facility will override the sensor signal. In this event, the ECM assumes a predetermined setting which will allow the fuel injection/ engine management system to run, albeit at reduced efficiency. When this occurs, the warning light on the instrument panel will come on, and a fault code will be stored by the systems self-diagnosis facility – the advice of an Audi dealer or specialist should be sought. The sensor itself can only be tested using special diagnostic equipment. *Do not* attempt to test the circuit using any other equipment, as there is a high risk of damaging the ECM.

Removal

Engine-mounted sensor

4 Either partially drain the cooling system to just below the level of the sensor (as described in Chapter 1A or 1B), or have a suitable plug which can be used to plug the sensor aperture whilst it is removed. If a plug is used, take great care not to damage the sensor unit aperture, and do not use anything which would allow foreign matter to enter the cooling system.

5 On diesel engines, undo the nuts and remove the plastic cover from the top of the engine.

6 Disconnect the sensor wiring plug, and identify whether the sensor is a push-fit or screw-fit.

7 On screw-fit sensors, unscrew the sensor from the engine and recover its sealing washer.

8 On push-fit sensors, press the sensor unit in, and slide out the retaining clip. Withdraw the sensor from the engine and recover the sealing ring **(see illustration 6.1b)**.

Radiator outlet pipe sensor

9 Drain the cooling system as described in Chapter 1A.

10 Disconnect the sensor wiring plug **(see illustration 6.1c)**.

11 Prise out the retaining clip and pull the sensor from the pipe.

Refitting

12 On screw-fit sensors, fit a new sealing washer, then fit the sensor, tightening it securely.

13 On push-fit sensors, fit a new sealing ring, then push the sensor fully into the aperture and slide in the retaining clip.

14 Reconnect the wiring plug, and refill the cooling system (Chapter 1A or 1B). On diesel engines, refit the cover to the top of the engine.

7 Coolant pump –
removal and refitting

Removal

1 Drain the cooling system as described in Chapter 1A or 1B.

2 Place the lock carrier in the Service position, as described in Chapter 11.

3 Remove the auxiliary drivebelt as described in Chapter 2A, 2B or 2C.

4 With reference to Chapter 2A, 2B or 2C remove the timing belt. **Note:** *On 1.8 litre and 2.0 litre indirect injection petrol engines, there is no need to remove the lower timing belt cover – the timing belt can be left in position on the crankshaft sprocket.*

5 Unscrew and remove the coolant pump securing bolts. Carefully withdraw the pump from the cylinder block and recover the sealing O-ring **(see illustrations)**.

7.5b Undo the pump retaining bolts

Refitting

6 Ensure that the pump and housing mating surfaces are clean and free from all traces of corrosion.

7 Obtain a new sealing O-ring and moisten it with undiluted antifreeze of the specified type (see *Lubricants and fluids*). Position the sealing ring on the pump.

8 Fit the coolant pump to the cylinder block, ensuring that the plug insert in the pump flange on the lower side **(see illustration)**.

9 Insert the mounting bolts and tighten them evenly and progressively to the specified torque.

10 Refit the timing belt as described in Chapter 2A, 2B or 2C.

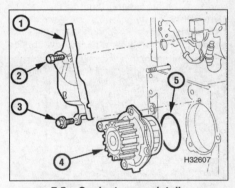

7.5a Coolant pump details

1	Timing belt cover	3	Bolt
2	Bolt	4	Coolant pump
		5	Seal

7.5c Renew the pump O-ring seal

7.8 Refit the coolant pump with the plug insert (arrowed) on the lower side

11 Refit the lock carrier and tighten the securing bolts (see Chapter 11).

12 On completion refill the cooling system as described in Chapter 1A or 1B.

8 Heating and ventilation system – general information

1 The heating/ventilation system consists of a fully-adjustable blower motor (housed behind the facia), face level vents in the centre and at each end of the facia, and air ducts to the front and rear footwells.

2 The heater control unit is located in the facia, and the controls operate flap valves to deflect and mix the air flowing through the various parts of the heating/ventilation system. The flap valves are contained in the air distribution housing, which acts as a central distribution

9.4 Reach through the audio unit aperture and push the control panel from position

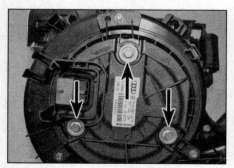

9.9 Undo the 3 bolts and lower the blower motor from the heater housing (arrowed)

unit, passing air to the various ducts and vents.

3 Cold air enters the system through the grille at the rear of the engine compartment. If required, the airflow is boosted by the blower, and then flows through the various ducts, according to the settings of the controls. Stale air is expelled through ducts at the rear of the vehicle. If warm air is required, the cold air is passed over the heater matrix, which is heated by the engine coolant.

4 The outside air supply to the vehicle can be closed off which is useful to prevent unpleasant odours entering from outside the vehicle. This is achieved either by setting the blower motor switch to position 0 or by operating the recirculation switch (depending on model). This facility should only be used briefly, as the recirculated air inside the vehicle will soon become stale.

5 On models with a solar sunroof, the sliding roof incorporates solar panels which energise the air conditioning blower motor to cool the interior of the car.

6 The heating and air conditioning systems fitted to the Audi A4 are equipped with a sophisticated self-diagnosis facility. Should a fault occur, before attempting a repair procedure, have the facility interrogated using Audi's diagnosis equipment (VAS 5051 or VAG 1551). This may reveal any stored fault codes, and pin-point the problem area. Consult an Audi dealer or suitably-equipped specialist. Note that the control unit communicates with the rest of the vehicle's electrical system by means of Databus

9.5 Disconnect the wiring plugs from the rear of the control panel

9.13a Undo the 2 cover bolts (arrowed) . . .

network. Traditional 'back-probing' of connectors should not be attempted without first identifying the Databus connections.

9 Heater/ventilation components – removal and refitting

General information

1 The information in this Section is applicable to heating/ventilation of the vehicle. The air conditioning is described in Section 12.

Heater/ventilation/ air conditioning control panel

Removal

2 Disconnect the battery negative lead (see Chapter 5A).

3 Reach beneath the control panel, and pull the unit rearwards to release the 4 retaining clips.

4 If the control panel is reluctant to move, remove the audio unit as described in Chapter 12, then push the control panel from position **(see illustration)**.

5 Note their fitted positions, then squeeze together the retaining tabs and disconnect the wiring plugs from the rear of the panel **(see illustration)**.

Refitting

6 Refitting is a reversal of removal. Note that if a new control panel has been fitted, it will be necessary to carry out the basic setting procedure. This procedure necessitates the use of Audi diagnostic equipment VAS5051/1. Consequently, this task should be entrusted to an Audi dealer or suitably-equipped specialist.

Blower motor/control unit

7 Remove the passenger's glovebox and lower A-pillar trim as described in Chapter 11.

8 Cut the cable ties securing the wiring harness, and disconnect the wiring plug from the blower motor/control unit.

9 Move the noise insulation/carpet towards the centre of the vehicle, then undo the 3 bolts and pull the motor/control unit from position **(see illustration)**.

10 Refitting is a reversal of removal. Note that the motor cannot be renewed separately from the control unit.

Heater matrix

Removal

11 Ensure that engine has cooled completely before starting work.

12 Remove the heater matrix/evaporator housing as described in Section 11. Note that it is not necessary to completely remove the housing, merely move it away from the pedal bracket a little.

13 Undo the 2 bolts and remove the cover from the coolant pipes, then undo the screw and remove the clamp at the front of the

9.13b . . . and the clamp screw (arrowed)

9.14 Undo the screws and remove the clamps (arrowed)

9.16 Slide the matrix from the housing

housing **(see illustrations)**. Unclip the wiring loom as the cover is removed.

14 Undo the clamps and pull the two coolant pipes from the matrix **(see illustration)**. Be prepared for coolant spillage.

15 On diesel models equipped with an auxiliary electrical heater element, disconnect the wiring plug.

16 Slide the matrix from the heater housing **(see illustration)**. Discard the coolant pipe seals – new ones must be fitted.

Refitting

17 Check the condition of the seals around the ends and sides of the matrix, and renew as necessary.

18 Moisten the new coolant pipe seals (normally supplied with a new matrix) with coolant, and fit them into the openings in the matrix **(see illustration)**.

19 Slide the new matrix into the heater housing.

20 Fit new clamps (normally supplied with a new matrix) onto the coolant pipes, and engage the pipes with the matrix. Fit the clamps around the pipe/matrix flanges, and tighten the bolts securely.

21 The remainder of refitting is a reversal of removal, remembering to top up the cooling system as described in Chapter 1A or 1B.

Fresh air/ recirculating airflaps motor

Removal

22 Remove the glovebox assembly as described in Chapter 11.

23 The flap valve motor is located on the right-hand side (LHD: left-hand side) of the blower motor housing.

24 Unplug the wiring connector from the side of the motor.

25 Undo the securing screws and carefully withdraw the motor from the housing, noting how the motor shaft engages **(see illustration)**.

26 The operation of the motor can be checked by connecting a 12 V DC source to contacts 5 and 6 of the motor's connector. The motor should move in one direction to the stop. Reversing the polarity of the power should alter the direction of rotation.

9.18 Renew the pipe seals in the matrix (arrowed)

Refitting

27 Refitting is a reversal of removal.

Defrost flap control motor

Removal

28 Remove the glovebox as described in Chapter 11.

29 Disconnect the motor wiring plug.

30 Undo the retaining bolts, and detach the motor from the mounting. Detach the connecting rod from the motor lever as the motor is withdrawn **(see illustration)**.

31 The operation of the motor can be checked by connecting a 12v DC source to contacts 5 and 6 of the motors connector. The motor should move in one direction to the stop. Reversing the polarity of the power should alter the direction of rotation.

Refitting

32 Refitting is a reversal of removal.

Temperature flap control motors

Removal

33 To remove the left-hand motor, remove the glovebox as described in Chapter 11. To remove the right-hand motor, remove the driver's side storage compartment as described in Chapter 11.

34 Disconnect the motor wiring plug.

35 Undo the retaining bolts, and detach the motor from the mounting. Detach the connecting rod from the motor lever as the motor is withdrawn **(see illustration 9.30)**.

36 The operation of the motor can be checked by connecting a 12 V DC source to

9.25 Recirculating airflap motor (arrowed)

contacts 5 and 6 of the motor's connector. The motor should move in one direction to the stop. Reversing the polarity of the power should alter the direction of rotation.

Refitting

37 Refitting is a reversal of removal.

Central flap control motor

Removal

38 Remove the glovebox as described in Chapter 11.

39 Disconnect the motor wiring plug.

40 Undo the retaining bolts, and detach the motor from the mounting **(see illustration 9.30)**.

41 The operation of the motor can be checked by connecting a 12 V DC source to contacts 5 and 6 of the motor's connector. The motor should move in one direction to

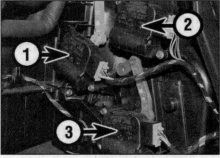

9.30 Heater distribution flap motors

1 *Defrost flap control motor*
2 *Central flap control motor*
3 *Temperature flap control motor*

9.45 Rotate the sensor 90° and remove the temperature sensor (arrowed)

9.52 Footwell vent air temperature sensors (arrowed)

9.54 Fresh air intake duct sensor (arrowed)

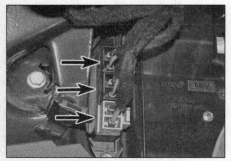

9.58 Disconnect the auxiliary heater element wiring plugs (arrowed)

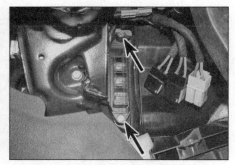

9.59 Undo the element retaining bolts (arrowed)

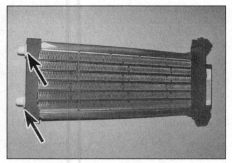

9.60 Check the rubber mountings (arrowed)

the stop. Reversing the polarity of the power should alter the direction of rotation.

Refitting

42 When refitting ensure the two lugs on the motor engage with the groove in the cam plate.
43 The remainder of refitting is a reversal of removal.

Air vent temperature sensors

Left-hand side

44 Remove the glovebox as described in Chapter 11.
45 Disconnect the sensor wiring plug, then rotate the sensor 90° and remove it from the air duct (see illustration).
46 Refitting is a reversal of removal.

Right-hand side

47 Remove the driver's side A-pillar trim as described in Chapter 11.
48 Rotate the sensor 90° and remove it from the air duct. Disconnect the wiring plug as the sensor is withdrawn (see illustration 9.45).
49 Refitting is a reversal of removal.

Footwell vent sensors

50 Remove the control panel as described in this Section.
51 Reach through the aperture and disconnect the sensor wiring plug (one sensor for the right-hand side, and one for the left).
52 Rotate the sensor 90° and pull it from the heater (see illustration).

Fresh air intake duct sensor

53 Remove the glovebox as described in Chapter 11.

54 Reach between the heater housing and the plenum chamber baseplate, and rotate the sensor 90° (see illustration). Disconnect the wiring plug as the sensor is withdrawn.
55 If the sensor is difficult to remove, remove the pollen filter as described in Chapter 1A or 1B. The sensor is accessible through the intake housing.
56 Refitting is a reversal of removal.

Auxiliary heater element

57 Diesel models may be fitted with an electrically-operated heating element, fitted into the heater housing alongside the heater matrix. To remove the element, first remove the driver's side storage compartment as described in Chapter 11.
58 Note their fitted positions, and disconnect the wiring plugs from the element (see illustration).
59 Undo the 2 bolts and pull the element from the heater housing (see illustration).
60 Upon refitting the element, ensure the rubber mountings are in place on the lugs at the end of the element (see illustration). The remainder of refitting is a reversal of removal.

10 Air conditioning system – general information and precautions

General information

1 Air conditioning is fitted as standard equipment to all models. It combines a conventional air heating system with an air cooling and dehumidifying system. This allows greater control over the temperature and humidity of the air inside the car, giving increased comfort and rapid window demisting.
2 The cooling side of the system works in the same way as a domestic refrigerator. Refrigerant gas, contained in a sealed network of alloy pipes, is drawn into a belt-driven compressor, and is forced through a condenser mounted on the front of the radiator. On entering the condenser, the refrigerant changes state from gas to liquid and releases heat, which is absorbed by the air flowing into the front of the engine compartment through the condenser. The liquid refrigerant passes through an expansion valve to an evaporator, where it changes from liquid under high pressure to gas under low pressure. This change in state is accompanied by a drop in temperature, which cools the evaporator. Air passing through the evaporator is cooled before flowing into the air distribution unit. The refrigerant then returns to the compressor, and the cycle begins again.
3 The cooled air passes to the air distribution unit/heater housing, where it is blended with hot air blown through the heater matrix, to achieve the desired temperature in the passenger compartment. When the air conditioning system is operating in Automatic mode, a series of air valves controlled by servo motors automatically regulate the cabin temperature by blending hot and cold air.
4 The heating side of the system operates as described in Section 8.
5 The operation of the air conditioning system is managed by an electronic

control unit, which controls the electric cooling fan, the compressor, and the facia-mounted warning light. The heating and air conditioning systems fitted to the Audi A4 are equipped with a sophisticated self-diagnosis facility. Should a fault occur, before attempting a repair procedure, have the facility interrogated using Audi's diagnosis equipment (VAS 5051 or VAG 1551). This may reveal any stored fault codes, and pin-point the problem area. Consult an Audi dealer or suitably-equipped specialist. Note that the control unit communicates with the rest of the vehicle's electrical system by means of Databus network. Traditional 'back-probing' of connectors should not be attempted without first identifying the Databus connections.

Precautions

6 When working on the air conditioning system, it is necessary to observe special precautions. If for any reason the refrigerant lines must be disconnected, you must entrust this task to a Audi dealer or an air conditioning specialist. Similarly, the system can only be evacuated and recharged by a dealer or air conditioning specialist. The refrigerant circuit service ports are located in the right-hand front corner of the engine compartment (see illustration and Tool tip).

⚠ *Warning: The air conditioning system contains a pressurised liquid refrigerant. If the system is discharged in an uncontrolled manner without the aid of specialist equipment, the refrigerant will boil as soon as it is exposed to the atmosphere, causing severe frostbite if it comes into contact with unprotected skin. In addition, certain refrigerants, in the presence of a naked flame (including a lit cigarette), will oxidise to form a highly poisonous gas. It is therefore extremely dangerous to disconnect any part of the air conditioning system without specialised knowledge and equipment.*

10.6 Air conditioning system refrigerant circuit service ports

7 Uncontrolled discharging of the refrigerant can also be damaging to the environment, as certain refrigerants contain CFCs.

8 As no clutch is fitted to the air conditioning compressor (the compressor operates continuously), do not operate the engine if it is known to be short of refrigerant, as this will damage the compressor.

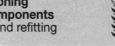
11 Air conditioning system components – removal and refitting

⚠ *Warning: Do not attempt to discharge the refrigerant circuit yourself (refer to the precautions given in Section 10). Have the air conditioning system discharged by a suitably-equipped specialist. On completion, have the engineer fit new O-rings to the line connections and evacuate and recharge the system.*

Compressor

Removal

1 Have the air conditioning system discharged by a suitably-equipped specialist.

2 Place the lock carrier in the Service position (see Chapter 11).

Many car accessory shops sell one-shot air conditioning recharge aerosols. These generally contain refrigerant, compressor oil, leak sealer and system conditioner. Some also have a dye to help pinpoint leaks.

⚠ *Warning: These products must only be used as directed by the manufacturer, and do not remove the need for regular maintenance.*

3 Remove the auxiliary drivebelt as described in the relevant part of Chapter 2A, 2B or 2C.

4 Unscrew the retaining bolts and disconnect the refrigerant lines from the compressor. Remove the O-ring seals and discard them – new ones must be used on reconnection. Plug the open pipes and ports to prevent the ingress of moisture.

5 Disconnect the wiring plug, then unscrew the retaining bolts from the compressor, then remove the compressor from its mounting bracket (see illustrations).

Refitting

6 Refitting is a reversal of the removal procedure; ensure that all fixings are tightened to the specified torque, where given. On completion, have the refrigerant engineer fit new O-rings to the line connections and then evacuate and recharge the refrigerant circuit.

11.5a Disconnect the compressor wiring plug (arrowed) . . .

11.5b . . . then unscrew the compressor mounting bolts (arrowed – viewed from beneath)

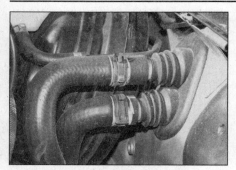

11.12 Release the clamps and disconnect the heater hoses from the pipes at the bulkhead . . .

11.15 . . . then prise out the grommet around the pipes

11.16 Undo the nut and disconnect the air conditioning pipes at the engine compartment bulkhead (arrowed)

Evaporator/heater matrix housing

Removal

7 Have the air conditioning system discharged by a suitably-equipped specialist.

8 Ensure that engine has cooled completely before starting work.

9 Move the front seats to their rearmost positions, then disconnect the battery as described in Chapter 5A.

10 Locate the heater matrix hoses and trace them back to the point where they connect to bulkhead stub pipes.

11 Place a draining container underneath the hoses, to catch the coolant that will escape when they are disconnected.

12 Apply proprietary hose clamps to both heater hoses, then release the clips and disconnect the hoses from the bulkhead stubs **(see illustration)**. Allow the coolant from the heater circuit to collect in the draining container.

13 If you have access to a source of compressed air, apply it carefully at *low pressure* to the upper bulkhead stub and blow the remainder of the coolant from the heater matrix.

 Warning: Always wear eye protection when working with compressed air.

14 If you do not have access to compressed air, bear in mind that a large volume of coolant will remain in the heater circuit and that this may escape as the heater unit is removed from the inside of the car.

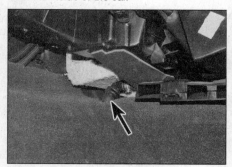

11.18 Disconnect the drain tube from the housing (arrowed)

15 Prise the rubber grommet from the bulkhead aperture, then slide it off the pipe stubs and remove it from the engine compartment **(see illustration)**.

16 Undo the retaining nut and disconnect the refrigerant pipes from the engine compartment bulkhead. Plug the openings to prevent contamination **(see illustration)**. Discard the O-ring seals – new ones must be fitted.

17 Remove the entire facia panel and crossmember as described in Chapter 11.

18 Detach the drain tube from the housing **(see illustration)**.

19 Unclip the rear passenger air ducts from the front of the footwell vent unit. Remove the securing screws and detach the footwell vent unit from the base of the heater unit **(see illustration)**.

20 Note their fitted positions, then unplug the wiring heater unit wiring at the multiway connectors. Label each connection to avoid confusion on refitting. Release the wiring from the support clips on the side of the heater unit.

21 Lift the heater unit away from the bulkhead, towards the passenger's side of the vehicle. The heater unit gasket may be stuck to the bulkhead – carefully rock the housing from side-to-side until the gasket releases. Note that if the heater housing is being removed to renew the matrix, the housing can be moved slightly forwards to provide the necessary access, rather than be completely removed.

22 Remove the unit from the vehicle, keeping it upright to avoid spilling the residual coolant.

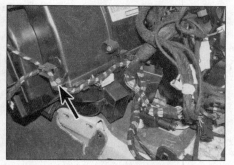

11.19 Undo the screws securing the footwell vent unit to the housing (left-hand screw arrowed)

Refitting

23 Refitting is the reverse of removal, noting the following points.

a) Use a new housing gasket if the original is damaged.

b) Ensure the ducts, elbows and gaiter are all securely joined to the housing and the wiring/cables are correctly routed before securing the housing in position.

c) Ensure the coolant hoses are securely reconnected to the matrix; the feed hose from the cylinder head must be connected to the lower union and the return hose to the coolant pump to the upper union.

d) Ensure that the rubber grommet is securely seated over the bulkhead stub pipes.

e) Reconnect the refrigerant pipes using new O-ring seals.

f) On completion, top-up and bleed the cooling system as described in the relevant part of Chapter 1.

Evaporator

Removal

24 Remove the evaporator/heater matrix housing as described in this Section.

25 Undo the 2 bolts and remove the cover from the coolant pipes **(see illustration 9.13a and 9.13b)**.

26 Slacken the clamps and pull the two coolant pipes from the heater matrix **(see illustration 9.14)**. Be prepared for coolant spillage.

27 On diesel models equipped with an auxiliary electrical heater element, disconnect the wiring plug.

28 Slide the heater matrix from the housing **(see illustration 9.16)**. Discard the coolant pipe seals – new ones must be fitted.

29 Detach the refrigerant pipe holder **(see illustration)**.

30 Undo the bolts, and detach the air duct assembly from the rear of the housing **(see illustration)**.

31 Lift the evaporator from position, and remove the seal **(see illustration)**.

11.29 Remove the refrigerant pipe clamp bolt (arrowed)

11.30 Detach the duct assembly from the rear of the housing

11.31 Slide the evaporator from position

11.34 Evaporator outflow temperature sensor (arrowed)

11.36 Sunlight sensor cover

11.37 Undo the sensor retaining screw (arrowed)

Refitting

32 Refitting is the reverse of removal, noting the following points.

a) Check the condition of the evaporator seal and renew it if necessary.

b) Reconnect the coolant pipes to the heater matrix using new seals.

c) Top-up and bleed the cooling system as described in the relevant part of Chapter 1.

d) On completion, have the refrigerant engineer fit new O-rings to the line connections and then evacuate and recharge the refrigerant circuit.

Evaporator outflow temperature sensor

33 Remove the passenger's side glovebox as described in Chapter 11.

34 Disconnect the wiring plug, then rotate the sensor 90° and pull it from the housing **(see illustration)**.

35 Refitting is a reversal of removal.

Sunlight photo-sensor

36 Carefully prise the sensor cover forwards and remove it from the vent **(see illustration)**.

11.41 Undo the Torx screws securing the pipes to the top of the receiver/drier . . .

37 Undo the retaining bolt and lift the sensor upwards from position **(see illustration)**. Disconnect the sensor wiring plug as it is withdrawn, and tie the connector back to prevent it from disappearing down inside the facia.

38 Refitting is a reversal of removal.

Receiver/drier

39 Have the air conditioning refrigerant discharged by a suitably-equipped specialist

11.42 . . . then slacken the clamp bolt (arrowed)

40 Remove the right-hand headlight as described in Chapter 12.

41 Undo the 2 Torx screws and detach the pipes from the top of the receiver/drier **(see illustration)**.

42 Undo the clamp bolt and remove the receiver/drier **(see illustration)**.

43 Refitting is a reversal of removal. Have the refrigerant recharged by a suitably-equipped specialist.

Chapter 4 Part A:
Fuel system – indirect petrol injection models

Contents

Section number

Air cleaner and intake ducts – removal and refitting 2
Engine management components – removal and refitting. 3
Fuel filter – renewal. 4
Fuel injection system – depressurisation 8
Fuel injection system – testing and adjustment 10
Fuel pump and gauge sender unit – testing, removal and refitting . . 6

Section number

Fuel system bleeding 5
Fuel tank – removal and refitting 7
General information and precautions. 1
Intake manifold – removal and refitting 9
Intercooler – removal and refitting 12
Turbocharger – general information, removal and refitting. 11

Degrees of difficulty

Easy, suitable for novice with little experience 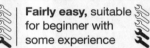	Fairly easy, suitable for beginner with some experience	Fairly difficult, suitable for competent DIY mechanic	Difficult, suitable for experienced DIY mechanic	Very difficult, suitable for expert DIY or professional

Specifications

General
Engine code*:
  1781 cc:
    Bosch Motronic ME7.5:

110 kW (143 bhp)	AVJ
125 kW (163 bhp)	AMB

    Bosch Motronic ME7.1:

120 kW (156 bhp)	BFB and BKB
140 kW (182 bhp)	BEX
1984 cc, Bosch Motronic ME7, 96 kW (125 bhp).	ALT

* **Note:** See 'Vehicle identification' for the location of the code marking on the engine.

Recommended fuel
Minimum octane rating.	95 RON unleaded
	(91 RON unleaded may be used, but with reduced performance)

Fuel system data
Fuel pump type	Electric, immersed in fuel tank
Fuel pump delivery rate (battery voltage 12 V).	380 cm³/15 secs (approximately)
Regulated fuel pressure at idling speed:	
All except engine code ALT	4.0 bar (approximately)
Engine code ALT:	
Vacuum hose connected	3.5 bar (approximately)
Vacuum hose disconnected	4.0 bar (approximately)
Minimum holding pressure (after 10 minutes)	2.5 bar
Engine idle speed (non-adjustable, electronically-controlled):	
All except ALT engine code	740 to 860 rpm
ALT engine code.	700 to 960 rpm
Injector electrical resistance (at room temperature):	
All except ALT engine code	12 to 13 ohms
ALT engine code.	14 to 17 ohms

Torque wrench settings

	Nm	lbf ft
Accelerator pedal/sensor	10	7
Air cleaner	10	7
Air temperature sensor.	10	7
Coolant pipe to intake manifold	10	7
Engine speed sensor	10	7
Fuel pump/sender unit ring	60	44
Fuel rail to intake manifold.	10	7
Fuel tank filler neck	25	18
Fuel tank mounting bolts	25	18
Intake manifold support brackets.	20	15
Intake manifold.	10	7
Oil return pipe to turbocharger.	10	7
Oil supply pipe to turbocharger	35	26
Oxygen sensor.	50	37
Throttle body	10	7
Turbocharger bracket:		
To turbocharger	30	22
To cylinder block.	25	18
Turbocharger to exhaust manifold*	35	26
Turbocharger to exhaust pipe/catalytic converter*	30	22

* *Do not re-use*

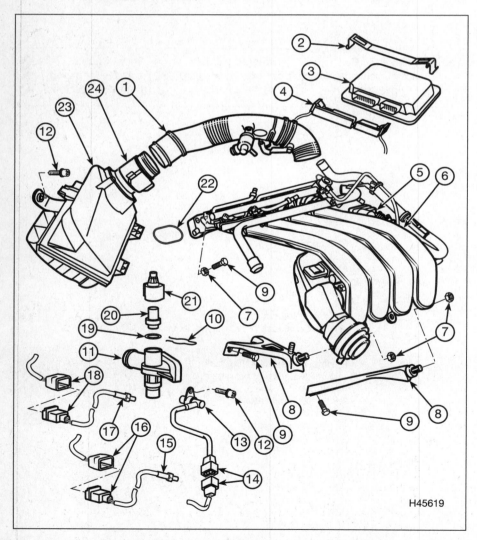

H45619

1 General information and precautions

General information

The sequential multipoint petrol injection systems described in this Chapter are self-contained engine management systems, which control both the fuel injection and ignition (see illustration). This Chapter deals with the fuel system components only; refer to Chapter 5B for details of the ignition system.

The fuel injection system consists of a fuel tank, an electric fuel pump, a fuel filter, fuel supply and return lines, a throttle body, an air mass sensor, a fuel rail and four electronic injectors, a fuel pressure regulator, and an electronic control module (ECM), together with its associated sensors, actuators and wiring. The component layout varies according to the system.

1.1 Engine management components – engine code ALT

1 Intake duct
2 Retaining plate
3 ECM
4 Wiring connector
5 Throttle valve control
6 Intake manifold
7 Nuts
8 Support brackets
9 Bolt
10 Spring clip
11 Elbow
12 Bolt
13 Engine speed sensor
14 Wiring connector
15 Oxygen sensor (post-catalytic converter)
16 Wiring connector
17 Oxygen sensor (pre-catalytic converter)
18 Wiring connector
19 O-ring
20 Coolant temperature sensor
21 Wiring connector
22 Gasket
23 Air cleaner
24 Airflow meter

A turbocharger is fitted to all engines apart from engine code ALT. Engine code ALT has a variable geometry intake manifold, where the length of the intake track is varied to emphasise the torque or power characteristics of the engine dependant on engine speed and load, etc. The intake path is controlled by a vacuum-operated valve which can operate in one of two positions. At low engine speed/high torque the valve position forces the incoming air through a long intake track, thus increasing the torque output and low speed driveability. At high engine speed/high power the valve position forces the incoming air through a short intake track, thus increasing the power output and throttle response. The vacuum supply to the valve is controlled by the engine management ECM. The other engines have fixed intake manifolds.

All models are equipped with an electronically-controlled throttle system referred to as Electronic Power Control (EPS). A sensor on the accelerator pedal informs the engine management ECM of the position and rate-of-change of the pedal, which then determines the optimum position for the throttle valve in the throttle body. There is no accelerator cable. The position of the accelerator pedal is transmitted to the engine control unit by two variable resistors, and the throttle valve is operated by an electric motor on the throttle body. When the engine is stopped but the ignition is switched on, the throttle valve moves exactly as dictated by the throttle pedal, however, when the engine is running, the control unit can open or close the throttle valve independently. The control unit calculates the most efficient opening of the throttle valve according to a number of parameters, so it is possible under certain conditions that the throttle valve may be completely open even though the pedal is only depressed half-way.

The air mass sensor is located on the air cleaner outlet to the throttle body. Fuel is supplied under pressure to a fuel rail, and then passes to four electronic injectors. The duration of the injection period is determined by the ECM which switches the injectors on and off as required.

The fuel pump delivers a constant supply of fuel through a cartridge filter. The fuel is supplied to a fuel rail, and the fuel pressure regulator maintains a constant fuel pressure to the fuel injectors and returns excess fuel to the tank via the return line. The constant fuel flow system helps to reduce fuel temperature and prevents vaporisation.

The ECM controls starting and warm-up enrichment together with idle speed regulation and lambda control. Idle speed control is achieved partly by an electronic throttle valve positioning module, on the side of the throttle body and partly by the ignition system. Manual adjustment of the idle speed is not possible.

Intake air is drawn into the engine through the air cleaner, which contains a renewable paper filter element.

2.1a Detach the carbon canister valve from the bracket on the air cleaner cover

The exhaust gas oxygen content is constantly monitored by the ECM via the two oxygen sensors, which are mounted each side of the catalytic converter. The ECM then uses this information to adjust the air/fuel ratio. Manual adjustment of the idle speed exhaust CO content is not possible. A catalytic converter is fitted to the exhaust system on all models. A fuel evaporative control system is fitted, and the ECM controls the operation of the activated charcoal canister – refer to Chapter 4D for further details.

It should be noted that fault diagnosis of all the engine management systems described in this Chapter is only possible with dedicated electronic test equipment. Problems with the system operation should therefore be referred to an Audi dealer or engine management specialist for assessment. Once the fault has been identified, the removal and refitting sequences detailed in the following Sections will then allow the appropriate component(s) to be renewed as required.

Precautions

⚠ **Warning: Many of the procedures in this Chapter require the removal of fuel lines and connections, which may result in some fuel spillage. Before carrying out any operation on the fuel system, refer to the precautions given in 'Safety first!' at the beginning of this manual, and follow them implicitly. Always switch off the ignition before working on the fuel system. Petrol is a highly dangerous and volatile liquid, and the precautions necessary when handling it cannot be overstressed.**

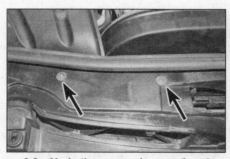

2.2a Undo the screws (arrowed) and detach the intake ducting from the lock carrier . . .

2.1b On 1.8 litre models, release the clip (arrowed) and disconnect the hose

Note: *Residual pressure will remain in the fuel lines long after the vehicle was last used. Before disconnecting any fuel line, first depressurise the fuel system as described in Section 8.*
Caution: *Before working on the fuel system components, always remove the fuel pump fuse (fuse 28), otherwise the fuel pump can be activated by the door contact switch.*

<table>
<tr><td>**2**</td><td>**Air cleaner and intake ducts**
– removal and refitting</td><td></td></tr>
</table>

Removal

1 Release the carbon canister solenoid valve from the bracket on the air cleaner housing, then on 1.8 litre models, release the clip and disconnect the hose from the valve **(see illustrations)**.
2 Remove the air cleaner ducts from the top of the housing/lock carrier panel **(see illustrations)**.
3 On turbo models, where fitted, undo the screws and remove the heat shield from the side of the air cleaner housing, then undo the carbon canister pipe brackets, and detach the pipe from the air cleaner housing **(see illustrations)**.
4 Squeeze together the sides of the collar and disconnect the secondary air injection pipe (where applicable) from the air cleaner housing **(see illustration)**.

2.2b . . . then pull the duct from the top of the air cleaner housing

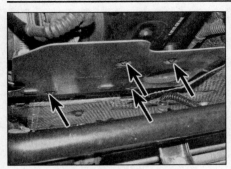

2.3a Undo the screws and remove the heat shield (arrowed) . . .

2.3b . . . then detach the pipe (arrowed) from the air cleaner housing

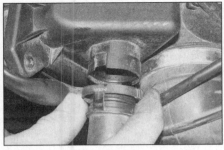

2.4 Squeeze together the sides of the secondary air injection pipe collar and pull it from the air cleaner housing

2.7 Air cleaner outlet pipe clamp (arrowed)

2.8 Prise out the top mounting centre pin

2.9 Fit the rubber mountings to the base of the air cleaner housing (arrowed)

5 Carefully prise the wiring harness clips (where fitted) from the housing.

6 Where fitted, disconnect the crankcase ventilation hoses.

7 Disconnect the wiring from the airflow meter, then slacken the clamp and detach the outlet pipe from the housing **(see illustration)**.

8 Prise out the upper mounting centre pin, pull the top of the housing away from the inner wing, then lift the complete assembly from place **(see illustration)**. Remove the rubber mountings from the body. Check the condition of the mountings and renew them if necessary.

Refitting

9 Refitting is a reversal of removal, noting that the rubber mountings should be fitted to the base of the housing prior to refitting **(see illustration)**.

3 Engine management components – removal and refitting

Note: *Observe the precautions in Section 1 before working on any component in the fuel system. The ignition must be switched off at all times.*

Airflow meter

Removal

1 The airflow meter is located in the intake ducting.

2 Disconnect the airflow meter wiring plug **(see illustration)**.

3 Release the clips and detach the air duct from the airflow meter **(see illustration 2.7)**.

4 On some models, the airflow meter may be available separately from the housing – check

with an Audi dealer. If this is the case, undo the screws and withdrawn the meter from the housing.

Refitting

5 Refitting is a reversal of removal, but fit a new gasket or O-ring as applicable.

Throttle valve potentiometer

Note: *The potentiometer is an integral part of the throttle body and cannot be renewed separately.*

Intake air temperature sensor

Removal

6 The sensor is located on the intake manifold **(see illustrations)**.

7 Unplug the harness connector from the sensor.

8 Unscrew the bolt and remove the sensor from the manifold. The sensor can be tested

3.2 Disconnect the airflow meter wiring plug

3.6a Intake air temperature sensor – 1.8 litre models

3.6b Intake air temperature sensor – 2.0 litre models

3.11 The coolant temperature sensor is located at the rear of the cylinder head

using a multimeter. Connect the multimeter leads to the terminals of the sensor and set the meter to measure resistance (ohms). As the temperature increases, the resistance of the sensor decreases. So at 30°C the resistance should be 1500 to 2000 ohms, and at 80°C the resistance should be 275 to 375 ohms (approximately). If the resistance value of the sensor does not match these values, or fails to change, it may be faulty.

Refitting

9 Refitting is a reversal of removal, however observe the correct tightening torque.

Throttle valve positioner

Note: *The throttle valve positioner is incorporated in the throttle body and is not available as a separate part.*

Vehicle speed sensor

Removal and refitting

10 On models up to 06/2002, the vehicle speed sensor is fitted into the back of the gearbox. Refer to Chapter 7A for the removal and refitting procedure. After this date, the vehicle speed data is provided by the ABS wheel speed sensors. Any fault with the sensor must be checked by an Audi dealer or specialist, and if necessary renewed.

Coolant temperature sensor

Removal

11 The coolant temperature sensor is located on the rear of the cylinder head on all engines **(see illustration)**.
12 Drain approximately one quarter of the

3.24 Undo the bolts and detach the throttle body – 1.8 litre model shown

3.21 Slacken the clip and disconnect the air ducting from the throttle body

coolant from the engine with reference to Chapter 1A.
13 Disconnect the wiring from the sensor.
14 Unscrew the sensor or extract the retaining clip and remove the sensor. Recover the sealing washer/O-ring.

Refitting

15 Refitting is a reversal of removal, but fit a new washer/O-ring. Where applicable, tighten the sensor securely. Refer to Chapter 1A and top-up the cooling system.

Engine speed sensor

Removal

16 The engine speed sensor is mounted on the rear, left-hand side of the cylinder block, adjacent to the mating surface of the block and transmission bellhousing, just behind the oil filter.
17 If necessary, drain the engine oil and remove the oil filter and cooler to improve access with reference to Chapter 1A.
18 Unplug the harness connector from the sensor.
19 Unscrew the retaining bolt and withdraw the sensor from the cylinder block.

Refitting

20 Refitting is a reversal of removal. Tighten the securing bolt to the specified torque.

Throttle body/control unit

Note: *In order for a new throttle body/control unit to function correctly, it must be matched to the engine management ECM using Audi diagnostic equipment.*

3.28a Fuel supply line union (arrowed) – 1.8 litre model shown

3.23 Throttle body coolant and vacuum hoses – 2.0 litre model shown

Removal

21 Loosen the clips and detach the air ducting from the throttle body **(see illustration)**.
22 Unplug the harness connector from the throttle body.
23 Note their fitted locations, disconnect the vacuum and coolant hoses (where fitted) from the throttle body. Where necessary release the wiring harness from the guide clip **(see illustration)**.
24 Unscrew and remove the securing bolts, then lift the throttle body/control unit away from the intake manifold. Recover and discard the seal **(see illustration)**.
25 Further dismantling of the throttle body is not recommended. No parts are available separately. If any part of the throttle body is defective, the completely assembly must be renewed.

Refitting

26 Refitting is a reversal of removal, noting the following:
a) *Use a new throttle body-to-intake manifold seal.*
b) *Ensure that all vacuum hoses, coolant hoses (where applicable) and electrical connectors are refitted securely.*

Fuel injectors and fuel rail

Removal

27 Disconnect the battery negative (earth) lead (see Chapter 5A). Undo the retaining fasteners (only applicable to 1.8 litre models) and remove the engine top cover.
28 Wrap some rag around the fuel supply line union located over the fuel rail **(see illustrations)**,

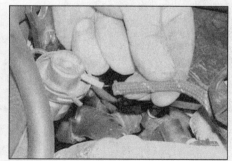

3.28b Disconnect the fuel pressure regulator vacuum hose – 2.0 litre models only

3.29a Press in the clip (arrowed) and pull the connector from the injector – 1.8 litre models

3.29b Squeeze together the tabs and pull the connector from the injector – 2.0 litre models

3.30a Fuel rail mounting bolts (arrowed) – 1.8 litre models

3.30b Fuel rail mounting bolts (arrowed) – 2.0 litre models

and also place a suitable container beneath the union to catch any spilt fuel. Unscrew the union nut while holding the union bolt with another spanner, and allow the fuel to drain into the container. Remove the rag. Where applicable, disconnect the fuel return hose from the fuel

rail, and the vacuum hose from the pressure regulator also on the fuel rail.

29 Note their fitted positions, then disconnect the wiring from each of the injectors, then the intake air temperature sensor, camshaft position sensor and throttle control unit.

The fuel injectors wiring plugs are released by pressing in the retaining clips (1.8 litre models), or squeezing together the clips (2.0 litre models) **(see illustrations)**.

30 Unscrew the mounting bolts, then carefully lift the fuel rail together with the injectors from the intake manifold **(see illustrations)**.

31 With the assembly on the bench, pull out the clips and release each of the injectors from the fuel rail. Recover the O-ring seals **(see illustrations)**.

Refitting

32 Refit the injectors and fuel rail by following the removal procedure in reverse, noting the following points:

a) Renew the injector O-ring seals, and smear them with a little clean engine oil before fitting them. When fitting the front O-ring, do not remove the plastic cap from the head of the injector but leave it in position and lift the O-ring over it.

b) Ensure that the injector retaining clips are securely seated.

c) Check that the fuel supply line is reconnected correctly.

d) Check that all electrical connections are remade correctly and securely.

e) Reconnect the battery as described in Chapter 5A.

f) On completion, start the engine and check for fuel leaks.

Camshaft position Hall sender

Removal

33 Remove the timing belt outer cover with reference to Chapter 2A.

34 Release the clip and disconnect the wiring multiplug from the Hall sender **(see illustration)**.

35 Unscrew the mounting bolts and withdraw the Hall sender from the front of the cylinder head. Recover the gasket.

Refitting

36 Refitting is a reversal of removal, but renew the gasket and tighten the mounting bolts securely.

Oxygen sensors

Removal

37 On all engines covered in this Manual,

3.31a Pull out the clips . . .

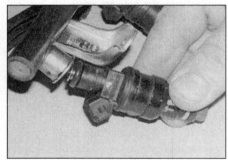

3.31b . . . and withdraw the injectors from the fuel rail

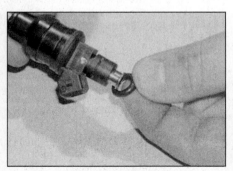

3.31c Remove the O-ring from the injectors

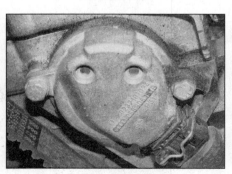

3.34 Camshaft position Hall sender

3.37 Pre-catalytic converter oxygen sensor – 1.8 litre model shown

3.45 Pull up the rubber sealing strip (arrowed)

3.47a Prise forward the 3 clips – one in the centre, one at each end (left-hand end clip arrowed) . . .

3.47b . . . then pull the scuttle trim panel upwards from the base of the windscreen

the two oxygen sensors are located at each end of the catalytic converter on the right-hand side of the engine. One is located on the front-top of the catalytic converter **(see illustration)**, and one on the rear-top of the catalytic converter. On the non-turbocharged engine, the catalytic converter is attached to the rear of the exhaust manifold. On the turbocharged engines, it is attached to the rear of the turbocharger.

38 The wiring connector for the oxygen sensors is located on the left-hand side of the bulkhead, beneath the coolant expansion tank. Undo the tank mounting screws and disconnect the low coolant wiring, then position the tank to one side. **Do not** disconnect any of the coolant hoses from the tank. Disconnect the oxygen sensor wiring and release the cables from the plastic ties.

39 Unscrew and remove the sensor, taking care to avoid damaging the sensor probe as it is removed. **Note:** *As the wiring flying lead remains connected to the sensor, a special slotted socket needs to be used to remove the sensor.*

Refitting

40 Apply a little anti-seize grease to the sensor threads, but avoid contaminating the probe tip. **Note:** *New oxygen sensors may be supplied with fitting paste on the threads.*

41 Refit the sensor and tighten it to the correct torque.

42 Reconnect the wiring and secure with the plastic ties.

Electronic control unit (ECM)

Caution: The ECM is programmed and identified specifically for the vehicle it is fitted to, and the identity coding must be transferred to any new unit. This process requires the use of dedicated Audi diagnostic equipment VAS 5051. For this reason, it is recommended that ECM renewal is carried out by an Audi dealer or suitably-equipped specialist, however removal and refitting of the original ECM is possible by the home mechanic. Note also that if the ECM is renewed, the identification of the new ECM must be transferred to the immobiliser control unit by an Audi dealer or specialist.

Caution: Always wait at least 30 seconds after switching off the ignition before disconnecting the wiring from the ECM. When the wiring is disconnected, all the learned values may be erased, although any contents of the fault memory are retained. After reconnecting the wiring, the vehicle must be driven for several miles so that the ECM can learn its basic settings. If the engine still runs erratically, the basic settings may be reinstated by an Audi dealer or specialist using a special test instrument.

Removal

43 The electronic control unit is located on the bulkhead at the rear of the engine compartment. On RHD models it is on the right-hand side, and on LHD models it is on the left-hand side.

44 Disconnect the battery negative (earth) lead (see Chapter 5A).

45 Pull of the rubber seal from the plenum chamber cover (where fitted), then undo the fasteners and remove the cover **(see illustration)**.

46 Remove the wiper arms as described in Chapter 12.

47 Release the clips and remove the windscreen scuttle trim panel **(see illustrations)**.

48 Undo the screws and lift off the cover **(see illustration)**.

49 Release the spring retainer with a screwdriver and lift up the electronic control unit **(see illustration)**.

50 Pull out the locking catches and disconnect the wiring connectors from the ECM. **Note:** *On some models, the ECM is fitted into a protective metal housing. The housing is secured to the ECM with shear bolts, which are coated with thread-locking compound* **(see illustration)**. *In order to remove the bolts, heat them with a hot-air gun, and use self-grip pliers to undo the shear bolts.*

> **Warning: Wait a minimum of 30 seconds after switching off the ignition before disconnecting the ECM wiring connector.**

51 Withdraw the ECM from the bulkhead.

Refitting

52 Refitting is a reversal of removal, but press the clip down until it snaps into position. On ECMs with the metal housing, apply thread-locking compound to the shear bolts,

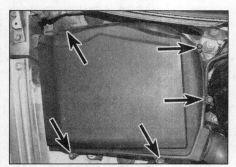

3.48 Undo the ECM cover screws (arrowed)

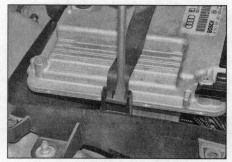

3.49 Release the ECM spring retainer

3.50 ECM housing shear bolts (arrowed)

3.56 Turbocharger boost pressure sensor (arrowed)

3.60 Accelerator pedal/position sensor retaining bolts (arrowed)

3.64 Disconnect the regulator vacuum hose (arrowed)

then tighten the bolts until the heads shear off. Reconnect the battery as described in Chapter 5A. Note that the vehicle must be driven for several miles so that the ECM can learn its basic settings. In order to store its learnt values (and faults where present), the ECM continues to be supplied with voltage for up to 15 minutes. Once this period is finished, the ECM disconnects the earth path.

Turbocharger boost pressure

53 The boost pressure sensor is located on the top of the intercooler. To remove the sensor, remove the plastic cover around the power steering fluid reservoir.
54 Slacken the clip and disconnect the air intake hose from the top of the intercooler.
55 Disconnect the sensor wiring plug.
56 Undo the bolts and pull the sensor from the intercooler **(see illustration)**.
57 Refitting is a reversal of removal.

Accelerator pedal/ position sensor

Removal

58 Remove the driver's side storage compartment as described in Chapter 11.
59 Disconnect the sensor wiring plug.
60 Undo the 3 bolts and remove the pedal/ sensor assembly **(see illustration)**. Note that the sensor is not available separately from the pedal assembly.

Refitting

61 Refitting is a reversal of removal,

remembering to tighten the retaining bolts to the specified torque. **Note:** *If the sensor has been renewed on vehicles with automatic transmission, the kick-down function must be adapted using Audi diagnostic equipment (VAS 5051). Entrust this task to an Audi dealer or suitably-equipped specialist.*

Fuel pressure regulator

Note: *This procedure applies to engine code ALT only. On other engines, the regulator is integral with the fuel filter.*
62 Pull the plastic cover upwards from the top of the engine.
63 Depressurise the fuel system as described in Section 8.
64 Disconnect the vacuum hose from the pressure regulator **(see illustration)**.
65 Place a cloth rag beneath the regulator to catch any spilt fuel.
66 Pull out the retaining clip, then lift the regulator from the fuel rail. Recover the O-ring seals.
67 Refitting is a reversal of removal, but renew the O-ring seals and ensure the retaining clip is secure.

4 Fuel filter – renewal

Note: *Observe the precautions in Section 1 before working on fuel system components.*
1 The fuel filter is situated underneath the rear of the vehicle, in front of the fuel tank.

To gain access to the filter, chock the front wheels, then jack up the rear of the vehicle and support it securely on axle stands. Undo the fasteners and remove the underbody trim panel.
2 If available, fit hose clamps to the filter intake and outlet hoses. These are not essential, but will reduce the amount of fuel spillage. Even with hose clamps fitted, the old filter will contain some fuel, so have some rags ready to soak up any spillage.
3 Wrap rags around the connections, then dissipate the fuel pressure by carefully depressing the release tabs and slowly disconnecting the fuel pipe connections to and from the filter **(see illustration)**. If the fuel hoses show any sign of perishing or cracking, particularly at the hose ends or where the hose enters the metal end fitting, renew the hoses.
4 Before removing the filter, note the direction-of-flow marking on the filter body, and check against the new filter – the arrow should point in the direction of fuel flow (towards the front of the car).
5 Undo the clamp bolt and slide the filter from the mounting bracket **(see illustration)**.
6 Fit the new filter into position, with the flow marking arrow correctly orientated. The arrow on the filter must also align with the mark on the mounting bracket. With the filter located in the mounting, insert and tighten the clamp bolt.
7 Reconnect the fuel hoses using new clips if necessary, ensuring they are fitted to their original positions. The connections are marked to indicated the fitting locations:

   RL = Return pipe
   VL = Fuel supply from tank
   MOTOR = Supply to engine
   E = Breather

Ensure that no dirt is allowed to enter the hoses or filter connections. Remove the hose clamps (where fitted).

Turbocharged models

8 As the fuel injection system on these models is not equipped with a return pipe from the fuel rail, it is now necessary to bleed the system as described on Section 5.

 Warning: Dispose the old filter safely; it will be highly flammable, and may explode if thrown on a fire.

4.3 Depress the tabs and disconnect the fuel pipes from each end of the filter (arrowed)

4.5 Undo the filter clamp bolt (arrowed)

5 Fuel system bleeding

1 Because the fuel injection system fitted to turbocharged models is not equipped with a return pipe from the fuel rail in the engine compartment, it is necessary to bleed the system after disconnecting any part of the pressurised fuel circuit. The bleed point is located at the rear of the fuel rail in the engine compartment. Due to the risk of damage to the catalytic converter, the engine must not be started until the fuel system has been bled. Prise out the caps, undo the nuts, and remove the plastic cover from the top of the engine.

2 Remove the protective cap from the end of the fuel rail (see illustration).

3 A special Audi tool (1318/21) may be available which attaches to the valve on the end of the fuel rail, depresses the pin in the valve, and allows the flow of fuel/air to be observed. In the absence of the special tool, position rags around the valve, then use a screwdriver to depress the pin in the centre of the valve (see illustration). Note that the fuel will emerge under some pressure. Take steps to reduce any possible fuel spray/spillage by the use of absorbent cloths, etc.

4 Turn the ignition on. The fuel pump will run for a few seconds. As soon as fuel emerges that is free of air bubbles, turn the ignition off. The system is now bled.

6 Fuel pump and gauge sender unit – testing, removal and refitting

Note: Observe the precautions in Section 1 before working on fuel system components.

Testing

1 Refer to Chapter 11, and remove the trim from the load space floor (Saloon models) or both rear luggage compartment side trims and the floor tray (Avant models). Slacken and remove the access hatch screws and lift the hatch away from the floorpan.

2 Disconnect the wiring connector from the pump/sender unit, then connect a hand-held multimeter to the middle two contacts in the sender/pump unit socket. With the float arm at its lower stop position (empty tank) the resistance should be approximately 65 ohms (vehicles up to 06/2001) or 300 to 310 ohms (vehicles from 06/2001). With the float arm at its upper stop position (full tank) the resistance should be approximately 275 ohms (vehicles up to 06/2001) or 53.5 to 590 ohms (vehicles from 06/2001). Note that these specifications are for the sender fitted in the tank. If the unit has been removed, the float arm will be able to travel further. The specifications for the sender when removed are 45 ohms (lower) and 295 ohms (upper) – models up to 06/2001, and 271 to 296 ohms (lower) and 55 to 69 ohms (upper) – models from 06/2001.

5.2 Unscrew the cap from the valve (arrowed)

Removal

Caution: The fuel tank must not be more than half full when carrying out this work, and ideally, nearly empty.

3 The fuel pump and gauge sender unit are combined in one assembly, mounted in the fuel tank. Access is via a hatch provided in the load space floor. Removal of the unit exposes the contents of the tank to the atmosphere, so extreme care must be exercised to prevent fire. The area inside and around the car must be well-ventilated to prevent a build-up of fuel fumes. If possible, remove the unit when the fuel tank is nearly empty, or alternatively syphon the fuel from the tank into a suitable container.

4 Ensure that the vehicle is parked on a level surface, then disconnect the battery negative (earth) lead (see Chapter 5A), and depressurise the fuel system as described in Section 8.

5 Refer to Chapter 11, Section 33, and remove

6.6 Undo the screws and lift away the access hatch

6.8 Using a home-made tool to unscrew the plastic support ring

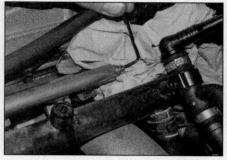

5.3 Use a tool to depress the pin in the centre of the valve

the trim from the load space floor (Saloon models) or both luggage compartment side trim panels and the floor tray (Avant models).

6 Slacken and remove the access hatch screws and lift the hatch away from the floorpan (see illustration), then unplug the wiring connector from the pump/sender unit.

7 Place rags beneath the fuel hoses to catch spilt fuel. Depress the retaining tabs and disconnect the fuel supply and return hoses (see illustration). Mark/Identify each hose for position.

8 Note the location of the arrows and support ring, then unscrew the plastic ring securing the pump/sender unit in the tank. Audi technicians use a special tool to unscrew the ring, however a home-made equivalent will suffice. Alternatively use a pair of large water pump pliers (see illustration).

9 Pull the flange upwards and sideways until the aperture seal can be removed (see illustration).

6.7 Depress the tab and disconnect the fuel hoses

6.9 Pull the flange upwards and remove the seal (arrowed)

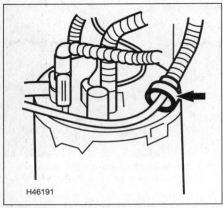

6.10 **Reach down and disconnect the auxiliary heater suction pipe connection (arrowed)**

10 On models from 02/2003 with an auxiliary heater, reach down alongside the delivery unit, depress the release tab and disconnect the suction pipe for the auxiliary heater **(see illustration)**.

11 On all models, reach down between the flange and the tank aperture, and squeeze together the retaining tabs and release the suction jet pump from the fuel delivery unit **(see illustration)**.

12 Pull the suction jet pump upwards, and disconnect it from the supply pipe **(see illustration)**.

13 Remove the suction jet pump and fuel pump/sender unit from the tank. Take great care not to bend or damage the sender unit float and arm as they are removed from the tank.

14 Inspect the float on the sender unit swinging arm for punctures and fuel ingress, and renew it if it appears damaged. Inspect the rubber seal from the fuel tank aperture and renew it if necessary. Inspect the sender unit wiper and track; clean off any dirt and debris that may have accumulated and look for breaks in the track.

Refitting

15 Refitting is a reversal of removal, noting the following points:

a) Renew the fuel tank aperture seal if necessary, and refit it dry.

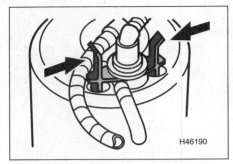

6.11 **Squeeze together the retaining tabs and release the suction jet pump (arrowed)**

b) Do not bend the float arm during refitting.
c) Ensure all hoses are securely reconnected to their original positions.
d) The arrow on the flange must align with the arrow on the fuel tank **(see illustration)**
e) Tighten the support ring to its original position using the arrows/marks noted on removal.
f) Reconnect the battery as described in Chapter 5A.

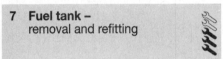

7 Fuel tank – removal and refitting

Note: Observe the precautions in Section 1 before working on fuel system components.

Removal

1 Before the tank can be removed, it must be drained of as much fuel as possible. As no drain plug is provided, it is preferable to remove the tank when it is nearly empty. Alternatively, syphon or hand-pump the fuel from the tank into a suitable safe container.

2 Disconnect the battery negative (earth) lead (see Chapter 5A).

3 Refer to Chapter 11, Section 33, and remove the trim from the load space floor (Saloon models) or the left-hand side luggage compartment side trim panel and floor tray (Avant models).

4 Slacken and remove the access hatch screws and lift the hatch away from the floorpan.

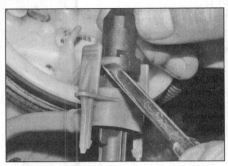

6.12 **Depress the tab and disconnect the suction jet pump from the supply pipe**

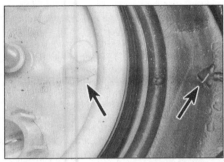

6.15 **The arrow on the flange must align with the arrow on the tank**

5 Unplug the wiring connector from the pump/sender unit. **Do not** disconnect the fuel supply and return hoses as they are disconnected later on the underbody in front of the fuel tank. However, working through the floor aperture, disconnect the breather pipe **(see illustration)**.

6 Chock the front wheels, then jack up the rear of the vehicle and support on axle stands (see Jacking and vehicle support). Remove the right-hand rear roadwheel.

7 Open the fuel tank filler flap and wipe clean the area around the filler neck. Unclip the 'loop' from the flap, then lever off the retaining ring and push the rubber cup inwards from the body panel **(see illustrations)**.

8 Remove the right-hand rear wheel arch liner with reference to Chapter 11.

9 Disconnect the breather pipe from the filler neck assembly, then undo the filler neck retaining bolt **(see illustrations)**.

7.5 **Depress the tab and disconnect the breather pipe**

7.7a **Lever out the retaining ring . . .**

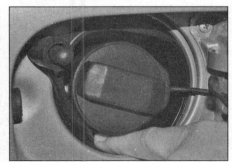

7.7b **. . . and push the rubber cup inwards**

7.9a Squeeze together the sides of the collar and disconnect the breather hose . . .

7.9b . . . then undo the retaining bolt

7.14 Disconnect the fuel supply, return and breather pipes from in front of the fuel tank

10 Working underneath the vehicle, release the fasteners and remove the panels from under the fuel tank and fuel cooler (where fitted).

11 Remove the rear section of the exhaust system as described in Chapter 4D.

12 Remove the rear axle assembly as described in Chapter 10.

13 Unclip the handbrake cable from the front-right-hand side of the fuel tank.

14 Depress the release tabs, and disconnect the fuel supply pipe from the filter, and the return and breather pipes **(see illustration)**. On models with an auxiliary heater, disconnect the pipe leading to the metering pump. Plug all openings to prevent contamination.

15 Support the fuel tank with a trolley jack and piece of wood.

16 Mark the positions of the support straps to ensure correct refitting, then unbolt and remove them **(see illustrations)**. Note the position of the earth cable filler neck.

17 With the help of an assistant, lower the fuel tank to the ground and remove from under the vehicle.

18 If the tank is contaminated with sediment or water, remove the fuel pump/sender unit (see Section 6) and swill the tank out with clean fuel. The tank is injection moulded from a synthetic material and if damaged, it should be renewed. However, in certain cases it may be possible to have small leaks or minor damage repaired by a suitable specialist.

Refitting

19 Refitting is the reverse of the removal procedure noting the following points:

a) When lifting the tank back into position take care to ensure none of the hoses get trapped between the tank and vehicle underbody.

b) Ensure that all pipes and hoses are correctly routed and secured.

c) It is important that the earth cable is correctly refitted to the strap and filler neck. Connect an ohmmeter between the metal ring on the filler neck and a bare metal part of the body, and check that the reading is zero resistance.

d) Tighten the tank retaining strap bolts.

e) On completion, refill the tank with fuel

and thoroughly check for signs of leakage prior to taking the vehicle out on the road.

f) Reconnect the battery as described in Chapter 5A.

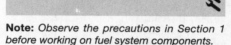

8 Fuel injection system – depressurisation

Note: *Observe the precautions in Section 1 before working on fuel system components.*

⚠️ **Warning: The following procedure will merely relieve the pressure in the fuel system – remember that fuel will still be present in the system components and take precautions accordingly before disconnecting any of them. Before working on the fuel system components, it is recommended that fuse 28 is removed, otherwise the fuel pump can be activated by the door contact switch.**

1 The fuel system referred to in this Section consists of the tank-mounted fuel pump and sender, the fuel filter, the fuel rail and injectors, and the metal pipes and flexible hoses of the fuel lines between these components. All these contain fuel which will be under pressure while the engine is running, while the ignition is switched on, or if a door contact switch is operated. The pressure will remain for some time after the ignition has been switched off and must be relieved before any of these components are disturbed for servicing work.

2 Disconnect the battery negative (earth) lead (see Chapter 5A).

3 Open the fuel filler flap and briefly remove

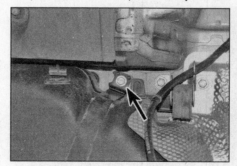

7.16a Fuel tank strap bolts at the front (arrowed) . . .

the filler cap to relieve any pressure in the fuel tank. Refit the cap.

4 Where applicable, undo the retaining fasteners and remove the engine top cover.

5 Place some cloth rags beneath the fuel supply pipe union located over the fuel rail on the intake manifold. Also wrap a cloth around the union.

6 Using two spanners, loosen the union nut and release the fuel pressure. Leave the union nut loose and the rags in position while working on the fuel system.

7 On completion of the work, tighten the union nut using the two spanners.

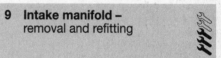

9 Intake manifold – removal and refitting

Note: *Observe the precautions in Section 1 before working on fuel system components.*

Removal

1 Where applicable, undo the retaining bolts, and remove the engine top cover(s).

2 Drain the cooling system as described in Chapter 1A. Alternatively on non-turbo models, fit hose clamps to the two hoses leading to the throttle body.

Turbocharged models

3 Release the clips, and disconnect the coolant hoses from the metal coolant pipe above the intake manifold. Undo the 2 retaining bolts and remove the coolant pipe **(see illustration)**.

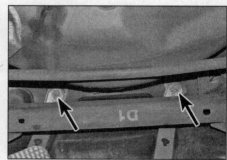

7.16b . . . and rear of the tank (arrowed)

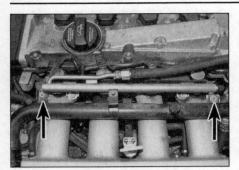

9.3 Coolant pipe retaining bolts (arrowed)

9.4 Note their positions, then disconnect the vacuum hoses from the intake manifold

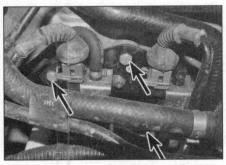

9.7 Viewed from underneath the intake manifold, undo the air recirculation valve and secondary air injection plate bolts (arrowed)

4 Note their fitted positions, and disconnect the various vacuum hoses from the intake manifold **(see illustration)**.

5 Slacken the clip and disconnect the air intake hose from the intake manifold **(see illustration 3.21)**.

6 Disconnect the wiring plugs from the throttle body/control unit and intake air temperature sensor.

7 Undo the 3 retaining bolts and remove the turbocharger air recirculation valve (where applicable) and secondary air injection plate from the underside of the manifold **(see illustration)**. There is no need to disconnect the vacuum pipes or wiring plugs – move the plate to one side.

8 Undo the bolts and remove the intake manifold support bracket.

9 Disconnect the wiring plug from the camshaft position Hall sender, then undo the fuel rail retaining bolts, and remove the fuel rail, complete with injectors and wiring harness. Lay the assembly clear of the manifold. Cover the injectors to prevent contamination.

10 Pull out the engine oil level dipstick, then undo the bolt and remove the dipstick guide tube bracket.

11 Undo the retaining nuts/bolts and remove the manifold from the cylinder head. Recover the gasket, and plug the ports in the cylinder head to prevent dirt ingress.

Non-turbocharged models

12 Release the retaining clips and disconnect

the air intake pipe from between the air cleaner and the throttle body intake duct.

13 Undo the retaining bolt, release the clip and remove the intake duct from the throttle body.

14 Disconnect the vacuum hose from the fuel pressure regulator **(see illustration 3.64)**.

15 Release the clips, disconnect the coolant hoses, then undo the bolts and remove the metal coolant hose from the top of the manifold **(see illustration)**.

16 Note their fitted positions, then disconnect the various vacuum hoses from the manifold.

17 Disconnect the wiring plug and coolant hose from the throttle body/control unit.

18 Note its fitted position then disconnect the charcoal canister solenoid valve vacuum hose.

19 Disconnect the wiring plugs from the intake air temperature sensor, and the variable intake manifold changeover valve **(see illustration)**.

20 Disconnect the camshaft position Hall sender wiring plug.

21 Undo the 2 retaining bolts, and remove the fuel rail, complete with injectors and wiring harness. Lay the assembly to one side, and cover to prevent dirt ingress.

22 Pull out the oil level dipstick, then undo the bolt and remove the dipstick guide tube.

23 Undo the nuts/bolts securing the manifold flange to the cylinder head, and the nuts securing the manifold to the support brackets. Remove the intake manifold.

24 The manifold is fitted with rubber connecting boots between the manifold and the manifold flange. If necessary, release the retaining clips and ease the manifold from the connecting boots. If split or damaged, the boots must be renewed.

25 Although the variable intake manifold vacuum control element and/or control solenoid can be removed with the intake manifold in place (by disconnecting the vacuum hoses, disconnecting the wiring plug and unscrewing the retaining screws), in order to remove the changeover barrel the intake manifold must be removed **(see illustration opposite)**.

Refitting

26 Refitting is the reverse of the removal procedure noting the following points:
  a) Clean the contact faces of the intake manifold, flange and cylinder head, and fit new gaskets.
  b) Tighten nuts and bolts to the specified torque.
  c) Refill/top-up the cooling system with reference to Chapter 1A.
  d) Reconnect the battery as described in Chapter 5A.

10 Fuel injection system – testing and adjustment

1 If a fault appears in the fuel injection system first ensure that all the system wiring connectors are securely connected and free of corrosion. Then ensure that the fault is not due to poor maintenance; ie, check that the air cleaner filter element is clean, the spark plugs are in good condition and correctly gapped, the cylinder compression pressures are correct, the ignition system wiring is in good condition and securely connected and the engine breather hoses are clear and undamaged, referring to Chapters 1A, 2A and 5B.

2 If these checks fail to reveal the cause of the problem the vehicle should be taken to an Audi dealer or specialist for testing. A diagnostic connector, located under the driver's side of the facia **(see illustration)**, into

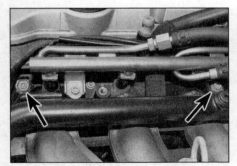

9.15 Coolant rail bolts (arrowed)

9.19 Disconnect the intake air temperature sensor and intake manifold changeover valve wiring plugs (arrowed)

which dedicated electronic test equipment can be plugged. The test equipment is capable of 'interrogating' the engine management system ECM electronically and accessing its internal fault log (reading fault codes).

3 Fault codes can only be extracted from the ECM using a dedicated fault code reader. An Audi dealer will obviously have such a reader, but they are also available from other suppliers. It is unlikely to be cost-effective for the private owner to purchase a fault code reader, but a well-equipped local garage or auto-electrical specialist will have one.

4 Using this equipment, faults can be pin-pointed quickly and simply, even if their occurrence is intermittent. Testing all the system components individually in an attempt to locate the fault by elimination is a time-consuming operation that is unlikely to be fruitful (particularly if the fault occurs dynamically), and carries a high risk of damage to the ECM's internal components.

5 Experienced home mechanics equipped with an accurate tachometer and a carefully-calibrated exhaust gas analyser may be able to check the exhaust gas CO content and the engine idle speed; if these are found to be out of specification, then the vehicle must be taken to a suitably-equipped Audi dealer or specialist for assessment. Neither the air/fuel mixture (exhaust gas CO content) nor the engine idle speed are manually adjustable; incorrect test results indicate the need for maintenance (possibly, injector cleaning) or a fault within the fuel injection system.

6 The engine management ECM communicates with the other control units fitted to the vehicle via a network known as a Databus. Do not attempt to 'back probe' connectors with a multimeter in the traditional manner, without first identifying the Databus wires.

11 Turbocharger – general information, removal and refitting

General information

1 The water-cooled turbocharger is mounted directly on the exhaust manifold. Lubrication is provided by an oil supply pipe that runs from the engine oil filter mounting. Oil is returned to the sump via a return pipe that connects to the side of the sump. The wastegate incorporates several internal vanes connected to a control ring; controlled by a vacuum actuator diaphragm by the engine management ECM in order to vary the boost pressure applied to the intake manifold **(see illustrations overleaf)**.

2 The turbocharger's internal components rotate at a very high speed, and as such are very sensitive to contamination; a great deal of damage can be caused by small particles of dirt, particularly if they strike the delicate turbine blades.

Caution: Thoroughly clean the area around all oil pipe unions before disconnecting them, to

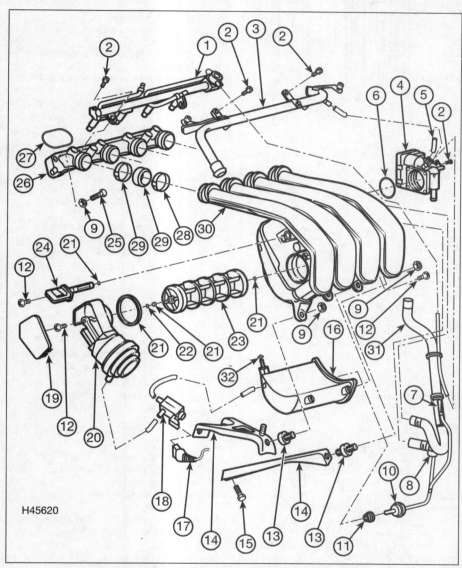

H45620

9.25 Variable manifold components – 2.0 litre engine

1 Fuel rail with injectors	12 Bolt	23 Changeover roller
2 Coolant pipe mounting bolts	13 Rubber mounting	24 Intake air temperature sensor
3 Coolant pipe	14 Intake manifold support	25 Clamp bolt
4 Throttle body/control unit	15 Support retaining bolt	26 Intake connecting pipe
5 From charcoal canister solenoid valve	16 Vacuum reservoir	27 Seal
6 Seal	17 Wiring connector	28 Clip
7 Vacuum booster	18 Intake manifold changeover valve	29 Connecting gaiters
8 Non-return valve	19 Cover	30 Intake manifold
9 Rubber mounting nut	20 Vacuum control element	31 From crankcase breather valve
10 Non-return valve	21 O-ring	32 Rubber bush
11 Gasket	22 Spring	

10.2 Diagnostic connector (arrowed)

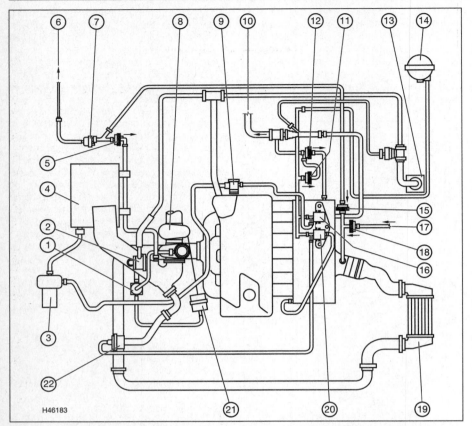

11.1a Turbocharger boost and vacuum control – vehicles up to 06/2002

1 Boost pressure control solenoid valve
2 Crankcase breather system pressure control valve
3 Secondary air injection pump
4 Air cleaner
5 Non return valve – arrow shows flow direction
6 To charcoal canister
7 Charcoal canister solenoid valve
8 Turbocharger
9 Secondary air injection combination valve
10 To brake servo
11 Non return valve – arrow shows flow direction
12 Non return valve – arrow shows flow direction
13 Crankcase breather
14 Vacuum reservoir
15 Non return valve – arrow shows flow direction
16 Secondary air injection inlet valve
17 Fuel system diagnostic pump (USA only)
18 Non return valve (USA only)
19 Intercooler
20 Turbocharger air recirculation valve
21 Boost pressure control vacuum unit
22 Mechanical air recirculation valve

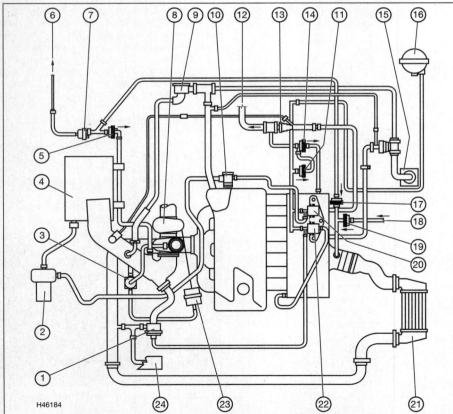

11.1b Turbocharger boost and vacuum control – vehicles from 07/2002

1 Mechanical air recirculation valve
2 Secondary air injection pump
3 Boost pressure control solenoid valve
4 Air cleaner
5 Non return valve – arrow shows flow direction
6 To charcoal canister
7 Charcoal canister solenoid valve
8 Turbocharger
9 Crankcase breather system pressure control valve
10 Secondary air injection combination valve
11 Non return valve – arrow shows flow direction
12 To brake servo
13 Vacuum booster
14 Non return valve – arrow shows flow direction
15 Crankcase breather
16 Vacuum reservoir
17 Non return valve – arrow shows flow direction
18 Fuel system diagnostic pump (USA only)
19 Non return valve (USA only)
20 Secondary air injection inlet valve
21 Intercooler
22 Turbocharger air recirculation valve
23 Boost pressure control vacuum unit
24 Resonator

11.5 Turbocharger support bracket (1) and oil return pipe (2)

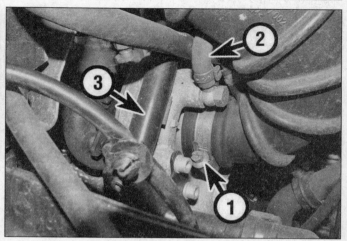

11.8 Turbocharger intake hose clip (1), coolant return hose (2) and secondary air pipe (3)

prevent the ingress of dirt. Store dismantled components in a sealed container to prevent contamination. Cover the turbocharger air intake ducts to prevent debris entering, and clean using lint-free cloths only.

Removal

3 Apply the handbrake, then jack up the front of the vehicle and support it on axle stands (see *Jacking and vehicle support*). Remove the engine compartment undershield.
4 Remove the engine top cover where applicable.
5 Undo the bolts and remove the turbocharger support bracket **(see illustration)**.
6 Undo the bolts securing the oil return pipe to the underside of the turbocharger, and position the pipe to one side **(see illustration 11.3)**. Recover the gasket.
7 Remove the air cleaner as described in Section 2.
8 Slacken the clip and disconnect the air intake hose from the turbocharger **(see illustration)**.
9 Undo the union securing the oil supply pipe to the turbocharger **(see illustration)**.
10 Disconnect the hose from the boost pressure regulating valve vacuum unit on the turbocharger.

11 Undo the bolts and remove the heat shield from the secondary air pipe and cylinder head.
12 Clamp off the coolant return hose, then disconnect it from the turbocharger **(see illustration 11.6)**.
13 Release the clips, undo the bolts, and remove the secondary air pipe **(see illustration 11.6)**.
14 Clamp off the hose, unscrew the union, and disconnect the coolant supply pipe from the top of the turbocharger **(see illustration 11.7)**.
15 Undo the nuts securing the catalytic converter/exhaust pipe to the turbocharger. Discard the nuts, new ones must be fitted.
16 Undo the retaining bolts, and detach the turbocharger from the manifold. Manoeuvre the turbocharger from the engine compartment, taking great care not to bend the exhaust flexible coupling more than 10°, or it will be damaged. Discard the gasket.

Refitting

17 Refit the turbocharger by following the removal procedure in reverse, noting the following points:
 a) *Renew all gaskets.*
 b) *Renew all self-locking nuts.*
 c) *Coat the turbocharger mounting bolts with high-temperature grease.*
 d) *Before tightening the turbocharger mounting bolts, refit the coolant supply hose bracket loosely to the boost pressure regulating valve vacuum unit, and tighten the banjo bolt to 35 Nm (26 lbf ft) – then tighten the bracket.*
 e) *Before reconnecting the oil supply pipe, fill the oil gallery in the turbocharger with fresh oil using an oil can.*
 f) *Tighten all nuts and bolts to the specified torque where given.*
 g) *When the engine is started after refitting, allow it to idle for approximately one minute to give the oil time to circulate around the turbine shaft bearings.*
 h) *Top-up and bleed the cooling system with reference to Chapter 1A.*

12 Intercooler – removal and refitting

Removal

1 Apply the handbrake, then jack up the front of the vehicle and support it on axle stands (see *Jacking and vehicle support*). Remove the engine compartment undershield.
2 The intercooler is located on the left-hand side of the engine compartment, and access to it is achieved by moving the complete front panel (the lock carrier assembly) away from the front of the car as far as possible, but without disconnecting the radiator hoses or electrical wiring – into the Service position. This procedure is described in Chapter 11.
3 Unclip and intercooler air duct **(see illustration)**.
4 Disengage the refrigerant pipe from the bracket at the base of the intercooler **(see illustration)**.
5 Disconnect the wiring plug from the sensor at the top of the intercooler **(see illustration 3.56)**.
6 Loosen the clips and disconnect the top,

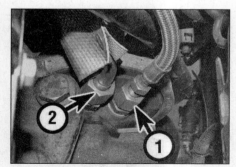

11.9 Turbocharger oil supply pipe union (1) and coolant supply pipe (2)

12.3 Unclip the intercooler air duct

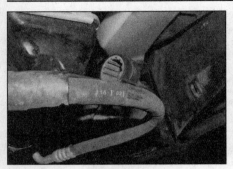

12.4 Detach the refrigerant pipe from the bracket at the base of the intercooler

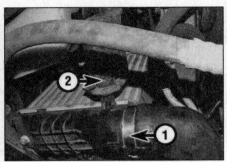

12.6 Intercooler bottom hose clip (1) and lower mounting grommet (2)

and bottom hoses from the intercooler **(see illustration)**.

7 Pull the bottom of the intercooler out from the mounting grommet, then unhook it from the upper mounting grommets **(see illustration 12.6)**. If necessary, remove the grommets from the mounting bracket.

Refitting

8 Refitting is a reversal of removal.

Chapter 4 Part B:
Fuel system –
direct petrol injection (FSI) models

Contents

Section number

Air cleaner and intake ducts – removal and refitting 2
Engine management components – removal and refitting. 3
Fuel filter – renewal. 4
Fuel injection system – depressurisation 8
Fuel injection system – testing and adjustment 10

Section number

Fuel pump and gauge sender unit – testing, removal and refitting . . 6
Fuel tank – removal and refitting 7
General information and precautions. 1
High-pressure pump – removal and refitting 5
Intake manifold – removal and refitting 9

Degrees of difficulty

Easy, suitable for novice with little experience		Fairly easy, suitable for beginner with some experience	Fairly difficult, suitable for competent DIY mechanic	Difficult, suitable for experienced DIY mechanic	Very difficult, suitable for expert DIY or professional	

Specifications

General
Engine code*:
  1984 cc, Bosch Motronic MED7.1, 110 kW (143 bhp) . . . . AWA
* **Note:** *See 'Vehicle identification' for the location of the code marking on the engine.*

Recommended fuel
Minimum octane rating. . . . . 95 RON unleaded
                                                    (91 RON unleaded may be used, but with reduced performance)

Fuel system data
Fuel pump type:
  Low-pressure pump . . . . Electric, immersed in fuel tank
  High-pressure pump. . . . . Mechanical, single piston, camshaft driven
Fuel pressure:
  Supplied to high-pressure pump at idle speed . . . . 6.0 bar (approximately)
  High pressure circuit:
    At idle speed. . . . . 39.0 bar (approximately)
    Maximum . . . . 110.0 bar (approximately)
Engine idle speed (non-adjustable, electronically-controlled) . . . . 640 to 800 rpm

Torque wrench settings

	Nm	lbf ft
Accelerator pedal/sensor	10	7
Air cleaner	10	7
Camshaft position Hall sensor	10	7
Coolant pipe to intake manifold	10	7
Engine speed sensor	10	7
Exhaust gas temperature sensor	45	33
Fuel pressure sensor	22	6
Fuel pump/sender unit ring	60	44
Fuel rail to intake manifold	10	7
Fuel tank filler neck	25	18
Fuel tank mounting bolts	25	18
Intake air temperature sensor	5	4
Intake manifold support brackets	20	15
Intake manifold nuts	10	7
High-pressure fuel pipe banjo bolts*	40	30
High-pressure pump bolts	10	7
Low-pressure fuel pipe banjo bolts*	18	13
Low-fuel pressure sensor	22	16
NOx sensor	63	46
Oil return pipe to turbocharger	10	7
Oil supply pipe to turbocharger	30	22
Oxygen sensor	55	41
Throttle body to EGR valve:		
Stage 1	5	4
Stage 2	Angle-tighten a further 180°	

Do not re-use

1 General information and precautions

General information

The direct injection systems described in this Chapter are self-contained engine management systems, which control both the fuel injection and ignition. This Chapter deals with the fuel system components only; refer to Chapter 5B for details of the ignition system.

The fuel injection system consists of a fuel tank, an electric fuel pump within the tank, a fuel filter, fuel supply lines, a throttle body, an air mass sensor, a camshaft-driven high-pressure pump, a fuel rail and four electronic injectors, a fuel pressure regulator, and an electronic control module (ECM), together with its associated sensors, actuators and wiring. The component layout varies according to the system.

The FSI (Fuel Stratified Injection) direct injection system differs from the traditional indirect systems in that the fuel is injected directly in the combustion chamber as opposed to into the intake manifold. The injection point is accurately controlled to maximise engine output, whilst minimising emissions. The combustion process can be operated in three different modes: Stratified charge mode, Homogenous lean charge mode, and Homogenous (evenly spread) mode. At low-to-medium engine loads the engine operates in Stratified charge mode, where fuel is only injected into the area around the spark plug in the centre of the combustion chamber during the compression stroke, resulting in an extremely lean mixture of lambda 1.6 to 3.0. In this mode the fuel is injected towards the piston crown, which is shaped in such a way that the fuel is directed upwards to the spark plug. At high engine speeds and loads the engine runs in Homogenous charge mode, which is the traditional method of injecting fuel during the intake piston stroke, and a resulting lambda value of 1.0. The transition zone between the two modes is known as Homogenous lean charge mode, where fuel is injected during the intake stroke, but is regulated by the ECM in such a way that the lambda value is approximately 1.55.

The engine has a variable geometry intake manifold, where the length of the intake track is varied to emphasise the torque or power characteristics of the engine dependant on engine speed and load, etc. The intake path is controlled by a vacuum-operated valve which can operate in one of two positions. At low engine speed/high torque the valve position forces the incoming air through a long intake track, thus increasing the torque output and low speed driveability. At high engine speed/high power the valve position forces the incoming air through a short intake track, thus increasing the power output and throttle response. The vacuum supply to the valve is controlled by the engine management ECM.

All models are equipped with an electronically-controlled throttle system referred to as Electronic Power Control (EPS). A sensor on the accelerator pedal informs the engine management ECM of the position and rate-of-change of the pedal, which then determines the optimum position for the throttle valve in the throttle body. There is no accelerator pedal is transmitted to the engine control unit by two variable resistors, and the throttle valve is operated by an electric motor on the throttle body. When the engine is stopped but the ignition is switched on, the throttle valve moves exactly as dictated by the throttle pedal, however, when the engine is running, the control unit can open or close the throttle valve independently. The control unit calculates the most efficient opening of the throttle valve according to a number of parameters, so it is possible under certain conditions that the throttle valve may be completely open even though the pedal is only depressed half-way.

The air mass sensor is located on the air cleaner outlet to the throttle body. Fuel is supplied under pressure to a high-pressure pump, where it is further pressurised, and delivered to the fuel rail, and then passes to four electronic injectors. The duration of the injection period is determined by the ECM which switches the injectors on and off as required.

The ECM controls starting and warm-up enrichment together with idle speed regulation and lambda control. Idle speed control is achieved partly by an electronic throttle valve positioning module, on the side of the throttle body and partly by the ignition system. Manual adjustment of the idle speed is not possible.

Intake air is drawn into the engine through the air cleaner, which contains a renewable paper filter element.

The exhaust gas oxygen content is constantly monitored by the ECM via oxygen sensors either side of the catalytic converter. The ECM then uses this information to adjust the air/fuel ratio. Manual adjustment of the idle speed exhaust CO content is not possible. A NOx sensor is also fitted downstream of the converter. A fuel evaporative control system is also fitted, and the ECM controls the operation of the activated charcoal canister – refer to Chapter 4D for further details.

It should be noted that fault diagnosis of all the engine management systems described in this Chapter is only possible with dedicated electronic test equipment. Problems with the system operation should therefore be referred to an Audi dealer or engine management specialist for assessment. Once the fault has been identified, the removal and refitting sequences detailed in the following Sections will then allow the appropriate component(s) to be renewed as required.

Precautions

⚠️ *Warning: Many of the procedures in this Chapter require the removal of fuel lines and connections, which may result in some fuel spillage. Before carrying out any operation on the fuel system, refer to the precautions given in 'Safety first!' at the beginning of this manual, and follow them implicitly. Always switch off the ignition before working on the fuel system. Petrol is a highly dangerous and volatile liquid, and the precautions necessary when handling it cannot be overstressed.*

Note: *Residual pressure will remain in the fuel lines long after the vehicle was last used. Before disconnecting any fuel line, first depressurise the fuel system as described in Section 8.*

Caution: Before working on the fuel system components, always remove the fuel pump fuse (no 28 in the passenger compartment fusebox), otherwise the fuel pump can be activated by the door contact switch.

2 Air cleaner and intake ducts – removal and refitting 🔧

Removal

1 Undo the 2 bolts and detach the intake ducting from the lock carrier, then detach the carbon canister purge valve from the ducting and pull the ducting from the top of the air cleaner housing **(see illustration)**.
2 Disconnect the airflow meter wiring plug.
3 Prise out the centre pin, then lever out the air cleaner top mounting **(see illustration)**.
4 Release the clamp and disconnect the air outlet pipe from the air cleaner.
5 Pull the air cleaner housing upwards from the engine compartment **(see illustration)**. If necessary remove the rubber mountings. Check the condition of the mountings and renew them if necessary.

2.1 Undo the ducting screws on the lock carrier (arrowed)

Refitting

6 Refitting is a reversal of removal.

3 Engine management components – removal and refitting 🔧

Note: *Observe the precautions in Section 1 before working on any component in the fuel system. The ignition must be switched off at all times.*

Airflow meter

Removal

1 The airflow meter is located in the intake ducting, downstream from the air filter housing.
2 Disconnect the airflow meter wiring plug.
3 Undo the 2 retaining screws and remove the air duct from the lock carrier panel **(see illustration 2.1)**.
4 Slacken the clip and disconnect the air hose from the airflow meter **(see illustration)**.
5 Undo the screws and pull the airflow meter from the housing **(see illustration)**.

Refitting

6 Refitting is a reversal of removal, but fit a new gasket or O-ring as applicable.

Throttle valve potentiometer

Note: *The potentiometer is an integral part of the throttle body and cannot be renewed separately.*

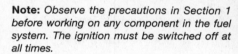

3.4 Use a pair of pipe grips to release the air duct clips

2.3 Prise out the centre pin and remove the mounting

2.5 Check the condition of the mounting rubbers (arrowed)

Throttle valve positioner

Note: *The throttle valve positioner is incorporated in the throttle body and is not available as a separate part.*

Coolant temperature sensor

7 One coolant temperature sensor is located on the rear of the cylinder head, and one is fitted to the radiator outlet pipe.

Engine mounted sensor removal

8 Drain approximately one quarter of the coolant from the engine with reference to Chapter 1A.
9 Disconnect the wiring from the sensor.
10 Extract the retaining clip and remove the sensor **(see illustration)**. Recover the sealing O-ring.

Radiator outlet sensor removal

11 Drain the cooling system as described in Chapter 1A.

3.5 Undo the two screws and remove the airflow meter

3.10 Prise out the clip (arrowed) and remove the coolant temperature sensor from the pipe at the rear of the cylinder head

12 Disconnect the sensor wiring plug **(see illustration)**.

13 Prise out the retaining clip, and pull the sensor from the outlet pipe.

Refitting

14 Refitting is a reversal of removal, but fit a new O-ring. Refer to Chapter 1A and top-up the cooling system.

Engine speed sensor

Removal

15 The engine speed sensor is mounted on the rear, left-hand side of the cylinder block, adjacent to the mating surface of the block and transmission bellhousing, just behind the oil filter **(see illustration)**.

16 If necessary, drain the engine oil and

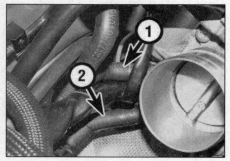

3.22 Disconnect the vacuum hose (1) and the coolant hose (2) from the throttle body

3.29 Disconnect the fuel supply and return hoses

3.12 The radiator outlet coolant temperature sensor (arrowed) is adjacent to the drain tap

remove the oil filter and cooler to improve access with reference to Chapter 1A.

17 Unplug the harness connector from the sensor.

18 Unscrew the retaining bolt and withdraw the sensor from the cylinder block.

Refitting

19 Refitting is a reversal of removal. Tighten the securing bolt to the specified torque.

Throttle body/control unit

Note: *In order for a new throttle body/control unit to function correctly, it must be matched to the engine management ECM using Audi diagnostic equipment (VAS 5051).*

Removal

20 Loosen the clips and detach the air ducting from the throttle body.

3.23 Undo the 4 Torx bolts (arrowed) and detach the throttle body from the manifold/EGR valve

3.30a Undo the banjo bolts and detach the pipes from the fuel rail (arrowed) . . .

3.15 The engine speed sensor is located just behind the oil filter housing, on the left-hand side of the engine block

21 Unplug the harness connector from the throttle body.

22 Note their fitted locations, disconnect the vacuum and coolant hoses (where fitted) from the throttle body **(see illustration)**. Where necessary release the wiring harness from the guide clip.

23 Unscrew and remove the securing Torx bolts, then lift the throttle body/control unit away from the intake manifold **(see illustration)**. Recover and discard the gasket.

24 Further dismantling of the throttle body is not recommended. It is unclear if any parts are available separately. If any part of the throttle body is defective, the completely assembly may need be renewed.

Refitting

25 Refitting is a reversal of removal, noting the following:
  a) Use a new throttle body-to-intake manifold seal.
  b) Ensure that all vacuum hoses, coolant hoses (where applicable) and electrical connectors are refitted securely.

Manifold flange/fuel rail

Removal

26 Disconnect the battery negative (earth) lead (see Chapter 5A). Pull the plastic cover on top of the engine upwards from its mountings.

27 Remove the intake manifold as described in Section 9.

28 If not already done, release the clip and remove the engine oil level dipstick guide tube.

29 Undo the union, release the clip and disconnect the fuel supply and return hoses **(see illustration)**.

30 Undo the banjo bolts, and the Allen screws, then remove the high-pressure and return fuel pipes from the manifold flange and fuel pump **(see illustrations)**. No washers are fitted. Discard the banjo bolts – new ones must be fitted.

31 Disconnect the manifold changeover flap motor wiring plug and the fuel pressure sensor wiring plug **(see illustrations)**.

32 Prise out the retaining clip, undo the

bolt and remove the oil separator **(see illustration)**.

33 Undo the nuts/bolts and remove the intake manifold flange, leaving the injectors in the cylinder head **(see illustration)**.

Refitting

34 Refitting is a reversal of removal, using a new manifold flange-to-cylinder head gasket **(see illustration)**.

Injectors

Removal

35 Remove the intake manifold flange/ fuel rail as described in this Section. Plug the open ends of the injectors to prevent contamination.

36 Disconnect the wiring plug from the relevant injector.

37 Use a screwdriver to bend the retaining tabs of the radial compensation element to one side, and pull the support ring from the injector **(see illustrations)**. Note that it's likely the tabs will break off from the radial compensation elements – renew them if this happens.

38 Carefully lever the injector from the cylinder head. If the injectors are reluctant to move, a slide hammer (Audi tool T10133) will be needed. This tool engages with a slot in the injector body, and pulls the injector from the cylinder head. Pull the injector from the cylinder head **(see illustration)**.

39 Remove the Teflon ring and O-ring seal from the injector body, then check the condition of the radial compensation ring, support ring and spacer ring – renew them if they show any

3.30b . . . and the fuel pump

3.31a Disconnect the intake manifold changeover motor wiring plug . . .

sign of damage **(see illustration)**. Note that the Teflon seal must be renewed regardless of its apparent condition – use a razor blade to cut the seal from position, ensuring that the injector groove surface is not scratched.

3.30c The pipe unions have a chamfer which locates in the fitting – no washers are fitted

3.31b . . . and the fuel pressure sensor wiring plug

If renewing the spacer ring, don't spread the ring to fit it – instead extend it slightly and 'screw' it into place **(see illustrations)**. Note that the flat face (non-stepped) of the spacer ring faces the O-ring.

3.32 Prise out the oil separator retaining clip (arrowed)

3.33 Undo the bolts/nuts and detach the manifold flange/fuel rail from the cylinder head

3.34 Fit a new gasket to the manifold flange

3.37a Bend the radial compensation element tabs outwards . . .

3.37b . . . and pull the support ring from the injector

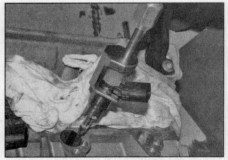

3.38 We used a slide hammer to pull the injectors from place

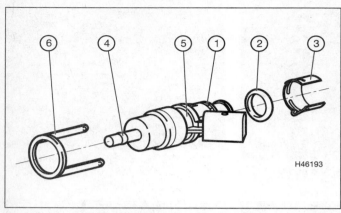

3.39a **Injector assembly**

1 *Spacer ring*
2 *O-ring*
3 *Support ring*
4 *Teflon ring*
5 *Removal groove*
6 *Radial compensation element*

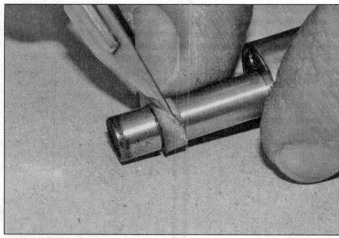

3.39b **Take great care not to mark the injector when cutting away the Teflon seal**

3.39c **'Screw' the new spacer ring into the injector**

3.41a **We used a cut-down sealant nozzle to spread the new Teflon seal . . .**

3.41b **. . . so that it slid onto the injector, and into the groove**

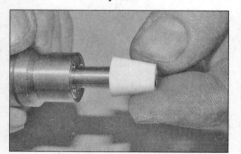

3.41c **Then we used another cut-down nozzle slid over the end of the injector to compress the seal into the groove**

3.44a **Fit the support ring over the injector . . .**

40 Carefully remove any combustion residue from the injector around the area of the Teflon ring groove and injector stem. Examine the condition of the ring groove. If it is damaged at all, the injector must be renewed.

Refitting

41 To renew the Teflon seal, Audi technicians use a number of special tools which spread the seal, and push it into place, and compress it into the groove afterwards. In the absence of these tools, it may be prudent to have the rings renewed by an Audi dealer or specialist. We managed to renew the seals using improvised tools fabricated from a couple of sealant tube nozzles **(see illustrations)**. Note that the seal must not be lubricated.

42 Use a nylon brush and a vacuum cleaner to thoroughly clean out the injector holes in the cylinder head. Take care not to let any debris fall into the combustion chamber.

43 Dip the new O-ring seal in clean engine oil then fit it to the end of the injector.

44 Fit the support ring onto the end of the injector, then clip the radial compensation element onto the support ring **(see illustrations)**.

45 Push the injector(s) into the hole in the cylinder head as far as it will go, ensure the electrical connector is correctly orientated. Note that the support web for the electrical

3.44b **. . . then fit the radial compensation element . . .**

3.44c **. . . and clip it to the support ring**

connector locates in a recess adjacent to the injector hole (see illustration).

46 With all the injectors refitted, the remainder of refitting is a reversal of removal. Note: *Remember to reconnect the injector wiring plugs before refitting the manifold flange.*

Camshaft position Hall sender

Removal

47 Release the clip and disconnect the wiring multiplug from the Hall sender (see illustration).
48 Unscrew the mounting bolt and withdraw the Hall sender from the front of the cylinder head. Recover the O-ring seal.

Refitting

49 Refitting is a reversal of removal, but renew the O-ring seal if it shows any sign of damage or deterioration, and tighten the mounting bolt to the specified torque.

Oxygen sensors

Removal

50 The two oxygen sensors are located at each end of the catalytic converter on the right-hand side of the engine. One is located on the front-top of the catalytic converter, and one on the rear-top of the catalytic converter (see illustrations). The catalytic converter is attached to the rear of the exhaust manifold.
51 The wiring connector for the oxygen sensors is located on the left-hand side of the engine, beneath the coolant expansion tank (see illustration). Undo the tank mounting screws and disconnect the low coolant wiring, then position the tank to one side. Do not disconnect any of the coolant hoses from the tank. Disconnect the oxygen sensor wiring and release the cables from the plastic ties.
52 Unscrew and remove the sensor, taking care to avoid damaging the sensor probe as it is removed. Note: *As the wiring flying lead remains connected to the sensor, a special slotted socket needs to be used to remove the sensor.*

Refitting

53 Apply a little anti-seize grease to the sensor threads, but avoid contaminating the probe tip. Note: *New oxygen sensors may be supplied with fitting paste on the threads.*
54 Refit the sensor and tighten it to the correct torque.
55 Reconnect the wiring and secure with the plastic ties.

Electronic control unit (ECM)

Caution: *The ECM is programmed and identified specifically for the vehicle it is fitted to, and the identity coding must be transferred to any new unit. This process requires the use of dedicated Audi diagnostic equipment VAS 5051. For this reason, it is recommended that ECM renewal is carried out by an Audi dealer or suitably-equipped specialist, however removal and refitting of the original ECM*

3.45 The electrical connector support web locates in a recess in the cylinder head (arrowed)

3.50a Pre-catalyst oxygen sensor . . .

3.51 Oxygen sensors wiring connectors (arrowed)

is possible by the home mechanic. Note also that if the ECM is renewed, the identification of the new ECM must be transferred to the immobiliser control unit by an Audi dealer or specialist.
Caution: *Always wait at least 30 seconds after switching off the ignition before disconnecting the wiring from the ECM. When the wiring is disconnected, all the learned values may be erased, although any contents of the fault memory are retained. After reconnecting the wiring, the vehicle must be driven for several miles so that the ECM can learn its basic settings. If the engine still runs erratically, the basic settings may be reinstated by an Audi dealer or specialist using a special test instrument.*

Removal

56 The electronic control unit is located

3.47 Disconnect the camshaft position Hall sender wiring plug (shown with the timing belt removed for clarity)

3.50b . . . and post-catalyst oxygen sensor (arrowed)

on the bulkhead at the rear of the engine compartment. On RHD models it is on the right-hand side, and on LHD models it is on the left-hand side.
57 Disconnect the battery negative (earth) lead (see Chapter 5A).
58 Pull of the rubber seal from the plenum chamber cover, then prise out the clips, and pull the cover forwards from place (see illustration).
59 Remove the wiper arms as described in Chapter 12.
60 Prise off the clips, and pull the scuttle trim panel upwards from the base of the windscreen (see illustrations).
61 Undo the screws and lift off the cover (see illustration).
62 Release the spring retainer with a screwdriver and lift up the electronic control unit (see illustration).
63 Pull out the locking catches and

3.58 Pull up the rubber seal (arrowed)

3.60a Prise off the 3 clips (arrowed – one at each end, one in the centre) . . .

3.60b . . . then pull the scuttle trim panel upwards

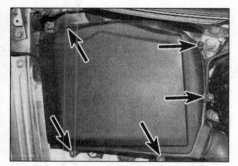

3.61 Undo the ECM cover screws (arrowed)

3.62 Use a screwdriver to release the ECM retaining clip

3.68 The manifold pressure/altitude/intake air temperature sensor is located on the front of the intake manifold

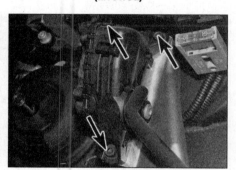

3.72 The accelerator pedal/position sensor is retained by 3 Allen screws (arrowed)

disconnect the wiring connectors from the ECM. **Note:** *On some models, the ECM is fitted into a protective metal housing. The housing is secured to the ECM with shear bolts, which are coated with thread-locking compound. In order to remove the bolts, heat them with a hot-air gun, and use self-grip pliers to undo the shear bolts.*

⚠️ **Warning: Wait a minimum of 30 seconds after switching off the ignition before disconnecting the ECM wiring connector.**

64 Withdraw the ECM from the bulkhead.

Refitting

65 Refitting is a reversal of removal, but press the clip down until it snaps into position. On ECMs with the metal housing, apply thread-locking compound to the shear bolts, then tighten the bolts until the heads shear off. Reconnect the battery as described in Chapter 5A. Note that the vehicle must be driven for several miles so that the ECM can learn its basic settings. In order to store its learnt values (and faults where present), the ECM continues to be supplied with voltage for up to 15 minutes. Once this period is finished, the ECM disconnects the earth path.

Intake manifold pressure/altitude/intake air temperature sensor

66 This sensor is located on the side of the intake manifold.
67 Disconnect the sensor wiring plug.

68 Undo the bolts and pull the sensor from the manifold **(see illustration).**
69 Refitting is a reversal of removal.

Accelerator pedal position sensor

Removal

70 Remove the driver's side storage compartment as described in Chapter 11.
71 Disconnect the sensor wiring plug.
72 Undo the 3 bolts and remove the pedal/sensor assembly **(see illustration).** Note that the sensor is not available separately from the pedal assembly.

Refitting

73 Refitting is a reversal of removal, remembering to tighten the retaining bolts to the specified torque. **Note:** *If the sensor has been renewed on vehicles with automatic*

4.3 Depress the clip and disconnect the hoses from the filter

transmission, the kick-down function must be adapted using Audi diagnostic equipment (VAS 5051). Entrust this task to an Audi dealer or suitably-equipped specialist.

4 Fuel filter – renewal

Note: *Observe the precautions in Section 1 before working on fuel system components.*
1 The fuel filter is situated underneath the rear of the vehicle, alongside the fuel tank. To gain access to the filter, chock the front wheels, then jack up the rear of the vehicle and support it securely on axle stands. Undo the fasteners and remove the plastic cover from below the filter.
2 If available, fit hose clamps to the filter intake and outlet hoses. These are not essential, but will reduce the amount of fuel spillage. Even with hose clamps fitted, the old filter will contain some fuel, so have some rags ready to soak up any spillage.
3 Wrap rags around the connections, then dissipate the fuel pressure by carefully depressing the release tabs and slowly disconnecting the fuel pipe connections to and from the filter **(see illustration).** If the fuel hoses show any sign of perishing or cracking, particularly at the hose ends or where the hose enters the metal end fitting, renew the hoses.
4 Before removing the filter, note the direction-of-flow marking on the filter body, and check against the new filter – the arrow should point

in the direction of fuel flow (towards the front of the car).

5 Undo the clamp bolt and slide the filter from the mounting bracket **(see illustration)**.

6 Fit the new filter into position, with the flow marking arrow correctly orientated. The arrow on the filter must also align with the mark on the mounting bracket **(see illustration)**. With the filter located in the mounting, insert and tighten the clamp bolt.

7 Reconnect the fuel hoses using new clips if necessary, ensuring they are fitted to their original positions. Ensure that no dirt is allowed to enter the hoses or filter connections. Remove the hose clamps (where fitted).

 Warning: Dispose the old filter safely; it will be highly flammable, and may explode if thrown on a fire.

5 High-pressure pump
– removal and refitting

Caution: The fuel system operates under high pressure. Before removing the pump it is essential that the system is depressurised as described in Section 8.

Removal

1 Pull up the plastic cover from the top of the engine, then disconnect the wiring plug for the fuel pressure regulating valve on the pump body **(see illustration)**.

2 Undo the unions and disconnect the fuel pipes from the pump **(see illustration 3.30b)**. **Note:** *Cover/plug the openings. It is absolutely essential that no dirt be allowed to enter the fuel system.*

3 Undo the 3 retaining Torx bolts and pull the pump from the cylinder head. If the sleeve remains in the cylinder head, carefully pull it from position **(see illustrations)**. No further dismantling of the pump is advised.

Refitting

4 Renew the sealing O-ring on the pump body, then refit the sleeve over the pump spring, fit the pump to the cylinder head **(see illustration)**. Tighten the Torx bolts to the specified torque.

5 Reconnect the fuel pipes to the pump using new banjo bolts, and tighten them to the specified torque.

6 Reconnect the wiring plugs.

6 Fuel pump and gauge sender unit –
testing, removal and refitting

Note: *Observe the precautions in Section 1 before working on fuel system components.*

Testing

1 Remove the carpet from the load space floor (Saloon models) or refer to Chapter 11 and remove the left-hand side luggage

4.5 Undo the clamp bolt (arrowed)

compartment side trim panel and anti-soiling tray (Avant models).

2 Slacken and remove the access hatch screws and lift the hatch away from the floorpan **(see illustration 6.9)**.

3 Disconnect the wiring connector from the pump/sender unit.

4 Connect a hand-held multimeter to the middle two contacts in the sender/pump unit socket. With the float arm at its lower stop position (empty tank) the resistance should be 300 to 310 ohms. With the float arm at its upper stop position (full tank) the resistance should be 53.5 to 590 ohms. Note that these specifications are for the sender fitted in the tank. If the unit has been removed, the float arm will be able to travel further. The specifications for the sender when removed are 271 to 296 ohms (lower) and 55 to 69 ohms (upper).

5.1 Disconnect the fuel pressure regulating valve wiring plug

5.3b Recover the sleeve from the cylinder head

4.6 Note the arrow indicates direction of flow

Removal

Caution: The fuel tank must not be more than half full when carrying out this work, and ideally, nearly empty.

5 The fuel pump and gauge sender unit are combined in one assembly, mounted in the fuel tank. Access is via a hatch provided in the load space floor. Removal of the unit exposes the contents of the tank to the atmosphere, so extreme care must be exercised to prevent fire. The area inside and around the car must be well-ventilated to prevent a build-up of fuel fumes. If possible, remove the unit when the fuel tank is nearly empty, or alternatively syphon the fuel from the tank into a suitable container.

6 Ensure that the vehicle is parked on a level surface, then disconnect the battery negative (earth) lead (see Chapter 5A).

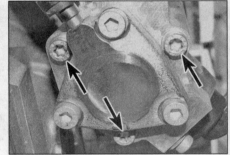

5.3a Undo the 3 Torx bolts on the underside of the pump (arrowed)

5.4 Renew the O-ring seal at the top of the pump

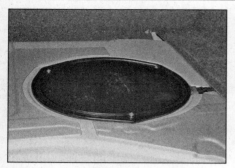

6.9 Undo the 3 screws and remove the access hatch from the floor

6.10 Depress the catch (arrowed) and disconnect the wiring plug

6.11 Depress the catch and disconnect the fuel lines

7 Depressurise the fuel system as described in Section 8.

8 Remove the carpet from the load space floor (Saloon models) or refer to Chapter 11, and remove the left-hand side luggage compartment side trim panel and anti-soiling tray (Avant models).

9 Slacken and remove the access hatch screws and lift the hatch away from the floorpan **(see illustration)**.

10 Unplug the wiring connector from the pump/sender unit **(see illustration)**.

11 Place rags beneath the fuel hoses to catch spilt fuel. Depress the retaining tabs and disconnect the fuel supply and return hoses **(see illustration)**. Mark/identify each hose for position. Note that on vehicles equipped with an auxiliary heater, a 3rd fuel pipe connection is made to the fuel sender/pump unit.

12 Make alignment marks between the plastic ring and the tank, then unscrew the

plastic ring securing the pump/sender unit in the tank. Audi technicians use a special tool to unscrew the ring, however a home-made equivalent will suffice. Alternatively use a pair of large water pump pliers **(see illustration)**.

13 Pull the flange upwards and sideways until the aperture seal can be removed **(see illustration)**.

14 On models from 02/2003 with an auxiliary heater, reach down alongside the delivery unit, depress the release tab and disconnect the suction pipe for the auxiliary heater **(see illustration)**.

15 On all models, reach down between the flange and the tank aperture, and squeeze together the retaining tabs and release the suction jet pump from the fuel delivery unit **(see illustration)**.

16 Pull the suction jet pump upwards, and disconnect it from the supply pipe **(see illustration)**.

17 Remove the suction jet pump and fuel pump/sender unit from the tank. Take great care not to bend or damage the sender unit float and arm as they are removed from the tank.

18 Inspect the float on the sender unit swinging arm for punctures and fuel ingress, and renew it if it appears damaged. Inspect the rubber seal from the fuel tank aperture and renew it if necessary. Inspect the sender unit wiper and track; clean off any dirt and debris that may have accumulated and look for breaks in the track.

Refitting

19 Refitting is a reversal of removal, noting the following points:

a) *Renew the fuel tank aperture seal if necessary, and refit it dry.*

b) *Do not bend the float arm during refitting.*

c) *Ensure all hoses are securely reconnected to their original positions.*

6.12 Using a home-made tool to unscrew the plastic ring

6.13 Pull the flange upwards to recover the seal

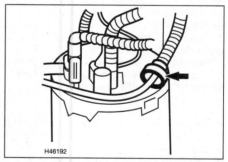

6.14 Depress the tab (arrowed) and disconnect the auxiliary heater suction pipe

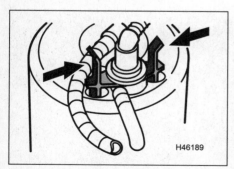

6.15 Squeeze together the tabs (arrowed) to release the suction pipe

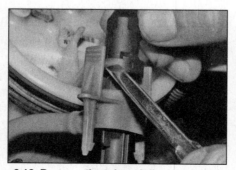

6.16 Depress the tab and disconnect the pipe from the fitting

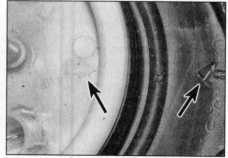

6.19 The arrow on the flange must align with the arrow on the tank (arrowed)

7.5 Depress the tab and disconnect the breather pipe

7.7a Lever out the retaining ring . . .

7.7b . . . and push the rubber cup inwards

d) The arrow on the flange must align with the arrow on the fuel tank (see illustration).

e) Tighten the support ring to its original position.

e) Reconnect the battery as described in Chapter 5A.

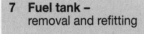

7 Fuel tank – removal and refitting

Note: Observe the precautions in Section 1 before working on fuel system components.

Removal

1 Before the tank can be removed, it must be drained of as much fuel as possible. As no drain plug is provided, it is preferable to remove the tank when it is nearly empty. Alternatively, syphon or hand-pump the fuel from the tank into a suitable safe container.

2 Disconnect the battery negative (earth) lead (see Chapter 5A).

3 Refer to Chapter 11, and remove the trim from the load space floor (Saloon models) or the left-hand side luggage compartment side trim panel and anti-soiling tray (Avant models).

4 Slacken and remove the access hatch screws and lift the hatch away from the floorpan (see illustration 6.9).

5 Unplug the wiring connector from the pump/sender unit. **Do not** disconnect the fuel supply and return hoses as they are disconnected later on the underbody in front of the fuel tank. However, working through the floor aperture, disconnect the breather pipe **(see illustration)**.

6 Chock the front wheels, then jack up the rear of the vehicle and support on axle stands (see *Jacking and vehicle support*). Remove the right-hand rear roadwheel.

7 Open the fuel tank filler flap and wipe clean the area around the filler neck. Unclip the 'loop' from the flap, then lever off the retaining ring and push the rubber cup inwards from the body panel **(see illustrations)**.

8 Remove the right-hand rear wheel arch liner with reference to Chapter 11.

9 Disconnect the breather pipe from the filler neck assembly, then undo the filler neck retaining bolt **(see illustrations)**.

10 Working underneath the vehicle, release the fasteners and remove the panels from under the fuel tank and fuel filter.

11 Remove the rear section of the exhaust system as described in Chapter 4D.

12 Remove the rear axle assembly as described in Chapter 10.

13 Unclip the handbrake cable from the front right-hand side of the fuel tank.

14 Depress the release tabs, and disconnect the fuel supply pipe from the filter, and the return and breather pipes **(see illustration)**. On models with an auxiliary heater, disconnect the pipe leading to the metering pump. Plug all openings to prevent contamination.

15 Support the fuel tank with a trolley jack and piece of wood.

16 Mark the positions of the support straps to ensure correct refitting, then unbolt and remove them **(see illustrations)**. Note the position of the earth cable at the filler neck.

17 With the help of an assistant, lower the fuel tank to the ground and remove from under the vehicle.

7.9a Squeeze together the sides of the collar and disconnect the breather hose . . .

7.9b . . . then undo the retaining bolt

7.14 Disconnect the fuel supply, return and breather pipes from in front of the fuel tank

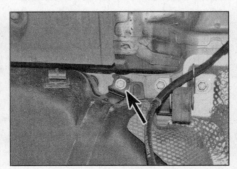

7.16a Fuel tank strap bolts at the front (arrowed) . . .

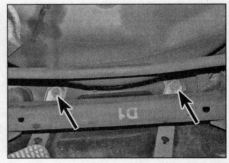

7.16b . . . and rear of the tank (arrowed)

9.3 Disconnect the EGR valve wiring plug

9.4 Disconnect the vacuum hose

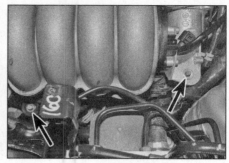

9.6 Undo the manifold retaining nuts (arrowed)

18 If the tank is contaminated with sediment or water, remove the fuel pump/sender unit (see Section 6) and swill the tank out with clean fuel. The tank is injection moulded from a synthetic material and if damaged, should be renewed. However, in certain cases it may be possible to have small leaks or minor damage repaired by a suitable specialist.

Refitting

19 Refitting is the reverse of the removal procedure noting the following points:
  a) When lifting the tank back into position take care to ensure none of the hoses get trapped between the tank and vehicle underbody.
  b) Ensure that all pipes and hoses are correctly routed and secured.
  c) It is important that the earth cable is correctly refitted to the strap and filler neck. Connect an ohmmeter between the metal ring on the filler neck and a bare metal part of the body, and check that the reading is zero resistance.
  d) Tighten the tank retaining strap bolts.
  e) On completion, refill the tank with fuel and thoroughly check for signs of leakage prior to taking the vehicle out on the road.
  f) Reconnect the battery as described in Chapter 5A.

8 Fuel injection system – depressurisation

Note: *Observe the precautions in Section 1 before working on fuel system components.*

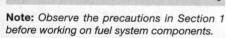

9.8 Release the metal clamps

⚠ *Warning: The following procedure will merely relieve the pressure in the fuel system – remember that fuel will still be present in the system components and take precautions accordingly before disconnecting any of them. Before working on the fuel system components, it is recommended that fuse 28 is removed, otherwise the fuel pump can be activated by the door contact switch.*

1 The fuel system referred to in this Section consists of the tank-mounted fuel pump and sender, the fuel filter, the fuel rail and injectors, and the metal pipes and flexible hoses of the fuel lines between these components. All these contain fuel which will be under pressure while the engine is running, while the ignition is switched on, or if a door contact switch is operated. The pressure will remain for some time after the ignition has been switched off and must be relieved before any of these components are disturbed for servicing work.

2 Disconnect the battery negative (earth) lead (see Chapter 5A).

3 Open the fuel filler flap and briefly remove the filler cap to relieve any pressure in the fuel tank. Refit the cap.

4 Where applicable, undo the retaining bolts and remove the engine top cover.

5 Place some cloth rags beneath the fuel supply pipe union located over the fuel rail on the intake manifold. Also wrap a cloth around the union.

6 Using two spanners, loosen the union nut and release the fuel pressure (see illustration 3.29). Leave the union nut loose and

9.9 Renew the gasket between the EGR valve and pipe

the rags in position while working on the fuel system.

7 On completion of the work, tighten the union nut using the two spanners.

9 Intake manifold – removal and refitting

Note: *Observe the precautions in Section 1 before working on fuel system components.*

Removal

1 Release the retaining clips and disconnect the air intake pipe from between the air cleaner and the throttle body intake duct. Pull the hose upwards from the retaining stud and release the harness cable tie.

2 Undo the retaining bolt, lift up the front edge, and pull the coolant expansion forwards. Disconnect the return hose from the rear of the tank, disconnect the wiring plug from the sensor on the tank underside, then position the tank to one side. Plug the openings to prevent spillage and contamination.

3 Release the catches and disconnect the wiring plug from the EGR valve **(see illustration)**.

4 Release the clip and disconnect the vacuum hose from the manifold **(see illustration)**.

5 Undo the 4 Torx bolts securing the throttle valve to the EGR valve **(see illustration 3.23)**.

6 Undo the 2 retaining nuts at the left-hand edge of the manifold **(see illustration)**.

7 Remove the engine oil level dipstick.

8 Using a small screwdriver, release the 4 intake rubber connectors clamps **(see illustration)**.

9 Undo the 2 Torx screws securing the EGR pipe to the underside of the EGR valve body **(see illustration)**.

10 Working around the manifold, note their fitted positions, and disconnect the wiring plugs from the manifold changeover solenoid valve, and intake air temperature sensor, then release the cable tie from the rear of the manifold.

11 Lift up the left-hand side of the manifold, then remove it complete with the EGR valve, leaving the throttle valve body in place.

12 Although the variable intake manifold

vacuum control element and/or control solenoid can be removed with the intake manifold in place (by disconnecting the vacuum hoses, disconnecting the wiring plug and unscrewing the retaining screws), in order to remove the changeover barrel the intake manifold must be removed.

Refitting

13 Refitting is the reverse of the removal procedure noting the following points:

  a) *Clean the contact faces of the intake manifold and flange.*
  b) *Tighten nuts and bolts to the specified torque.*
  c) *Refill/top-up the cooling system with reference to Chapter 1A.*
  d) *Reconnect the battery as described in Chapter 5A.*

10 Fuel injection system – testing and adjustment

1 If a fault appears in the fuel injection system first ensure that all the system wiring connectors are securely connected and free of corrosion. Then ensure that the fault is not due to poor maintenance; ie, check that the air cleaner filter element is clean, the spark plugs are in good condition and correctly gapped, the cylinder compression pressures are correct, the ignition system wiring is in good condition and

securely connected and the engine breather hoses are clear and undamaged, referring to Chapters 1A, 2B and 5B.

2 If these checks fail to reveal the cause of the problem the vehicle should be taken to a Audi dealer or specialist for testing. A diagnostic connector, located under the driver's side facia panel, is incorporated in the engine management system wiring harness, into which dedicated electronic test equipment can be plugged **(see illustration)**. The test equipment is capable of 'interrogating' the engine management system ECM electronically and accessing its internal fault log (reading fault codes).

3 Fault codes can only be extracted from the ECM using a dedicated fault code reader. An Audi dealer will obviously have such a reader, but they are also available from other suppliers. It is unlikely to be cost-effective for the private owner to purchase a fault code reader, but a well-equipped local garage or auto-electrical specialist will have one.

4 Using this equipment, faults can be pin-pointed quickly and simply, even if their occurrence is intermittent. Testing all the system components individually in an attempt to locate the fault by elimination is a time-consuming operation that is unlikely to be fruitful (particularly if the fault occurs dynamically), and carries a high risk of damage to the ECM's internal components.

5 Experienced home mechanics equipped with an accurate tachometer and a carefully-

10.2 Fault finding diagnostic connector (arrowed)

calibrated exhaust gas analyser may be able to check the exhaust gas CO content and the engine idle speed; if these are found to be out of specification, then the vehicle must be taken to a suitably-equipped Audi dealer or specialist for assessment. Neither the air/fuel mixture (exhaust gas CO content) nor the engine idle speed are manually adjustable; incorrect test results indicate the need for maintenance (possibly, injector cleaning) or a fault within the fuel injection system.

6 The engine management ECM communicates with the other control units fitted to the vehicle via a network known as a Databus. Do not attempt to 'back probe' connectors with a multimeter in the traditional manner, without first identifying the Databus wires.

Chapter 4 Part C:
Fuel system – diesel models

Contents

Section number

Accelerator pedal position sender – removal, refitting and
    adjustment 3
Air cleaner and intake ducts – removal and refitting 2
Diesel engine management components – removal and refitting . . . 7
Fuel cooler – removal and refitting 13
Fuel gauge sender unit – testing, removal and refitting 4
Fuel tank – removal and refitting 5

Section number

General information and precautions 1
Injectors – general information, removal and refitting 6
Intake manifold – removal and refitting 10
Intake manifold flap and valve – removal and refitting 12
Intercooler – removal and refitting 9
Tandem fuel pump – removal and refitting 11
Turbocharger – general information, removal and refitting 8

Degrees of difficulty

Easy, suitable for novice with little experience	**Fairly easy,** suitable for beginner with some experience	**Fairly difficult,** suitable for competent DIY mechanic	**Difficult,** suitable for experienced DIY mechanic	**Very difficult,** suitable for expert DIY or professional

Specifications

General

Engine code*:	
74 kW (96 bhp)	AVB
85 kW (111 bhp)	BKE and BRB
96 kW (125 bhp)	AVF and AWX
Maximum engine speed	Non-adjustable (ECM controlled)
Engine idle speed	820 to 900 rpm

* Note: *See 'Vehicle identification' for the location of the code marking on the engine.*

Fuel injectors

Injection pressure	180 to 2050 bar

Tandem pump

Fuel pressure at 1500 rpm	3.5 bar

Turbocharger

Type	Garrett
Maximum boost pressure	1.7 to 2.2 bar

Torque wrench settings

	Nm	lbf ft
Accelerator pedal position sender	10	7
Camshaft position sensor	10	7
EGR pipe to exhaust manifold*	25	18
EGR valve to intake manifold	10	7
Fuel filler neck	10	7
Fuel pump/sender retaining ring	80	59
Fuel tank retaining strap bolts	25	18
Heat shield to exhaust manifold	25	18
Injector clamp bolt*:		
Stage 1	12	9
Stage 2	Angle-tighten a further 270°	
Injector rocker arm adjustment screw locknut	30	22
Injector rocker shaft bolts*:		
Stage 1	20	15
Stage 2	Angle-tighten a further 90°	
Intake manifold flap housing	10	7
Intake manifold to cylinder head:		
Engine codes AVF, AVB, AWX	25	18
Engine codes BKE and BRB	21	15
Intercooler	10	7
Oil supply pipe to turbocharger	25	18
Tandem pump bolts:		
Upper	20	15
Lower	10	7
Turbocharger oil return pipe to cylinder block	40	30
Turbocharger oil return pipe to turbocharger	15	11
Turbocharger to catalytic converter/front exhaust pipe*	25	18
Turbocharger to exhaust manifold*	25	18

* Do not re-use

1 General information and precautions

General information

The fuel system consists of a rear-mounted fuel tank, an engine-bay mounted fuel filter with an integral water separator, fuel supply and return lines and four pump injectors (one for each cylinder) operated mechanically by a separate camshaft and electronically by a solenoid. The fuel is delivered to the injectors (known as 'Unit injectors') by a camshaft driven tandem pump – the pump is called a 'tandem pump' as it also incorporates the brake vacuum pump. From the pump, the fuel is channelled through a distributor pipe located within the cylinder head to the injectors. A 'roller rocker' assembly, mounted above the camshaft bearing caps, uses an extra set of camshaft lobes to compress the top of each injector once per firing cycle. This arrangement creates far higher injection pressures. The injection lobes incorporate a steep leading edge and a flat trailing edge in order to achieve high injection pressure quickly and allow good recharging. The precise timing of the pre-injection and main injection is controlled by the engine management ECM and a solenoid on each injector – in its normal open position, the solenoid effectively diverts the fuel to the tank return circuit, however, when the solenoid is activated, it closes the return to enable the fuel pressure necessary for

injection to be achieved. The resultant effect of this system is improved engine torque and power output, greater combustion efficiency, and lower exhaust emissions. Because the fuel injection pressures are very high, the fuel is heated considerably, and therefore it is channelled through a cooler located under the right-hand side of the vehicle before it is returned to the fuel tank.

All engines are fitted with a turbocharger and an intercooler.

The direct injection fuelling system is controlled electronically by a diesel engine management system, consisting of an Electronic Control Module (ECM) and its associated sensors, actuators and wiring.

Injection timing and duration are controlled by the ECM and are dependant on engine speed, throttle position and rate of opening, intake air flow, intake air temperature, coolant temperature, fuel temperature, ambient pressure (altitude) and manifold depression information, received from sensors mounted on and around the engine.

On all engines, the ECM also manages the operation of the Exhaust Gas Recirculation (EGR) emission control system, the turbocharger boost pressure control system and the glow plug control system.

It should be noted that fault diagnosis of the diesel engine management system is only possible with dedicated electronic test equipment. Problems with the system's operation should therefore be referred to an Audi dealer or suitably-equipped specialist for assessment. Once the fault has been

identified, the removal/refitting sequences detailed in the following Sections will then allow the appropriate component(s) to be renewed as required.

Precautions

Many of the operations described in this Chapter involve the disconnection of fuel lines, which may cause an amount of fuel spillage. Before commencing work, refer to the warnings below and the information in *Safety first!* at the beginning of this manual.

⚠️ *Warning: When working on any part of the fuel system, avoid direct contact skin contact with diesel fuel – wear protective clothing and gloves when handling fuel system components. Ensure that the work area is well-ventilated to prevent the build-up of diesel fuel vapour.*

• *Fuel injectors operate at extremely high pressures and the jet of fuel produced at the nozzle is capable of piercing skin, with potentially fatal results. However, note that with the pump injector system fitted to all diesel engines in this manual the injectors can only be operated when fully fitted in the cylinder head, so there is no real danger of personal injury as they cannot be operated while connected to a fuel line away from the engine (as is the case with injectors on an engine with an injector pump). Nevertheless, where pressure testing of the fuel system components is involved, it is highly recommended that a diesel fuel systems specialist carries out this work.*

2.1 Undo the screws (arrowed) securing the air intake duct to the lock carrier

2.2 Disconnect the airflow meter wiring plug

2.4 Prise out the top mounting centre pin

• Under no circumstances should diesel fuel be allowed to come into contact with coolant hoses – wipe off accidental spillage immediately. Hoses that have been contaminated with fuel for an extended period should be renewed. Diesel fuel systems are particularly sensitive to contamination from dirt, air and water. Pay particular attention to cleanliness when working on any part of the fuel system, to prevent the ingress of dirt. Thoroughly clean the area around fuel unions before disconnecting them. Store dismantled components in sealed containers to prevent contamination and the formation of condensation. Only use lint-free cloths and clean fuel for component cleansing.

2.7 Intercooler air pipe clip (arrowed)

2.10 Air cleaner housing drain hole (arrowed)

2 Air cleaner and intake ducts – removal and refitting

Removal

1 Undo the two bolts at the bonnet slam panel, then remove the air intake ducts **(see illustration)**.
2 Disconnect the wiring from the airflow meter **(see illustration)**.
3 Release the clip and disconnect the air hose from the airflow meter to the turbocharger, then prise out the wiring harness retaining clips at the top of the air cleaner housing.
4 Prise out the centre pin and remove the plastic rivet at the upper edge of the air cleaner housing **(see illustration)**.
5 Pull the air cleaner housing upwards to release it from the rubber mountings on the underside.
6 To remove the remaining ducting, apply the handbrake, then jack up the front of the vehicle and support it on axle stands (see *Jacking and vehicle support*). Release the fasteners and remove the engine undershield.
7 Loosen the clips and disconnect the U-shaped hose from the intercooler and air pipe on the left-hand side of the engine compartment **(see illustration)**.
8 Loosen the clip and disconnect the air cleaner hose from the right-hand side of the air pipe, then unbolt and remove the air pipe.

9 Loosen the clips and disconnect the rear air ducts from the intercooler and intake manifold. Disconnect the wiring and hoses as applicable, then unscrew the mounting bolts and remove the ducts.

Refitting

10 Refitting is a reversal of removal, noting the following:
a) *All air hose/duct connections must be free of oil or grease before assembly. Do not use any lubricant containing silicone.*
b) *The air cleaner housing must be clean and dry before refitting.*
c) *Clean out the drain hole in the bottom of the air cleaner housing* **(see illustration)**.
d) *Prise the rubber mounting grommets from the chassis channel, and fit them to the base of the air cleaner housing prior to refitting.*

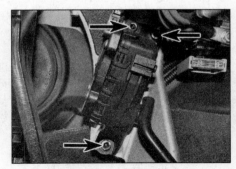

3.3 Accelerator pedal position sensor retaining Allen screws (arrowed)

3 Accelerator pedal position sender – removal, refitting and adjustment

Note: *In order for a new accelerator position sender to function correctly, it must be matched to the engine management ECM using a dealer scan tool. Consult an Audi dealer or suitably-equipped specialist.*

Removal

1 Refer to Chapter 11, remove the driver's side storage compartment.
2 Disconnect the wiring from the accelerator position sender.
3 Undo the three Allen screws, and remove the sender from its mounting bracket **(see illustration)**.
4 No further dismantling of the sender is recommended – no component parts are available. If the sender i faulty, a new one must be fitted.

Refitting

5 Position the sender on the mounting bracket, ensuring that the two locating pins engage with their corresponding holes in the bracket.
6 Insert and tighten the three Allen screws to the specified torque. Reconnect the wiring plug, and refit driver's side storage compartment.

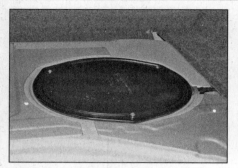

4.8 Undo the screws and remove the access hatch

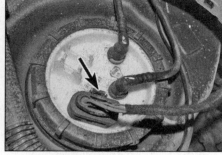

4.9 Depress the clip (arrowed) and disconnect the wiring plug

4.10 Depress the tab and disconnect the hose

4.11 Using a home-made tool to unscrew the plastic ring

4.12 Aperture seal (arrowed)

4 Fuel gauge sender unit – testing, removal and refitting

Note: *Observe the precautions in Section 1 before working on fuel system components.*

Testing

1 Refer to Chapter 11, and remove the trim from the load space floor (Saloon models) or the left-hand side luggage compartment side trim panel and floor tray (Avant models).
2 Slacken and remove the access hatch screws and lift the hatch away from the floorpan **(see illustration 4.8)**.

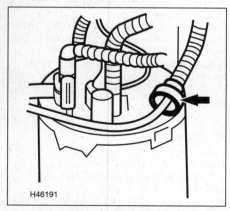

4.13 Reach down and disconnect the auxiliary heater suction pipe connection (arrowed)

3 Disconnect the wiring connector from the pump/sender unit.
4 Connect a hand-held multimeter to the middle two contacts in the sender/pump unit socket. With the float arm at its lower stop position (empty tank) the resistance should be approximately 65 ohms (vehicles up to 06/2001) or 300 to 310 ohms (vehicles from 06/2001). With the float arm at its upper stop position (full tank) the resistance should be approximately 275 ohms (vehicles up to 06/2001) or 53.5 to 590 ohms (vehicles from 06/2001). Note that these specifications are for the sender fitted in the tank. If the unit has been removed, the float arm will be able to travel further. The specifications for the sender when removed are 45 ohms (lower) and 295 ohms (upper) – models up to 06/2001, and 271 to 296 ohms (lower) and 55 to 69 ohms (upper) – models from 06/2001.

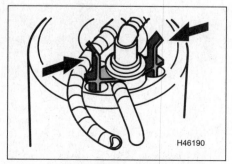

4.14 Squeeze together the retaining tabs and release the suction jet pump (arrowed)

Removal

5 The fuel gauge sender unit is mounted in the fuel tank. Access is via a hatch provided in the load space floor. Removal of the unit exposes the contents of the tank to the atmosphere, so extreme care must be exercised to prevent fire. The area inside and around the car must be well-ventilated to prevent a build-up of fuel fumes. If possible, remove the unit when the fuel tank is nearly empty, or alternatively syphon the fuel from the tank into a suitable container.
6 Ensure that the vehicle is parked on a level surface, then disconnect the battery negative (earth) lead (see Chapter 5A).
7 Refer to Chapter 11, and remove the trim from the load space floor (Saloon models), or the left-hand side luggage compartment trim and anti-soiling tray.
8 Unscrew and remove the access hatch screws and lift the hatch away from the floorpan **(see illustration)**.
9 Unplug the wiring connector from the sender cover **(see illustration)**.
10 Place rags beneath the fuel supply and return hoses to catch spilt fuel. Press-in the retaining tabs and disconnect the fuel supply and return hoses. Identify each hose for position **(see illustration)**. On models with an auxiliary heater, a 3rd fuel hose must be disconnected from the sender cover.
11 Note the location of the arrows and then unscrew the plastic ring securing the tank hatch to the tank. Audi technicians use a special tool to unscrew the ring, however a home-made equivalent will suffice. Alternatively use a pair of large water pump pliers **(see illustration)**.
12 Pull the cover upwards and sideways until the aperture seal can be removed **(see illustration)**.
13 On models from 02/2003 with an auxiliary heater, reach down alongside the delivery unit, depress the release tab and disconnect the suction pipe for the auxiliary heater **(see illustration)**.
14 On all models, reach down between the cover and the tank aperture, and squeeze together the retaining tabs and release the suction jet pump from the fuel delivery unit **(see illustration)**.
15 Pull the suction jet pump upwards, and

disconnect it from the supply pipe **(see illustration)**.

16 Remove the suction jet pump and fuel pump/sender unit from the tank. Take great care not to bend or damage the sender unit float and arm as they are removed from the tank.

17 Inspect the float on the sender unit swinging arm for punctures and fuel ingress, and renew it if it appears damaged. Inspect the rubber seal from the fuel tank aperture and renew it if necessary. Inspect the sender unit wiper and track; clean off any dirt and debris that may have accumulated and look for breaks in the track.

Refitting

18 Refitting is a reversal of removal, noting the following points:

a) *Renew the fuel tank aperture seal if necessary, and refit it dry.*

b) *Do not bend the float arm during refitting.*

c) *Fit the sender cover so the arrow aligns with the arrow on the tank (see illustration).*

d) *Ensure all hoses are securely reconnected to their original positions.*

e) *Tighten the support ring to its original position – the lug on the ring must be between the tabs on the tank.*

f) *Reconnect the battery as described in Chapter 5A.*

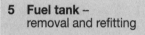

5 Fuel tank – removal and refitting

Note: *Observe the precautions in Section 1 before working on fuel system components.*

Removal

1 Before the tank can be removed, it must be drained of as much fuel as possible. As no drain plug is provided, it is preferable to remove the tank when it is nearly empty. Alternatively, syphon or hand-pump the fuel from the tank into a suitable safe container.

2 Disconnect the battery negative (earth) lead (see Chapter 5A).

3 Refer to Chapter 11, and remove the trim from the load space floor (Saloon models) or the left-hand side luggage compartment side trim panel and floor tray (Avant models).

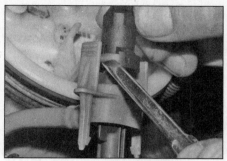

4.15 Press in the tab and disconnect the supply pipe from the jet pump

4 Slacken and remove the access hatch screws and lift the hatch away from the floorpan **(see illustration 4.8)**.

5 Unplug the wiring connector from the pump/sender unit. **Do not** disconnect the fuel supply and return hoses as they are disconnected later on the underbody in front of the fuel tank. However, working through the floor aperture, disconnect the breather pipe **(see illustration)**.

6 Chock the front wheels, then jack up the rear of the vehicle and support on axle stands (see *Jacking and vehicle support*). Remove the right-hand rear roadwheel.

7 Open the fuel tank filler flap and wipe clean the area around the filler neck. Unclip the 'loop' from the flap, then lever off the retaining ring and push the rubber cup inwards from the body panel **(see illustrations)**.

8 Remove the right-hand rear wheel arch liner with reference to Chapter 11.

5.5 Depress the tab and disconnect the breather hose

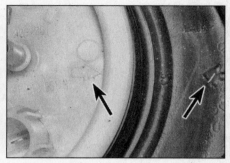

4.18 The arrow on the sender cover must align with the arrow on the tank

9 Disconnect the breather pipe from the filler neck assembly, then undo the filler neck retaining bolt **(see illustrations)**.

10 Working underneath the vehicle, release the fasteners and remove the panels from under the fuel tank and fuel cooler.

11 Remove the rear section of the exhaust system as described in Chapter 4D.

12 Remove the rear axle assembly as described in Chapter 10.

13 Unclip the handbrake cable from the front right-hand side of the fuel tank.

14 Depress the release tabs, and disconnect the fuel supply pipe (black), and the return pipe (blue) **(see illustration)**. On models with an auxiliary heater, disconnect the pipe leading to the metering pump. Plug all openings to prevent contamination.

15 Support the fuel tank with a trolley jack and piece of wood.

16 Mark the positions of the support straps

5.7a Lever out the retaining ring . . .

5.7b . . . and push the rubber cup inwards

5.9a Squeeze together the sides of the collar and disconnect the breather hose . . .

5.9b . . . then undo the retaining bolt

5.14 Disconnect the fuel supply, return and breather pipes from in front of the fuel tank

5.16a Fuel tank strap bolts at the front (arrowed) . . .

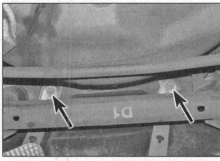

5.16b . . . and rear of the tank (arrowed)

to ensure correct refitting, then unbolt and remove them **(see illustrations)**. Note the position of the earth cable filler neck.

17 With the help of an assistant, lower the fuel tank to the ground and remove from under the vehicle.

18 If the tank is contaminated with sediment or water, remove the fuel sender unit (see Section 4) and swill the tank out with clean fuel. The tank is injection moulded from a synthetic material and if damaged, should be renewed. However, in certain cases it may be possible to have small leaks or minor damage repaired by a suitable specialist.

Refitting

19 Refitting is the reverse of the removal procedure noting the following points:

a) When lifting the tank back into position take care to ensure none of the hoses get trapped between the tank and vehicle underbody.

b) Ensure that all pipes and hoses are correctly routed and secured.

c) It is important that the earth cable is correctly refitted to the strap and filler neck. Connect an ohmmeter between the metal ring on the filler neck and a bare metal part of the body, and check that the reading is zero resistance.

d) Tighten the tank retaining strap bolts.

e) On completion, refill the tank with fuel and thoroughly check for signs of leakage prior to taking the vehicle out on the road.

f) Reconnect the battery as described in Chapter 5A.

6 Injectors – general information, removal and refitting

Note: Observe the precautions in Section 1 before working on fuel system components.

General information

1 Injectors deteriorate with prolonged use and it is reasonable to expect them to need reconditioning or renewal after 100 000 miles or so. Accurate testing, overhaul and calibration of the injectors must be left to a specialist.

Removal

Note: Take care not to allow dirt into the injectors or fuel pipes during this procedure. Do not drop the injectors or allow the needles at their tips to become damaged. The injectors are precision-made to fine limits and must not be handled roughly.

2 With reference to Chapter 2C, remove the upper timing belt cover and camshaft cover.

3 Using a spanner or socket, turn the crankshaft pulley until the rocker arm for the injector which is to be removed is at its highest, ie, the injector plunger spring is under the least amount of tension.

4 Slacken the locknut of the adjustment screw on the end of the rocker arm above the injector, and undo the adjustment screw until the rocker arm lies against the plunger pin of the injector **(see illustration)**.

5 Starting at the outside and working in, gradually and evenly slacken and remove the rocker shaft retaining bolts. Lift off the rocker shaft. Check the contact face of each adjustment screw, and renew any that show signs of wear.

6 Undo the clamping block securing bolt and remove the block from the side of the injector **(see illustration)**.

7 Using a small screwdriver, carefully prise the wiring connector from the injector.

8 Audi technicians use a slide hammer (tool T10055) to pull the injector from the cylinder head. This is a slide hammer which engages in the side of the injector. If this tool is not available, it is possible to fabricate an equivalent using a short section of angle-iron, a length of threaded rod, a cylindrical weight,

6.4 Undo the adjustment screw until the rocker arm lies against the plunger pin of the injector

6.6 Remove the clamping block securing bolt (arrowed)

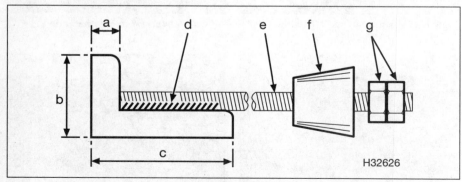

6.8a Unit injector removal tool

a 5 mm	d Weld/braze the rod to the angle iron	f Cylindrical weight
b 15 mm	e Threaded rod	g Locknuts
c 25 mm		

6.8b Seat the slide hammer/tool in the slot on the side of the injector, and pull the injector out

6.9a Undo the two nuts at the back of the head and slide the injector loom/rail out

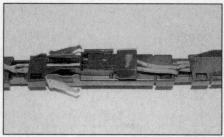

6.9b The injector connectors will slide into the loom/rail to prevent them from being damaged as the assembly is withdrawn/ inserted into the cylinder head

and two locknuts. Weld/braze the rod to the angle-iron, slide the weight over the rod, and lock the two nuts together at the end of the rod to provide the stop for the weight **(see illustration)**. Seat the slide hammer/tool in the slot on the side on the injector, and pull the injector out using a few gentle taps. Recover the circlip, the heat shield and O-rings and discard. New ones must be used for refitting **(see illustration)**.

9 If required, the injector wiring loom/rail can be removed from the cylinder head by undoing the two retaining nuts/bolts at the back of the head. To prevent the wiring connectors fouling the cylinder head casting as the assembly is withdrawn, insert the connectors into the storage slots in the plastic wiring rail. Carefully push the assembly to the rear, and out of the casting **(see illustrations)**.

Refitting

10 Prior to refitting the injectors, the three O-rings, heat insulation washer and clip must be renewed. Due to the high injection pressures, it is essential that the O-rings are fitted without being twisted. Audi recommend the use of three special assembly sleeves to install the O-rings squarely. It may be prudent to entrust O-ring renewal to a Audi dealer or suitably-equipped injection specialist, rather than risk subsequent leaks **(see illustration)**. If a new pump injector is fitted, the adjustment screw in the rocker arm must also be renewed. Whenever the pump injector is adjusted, the adjustment

6.10 Great care must be used to ensure that the injector O-rings are fitted without being twisted

screw and the pump injector ball-pin must be examined for wear, and if necessary renewed.

11 After renewing the O-rings, fit the heat shield and secure it in place with the circlip **(see illustration)**.

12 Smear clean engine oil onto the O-rings,

and push the injector evenly down into the cylinder head onto its stop.

13 Fit the clamping block alongside the injector, but only hand-tighten the new retaining bolt at this stage.

14 It is essential that the injectors are fitted at right-angles to the clamping block. In order

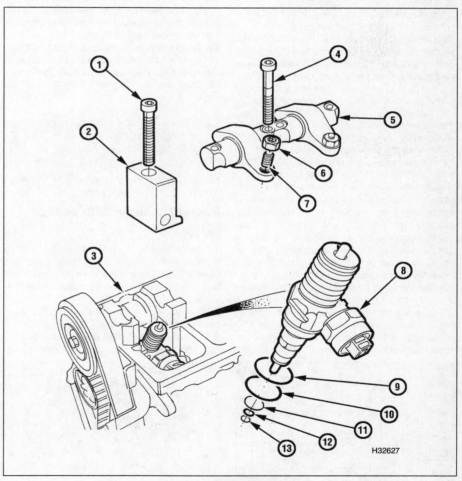

6.11 Unit injector

1 Bolt	4 Bolt	7 Adjuster	10 O-ring
2 Clamping	5 Rocker	8 Unit	11 O-ring
block	arm	injector	12 Heat shield
3 Cylinder head	6 Nut	9 O-ring	13 Circlip

H32627

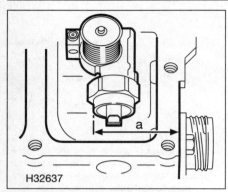

6.14a Measure the distance (a) from the rear of the cylinder head to the rounded section of the injector

to achieve this, measure the distance from the rear face of the cylinder head to the rounded section of the injector **(see illustrations)**. The dimensions (a) are as follows:

Cylinder 1 = 333.0 ± 0.08 mm
Cylinder 2 = 245.0 ± 0.08 mm
Cylinder 3 = 153.6 ± 0.08 mm
Cylinder 4 = 65.6 ± 0.08 mm

15 Once the injector(s) are aligned correctly, tighten the clamping bolt to the specified Stage one torque setting, and the Stage two angle tightening setting. **Note:** *If an injector has been renewed, it is essential that the adjustment screw, locknut of the corresponding rocker and ball-pin are renewed at the same time. The ball-pins simply pull out of the injector spring cap. There is an O-ring in each spring cap to stop the ball-pins from falling out.*

16 Smear some grease (Audi G000 100) onto the contact face of each rocker arm adjustment screw, and refit the rocker shaft assembly to the camshaft bearing caps, tightening the retaining bolts as follows. Starting from the inside out, hand-tighten the bolts. Again, from the inside out, tighten the bolts to the Stage one torque setting. Finally, from the inside out, tighten the bolts to the Stage two angle tightening setting.

17 The following procedure is only necessary if an injector has been removed. Attach a DTI (Dial Test Indicator) gauge to the cylinder head upper surface, and position the DTI probe against the top of the adjustment screw **(see illustration)**. Turn the crankshaft until

7.1 Coolant temperature sensor retaining clip (arrowed)

6.14b Use a set square against the rounded edge of the injector . . .

the rocker arm roller is on the highest point of its corresponding camshaft lobe, and the adjustment screw is at its lowest. Once this position has been established, remove the DTI gauge, screw the adjustment screw in until firm resistance is felt and the injector spring cannot be compressed further. Turn the adjustment screw **anti-clockwise** 180°, and tighten the locknut to the specified torque. Repeat this procedure for any other injectors that have been removed.

18 Reconnect the wiring plug to the injector.
19 Refit the camshaft cover and upper timing belt cover, as described in Chapter 2C.
20 Start the engine and check that it runs correctly.

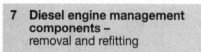

7	**Diesel engine management components –** removal and refitting

Note: *Observe the precautions in Section 1 before working on the fuel system.*

Coolant temperature sensor

Removal

1 The coolant temperature sensor is located on the rear of the cylinder head **(see illustration)**. Prise out the cover caps, undo the retaining nuts and remove the engine cover.
2 Refer to Chapter 1B and drain approximately one quarter of the coolant from the engine.
3 Disconnect the wiring, pull out the retaining clip, and remove the sensor. The sensor can be

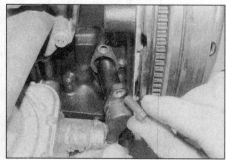

7.5 Engine speed sensor (engine removed for clarity)

6.14c . . . and measure the distance to the rear of the cylinder head

6.17 Attach a DTI (Dial Test Indicator) gauge to the cylinder head upper surface, and position the DTI probe against the top of the adjustment screw

tested using a multimeter. Connect the multimeter leads to the terminals of the sensor and set the meter to measure resistance (ohms). As the temperature increases, the resistance of the sensor decreases. So at 30°C the resistance should be 1500 to 2000 ohms, and at 80°C the resistance should be 275 to 375 ohms. If the resistance value of the sensor does not match these values, or fails to change, it may be faulty.

Refitting

4 Refitting is a reversal of removal. Top-up the cooling system with reference to Chapter 1B.

Engine speed sensor

Removal

5 The engine speed sensor is mounted on the rear left-hand side of the cylinder block, adjacent to the mating surface of the block and transmission bellhousing **(see illustration)**. Prise out the cover caps, undo the retaining nuts and remove the engine cover.
6 Trace the wiring back from the sensor to the connector and disconnect it.
7 Undo the retaining screw and withdraw the sensor from the cylinder block. The sensor can be tested using a multimeter. Connect the multimeter leads to terminals 1 (adjacent to the square side of the plug) and 2 (centre terminal) of the sensor plug, and set the meter to measure resistance (ohms). If the sensor is usable, the resistance should 450 to 550 ohms. If the sensor resistance is outside this range, renew the sensor.

7.9 Charge pressure control valve

7.14 Air intake charge pressure/
temperature sensor

7.20 Airflow meter

Refitting

8 Refitting is a reversal of removal.

Charge pressure control valve

Removal

9 The charge pressure control valve is located to the front, right-hand side of the engine (see illustration).
10 Disconnect the wiring from the valve.
11 Remove the vacuum hoses, noting their order of connection carefully to aid correct refitting.
12 Unscrew the mounting nuts and withdraw the valve.

Refitting

13 Refitting is a reversal of removal.

Air intake charge pressure/ temperature sensor

Removal

14 The air intake charge pressure/temperature sensor is located on the air duct leading from the intercooler to the intake manifold, at the left-hand rear of the engine compartment (see illustration). First disconnect the wiring.
15 Undo the screws and remove the sensor from the air duct.

Refitting

16 Refitting is a reversal of removal.

Airflow meter

Removal

17 Undo the two bolts and remove the air ducts from the bonnet slam panel to the air cleaner housing upper cover (see illustration 2.1).
18 Disconnect the airflow meter wiring plug.
19 Loosen the clip and disconnect the air intake hose from the airflow meter.
20 Undo the two bolts and pull the airflow meter from the guide on the air cleaner housing (see illustration). Handle the airflow meter carefully, as it is a delicate component.

Refitting

21 Refitting is a reversal of removal.

Electronic control module (ECM)

Caution: Always wait at least 30 seconds after switching off the ignition before disconnecting the wiring from the ECM.

When the wiring is disconnected, all the learned values may be erased, although any contents of the fault memory are retained. After reconnecting the wiring, the basic settings may be reinstated by an Audi dealer or specialist using a special test instrument. Note also that if the ECM is renewed, the identification of the new ECM must be transferred to the immobiliser control unit by an Audi dealer or specialist.

Removal

22 The electronic control unit is located on the bulkhead at the rear of the engine compartment. On RHD models it is on the right-hand side, and on LHD models it is on the left-hand side.
23 Disconnect the battery negative (earth) lead (see Chapter 5A).
24 Pull of the rubber seal from the plenum

7.24 Pull the up the rubber seal (arrowed)

7.26b . . . then pull the scuttle trim upwards from the base of the windscreen

chamber cover (where fitted), then undo the fasteners and remove the cover (see illustration).
25 Remove the wiper arms as described in Chapter 12.
26 Release the clips and remove the windscreen scuttle trim panel (see illustrations).
27 Undo the screws and lift off the cover (see illustration).
28 Release the spring retainer with a screwdriver and lift up the electronic control unit (see illustration).
29 Pull out the locking catches and disconnect the wiring connectors from the ECM. Note: *On some models, the ECM is fitted into a protective metal housing. The housing is secured to the ECM with shear bolts, which are coated with thread-locking compound (see illustration). In order to remove the bolts, heat the housing around the*

7.26a Prise forwards the 3 clips – one in the centre, and one at each end (left-hand clip arrowed) . . .

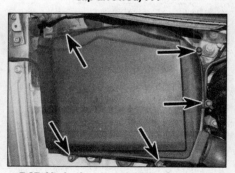

7.27 Undo the cover screws (arrowed)

7.28 Use a screwdriver to release the ECM retaining clip

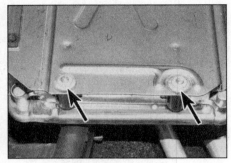

7.29 ECM housing shear bolts (arrowed)

7.37 Fuel temperature sensor (arrowed)

shear bolts with a hot-air gun, and use self-grip pliers to undo the shear bolts.

 Warning: Wait a minimum of 30 seconds after switching off the ignition before disconnecting the ECM wiring connector.

30 Withdraw the ECM from the bulkhead.

Refitting

31 Refitting is a reversal of removal, but press the clip down until it snaps into position. On ECMs with the metal housing, apply thread-locking compound to the shear bolts, then tighten the bolts until the heads shear off. Reconnect the battery as described in Chapter 5A. Note that the vehicle must be driven for several miles so that the ECM can learn its basic settings. In order to store its learnt values (and faults where present), the ECM continues to be supplied with voltage for up to 15 minutes. Once this period is finished, the ECM disconnects the earth path.

System relay and glow plug fusebox

Removal

32 The system relay is located beneath the ECM cover. First disconnect the battery negative (earth) lead (see Chapter 5A).
33 Remove the ECM cover as described in paragraphs 24 to 27.
34 To remove the relay, pull it directly from the fusebox. To remove the fusebox, remove the ECM (without disconnecting it), and slide the fusebox up.

7.45 The camshaft position sensor has a locating leg which must be fitted into the hole in the cylinder head

Refitting

35 Refitting is a reversal of removal.

Clutch and brake pedal switches

Removal and refitting

36 The clutch and brake pedal switches send signals to the ECM which automatically adjusts the injection pump timing. Refer to Chapters 6 and 9 for information on their removal and refitting.

Fuel temperature sensor

37 The fuel temperature sensor is located in the fuel return pipe beside the fuel filter assembly on the left-hand side of the engine compartment **(see illustration)**. Clamp the fuel return hoses either side of the sensor.
38 Release the retaining clips and disconnect the hoses from the sensor. Be prepared for fuel spillage.
39 Disconnect the wiring plug from the sensor. The sensor can be tested using a multimeter. Connect the multimeter leads to the terminals of the sensor and set the meter to measure resistance (ohms). As the temperature increases, the resistance of the sensor decreases. So at 30°C the resistance should be 1500 to 2000 ohms, and at 80°C the resistance should be 275 to 375 ohms. If the resistance value of the sensor does not match these values, or fails to change, it may be faulty.
40 Refitting is a reversal of removal.

Camshaft position sensor

Removal

41 With reference to Chapter 2C, remove the timing belt upper cover.
42 Undo the retaining bolt, and remove the sensor from the cylinder head.
43 Trace the sensor wiring back to the connector on the engine bulkhead and unplug.
44 Prise out the grommet in the timing belt rear cover and manoeuvre the sensor out through the hole.

Refitting

45 Refitting is a reversal of removal, noting that the sensor has a locating peg which must

be fitted into the hole in the cylinder head **(see illustration)**. Tighten the sensor retaining bolt to the specified torque.

8 Turbocharger – general information, removal and refitting

General information

1 A turbocharger is fitted to all diesel engines in this Manual, and it is mounted directly on the exhaust manifold. Lubrication is provided by an oil supply pipe that runs from the engine oil filter mounting. Oil is returned to the sump by a return pipe that connects to the side of the cylinder block. The turbocharger unit has an integral wastegate valve and vacuum actuator diaphragm, which is used to control the boost pressure applied to the intake manifold.
2 The turbocharger's internal components rotate at a very high speed, and as such are very sensitive to contamination; a great deal of damage can be caused by small particles of dirt, particularly if they strike the delicate turbine blades.
Caution: Thoroughly clean the area around all oil pipe unions before disconnecting them, to prevent the ingress of dirt. Store dismantled components in a sealed container to prevent contamination. Cover the turbocharger air intake ducts to prevent debris entering, and clean using lint-free cloths only.

Removal

Engine codes AVB, AVF, AWX and BKE

3 Apply the handbrake, then jack up the front of the vehicle and support it on axle stands (see *Jacking and vehicle support*). Remove the engine compartment undershield.
4 Remove the air cleaner housing as described in Section 2.
5 Prise out the cover caps, undo the retaining nuts and remove the engine top cover.
6 On models with air conditioning, loosen the pivot and tension bolts and move the tensioner roller upwards to release the tension on the drivebelt. Slip the drivebelt from the crankshaft, compressor and tensioner pulleys.

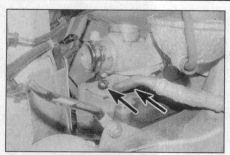

8.9 Undo the bolts (arrowed) and disconnect the oil return pipe from the base of the turbocharger

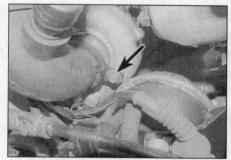

8.13 The turbocharger air inlet pipe is secured by bolts as well as a clip (arrowed)

8.14 Turbocharger wastegate control unit vacuum pipe (arrowed)

Unbolt the compressor and tie it to one side with reference to Chapter 3. **Do not** disconnect the refrigerant lines from the compressor.

7 Working under the engine, unbolt the refrigerant pipe bracket from the sump, then unclip the refrigerant pipe from the bracket on the other side of the sump.

8 Prise up the retaining clip and remove the air outlet hose from the base of the turbocharger.

9 On vehicles with 6-speed manual transmission, undo the union nut and disconnect the oil return pipe from the cylinder block. On all other models, undo the two bolts and disconnect the oil return pipe from the underside of the turbocharger **(see illustration)**. Plug or cover the pipe and aperture to prevent entry of dust and dirt.

10 Undo the bolts/nuts, and remove the support bracket from the underside of the turbocharger.

11 Whilst still underneath the vehicle, remove the two lower nuts securing the turbocharger to the exhaust manifold.

12 On vehicles with engine code BKE, remove the intake manifold, complete with the EGR cooler, as described in Section 10. Note there is no need to disconnect the EGR cooler coolant hoses.

13 Slacken the clip, undo the bolt and disconnect the air intake hose from the turbocharger **(see illustration)**.

14 Note the location of the vacuum hose then disconnect it from the wastegate/vane control unit **(see illustration)**.

15 Unscrew the union nut and disconnect the oil supply pipe from the turbocharger **(see illustration)**. Release the oil supply pipe supporting bracket from its mounting point.

16 Unscrew and remove the nuts securing the turbocharger to the catalytic converter/front exhaust pipe/particulate filter **(see illustration)**.

17 Undo the remaining nut and detach the turbocharger from the manifold. Manoeuvre the turbocharger from the engine compartment. Recover the gasket.

Engine code BRB

18 Remove the front exhaust pipe and particulate filter as described in Chapter 4D.

19 Release the clip and disconnect the air intake hose from the base of the turbocharger.

20 On models with Multitronic transmission, undo the two bolts and detach the oil return pipe from the underside of the turbocharger. Plug all openings to prevent dirt ingress.

21 On models with manual transmission, undo the union nut and detach the oil return hose from the cylinder block. Plug all openings to prevent dirt ingress.

22 On all models, undo the nuts/bolts and remove the support bracket from underside the turbocharger.

23 Whilst still underneath the vehicle, remove the two lower nuts securing the turbocharger to the exhaust manifold.

24 Squeeze together the sides of the collar and disconnect the breather hose from the cylinder head cover, then undo the two bolts and detach the turbocharger-to-intercooler air outlet hose from the turbocharger.

25 Remove the intake manifold, complete with EGR cooler, as described in Section 10. Note there is no need to disconnect the coolant hoses from the EGR cooler.

26 Note the location of the vacuum hose then disconnect it from the wastegate/vane control unit.

27 Undo the union nut and disconnect the oil supply pipe from the top of the turbocharger, then undo the bolt securing the oil supply pipe to the exhaust manifold.

28 Undo the remaining nut securing the turbocharger to the exhaust manifold, and manoeuvre the turbocharger from the engine compartment.

Refitting

29 Refit the turbocharger by following the

8.15 Turbocharger oil supply pipe union (arrowed)

removal procedure in reverse, noting the following points:

a) *Renew the gasket.*

b) *Renew all self-locking nuts.*

c) *Before reconnecting the oil supply pipe, fill the turbocharger with fresh oil using an oil can.*

d) *Apply high-temperature grease to the turbocharger mounting studs.*

e) *Tighten all nuts and bolts to the specified torque where given.*

f) *When the engine is started after refitting, allow it to idle for approximately one minute to give the oil time to circulate around the turbine shaft bearings.*

9 Intercooler – removal and refitting

Removal

1 Apply the handbrake, then jack up the front of the vehicle and support it on axle stands (see *Jacking and vehicle support*). Remove the engine compartment undershield.

2 The intercooler is located on the left-hand side of the engine compartment, and access to it is achieved by moving the complete front panel (the lock carrier assembly) away from the front of the car as far as possible, but without disconnecting the radiator hoses or electrical wiring. To do this, place the lock carrier in the Service position as described in Chapter 11.

8.16 Turbocharger-to-exhaust pipe/catalytic converter nuts

9.3 Looking downwards in the front, left-hand corner of the engine compartment, slacken the clip (arrowed) and disconnect the top hose from the intercooler

3 Loosen the clip and disconnect the top hose from the intercooler **(see illustration)**.
4 Remove the air duct from the front of the intercooler **(see illustrations)**.
5 Loosen the clip and disconnect the bottom hose from the intercooler **(see illustration)**.
6 Unclip the refrigerant pipe from the underside of the intercooler.
7 Pull the bottom of the intercooler out from the mounting grommet, then unhook it from the upper mounting grommets. Withdraw it downwards from under the car. If necessary, remove the grommets from the mounting bracket.

Refitting

8 Refitting is a reversal of removal.

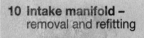

10 Intake manifold – removal and refitting

Removal

1 Pull out the engine oil level dipstick, then prise out the cover caps, undo the retaining nuts and remove the engine top cover. Refit the dipstick.

Engine codes AVB, AVF and AWX

2 Remove the air cleaner housing as described in Section 2.
3 Undo the bolts securing the EGR pipe to the intake manifold flap assembly, and the exhaust manifold.

10.5 Disconnect the vacuum hoses from the EGR valve and manifold flap

---

9.4a Release the clip at the base of the intercooler (arrowed) . . .

4 Release the clip and disconnect the intake hose from the manifold flap assembly.
5 Note their fitted positions, then disconnect the vacuum hoses from the EGR valve and manifold flap valve **(see illustration)**.
6 Undo the retaining bolts and manoeuvre the manifold from position **(see illustration)**.

Engine codes BKE and BRB

7 Drain the cooling system as described in Chapter 1B.
8 Disconnect the intake air charger pressure sensor wiring plug, then undo the retaining bolt, release the retaining clips, and remove the air intake pipe from the intake manifold flap to the intercooler hose.
9 Remove the air cleaner housing as described in Section 2.
10 Note their fitted positions, and the harness routing, then disconnect the wiring plugs from the EGR valve potentiometer, and the intake manifold flap motor.
11 Release the clips and disconnect the coolant hoses from the EGR cooler.
12 Undo the two nuts and disconnect the EGR pipe from the exhaust manifold.
13 Undo the retaining bolts, and manoeuvre the manifold, complete with EGR cooler and flap assembly, from position.

Refitting

14 Refitting is a reversal of removal, using new manifold, EGR pipe and manifold flap assembly gaskets. Remember to renew any self-locking nuts.

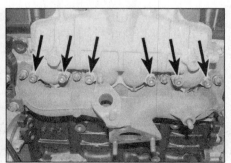

10.6 Undo the intake manifold mounting bolts (arrowed)

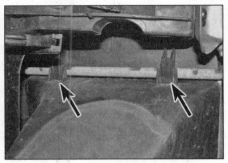

9.4b . . . then unclip the top of the air duct (arrowed)

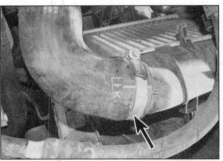

9.5 Slacken the clip (arrowed) and disconnect the intercooler bottom hose

11 Tandem fuel pump – removal and refitting

Note: *Disconnecting the central connector for the unit injectors may cause a fault code to be logged by the engine management ECM. This code can only be erased by an Audi dealer or suitably-equipped specialist.*

Removal

1 Pull out the engine oil level dipstick, then prise out the cover caps, unscrew the retaining nuts/bolts and remove the engine top cover. Refit the dipstick.
2 Disconnect the charge air pipe at the back of the cylinder head, and place it to one side. Rotate the collar anti-clockwise, and disconnect the central connector for the unit injectors **(see illustration)**.

11.2 Disconnect the injector connector

3 Release the retaining clip (where fitted) and disconnect the brake servo pipe from the tandem pump **(see illustration)**.
4 Disconnect the fuel supply hose (marked white) from the tandem pump **(see illustration 11.3)**. Be prepared for fuel spillage.
5 Unscrew the four retaining bolts and move the tandem pump away from the cylinder head **(see illustration 11.3)**. As the pump is lifted up, disconnect the fuel return hose (marked blue). Be prepared for fuel spillage. There are no serviceable parts within the tandem pump. If the pump is faulty, it must be renewed.

Refitting

6 Reconnect the fuel return hose to the pump and refit the pump to the cylinder head, using new rubber seals, and ensuring that the pump pinion engages correctly with the drive slot in the camshaft **(see illustration)**.
7 Refit the pump retaining bolts, and tighten them to the specified torque.
8 Re-attach the fuel supply hose and brake servo hose to the pump.
9 Reconnect the central connector for the unit injectors.
10 Refit the charge air pipe.
11 Disconnect the fuel filter return hose (marked blue), and connect the hose to a hand vacuum pump. Operate the vacuum pump until fuel comes out of the return hose. This primes the tandem pump. Take care not to suck any fuel into the vacuum pump. Reconnect the return hose to the fuel filter.
12 Refit the engine top cover.
13 If necessary, have the engine management ECM's fault memory interrogated and erased by an Audi dealer or suitably-equipped specialist.

---

12 Intake manifold flap and valve – removal and refitting

Intake manifold flap housing and vacuum control element

1 As diesel engines have a very high compression ratio, when the engine is turned off, the pistons still compress a large quantity of air for a few revolutions and cause the engine unit to shudder. The intake manifold changeover flap is located in the intake flange housing bolted to the intake manifold. When the ignition switch is turned to the 'off' position, the engine management ECM-controlled valve actuates the flap, which shuts off the air supply to the cylinders. This allows the pistons to compress very little air, and the engine runs softly to a halt. The flap must open again approximately 3 seconds after switching off the ignition switch. On engine codes AVB, AVF and AWX, the EGR (Exhaust Gas Recirculation) valve is also incorporated into the flap housing.
2 Pull out the engine oil level dipstick, prise out the cover caps, undo the retaining nuts,

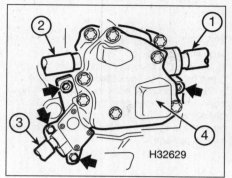

11.3 Fuel tandem pump securing bolts (arrowed)

 1 *Brake servo hose*
 2 *Fuel supply hose*
 3 *Fuel return hose*
 4 *Tandem pump*

and remove the engine top cover. Refit the dipstick.
3 Release the retaining clips, and disconnect the air intake trucking from the intake manifold flap housing.

Engine codes AVB, AVF and AWX

4 Undo the two retaining bolts and disconnect the EGR pipe from the underside of the intake flap housing. Recover the gasket.
5 Disconnect the vacuum pipe to the actuator. Disconnect the vacuum pipe for the EGR valve.
6 Unscrew the three retaining bolts and remove the intake manifold flap housing. Discard the sealing O-ring, a new one must be used **(see illustration)**.
7 Although it is possible to remove the vacuum actuator from the intake flap housing, by unscrewing the two bracket retaining bolts and disengaging the actuating arm from the flap spindle, at the time of writing the intake manifold flange was only available as a unit complete with the vacuum actuator and EGR valve. Consult your Audi dealer or parts specialist.
8 Refitting is a reversal of removal. Tighten the intake manifold flap housing bolts to the specified torque.

Engine codes BKE and BRB

9 Disconnect the wiring plug from the intake

12.6 Undo the manifold flap housing retaining bolts (two upper bolts arrowed)

11.6 Ensure that the tandem pump pinion engages correctly with the drive slot in the camshaft

manifold flap motor. Undo the two bolts, and remove the flap motor from the manifold. Discard the O-ring seal, a new one must be fitted.
10 Refitting is a reversal of removal. Tighten the intake manifold flap housing bolts to the specified torque.

Control valve

11 This valve controls the supply of vacuum to the manifold flap vacuum unit. The electrical supply to the valve is controlled by the engine management ECM. When the ignition key is turned to the 'off' position, the ECM signals the valve, which allows vacuum to pull the flap shut. Approximately three seconds later, the power supply to the valve is cut, the vacuum to the actuator collapses, and the flap opens.
12 The valve is located on the front right-hand side of the engine compartment. Note their fitted positions and disconnect the vacuum pipes from the valve **(see illustration)**.
13 Disconnect the wiring plug from the valve.
14 Undo the retaining screw and remove the valve.
15 Refitting is a reversal of removal.

---

13 Fuel cooler – removal and refitting

⚠ *Warning: The temperature of the fuel in the cooler can exceed 100°C in extreme cases. Allow the fuel circuit to cool before starting work.*

12.12 Manifold flap control valve (arrowed)

13.2 Undo the fasteners and remove the panels around the fuel cooler

Removal

1 Jack up the rear of the vehicle, and support it securely on axle stands (see *Jacking and vehicle support*).

2 Release the fasteners and remove the cover panel around the cooler **(see illustration)**.

3 Place a container beneath the fuel tank hose connections, then press the release tabs, and disconnect the fuel supply pipe (black) and the return pipe (blue) from the tank. Be prepared for fuel spillage.

4 Release the clips and disconnect the fuel supply and return pipes from the front of the fuel cooler.

5 Undo the fasteners, and remove the fuel cooler.

Refitting

6 Refitting is a reversal of removal, ensuring the all fuel pipes are securely reconnected.

Chapter 4 Part D:
Emission control and exhaust systems

Contents

	Section number			Section number
Catalytic converter – general information and precautions	7		Exhaust manifold – removal and refitting	5
Crankcase emission system – general information	3		Exhaust system – component renewal	6
Evaporative loss emission control system – information and component renewal	2		General information	1
			Secondary air injection system – information and component	
Exhaust Gas Recirculation (EGR) system – information and component removal	4		renewal	8

Degrees of difficulty

Easy, suitable for novice with little experience	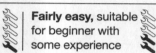	Fairly easy, suitable for beginner with some experience		Fairly difficult, suitable for competent DIY mechanic		Difficult, suitable for experienced DIY mechanic		Very difficult, suitable for expert DIY or professional	

Specifications

Engine codes*

1781 cc:
  Bosch Motronic ME7.5:
    110 kW (143 bhp) .... AVJ
    125 kW (163 bhp) .... AMB
  Bosch Motronic ME7.1:
    120 kW (156 bhp) .... BFB and BKB
    140 kW (182 bhp) .... BEX
    1984 cc, Bosch Motronic ME7, 96 kW (125 bhp)............... ALT
1984 cc:
  Bosch Motronic ME7, 96 kW (125 bhp) .... ALT
  Bosch Motronic MED7.1, 110 kW (143 bhp) .... AWA

Diesel engines

74 kW (96 bhp).. AVB
85 kW (111 bhp)... BKE and BRB
96 kW (125 bhp)... AVF and AWX

*** Note:** *See 'Vehicle identification' for the location of the code marking on the engine.*

Torque wrench settings	**Nm**	**lbf ft**
Catalytic converter to front pipe:		
Engine code AWA	25	18
Diesel engines	25	18
Catalytic converter to manifold*:		
Engine code AWA	40	30
Engine code ALT	30	22
Catalytic converter to turbocharger*:	30	22
Combination valve to cylinder head	10	7
EGR valve to intake manifold	10	7
Exhaust manifold*	25	18
Exhaust mounting brackets to underbody	25	18
Exhaust gas temperature sensor	45	33
Front pipe to bracket on gearbox	25	18
NOx sensor	52	38
Oxygen sensor	55	41
Particulate filter to front exhaust pipe*	25	18
Particulate filter to turbocharger*	27	20
Secondary air injection pump motor	10	7

*** Do not re-use fasteners*

1 General information

Emission control systems

All petrol engine models are designed to use unleaded petrol and are controlled by engine management systems that are programmed to give the best compromise between driveability, fuel consumption and exhaust emission production. In addition, a number of systems are fitted that help to minimise other harmful emissions. A crankcase emission control system is fitted, which reduces the release of pollutants from the engine's lubrication system, and a catalytic converter is fitted which reduces exhaust gas pollutant. An evaporative loss emission control system reduces the release of gaseous hydrocarbons from the fuel tank, and a secondary injection system is fitted to some models to reduce the catalytic converter warm-up time.

All diesel-engined models have a crankcase emission control system, and in addition are fitted with a catalytic converter or particulate filter, and an Exhaust Gas Recirculation (EGR) system to reduce exhaust emissions.

Crankcase emission control

To reduce the emission of unburned hydrocarbons from the crankcase into the atmosphere the engine is sealed and the blow-by gases and oil vapour are drawn from inside the crankcase, through a wire mesh oil separator, into the intake tract to be burned by the engine during normal combustion.

Under all conditions the gases are forced out of the crankcase by the (relatively) higher crankcase pressure. All diesel engines have a pressure-regulating valve on the camshaft cover to control the flow of gases from the crankcase.

Exhaust emission control

Petrol models

To minimise the amount of pollutants which escape into the atmosphere, all petrol models are fitted with a three-way catalytic converter in the exhaust system. On engine code AWA, 2 catalytic converters are fitted – a main converter, and a starter converter. The fuelling system is of the closed-loop type, in which an oxygen sensor in the exhaust system provides the engine management system ECM with constant feedback, enabling the ECM to adjust the air/fuel mixture to optimise combustion. A second oxygen sensor is also fitted after the catalytic converter, to inform the ECM of the oxygen content of the post-catalyst gases.

The oxygen sensors have a heating element built-in that is controlled by the ECM through the oxygen sensor relay to quickly bring the sensor's tip to its optimum operating temperature. The sensor's tip is sensitive to oxygen and relays a voltage signal to the ECM that varies according on the amount of oxygen in the exhaust gas. If the intake air/fuel mixture is too rich, the exhaust gases are low in oxygen so the sensor sends a low-voltage signal, the voltage rising as the mixture weakens and the amount of oxygen rises in the exhaust gases. On non-direct injection engines, peak conversion efficiency of all major pollutants occurs if the intake air/fuel mixture is maintained at the chemically-correct ratio for the complete combustion of petrol of 14.7 parts (by weight) of air to 1 part of fuel (the stoichiometric ratio – lambda value 1.0). The sensor output voltage alters in a large step at this point, the ECM using the signal change as a reference point and correcting the intake air/fuel mixture accordingly by altering the fuel injector pulse width. On direct injection engine, the lambda value can vary from 1.0 to 3.0 depending on its mode of operation. Details of the oxygen sensor removal and refitting are given in Chapter 4A and 4B.

In order to work efficiently, the catalytic converter needs to be heated to a temperature of at least 300°C. So that the exhaust gases can heat the catalyst up faster, some models are equipped with a secondary air injection system. During the initial warm-up stage, fresh air is injected behind the exhaust valves, this enriches the exhaust gases with oxygen, which causes an 'afterburning' effect, which shortens the catalyst warm-up phase. The activation of the secondary air injection pump and intake valve, is controlled by the engine management ECM.

On FSI petrol models (engine code AWA), a nitrogen oxide (NOx) storage catalyst is also fitted. When FSI engines are running is stratified charge mode (light throttle situations), the combustion process produces a greater-than-normal amount of NOx, which is harmful to the atmosphere. Consequently, a catalyst is fitted to store these gases, after the normal catalyst. When the storage catalyst is saturated, a sensor fitted downstream signals the engine management ECM which then operates the engine in full homogenous mode (conventional combustion mode) until the stored NOx is harmlessly burnt off.

Diesel models

An oxidation catalyst is fitted in the exhaust system of some diesel engined models. This has the effect of removing a large proportion of the gaseous hydrocarbons, carbon monoxide and particulates present in the exhaust gas. On other models, a particulate filter is fitted.

An Exhaust Gas Recirculation (EGR) system is also fitted to all diesel engined models. This reduces the level of nitrogen oxides produced during combustion by introducing a proportion of the exhaust gas back into the intake manifold, under certain engine operating conditions, via a plunger valve. The system is controlled electronically by the diesel engine management ECM.

Evaporative emission control

Petrol models

To minimise the escape of unburned hydrocarbons into the atmosphere, an evaporative loss emission control system (EVAP) is fitted to all petrol models. The fuel tank filler cap is sealed and a charcoal canister is mounted underneath the right-hand wing to collect the petrol vapours released from the fuel contained in the fuel tank. It stores them until they can be drawn from the canister (under the control of the engine management system ECM) via the purge valve(s) into the intake tract, where they are then burned by the engine during normal combustion.

To ensure that the engine runs correctly when it is cold and/or idling and to protect the catalytic converter from the effects of an over-rich mixture, the purge control valve(s) are not opened by the ECM until the engine has warmed-up, and the engine is under load; the valve solenoid is then modulated on and off to allow the stored vapour to pass into the intake tract.

Exhaust systems

On petrol models the exhaust system consists of the exhaust manifold, turbocharger (where applicable), catalytic converter(s) (with 'before' and 'after' oxygen sensors), front pipe, intermediate pipe and silencer, and tailpipe and silencer.

On all diesel models, the exhaust system consists of the exhaust manifold, turbocharger, front pipe and integral catalytic converter/particulate filter, a short connecting pipe, intermediate pipe and silencer, and tailpipe and silencer. The system is supported by rubber bushes and/or rubber mounting rings.

Initially, the exhaust intermediate and rear sections are fitted as one unit, however they are available separately as service items.

2 Evaporative loss emission control system – information and component renewal

Information

1 The evaporative loss emission control system is only fitted to petrol models, and consists of a purge valve, activated charcoal filter canister and a series of connecting vacuum hoses.

2 The purge valve is located in the front right-hand corner of the engine compartment, in the vacuum line between the charcoal canister and the intake manifold. The charcoal canister is mounted inside the right-hand front wheel housing behind the wheel arch liner, in front of the A-pillar.

Component renewal

Purge valve

3 Ensure that the ignition is switched off, then unplug the wiring harness from the purge valve at the connector.

4 Loosen the clips and disconnect the vacuum hoses. Note which way round the valve is fitted.

5 Refitting is a reversal of removal.

2.10 Charcoal canister solenoid valve (arrowed)

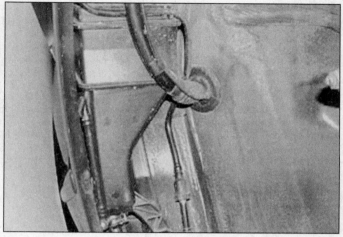

2.11 The charcoal canister is located behind the right-hand front inner wing

Charcoal canister

6 Apply the handbrake, then jack up the front of the vehicle and support it on axle stands (see *Jacking and vehicle support*). Remove the right-hand front roadwheel.

7 Refer to Chapter 11, and partially remove the rear of the right-hand front wheel arch liner to give access to the charcoal canister.

8 Remove the fasteners, and the cover panel from the front-right of the vehicle underbody.

9 Disconnect the vacuum and breather hoses at the base of the wheel arch.

10 Disconnect the hose from the solenoid valve on the right-hand inner wing in the engine compartment **(see illustration)**.

11 Undo the mounting screw and remove the charcoal canister **(see illustration)**.

12 Refitting is a reversal of removal.

3 Crankcase emission system – general information

1 The crankcase emission control system consists of hoses connecting the crankcase to the air cleaner or intake manifold. A pressure regulating valve is fitted to all diesel engines. Oil separator units are fitted to some petrol engines.

2 The system requires no attention other than to check at regular intervals that the hoses, valve and oil separator are free of blockages and in good condition.

4 Exhaust Gas Recirculation (EGR) system – information and component removal

Information

1 An Exhaust Gas Recirculation (EGR) system is fitted to all diesel engines; it consists of an EGR valve, modulator valve, delivery pipe(s), and a series of connecting vacuum hoses **(see illustrations)**.

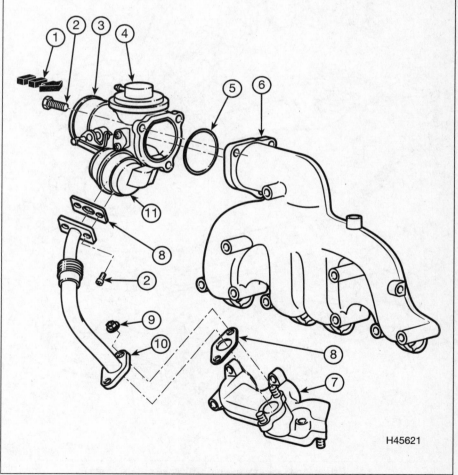

H45621

4.1a Exhaust gas recirculation (EGR) valve components – manual transmission models

1 Air from intercooler	4 EGR valve	8 Gasket
2 Bolt	5 O-ring	9 Nut
3 Inlet connecting pipe	6 Intake manifold	10 EGR connecting pipe
	7 Exhaust manifold	11 Vacuum actuator

2 The EGR valve is controlled by the engine management control unit (ECM), and is incorporated into the intake manifold flap housing on engine codes AVB, AVF and AWX. On engine codes BKE and BRB, the EGR valve is separate from the intake flap housing.

EGR valve renewal

3 Pull out the engine oil level dipstick, then prise out the caps, undo the nuts and remove the plastic cover from the top of the engine. Refit the dipstick.

Engine codes AVB, AVF and AWX

4 Disconnect the vacuum hose from the port on the EGR valve.
5 Unscrew the bolts securing the EGR flexible pipe to the underside of the intake manifold flange housing. Recover the gasket **(see illustration)**.
6 Disconnect the vacuum pipe to the intake manifold flap actuator.
7 Release the retaining clips and disconnect the intake trunking from the intake manifold flange housing.

8 Undo the three retaining bolts and remove the intake manifold flange housing, complete with EGR valve **(see illustration)**. As the EGR valve is integral with the intake manifold flange housing, it is not available as a separate part.
9 Refitting is a reversal of removal, but use new flange joint gaskets and self-locking nuts.

Engine codes BKE and BRB

10 Disconnect the EGR valve wiring plug.
11 Undo the bolts and detach the valve from the intake manifold. Discard the O-ring seal, a new one must be fitted.
12 Refitting is a reversal of removal, using a new EGR valve O-ring seal, and tightening the retaining bolts to the specified torque.

EGR control valve renewal

Engine codes AVB, AVF and AWX

13 The EGR control valve is located on the connecting pipe between the intercooler and the intake manifold to the left of the engine. The valve controls the vacuum supply to the EGR valve. The EGR control valve is in turn controlled by the engine management ECM.
14 Note their fitted locations, and disconnect the vacuum pipes from the control valve **(see illustration)**.
15 Disconnect the wiring plug from the control valve.

4.5 Unscrew the bolts securing the EGR flexible pipe to the underside of the intake manifold flange housing and recover the gasket

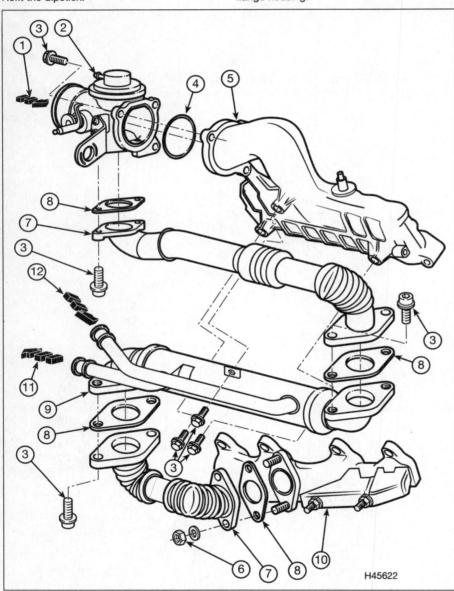

4.1b Exhaust gas recirculation (EGR) valve components – automatic transmission models

1 Air from intercooler	*6 Nut*	*10 Exhaust manifold*
2 EGR valve	*7 EGR connecting*	*11 To heat exchanger*
3 Retaining bolt	*pipes*	*12 From connection*
4 O-ring	*8 Gasket*	*13 Intake connecting*
5 Intake manifold	*9 Cooling radiator*	*pipe*

4.8 Undo the three retaining bolts and remove the intake manifold flange, complete with EGR valve

16 Undo the two retaining bolts and remove the control valve **(see illustration)**.
17 Refitting is a reversal of removal.

5 Exhaust manifold – removal and refitting

Petrol engine models

Removal

1 Apply the handbrake, then jack up the front of the vehicle and support it on axle stands (see *Jacking and vehicle support*). Remove the splash guard from the bottom of the engine compartment.
2 Remove the air cleaner and trunking as described in Chapters 4A or 4B. Also, undo the retaining fasteners and remove the engine top cover where necessary.
3 On turbocharged engines, unscrew the turbocharger support bracket bolts several turns only. Also unbolt the oil supply pipe from the heat shield.
4 Unbolt the heat shield from over the exhaust manifold where necessary.
5 On non-turbocharged engines, unscrew the nuts and disconnect the exhaust front pipe/catalytic converter from the exhaust manifold. Recover the gasket and push the front pipe/catalytic converter to the rear away from the manifold. If greater access is required, remove the front pipe/catalytic converter as described in Section 6.
6 On turbocharged engines, unscrew the three bolts securing the turbocharger to the exhaust manifold, and lower the turbocharger, then recover the gasket. Plug the opening in the turbocharger with rag to prevent entry of any foreign objects.
7 Progressively unscrew and remove the nuts and washers, and withdraw the exhaust manifold from the studs on the cylinder head. Recover the gasket(s).

Refitting

8 Clean thoroughly the mating surfaces of the manifold and cylinder head.
9 Refitting is a reversal of removal, but fit new gaskets, renew self-locking nuts, and tighten the nuts to the specified torque. Apply high-temperature grease to the manifold studs. On turbocharged engines, fit the exhaust manifold, then the turbocharger to the manifold, and finally the turbocharger to the cylinder block. Refer to Chapter 4A or 4B for additional tightening torques.

Diesel engine models

Removal

10 Remove the turbocharger as described in Chapter 4C.
11 Unbolt and remove the heat shield.
12 Remove the intake manifold as described in Chapter 4C.
13 Unscrew the bolt securing the oil supply pipe to the exhaust manifold.

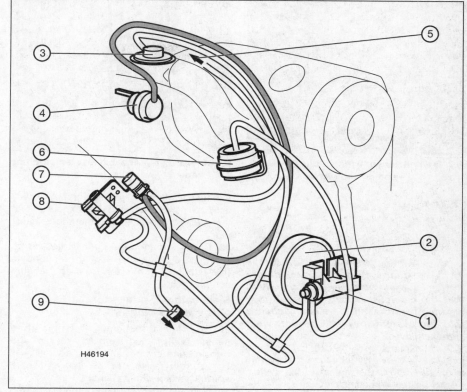

4.14 EGR and turbocharger vacuum hose layout – engine codes AVB, AVF and AWX

1 *Charge pressure control solenoid valve*	5 *To tandem pump*
2 *Vacuum reservoir*	6 *Charge pressure control vacuum unit*
3 *EGR valve*	7 *Intake manifold flap valve*
4 *Intake manifold flap vacuum unit*	8 *EGR solenoid valve*
	9 *One-way valve*

14 Unbolt and remove the EGR pipe **(see illustration)**. Recover the gaskets. **Note:** *On models fitted with automatic transmission, undo the bolts securing the EGR flexible pipe to the intake flange housing and the exhaust manifold, undo the bolts securing the EGR cooler to the intake manifold and position it to one side.*
15 On models with engine code BRB, unbolt the exhaust gas temperature sensor from the manifold.
16 Progressively unscrew and remove the nuts and washers, and withdraw the exhaust manifold from the studs on the cylinder head. Recover the gaskets.

Refitting

17 Clean thoroughly the mating surfaces of the manifold and cylinder head.
18 Refitting is a reversal of removal, but fit new gaskets, apply a little high-temperature grease to the manifold studs, renew self-locking nuts, and tighten the nuts to the specified torque.

4.16 Undo the two retaining nuts and remove the EGR control valve

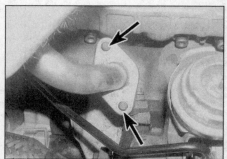

5.14 EGR pipe-to-manifold bolts (arrowed)

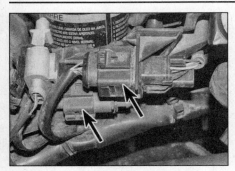

6.7 Oxygen sensor wiring plugs (arrowed) – engine code AWA

6.14a Disconnect the exhaust temperature sensor wiring plug (arrowed) . . .

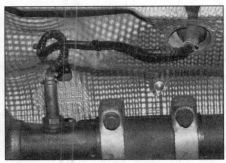

6.14b . . . and unscrew the NOx sensor

6 Exhaust system – component renewal

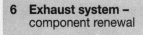

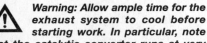

⚠️ **Warning: Allow ample time for the exhaust system to cool before starting work. In particular, note that the catalytic converter runs at very high temperatures. If there is any chance that the system may still be hot, wear suitable gloves.**

1 Each exhaust section can be removed individually, however because the system is located above the rear axle, the system cannot be removed complete.

2 To remove part of the system, first jack up the front or rear of the car and support it on axle stands (see *Jacking and vehicle support*). Alternatively, position the car over an inspection pit or on car ramps.

Catalytic converter removal – engine code AWA

Note: *Handle the flexible, braided section of the front pipe carefully, and do not bend it more than 10°.*

3 Two catalytic converters are fitted to this model.

Starter catalytic converter

4 Carefully pull the plastic cover on top of the engine upwards to release it from its mountings.

5 Remove the air cleaner housing as described in Chapter 4B.

6 Unbolt the coolant expansion tank and move it to one side.

7 Disconnect both oxygen sensor wiring plugs **(see illustration)**. Note their routing, then release their harnesses from any retaining clips.

8 Undo the fasteners and remove the engine undershield.

9 Working under the car, undo the bolt(s) and remove the heat shield over the right-hand driveshaft.

10 Undo the nuts, securing the catalytic converter to the exhaust manifold.

11 Disconnect the EGR connecting pipe at the starter catalytic converter.

12 Support the intermediate section of the exhaust system on axle stands or trolley jacks. Unscrew the flange bolts and separate the catalytic converter from the front exhaust pipe.

13 Undo the mounting nut adjacent to the front pipe flexible section. Manoeuvre the catalytic converter from the engine compartment.

Main catalytic converter/ NOx storage catalyst

14 Disconnect the exhaust temperature sensor wiring plug from the rear of the transmission casing, and unscrew the NOx sensor from the rear of the catalyst (where applicable) **(see illustrations)**.

15 Note the fitted position of the clamp (the bolts should be on the left-hand side of the clamp, and the lower ends of the bolts should not be below the bottom of the intermediate pipe), then unscrew the clamp bolts and separate the catalytic converter from the intermediate section.

16 Undo the flange nuts and detach the catalytic converter from the front pipe. Discard the nuts, new ones must be fitted.

Catalytic converter removal – engine code ALT

Note: *Handle the flexible, braided section of the front pipe carefully, and do not bend it more than 10°.*

17 Carefully pull the plastic cover on top of the engine upwards to release it from its mountings.

6.20 Oxygen sensor wiring plugs – non-FSI models (arrowed – brown plug is the rear sensor, and the black plug is the front sensor)

18 Remove the air cleaner housing as described in Chapter 4A.

19 Unbolt the coolant expansion tank and move it to one side.

20 Disconnect the oxygen sensor wiring plugs from the engine compartment bulkhead **(see illustration)**.

21 Undo the fasteners and remove the engine undershield.

22 Working under the car, undo the bolt(s) and remove the heat shield over the right-hand driveshaft.

23 Unscrew the flange nuts securing the catalytic converter to the exhaust manifold. Note that the nuts should be unscrewed from the catalytic converter side.

24 Undo the mounting nut adjacent to the front pipe flexible section.

25 Note the fitted position of the clamp (the bolts should be on the left-hand side of the clamp, and the lower ends of the bolts should not be below the bottom of the intermediate pipe), then unscrew the clamp bolts and separate the catalytic converter from the intermediate section.

26 Remove the catalytic converter.

Catalytic converter removal – turbo petrol engines

Note: *Handle the flexible, braided section of the front pipe carefully, and do not bend it more than 10°.*

27 Undo the fasteners and remove the plastic over on the top of the engine.

28 Remove the air cleaner housing as described in Chapter 4A.

29 Unbolt the coolant expansion tank and move it to one side.

30 Disconnect the oxygen sensor wiring plugs at the engine compartment bulkhead **(see illustration 6.20)**.

31 Undo the 3 nuts securing the catalytic converter to the turbocharger.

32 Undo the fasteners and remove the engine undershield.

33 Working under the car, undo the bolt(s) and remove the heat shield over the right-hand driveshaft.

34 Undo the mounting nut adjacent to the front pipe flexible section.

35 Note the fitted position of the clamp (the bolts should be on the left-hand side of the clamp, and the lower ends of the bolts should not be below the bottom of the intermediate pipe), then unscrew the clamp bolts and separate the catalytic converter from the intermediate section.

Catalytic converter removal – diesel engines

Note: *On some diesel models, a particulate filter is fitted in place of the catalytic converter.*

36 Remove the air cleaner housing as described in Chapter 4C.

37 Undo the 3 nuts securing the catalytic converter to the turbocharger.

38 Release the fasteners and remove the engine undershield.

39 Slacken the clamp bolts and slide the connecting sleeve between the catalytic converter and exhaust pipe rearwards. Remove the catalytic converter.

Particulate filter removal

Note: *On some versions of models with engine code BRB a particulate filter is fitted in place of the catalytic converter.*

40 Remove the air cleaner housing as described in Chapter 4C.

41 Unbolt the coolant expansion tank and move it to one side.

42 Slacken the clamps and move the air intake pipe at the rear of the engine to one side.

43 At the engine compartment bulkhead, disconnect the exhaust temperature sensor and exhaust gas pressure sensor wiring plugs, then undo the nut and detach the exhaust gas pressure sensor from its bracket. Leave the hoses connected and move the gas pressure sensor clear towards the bottom of the vehicle.

44 Undo the nuts securing the particulate filter to the turbocharger.

45 Release the fasteners and remove the engine undershield.

46 Remove the right-hand front roadwheel.

47 Undo the nuts and detach the mounting bracket from the front exhaust pipe.

48 Undo the union nut and remove the post-particulate filter temperature sensor.

49 Slacken the clamps, then slide the connecting sleeve between the front and intermediate pipes rearwards, and remove the front exhaust pipe.

50 Detach the right-hand side driveshaft from the gearbox flange as described in Chapter 8, and move the shaft to one side.

51 Undo the bolts and detach the front exhaust pipe mounting bracket from the gearbox casing.

52 Detach the particulate filter from the turbocharger and manoeuvre it from place.

Intermediate pipe and silencer removal

53 Working under the car, support the front pipe on an axle stand or trolley jack.

54 If the original intermediate/tail pipe is fitted, it will be necessary to cut through the middle pipe in order to separate it from the tailpipe and silencer. The pipe may have an indentation to indicate where the cut must be made approximately 160 to 180 mm before the rear silencer. Using a hacksaw, cut through the pipe at right-angles.

55 If the service pipe has been fitted, unscrew the clamp bolts and separate the intermediate pipe from the tailpipe.

56 Note the fitted position of the clamp attaching the intermediate pipe to the catalytic converter or short pipe (the bolts should be on the left-hand side of the clamp, and the lower ends of the bolts should not be below the bottom of the pipe), then unscrew the clamp bolts and separate the catalytic converter.

57 Disconnect the rubber mounting and withdraw the intermediate pipe and silencer from under the car.

Tailpipe and silencer removal

58 If the original intermediate/tail pipe is fitted, it will be necessary to cut through the middle pipe in order to separate it from the tailpipe and silencer. The pipe has an indentation to indicate where the cut must be made. Using a hacksaw, cut through the pipe at right-angles.

59 If the service pipe has been fitted, unscrew the clamp bolts and separate the tailpipe from the intermediate pipe. Note that the fitted position of the clamp should be with the bolts facing the rear of the car, and the bolt ends should not be below the bottom of the pipe.

60 Disconnect the rubber mountings and withdraw the tailpipe and silencer from under the car **(see illustration)**.

Refitting

61 Each section is refitted by a reversal of the removal sequence, noting the following points.

a) Ensure that all traces of corrosion have been removed from the flanges or pipe ends and renew all necessary gaskets.

b) Inspect the rubber mountings for signs of damage or deterioration and renew as necessary.

c) Prior to tightening the exhaust system mounting, ensure that all rubber mountings are correctly located and that there is adequate clearance between the exhaust system and vehicle underbody.

d) Renew all self-locking nuts.

e) Apply high-temperature grease to all mounting studs.

7 Catalytic converter – general information and precautions

1 The catalytic converter is a reliable and simple device which needs no maintenance in itself, but there are some facts which an owner should be aware of if the converter is to function properly for its full service life.

6.60 Release the system from the rubber mountings

Petrol models

a) DO NOT use leaded petrol (or LRP) – the lead will coat the internal precious metals, reducing their converting efficiency and will eventually destroy the converter.

b) Always keep the ignition and fuel systems well-maintained in accordance with the manufacturer's schedule.

c) If the engine develops a misfire, do not drive the car at all (or at least as little as possible) until the fault is cured.

d) DO NOT push- or tow-start the car – this will soak the catalytic converter in unburned fuel, causing it to overheat when the engine does start.

e) DO NOT switch off the ignition at high engine speeds.

f) The catalytic converter, used on a well-maintained and well-driven car, should last between 50 000 and 100 000 miles – if the converter is no longer effective it must be renewed.

Petrol and diesel models

a) DO NOT use fuel or engine oil additives – these may contain substances harmful to the catalytic converter.

b) Remember that the catalytic converter operates at very high temperatures. DO NOT, therefore, park the car in dry undergrowth, over long grass or piles of dead leaves after a long run.

c) Remember that the catalytic converter is FRAGILE – do not strike it with tools during servicing work.

8 Secondary air injection system – information and component renewal

Information

1 1.8 litre engines with codes AVJ, AMB, BEX and BFB are equipped with a secondary air injection system which is designed to reduce the amount of time the catalytic converter takes to warm-up, thus reducing harmful emissions. In order to function correctly, the catalytic converter needs to be at a temperature of at least 300°C, and this temperature level is normally achieved by the action of the exhaust gases passing through. In order to reduce

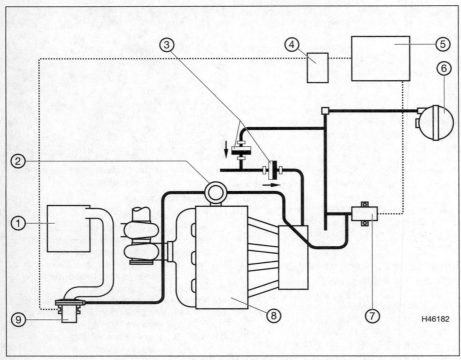

8.1 Secondary air injection

1 *Air cleaner*
2 *Combination valve – right rear of cylinder head*
3 *One-way valves – arrows indicate direction of flow*
4 *Secondary air pump relay – in electronic box in plenum chamber (alongside Motronic control unit)*
5 *Motronic control unit*
6 *Vacuum reservoir – behind front-left wheel arch liner*
7 *Secondary air inlet valve – beneath intake manifold*
8 *Cylinder head*
9 *Air pump – front-right underside of engine compartment*

the catalyst warm-up phase, a secondary air injection pump injects fresh air just behind the exhaust valves in the cylinder head. This oxygen rich mixture causes an 'afterburning' effect in the exhaust, and greatly increases the gas temperature, and therefore the catalyst temperature. The system is only active during cold starts (up to 33°C coolant temperature), and only operates for approximately 2 minutes **(see illustration)**.

8.8 The secondary air injection pump is located under the front, right-hand corner of the engine compartment

Component renewal

Combination valve

2 Release the fasteners and remove the plastic cover from the top of the engine.
3 Release the clamps and disconnect the hoses from the valve, located at the rear of the cylinder head.
4 Undo the 3 bolts and remove the valve from the cylinder head.
5 Refitting is a reversal of removal, ensuring that all seals and gaskets are renewed, and the bolts tightened to their specified torque.

Air pump motor

6 Remove the air cleaner housing as described in Chapter 4A.
7 Jack up the front of the vehicle, and support it securely on axle stands (see *Jacking and vehicle support*). Release the fasteners and remove the engine undershield.
8 Disconnect the wiring plugs from the pump **(see illustration)**.
9 Disconnect the air hoses from the pump, then undo the mounting bolts and remove the air pump.
10 Refitting is a reversal of removal, ensuring the bolts are tightened to their specified torque.

Chapter 5 Part A:
Starting and charging systems

Contents

Section number

Alternator – brush holder/voltage regulator module renewal 6
Alternator – removal and refitting 5
Alternator/charging system – testing in vehicle 4
Battery – disconnection, reconnection, removal and refitting 3
Battery – testing and charging 2
Battery check . . . . .See *Weekly checks*
Electrical system check . . . . .See *Weekly checks*

Section number

General information and precautions 1
Oil level/temperature sensor – removal and refitting 11
Oil pressure warning light switch – removal and refitting 10
Starter motor – removal and refitting 8
Starter motor – testing and overhaul 9
Starting system – testing 7

Degrees of difficulty

Easy, suitable for novice with little experience	Fairly easy, suitable for beginner with some experience	Fairly difficult, suitable for competent DIY mechanic	Difficult, suitable for experienced DIY mechanic	Very difficult, suitable for expert DIY or professional

Specifications

General
System type . . . . 12 volt, negative earth

Starter motor
Type . . . . Pre-engaged

Battery
Rating . . . . 44 to 80 Ah (depending on model and market)

Alternator
Type . . . . Bosch or Valeo
Rating . . . . 70, 90 or 120 amp
Minimum brush length . . . . 5.0 mm

Torque wrench settings

	Nm	lbf ft
Alternator connections:		
B+ connection	15	11
D+ connection (where applicable)	3	2
Alternator mounting bolt	25	18
Battery clamp bolt	15	11
Oil level/temperature sensor bolts	10	7
Oil pressure switch	20	15
Starter motor:		
M10	45	33
M12	65	48

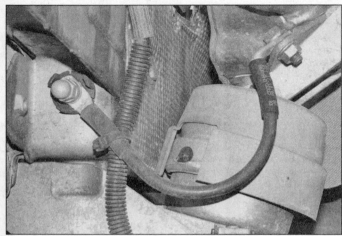

1.1a Main earth straps are fitted from the right-hand engine mounting to the chassis leg . . .

1.1b . . . and from the battery negative terminal to the body (arrowed)

1 General information and precautions

General information

The engine electrical system consists mainly of the charging and starting systems. Because of their engine-related functions, these are covered separately from the body electrical devices such as the lights, instruments, etc, which are covered in Chapter 12. On petrol engine models refer to Part B of this Chapter for information on the ignition system, and on diesel models refer to Part C for the preheating system.

The electrical system is of the 12 volt negative earth type.

The battery, which may be of the low maintenance or maintenance-free (sealed for life) type, is charged by the alternator, which is belt-driven from the crankshaft pulley.

The starter motor is of the pre-engaged type, with an integral solenoid. On starting, the solenoid moves the drive pinion into engagement with the flywheel/driveplate ring gear before the starter motor is energised. Once the engine has started, a one-way clutch prevents the motor armature being driven by the engine until the pinion disengages from the flywheel.

Two primary earth straps are fitted; one from the battery negative terminal to the body, and one from the engine to the body (see illustrations).

Further details of the various systems are given in the relevant Sections of this Chapter. While some repair procedures are given, the usual course of action is to renew the component concerned. The owner whose interest extends beyond mere component renewal should obtain a copy of the *Automotive Electrical & Electronic Systems Manual*, available from the publishers of this manual.

Precautions

⚠ *Warning: It is necessary to take extra care when working on the electrical system to avoid damage to semi-conductor devices (diodes and transistors), and to avoid the risk of personal injury. In addition to the precautions given in 'Safety first!', observe the following when working on the system:*
• *Always remove rings, watches, etc, before working on the electrical system.* Even with the battery disconnected, capacitive discharge could occur if a component's live terminal is earthed through a metal object. This could cause a shock or nasty burn.
• *Do not reverse the battery connections.* Components such as the alternator, electronic control units, or any other components having semi-conductor circuitry could be irreparably damaged.
• *Never disconnect the battery terminals, the alternator, any electrical wiring or any test instruments when the engine is running.*
• *Do not allow the engine to turn the alternator when the alternator is not connected.*
• *Never test for alternator output by 'flashing' the output lead to earth.*
• Always ensure that the battery negative lead is disconnected when working on the electrical system.
• If the engine is being started using jump leads and a slave battery, connect the batteries *negative-to-negative* and *positive-to-positive* (see *Jump starting* at the beginning of the manual). This also applies when connecting a battery charger.
• Before using electric-arc welding equipment on the car, *disconnect the battery, alternator and components such as electronic control units to protect them from the risk of damage.*
Caution: The radio fitted as standard equipment has a built-in security code to deter thieves. If the power source to the unit is cut, the anti-theft system will activate.

Even if the power source is immediately reconnected, the radio will not function until the correct security code has been entered. Therefore, if you do not know the correct security code for the radio, do not disconnect the battery negative terminal or remove the radio from the vehicle.

2 Battery – testing and charging

Testing

Standard and low-maintenance battery

1 If the vehicle covers a small annual mileage, it is worthwhile checking the specific gravity of the electrolyte every three months to determine the state of charge of the battery. Use a hydrometer to make the check, and compare the results with the following table. Note that the specific gravity readings assume an electrolyte temperature of 15°C; for every 10°C below 15°C subtract 0.007. For every 10°C above 15°C add 0.007.

	Above 25°C	Below 25°C
Fully-charged	1.210 to 1.230	1.270 to 1.290
70% charged	1.170 to 1.190	1.230 to 1.250
Discharged	1.050 to 1.070	1.110 to 1.130

2 If the battery condition is suspect, first check the specific gravity of electrolyte in each cell. A variation of 0.040 or more between any cells indicates loss of electrolyte or deterioration of the internal plates.

3 If the specific gravity variation is 0.040 or more, the battery should be renewed. If the cell variation is satisfactory but the battery is discharged, it should be charged as described later in this Section.

Maintenance-free battery

4 In cases where a sealed for life maintenance-free battery is fitted, topping-up and testing of the electrolyte in each cell is not possible. The

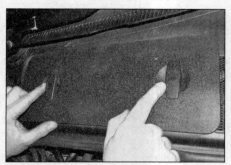

3.2 Slide the battery cover in the direction of the arrows

3.3a Slacken the negative terminal clamp nut

3.3b . . . and lift the negative lead clamp from the battery terminal

condition of the battery can therefore only be tested using a battery condition indicator or a voltmeter.

5 Certain models may be fitted with a maintenance-free battery with a built-in charge condition indicator. The indicator is located in the top of the battery casing and indicates the condition of the battery from its colour. If the indicator shows green, then the battery is in a good state of charge. If the indicator turns darker, eventually to black, then the battery requires charging, as described later in this Section. If the indicator shows clear/yellow, then the electrolyte level in the battery is too low to allow further use, and the battery should be renewed. **Do not** attempt to charge, load or jump start a battery when the indicator shows clear/yellow.

All battery types

6 If testing the battery using a voltmeter, connect the voltmeter across the battery and note the voltage. The test is only accurate if the battery has not been subjected to any kind of charge for the previous six hours. If this is not the case, switch on the headlights for 30 seconds, then wait four to five minutes before testing the battery after switching off the headlights. All other electrical circuits must be switched off, so check that the doors and tailgate are fully shut when making the test.

7 If the voltage reading is less than 12.2 volts, then the battery is discharged, whilst a reading of 12.2 to 12.4 volts indicates a partially-discharged condition.

8 If the battery is to be charged, remove it from the vehicle and charge it as described later in this Section.

Charging

Note: *The following is intended as a guide only. Always refer to the manufacturer's recommendations (often printed on a label attached to the battery) before charging a battery.*

Standard and low-maintenance battery

9 Charge the battery at a rate equivalent to 10% of the battery capacity (eg, for a 45 Ah battery charge at 4.5 A) and continue to charge the battery at this rate until no further

rise in specific gravity is noted over a four-hour period.

10 Alternatively, a trickle charger charging at the rate of 1.5 amps can safely be used overnight.

11 Specially rapid boost charges which are claimed to restore the power of the battery in 1 to 2 hours are not recommended, as they can cause serious damage to the battery plates through overheating.

12 While charging the battery, note that the temperature of the electrolyte should never exceed 38°C.

Maintenance-free battery

13 This battery type takes considerably longer to fully recharge than the standard type, the time taken being dependent on the extent of discharge, but it can take anything up to three days.

14 A constant voltage type charger is required, to be set, when connected, to 13.9 to 14.9 volts with a charger current below 25 amps. Using this method, the battery should be useable within three hours, giving a voltage reading of 12.5 volts, but this is for a partially-discharged battery and, as mentioned, full charging can take far longer.

15 If the battery is to be charged from a fully-discharged state (condition reading less than 12.2 volts), have it recharged by your local automotive electrician, as the charge rate is higher and constant supervision during charging is necessary.

3 Battery – disconnection, reconnection, removal and refitting

Note: *If the vehicle has a security-coded radio, check that you have a copy of the code number before disconnecting the battery cable; refer to the caution in Section 1.*

Note: *If the vehicle is equipped with Telematics, including the factory option of a phone, place the system in service mode before disconnecting the battery, otherwise the Telematics emergency battery will be drained. Switch on the Telematics system and the following sequence of buttons on the telephone handset: #4610# then press the 'Navi' button.*

Disconnection and reconnection

1 The battery is located at the rear of the engine compartment, in the plenum chamber.

2 Slide the battery cover to the right-hand side, and lift it from position **(see illustration)**.

3 Loosen the clamp nut and disconnect the battery negative (-) lead from the terminal **(see illustrations)**.

4 Lift the plastic flap where fitted, then loosen the clamp nut and disconnect the battery positive (+) lead from the terminal.

5 Reconnection is a reversal of disconnection, ensuring the battery positive (+) lead is reconnected first.

6 After both leads have been reconnected, note the following:

a) *Re-activate the radio by inserting the security code.*

b) *The ESP warning light on the instrument panel may illuminate until the vehicle has be driven several metres.*

c) *On models with Telematics, de-activate the service mode by pressing the 'Navi' button on the telephone handset.*

Removal

7 Pull the rubber seal from the front edge of the plenum chamber trim panel, then pull the panel forwards and remove it (where fitted) **(see illustration)**.

8 Loosen the clamp nut and disconnect the battery negative (-) lead from the terminal **(see illustrations 3.3a and 3.3b)**.

9 Lift the plastic flap where fitted, then loosen the clamp nut and disconnect the battery positive (+) lead from the terminal.

3.7 Pull the rubber seal upwards from the front edge of the plenum chamber (arrowed)

3.10a Release the clips and lift up the wiring loom . . .

3.10b . . . then undo the battery clamp bolt (arrowed)

5 Alternator – removal and refitting

10 Lift out the wiring loom, then at the base of the battery, unscrew the retaining clamp bolt and remove the clamp **(see illustrations)**.

11 Where fitted, disconnect the vent pipe from the battery. Note on some models the vent incorporates a flashback arrester.

12 Lift out the battery and withdraw it from the engine compartment.

Refitting

13 Clean the battery mounting, then refit the battery in position and refit the clamp. Tighten the bolt to the specified torque.

14 Where fitted, refit the vent pipe.

15 Reconnect the battery positive (+) lead to the terminal and tighten the clamp nut.

16 Reconnect the battery negative (-) lead to the terminal and tighten the clamp nut.

17 Audi state that the terminals should not be greased.

18 Refit the plenum chamber trim panel and refit the rubber strip.

19 Re-activate the radio by inserting the security code.

4 Alternator/charging system – testing in vehicle

Note: *Refer to Section 1 of this Chapter before starting work.*

1 If the charge warning light fails to illuminate when the ignition is switched on, first check the alternator wiring connections for security. Check the condition of the auxiliary drivebelt. If all is satisfactory, the alternator may be at

fault and should be renewed or taken to an auto-electrician for testing and repair.

2 Similarly, if the charge warning light comes on with the ignition, but is then slow to go out when the engine is started, this may indicate an impending alternator problem. Check all the items listed in the preceding paragraph, and refer to an auto-electrical specialist if no obvious faults are found.

3 If the charge warning light illuminates when the engine is running, stop the engine and check that the drivebelt is correctly tensioned (see Chapter 2A, 2B or 2C) and that the alternator connections are secure. If the fault persists, the alternator should be renewed, or taken to an auto-electrician for testing and repair.

4 If the alternator output is suspect even though the warning light functions correctly, the regulated voltage may be checked as follows.

5 Connect a voltmeter across the battery terminals, and start the engine.

6 Increase the engine speed until the voltmeter reading remains steady; the reading should be approximately 12 to 13 volts, and no more than 14 volts.

7 Switch on as many electrical accessories (eg, the headlights, heated rear window and heater blower) as possible, and check that the alternator maintains the regulated voltage at around 13 to 14 volts.

8 If the regulated voltage is not as stated, this may be due to worn brushes, weak brush springs, a faulty voltage regulator, a faulty diode, a severed phase winding or worn or damaged slip-rings. Have the alternator checked and tested by an auto-electrician.

1 The alternator is fitted to the left-hand front of the engine. First, disconnect the battery negative lead and position it away from the terminal – refer to Section 3. Where applicable, prise out the cover caps, undo the retaining nuts/bolts, and remove the engine top cover.

Petrol engines – removal

1.8 litre models

2 Drain the cooling system as described in Chapter 1A.

3 Release the clip and disconnect the hose from the coolant pipe above the alternator.

4 Undo the retaining bolt, and position the radiator fan control unit (located on the lock carrier panel) to one side.

All models

5 Remove the auxiliary drivebelt as described in Chapter 2A or 2B as applicable.

6 On 2.0 litre models, disconnect the electrical plugs adjacent to the alternator to give sufficient clearance.

7 Unscrew and remove the alternator upper and lower mounting bolts, and manoeuvre the alternator forwards **(see illustration)**.

8 Note their fitted positions, then disconnect the wiring from the rear of the alternator **(see illustration)**. Withdraw the alternator from the engine compartment.

Diesel engines – removal

9 Remove the auxiliary drivebelt as described in Chapter 1B.

10 Remove the viscous fan unit with reference to Chapter 3. Briefly, it is removed by inserting an Allen key from behind, while holding the unit stationary with a temporary bolt inserted from behind, resting on the cylinder block, or a strap wrench around the pulley. Once release, place the fan and coupling in the radiator shroud.

11 Note their fitted positions, then disconnect the wiring from the rear of the alternator **(see illustration 5.8)**.

12 Support the alternator, then unscrew and remove the mounting bolts **(see illustration)**.

5.7 Alternator mounting bolts

5.8 Disconnect the wiring from the rear of the alternator

5.12 Undo the mounting bolts and remove the alternator

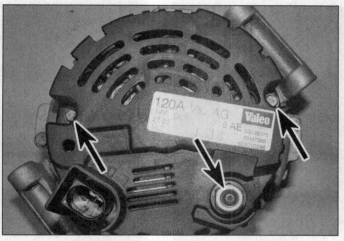

6.2 Undo the screws and the nut (arrowed)

6.3 Undo the three brush holder/regulator screws

Refitting

13 Refitting is a reversal of removal. Refer to Chapter 2A, 2B or 2C as applicable for details of refitting the main drivebelt. Tighten the alternator mounting bolts, and the alternator wiring connections to the specified torque.

6 Alternator – brush holder/voltage regulator module renewal

1 Remove the alternator as described in Section 5.
2 Undo the nuts or bolts as applicable, and remove the protective cover from the alternator **(see illustration)**.
3 Undo the three screws, and withdraw the brush holder/voltage regulator module from the alternator **(see illustrations)**.
4 Inspect the brushes for wear and damage. No specifications for brush length are given by Audi, but excessive wear should be obvious.
5 Clean and inspect the surfaces of the slip-rings on the end of the alternator shaft, working through the module location hole. If they are excessively worn, or damaged, the alternator must be renewed.
6 To refit the brush holder/voltage regulator module, push the brushes back into their holders, then insert a paper clip through the hole in the brush cover to hold the brushes in their retracted positions **(see illustration)**.
7 Lower the brush holder/voltage regulator module over the slip-rings and securely tighten the retaining screws. Remove the paper clip.
8 Refit the protective cover, tighten the retaining screws, and refit the alternator.

7 Starting system – testing

Note: *Refer to Section 1 of this Chapter before starting work.*

1 If the starter motor fails to operate when the ignition key is turned to the appropriate position, the following possible causes may be to blame:
  a) *The battery is faulty.*
  b) *The electrical connections between the switch, solenoid, battery and starter motor are somewhere failing to pass the necessary current from the battery through the starter to earth.*
  c) *The solenoid is faulty.*
  d) *The starter motor is mechanically or electrically defective.*
2 To check the battery, switch on the headlights. If they dim after a few seconds, this indicates that the battery is discharged – recharge (see Section 2) or renew the battery. If the headlights glow brightly, operate the ignition switch and observe the lights. If they dim, then this indicates that current is reaching the starter motor, therefore the fault must lie in the starter motor. If the lights continue to glow brightly (and no clicking sound can be heard from the starter motor solenoid), this indicates that there is a fault in the circuit or solenoid – see following paragraphs. If the starter motor turns slowly when operated, but the battery is in good condition, then this indicates that either the starter motor is faulty, or there is considerable resistance somewhere in the circuit.
3 If a fault in the circuit is suspected, disconnect the battery leads (including the earth connection to the body), the starter/solenoid wiring and the engine/transmission earth strap. Thoroughly clean the connections, and reconnect the leads and wiring, then use a voltmeter or test light to check that full battery voltage is available at the battery positive lead connection to the solenoid, and that the earth is sound.
4 If the battery and all connections are in good condition, check the circuit by disconnecting the wire from the solenoid blade terminal. Connect a voltmeter or test light between the wire end and a good earth (such as the battery

negative terminal), and check that the wire is live when the ignition switch is turned to the start position. If it is, then the circuit is sound – if not the circuit wiring can be checked as described in Chapter 12.
5 The solenoid contacts can be checked by connecting a voltmeter or test light between the battery positive feed connection on the starter side of the solenoid and earth. When the ignition switch is turned to the start position, there should be a reading or lighted bulb, as applicable. If there is no reading or lighted bulb, the solenoid is faulty and should be renewed.
6 If the circuit and solenoid are proved sound, the fault must lie in the starter motor. Remove the starter motor, and have it inspected by an auto-electrician.

8 Starter motor – removal and refitting

Removal

1 Disconnect the battery negative lead as described in Section 3.
2 Apply the handbrake, then jack up the front of the vehicle and support it on axle stands

6.6 Insert a paper clip through the hole in the top of the brush holder to hold back the brushes

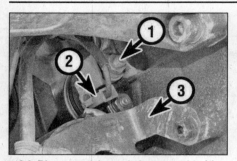

8.3 Disconnect the main battery cable (1), and the trigger wire (2), then undo the nuts/bolt and remove the bracket (3) from the front of the starter motor

(see *Jacking and vehicle support*). Undo the fasteners and remove the engine undershield.
3 The starter motor is located on the right-hand side of the engine. Note their fitted positions, then undo the fasteners and disconnect the wiring from the starter motor **(see illustration)**.
4 Undo the nuts/bolts, detach the cable bracket from the starter, and the mounting bracket from the front of the starter motor **(see illustration 8.3)**.
5 Undo the 2 bolts securing the starter to the transmission bellhousing, and manoeuvre the starter downwards and withdraw it from under the vehicle.

Diesel engines

6 Note their fitted positions, and disconnect the wiring from the starter.
7 Undo the nut securing the cable clamp at the front of the starter.
8 Remove the bolts securing the starter to the transmission bellhousing, and manoeuvre the starter downwards and out from under the vehicle.

Refitting

9 Refit the starter motor by following the removal procedure in reverse. Tighten the mounting bolts to the specified torque.

9 Starter motor – testing and overhaul

If the starter motor is thought to be defective,

11.4 Undo the bolts and lower the sensor from the sump

it should be removed from the vehicle and taken to an auto-electrician for assessment. In the majority of cases, new starter motor brushes can be fitted at a reasonable cost. However, check the cost of repairs first as it may prove more economical to purchase a new or exchange motor.

10 Oil pressure warning light switch – removal and refitting

Removal

Non-FSI petrol engines

1 The oil pressure light switch is screwed into the oil filter housing, located on the left-hand side of the engine block. Release the fasteners and remove the engine top cover.
2 Unbolt the coolant expansion tank and move it to one side. There's no need to disconnect the coolant hoses.
3 Disconnect the switch wiring plug.
4 Unscrew the switch from the housing and (where fitted) recover the sealing washer **(see illustration)**. Be prepared for fluid spillage, and if the switch is to be left removed from the engine for any length of time, plug the switch aperture.

FSI engines

5 The oil pressure light switch is screwed into the oil filter housing, located on the left-hand side of the engine block. Remove the intake manifold as described in Chapter 4B.
6 Disconnect the switch wiring plug.
7 Unscrew the switch from the housing and recover the sealing washer **(see illustration)**. Be prepared for fluid spillage, and if the switch is to be left removed from the engine for any length of time, plug the switch aperture.

Diesel engines

8 The oil pressure light switch is screwed into the oil filter housing on the left-hand side of the engine block. Prise out the caps, undo the nuts and remove the plastic cover on top of the engine. Remove the insulation beneath the cover (where fitted).
9 Disconnect the wiring plug from the switch.
10 Unscrew the switch from the housing and recover the sealing washer. Be prepared

10.4 Unscrew the oil pressure switch from the filter housing – non-FSI engines

10.7 Oil pressure switch – FSI engines

for fluid spillage, and if the switch is to be left removed for some time, plug the switch aperture.

Refitting

11 Examine the sealing washer for signs of damage or deterioration and if necessary renew it.
12 Refit the switch and washer, tightening it to the specified torque, and reconnecting the wiring plug.
13 The remainder of refitting is a reversal of removal. If necessary, top-up the engine oil level.

11 Oil level/temperature sensor – removal and refitting

Removal

1 Where fitted, the engine oil level/temperature sensor is located in the base of the oil sump. Apply the handbrake, then jack up the front of the vehicle and support it on axle stands (see *Jacking and vehicle support*). Undo the fasteners, and remove the engine undershield.
2 Position a container beneath the sump, then unscrew the drain plug (refer to the relevant part of Chapter 1) and drain the engine oil. Clean, refit, and tighten the plug after all the oil has drained.
3 Disconnect the oil level/temperature sensor wiring plug.
4 Undo the securing bolts, and lower the sensor from the sump. Discard the O-ring seal, a new one must be fitted **(see illustration)**.

Refitting

5 Clean the mating surfaces of the sensor and the sump. Smear the new O-ring seal with clean engine oil, and position it on the sensor.
6 Fit the sensor to the sump, insert the securing bolts and tighten them to the specified torque.
7 Reconnect the sensor wiring plug
8 Refit the engine undershield, lower the vehicle to the ground.
9 Refill the engine with new oil as described in the relevant part of Chapter 1. Start the engine and check for leaks.

Chapter 5 Part B:
Ignition system – petrol engine models

Contents

Section number

General information 1
HT coils – removal and refitting 3
Ignition switch removal and refitting................See Chapter 10
Ignition system – testing.................................... 2

Section number

Ignition timing – checking and adjusting 4
Knock sensors – removal and refitting........................ 5
Spark plug renewal...........................See Chapter 1A

Degrees of difficulty

| Easy, suitable for novice with little experience | Fairly easy, suitable for beginner with some experience | Fairly difficult, suitable for competent DIY mechanic | Difficult, suitable for experienced DIY mechanic | Very difficult, suitable for expert DIY or professional |

Specifications

General

Ignition type	One coil per plug
Coil winding resistance:	
Primary	N/A
Secondary	N/A
Firing order	1 – 3 – 4 – 2

Ignition timing

All engines	Controlled by engine management system

Spark plugs

See Chapter 1A Specifications

Torque wrench setting

	Nm	lbf ft
Knock sensor mounting bolt	20	15

1 General information

The vehicles covered by this manual are equipped with self-contained engine management systems, which control both the fuel injection and ignition. This Chapter deals with the ignition system components only – refer to Chapter 4A or 4B for details of the fuel system components.

The ignition system includes four separate coils, one fitted to each spark plug. The ignition timing is adjusted automatically by the Electronic Control Module (ECM). The ECM calculates and controls the ignition timing according to engine speed, crankshaft position, camshaft position, and intake airflow rate information, received from sensors mounted on and around the engine. Other parameters that affect ignition timing are throttle position and rate of opening, intake air temperature, coolant temperature and engine knock. Note that most of these sensors have a dual role, in that the information they provide is equally useful in determining the fuelling requirements as in deciding the optimum ignition or firing point – therefore, removal of some of the sensors mentioned below is described in Chapter 4A or 4B.

Knock sensors are mounted on the cylinder block in order to detect engine pre-ignition (or 'pinking') before it actually becomes audible. If pre-ignition occurs, the ECM retards the ignition timing of the cylinder that is pre-igniting in steps until the pre-ignition ceases. The ECM then advances the ignition timing of that cylinder in steps until it is restored to normal, or until pre-ignition occurs again.

Idle speed control is achieved partly by an electronic throttle valve positioning module, mounted on the side of the throttle body and partly by the ignition system, which gives fine control of the idle speed by altering the ignition timing. On direct injection engines, idle speed control is also achieved by adjusting the quantity of fuel injected – at idle speed in Stratified charge mode, the throttle valve is held fully open to reduce pumping losses, and therefore fuel consumption and emissions. Manual adjustment of the engine idle speed is not necessary or possible.

In the event of a fault in the system due to loss of a signal from one of the sensors, the ECM reverts to an emergency ('limp-home') program. This will allow the car to be driven, although engine operation and performance will be limited. A warning light on the instrument panel will illuminate if the fault is likely to cause an increase in harmful exhaust emissions.

1.6 The diagnostic connector (arrowed) is located under the driver's side of the facia

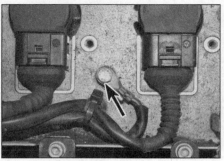

3.2 Coil wiring harness earth connection (arrowed)

3.5 Undo the harness screws (arrowed)

It should be noted that comprehensive fault diagnosis of all the engine management systems described in this Chapter is only possible with dedicated electronic test equipment. In the event of a sensor failing or other fault occurring, a fault code will be stored in the ECM's fault log, which can only be extracted from the ECM using a dedicated fault code reader. An Audi dealer will obviously have such a reader, but they are also available from other suppliers. It is unlikely to be cost-effective for the private owner to purchase a fault code reader, but a well-equipped local garage or auto-electrical specialist will have one. Once the fault has been identified, the removal and refitting sequences detailed in the following Sections will then allow the appropriate component(s) to be renewed as required. The diagnostic connector is located under the driver's side of the facia **(see illustration)**.

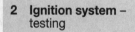

2 Ignition system – testing

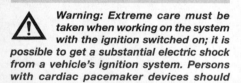

⚠️ **Warning: Extreme care must be taken when working on the system with the ignition switched on; it is possible to get a substantial electric shock from a vehicle's ignition system. Persons with cardiac pacemaker devices should** *keep well clear of the ignition circuits, components and test equipment. Always switch off the ignition before disconnecting or connecting any component and when using a multimeter to check resistances.*

1 If a fault appears in the engine management (fuel injection/ignition) system which is thought to ignition related, first ensure that the fault is not due to a poor electrical connection or poor maintenance; ie, check that the air cleaner filter element is clean, the spark plugs are in good condition and correctly gapped, that the engine breather hoses are clear and undamaged, referring to Chapter 1A for further information. If the engine is running very roughly, check the compression pressures as described in Chapter 2A or 2B (as applicable).

2 If these checks fail to reveal the cause of the problem the vehicle should be taken to a suitably-equipped Audi dealer or specialist for testing. A diagnostic connector is incorporated in the engine management circuit into which a special electronic diagnostic tester can be plugged (see Chapter 4A or 4B). The tester will locate the fault quickly and simply, alleviating the need to test all the system components individually which is a time-consuming operation that carries a high risk of damaging the ECM.

3 The only ignition system checks which can be carried out by the home mechanic are those described in Chapter 1A, relating to the spark plugs.

3 HT coils – removal and refitting

Removal

1 Release the fasteners (where applicable) and remove the plastic cover from the top of the engine.

1.8 litre engines

2 Unscrew the coil wiring harness earth connection from the cylinder head cover **(see illustration)**.

3 Release the retaining tabs and disconnect the wiring plugs from the each of the ignition coils.

4 Carefully lever up the coils from the cylinder head cover. A special Audi tool (T40039) is available to remove the coils.

2.0 litre engines

5 Undo the screws securing the coil wiring harness rail to the cylinder head cover **(see illustration)**.

6 Release the retaining tabs and disconnect the wiring plugs from each coil, then carefully lever up the coils from the cylinder

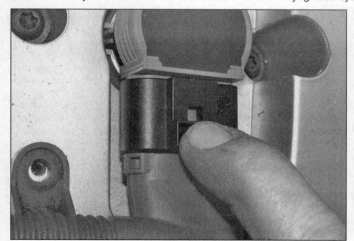

3.6a Depress the tabs and disconnect the coil plugs

3.6b Only lever under the thick rib on the coil top . . .

3.6c . . . and remove the coil

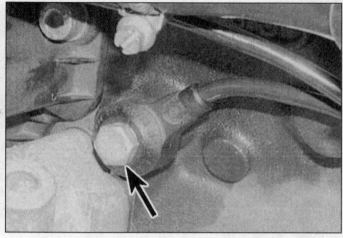

5.3 Unscrew the knock sensor mounting bolt (arrowed)

head cover **(see illustrations)**. A special Audi tool (T40039) is available to remove the coils. Remove the coils.

Refitting

7 Refitting is a reversal of the relevant removal procedure.

4 Ignition timing – checking and adjusting

The ignition timing is controlled by the engine management system ECM and cannot be adjusted manually. The vehicle must be taken to an Audi dealer if the timing requires checking.

5 Knock sensors – removal and refitting

Removal

1 The two knock sensors are located on the left-hand side of the cylinder block.

2 Unplug the wiring from the sensor at the connector.
3 Unscrew the mounting bolt and remove the sensor **(see illustration)**.

Refitting

4 Refitting is a reversal of removal, but note that the sensor's operation will be affected if its mounting bolt is not tightened to exactly the right torque.

Chapter 5 Part C:
Pre/post-heating system – diesel engine models

Contents

General description 1   Glow plugs – testing, removal and refitting 2

Degrees of difficulty

Easy, suitable for novice with little experience	**Fairly easy,** suitable for beginner with some experience	**Fairly difficult,** suitable for competent DIY mechanic	**Difficult,** suitable for experienced DIY mechanic	**Very difficult,** suitable for expert DIY or professional

Specifications

General

Engine code*:
74 kW (96 bhp)	AVB
85 kW (111 bhp)	BKE and BRB
96 kW (125 bhp)	AVF and AWX

* Note: *See 'Vehicle identification' for the location of the code marking on the engine.*

Glow plugs

Current consumption	8 amps per glow plug

Torque wrench settings

	Nm	lbf ft
Glow plug to cylinder head:		
Metal glow plugs	15	11
Ceramic glow plugs	12	9

1 General information

To assist cold starting, diesel engined models are fitted with a preheating system, which consists of four glow plugs, a glow plug control unit (incorporated in the ECM), a facia-mounted warning lamp and the associated electrical wiring.

The glow plugs are miniature electric heating elements, encapsulated in a metal or ceramic case with a probe at one end and electrical connection at the other. Each combustion chamber has a glow plug threaded into it, which is positioned directly in line with the incoming spray of fuel. When the glow plug is energised, the air in the combustion chamber is heated, allowing optimum combustion temperature to be achieved more quickly.

The duration of the preheating period is governed by the ECM, which monitors the temperature of the engine via the coolant temperature sensor and alters the preheating time to suit the conditions. Preheating only takes place at coolant temperatures below 9°C.

A facia-mounted warning light informs the driver that preheating is taking place. The light extinguishes when sufficient preheating has taken place to allow the engine to be started, but power will still be supplied to the glow plugs for a further period until the engine is started. If no attempt is made to start the engine, the power supply to the glow plugs is switched off to prevent battery drain and glow plug burn-out. After the engine is started, there is a period of post-heating which takes place irrespective of whether it is preceded by preheating or not. This period lasts for a maximum of 4 minutes after the engine has been started, at engine speeds of under 2500 rpm. The heating is switched off after this period, or if the engine speed exceeds 2500 rpm. Post-heating reduces combustion noise and improves idling quality, and additionally reduces hydrocarbon emissions.

The warning light comes on when the ignition is initially switched on with a cold engine, and indicates that the glow plugs are being energised. If the light does not come on in these conditions, there is a defect in the glow plug system which should be investigated. When the engine is warm, the light may not come on, and the engine can be started straight away; any post-heating will take place automatically.

2 Glow plugs – testing, removal and refitting

Testing

1 If the system malfunctions, testing is ultimately by substitution of known good units, but some preliminary checks may be made as described in the following paragraphs.

2 Before testing the system, check that the battery voltage is at least 11.5 volts, using a voltmeter. Switch off the ignition.

3 Where necessary for access, remove the engine top cover(s). Removal details vary according to model, but the cover retaining nuts are concealed under circular covers, which are prised out of the main cover. Remove the nuts, and lift the cover from the engine, releasing any wiring or hoses attached.

4 Disconnect the wiring plug from the coolant temperature sender at the rear of the engine. Disconnecting the sender in this way simulates a cold engine, which is a requirement for the glow plug system to activate.

5 Disconnect the wiring connector from the most convenient glow plug, and connect a suitable voltmeter between the wiring connector and a good earth.

6 Have an assistant switch on the ignition. Battery voltage should be displayed for approximately 20 seconds – note that the voltage will drop to zero when the pre- and post-heating periods end.

7 If no supply voltage can be detected at the glow plug, then either the glow plug relay (where applicable) or the supply wiring must be faulty. Also check that the glow plug fuse or fusible link (usually located on top of the battery) has not blown – if it has, this may indicate a serious wiring fault; consult an Audi dealer or specialist for advice.

8 To locate a faulty glow plug, first disconnect the battery negative cable and position it away from the terminal (see Chapter 5A).

9 Disconnect the wiring plug from the glow plug terminal. Measure the electrical resistance between the glow plug terminal and the engine earth. Ceramic glow plugs should have a resistance of no more than 1 ohm, and as a guide on metal glow plugs, more than a few ohms indicates that the plug is defective. Ceramic glow plugs are identified by a white or silver seal around the top of the plug. Metal plugs have a red seal around the top of the plug.

10 If a suitable ammeter is available, connect it between the glow plug and its wiring connector, and measure the steady-state current consumption (ignore the initial current surge, which will be about 50% higher). As a guide, high current consumption (or no current draw at all) indicates a faulty glow plug.

11 As a final check, remove the glow plugs and inspect their stems for signs of damage. A badly burned or charred stem may be an indication of a faulty fuel injector.

Removal

Ceramic glow plugs

12 Ceramic glow plugs may be fitted to engine code BKE. They are identified by a white or silver seal at the top of the plug. Due to the materials used in their construction, special rules must be followed regarding their handling:

a) *Do not remove the plugs from the packaging until you are ready to fit them.*

b) *Ceramic plugs are very delicate. Protect them from knocks. Audi claim that plugs which have been dropped (even from 2.0 cm) must not be fitted.*

c) *Damaged glow plugs may cause engine damage. Remove any fragments of damaged ceramic heater tips from the combustion chamber.*

d) *The software within the ECM is specific to ceramic plugs. Therefore, these type of plugs are not interchangeable with metal plugs.*

13 Audi state that before ceramic plugs can be removed, they must be burnt clean using a function of their VAS 5051 diagnostic tester. Unless access to this equipment is available, it may be prudent to entrust plug renewal to an Audi dealer or suitably-equipped specialist.

14 Pull out the engine oil level dipstick, then prise out the caps, undo the nuts, and remove the plastic cover from the top of the engine. Refit the dipstick.

15 To improve access to No 4 glow plug, undo the clamp screw, and slide the fuel filter up and out of the bracket (see Chapter 1B). There is no need to disconnect the fuel hoses.

16 Carefully pull the connector(s) from the top of the glow plug(s).

17 Using a universal joint, extension and a deep 10 mm socket, unscrew and remove the glow plug(s) from the cylinder head. Note that the plug must be kept 'straight' when being removed – if the ceramic heater tip touches the cylinder head, etc, it may easily be damaged.

Caution: Do not exceed the maximum release torque of 20 Nm (15 lbf ft). If the plug will not release, apply releasing agent (Plus Gas, etc) to the area of the plug threads/cylinder head. Wait a few minutes and try again. Exceeding the release torque may cause damage to the ceramic heater tip, and therefore fragments to enter the combustion chamber. These fragments could cause engine damage. If it is still not possible to unscrew the plugs, Audi insist that the cylinder head must be removed, and the plugs unscrewed.

Metal glow plugs

18 Pull out the engine oil level dipstick, then prise out the caps, undo the nuts, and remove the plastic cover from the top of the engine. Refit the dipstick.

19 To improve access to No 4 glow plug, undo the clamp screw, and slide the fuel filter up and out of the bracket (see Chapter 1B) **(see illustration)**. There is no need to disconnect the fuel hoses.

20 Carefully pull the connector(s) from the top of the glow plug(s).

21 Using a universal joint, extension and a deep 10 mm socket, unscrew and remove the glow plug(s) from the cylinder head **(see illustrations)**.

Refitting

Ceramic glow plugs

22 Ensure the threads in the cylinder head and on the glow plugs are clean and dry, and free of oil or grease. Clean any combustion deposits from the area around the glow plug apertures in the cylinder head.

23 Fit the glow plugs finger tight only, taking great care not to allow the ceramic heater tips to contact any part of the cylinder head, etc.

24 Tighten the plugs to the specified torque.

25 Using a hand-held multimeter, check the resistance of the plugs. If the resistance of any of the plugs exceeds 1 ohm, remove it and check the ceramic heater tip is not damaged. If any of the tips are damaged, the ceramic fragments must be removed from the combustion chamber before the engine is started, otherwise extensive engine damage may result.

26 Reconnect the glow plug wiring plugs.

27 Audi insist that the engine management ECM self-diagnosis system must be interrogated for any stored faults relating to the glow plugs before the engine is started. If any glow plug related faults are stored, do not start the engine. Remove the plugs and inspect them for damage.

28 The remainder of refitting is a reversal of removal.

Metal glow plugs

29 Ensure the threads in the cylinder head and glow plugs are clean, then refit the plugs to the cylinder head.

30 Tighten the plugs to the specified torque.

31 Reconnect the glow plug wiring plugs.

32 The remainder of refitting is a reversal of removal.

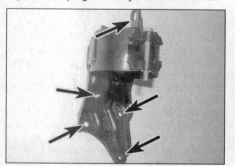

2.19 The fuel filter bracket is attached to the cylinder block/head at five points (arrowed)

2.21a Glow plug location in the cylinder head (arrowed)

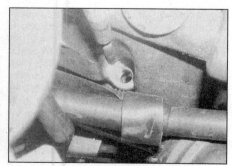

2.21b Removing No 4 glow plug

Chapter 6
Clutch

Contents

Section number

Clutch friction disc and pressure plate – removal, inspection and
  refitting 6
Clutch pedal – removal and refitting. 3
Clutch pedal switch – removal and refitting 8
General information 1

Section number

Hydraulic system – bleeding 2
Master cylinder – removal, overhaul and refitting 4
Release bearing and lever – removal, inspection and refitting...... 7
Slave cylinder – removal, overhaul and refitting 5

Degrees of difficulty

Easy, suitable for novice with little experience	**Fairly easy,** suitable for beginner with some experience	**Fairly difficult,** suitable for competent DIY mechanic	**Difficult,** suitable for experienced DIY mechanic	**Very difficult,** suitable for expert DIY or professional

Specifications

General

Type	Single dry friction disc, diaphragm spring with spring-loaded hub, self-adjusting pressure plate (SAC)*
Operation	Hydraulic with slave and master cylinders

Friction disc diameter:
  6-speed transmission.................................... 240 mm
  5-speed transmission:
    Except 85 or 96 kW diesel models...................... 228 mm
    85 or 96kW diesel models .... 240 mm
* Optional

Torque wrench settings

	Nm	lbf ft
Clutch master cylinder mounting bolts	20	15
Clutch pedal bracket mounting bolts (from inside engine compartment):		
Long Torx bolt (also secures brake master cylinder and servo).....	25	18
Short hex socket-head bolt	25	18
Clutch release lever leaf spring retaining bolt*:		
01E and 0A1 transmissions	25	18
Clutch slave cylinder mounting bolt*	23	17
Hydraulic pipe unions.....................................	15	11
Pressure plate-to-flywheel bolt:		
5-speed transmission.....................................	25	18
6-speed transmission.....................................	22	16

* Use new fasteners

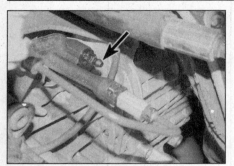

2.10 Use a length of plastic or rubber tubing that is a tight fit over the end of the bleed screw (arrowed)

1 General information

The clutch is of single dry plate type, incorporating a diaphragm spring pressure plate, and is hydraulically-operated.

The clutch cover (pressure plate) is bolted to the rear face of the flywheel, and the friction disc is located between the pressure plate and the flywheel friction surface. The disc hub is splined to the transmission input shaft and is free to slide along the splines. Friction lining material is riveted to each side of the disc and the disc hub incorporates cushioning springs to absorb transmission shocks and ensure a smooth take-up of drive. The flywheel is manufactured in two parts instead of the conventional single unit; the friction surface has a limited buffered movement in relation to the main flywheel mass bolted to the rear of the crankshaft. This has the effect of absorbing the initial clutch engagement shock and makes for a smoother gearchange.

When the clutch pedal is depressed, the slave cylinder pushrod moves the release lever forwards, and the release bearing is forced onto the diaphragm spring fingers. As the centre of the spring is pushed in, the outer part of the spring moves out and releases the pressure plate from the friction disc. Drive then ceases to be transmitted to the transmission.

When the clutch pedal is released, the diaphragm spring forces the pressure plate into contact with the linings on the friction disc, and at the same time pushes the disc slightly forward along the input shaft splines into engagement with the flywheel. The friction disc is now firmly sandwiched between the pressure plate and flywheel. This causes drive to be taken up.

An over-centre spring is fitted to the clutch pedal to equalise the operating effort over the full pedal stroke.

As the linings wear on the friction disc, the pressure plate rest position moves closer to the flywheel resulting in the 'rest' position of the diaphragm spring fingers being raised. Some vehicles equipped with 6-speed transmission, may have a Self-adjusting clutch

(SAC) fitted. On these units, as the friction disc wears, an adjustment ring of varied thickness within the pressure plate assembly, rotates slightly to compensate. This should ensure a more consistent feel to the clutch pedal. The hydraulic system requires no adjustment since the quantity of hydraulic fluid in the circuit automatically compensates for wear every time the clutch pedal is operated.

2 Hydraulic system – bleeding

⚠️ *Warning: Hydraulic fluid is poisonous; thoroughly wash off spills from bare skin without delay. Seek immediate medical advice if any fluid is swallowed or gets into the eyes. Certain types of hydraulic fluid are inflammable and may ignite when brought into contact with hot components. Hydraulic fluid is also an effective paint stripper. If spillage occurs onto painted bodywork or fittings, it should be washed off immediately, using copious quantities of cold water. It is also hygroscopic (it absorbs moisture from the air) therefore old fluid should never be re-used.*

1 The correct operation of any hydraulic system is only possible after removing all air from the components and circuit; this is achieved by bleeding the system.

2 During the bleeding procedure, add only clean, unused hydraulic fluid of the recommended type; never re-use fluid that has already been bled from the system. Ensure that sufficient fluid is available before starting work.

3 If there is any possibility of incorrect fluid being already in the system, the hydraulic circuit must be flushed completely with uncontaminated, correct fluid.

4 If hydraulic fluid has been lost from the system, or air has entered because of a leak, ensure that the fault is cured before continuing further.

5 The bleed screw is located on the slave cylinder located on the left-hand upper side of the transmission. As access to the bleed screw is limited it will be necessary to jack up the front of the vehicle and support it on axle stands so that the screw can be reached from below. Release the fasteners and remove the transmission undershield (where fitted).

6 Check that all pipes and hoses are secure, unions tight and the bleed screw is closed. Clean any dirt from around the bleed screw.

7 Unscrew the master cylinder fluid reservoir cap (the clutch shares the same fluid reservoir as the braking system), and top the master cylinder reservoir up to the upper (MAX) level line. Refit the cap loosely, and remember to maintain the fluid level at least above the lower (MIN) level line throughout the procedure, or there is a risk of further air entering the system.

8 There is a number of one-man, do-it-yourself bleeding kits currently available from motor accessory shops. It is recommended that one of these kits is used whenever possible, as they greatly simplify the bleeding operation, and reduce the risk of expelled air and fluid being drawn back into the system. If such a kit is not available, the basic (two-man) method must be used, which is described in detail below.

9 If a kit is to be used, prepare the vehicle as described previously, and follow the kit manufacturer's instructions, as the procedure may vary slightly according to the type being used; generally, they are as outlined below in the relevant sub-section.

Bleeding

Basic (two-man) method

10 Collect a clean glass jar, a suitable length of plastic or rubber tubing which is a tight fit over the bleed screw **(see illustration)**, and a ring spanner to fit the screw. The help of an assistant will also be required.

11 Remove the dust cap from the bleed screw. Fit the spanner and tube to the screw, place the other end of the tube in the jar, and pour in sufficient fluid to cover the end of the tube.

12 Ensure that the fluid level is maintained at least above the lower level line in the reservoir throughout the procedure.

13 Have the assistant fully depress the clutch pedal several times to build-up pressure, then maintain it on the final downstroke.

14 While pedal pressure is maintained, unscrew the bleed screw (approximately one turn) and allow the compressed fluid and air to flow into the jar. The assistant should maintain pedal pressure and should not release it until instructed to do so. When the flow stops, tighten the bleed screw again, have the assistant release the pedal slowly, and recheck the reservoir fluid level.

15 Repeat the steps given in paragraphs 13 and 14 until the fluid emerging from the bleed screw is free from air bubbles. If the master cylinder has been drained and refilled allow approximately five seconds between cycles for the master cylinder passages to refill.

16 When no more air bubbles appear, tighten the bleed screw securely, remove the tube and spanner, and refit the dust cap. Do not overtighten the bleed screw.

Using a one-way valve kit

17 As their name implies, these kits consist of a length of tubing with a one-way valve fitted, to prevent expelled air and fluid being drawn back into the system; some kits include a translucent container, which can be positioned so that the air bubbles can be more easily seen flowing from the end of the tube.

18 The kit is connected to the bleed screw, which is then opened. The user returns to the driver's seat, depresses the clutch pedal with a smooth, steady stroke, and slowly releases it; this is repeated until the expelled fluid is clear of air bubbles.

19 Note that these kits simplify work so much that it is easy to forget the fluid reservoir level; ensure that this is maintained at least above the lower level line at all times.

Using a pressure-bleeding kit

20 These kits are usually operated by the reservoir of pressurised air contained in the spare tyre. However, note that it will probably be necessary to reduce the pressure to a lower level than normal; refer to the instructions supplied with the kit.

21 By connecting a pressurised, fluid-filled container to the fluid reservoir, bleeding can be carried out simply by opening the bleed screw and allowing the fluid to flow out until no more air bubbles can be seen in the expelled fluid.

22 This method has the advantage that the large reservoir of fluid provides an additional safeguard against air being drawn into the system during bleeding.

All methods

23 When bleeding is complete, and correct pedal feel is restored, tighten the bleed screw securely and wash off any spilt fluid. Refit the dust cap to the bleed screw.

24 Check the hydraulic fluid level in the master cylinder reservoir, and top-up if necessary (see *Weekly Checks*).

25 Discard any hydraulic fluid that has been bled from the system; it will not be fit for re-use.

26 Check the operation of the clutch pedal. If the clutch is still not operating correctly, air must still be present in the system, and further bleeding is required. Failure to bleed satisfactorily after a reasonable repetition of the bleeding procedure may be due to worn master cylinder/release cylinder seals.

---

3 Clutch pedal –
removal and refitting

Removal

1 Remove the storage compartment/panel from below the steering column. Unclip the cover then undo the retaining screws and pull the storage compartment from the clips in the facia. This will allow access to the pedal bracket.

2 Where fitted, disconnect the wiring and rotate the switch above the clutch pedal anti-clockwise 90°, then remove it **(see illustration)**.

3 Undo the pivot bolt at the left-hand end of the pedal bracket, and slide the brake pedal to the right **(see illustration)**. As the brake pedal moves, the arm at the left-hand end and the clutch pedal will be unsupported. Note the position of the over-centre spring.

4 Lower the clutch pedal, depress the clip each side, and disconnect the master cylinder pushrod from the pedal.

Refitting

6 Refitting is a reversal of removal. Apply

3.2 Disconnect the plug, then rotate the clutch switch 90° (arrowed)

locking fluid to the pivot bolt before tightening it to the specified torque. Refer to Chapter 9 and make sure that the brake pedal is refitted correctly.

---

4 Master cylinder –
removal, overhaul and refitting

Note: *Refer to the warning at the beginning of Section 2 regarding the hazards of working with hydraulic fluid.*

Removal

1 Remove the engine management ECM as described in the relevant part of Chapter 4.

2 Note their fitted positions, and disconnect the wiring plugs within the plenum chamber electronics box.

3 Release the retaining clips and pull the auxiliary relay carrier upwards, then pull

4.3 Release the clips and remove the auxiliary relay carrier

4.5 Disconnect the fluid supply hose (arrowed)

3.3 Brake/clutch pedal pivot bolt (arrowed)

the engine wiring harness (complete with rubber grommet) through the opening in the electronics box **(see illustration)**.

4 Undo the 3 nuts and lift the electronics box out from the plenum chamber **(see illustration)**.

5 Place cloth rags beneath the clutch master cylinder fluid supply hose, then fit a hose clamp to the hose and disconnect it from the master cylinder **(see illustration)**. Plug the open end of the hose to prevent dirt ingress. The hose supplies the master cylinder with fluid from the brake master cylinder reservoir. Be prepared for fluid spillage.

6 Remove the rubber grommet over the supply hose from the bulkhead.

7 Prise out the retaining clip and pull the fluid pressure pipe from the clutch master cylinder **(see illustration)**.

8 Disconnect the brake fluid level sensor wiring plug, then unscrew the pin securing

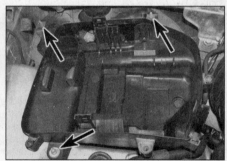

4.4 Undo the nuts (arrowed) and remove the electronics box

4.7 Prise out the retaining clip (arrowed) and disconnect the pressure pipe from the master cylinder

4.15 Slacken the retaining bolt (arrowed) above the brake pedal

the brake fluid reservoir to the brake master cylinder. Do not remove the reservoir.

9 Prise the brake servo vacuum hose from the servo.

10 Slacken the nuts then undo the 2 Torx screws securing the brake master cylinder/servo to the bulkhead/pedal bracket. To access the upper screw, it will be necessary to move the fluid reservoir slightly to one side.

11 Inside the car, remove the storage compartment/panel from below the steering column (see Chapter 11).

12 Separate the brake pedal pushrod from the servo (see Chapter 9).

13 Make alignment marks between the steering rack pinion and the lower part of the steering column universal joint, then unscrew the pinch-bolt, and pull the joint upwards and off the pinion.

14 Note their fitted positions, then disconnect the wiring plugs from the clutch pedal switch, brake pedal switch and accelerator pedal position sender assembly.

15 Slacken the retaining bolt above the brake pedal, and slide the entire foot pedal assembly rearwards **(see illustration)**. Be prepared for fluid spillage.

16 Depress the clutch pedal and use Audi tool T40025 to retain the over-centre spring in the tension position, then release the pedal and remove the over-centre spring.

17 Compress the clips each side and separate the clutch master cylinder pushrod from the pedal **(see illustration)**. Take great care not to damage the mounting clip for the clutch pedal switch.

18 Undo the 2 bolts and detach the clutch

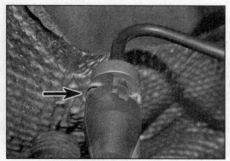

5.5 Prise out the clip (arrowed) and pull the pipe from the slave cylinder

4.17 Depress the pushrod retaining clips (arrowed)

master cylinder from the pedal bracket assembly **(see illustration)**.

Overhaul

19 At the time of writing, it would appear repair kits are not available. Check with your local Audi dealer or parts specialist.

Refitting

20 Refitting is a reversal of removal, but tighten all nuts and bolts to the specified torques where given. When repositioning the pedal bracket onto the bulkhead, have an assistant guide the clutch master cylinder pipe through the location hole from the engine compartment side. When reconnecting the fluid pressure line, the clip must engage audibly. Bleed the clutch hydraulic system as described in Section 2.

| 5 | Slave cylinder – removal, overhaul and refitting |

Note: *Refer to the warning at the beginning of Section 2 regarding the hazards of working with hydraulic fluid.*
Note: *A new slave cylinder mounting bolt will be required.*

Removal

1 The slave cylinder is located on top of the transmission on the left-hand side.

2 Apply the handbrake, then jack up the front of the vehicle and support it on axle stands (see *Jacking and vehicle support*). Remove the engine undertray.

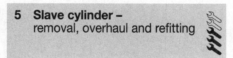

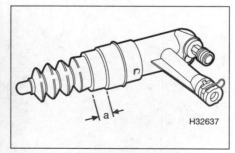

5.7 Apply a thin layer of lithium grease to the area (a) of the slave cylinder before inserting it into the transmission housing

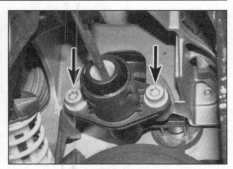

4.18 Clutch master cylinder bolts (arrowed)

3 Clamp the rubber section of the hydraulic hose leading from the master cylinder to the slave cylinder using a brake hose clamp, to prevent loss of hydraulic fluid.

4 Unscrew the mounting bolt and withdraw the slave cylinder. As the cylinder is being removed, recover the hose support bracket.

5 Using a screwdriver, prise out the spring clip and disconnect the hydraulic line from the slave cylinder. Tape over or plug the end of the line and the slave cylinder aperture **(see illustration)**.
Caution: Do not depress the clutch pedal with the slave cylinder removed.

Overhaul

6 At the time of writing, it would appear that slave cylinder overhaul kits are not available. Check with your local Audi dealer or spare parts specialist.

Refitting

7 Refitting is a reversal of removal, but smear a little lithium-based grease to the outer surface of the rubber boot before locating the slave cylinder in the transmission aperture **(see illustration)**. Tighten the new mounting bolt and union to the specified torque and finally bleed the system as described in Section 2. The end of the pushrod which contacts the release lever should be lightly lubricated with a molybdenum disulphide grease and care must be taken to ensure that the pushrod actually engages with the depression in the lever. The slave cylinder must be pressed into the transmission casing before the mounting bolt can be inserted. Due to the limited access and the fact that the slave cylinder must be pushed against the considerable force of the internal return spring, refitting should be made in stages. First fully insert the cylinder (without the hose support bracket), ensuring that the bolt hole is correctly aligned, then refit the hose support bracket so that the front tags are engaged with the cut-out in the cylinder. With the cylinder held in this position, insert the mounting bolt and tighten to the specified torque. Finally locate the hydraulic line on the support bracket. Upon completion, check the action of the clutch pedal. If usually strong resistance is felt, it is possible that the slave cylinder operating rod has been guided past the release lever. Do not apply excessive pressure on the clutch pedal – Audi state that the slave cylinder will be damaged if the applied force exceeds 300 N – normal pedal force is approximately 115 N.

6 Clutch friction disc and pressure plate – removal, inspection and refitting

⚠️ *Warning: Dust created by clutch wear and deposited on the clutch components may contain asbestos, which is a health hazard. DO NOT blow it out with compressed air or inhale any of it. DO NOT use petrol or petroleum-based solvents to clean off the dust. Brake system cleaner or methylated spirit should be used to flush the dust into a suitable receptacle. After the clutch components are wiped clean with clean rags, dispose of the contaminated rags and cleaner in a sealed container.*

Removal

1 Access to the clutch is obtained by removing the transmission as described in Chapter 7A.
2 Mark the clutch pressure plate and flywheel in relation to each other. Note that on some models, Audi used a white spot on the flywheel and pressure plate cover to indicate the correct assembly position.
3 Hold the flywheel stationary, then unscrew the clutch pressure plate bolts one quarter of a turn at a time, in a clockwise direction using an Allen key **(see illustrations)**. With the bolts unscrewed two or three turns, check that the pressure plate is not binding on the dowel pins. If necessary, use a screwdriver to release the pressure plate.
4 Remove all the bolts, then lift the clutch pressure plate and friction disc from the flywheel.

Inspection

Note: *Due to the amount of work necessary to remove and refit clutch components, it is usually considered good practice to renew the clutch friction disc, pressure plate assembly and release bearing as a matched set, even if only one of these is actually worn enough to require renewal. It is also worth considering the renewal of the clutch components on a preventative basis if the engine and/or transmission have been removed for some other reason.*

5 Clean the pressure plate friction surface, clutch friction disc and flywheel. Do not inhale the dust, as it may contain asbestos which is dangerous to health.
6 Examine the fingers of the diaphragm spring for wear or scoring **(see illustration)**. If the depth of wear exceeds half the thickness of the fingers, a new pressure plate assembly must be fitted.
7 Examine the pressure plate for scoring, cracking, distortion and discoloration. Light scoring is acceptable, but if excessive, a new pressure plate assembly must be fitted. If the distortion of the friction surface exceeds 1.0 mm, renew it.
8 Examine the friction disc linings for wear and cracking, and for contamination with oil or grease **(see illustration)**. The linings are worn excessively if they are worn down to, or near, the rivets. Check the disc hub and splines for wear by temporarily fitting it on the transmission input shaft. Renew the friction disc as necessary.
9 Examine the flywheel friction surface for scoring, cracking and discoloration (caused by overheating). If excessive, it may be possible to have the flywheel machined by an engineering works, otherwise it should be renewed.
10 Ensure that all parts are clean, and free of oil or grease, before reassembling. Apply just a small amount of lithium-based grease to the splines of the friction disc hub. **Do not** use copper-based grease. Note that new pressure plates and clutch covers may be coated with protective grease. It is only permissible to clean the grease away from the friction disc lining contact area. Removal of the grease from other areas will shorten the service life of the clutch.

Refitting

11 Commence reassembly by locating the friction disc on the flywheel, with the raised side of the hub facing outwards (normally marked Getriebeseite or Gearbox side). If possible, the centralising tool (see paragraph 19) should be used to hold the disc on the flywheel at this stage **(see illustrations)**.

Models with self-adjusting clutch

12 On models with a self-adjusting clutch (SAC), where a new friction disc is fitted,

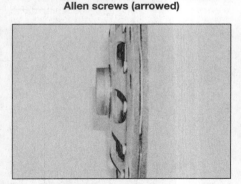

6.3a Undo the pressure plate retaining Allen screws (arrowed)

6.3b It may be necessary to prise the plate from the dowel pins

6.6 Examine the fingers of the diaphragm spring for wear or scoring

6.8 Examine the friction disc linings for wear and cracking

6.11a Install the clutch friction disc with the raised centre section facing away from the flywheel

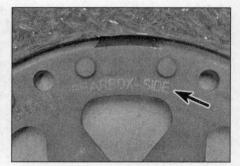

6.11b The friction disc is normally marked to indicated the gearbox side (arrowed)

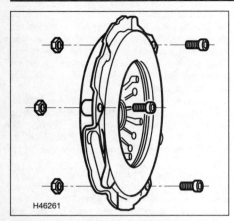

6.13 Insert three 8 mm bolts from the flywheel side, and secure with nuts

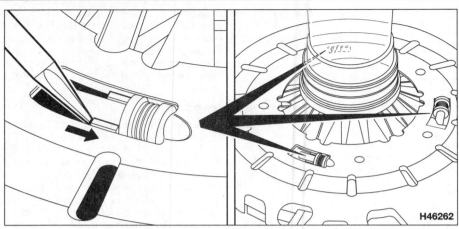

6.15 Move the adjuster ring anti-clockwise to the stop

6.17 Fit the pressure plate over the locating dowel pins (arrowed)

but the pressure plate is to be re-used, it is necessary to reset the pressure plate adjusting ring prior to assembly as follows. **Note:** *On models equipped with a Sachs SAC, the friction disc and pressure plate can only be renewed together.*

13 Insert three 8 mm bolts into the pressure plate mounting holes at intervals of 120°. The bolts should be inserted from the flywheel side, and retained by nuts **(see illustration)**.

14 Place the pressure plate face down on the bed of an hydraulic press so that only the heads of the bolts make contact with the press bed, then place a circular spacer over the ends of the diaphragm springs fingers.

15 Use 2 screwdrivers to attempt to rotate the adjuster ring anti-clockwise. Apply just enough pressure with the hydraulic press until it's just possible to move the adjuster ring **(see illustration)**.

16 Once the adjuster ring is against its stop, relieve the pressure. The ring is now reset. **Note:** *New pressure plates are supplied in this reset position.*

All models

17 Locate the clutch pressure plate on the disc, and fit it onto the location dowels **(see illustration)**. If refitting the original pressure plate, make sure that the previously-made marks are aligned.

18 Insert the bolts finger-tight to hold the pressure plate in position. On models with the Sachs SAC, ensure the position sensor stop mechanism is free to move **(see illustration)**.

19 The friction disc must now be centralised, to ensure correct alignment of the transmission input shaft with the spigot bearing in the crankshaft. To do this, a proprietary tool may be used, or alternatively, use a wooden mandrel made to fit inside the friction disc and flywheel spigot bearing. Insert the tool through the friction disc into the spigot bearing, and make sure that it is central.

20 Tighten the pressure plate bolts progressively and in diagonal sequence, until the specified torque setting is achieved, then remove the centralising tool **(see illustration)**.

6.20 With the pressure plate bolts tightened, remove the centralising tool

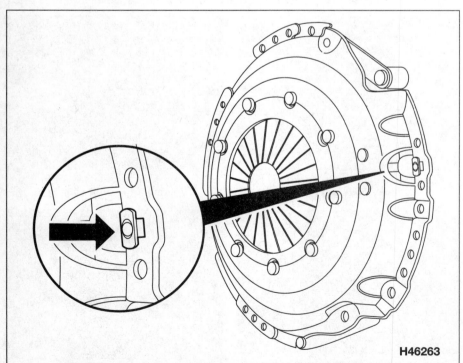

6.18 Ensure the position sensor stop mechanism is free to move (arrowed) – Sachs SAC only

On models with the Sachs SAC, the position sensor stop pin should lift away from the pressure plate as the bolts are tightened.

21 Check the release bearing in the transmission bellhousing for smooth operation, and if necessary renew it with reference to Section 7.

22 Refit the transmission with reference to Chapter 7A.

7 Release bearing and lever – removal, inspection and refitting

Removal

1 Remove the transmission as described in Chapter 7A.

2 On 012/01W and 01X transmissions, use a screwdriver to prise the release lever from the ball-stud inside the transmission bellhousing. If this proves difficult, push the spring clip from the pivot end of the release lever by pushing it through the hole. This will release the pivot end of the lever from the ball-stud. Now withdraw the lever together with the release bearing from the guide sleeve **(see illustrations)**. On 01E and 0A1 transmissions, undo the single bolt and remove the leaf spring. Withdraw the release lever complete with release bearing and intermediate piece.

3 Use a screwdriver to depress the plastic tabs and separate the bearing from the lever **(see illustrations)**.

4 On 012/01W and 01X transmissions, remove the plastic pivot from the ball-stud. The release lever locates on the plastic pivot.

Inspection

5 Spin the release bearing by hand, and check it for smooth running. Any tendency to seize or run rough will necessitate renewal of the bearing. If it is to be re-used, wipe it clean with a dry cloth; on no account should the bearing be washed in a liquid solvent, otherwise the internal grease will be removed.

Refitting

6 On 012/01W and 01X transmissions, commence refitting by lubricating the ball-stud and plastic pivot with a little lithium-based grease **(see illustration)**. On all transmissions, smear a little grease on the release bearing surface which contacts the diaphragm spring fingers and the release lever, and also on the guide sleeve. Wipe off any excess grease.

7 On 012/01W and 01X transmissions, fit the spring onto the release lever, and make sure the plastic pivot is in place on the ball-stud. Refit the lever together with the bearing and press the release lever onto the ball-stud until the spring holds it in position **(see illustrations)**. On 01E and 0A1 transmissions, re-glue the plastic ring to the

bearing race, and engage the retaining lugs of the release bearing with the release lever. Set the release lever on the intermediate

piece, fit the leaf spring, and tighten the retaining bolt to the specified torque **(see illustration overleaf)**.

7.2a Push the spring clip to release the arm from the pivot stud – 012 transmission

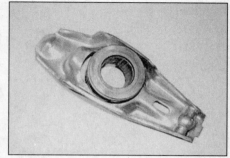

7.2b Release lever and bearing removed from the 012 transmission

7.3a Depress the plastic tabs . . .

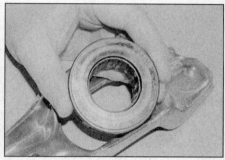

7.3b . . . and remove the bearing from the arm

7.6 Lubricate the ball-stud and pivot with a little lithium grease

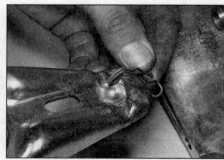

7.7a Locate the spring over the end of the release lever . . .

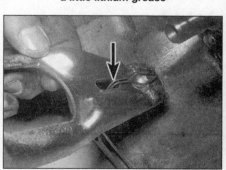

7.7b . . . and press the spring into the hole (arrowed) . . .

7.7c . . . then press the release lever onto the ball-stud until the spring clip holds it in position

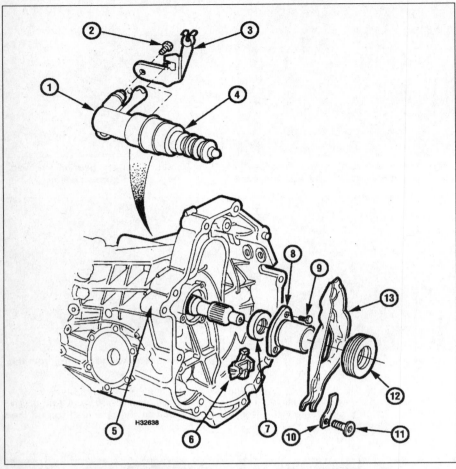

7.7d Clutch release mechanism – 01E transmission

1 Slave cylinder	5 Gearbox	9 Bolt
2 Bolt	6 Intermediate	10 Leaf spring
3 Hose support	piece	11 Bolt
bracket	7 Oil seal	12 Release bearing
4 Plunger	8 Guide sleeve	13 Release lever

8 Clutch pedal switch
– removal and refitting

Removal

1 Inside the car, remove the driver's side storage compartment. Unclip the cover then undo the retaining screws and pull the storage compartment from the clips in the facia. This will allow access to the pedal switch.
2 Disconnect the wiring plug, then rotate the switch 45° anti-clockwise and pull it from the bracket **(see illustration 3.2)**.

Refitting

3 Pull the operating rod out all the way from the switch.
4 With the clutch pedal fully up in the 'at rest' position, insert the switch into the bracket, pressing the operating rod against the clutch pedal, and twist the switch 45° clockwise.
5 Reconnect the wiring plug. The remainder of refitting is a reversal of removal.

Chapter 7 Part A:
Manual transmission

Contents

Section number

Gearchange linkage – adjustment 2
General information 1
Manual transmission – removal and refitting 3
Manual transmission oil level check . . . . See Chapter 1A or 1B

Section number

Manual transmission overhaul – general information 4
Oil seals – renewal 7
Roadspeed sensor – removal and refitting 6
Transmission switches – renewal 5

Degrees of difficulty

| Easy, suitable for novice with little experience 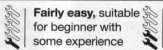 | Fairly easy, suitable for beginner with some experience 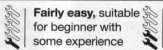 | Fairly difficult, suitable for competent DIY mechanic 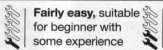 | Difficult, suitable for experienced DIY mechanic 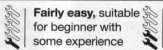 | Very difficult, suitable for expert DIY or professional |

Specifications

General

Type . . . . Transmission mounted on rear of engine, with drive flanges to front wheels. Five or six forward speeds and reverse, synchromesh on all gears, integral final drive

Application:
  1.8 litre petrol:
    110 kW (149 bhp) 09/00 to 06/02 . . . . 012/01W 5-speed
    120 kW (156 bhp) 05/03-on 012/01W 5-speed
    125 kW (163 bhp) 07/02 to 05/03 . . . . 012/01W 5-speed
    140 kW (182 bhp) 07/02-on 0A1 6-speed
  2.0 litre petrol:
    96 kW (125 bhp) 09/00-on 012/01W 5-speed
    110 kW (143 bhp) 05/03-on 012/01W 5-speed
  Diesel:
    74 kW (100 bhp) and 85 kW (115 bhp) 012/01W 5-speed
    96 kW (125 bhp) 08/01-on 01E 6-speed
    96 kW (125 bhp) 04/03-on 01X 6-speed
Lubricant capacities . . . . See Chapter 1A or 1B

Torque wrench settings

	Nm	lbf ft
Drive flange:		
Stage 1	10	7
Stage 2	Angle-tighten a further 90°	
Driveshaft cover plates	25	18
Engine speed/crankshaft position sensor	10	7
Engine-to-transmission bolts:		
M10	45	33
M12	65	48
Gearchange adjustment bolt	23	17
Guide sleeve bolt:		
012/01W 5-speed transmission*:		
Aluminium casing	35	26
Magnesium casing	25	18
01E and 0A1 6-speed transmissions	15	11
01X transmission	35	26
Multifunction switch*:		
Aluminium casing	25	18
Magnesium casing	15	11

Torque wrench settings (continued)	Nm	lbf ft
Oil drain plug:		
01E and 0A1 transmissions	40	30
01X transmission	45	33
Oil filler plug:		
01E and 0A1 transmissions	40	30
012/01W transmission	25	18
01X transmission	45	33
Reversing light switch	20	15
Selector lever bolt	25	18
Transmission crossmember-to-body bolts (renew):		
M12:		
Stage 1	110	81
Stage 2	Angle-tighten a further 90°	
M10	55	41

* On magnesium casings the code MgAl9Zn1 appears just in front of the left-hand driveshaft, and on the bottom of the casing behind the left-hand driveshaft

1 General information

Four different transmissions may be fitted to vehicles covered by this manual – 012/01W is a five-speed transmission, 01E, 0A1 and 01X are six-speed transmissions. All units may have aluminium or magnesium casings. The transmission identification marks are stamped into the casing on the mounting flange in front of the left-hand driveshaft. Note that on magnesium casings, it's essential that the correct type of bolts/nuts are fitted, or corrosion will result. If a fastener needs renewing, consult an Audi dealer or parts specialist.

The transmissions are bolted to the rear of the in-line engines. The front-wheel-drive configuration transmits the power to a differential unit located at the front of the transmission, through driveshafts, to the front wheels. All gears, including reverse, incorporate a synchromesh engagement.

Gearchange is by a floor-mounted lever.

A rod connects the bottom of the lever to a shift rod which protrudes from the rear of the transmission **(see illustrations)**.

2 Gearchange linkage – adjustment

1 Working inside the car, ensure the transmission is in the neutral position, then prise up the gear lever gaiter surround from the centre console, and pull the surround and gaiter up around the gear lever knob. Note that the knob must be removed with the gaiter and surround.

2 To remove the knob with a locking mechanism, rotate the collar clockwise and lift pull the knob upwards and remove it with the gaiter/surround. To remove a knob with a securing clip, cut the clip with a pair of pliers, and pull the knob

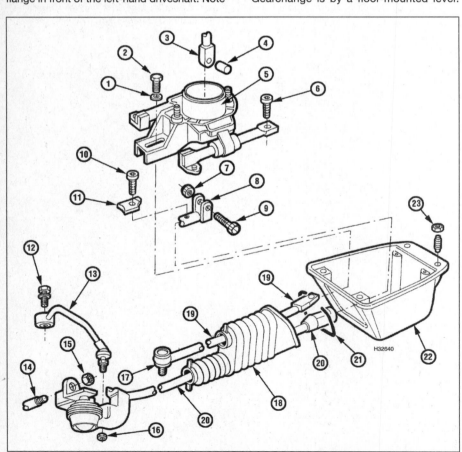

1.3a 01E and 0A1 transmissions selector components

1 Washer
2 Bolt
3 Gear lever
4 Spacer
5 Rear housing with pushrod
6 Bolt
7 Nut*
8 Selector fork
9 Bolt
10 Bolt
11 Clamp
12 Bolt
13 Connecting rod
14 Transmission selector shaft
15 Nut*
16 Nut
17 Washer
18 Bellows
19 Front pushrod
20 Selector rod
21 Tensioning ring
22 Gear lever housing
23 Nut
* Always renew

1.3b 012/01W transmission selector components

1	Gear knob	21	Buffer
2	Gaiter	22	Rear housing
3	Clip*		and pushrod
4	Spacer	23	Nut
5	Spring	24	Stud
6	Ball stop	25	Gear lever
7	Spring		housing
8	Bush	26	Nut*
9	Nut	27	Bolt
10	Nut	28	Selector fork
11	Cover	29	Selector rod
12	Gear lever	30	Clamp
13	Circlip*	31	Bolt
14	Ball housing	32	Front pushrod
15	Buffer	33	Tensioning
16	Nut		ring
17	Connecting	34	Bellows
	piece	35	Bolt*
18	Spacer	36	Bolt
19	Nut	37	Washer
20	Connecting	38	Washer
	piece		* Always renew

1.3c 01X transmission selector components

1 Selector shaft lever
2 Gaiter
3 Washer
4 Ball socket
5 Cap nut
6 Ball-stud
7 Ball socket
8 Connecting rod
9 Bush
10 Bush
11 Bolt
12 Sleeve
13 Clip
14 Bolt
15 Pushrod
16 Bolt
17 Washer
18 Gearlever housing
19 Retaining clip
20 Gaiter
21 Bolt
22 Clamp
23 Selector rod
24 Joint
25 Nut

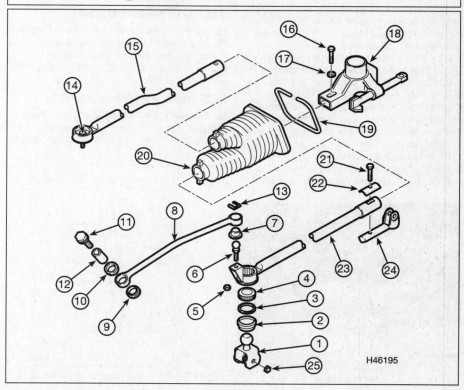

H32641

H46195

2.2 Release the retaining clip and pull the knob and gaiter from the lever

2.4 Release the clips at the edge and remove the panel beneath the air conditioning control panel

2.5 Undo the two bolts (arrowed) and remove the ashtray

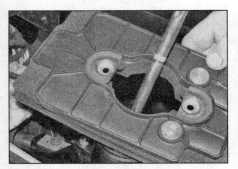

2.7 Undo the nuts and lift away the noise insulation pad

2.8 Measure between the two studs

2.9 Slacken the pushrod screw (arrowed) and move the rod in relation to the housing

upwards and remove it complete with the gaiter/surround **(see illustration)**.

3 On models with a large radio 'slot' remove the air conditioning control panel as described in Chapter 3.

4 On models with a small radio 'slot', carefully prise up the rear edge of the panel below the air conditioning control panel, and pull it rearwards **(see illustration)**.

5 On all models, undo the two bolts and remove the front ashtray **(see illustration)**.

6 Lift out the noise insulation and damper washer from around the gearchange lever.

7 Undo the two nuts and lift out the insulation pad around the lever **(see illustration)**.

8 Measure the distance between the stud in front of the lever, and the stud on the mechanism **(see illustration)**.

9 The correct dimension is 85 mm. If this is not the measurement obtained, slacken the

push rod screw, and move the pushrod in relation to the lever housing until the correct measurement is obtained **(see illustration)**. Hold it in this position and tighten the push rod bolt securely.

012/01W transmission

10 Slacken the selector rod bolt, and position the gearchange lever in the dead centre of the ball socket **(see illustration)**. Hold the lever in this position and tighten the selector rod bolt securely.

01E and 0A1 transmissions

11 Slacken the selector rod bolt, and position the gearchange lever in the dead centre of the ball socket. Now move the lever slightly to

the right, so that it is 3° from the vertical **(see illustration)**. Hold the lever in this position and tighten the selector rod bolt securely.

01X transmission

12 Slacken the selector rod bolt, and position the gearchange lever in the dead centre of the ball socket. Now move the lever slightly to the right, so that it is 1.5° from the vertical **(see illustration)**. Hold the lever in this position and tighten the selector rod bolt securely.

All transmissions

13 Check the correct operation of the selector mechanism, and refit the gear lever surround, gaiter and gear knob (use a new clip where applicable).

2.10 Slacken the selector rod bolt (arrowed)

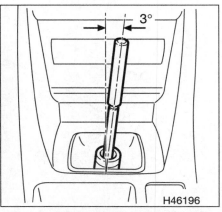

2.11 Position the lever 3° from vertical

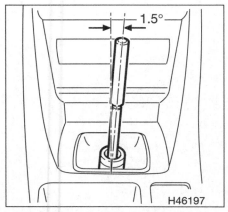

2.12 Position the lever 1.5° from vertical

3 Manual transmission – removal and refitting

Removal

1 Select a solid, level surface to park the vehicle upon. Give yourself enough space to move around it easily. Apply the handbrake and chock the rear wheels.

2 Apply the handbrake, then jack up the front of the vehicle and support it on axle stands (see *Jacking and vehicle support*). Remove the undershields from the engine and transmission.

3 Disconnect the battery negative (earth) lead (see Chapter 5A). Remove the engine cover.

4 Attach an engine compartment crossbrace or hoist to the cylinder head, to steady the engine when the transmission is removed.

5 Remove the air cleaner assembly as described in Chapter 4A, 4B or 4C. On diesel models, remove the air intake pipe at the back of the cylinder head.

6 On diesel models, undo the screws and lift the coolant expansion tank from its location and move it to one side without disconnecting the coolant hoses.

7 Remove the front crossmember from the exhaust tunnel under the body **(see illustration)**.

8 Refer to Chapter 4D, and remove the exhaust front pipe and catalytic converter. Take care not to bend excessively the flexible section of the front pipe.

9 Unbolt the undershield bracket from under the transmission.

10 Using an Allen key, unbolt the heat shields from over the inner end of the right-hand driveshaft and left-hand driveshaft (if fitted).

11 Remove the heat shield above the exhaust front pipe.

Cabriolet models

12 On petrol models, undo the 3 bolts securing the torque reaction support to the engine.

13 Undo the front anti-roll bar clamp nuts and allow the anti-roll bar to swing down.

14 Slacken the nuts on the base of the left- and right-hand engine mountings, until they are flush with the bottom of the mounting studs.

3.7 Undo the bolts and remove the crossmember from the front of the exhaust tunnel

15 Use a hoist to left the engine until the mounting nuts contact the underside of the mounting.

All models

16 Undo the 3 lower screws securing the transmission to the engine. On Cabriolet models, lower the engine back to its original position.

17 Remove the left- and right-hand driveshafts with reference to Chapter 8. Note that it is permissible to disconnect the shafts from the drive flanges and tie them to one side.

18 Position a trolley jack under the transmission and take the weight.

19 Undo the bolts securing the transmission crossmember to the vehicle underbody, then undo the nuts securing the crossmember to the transmission. Remove the crossmember. Insert and lightly tighten the subframe rear mounting bolts to prevent excessive strain being placed on the front mounting bolts **(see illustrations)**.

20 Disconnect the selector rod and pushrod from the transmission **(see illustration)**.

21 Note their fitted positions and disconnect all wiring plugs from the transmission.

22 Unbolt the starter motor from the engine and move it to one side. There is no need to disconnect the starter wiring.

23 Ensure the transmission is adequately supported, then remove the remaining bolts securing the transmission to the engine.

24 Carefully pull the transmission from the locating dowels on the engine, and lower

it sufficiently to access the slave cylinder retaining bolt. Undo the bolt and position the slave cylinder to one side. There is no need to disconnect the fluid pipe.

Caution: Take care to steady the engine during this procedure. Enlist the help of an assistant.

25 Lower the transmission and manoeuvre it from the underside of the vehicle. Note that the transmission is heavy.

Refitting

26 Before refitting the transmission, make sure that the location dowels are correctly positioned in the engine cylinder block rear face. It is recommended that the clutch friction disc, pressure plate and release bearing are checked as described in Chapter 6, and renewed if necessary.

27 Refitting the transmission is a reversal of the removal procedure, but note the following points:

a) *Check the rear rubber mountings and renew them if necessary.*

b) *Apply a little clutch assembly grease to the splines of the transmission input shaft. Wipe off any excess.*

c) *Tighten all nuts and bolts to the specified torque where given.*

d) *On completion, refer to Section 2 and check the gearchange linkage adjustment.*

4 Manual transmission overhaul – general information

1 Overhauling a manual transmission unit is a difficult and involved job for the DIY home mechanic. In addition to dismantling and reassembling many small parts, clearances must be precisely measured and, if necessary, changed by selecting shims and spacers. Internal transmission components are also often difficult to obtain and in many instances, extremely expensive. Because of this, if the transmission develops a fault or becomes noisy, the best course of action is to have the unit overhauled by a specialist repairer or to obtain an exchange reconditioned unit.

2 Nevertheless, it is not impossible for the more experienced mechanic to overhaul the transmission if the special tools are available

3.19a Undo the bolts at the ends of the crossmember . . .

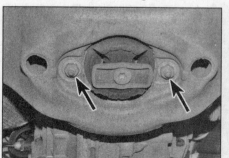

3.19b . . . and the nuts (arrowed) in the centre

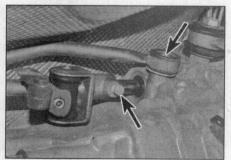

3.20 Undo the bolt and detach the selector rod, followed by the pushrod bolt (arrowed)

5.1 Multifunction switch

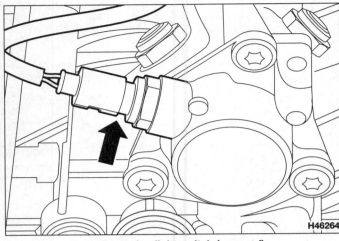

5.13 Reversing light switch (arrowed) –
01X 6-speed transmission only

and the job is carried out in a deliberate step-by-step manner, to ensure that nothing is overlooked.

3 The tools necessary for an overhaul include internal and external circlip pliers, bearing pullers, a slide hammer, a set of pin punches, a dial test indicator and possibly a hydraulic press. In addition, a large, sturdy workbench and a vice will be required.

4 During dismantling of the transmission, make careful notes of how each component is fitted to make reassembly easier and accurate.

5 Before dismantling the transmission, it will help if you have some idea of where the problem lies. Certain problems can be closely related to specific areas in the transmission which can make component examination and renewal easier. Refer to the *Fault finding* Section in this manual for more information.

5 Transmission switches – renewal

Multifunction switch

1 The multifunction switch is located on top of the 012/01W transmission only **(see illustration)**.

2 Apply the handbrake, then jack up the front

6.1 The roadspeed sensor is located on the left-hand side of the transmission

of the vehicle and support it on axle stands (see *Jacking and vehicle support*). Remove the transmission undershield.

3 Disconnect the wiring connector, then unscrew the bolts securing the switch lead to the top of the transmission.

4 Note the fitted position of the switch, then unscrew the bolt and remove the switch retainer plate.

5 Withdraw the multifunction switch from the transmission. Recover the O-ring seal.

6 To refit the switch, first clean the switch location in the transmission. Fit a new O-ring seal, then insert the switch in the previously noted position.

7 Refit the retainer plate and tighten the bolt.

8 Secure the lead to the top of the transmission and tighten the bolts.

9 Reconnect the wiring, refit the undershield, then lower the vehicle to the ground.

Reversing light switch

10 A reversing light switch is fitted to 6-speed 01X transmissions only.

11 Apply the handbrake, then jack up the front of the vehicle and support it on axle stands (see *Jacking and vehicle support*). Remove the transmission undershield.

12 The switch is located on the right-hand side of the transmission. Disconnect the switch wiring plug.

13 Unscrew the switch from the selector shaft cover **(see illustration)**.

14 Clean the switch location in the cover, then refit the switch and tighten it to the specified torque.

6 Roadspeed sensor – removal and refitting

Note: *Roadspeed sensors are fitted to 012/01W, 01E and 0A1 transmissions up to 07/2002. After this date, vehicle speed data is derived from information supplied by the wheel speed sensors.*

Removal

1 The electronic roadspeed sensor on the left-hand side of the transmission, just above the driveshaft drive flange **(see illustration)**. This device measures the rotational speed of the transmission final drive and converts the information into an electronic signal, which is then sent to the speedometer module in the instrument panel. On certain models, the signal is also used as an input by the engine management system ECM.

2 Apply the handbrake, then jack up the front of the vehicle and support it on axle stands (see *Jacking and vehicle support*). Remove the transmission undershield.

3 Remove the left-front road wheel, and the cover above the left-hand driveshaft.

4 Disconnect the wiring plug from the sensor.

5 Depress the retainer, then turn the sensor and withdraw it from the transmission. Take care not to damage the drive, as the electronic components are delicate. Recover the seal **(see illustration)**.

Refitting

6 Refitting is a reversal of removal, but renew the seal.

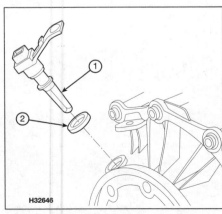

6.5 Roadspeed sensor (1) and seal (2)

7.4 Screw a bolt through the driveshaft flange and onto a distance piece placed against the transmission casing

7.5 Note the depth of the fitted seal, then prise it out using a flat-bladed screwdriver

7.7 Using a suitable tubular drift (such as a socket), tap the seal squarely into position

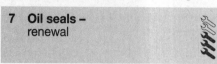

7 Oil seals – renewal

Driveshaft flange oil seals

1 Apply the handbrake, then jack up the front of the vehicle and support it on axle stands (see *Jacking and vehicle support*). Remove the relevant roadwheel. Undo the retaining bolts/nuts and remove the engine undertray.
2 Refer to Chapter 8 and unbolt the heat shield, then unscrew the bolts and remove the relevant driveshaft from the transmission drive flange. Tie the driveshaft away from the transmission, and wrap the inner joint in a plastic bag, in order to prevent entry of dust and dirt. Turn the steering as necessary to move the driveshaft away from the flange.
3 Position a suitable container beneath the transmission to catch spilled oil.

012/01W and 01X transmissions

4 The drive flange is held in the differential sun gear by an internal circlip, and the flange must be pulled outwards to release the circlip. To do this, locate a suitable distance piece (such as a chisel) between the flange and the final drive cover or transmission casing (as applicable), then screw a bolt through the flange onto the distance piece. As the bolt is tightened, the flange will be forced outwards and the circlip released from its groove **(see illustration)**. If the flange is tight, turn it 180° and repeat the removal procedure.
5 With the flange out, note the fitted depth of the oil seal in the housing, then prise it out using a large flat-bladed screwdriver **(see illustration)**.
6 Clean all traces of dirt from the area around the oil seal aperture, then apply a smear of grease to the lips of the new oil seal.
7 Ensure the seal is correctly positioned, with its sealing lip facing inwards, and tap it squarely into position, using a suitable tubular drift (such as a socket) which bears only on the hard outer edge of the seal **(see illustration)**. If the surface of the flange is good, make sure the seal is fitted at the same depth in its housing as originally noted; it should be 5.5 mm below the outer edge of the

transmission. On 012/01W transmissions, if the surface of the flange is worn, fit the oil seal at a depth of 6.5 mm.
8 Clean the oil seal and apply a smear of multi-purpose grease to its lips.
9 It is recommended that the circlip on the inner end of the drive flange is renewed whenever the flange is removed. To do this, mount the flange in a soft-jawed vice, then prise off the old circlip and fit the new one **(see illustration)**. Lightly grease the circlip.
10 Insert the drive flange through the oil seal and engage it with the differential gear. Using a suitable drift, drive the flange fully into the gear until the circlip is felt to engage.

01E and 0A1 transmissions

11 The drive flange is held in place by a M8 or M10 bolt. Undo the bolt and pull the flange out. If necessary, counterhold the flange by inserting two bolts into its circumference and using a lever.
12 With the flange out, note the fitted depth of the oil seal in the housing, then prise it out using a large flat-bladed screwdriver.
13 Clean all traces of dirt from the area around the oil seal aperture, then apply a smear of grease to the lips of the new oil seal.
14 Ensure the seal is correctly positioned, with its sealing lip facing inwards, and tap it squarely into position, using a suitable tubular drift (such as a socket) which bears only on the hard outer edge of the seal. If the surface of the flange is good, make sure the seal is fitted at the same depth in its housing as

originally noted; it should be 5.5 mm below the outer edge of the transmission. If the surface of the flange is worn, fit the oil seal at a depth of 6.5 mm.
15 Clean the oil seal and apply a smear of multi-purpose grease to its lips. Refit the drive flange and tighten the retaining bolt to the specified torque setting.

All transmissions

16 Refit the driveshaft (see Chapter 8), and the transmission undershield.
17 Refit the roadwheel, then lower the vehicle to the ground. Check and if necessary top-up the transmission oil level (refer to the relevant part of Chapter 1).

Input shaft oil seal

18 The transmission must be removed for access to the input shaft oil seal. Refer to Section 3 of this Chapter.
19 Remove the clutch release bearing and lever with reference to Chapter 6.

012/01W transmission

20 Unscrew the bolts and remove the guide sleeve from inside the bellhousing. Recover the O-ring. Do not disturb any shims located on the input shaft. Discard the O-ring, a new one must be fitted **(see illustration)**.
21 The oil seal is only supplied with a new guide sleeve.
22 Using a new O-ring and new bolts, fit the guide sleeve to the transmission, tightening the bolts to the specified torque.

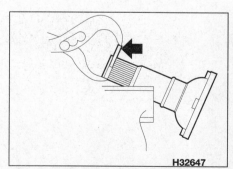

7.9 Fit a new circlip (arrowed) to the groove in the transmission's drive flange

7.20 Unscrew the bolts and remove the guide sleeve from inside the bellhousing

7.24 Carefully drive the input shaft oil seal from the guide tube

01X transmission

23 Unscrew the bolts and remove the guide sleeve from inside the bellhousing. Recover the O-ring. Do not disturb any shims located on the input shaft. Discard the O-ring, a new one must be fitted.

24 Using a punch or drift, carefully drive the oil seal from its fitted position in the guide sleeve **(see illustration)**.

25 Wipe clean the oil seal seating.

26 Smear a little multi-purpose grease on the lips of the new oil seal, and locate the seal in the guide sleeve with the sealing lip facing the gearbox side **(see illustration)**. Tap the seal squarely into position, using a suitable drift which bears only on the hard outer edge of the seal, until it is against the stop.

27 Using a new O-ring and new bolts, refit the guide sleeve to the transmission, tightening the bolts to the specified torque.

01E and 0A1 transmissions

28 Unscrew the bolts and remove the guide sleeve from inside the bellhousing. Recover the gasket. Do not disturb any shims located on the input shaft.

29 Note the fitted depth of the oil seal in the transmission housing, then use a screwdriver to prise it out taking care not to damage the input shaft.

7.26 Locate the seal in the guide sleeve with the sealing lip facing the gearbox side

30 Wipe clean the oil seal seating and input shaft.

31 Smear a little multi-purpose grease on the lips of the new oil seal, then locate the seal over the input shaft with its sealing lip facing inwards. Tap the oil seal squarely into position to a depth of 3.5 mm, using a suitable tubular drift which bears only on the hard outer edge of the seal. If the surface of the input shaft is worn excessively, position the oil seal at a depth of 4.5 mm.

32 Refit the guide sleeve, and tighten the bolts to the specified torque.

All transmissions

33 Refit the clutch release bearing and lever with reference to Chapter 6.

34 Refit the transmission with reference to Section 3 of this Chapter.

Selector shaft oil seal

35 Apply the handbrake, then jack up the front of the vehicle and support it on axle stands (see *Jacking and vehicle support*). Remove the transmission undershield.

012/01W transmission

36 Unscrew the locking bolt and slide the gear lever coupling from the transmission selector shaft.

37 Using a small screwdriver, carefully prise the oil seal from the transmission housing taking care not to damage the surface of the selector shaft or housing.

38 Wipe clean the oil seal seating and selector shaft, then smear a little multi-purpose grease on the new oil seal lips and locate the seal over the end of the shaft. Make sure the closed side of the seal faces outwards. To prevent damage to the oil seal, temporarily wrap some adhesive tape around the end of the shaft.

39 Tap the oil seal squarely into position, using a suitable tubular drift which bears only on the hard outer edge of the seal. The seal should be inserted until it is 1.0 mm below the surface of the transmission.

40 Refit the gear lever coupling and tighten the locking bolt.

01E, 0A1 and 01X transmissions

41 Unscrew the retaining nut, and pull the selector lever from the selector shaft. **Note:** *Access to the selector lever with the transmission fitted is limited. It may be improved by lowering the transmission a little – see Section 3.*

42 Using a small screwdriver, carefully prise the oil seal from the housing, taking care not to damage the surface of the selector shaft or housing.

43 Wipe clean the oil seal seating and selector shaft, then smear a little multi-purpose grease on the new oil seal lips and locate the seal over the end of the shaft. Make sure the closed side of the seal faces outwards.

44 Tap the seal squarely into position, using a suitable drift which bears only on the outer edge of the seal.

45 Refit the selector lever to the shaft and tighten the nut to the specified torque.

All transmissions

46 Refit the transmission undershield.

47 Lower the vehicle to the ground.

Chapter 7 Part B:
Automatic transmission

Contents

	Section number		Section number
Automatic transmission – removal and refitting	2	General information	1
Automatic transmission fluid – renewal	See Chapter 1A	Locking cable – removal, refitting and adjustment	5
Automatic transmission overhaul – general information	3	Selector cable – removal, refitting and adjustment	4

Degrees of difficulty

Easy, suitable for novice with little experience	**Fairly easy,** suitable for beginner with some experience	**Fairly difficult,** suitable for competent DIY mechanic	**Difficult,** suitable for experienced DIY mechanic	**Very difficult,** suitable for expert DIY or professional

Specifications

General

Type	Electro-hydraulically controlled planetary gearbox providing five forward speeds and one reverse speed. Drive transmitted through hydrodynamic torque converter
Designation	01V
Automatic transmission fluid capacity	See Chapter 1A

Torque wrench settings

	Nm	lbf ft
Automatic transmission selector cable support bolt	23	17
Bracket for fluid pipe	10	7
Fluid pipe union	25	18
Fluid pipes to transmission	20	15
Front crossmember to vehicle floor	55	41
Rear crossmember to vehicle floor	55	41
Selector cable clamping screw	13	10
Torque converter to driveplate*	85	63
Transmission bellhousing-to-engine bolts:		
M10	45	33
M12	65	48
Transmission mounting:		
Centre bolt	40	30
To body	23	17
To transmission	40	30

Do not re-use

1 General information

The automatic transmission is a five-speed unit, incorporating a hydrodynamic torque converter with a lock-up function and a planetary gearbox.

Gear selection is achieved by means of a floor-mounted, seven position selector lever. The positions are P (Park), R (Reverse), N (Neutral), D (Drive), 3 (3rd gear lock), 2 (2nd gear lock), 1 (1st gear lock). The transmission has a kick-down feature which provides greater acceleration when the accelerator pedal is depressed to the floor.

The overall operation of the transmission is managed by the engine management electronic control module (ECM) and as a result there are no manual adjustments. Comprehensive fault diagnosis can therefore only be carried out using dedicated electronic test equipment.

Due to the complexity of the transmission and its control system, major repairs and overhaul operations should be left to an Audi dealer or transmission specialist, who will be equipped to carry out fault diagnosis and repair. The information in this Chapter is therefore limited to a description of the removal and refitting of the transmission as a complete unit. The removal, refitting and adjustment of the selector cable is also described.

2 Automatic transmission – removal and refitting

Removal

1 Select a solid, level surface to park the vehicle upon. Give yourself enough space to move around it easily. Apply the handbrake and chock the rear wheels.

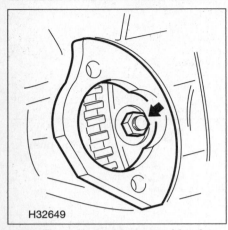

2.16 The torque converter-to-driveplate nuts are accessed through the starter motor aperture

2 Apply the handbrake, then jack up the front of the vehicle and support it on axle stands (see *Jacking and vehicle support*). Remove both front roadwheels.

3 Remove the engine/transmission undershield panel and remove the noise insulation and bracket.

4 Disconnect the battery negative (earth) lead (see Chapter 5A) and position it away from the terminal.

5 Where necessary, unscrew the nuts/bolts and remove the top cover from the engine.

6 Remove the air cleaner housing and intake ducting (see the relevant part of Chapter 4).

7 Support the engine with a hoist or support bar located on the front wing inner channels. If necessary, remove the bonnet as described in Chapter 11 in order to position the hoist over the engine. Due to the weight of the automatic transmission, the engine should be supported using both the front and rear lifting eyes. Depending on the engine, temporarily remove components as necessary to attach the hoist.

8 Undo the bolts and remove the heat shields above the left- and right-hand driveshaft flanges.

9 Refer to Chapter 8 and detach the driveshafts from the transmission flanges. Tie the driveshafts away from the transmission.

10 Remove the exhaust front downpipe and catalytic converter with reference to Chapter 4D,

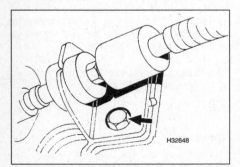

2.17 Undo the bolt (arrowed) and release the selector cable support bracket

taking care not to bend the flexible coupling. Also, where necessary, unbolt the downpipe mounting bracket from the transmission.

11 Note their fitted positions and the harness routing, then disconnect all electrical wiring plugs from the transmission.

12 Undo the bolts securing the automatic transmission fluid (ATF) pipes bracket to the engine sump.

13 Position a suitable container beneath the transmission to collect spilt hydraulic fluid.

14 Make identification marks on the ATF pipes adjacent to the right-hand driveshaft flange using paint or similar, then undo the unions. Be prepared for fluid spillage. Plug the pipe openings to prevent dirt ingress.

15 Remove the starter as described in Chapter 5A.

16 Turn the engine to locate one of the torque converter-to-driveplate bolts in the starter motor aperture **(see illustration)**. Unscrew and remove the bolt while preventing the engine from turning using a wide-bladed screwdriver engaged with the ring gear teeth on the driveplate. Unscrew the remaining two bolts, turning the engine a third of a turn at a time to locate them.

17 With the selector lever in position P, carefully disconnect the inner cable from the transmission lever, then make alignment marks and unbolt the support bracket **(see illustration)**. Position the cable to one side.

18 Undo the screws and remove the multifunction switch from the left-hand side of the transmission housing. Position the switch and harness to one side.

19 Undo the nuts securing the left- and right-hand engine mountings to their brackets.

20 Unscrew the transmission-to-engine mounting bolts accessible from under the car.

21 Support the transmission with a trolley jack, and take the weight.

22 Mark the location of the subframe beneath the engine compartment, then loosen only the front subframe bolts. Remove the remaining subframe bolts and lower the rear of the subframe. **Note:** *It is important that the subframe is refitted in its correct position otherwise the handling of the car will be affected and excessive tyre wear will occur.*

23 Unscrew and remove the remaining transmission-to-engine mounting bolts.

24 With the help of an assistant, lower the engine and transmission approximately 30 mm. Check that no components are trapped or damaged.

25 With the help of an assistant, withdraw the transmission from the locating dowels on the rear of the engine, making sure that the torque converter remains fully engaged with the transmission input shaft. If necessary, use a lever to release the torque converter from the driveplate.

26 When the locating dowels are clear of their mounting holes, lower the transmission to the ground using the jack. Strap a restraining bar across the front of the bellhousing to keep the torque converter in position.

⚠ Warning: The transmission is heavy. Make sure that the transmission remains steady on the jack head. Take care to prevent the torque converter from falling out as the transmission is removed.

Refitting

27 Refitting the transmission is a reversal of the removal procedure, but note the following points:

a) *As the torque converter is refitted, ensure that the drive pins at the centre of the torque converter hub engage with the recesses in the automatic transmission fluid pump inner wheel. When the converter is fully inserted, the distance between the surface of the converter mounting holes and the transmission bellhousing mating face must be at least 23 mm.*

b) *Tighten the bellhousing bolts and torque converter-to-driveplate nuts to the specified torque. Always renew self-locking nuts and bolts.*

c) *Renew the O-ring seals on the fluid pipes and filler tube attached to the transmission casing.*

d) *Tighten the transmission mounting bolts to the correct torque.*

e) *Check the final drive oil level and transmission fluid level as described in Chapter 1A.*

f) *On completion, refer to Section 4 and check the gear selector cable adjustment.*

g) *Renew the front subframe bolts and make sure that the front subframe is positioned exactly as removed. Finally have the wheel alignment checked and if necessary adjusted.*

h) *If the transmission does not perform as expected after refitting, have the ECM basic setting re-introduced by an Audi dealer or automatic transmission specialist.*

---

3 Automatic transmission overhaul – general information

In the event of a fault occurring, it will be necessary to establish whether the fault is electrical, mechanical or hydraulic in nature, before repair work can be contemplated. Diagnosis requires detailed knowledge of the transmission's operation and construction, as well as access to specialised test equipment, and so is deemed to be beyond the scope of this manual. It is therefore essential that problems with the automatic transmission are referred to a Audi dealer for assessment.

Note that a faulty transmission should not be removed before the vehicle has been assessed by a dealer, as fault diagnosis is carried out with the transmission *in situ*.

4 Selector cable – removal, refitting and adjustment

Removal

1 Move the selector lever to the P position.

2 Apply the handbrake, then jack up the front of the vehicle and support it on axle stands (see *Jacking and vehicle support*). Remove the left-hand front roadwheel, and the transmission undershield.

3 Working under the vehicle, undo the screws and remove the crossmember from under the exhaust system.

4 Undo the screws and lower the heat shield from the gear selector mounting bracket.

5 Remove the rear crossmember from under the exhaust system, and release the rear section of the exhaust system from its mounting clamps, to access the exhaust heat shield.

6 Undo the fasteners and remove the left- and right-hand inner vehicle floor covers, followed by the exhaust heat shield.

7 Remove the front section of the exhaust system as described in Chapter 4D.

8 Undo the bolt securing the selector cable support bracket to the transmission casing **(see illustration)**.

9 Carefully lever the end of the selector cable from the lever on the transmission.

10 Undo the four nuts securing the selector housing lower cover, then detach the cable sleeve from the bottom cover and slide the cover and sleeve along the cable **(see illustration)**.

11 Pull out the clip securing the outer cable to the selector housing, then pull the plastic securing spring slightly forward, then press the retaining pin upwards only as far as necessary to be able to pull the cable from the

4.8 Selector components

1 Selector lever handle
2 Sleeve
3 Cover moulding
4 Trim piece
5 Symbol panel
6 Masking panel
7 Guide
8 Spring
9 Pull-rod
10 Locking clip
11 Mounting bush
12 Mounting bush
13 Locking clip
14 Stop buffer
15 Cable lever
16 Detent
17 Frame
18 Fulcrum pin
19 Spring clip with roller
20 Spring clip with roller
21 Mounting bracket
22 Fulcrum pin
23 Locking pawl
24 Fulcrum pin
25 Selector lever lock solenoid
27 Securing clip
28 Locking cable
29 Selector lever cable
30 Locking lever
31 Securing spring
32 Mounting
33 Locking cable
34 Ignition/starter switch
35 Cable tie
36 Locking cable
37 Support bracket
38 Cover
39 Nut

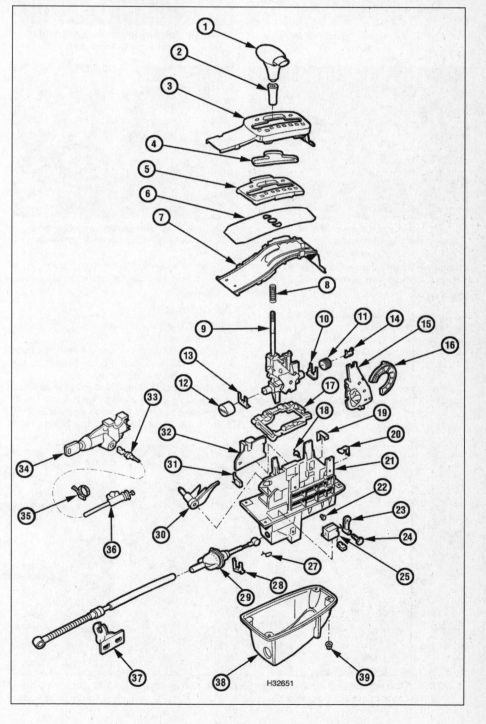

H32651

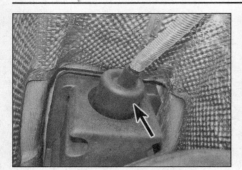

4.10 Pull the sleeve (arrowed) from the cover

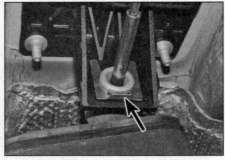

4.11a Pull the down the outer cable securing clip (arrowed)

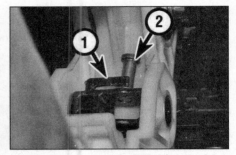

4.11b Pull forward the clip (1) and push the pin (2) upwards just enough to free the cable

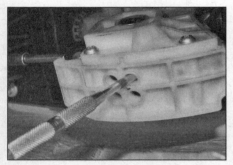

4.11c Insert a rod though the hole in the base of the selector assembly to push the pin upwards

fitting **(see illustrations)**. Do not push the pin fully out. Withdraw the cable.

Refitting

12 Refitting is a reversal of removal, noting the following points:
  a) Fit a new outer cable retaining clip.
  b) Push the end of the cable into the selector lever fitting, and press the pin downwards, ensuring the securing spring has locked into place.
  c) Check the operation of the selector lever before reconnecting the cable at the transmission end.

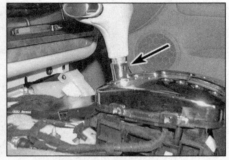

4.14 Rotate the sleeve (arrowed) anti-clockwise and push it downwards

  d) Before lowering the car to the ground, carry out the adjustment procedure as follows:

Adjustment

13 Move the selector lever inside the car to the D position.
14 Rotate the sleeve under the selector lever knob anti-clockwise, and push it down as far as it will go **(see illustration)**.
15 Carefully pull out the button in the selector lever knob just far enough for a cable tie to be inserted between the knob and the button. Secure the cable tie around the button **(see**

illustration). Do not pull the button out any further then necessary, or it will be damaged.
16 Pull the selector lever knob upwards and detach it from the lever.
17 Open the front ashtray, then starting at the front edge, lever up and remove the selector lever panel surround trim.
18 Undo the bolts and remove the ashtray.
19 Release the 4 clips and lift the selector lever surround upwards and over the lever. Disconnect any wiring plugs as the surround is withdrawn.
20 Move the selector lever to the S position (fully rearward).
21 Insert Audi special tool T40031 down through the hole in the selector mechanism, and check that the inner cable clamping screw is tight **(see illustration)**. In the absence of the special tool, a 5 mm Allen key, at least 140 mm long will suffice.
22 Move the selector lever to the P position (fully forward).
23 Undo the bolts securing the heat shield over the selector lever on the transmission casing, and the bolt(s) securing the selector lever support bracket on the transmission housing.
24 Move the selector lever on the transmission to the P position, which is the rear stop. Make sure that both front wheels

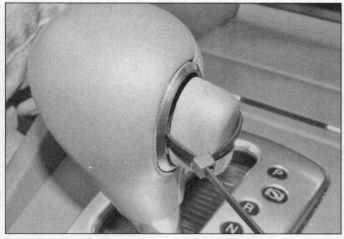

4.15 Pull the knob out just far enough to be able to secure it with a cable tie

4.21 Insert a 5 mm Allen key, at least 140 mm long, down through the hole to access the inner cable clamping screw (arrowed)

are locked by attempting to turn them in the same direction at the same time. **Note:** *Even though the transmission is locked, it will still be possible to turn the front wheels in* **opposite** *directions, since the differential gears are able move in relation to each other.*

25 Refit the selector cable support bracket and heat shield.

26 Working inside the vehicle, move the selector lever to position S.

27 Using Audi tool T40031 or equivalent, slacken the selector cable clamping screw approximately 1 complete turn – no more **(see illustration 4.21).**

28 Carefully move the selector lever backwards and forwards a little to 'settle' it in position. Do not shift the lever to another position. Finally pull the lever back to the stop in the S position, then gently release it.

29 Tighten the cable clamping screw to the specified torque. The adjustment is now set.

30 Refit the lever surround, trim and knob in a reversal of removal.

5 Locking cable – removal, refitting and adjustment

Note: *Audi tool number 3352A will be required to adjust the locking cable.*

Removal

1 Disconnect the battery negative terminal (see Chapter 5A).

2 Remove the driver's side storage compartment as described in Chapter 11.

3 Remove the steering column shrouds as described in Chapter 10.

4 Remove the air conditioning control panel as described in Chapter 3.

5 Open the front ashtray, take out the ashtray insert, undo the bolts and remove the ashtray.

6 Starting at the front edge, lever up and remove the selector lever panel surround trim.

7 Release the 4 clips and lift the selector lever surround upwards and over the lever.

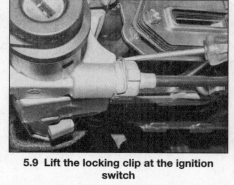

5.9 Lift the locking clip at the ignition switch

Disconnect any wiring plugs as the surround is withdrawn.

8 Turn the ignition switch to the 'on' position, and move the selector lever to position P.

9 Lift up the locking clip on the outer cable at the ignition switch, and pull the cable from the ignition switch **(see illustration)**.

10 Lift the securing spring slightly, and unclip the locking cable. Release the cable clamp and pull the cable sideways from the lever pin **(see illustration)**.

11 Note the routing of the cable and withdraw it from the passenger compartment.

Refitting

12 Refit the cable, using the routing noted during removal.

13 Ensure that the ignition switch is in the 'on' position, and the selector lever is in the P position.

14 Fit the cable to the ignition switch, ensuring that the locking device engages correctly. Turn the ignition switch to the 'off' position.

15 Clip the locking cable into the securing spring in the mounting bracket.

16 Engage the locking cable support bracket into the selector mechanism, and the locking inner cable eye over the lever pin. Carry out the following adjustment procedure.

17 The remainder of refitting is a reversal of removal.

5.10 Lift the securing spring and unclip the locking cable

Adjustment

18 Loosen the support bracket clamp bolt **(see illustration)**. It must be possible to move the support bracket forward by hand.

19 With the battery negative lead disconnected (see Chapter 5A), move the selector lever to position P, and the ignition key to the removal position.

20 Audi specify the use of a setting bar (tool 3352A) to set the position of the cable eye over the lever pin. This tool ensures the lever pin is accurately in the centre of the cable eye. Slide the tool over the lever pin and into the cable eye. In the absence of the special tool, we improvised using a plastic nozzle from a sealant tube, gradually trimming the nozzle until a good fit between the cable eye and pin was achieved. The internal and external diameters of the nozzle end are approximately 5.0 mm and 6.0 mm respectively **(see illustrations)**.

21 Pull the outer cable forwards towards the engine, and tighten the support bracket clamp bolt securely. Remove the setting bar. If the tool is not available, then ensure the selector lever pin is accurately in the centre of the cable eye, with the outer cable pulled forwards. Tighten the outer cable clamp bolt, and check the position of the cable eye/lever pin again.

22 Check the operation of the locking cable.

5.18 Support bracket clamp bolt (arrowed)

5.20a Improvised tool using a sealant tube nozzle and a roll-pin

5.20b Slide the tool over the lever pin, and centralise the cable eye (arrowed)

Chapter 7 Part C:
Multitronic transmission

Contents

	Section number			Section number
Multitronic damper unit – removal and refitting	4	General information		1
Multitronic transmission – removal and refitting	2	Locking cable – removal, refitting and adjustment		6
Multitronic transmission fluid – renewal	See Chapter 1A or 1B	Selector cable – removal, refitting and adjustment		5
Multitronic transmission overhaul – general information	3			

Degrees of difficulty

Easy, suitable for novice with little experience	**Fairly easy,** suitable for beginner with some experience	**Fairly difficult,** suitable for competent DIY mechanic	**Difficult,** suitable for experienced DIY mechanic	**Very difficult,** suitable for expert DIY or professional

Specifications

General

Type	Constantly variable transmission with multi-link steel belt and multiplate clutch, in a magnesium casing
Designation	O1J
Multitronic transmission fluid capacity	See Chapter 1A or 1B

Torque wrench settings

	Nm	lbf ft
Bracket for fluid pipe	10	7
Damper unit to flywheel	25	18
Fluid pipe union	25	18
Fluid pipes to transmission	20	15
Multitronic transmission selector cable support bolt	23	17
Selector cable clamping screw	13	10
Torque converter to driveplate	85	63
Transmission bellhousing-to-engine bolts:*		
M10	45	33
M12	65	48
Transmission mounting:		
Centre bolt	40	30
To body	23	17
To transmission	40	30

* Do not re-use

1 General information

The Multitronic transmission is a continuously variable transmission, with a steel link-plate chain running under tension between two pairs of hydraulically adjustable pulley halves. As the pulley halves move towards or away from each other, the ratio between them changes. This provides a wide range of effective ratios that transfers the engine power in a seamless manner, and allows the engine to always operate in its most economical speed range. Drive between the engine and transmission input shaft is controlled by a multiplate clutch, and the differential is enclosed in the same transmission casing. The operation of the whole system is controlled electronically by a dedicated electronic control module (ECM) located behind the transmission end cover.

Due to the complexity of the transmission and its control system, major repairs and overhaul operations should be left to an Audi dealer or transmission specialist, who will be equipped to carry out fault diagnosis and repair. The information in this Chapter is therefore limited to a description of the removal and refitting of the transmission as a complete unit. The removal, refitting and adjustment of the selector cable and locking cable; removal and refitting of the damper unit is also described.

Caution: The Multitronic transmission is fitted into a casing made from a magnesium alloy. In order to eliminate the possibility of contact corrosion, only renew fasteners with those approved by Audi – consult your dealer or spares specialist.

2.17 Some models have a round wiring plug at the rear of the transmission, some have square plugs

2.18 Selector cable support bracket retaining bolts (arrowed) at the rear of the transmission

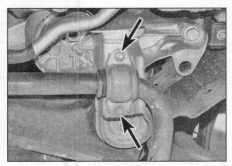

2.23 On Cabriolet models, undo the 2 nuts and remove the front anti-roll bar clamps each side (arrowed)

2 Multitronic transmission – removal and refitting

Removal

1 Select a solid, level surface to park the vehicle upon. Give yourself enough space to move around it easily. Apply the handbrake and chock the rear wheels.

2 Apply the handbrake, then jack up the front of the vehicle and support it on axle stands (see *Jacking and vehicle support*). Remove both front roadwheels.

3 Place the selector lever in position P.

4 Remove the engine/transmission undershields and remove the noise insulation and bracket.

5 Disconnect the battery negative (earth) lead (see Chapter 5A) and position it away from the terminal.

6 Remove the plastic cover from the top of the engine (where fitted).

7 To improve access, remove the air cleaner housing as described in the relevant part of Chapter 4.

8 Support the engine with a hoist or support bar located on the front wing inner channels. If necessary, remove the bonnet as described in Chapter 11 in order to position the hoist over the engine. Due to the weight of the transmission, the engine should be supported using both the front and rear lifting eyes. Depending on the engine, temporarily remove components as necessary to attach the hoist.

9 Undo the fasteners, and remove the left- and right-hand side vehicle underbody inner covers either side of the exhaust pipe tunnel.

10 Undo the bolts, and remove the front and rear tunnel crossmembers under the exhaust pipe.

11 Remove the front section of the exhaust pipe as described in Chapter 4D, taking care not to bend the flexible coupling. Also, where necessary, unbolt the downpipe mounting bracket from the transmission.

12 Position a workshop trolley jack beneath the transmission casing, then undo the bolts/nuts and detach the transmission crossmember from the vehicle body and transmission mounting.

13 Undo the bolts and remove the heat shields from above the driveshaft flanges.

14 Refer to Chapter 8 and detach the driveshafts from the transmission flanges. Tie the driveshafts away from the transmission.

15 Position a suitable container beneath the transmission to collect spilt hydraulic fluid.

16 Undo the ATF fluid union nuts, release the retaining brackets and remove the ATF pipes from under the transmission.

17 Note their fitted positions, and the harness routing, then disconnect all wiring plugs from the transmission **(see illustration)**.

18 Undo the bolts and detach the selector cable support bracket from the transmission casing **(see illustration)**.

19 Carefully prise the end of the selector cable from the lever on the transmission.

20 Undo the bolts and remove the mounting assembly from the rear of the transmission casing.

Cabriolet models

21 Raise the transmission slightly using the trolley jack.

22 Unbolts the torque reaction support arm from the engine sump.

23 Undo the front anti-roll bar clamp bolts and allow the bar to swing down **(see illustration)**.

24 Slacken the nuts on the base of the left- and right-hand engine mountings, until they are flush with the bottom of the mounting studs.

25 Use a hoist to left the engine until the mounting nuts contact the underside of the mounting.

All models

26 Undo and remove the bolts securing the transmission to the engine. On Cabriolet models, lower the engine back down.

27 Carefully pull the transmission from the locating dowels on the engine, and lower it carefully. Manoeuvre the transmission from under the vehicle.

 Warning: The transmission is heavy – enlist the help of an assistant.

Refitting

28 Refitting the transmission is a reversal of the removal procedure, but note the following points:

a) Clean the gearbox input shaft splines and damper unit splines, and apply a little clutch assembly grease to the splines – wipe off any excess grease.

b) Tighten the new bellhousing bolts to the specified torque. Always renew self-locking nuts and bolts.

c) Renew the O-ring seals on the fluid pipes attached to the transmission casing.

d) Tighten the transmission mounting bolts to the correct torque.

e) Check the final drive oil level and transmission fluid level as described in Chapter 1A or 1B.

f) On completion, refer to Section 5 and check the gear selector cable adjustment.

g) Make sure that the front subframe is positioned exactly as removed. Finally have the wheel alignment checked and if necessary adjusted.

3 Multitronic transmission overhaul – general information

In the event of a fault occurring, it will be necessary to establish whether the fault is electrical, mechanical or hydraulic in nature, before repair work can be contemplated. Diagnosis requires detailed knowledge of the transmission's operation and construction, as well as access to specialised test equipment, and so is deemed to be beyond the scope of this manual. It is therefore essential that problems with the transmission are referred to an Audi dealer or specialist for assessment.

Note that a faulty transmission should not be removed before the vehicle has been assessed by a dealer, as fault diagnosis is carried out with the transmission *in situ*.

4 Multitronic damper unit – removal and refitting

Removal

1 In order to dampen the torsional vibration caused by the engine's firing pulses, a damper unit is bolted to the flywheel. This unit transmits drive from the flywheel to the gearbox input shaft, and incorporates coil springs much like those fitted to traditional clutch friction discs. To remove the damper unit, first remove the transmission as described in Section 2.

2 Hold the flywheel stationary, then unscrew the damper unit bolts progressively in diagonal sequence.

3 Remove all the bolts, then lift the damper unit from the flywheel.

4 Check the condition of the damper unit for signs of wear or damage. Check the springs are not loose in the unit.

Refitting

5 Position the damper unit on the flywheel, noting that the locating pin on the flywheel must align with the corresponding hole in the damper unit **(see illustration)**.

6 Fit the bolts, and tighten them evenly and gradually, in a diagonal pattern, to the specified torque.

7 Refit the transmission as described in Section 2.

5	Selector cable – removal, refitting and adjustment

Removal

1 Move the selector lever to the P position.

2 Apply the handbrake, then jack up the front of the vehicle and support it on axle stands (see *Jacking and vehicle support*). Undo the fasteners and remove the transmission undershield **(see illustration)**.

3 Undo the fasteners and remove the left- and right-hand inner vehicle floor covers each side of the central floor tunnel.

4 Undo the screws and remove the cross-members from under the exhaust system.

5 Slacken the clamp bolts, and slide the sleeve rearwards, to disconnect the front section of the exhaust pipe from the rear section.

6 Undo the screws and lower the heat shield from below the selector cable.

7 Undo the 3 bolts securing the selector cable support bracket to the transmission casing **(see illustration 2.18)**.

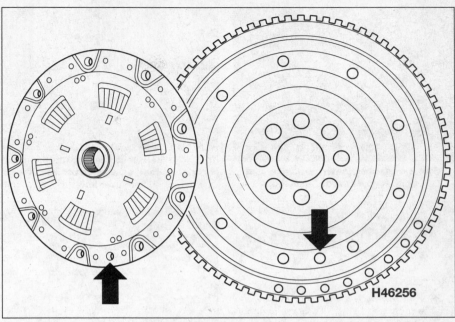

4.5 The locating pin on the flywheel must align with the corresponding hole in the damper unit (arrowed)

8 Carefully lever the end of the selector cable from the lever on the transmission.

9 Undo the four nuts securing the selector housing lower cover, then pull the cable sleeve forward from the housing cover, then slide the housing cover along the cable **(see illustration)**.

10 Pull out the clip securing the outer cable to the selector housing, then pull the plastic securing spring slightly forward, and press the retaining pin upwards only as far as necessary to be able to pull the cable from the fitting **(see illustrations)**. Do not push the pin fully out. Withdraw the cable.

11 If required, slacken the locknuts and detach the support bracket from the cable.

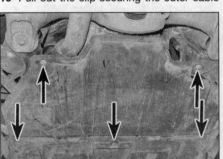

5.2 Undo the fasteners and remove the transmission undershield (arrowed)

5.9 Pull the rubber sleeve out of the housing cover and slide it along the cable (arrowed)

5.10a Slide the retaining clip downwards (arrowed)

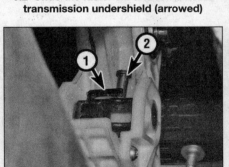

5.10b Pull the spring clip (1) forwards slightly, and push the pin (2) upwards . . .

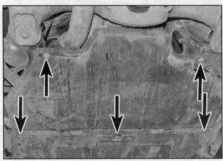

5.10c . . . using a small screwdriver from below

5.14 Rotate the sleeve clockwise, and push it downwards (arrowed)

5.17 Pull the selector lever panel surround trim upwards to release the clips

5.15 Pull the selector lever button out just enough to feed a cable tie between it and the lever knob

5.18 Undo the two bolts and remove the ashtray (arrowed)

Refitting

12 Refitting is a reversal of removal, noting the following points:

a) *Fit a new outer cable retaining clip.*

b) *Push the end of the cable into the selector lever fitting, and press the pin downwards, ensuring the securing spring has locked into place.*

c) *Check the operation of the selector lever before reconnecting the cable at the transmission end.*

d) *Before lowering the car to the ground carry out the adjustment as follows:*

Adjustment

13 Move the selector lever inside the car to the D position.

14 Rotate the sleeve under the selector lever knob clockwise approximately 45°, and push it down as far as it will go (see illustration).

15 Carefully pull out the button in the selector lever knob just far enough for a cable tie to be inserted between the knob and the button. Secure the cable tie around the button (see illustration). Do not pull the button out any further then necessary, or it will be damaged.

16 Pull the selector lever knob upwards and detach it from the lever.

17 Open the front ashtray, then starting at the front edge, lever up and remove the selector lever panel surround trim (see illustration).

18 Undo the bolts and remove the ashtray (see illustration).

19 Release the 4 clips and lift the selector lever surround upwards and over the lever (see illustration). Disconnect any wiring plugs as the surround is withdrawn.

Models with PRND selector

20 Move the selector lever to the D position (fully rearwards).

21 Insert Audi special tool T40031 down through the hole in the selector mechanism, and check that the inner cable clamping screw is tight (see illustration 5.32). In the absence of the special tool, a 5.0 mm Allen key at least 140 mm long will suffice.

22 Move the selector lever to the P position (fully forward).

23 Undo the nut securing the bracket on the selector cable to the support bracket on the transmission casing (see illustration).

24 Move the lever on the transmission as far rearwards as possible. This should place the transmission in park P. Make sure that both front wheels are locked by attempting to turn them in the same direction at the same time. **Note:** *Even though the transmission is locked, it will still be possible to turn the front wheels in* **opposite** *directions, since the differential gears are able move in relation to each other.*

25 Refit the cable bracket to the support bracket and tighten the nut securely.

26 Working inside the vehicle, move the selector lever to position D.

27 Using Audi tool T40031 or equivalent, slacken the selector cable clamping screw approximately 1 complete turn – no more (see illustration 5.32).

28 Carefully move the selector lever backwards and forwards a little to 'settle' it in position. Do not shift the lever to another position. Finally pull the lever back to the stop in the D position, then gently release it.

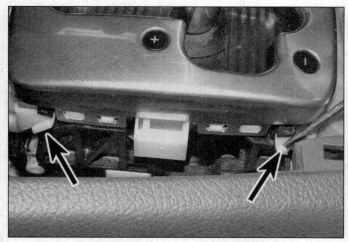

5.19 Press the clips outwards to release them (arrowed)

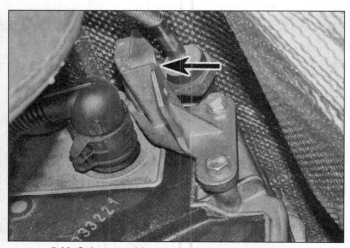

5.23 Selector cable support bracket retaining nut (arrowed)

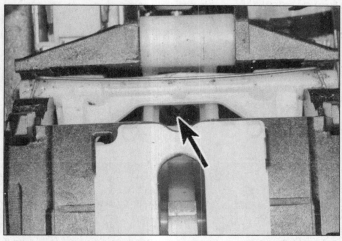

5.32 Insert a 5.0 mm Allen key, at least 140 mm long, down through the hole (arrowed) to check the inner cable clamping screw

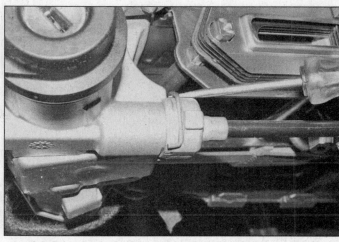

6.9 Prise up the locking cable clip at the ignition switch

29 Tighten the cable clamping screw to the specified torque. The adjustment is now set.
30 Refit the lever surround, trim and knob in a reversal of removal.

Models with PRNDS selector

31 Move the selector lever to the S position (fully rearward).
32 Insert Audi special tool T40031 down through the hole in the selector mechanism, and check that the inner cable clamping screw is tight **(see illustration)**. In the absence of the special tool, a 5.0 mm Allen key at least 140 mm long will suffice.
33 Move the selector lever to the P position (fully forward).
34 Undo the nut securing the bracket on the selector cable to the support bracket on the transmission casing **(see illustration 5.23)**.
35 Move the lever on the transmission as far rearwards as possible. This should place the transmission in park P. Make sure that both front wheels are locked by attempting to turn them in the same direction at the same time. **Note:** *Even though the transmission is locked, it will still be possible to turn the front wheels in opposite directions, since the differential gears are able move in relation to each other.*
36 Refit the cable bracket to the support bracket and tighten the nut securely.
37 Working inside the vehicle, move the selector lever to position S.
38 Using Audi tool T40031 or equivalent, slacken the selector cable clamping screw approximately 1 complete turn – no more **(see illustration 5.32)**.
39 Carefully move the selector lever backwards and forwards a little to 'settle' it in position. Do not shift the lever to another position. Finally pull the lever back to the stop in the S position, then gently release it.
40 Tighten the cable clamping screw to the specified torque. The adjustment is now set.
41 Refit the lever surround, trim and knob in a reversal of removal.

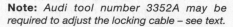

6 Locking cable –
removal, refitting and adjustment

Note: *Audi tool number 3352A may be required to adjust the locking cable – see text.*

Removal

1 Disconnect the battery negative terminal (see Chapter 5A).
2 Remove the driver's side storage compartment as described in Chapter 11.
3 Remove the steering column shrouds as described in Chapter 10.
4 Remove the air conditioning control panel as described in Chapter 3.
5 Open the front ashtray, undo the bolts and remove the ashtray.
6 Starting at the front edge, lever up and remove the selector lever panel surround trim **(see illustration 5.17)**.
7 Release the 4 clips and lift the selector lever surround upwards and over the lever **(see illustration 5.19)**. Disconnect any wiring plugs as the surround is withdrawn.
8 Turn the ignition switch to the 'on' position, and move the selector lever to position P.
9 Lift up the locking clip on the outer cable at

6.10 Prise up the spring clip and slide the cable from the lever pin

the ignition switch, and pull the cable from the ignition switch **(see illustration)**.
10 Lift the securing spring slightly, and unclip the locking cable. Pull the cable sideways from the lever pin **(see illustration)**.
11 Note the routing of the cable and withdraw it from the passenger compartment.

Refitting

12 Refit the cable, using the routing noted during removal.
13 Ensure that the ignition switch is in the 'on' position, and the selector lever is in the P position.
14 Fit the cable to the ignition switch, ensuring that the locking device engages correctly. Turn the ignition switch to the 'off' position.
15 Clip the locking cable into the securing spring in the mounting bracket.
16 Engage the locking cable support bracket into the selector mechanism, and the locking inner cable eye over the lever pin. Carry out the following adjustment procedure.
17 The remainder of refitting is a reversal of removal.

Adjustment

18 Loosen the support bracket clamp bolt **(see illustration)**. It must be possible to move the support bracket forward by hand.

6.18 Slacken the support bracket bolt (arrowed)

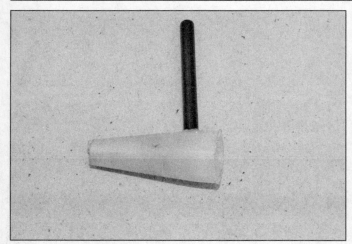

6.20a Improvised tool using a sealant tube nozzle and a roll-pin

6.20b Slide the tool over the lever pin, and centralise the cable eye (arrowed)

19 With the battery negative lead disconnected (see Chapter 5A), move the selector lever to position P, and the ignition key to the removal position.

20 Audi specify the use of a setting bar (tool 3352A) to set the position of the cable eye over the lever pin. This tool ensures the lever pin is accurately in the centre of the cable eye. Slide the tool over the lever pin and into the cable eye. In the absence of the special tool, we improvised using a plastic nozzle from a sealant tube, gradually trimming the nozzle until a good fit between the cable eye and pin was achieved. The internal and external diameters of the nozzle end are approximately 5.0 mm and 6.0 mm respectively **(see illustrations)**.

21 Pull the outer cable gently forwards towards the engine, and tighten the support bracket clamp bolt securely. Remove the setting bar/special tool. If no tool is available, then ensure the selector lever pin is accurately in the centre of the cable eye, with the outer cable pulled forwards. Tighten the outer cable clamp bolt, and check the position of the cable eye/lever pin again.

22 Check the operation of the locking cable.

Chapter 8
Driveshafts

Contents

Driveshaft and CV joint check . . . . See Chapter 1A or 1B
Driveshaft overhaul – general information 4
Driveshafts – overhaul 3

Section number

Driveshafts – removal and refitting. 2
General information 1

Section number

Degrees of difficulty

Easy, suitable for novice with little experience	**Fairly easy,** suitable for beginner with some experience	**Fairly difficult,** suitable for competent DIY mechanic	**Difficult,** suitable for experienced DIY mechanic	**Very difficult,** suitable for expert DIY or professional

Specifications

Lubrication

Type:
Outer constant velocity joints	G 000 603 grease
Inner constant velocity joints	G 000 603 grease
Inner tripod triple roller joints	G 000 605 grease

Amount per joint:
Outer joint:
88 mm diameter joint	90 g
100 mm diameter joint	120 g

Inner joint:
Constant velocity joint:
100 mm diameter joint	80 g
108 mm diameter joint	120 g

Triple roller tripod joint:
AAR 2000 driveshaft	110 g
AAR 2600 i/3300 i driveshaft	130 g

Torque wrench settings

	Nm	lbf ft
Driveshaft-to-transmission flange socket-head bolts:		
Stage 1	15	11
Stage 2:		
M8 bolts	40	30
M10 bolts	77	57
Hub bolt*:		
M14 bolt:		
Stage 1	115	85
Stage 2	Angle-tighten a further 180°	
M16 bolt:		
Stage 1	200	148
Stage 2	Angle-tighten a further 180°	
Roadwheel bolts.	120	89
Upper suspension link arm pinch-bolt/nut*	40	30

* Do not re-use

---

1 General information

Drive is transmitted from the differential to the front wheels by means of two steel driveshafts of either solid or hollow construction (depending on model). Both driveshafts are splined at their outer ends to accept the wheel hubs, and are secured to the hub by a large bolt. The inner end of each driveshaft is bolted to the transmission drive flanges.

Constant velocity (CV) joints are fitted to each end of the driveshafts, to ensure the smooth and efficient transmission of drive at all the angles possible as the roadwheels move up-and-down with the suspension, and as they turn from side-to-side under steering.

On some models, both inner and outer constant velocity joints are of the ball-and-cage type, whilst on others the outer joint is of the ball-and-cage type, but the inner joint is of the tripod type.

Rubber or plastic gaiters are secured over both CV joints with steel clips. These contain the grease that is packed into the joint, and also protect the joint from the ingress of dirt and debris.

2.1 Prise out the cap in the centre of the wheel

2 Driveshafts –
removal and refitting

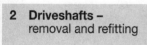

Removal

1 Remove the wheel trim/hub cap (as applicable) then slacken the hub bolt 90° (one quarter of a turn) with the vehicle resting on its wheels **(see illustration)**. Also slacken the wheel bolts.

2 Chock the rear wheels of the car, firmly apply the handbrake, then jack up the front of the car and support it on axle stands (see *Jacking and vehicle support*). Remove the appropriate front roadwheel. Whilst the wheel is removed, refit at least one of the wheel bolts to ensure the brake disc remains correctly positioned on the hub.

3 Remove the retaining fasteners and remove the transmission undershield to gain access to the driveshafts.

4 Remove the hub bolt. If the bolt was not slackened with the wheels on the ground, refit at least two roadwheel bolts to the front hub, tightening them securely, then have an assistant firmly depress the brake pedal to prevent the front hub from rotating, whilst you slacken and remove the hub bolt.

5 Slacken and remove the bolts securing the inner driveshaft joint to the transmission drive flange and recover the reinforcing plates (where fitted) from underneath the bolts. Support the driveshaft by suspending it with

2.9 Fit a new driveshaft retaining bolt

2.6 If necessary, remove the pinch-bolt (arrowed) and pull up the two balljoints

wire or string – do not allow it to hang under its weight, or the joint may be damaged.

6 Depending on the model, it may now be possible to pull the inner end of the driveshaft downwards, and slide it from the wheel hub. However, where there is insufficient clearance, remove the upper link arms pinch-bolt, and pull out both upper link arms' balljoints from the hub carrier **(see illustration)**. It should now be possible to pull the upper end of the hub carrier outwards slightly, and slide the driveshaft from place. Discard the pinch-bolt, a new one must be fitted.

Caution: Do not unbolt the steering track rod from the hub carrier.

Caution: Do not allow the vehicle to rest on its wheels with one or both driveshafts removed, as damage to the wheel bearings may result. If moving the vehicle is unavoidable, temporarily insert the outer end of the driveshaft in the hubs and tighten the driveshaft bolts. Support the inner ends of the driveshafts to avoid damage.

Refitting

7 Before installing the driveshaft, examine the driveshaft oil seal in the transmission for signs of damage or deterioration. If necessary, on manual transmissions, renew it as described in Chapter 7A.

8 Thoroughly clean the driveshaft outer joint and hub splines and the mating surfaces of the inner joint and transmission flange. Check that all gaiter clips are securely fastened.

2.10 Tighten the inner joint-to-transmission flange bolts to the specified torque

9 Manoeuvre the driveshaft into position, engaging the splines with those of the hub, and slide the outer joint into position. Fit the new hub bolt, tightening it by hand only at this stage **(see illustration)**. Note that the right-hand side driveshaft is slightly longer than the left-hand side.

10 Align the driveshaft inner joint with the transmission flange then refit the retaining bolts and, where fitted, the reinforcing plates. Tighten all bolts by hand then, working in a diagonal sequence, tighten them to the specified torque **(see illustration)**.

11 Where applicable, refit the front and rear upper suspension links arms to top of the hub, insert the new pinch-bolt, then fit the new retaining nut and tighten it to the specified torque.

12 Tighten the new hub bolt to the stage one torque setting. Prevent the driveshaft/hub from rotating by having an assistant depress the brake pedal.

13 Refit the undershield and roadwheel then lower the vehicle to the ground and tighten the wheel bolts to the specified torque.

14 With the vehicle resting on its wheels, tighten the hub bolt to the specified Stage 2 torque angle, using an angle-measuring gauge to ensure accuracy. If an angle gauge is not available, use white paint to make alignment marks between the bolt head and hub/wheel prior to tightening; the marks can then be used to check that the bolt has been rotated through the correct angle.

15 Refit the wheel trim/hub cap (as applicable).

3 Driveshafts –
overhaul

1 Remove the driveshaft from the vehicle as described in Section 2 and proceed as described under the relevant sub-heading. Note that several different types of driveshaft may be fitted **(see illustrations)**.

Outer joint

2 Secure the driveshaft in a vice equipped with soft jaws, and release the gaiter retaining clips. If necessary, the retaining clips can be cut to release them.

3 Fold back the rubber gaiter to expose the outer constant velocity joint. Scoop out the excess grease and dispose of it. If necessary, cut the boot from the shaft.

4 Use a hammer and suitable soft metal drift to sharply strike the inner member of the outer joint to drive it off the end of the shaft, taking great care not to damage the joint. On models with hollow driveshafts, it will first be necessary to displace the inner circlip (using circlip pliers) from its groove at the inner surface of the joint, to allow the dished washer and the plastic spacer ring to be slid along the driveshaft, away from the joint **(see illustration)**. Note that the dished washer and spacer ring are not fitted to all driveshafts.

3.1a Driveshaft details –
type AAR 2000

1 Clip
2 Gaiter
3 Clip
4 Multipoint socket bolt
5 Inner joint body
6 Triple roller tripod
7 Circlip
8 O-ring
9 Cover
10 Clip
11 Gaiter
12 Driveshaft
13 Circlip
14 Outer constant velocity joint
15 Hub bolt

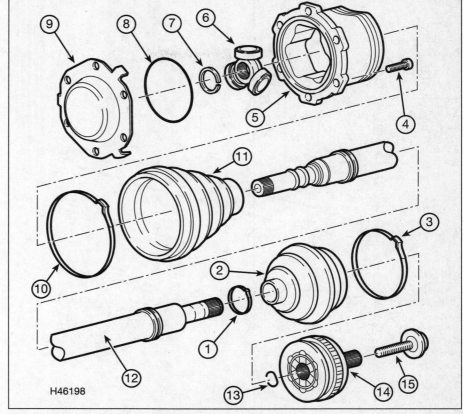

3.1b Driveshaft details –
type AAR 2600 i/3300 i

1 Gaiter
2 Clip
3 Circlip
4 Dished washer
5 Spacer
6 Circlip
7 Outer constant velocity joint
8 Hub bolt
9 Clip
10 Gaiter
11 Clip
12 Driveshaft
13 Circlip
14 Triple roller tripod
15 Circlip
16 Multipoint socket head bolts
17 Joint housing
18 Clip

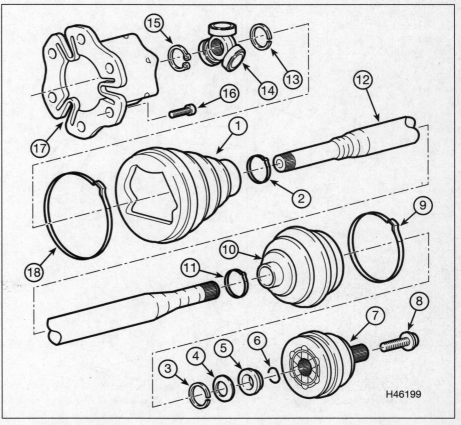

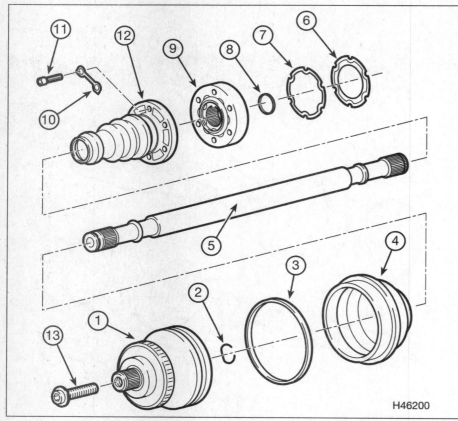

**3.1c Driveshaft details –
with 100 mm diameter inner CV joint**

1 Outer constant velocity joint
2 Circlip
3 Clip
4 Gaiter
5 Driveshaft
6 Cover
7 Gasket
8 Circlip
9 Inner constant velocity joint
10 Reinforcing plate
11 Multipoint socket head bolt
12 Gaiter with cap
13 Hub bolt

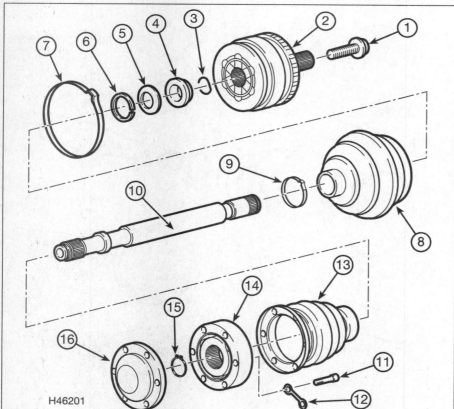

**3.1d Driveshaft details –
with 108 mm diameter inner CV joint**

1 Hub bolt
2 Outer constant velocity joint
3 Circlip
4 Spacer
5 Dished washer
6 Circlip
7 Clip
8 Gaiter
9 Clip
10 Driveshaft
11 Multipoint socket head bolt
12 Reinforcement plate
13 Gaiter with cap
14 Inner constant velocity joint
15 Circlip
16 Cover

5 Once the joint assembly has been removed, remove the circlip from the groove in the driveshaft splines, and discard it. A new circlip must be fitted on reassembly.

6 Slide the spacer, dished washer and circlip (where fitted) off from the driveshaft, noting their correct fitted locations, and remove the rubber gaiter.

7 With the constant velocity joint removed from the driveshaft, thoroughly clean the joint using paraffin, or a suitable solvent, and dry it thoroughly. Carry out a visual inspection of the joint.

8 Move the inner splined driving member from side-to-side, to expose each ball in turn at the top of its track. Examine the balls for cracks, flat spots, or signs of surface pitting.

9 Inspect the ball tracks on the inner and outer members. If the tracks have widened, the balls will no longer be a tight fit. At the same time, check the ball cage windows for wear or cracking between the windows.

10 If the constant velocity joint is found to be worn or damaged, it will be necessary to renew the joint, or the complete driveshaft (where the joint is not available separately). Refer to your Audi dealer or parts specialist for further information on parts availability. If the joint is in satisfactory condition, obtain a repair kit; the genuine Audi kit consists of a new gaiter, circlips, spring washer and spacer (where applicable), retaining clips, and the correct type and quantity of grease.

11 Tape over the splines on the end of the driveshaft, then fit the retaining clip to the small diameter, and slide the new gaiter onto the shaft **(see illustration)**. Remove the tape.

12 Fit the dished washer, ensuring its convex surface is facing inwards, then slide on the spacer with its flatter surface facing the dished washer (where fitted).

13 Fit the new circlip, making sure it is correctly located in the driveshaft groove **(see illustration)**.

14 Work the half of the grease supplied well into the ball tracks of the outer joint then fill the gaiter with any excess **(see illustration)**.

15 Locate the outer joint on the driveshaft splines and slide it on until the inner member abuts the circlip. Compress the circlip into the outer shaft groove with screwdrivers or pliers, and at the same time tap the joint outer member sharply with hammer and soft-metal drift to force the inner member over the circlip and fully onto the driveshaft. Pull on the joint assembly to make sure the joint is securely retained by the circlip.

16 Squeeze the remainder of the supplied into the gaiter, then locate the outer lip of the gaiter in the groove on the joint outer member and lift the inner lip of the gaiter to equalise the air pressure inside **(see illustration)**.

17 Fit the outer retaining clip to the gaiter and secure both clips in position by compressing its raised section. In the absence of the special tool, carefully compress each clip using a pair of side-cutters, taking great care not to cut through the clip **(see illustrations)**.

3.4 Drive the inner member of the outer joint from the end of the driveshaft

3.13 Fit a new circlip to the shaft

18 Check that the constant velocity joint moves freely in all directions, then refit the driveshaft to the vehicle as described in Section 2.

3.16 Lift the inner lip of the gaiter to equalise air pressure

3.17b . . . and compress its raised section . . .

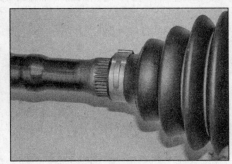

3.11 Slide the new gaiter onto the shaft

3.14 Work the grease well into the ball tracks of the outer joint

Inner joint

Note: *The inner joint is a very tight fit on the driveshaft and removal/refitting will therefore require the use of a hydraulic press and suitable*

3.17a Fit the new clip to the gaiter . . .

3.17c . . . until it looks like this

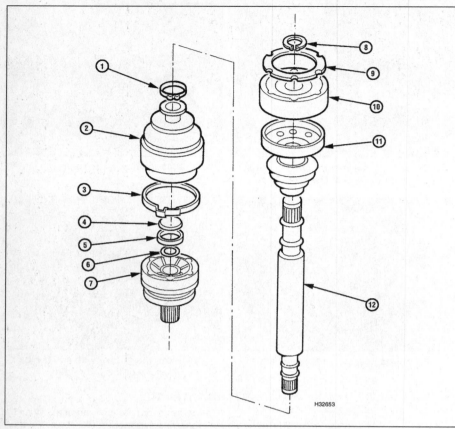

3.19 Driveshaft with 'ball-and-cage' type inner joint

1 Retaining clip	6 Circlip	10 Inner constant velocity
2 Outer gaiter	7 Outer constant velocity	joint
3 Retaining clip	joint	11 Locking plate and
4 Dished washer	8 Circlip	gaiter
5 Spacer	9 Gasket	12 Driveshaft

adapters. If this equipment is not available, gaiter renewal must be entrusted to an Audi dealer or other suitably-equipped garage.

Ball-and-cage type

19 Secure the driveshaft in a vice equipped with soft jaws then, using a hammer and punch, carefully tap the gaiter locking plate off from the inner constant velocity joint outer member **(see illustration).**

20 Prise the cap, and remove the gasket (where fitted) from the end of the joint.

21 Remove the circlip from the inner end of the driveshaft.

22 Remove the inner constant velocity joint from the driveshaft by securely supporting the joint outer member and pressing the driveshaft out from the inner member. Note which way around the joint outer member is fitted.

23 Release the gaiter inner retaining clip and remove the gaiter from the driveshaft.

24 Clean and inspect the inner joint as described in paragraphs 7 to 9.

25 If the constant velocity joint is found to be worn or damaged, it will be necessary to renew the joint, or the complete driveshaft (where no joint components are available separately).

Refer to your Audi dealer or parts specialist for further information on parts availability. If the joint is in satisfactory condition, obtain a repair kit; the genuine Audi kit consists of a new gaiter, locating plate, circlip, retaining clips, gasket, cap (where applicable) and the correct type and quantity of grease.

26 Tape over the splines on the end of the driveshaft, then slide the new gaiter onto the shaft. Remove the tape and fit the locating plate to the driveshaft gaiter.

3.35 Check the inner joint rollers and bearings for wear

27 Securely clamp the driveshaft then press the inner joint onto the shaft, ensuring it is fitted the right way around. Secure the joint in position with the new circlip making sure it is correctly located in the driveshaft groove, then fit the gasket and cap (where applicable).

28 Work the grease well into the ball tracks of the joint then fill the gaiter with any excess.

29 Wipe clean the mating surfaces of the gaiter locating plate and joint. Apply a smear of sealant (Audi recommend D 454 300 A2 sealant – available from your Audi dealer) to the locating plate then align the locating plate holes with those on the joint outer member and tap the plate firmly onto the joint.

30 Ensure the outer lip is correctly engaged with the locating plate then lift the inner lip of the gaiter to equalise the air pressure inside.

31 Fit both the inner and outer retaining clips to the gaiter and secure each one in position by compressing its raised section. In the absence of the special tool, carefully compress each clip using a pair of side-cutters taking great care not to cut through the clip.

32 Check that the constant velocity joint moves freely in all directions, then refit the driveshaft to the vehicle as described in Section 2.

Tripod type

33 On AAR 2000 driveshafts **(see illustration 3.1a)**, loosen the clips and slide the gaiter away from the joint, then use a screwdriver to lever off the joint protective cover. If necessary remove the large O-ring seal from the groove. Mark the driveshaft, tripod and joint housing in relation to each other, then slowly withdraw the housing from the tripod, making sure that the rollers remain in position – if necessary, mark the rollers to ensure correct refitting. Extract the circlip, then press or drive off the tripod from the driveshaft, and finally remove the gaiter.

34 On AAR 2600 i/3300 i driveshafts **(see illustration 3.1b)**, remove the outer constant velocity joint as described above in paragraphs 2 to 6, then release the retaining clips and slide the inner gaiter from the driveshaft. If necessary, cut the gaiter to release it from the shaft. Note that the joint cannot be dismantled without access to an hydraulic press and special pullers.

35 Thoroughly clean the joint using paraffin, or a suitable solvent, and dry it thoroughly. Check the tripod joint bearings and joint outer member for signs of wear, pitting or scuffing on their bearing surfaces. Check that the bearing rollers rotate smoothly and easily around the tripod joint, with no traces of roughness **(see illustration)**.

36 If on inspection the tripod joint or outer member reveal signs of wear or damage, it will be necessary to renew the complete driveshaft assembly, since the joint is not available separately. If the joint is in satisfactory condition, obtain a repair kit consisting of a new gaiter, retaining clips, and the correct type and quantity of grease. Although not strictly

3.37 Work the grease well into the bearing tracks and rollers

3.39a Tape over the splines and slide the inner gaiter into position . . .

3.39b . . . levering it carefully over the driveshaft ridge

3.42a Lift the inner lip to equalise pressure

3.42b Fit the retaining clips to the gaiter . . .

3.42c . . . and secure them in position by carefully compressing their raised sections

necessary, it is also recommended that the outer constant velocity joint gaiter is renewed, regardless of its apparent condition.

37 On reassembly, pack the inner joint with the grease supplied. Work the grease well into the bearing tracks and rollers, while twisting the joint **(see illustration)**.

38 Clean the shaft, using emery cloth to remove any rust or sharp edges which may damage the gaiter. Tape over the splines on the end of the driveshaft and grease the driveshaft ridges to prevent possible damage to the inner gaiter on installation.

39 Ease the inner gaiter and small clip onto and along the driveshaft and carefully lever it over the driveshaft ridge, taking care not to damage it **(see illustrations)**.

40 On AAR 2000 driveshafts, refit the tripod on the driveshaft splines in its previously-noted position, and fit the circlip. Locate the housing over the tripod and rollers, again in its previously-noted position. Fit a new O-ring seal and press on the cover.

41 On AAR 2600 i/3300 i driveshafts, locate

the outer lip in the groove on the joint outer member and seat the inner lip correctly on the driveshaft.

42 Lift the inner lip of the gaiter to equalise the air pressure inside then fit both the inner and outer retaining clips. Secure each clip in position by compressing its raised section **(see illustrations)**. In the absence of the special tool, carefully compress each clip using a pair of side-cutters taking great care not to cut through the clip.

43 Refit the outer constant velocity joint as described in paragraphs 11 to 17.

44 Check that both constant velocity joints move freely in all directions, then refit the driveshaft to the vehicle as described in Section 2.

4 Driveshaft overhaul – general information

If any of the checks described in Chapter 1A

or 1B reveal wear in any driveshaft joint, first remove the roadwheel trim or centre cap (as appropriate) and check that the hub bolt is tight. If the bolt is loose, obtain a new bolt and tighten it to the specified torque (see Section 2). If the bolt is tight, refit the centre cap/trim and repeat the check on the other hub bolt.

Road test the vehicle, and listen for a metallic clicking from the front as the vehicle is driven slowly in a circle on full-lock. If a clicking noise is heard, this indicates wear in the outer constant velocity joint; this means that the joint must be renewed.

If vibration, consistent with roadspeed, is felt through the car when accelerating, there is a possibility of wear in the inner constant velocity joints.

To check the joints for wear, remove the driveshafts, then dismantle them as described in Section 3; if any wear or free play is found, the affected joint must be renewed. Refer to your Audi dealer or parts specialist for information on the availability of driveshaft components.

Chapter 9
Braking system

Contents

	Section number
Anti-lock braking system (ABS) – general information	18
Anti-lock braking system (ABS) components – removal and refitting	19
Brake pedal – removal and refitting	11
ESP system components – removal and refitting	21
Front brake caliper – removal, overhaul and refitting	8
Front brake disc – inspection, removal and refitting	6
Front brake pad wear check	See Chapter 1A or 1B
Front brake pads – renewal	4
General information	1
Handbrake – adjustment	14
Handbrake cables – removal and refitting	16
Handbrake lever – removal and refitting	15
Hydraulic fluid – level check	See Weekly checks
Hydraulic fluid – renewal	See Chapter 1A or 1B

	Section number
Hydraulic pipes and hoses – renewal	3
Hydraulic system – bleeding	2
Master cylinder – removal, overhaul and refitting	10
Rear brake caliper – removal, overhaul and refitting	9
Rear brake disc – inspection, removal and refitting	7
Rear brake pad wear check	See Chapter 1A or 1B
Rear brake pads – renewal	5
Stop-light and brake pedal switches – removal, refitting and adjustment	17
Vacuum pump (diesel engine models) – removal and refitting	20
Vacuum pump (petrol engine models) – removal and refitting	22
Vacuum sensor – renewal	23
Vacuum servo unit – testing, removal and refitting	12
Vacuum servo unit check valve – removal, testing and refitting	13

Degrees of difficulty

Easy, suitable for novice with little experience 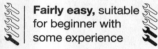	**Fairly easy,** suitable for beginner with some experience	**Fairly difficult,** suitable for competent DIY mechanic	**Difficult,** suitable for experienced DIY mechanic	**Very difficult,** suitable for expert DIY or professional

Specifications

Front brakes

Type	Disc, with single-piston sliding FN3 (ATE) calipers
Disc diameter	288 or 312 mm
Disc thickness:	
New	25 mm
Minimum	23 mm
Maximum disc run-out	0.05 mm
Brake pad wear limit (friction material only – not including backing plate)	2 mm

Rear brakes

Type	Disc, with single-piston sliding C38 caliper
Disc diameter	245, 255 or 288 mm
Disc thickness:	
New:	
245 mm diameter	10 mm
255 and 288 mm diameter	12 mm
Minimum thickness:	
245 mm diameter	8 mm
255 and 288 mm diameter	10 mm
Maximum disc run-out	0.05 mm
Brake pad wear limit (friction material only – not including backing plate)	2 mm

ABS systems

Type	Bosch 5.7 or Bosch 8.0 with EBD and ESP

Brake fluid

Type	DOT 4

Servo

Pushrod balljoint-to-servo unit mating surface dimension:	
LHD models	159.0 ± 0.5 mm
RHD models	173.5 ± 0.5 mm

Torque wrench settings

	Nm	lbf ft
ABS hydraulic unit mounting bolts............................	10	7
Brake pedal shaft to operating lever bolt*......................	25	18
Cross-piece bolts..	25	18
Front brake caliper:		
Guide pins	25	18
Mounting bracket bolts*.................................	190	140
Wiring/brake hose bracket bolt	10	7
Handbrake lever mounting nuts............................	25	18
Hydraulic pipe union nuts.................................	12	9
Lateral acceleration/yaw rate sensor nuts	10	7
Master cylinder retaining nuts*...........................	49	36
Rear brake caliper:		
Guide pin bolts*.......................................	35	26
Mounting bracket bolt*..................................	75	55
Roadwheel bolt	120	89
Tandem vacuum/fuel pump bolts:		
Upper	20	15
Lower	10	7
Vacuum servo-to-bulkhead/pedal bracket through-bolts	25	18
Wheel speed sensor......................................	10	7

Use new fasteners

1 General information

All models have disc brakes fitted at the front and rear wheels as standard. ABS (Anti-lock Braking System) is also fitted as standard on all models (refer to Section 18 for further information on ABS operation).

The front and rear disc brakes are actuated by single-piston sliding type calipers, which ensure that equal pressure is applied to each disc pad. The handbrake mechanism is built into the rear calipers.

On all models, the handbrake provides an independent mechanical (rather than hydraulic) means of rear brake application.

Because the diesel engines have no throttle valve, there is insufficient vacuum in the inlet manifold to operate the braking system servo effectively at all times. This also applies to direct injection petrol engines, operating in Stratified charge mode. To overcome this problem, a vacuum pump is fitted to these models, to provide sufficient vacuum to operate the servo unit. The vacuum pump is mounted on the rear of the cylinder head and driven by the camshaft. On petrol models to emission standard EU4 with automatic transmission, an electric vacuum pump is fitted to supplement the vacuum supplied to the brake servo. On these models, under certain conditions (cold start, idling, etc) there is insufficient vacuum in the intake manifold. Consequently, an electric pump is fitted, monitored by a pressure sensor, and controlled by the engine management ECM.

ESP (Electronic Stability Program) is fitted to all models. The ESP (Electronic Stability Program) incorporates the ABS, EBS (Electronic Brake Assist) system and TCS (Traction Control System). It stabilises the vehicle when oversteering or understeering by applying the brake, or applying increased power to the relevant roadwheel, to increase the driver's control of the vehicle. In order for the ESP system to function, it utilises sensors which provide data concerning the speed of the vehicle around a vertical axis, the lateral movement of the vehicle, the brake pressure and the angle of the front wheels.

Note: *When servicing any part of the system, work carefully and methodically; also observe scrupulous cleanliness when overhauling any part of the hydraulic system. Always renew components (in axle sets, where applicable) if in doubt about their condition, and use only genuine Audi parts, or at least those of known good quality. Note the warnings given in 'Safety first!' and at relevant points in this Chapter concerning the dangers of asbestos dust and hydraulic fluid.*

2 Hydraulic system – bleeding

⚠️ *Warning: Hydraulic fluid is poisonous; wash off immediately and thoroughly in the case of skin contact, and seek immediate medical advice if any fluid is swallowed or gets into the eyes. Certain types of hydraulic fluid are inflammable, and may ignite when allowed into contact with hot components; when servicing any hydraulic system, it is safest to assume that the fluid is inflammable, and to take precautions against the risk of fire as though it is petrol that is being handled. Hydraulic fluid is also an effective paint stripper, and will attack plastics; if any is spilt, it should be washed off immediately, using copious quantities of fresh water. Finally, it is hygroscopic (it absorbs moisture from the air) – old fluid may be contaminated and unfit for further use. When topping-up or renewing the fluid, always use the recommended type, and ensure that it comes from a freshly-opened sealed container.*

Note: *If the hydraulic circuit upstream of the ABS modulator has been disturbed, the system may need to be bled using Audi diagnostic equipment. Entrust this task to an Audi dealer or suitably-equipped specialist.*

General

1 The correct operation of any hydraulic system is only possible after removing all air from the components and circuit; this is achieved by bleeding the system.

2 During the bleeding procedure, add only clean, unused hydraulic fluid of the recommended type; *never* re-use fluid that has already been bled from the system. Ensure that a sufficient quantity of new fluid is available before starting work.

3 If there is any possibility of incorrect fluid being already in the system, the brake components and circuit must be flushed completely with uncontaminated, correct fluid, and new seals should be fitted to the various components.

4 If hydraulic fluid has been lost from the system, or air has entered because of a leak, ensure that the fault is cured before proceeding further.

5 Park the vehicle on level ground, securely chock the wheel then release the handbrake.

6 Check that all pipes and hoses are secure, unions tight and bleed screws closed. Clean any dirt from around the bleed screws.

7 Unscrew the master cylinder reservoir cap, and top the master cylinder reservoir up to the MAX level line; refit the cap loosely, and remember to maintain the fluid level at least above the MIN level line throughout the procedure, or there is a risk of further air entering the system.

8 There is a number of one-man, do-it-yourself brake bleeding kits currently available from motor accessory shops. It is recommended that one of these kits is used whenever possible, as they greatly simplify the bleeding operation, and also reduce the risk of expelled air and fluid being drawn back into the system. If such a kit is not available, the basic (two-man) method must be used, which is described in detail below.

9 If a kit is to be used, prepare the vehicle as described previously, and follow the kit manufacturer's instructions, as the procedure may vary slightly according to the type being used; generally, they are as outlined below in the relevant sub-section.

10 Whichever method is used, the same sequence must be followed (see paragraphs 11 and 12) to ensure the removal of all air from the system.

Bleeding

Sequence

11 If the system has been only partially disconnected, and suitable precautions were taken to minimise fluid loss, it should be necessary only to bleed that part of the system (ie, the primary or secondary circuit).

12 If the complete system is to be bled, then it should be done working in the following sequence:

 a) Left-hand front brake.
 b) Right-hand front brake.
 c) Left-hand rear brake.
 d) Right-hand rear brake.

Basic (two-man) method

13 Collect a clean glass jar, a suitable length of plastic or rubber tubing which is a tight fit over the bleed screw, and a ring spanner to fit the screw. The help of an assistant will also be required.

14 Remove the dust cap from the first screw in the sequence. Fit the spanner and tube to the screw, place the other end of the tube in the jar, and pour in sufficient fluid to cover the end of the tube.

15 Ensure that the master cylinder reservoir fluid level is maintained at least above the MIN level line throughout the procedure.

16 Have the assistant fully depress the brake pedal several times to build-up pressure, then maintain it on the final downstroke.

17 While pedal pressure is maintained, unscrew the bleed screw (approximately one turn) and allow the compressed fluid and air to flow into the jar.

18 The assistant should maintain pedal pressure, following it down to the floor if necessary, and should not release it until instructed to do so. When the flow stops, tighten the bleed screw again, have the assistant release the pedal slowly, and recheck the reservoir fluid level.

19 Repeat the steps given in paragraphs 16 to 18 inclusive until the fluid emerging from the bleed screw is free from air bubbles. If the master cylinder has been drained and refilled,

and air is being bled from the first screw in the sequence, allow approximately five seconds between cycles for the master cylinder passages to refill.

20 When no more air bubbles appear, tighten the bleed screw securely, remove the tube and spanner, and refit the dust cap. Do not overtighten the bleed screw.

21 Repeat the procedure on the remaining screws in the sequence, until all air is removed from the system and the brake pedal feels firm again. On completion, lower the vehicle to the ground (where necessary).

Using a one-way valve kit

22 As their name implies, these kits consist of a length of tubing with a one-way valve fitted, to prevent expelled air and fluid being drawn back into the system; some kits include a translucent container, which can be positioned so that the air bubbles can be more easily seen flowing from the end of the tube.

23 The kit is connected to the bleed screw, which is then opened **(see illustration)**. The user returns to the driver's seat, depresses the brake pedal with a smooth, steady stroke, and slowly releases it; this is repeated until the expelled fluid is clear of air bubbles.

24 Note that these kits simplify work so much that it is easy to forget to watch the master cylinder reservoir fluid level; ensure that this is maintained at least above the MIN level line at all times, otherwise air will be reintroduced into the system.

Using a pressure-bleeding kit

25 These kits are usually operated by the reservoir of pressurised air contained in the spare tyre. However, note that it will probably be necessary to reduce the pressure to a lower level than normal; refer to the instructions supplied with the kit.

26 By connecting a pressurised, fluid-filled container to the master cylinder reservoir, bleeding can be carried out simply by opening each screw in turn (in the specified sequence), and allowing the fluid to flow out until no more air bubbles can be seen in the expelled fluid.

27 This method has the advantage that the large reservoir of fluid provides an additional safeguard against air being drawn into the system during bleeding.

28 Pressure-bleeding is particularly effective when bleeding difficult systems, or when bleeding the complete system at the time of routine fluid renewal.

All methods

29 When bleeding is complete, and firm pedal feel is restored, wash off any spilt fluid, tighten the bleed screws securely, and refit their dust caps.

30 Check the hydraulic fluid level in the master cylinder reservoir, and top-up if necessary (see *Weekly checks*).

31 Discard any hydraulic fluid that has been bled from the system; it will not be fit for re-use.

32 Check the feel of the brake pedal. If it feels at all spongy, air must still be present in

2.23 Connect the brake bleeding kit hose to the caliper bleed screw, then use a spanner to open the screw

the system, and further bleeding is required. Failure to bleed satisfactorily after a reasonable repetition of the bleeding procedure may be due to worn master cylinder seals.

33 Because the clutch hydraulic system shares the same fluid reservoir, we recommend that the clutch is bled at the same time (see Chapter 6).

3 Hydraulic pipes and hoses – renewal

Note: *Before starting work, refer to the note at the beginning of Section 2 concerning the dangers of hydraulic fluid.*

1 If any pipe or hose is to be renewed, minimise fluid loss by first removing the master cylinder reservoir cap, then tightening it down onto a piece of polythene to obtain an airtight seal. Alternatively, flexible hoses can be sealed, if required, using a proprietary brake hose clamp; metal brake pipe unions can be plugged (if care is taken not to allow dirt into the system) or capped immediately they are disconnected. Place a wad of rag under any union that is to be disconnected, to catch any spilt fluid.

2 If a flexible hose is to be disconnected, unscrew the brake pipe union nut and remove the spring clip which secures the hose to its mounting bracket **(see illustration)**.

3 To unscrew the union nuts, it is preferable to obtain a brake pipe spanner of the correct size; these are available from most large motor

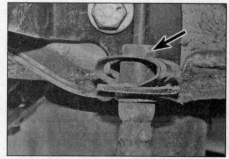

3.2 Undo the union nut (arrowed) and remove the spring clip

accessory shops. Failing this, a close-fitting open-ended spanner will be required, though if the nuts are tight or corroded, their flats may be rounded-off if the spanner slips. In such a case, a self-locking wrench is often the only way to unscrew a stubborn union, but it follows that the pipe and the damaged nuts must be renewed on reassembly. Always clean a union and surrounding area before disconnecting it. If disconnecting a component with more than one union, make a careful note of the connections before disturbing any of them.

4 If a brake pipe is to be renewed, it can be obtained, cut to length with the union nuts and end flares in place, from Audi dealers. All that is then necessary is to bend it to shape, following the line of the original, before fitting it to the car. Alternatively, most motor accessory shops can make up brake pipes from kits, but this requires very careful measurement of the original, to ensure that the new one is of the correct length. The safest answer is usually to take the original to the shop as a pattern.

5 On refitting, do not overtighten the union nuts. It is not necessary to exercise brute force to obtain a sound joint.

6 Ensure that the pipes and hoses are correctly routed, with no kinks, and that they are secured in the clips or brackets provided. After fitting, remove the polythene from the reservoir, and bleed the hydraulic system as described in Section 2. Wash off any spilt fluid, and check carefully for fluid leaks.

4 Front brake pads – renewal

![warning triangle] **Warning: Renew both sets of front brake pads at the same time – never renew the pads on only one wheel,** *as uneven braking may result. Note that the dust created by wear of the pads may contain asbestos, which is a health hazard. Never blow it out with compressed air, and don't inhale any of it. An approved filtering mask should be worn when working on the brakes. DO NOT use petrol or petroleum-based solvents to clean brake parts; use brake cleaner or methylated spirit only.*

1 Apply the handbrake, then loosen the front roadwheel nuts. Jack up the front of the vehicle and support it on axle stands. Remove both front roadwheels.

2 Follow the accompanying photos (**illustrations 4.2a to 4.2t**) for the actual pad renewal procedure. Be sure to stay in order and read the caption under each illustration, and note the following points:

a) *The inner pad (with a spring) is marked with an arrow. The arrow must point in the direction of brake disc rotation.*

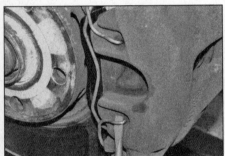
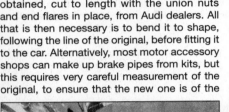
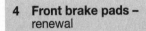

4.2a Use a screwdriver to prise out the ends of the retaining spring . . .

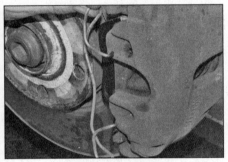

4.2b . . . and remove it from the caliper

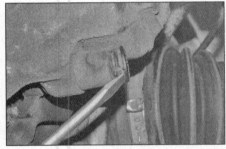

4.2c Prise out the rubber caps over the guide pins at the top and bottom of the caliper

4.2d Use a 7 mm Allen bit to undo both guide pins

4.2e Using a small screwdriver to release the clip . . .

4.2f . . . disconnect the pad wear sensor wiring plug

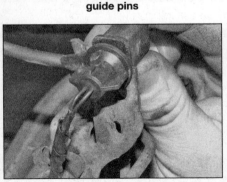

4.2g Turn the connector 90° and slide it up from the mounting bracket

4.2h Slide the caliper from the brake disc

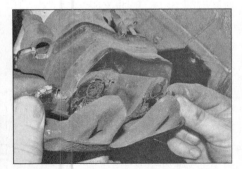

4.2i Remove the outer pad from the caliper . . .

4.2j . . . then pull the inner pad from the piston

4.2k Use wire to suspend the caliper from the suspension arm, so as not to strain the brake hose

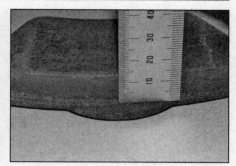

4.2l Measure the thickness of the pad's friction material – the minimum is 2.0 mm

4.2m If new pads are to be fitted, use a retraction tool to push the piston back into the caliper. Check the fluid level in the master cylinder reservoir doesn't overflow

4.2n Fit the outer pad to the caliper mounting bracket, ensuring the friction material is against the disc face . . .

4.2o . . . then clip the inner pad into the piston

4.2p Slide the pad wear sensor wiring connector into the bracket, and rotate it 90° to lock it in place

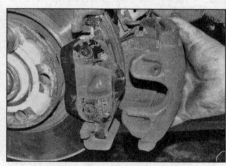

4.2q Fit the caliper into position . . .

4.2r . . . then refit the guide pins, tighten them to the specified torque, and refit the rubber caps

b) New pads may have an adhesive foil on the backplates. Remove this foil prior to installation.

c) Thoroughly clean the caliper guide surfaces, and apply a little brake assembly (polycarbamide) grease.

d) When pushing the caliper piston back to accommodate new pads, keep a close eye on the fluid lever in the reservoir.

3 Depress the brake pedal repeatedly, until the pads are pressed into firm contact with the brake disc, and normal (non-assisted) pedal pressure is restored.

4 Repeat the above procedure on the remaining front brake caliper.

5 Refit the roadwheels, then lower the vehicle to the ground and tighten the roadwheel bolts to the specified torque.

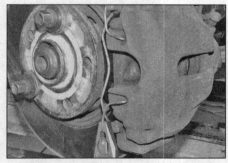

4.2s Insert the ends of the retaining spring into the corresponding holes in the caliper body, then use a pair of pliers to ease the 'ears' of the spring in front of the lugs on the mounting bracket

4.2t Don't forget to reconnect the pad wear sensor wiring plug

6 Check the hydraulic fluid level as described in *Weekly checks*.

Caution: New pads will not give full braking efficiency until they have bedded-in. Be prepared for this, and avoid hard braking as far as possible for the first hundred miles or so after pad renewal.

5 Rear brake pads – renewal

⚠️ **Warning: Renew both sets of rear brake pads at the same time – never renew the pads on only one wheel, as uneven braking may result. Note that the dust created by wear of the pads may contain asbestos, which is a health hazard. Never blow it out with compressed air, and** *don't inhale any of it. An approved filtering mask should be worn when working on the brakes. DO NOT use petrol or petroleum-based solvents to clean brake parts; use brake cleaner or methylated spirit only.*

Note: *The caliper guide pin bolts must be renewed whenever they are unscrewed.*

1 Chock the front wheels, then jack up the rear of the vehicle and support it on axle stands (see *Jacking and vehicle support*).

2 Remove the rear wheels. Whilst the wheels are removed, refit at least one wheel bolt to each hub to ensure the brake discs remain correctly positioned on the hubs.

3 With the handbrake lever fully released, follow the accompanying photos **(see illustrations 5.3a to 5.3k)** for the actual pad renewal procedure. Be sure to stay in order and read the caption under each illustration, and note the following points:

a) *If re-installing the original pads, ensure they are fitted to their original positions.*
b) *Guide pins and protective caps are available as a repair kit.*
c) *Thoroughly clean the caliper guide surfaces, and apply a little brake assembly (polycarbamide) grease.*
d) *If new pads are to be fitted, use a piston retraction tool to push the piston back and twist it clockwise at the same time – keep an eye on the fluid level in the reservoir whilst retracting the piston.*
e) *Fit new caliper guide pin bolts – included in the Audi repair kit.*

4 Depress the brake pedal repeatedly, until the pads are pressed into firm contact with the brake disc, and normal (non-assisted) pedal pressure is restored.

5 Repeat the above procedure on the remaining brake caliper.

5.3a Remove the caliper guide pin bolts at the top and bottom of the caliper – use an open-ended spanner to prevent the guide pin from rotating

5.3b Slide the caliper from position, and use wire to suspend it from the vehicle bodywork – don't strain the brake hose

5.3c Pull the inner pad from the mounting bracket . . .

5.3d . . . and the outer pad

5.3e If new pads are to be fitted, push the piston back into the caliper housing using a tool that rotates the piston clockwise at the same time as exerting pressure

5.3f Fit the inner pad, ensuring the friction material is against the disc face . . .

5.3g . . . followed by the outer pad

5.3h Check the condition of the guide pin gaiters – renew them if they show signs of deterioration or damage

5.3i Refit the caliper to the mounting bracket, ensuring it locates correctly over the ends of the guide pins

6 If necessary, adjust the handbrake as described in Section 14.
7 Refit the roadwheels, then lower the vehicle to the ground and tighten the roadwheel bolts to the specified torque.
8 Check the hydraulic fluid level as described in *Weekly checks*.
Caution: New pads will not give full braking efficiency until they have bedded-in. Be prepared for this, and avoid hard braking as far as possible for the first hundred miles or so after pad renewal.

6 Front brake disc –
inspection, removal and refitting

Note: Before starting work, refer to the note at the beginning of Section 4 concerning the dangers of asbestos dust.

Inspection

Note: If either disc requires renewal, BOTH should be renewed at the same time, to ensure even and consistent braking. New brake pads should also be fitted.

1 Apply the handbrake, then jack up the front of the car and support it on axle stands (see *Jacking and vehicle support*). Remove the appropriate front roadwheel. Whilst the wheel is removed, refit at least one of the wheel bolts to ensure the brake disc remains correctly positioned on the hub; if necessary fit spacers to the wheel bolts to clamp the disc firmly in position **(see illustration)**.
2 Slowly rotate the brake disc so that the full area of both sides can be checked; remove the brake pads if better access is required to the inboard surface. Light scoring is normal in the area swept by the brake pads, but if heavy scoring or cracks are found, the disc must be renewed.
3 It is normal to find a lip of rust and brake dust around the disc's perimeter; this can be scraped off if required. If, however, a lip has formed due to excessive wear of the brake pad swept area, then the disc's thickness must be measured using a micrometer. Take measurements at several places around the disc, at the inside and outside of the pad swept area; if the disc has worn at any point

5.3j Fit new guide pin bolts . . .

5.3k . . . and tighten them to the specified torque. Use an open-ended spanner to prevent the guide pins from rotating

to the specified minimum thickness or less, the disc must be renewed **(see illustration)**.
4 If the disc is thought to be warped, it can be checked for run-out. Secure the disc firmly to the hub by refitting at least two roadwheel bolts – fit plain washers to the roadwheel bolts to ensure that the disc is properly seated on the hub.
5 Either use a dial gauge mounted on any convenient fixed point, while the disc is slowly rotated, or use feeler blades to measure (at several points all around the disc) the clearance between the disc and a fixed point, such as the caliper mounting bracket **(see illustration)**. If the measurements obtained are at the specified maximum or beyond, the disc is excessively warped, and must be renewed, however, it is worth checking first that the hub bearing is in good condition (Chapter 10).
6 Check the disc for cracks, especially around

the wheel bolt holes, and any other wear or damage, and renew if necessary.

Removal

7 Unscrew and remove the two bolts securing the brake caliper mounting bracket to the hub carrier. Slide the whole caliper assembly off the hub and away from the disc and tie the assembly to the front coil spring, using a piece of wire or string, to avoid placing any strain on the hydraulic brake hose **(see illustrations)**. The caliper mounting bracket can be unbolted and removed separately if required (see Section 8).
8 Use chalk or paint to mark the relationship of the disc to the hub, then remove all the wheel bolts and washers used to secure the disc in position and remove the disc. If it is tight, lightly tap its rear face with a hide or plastic mallet to free it from the hub.

6.1 Refit at least one of the wheel bolts to retain the disc

6.3 Use a micrometer to measure the thickness of the disc

6.5 Use a DTI gauge to measure disc run-out

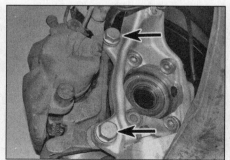
6.7a Undo the caliper mounting bracket bolts (arrowed)

6.7b Slide the caliper and mounting bracket from the hub carrier

7.4 Remove the rear brake disc

Refitting

9 Refitting is the reverse of the removal procedure, noting the following points:
  a) Ensure that the mating surfaces of the disc and hub are clean and flat.
  b) On refitting, align (if applicable) the marks made on removal.
  c) If a new disc has been fitted, use a suitable solvent to wipe any preservative coating from the disc, before refitting the caliper. Note that new brake pads should always be fitted when the disc is renewed.
  d) Prior to installation, renew the caliper mounting bracket bolts. Slide the caliper into position, making sure the pads pass either side of the disc, and tighten the caliper bracket bolts to the specified torque setting.
  e) Refit the roadwheel then lower the vehicle to the ground and tighten the wheel bolts to the specified torque. Apply the footbrake several times to force the pads back into contact with the disc before driving the vehicle.

7 Rear brake disc – inspection, removal and refitting

Note: Before starting work, refer to the note at the beginning of Section 5 concerning the dangers of asbestos dust.

Inspection

Note: If either disc requires renewal, BOTH should be renewed at the same time, to ensure even and consistent braking. New brake pads should be fitted also.

1 Firmly chock the front wheels, engage 1st gear (or P), then jack up the rear of the car and support it on axle stands (see Jacking and vehicle support). Remove the appropriate rear roadwheel.
2 Inspect the disc as described in Section 6.

Removal

3 Unscrew the two bolts securing the brake caliper mounting bracket in position, then slide the whole caliper, bracket and pads off the disc. To improve access to the mounting bracket Allen screws, disconnect the lower

end of the shock absorber as described in Chapter 10. If preferred, the caliper and pads can be removed separately before unbolting the mounting bracket. Using a piece of wire or string, tie the caliper to the exhaust hanger/ vehicle body, to avoid placing any strain on the hydraulic brake hose.
4 Use chalk or paint to mark the relationship of the disc to the hub, then remove the disc **(see illustration)**. If it is tight, lightly tap its rear face with a hide or plastic mallet to free it from the hub.

Refitting

5 Refitting is the reverse of the removal procedure, noting the following points:
  a) Ensure that the mating surfaces of the disc and hub are clean and flat.
  b) On refitting, align (if applicable) the marks made on removal.
  c) If a new disc has been fitted, use a suitable solvent to wipe any preservative coating from the disc, before refitting the caliper. Note that new brake pads should always be fitted when the disc is renewed.
  d) Prior to installation, renew the caliper bracket mounting bolts – note that the shorter bolt is fitted to the upper hole in the bracket. Slide the caliper into position, making sure the pads pass either side of the disc, and tighten the caliper bracket bolts to the specified torque setting.
  e) Refit the roadwheel then lower the vehicle to the ground and tighten the wheel bolts to the specified torque. Apply the footbrake several times to force the pads back into contact with the disc before driving the vehicle.

8 Front brake caliper – removal, overhaul and refitting

Note: Before starting work, refer to the note at the beginning of Section 2 concerning the dangers of hydraulic fluid, and to the warning at the beginning of Section 4 concerning the dangers of asbestos dust.

Removal

1 Apply the handbrake, then jack up the front of the vehicle and support it on axle stands (see Jacking and vehicle support). Remove the front roadwheels. Whilst the wheels are removed, refit at least one wheel bolt to the hub to ensure the brake disc remains correctly positioned on the hub.
2 Minimise fluid loss by first removing the master cylinder reservoir cap, and then tightening it down onto a piece of polythene, to obtain an airtight seal. Alternatively, use a brake hose clamp to clamp the flexible hose.
3 Where applicable, disconnect the wiring connector from the brake pad wear sensor connector. Unclip the connector from the caliper bracket.

4 Clean the area around the caliper brake pipe union then unscrew the union nut. Unbolt the mounting bracket from the caliper and position the pipe clear. Plug/cover the pipe end and caliper union to minimise fluid loss and prevent the entry of dirt into the hydraulic system. Wash off any spilt fluid immediately with cold water.
5 Carefully lever the pad retaining spring out position and remove it from the brake caliper using a flat-bladed screwdriver.
6 Remove the end caps from the guide bushes then unscrew and remove the caliper guide pins.
7 Lift the caliper out of position, freeing it from the pad wear sensor wiring (where applicable). Remove the inner and outer brake pads with reference to Section 4, then if required, unbolt and remove the caliper mounting bracket.

Overhaul

Note: At the time of writing, it would appear that caliper overhaul kits are available. However, it would be prudent to check with an Audi dealer or parts specialist prior to commencing work.

8 With the caliper on the bench, wipe away all traces of dust and dirt, but avoid inhaling the dust, as it is injurious to health.
9 Withdraw the partially ejected piston from the caliper body, and remove the dust seal. If the caliper piston is reluctant to move, apply low air pressure (eg, from a foot pump) to the fluid inlet, but note that the piston may be ejected with some force.
10 Using a soft flat-bladed instrument, such as a plastic spatula, extract the piston hydraulic seal, taking great care not to damage the caliper bore.
11 Thoroughly clean all components, using only methylated spirit, isopropyl alcohol or clean brake fluid as a cleaning medium. Never use mineral-based solvents such as petrol or paraffin, as they will attack the hydraulic system's rubber components. Dry the components immediately, using compressed air or a clean, lint-free cloth. Use compressed air to blow clear the fluid passages.
12 Check all components, and renew any that are worn or damaged. Check particularly the cylinder bore and piston; these should be renewed if they are scratched, worn or corroded in any way (note that this means the renewal of the complete body assembly). Similarly check the condition of the guide pins and the bushes in the caliper body; both pins should be undamaged and (when cleaned) a reasonably tight sliding fit in the bushes. If there is any doubt about the condition of any component, renew it.
13 If the caliper is fit for further use, obtain the appropriate repair kit. All rubber seals should be renewed as a matter of course; these should never be re-used.
14 On commencement of reassembly, ensure that all components are clean and dry **(see illustrations)**.

15 The seals must be soaked in the special fluid provided in the overhaul kit for at least 45 minutes – check with the instructions provided in the kit. Smear some of the special fluid on the cylinder bore surface.

16 Fit the new piston (fluid) seal, using only your fingers (no tools) to manipulate it into the cylinder bore groove.

17 Fit the new dust seal to the rear of the piston and seat the outer lip of the seal in the caliper body groove. Carefully ease the piston squarely into the cylinder bore using a twisting motion. Press the piston fully into position and seat the inner lip of the dust seal in the piston groove.

18 If the guide bushes are being renewed, push the old bushes out from the body and press the new ones into position, making sure they are correctly seated.

19 Prior to refitting, fill the caliper with fresh hydraulic fluid by unscrewing the bleed screw and pumping the fluid through the caliper until bubble-free fluid is expelled from the union hole.

Refitting

20 Refit the caliper mounting bracket to the hub carrier using new bolts, and tighten them to the specified torque **(see illustration 6.7a)**. Refit the brake pads with reference to Section 4, then manoeuvre the caliper into position over the brake pads.

21 Fit the caliper guide pins, tightening them to the specified torque setting, and refit the end caps to the guide bushes.

22 Reconnect the brake pipe to the caliper and refit the mounting bracket to the caliper. Tighten the bracket retaining bolt and the brake pipe union nut to their specified torque settings.

23 Refit the pad retaining spring, ensuring its ends are correctly located in the caliper body holes.

24 Ensure the wiring is correctly routed through the loop on the lower cap then clip the pad wear sensor wiring connector onto its bracket on the caliper. Securely reconnect the wiring connector.

25 Remove the brake hose clamp or polythene (where fitted) and bleed the hydraulic system as described in Section 2. Note that, providing the precautions described were taken to minimise brake fluid loss, it should only be necessary to bleed the relevant front brake.

26 Refit the roadwheel, then lower the vehicle to the ground and tighten the roadwheel bolts to the specified torque.

---

9 Rear brake caliper –
removal, overhaul and refitting

Note: *Before starting work, refer to the note at the beginning of Section 2 concerning the dangers of hydraulic fluid, and to the warning at the beginning of Section 5 concerning the dangers of asbestos dust.*

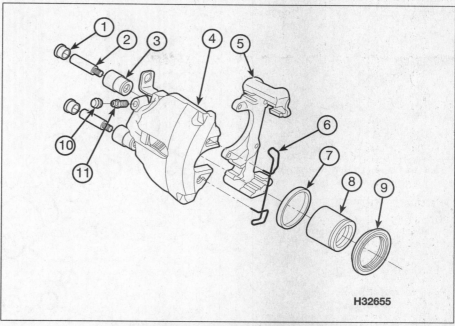

H32655

8.14 Exploded view of the front brake caliper

1 Dust cap	5 Caliper mounting	8 Piston
2 Guide pins	bracket	9 Dust seal
3 Guide sleeves	6 Pad retaining spring	10 Dust cap
4 Caliper	7 Piston seal	11 Bleed screw

Note: *New guide pin bolts must be used on refitting.*

Removal

1 Chock the front wheels, then jack up the rear of the vehicle and support it on axle stands (see *Jacking and vehicle support*). Remove the relevant rear wheel. Whilst the wheel is removed, refit at least one wheel bolt to the hub to ensure the brake disc remains in position.

2 With the handbrake lever fully released, disconnect the handbrake cable from the rear brake caliper by pulling out the outer cable retaining circlip and unhooking the inner cable from the lever on the caliper.

3 Minimise fluid loss by first removing the master cylinder reservoir cap, and then tightening it down onto a piece of polythene,

9.3 Use a brake hose clamp to clamp the flexible hose

to obtain an airtight seal. Alternatively, use a brake hose clamp, a G-clamp or a similar tool to clamp the flexible hose **(see illustration)**.

4 Clean the area around the caliper brake hose then unscrew the union.

5 Unscrew and remove the caliper guide pin bolts, using a slim open-ended spanner to prevent the guide pins from rotating. Discard the guide pin bolts – new bolts must be used on refitting.

6 Lift the brake caliper away from the its mounting bracket and unscrew it from the end of the brake hose. Plug/cover the hose end and caliper union to minimise fluid loss and prevent the entry of dirt into the hydraulic system. Wash off any spilt fluid immediately with cold water. Remove the inner and outer brake pads from the caliper mounting bracket. If required, unbolt and remove the caliper mounting bracket.

Overhaul

Note: *It is not possible to overhaul the brake caliper handbrake mechanism. If the mechanism is faulty, or fluid is leaking from the handbrake lever seal the caliper assembly must be renewed.*

7 With the caliper on the bench, wipe away all traces of dust and dirt, but avoid inhaling the dust, as it is injurious to health.

8 Remove the piston from the caliper bore by rotating it in an anti-clockwise direction **(see illustration)**. This can be achieved using a suitable pair of circlip pliers engaged in the caliper piston slots, or using a piston retraction

9.8 Use a pair of thin-nosed pliers to unscrew the piston

9.9 Use a blunt tool to extract the piston seal

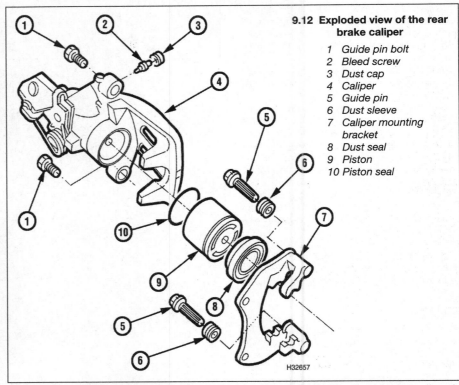

9.12 Exploded view of the rear brake caliper

1 Guide pin bolt
2 Bleed screw
3 Dust cap
4 Caliper
5 Guide pin
6 Dust sleeve
7 Caliper mounting bracket
8 Dust seal
9 Piston
10 Piston seal

H32657

tool. Once the piston turns freely but does not come out any further, the piston is held in only by its seal and can be withdrawn by hand.

9 Remove the dust seal from the piston then, using a blunt flat-bladed instrument, carefully extract the piston hydraulic seal from the caliper bore **(see illustration)**. Take great care not to mark the caliper surface.

10 Withdraw the guide pins from the caliper mounting bracket, and remove the guide sleeve gaiters.

11 Inspect all the caliper components (as described for the front brake caliper in Section 8), and renew as necessary, noting that the handbrake mechanism must **not** be dismantled.

12 On reassembly, ensure all components are clean and dry **(see illustration)**.

13 Soak the new seals in the special fluid provided in the overhaul kit for at least 45 minutes. Smear some of the special fluid on the cylinder bore surface. Fit the new piston (fluid) seal, using only your fingers (not tools) to manipulate it into the cylinder bore groove **(see illustration)**. Follow any instructions provided in the overhaul kit.

14 Fit the new dust seal to the rear of the piston and seat the outer lip of the seal in the caliper body groove. Carefully ease the piston squarely into the cylinder bore using a twisting motion **(see illustrations)**. Turn and push the piston in a clockwise direction, using the method employed on dismantling, until

9.13 Only use fingers to fit the new piston seal

9.14a Fit the new dust seal to the rear of the piston . . .

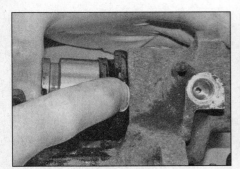

9.14b . . . then seat the outer lip of the seal in the caliper body groove

9.14c Push the piston in and turn it clockwise at the same time . . .

9.14d . . . until it's fully home, then seat the inner lip in the piston groove

it is fully retracted into the caliper bore then seat the inner lip of the dust seal in the piston groove.

15 Apply the grease supplied in the repair kit to the guide pins. Fit the new gaiters to the guide pins and fit the pins to the caliper mounting bracket, ensuring that the gaiters are correctly located in the grooves on both the pins and caliper bracket.

16 Prior to refitting, fill the caliper with fresh hydraulic fluid by unscrewing the bleed screw and pumping the fluid through the caliper until bubble-free fluid is expelled from the union hole.

Refitting

17 Where applicable, refit the caliper mounting bracket to the rear hub carrier using new bolts, and tighten them to the specified torque. Refit the brake pads to the caliper mounting bracket with reference to Section 5.

18 Screw the caliper fully onto the brake hose, then manoeuvre the caliper into position over the pads then fit the new guide pin bolts, tightening them to the specified torque setting.

19 Remove the brake hose clamp or polythene (where used) and securely tighten the brake hose union.

20 Bleed the hydraulic system as described in Section 2. Note that, providing the precautions described were taken to minimise brake fluid loss, it should only be necessary to bleed the relevant rear brake.

21 Reconnect the handbrake cable to the caliper, securing it in position with the retaining clip, and adjust the cable as described in Section 14.

22 Refit the roadwheel, then lower the vehicle to the ground and tighten the roadwheel bolts to the specified torque.

10 Master cylinder –
removal, overhaul and refitting

1 The master cylinder must be removed along with the servo unit – see Section 12.

11 Brake pedal –
removal and refitting

Removal

1 Remove the driver's side storage compartment as described in Chapter 11.

2 Release the stop-light switch from its mounting bracket and position it to one side. Also, where fitted, remove the brake pedal/ cruise control switches.

3 On right-hand drive models, unscrew the brake pedal pivot bolt, and push the pedal to the right and remove it (**see illustration**). Note that the pivot bolt is locked with locking fluid.

4 On left-hand drive models, pull off the securing clip from the right-hand end of the

11.3 Brake pedal pivot bolt

pedal pivot pin, unscrew the pivot pin securing bolt, and slide the pivot pin to the left.

5 On right-hand drive models, the brake pedal pivot pin is connected to a remote operating lever to the left of the clutch pedal, which then acts upon the brake servo pushrod. On left-hand drive models the brake pedal acts directly upon the servo pushrod. On both models it is necessary to separate the servo pushrod from the pedal/remote lever. The end of the pushrod is shaped as a ball, and engages with a retaining clip in the back of the lever/pedal. To release the clip a special Audi tool is available, but a suitable alternative can be improvised as shown. Note that the plastic lugs are very stiff, and it will not be possible to release them by hand. Using the tool, release the securing lugs and pull the pedal/lever from the servo pushrod (**see illustrations**).

6 Examine all components for signs of wear or damage, renewing them as necessary.

Refitting

7 Apply a smear of multi-purpose grease to the pedal pivot bore and the pushrod ball.

8 The remainder of the refitting procedure is a reversal of the removal procedure, noting the following points:

a) Apply locking fluid to the threads of the brake pedal pivot bolt before tightening it to the specified torque.

b) Tighten all fixings to the correct torque, where specified.

c) Refit and adjust the stop-light and pedal switch as described in Section 17.

d) Refit the cruise control system vacuum valves.

12.5 Disconnect the fluid level sensor wiring plug

11.5a The end of the servo pushrod is shaped as a ball, and engages in the back of the lever

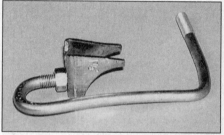

11.5b Improvised special tool constructed from a modified exhaust clamp, used to release the brake lever from the servo pushrod

12 Vacuum servo unit –
testing, removal and refitting

Testing

1 To test the operation of the servo unit, depress the footbrake several times to exhaust the vacuum, then start the engine whilst keeping the pedal firmly depressed. As the engine starts, there should be a noticeable give in the brake pedal as the vacuum builds-up. Allow the engine to run for at least two minutes, then switch it off. If the brake pedal is now depressed it should feel normal, but further applications should result in the pedal feeling firmer, with the pedal stroke decreasing with each application.

2 If the servo does not operate as described, first inspect the servo unit check valve as described in Section 13. On diesel engine models, also check the vacuum pump as described in Section 20.

3 If the servo unit still fails to operate satisfactorily, the fault may lie within the unit itself. Repairs to the unit are not possible – if faulty, the servo unit must be renewed.

Removal

Note: The servo can only be removed along with the master cylinder.

4 Disconnect the clutch master cylinder feed hose from the side of the brake master cylinder reservoir. Tape over or plug the outlet.

5 Disconnect the wiring plug from the brake fluid level sender unit (**see illustration**).

12.6 Unscrew the reservoir retaining bolt (arrowed)

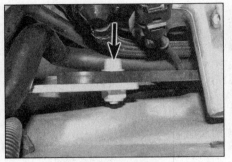

12.8a The cross-piece is secured by bolts at each end (arrowed) . . .

12.8b . . . and one in the middle (arrowed)

6 Unscrew the Torx bolt which secures the reservoir, and pull the reservoir from the top of the master cylinder **(see illustration)**. The reservoir will be quite tight in the rubber seals.

7 Wipe clean the area around the brake pipe unions on the side of the master cylinder, and make a note of the correct fitted positions of the unions, then unscrew the union nuts and carefully withdraw the pipes. Plug or tape over the pipe ends and master cylinder apertures, to minimise the loss of brake fluid, and to prevent the entry of dirt into the system. Wash off any spilt fluid immediately with cold water.

8 Unclip the wiring loom then undo the bolts and remove the cross-piece from in front of the master cylinder (where fitted) **(see illustrations)**.

9 The master cylinder is secured to the vacuum servo by two large hexagon nuts, and the vacuum servo is secured to the bulkhead by two long through-bolts. Unscrew the nuts **(see illustration)**.

10 Carefully ease the vacuum hose connection out from the servo unit, taking care not to damage the grommet.

11 Undo the retaining screws and remove the storage compartment panel from the driver's side of the facia (see Chapter 11).

12 Release the stop-light switch from its mounting bracket and position it to one side (see Section 17). Also, where fitted, remove the cruise control switch.

13 Working underneath the facia, locate the servo unit pushrod and note how it is connected to the brake pedal. On right-

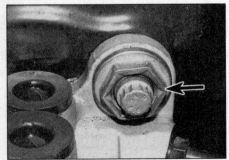

12.9 Undo the nuts (arrowed) securing the master cylinder to the servo

hand drive models, the pushrod connects to a remote operating lever, which is located to the left of the clutch pedal. On left-hand drive models it is connected directly to the rear of the brake pedal. In both installations, the pushrod is equipped with a balljoint. To disconnect the pushrod from the remote operating lever/pedal, depress the locking tabs of the balljoint retaining clip and raise the brake pedal, until the pushrod balljoint can be felt to disengage (refer to Section 11).

14 Undo the long through-bolts and manoeuvre the servo unit and master cylinder out of position. Recover the gasket which is fitted between the servo and bulkhead. Examine the gasket for signs of wear or damage and renew if necessary. Recover the sealing ring fitted to the rear of the master cylinder and discard it; a new one must be used on refitting.

Overhaul

15 If the master cylinder is faulty, it must be renewed. Repair kits are not available from Audi dealers, so the cylinder must be treated as a sealed unit.

16 The only items which can be renewed are the mounting seals for the fluid reservoir; if these show signs of deterioration, carefully lever out the old seals with the aid of a screwdriver. Lubricate the new seals with clean brake fluid, and ease them into the master cylinder ports. When fitting the rear seal, take care to ensure that the seal engages correctly with the pushrod circuit filling tube and ensure that the seal projects from the rear of its housing by approximately 1 mm. Once both seals are correctly fitted, ease the fluid reservoir into position and push it fully home.

Refitting

17 Ensure the servo unit and bulkhead mating surfaces are clean, fit the gasket to the rear of the servo unit, and then sealing ring between the master cylinder and servo. Position the master cylinder on the servo and manoeuvre the assembly into position.

18 From inside the vehicle, make sure the pushrod is correctly engaged with the rear of the pedal, or the remote operating lever (as applicable) then press the pushrod

firmly into position until the balljoint can be felt to engage. Lift the brake pedal by hand to check that the pushrod is securely reconnected.

19 Refit the through-bolts and tighten them to the specified torque.

20 Fit the new master cylinder mounting nuts and tighten them to the specified torque.

21 Wipe clean the brake pipe unions, then refit them to the master cylinder ports and tighten them to the specified torque.

22 Refit the fluid reservoir making sure that the outlets are fully entered in the rubber seals, then refit and tighten the retaining bolt.

23 Reconnect the clutch master cylinder hose to the fluid reservoir and securely tighten the retaining clip.

24 Reconnect the fluid level sender unit wiring connector.

25 Refit the cross-piece and tighten the bolts to the specified torque.

26 Clip the wiring loom into position and refit the sealing strip to the upper edge of the bulkhead.

27 Refill the master cylinder reservoir with new fluid, and bleed the brake and (if necessary) the clutch hydraulic systems, as described in Section 2 and Chapter 6 respectively.

28 Refit the stop-light as described in Section 17.

29 Refit the storage compartment panel to the underside of the facia.

30 Ease the vacuum hose end fitting into position in the servo unit, taking care not to displace the rubber grommet.

13 Vacuum servo unit check valve – removal, testing and refitting

Note: *The valve is an integral part of the servo unit vacuum hose and is not available separately.*

Removal

1 Carefully ease the vacuum hose connection out from the servo unit, taking care not to damage the grommet **(see illustration)**.

2 Work back along the hose, freeing it from all the relevant retaining clips whilst noting its correct routing.

3 Slacken the retaining clip then disconnect the vacuum hose from the manifold and/or vacuum pump (as applicable) and remove it from the vehicle.

Testing

4 Examine the vacuum hose for signs of damage, and renew if necessary. The valve may be tested by blowing through it in both directions. Air should flow through the valve in one direction only – when blown through from the servo unit end of the valve. Renew the valve if this is not the case.
5 Examine the servo unit rubber sealing grommet and hose(s) linking the main hose to the manifold/pump (as applicable) for signs of damage or deterioration, and renew as necessary.

Refitting

6 Ensure the sealing grommet is in position in the servo unit then carefully ease the vacuum hose end fitting into position, taking care not to displace or damage the grommet.
7 Ensure the hose is correctly routed then connect it to the pump/manifold and securely tighten the retaining clip.
8 On completion, start the engine and check the check valve-to-servo unit connection for signs of air leaks.

14 Handbrake – adjustment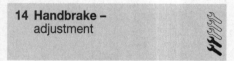

Note: *Handbrake adjustment is normally only required after renewing the cables, brake calipers or brake discs.*
1 Depress the brake pedal firmly, to settle the rear brake self-adjustment mechanism.
2 Chock the front wheels, then jack up the rear of the vehicle and support it on axle stands (see *Jacking and vehicle support*). Fully release the handbrake lever.
3 Remove the rear section of the centre console as described in Chapter 11.
4 Working underneath the vehicle, insert feeler gauges to set the gap between the operating arm and stop lever to 1.5 mm **(see illustration)**. Depress the brake pedal at least three times.

15.3 Disengage the cables from the hooks

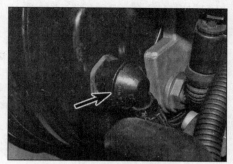
13.1 Pull the valve from the servo (arrowed)

5 Use a screwdriver to press the release button on the equaliser mechanism at the base of the handbrake lever **(see illustration)**.
6 Release the button, and firmly apply the handbrake at lease three times.
7 Place the hand brake lever in the 'at rest' position, then depress the release button – the spring-loaded hooks of the equalise mechanism must catch the cable eyelets.
8 Release the button, and remove the feeler gauge(s) from the caliper.
9 Check the gap between the caliper lever and the stop is between 0 and 1.5 mm.
10 Check the operation of the handbrake and repeat the adjustment procedure as necessary.
11 Once the handbrake is correctly adjusted (both brakes securely lock the wheels with the lever applied and spin freely when the lever is released), lower the vehicle to the ground.

14.4 Position a feeler gauge 1.5 mm thick between the caliper lever and the stop

15.4 Undo the two nuts (arrowed) and remove the lever

15 Handbrake lever – removal and refitting

Removal

1 Remove the centre console as described in Chapter 11.
2 Insert a screwdriver into the release opening in the equaliser mechanism at the base of the lever, and push the screwdriver forwards to release the mechanism **(see illustration 14.5)**.
3 Slowly operate the lever, making sure the cable eyelets remain on the hooks, then remove the screwdriver and unhook the cable eyelets **(see illustration)**.
4 Unscrew the two nuts that secure the handbrake lever to the floorpan **(see illustration)**.
5 Disconnect the handbrake warning light switch, then free the handbrake lever from its mountings and remove it from the vehicle.

Refitting

6 Prior to refitting the lever assembly, reset the equaliser mechanism by gripping one of the cable hooks in a vice, depressing the release button with a screwdriver, and pressing back the other hook **(see illustration)**.
7 The remainder of refitting is a reversal of removal, but adjust the handbrake, as described in Section 14, before the rear section of the centre console is refitted.

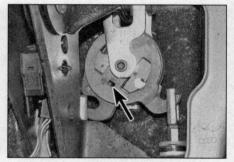
14.5 Use a small screwdriver to depress the release button (arrowed)

15.6 With one of the hooks held in a vice, depress the release button and push the other hook back

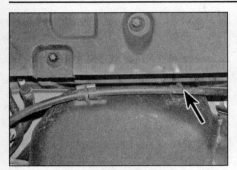

16.3a Release the handbrake cables from any clips (arrowed) . . .

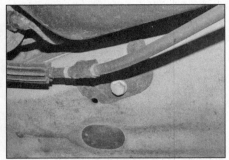

16.3b . . . on the vehicle underside

16 Handbrake cables – removal and refitting

Removal

1 The handbrake cable consists of two sections, a right- and a left-hand section, which are linked to the lever by an equaliser mechanism. Each section can be removed individually as follows. Chock the front wheels, then jack up the rear of the vehicle, support it on axle stands (see *Jacking and vehicle support*), and remove the rear wheels. Fully release the handbrake lever.
2 Remove the centre console as described in Chapter 11.
3 Release the fasteners, remove the left- and right-hand underbody panels, and unclip the handbrake cables **(see illustrations)**.

16.5a Slide off the outer cable clip . . .

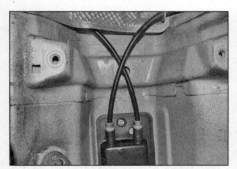

16.10 The left-hand handbrake cable is routed over the right-hand cable

4 Detach the rear section of the exhaust system, and release it from its mountings as described in Chapter 4D.
5 Pull the retaining clips, and detach the cables from the caliper brackets and levers **(see illustrations)**.
6 Work back along the length of each handbrake cable, noting its correct routing, and free it from all the relevant retaining clips and fixings, including those on the rear suspension beam. Note the location of the ABS sensor wiring on the clips.
7 Remove and reset the handbrake lever as described in Section 15.
8 Where necessary, remove the exhaust heat shield to gain access to the front of the cables.
9 Note the cables' routing, and manoeuvre them from under the vehicle.

Refitting

10 Refitting is a reversal of the removal

16.5b . . . and disengage the inner cable end from the lever

17.3 Depress the tabs (arrowed) and disconnect the stop-light wiring plug

procedure, ensuring that the cable is correctly routed and retained by all the necessary clips and ties. In particular, make sure that the cable grommets seat correctly in the underside of the handbrake lever housing, and note that the left-hand wheel cable is routed over the right-hand cable **(see illustration)**. On completion, adjust the operation of the handbrake as described in Section 14.

17 Stop-light and brake pedal switches – removal, refitting and adjustment

Note: *Audi recommend that the switch is renewed every time it is removed, to ensure secure fitment.*

Removal

1 The stop-light and brake pedal switches are located on the pedal bracket behind the facia.
2 Undo the retaining screws and remove the storage compartment panel/trim panel from the underside of the facia on the driver's side (see Chapter 11).
3 Disconnect the wiring connector from the switch body **(see illustration)**.
4 Turn the switch 45° anti-clockwise and remove it.

Refitting and adjustment

5 Pull the plunger fully out of the switch, then, with the brake pedal released, guide the plunger through the hole against the pedal, and secure by turning it 45° clockwise.
6 Reconnect the wiring connector, and check the operation of the stop-lights.
7 Refit the storage compartment panel/trim panel to the facia.

18 Anti-lock braking system (ABS) – general information

1 ABS is fitted as standard to all models in the range. The system consists of a hydraulic unit, an electronic control unit (ECU) and four roadwheel sensors. The hydraulic unit contains the eight hydraulic solenoid valves (two for each brake – one inlet and one outlet) and the electrically-driven return pump. The purpose of the system is to prevent the roadwheels locking during heavy braking. This is achieved by automatic release of the brake on the relevant wheel, followed by re-application of the brake. In the case of the rear wheels, both rear brakes are released and applied at the same time.
2 The solenoid valves are controlled by the ECU, which itself receives signals from the four wheel sensors (front sensors are fitted to the hubs and the rear sensors are fitted to the rear axle), which monitor the speed of rotation of each wheel. By comparing these signals, the ECU can determine the speed at which the vehicle is travelling. It

can then use this speed to determine when a wheel is decelerating at an abnormal rate, compared to the speed of the vehicle, and therefore predicts when a wheel is about to lock. During normal operation, the system functions in the same way as a non-ABS braking system.

3 If the ECU senses that a wheel is about to lock, it closes the relevant outlet solenoid valves in the hydraulic unit, which then isolates the relevant brake on the wheel which is about to lock from the master cylinder, effectively sealing-in the hydraulic pressure.

4 If the speed of rotation of the wheel continues to decrease at an abnormal rate, the ECU opens the inlet solenoid valves on the relevant brake and operates the electrically-driven return pump which pumps the hydraulic fluid back into the master cylinder, releasing the brake. Once the speed of rotation of the wheel returns to an acceptable rate, the pump stops; the solenoid valves switch again, allowing the hydraulic master cylinder pressure to return to the caliper, which then re-applies the brake. This cycle can be carried out many times a second.

5 The action of the solenoid valves and return pump creates pulses in the hydraulic circuit. When the ABS system is functioning, these pulses can be felt through the brake pedal.

6 The operation of the ABS system is entirely dependent on electrical signals. To prevent the system responding to any inaccurate signals, a built-in safety circuit monitors all signals received by the ECU. If an inaccurate signal or low battery voltage is detected, the ABS system is automatically shut down, and the warning light on the instrument panel is illuminated, to inform the driver that the ABS system is not operational. Normal braking should still be available, however.

7 On all models, the ABS system also includes Electronic Differential Lock (EDL) and traction control/Anti-Slip Regulation (ASR) functions. If under acceleration the ECU senses that a wheel is spinning, it uses the hydraulic unit to gradually apply the brake on that wheel until traction is regained. Once the wheel regains traction, the brake is released.

8 The ESP (Electronic Stability Program) function is a further expansion of the ABS system which takes into consideration the angle of the steering wheel, using a steering angle sender and Yaw Rate Sender. Additionally, the system monitors lateral acceleration with a Lateral Acceleration Sender.

9 Models covered in this Manual are fitted with Bosch type 5.7 or 8.0 ABS where the ECU and hydraulic unit are combined into one unit.

10 If a fault does develop in the ABS system, the vehicle must be taken to an Audi dealer or suitably-equipped specialist for fault diagnosis and repair.

19 Anti-lock braking system (ABS) components – removal and refitting

Hydraulic unit

Note: *Audi state that the operation of the hydraulic unit should be checked using special test equipment after refitting. Bearing this in mind, it is recommended that removal and refitting of the unit is entrusted to an Audi dealer or specialist. If you decide to remove/ refit the unit yourself, ensure that the operation of the braking system is checked at the earliest opportunity by an Audi dealer or specialist.*

Removal

1 Disconnect the battery negative terminal (see Chapter 5A). Where necessary, remove the engine plastic cover.

2 Release the locking bar and disconnect the main wiring connector from the hydraulic unit.

3 Raise the front of the vehicle and rest it securely on axle stands (see *Jacking and vehicle support*), then remove the left-hand front roadwheel.

4 Connect a length of hose to the left-hand front brake caliper bleed screw, then direct the other end of the hose into a suitable receptacle, as described in Section 2. Open the bleed screw and then depress the brake pedal through one full stroke and hold it in this position, using a suitable weight, or a wedge such as a block of wood. When the expelled brake fluid has collected into the receptacle, close the bleed screw. **Note:** *The brake pedal must be held in the depressed position until the brake pipes have been reconnected to the hydraulic unit, at the end of this procedure.*

5 Wipe clean the area around all the pipes unions and mark the locations of the hydraulic fluid pipes to ensure correct refitting. Unscrew the union nuts and disconnect the pipes from the regulator assembly. Be prepared for fluid spillage, and plug the open ends of the pipes and the hydraulic unit unions to prevent dirt ingress and further fluid loss.

6 Unscrew the hydraulic unit mounting bracket bolts and remove the assembly from the engine compartment. If necessary, the mounting bracket can then be unbolted and removed from the vehicle. Renew the regulator mountings if they show signs of wear or damage. **Note:** *Keep the hydraulic unit upright to minimise the risk of fluid loss, and to prevent air locks inside the unit.*

Refitting

Note: *New hydraulic units are supplied pre-filled with brake fluid and fully bled; it is vitally important that the union plugs are not removed until the brake pipes are reconnected as loss of fluid will introduce air into the unit.*

7 Manoeuvre the hydraulic unit into position in the mounting bracket and tighten the mounting bolts to the specified torque setting.

8 Remove the plugs and reconnect the hydraulic pipes to the correct unions on the

19.13 Prise out the grommet from the wheel arch, and disconnect the sensor wiring plug

hydraulic unit and tighten the union nuts to the specified torque.

9 Securely reconnect the wiring connector to the hydraulic unit.

10 Fill the brake fluid reservoir with fresh fluid (see *Weekly checks*) and reconnect the battery.

11 Remove the weight/wedge from the brake pedal and then bleed the entire braking hydraulic system as described in Section 2. Thoroughly check the operation of the braking system before using the vehicle on the road. Have the operation of the ABS system checked by an Audi dealer or specialist at the earliest possible opportunity.

Front wheel sensor

Removal

12 Apply the handbrake, then jack up the front of the vehicle and support securely on axle stands (see *Jacking and vehicle support*). To improve access, remove the roadwheel.

13 Trace the wiring back from the sensor, releasing it from all the relevant clips and ties whilst noting its correct routing, and disconnect the wiring connector **(see illustration)**.

14 Undo the retaining screw, then carefully pull the sensor out from the hub carrier assembly and remove it from the vehicle **(see illustration)**.

Refitting

15 Ensure that the mating faces of the sensor, clamping ring and hub carrier are clean and dry then lubricate clamping sleeve and wheel sensor surfaces with a small quantity of copper-based grease.

19.14 Undo the Allen screw and pull out the sensor

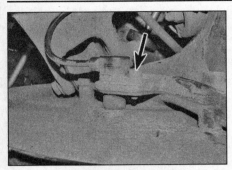

19.22 Rear wheel sensor retaining bolt (arrowed)

16 Ensure the sensor wiring is correctly positioned then push the sensor firmly into position until it is fully home in the hub carrier, and tighten the retaining screw to the specified torque.

17 Ensure the sensor is securely retained then work along the sensor wiring, making sure it is correctly routed, securing it in position with all the relevant clips and ties. Reconnect the wiring connector.

18 Refit the wheel then lower the vehicle and tighten the wheel bolts to the specified torque.

Rear wheel sensor

Removal

19 Remove the rear seat cushion and side trim (see Chapter 11), and locate the rear wheel sensor ABS wiring connectors. Unplug the relevant connector and free the wiring from its retaining clips.

20 Chock the front wheels, then jack up the rear of the vehicle and support it on axle stands (see *Jacking and vehicle support*). To improve access, remove the appropriate roadwheel.

21 Working underneath the vehicle, trace the wiring back from the sensor, releasing it from all the relevant clips. Undo the retaining bolts and remove the wiring protective cover from the rear axle (where fitted) then release the wiring grommet from body and pull the wiring through so that it is free to be removed with the sensor.

22 Note the fitted position of the speed sensor, then undo the retaining bolt and

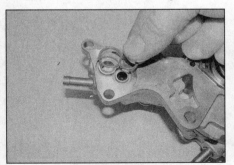

carefully prise the sensor from the axle assembly **(see illustration)**.

Refitting

23 Ensure that the mating faces of the sensor and axle are clean and dry, then lubricate the wheel sensor surfaces with a little copper-based grease.

24 Ensure the sensor wiring is correctly positioned then push the sensor firmly into position until it is fully home in the axle, and tighten the retaining bolt to the specified torque.

25 Work along the sensor wiring, making sure it is correctly routed, securing it in position with all the relevant clips and ties. Refit the wiring protective cover to the axle (where fitted), tighten its retaining screws securely, then feed the wiring connector up through the body and seat the wiring grommet correctly in position.

26 Refit the roadwheel then lower the vehicle to the ground and tighten the wheel bolts to the specified torque.

27 Reconnect the sensor wiring connect then refit the seat cushion and trim panel.

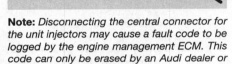

20 Vacuum pump (diesel engine models) – removal and refitting

Note: *Disconnecting the central connector for the unit injectors may cause a fault code to be logged by the engine management ECM. This code can only be erased by an Audi dealer or suitably-equipped specialist.*

Removal

1 Prise out the cover caps, unscrew the retaining nuts/bolts and remove the engine top cover.

2 Disconnect the charge air pipe at the back of the cylinder head, and place it to one side. Rotate the collar anti-clockwise and disconnect the central connector for the unit injectors.

3 Release the retaining clip (where fitted) and disconnect the brake servo pipe from the tandem pump.

4 Disconnect the fuel supply hose (marked white) from the tandem pump. Be prepared for fuel spillage.

20.6a Fit new rubber seals . . .

20.6b . . . and ensure the pump drive aligns with the slot in the camshaft

5 Unscrew the four retaining bolts and move the tandem pump away from the cylinder head. As the pump is lifted up, disconnect the fuel return hose (marked blue). Be prepared for fuel spillage. There are no serviceable parts within the tandem pump. If the pump is faulty, it must be renewed.

Refitting

6 Reconnect the fuel return hose to the pump and refit the pump to the cylinder head, using new rubber seals, and ensuring that the pump pinion engages correctly with the drive slot in the camshaft **(see illustrations)**.

7 Refit the pump retaining bolts, and tighten them to the specified torque.

8 Re-attach the fuel supply hose and brake servo hose to the pump.

9 Reconnect the central connector for the unit injectors.

10 Refit the charge air pipe.

11 Disconnect the fuel filter return hose (marked blue), and connect the hose to a hand vacuum pump. Operate the vacuum pump until fuel comes out of the return hose. This primes the tandem pump. Take care not to suck any fuel into the vacuum pump. Reconnect the return hose to the fuel filter.

12 Refit the engine top cover.

13 Where necessary, have the engine management ECU's fault memory interrogated and erased by an Audi dealer or suitably-equipped specialist.

21 ESP system components – removal and refitting

1 The ESP system consists of the ABS, TCS and EDL system. The ESP, TCS and EDL systems rely on the ABS system components for measuring and reducing wheel speed. In addition to the wheel speed sensors and brake pressure sensors, the ESP receives information concerning the steering wheel angle, lateral acceleration and vehicle rotational speed (yaw rate). Testing of the various system components should be entrusted to an Audi dealer or specialist.

Lateral acceleration sensor/ yaw rate sensor

⚠️ *Warning: Handle the sensor with great care. Severe shakes/jolts can destroy the sensors.*

2 The lateral acceleration sensor and the yaw rate sensor are integrated in one housing, located under the front section of the centre console. Remove the centre console as described in Chapter 11.

3 Disconnect the wiring plug, unscrew the two retaining nuts and remove the housing **(see illustration)**. No further dismantling is possible.

4 Refitting is a reversal of removal. Ensure the housing is correctly seated tightening the retaining nuts to the specified torque.

Brake pressure sensor

5 The brake pressure sensor is fitted to the ABS hydraulic control unit. To remove the sensor, undo the bolt and move the coolant expansion tank to one side. There is no need to disconnect the hose(s).

6 Disconnect the wiring plus, then unscrew the sensor.

7 Refitting is a reversal of removal, but bleed the system as described in Section 2.

Steering angle sensor

8 The steering angle sensor is incorporated into the airbag contact unit between the steering wheel and column switch **(see illustration)**. To remove the sensor, refer to Chapter 12, and remove the contact unit. Note that if the contact unit has been renewed, specialist equipment is required to perform a 'zero comparison'. This must be entrusted to an Audi dealer or specialist.

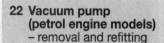

22 Vacuum pump (petrol engine models) – removal and refitting

Removal

1 The vacuum pump is located on the rear

21.3 Undo the two nuts and remove the lateral acceleration/yaw rate sensor

of the cylinder head, and driven by the intake camshaft.

2 Remove the plastic cover from the top of the engine (where fitted).

3 Release the clip and disconnect the vacuum pipe from the pump.

4 Undo the 3 Torx bolts and remove the pump. Note the dual earth leads attached to the top mounting bolt **(see illustration)**. Note that no parts are available for the pump. If faulty, it must be renewed.

Refitting

5 Refitting is a reversal of removal, using a new O-ring seal **(see illustrations)**.

21.8 Steering angle sensor retaining screws (arrowed)

23 Vacuum sensor – renewal

1 One some models, a vacuum sensor is fitted into the pipe connected to the brake servo unit. Remove the plenum chamber cover.

2 Disconnect the sensor wiring plug.

3 Undo the retaining screws/release the clips, and detach the sensor from the pipe.

4 Refitting is a reversal of removal, ensuring the sensor is an air-tight fit on the vacuum hose.

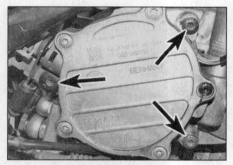

22.4 Pump mounting bolts (arrowed). Note the earth leads on the top pump mounting bolt

22.5a Fit a new O-ring seal to the pump

22.5b Align the pump drive with the slot in the end of the camshaft

Chapter 10
Suspension and steering

Contents

Section number

Front hub bearings and hub carrier – renewal 2
Front suspension anti-roll bar – removal and refitting 6
Front suspension strut – overhaul 4
Front suspension strut – removal and refitting 3
Front suspension subframe – removal and refitting 7
Front suspension transverse arms – removal, overhaul and refitting 5
General information 1
Ignition switch/steering column lock – removal and refitting 18
Power steering pump – removal and refitting 22
Power steering pump drivebelt check, adjustment and
    renewal . . . . See Chapter 1A or 1B
Power steering system – level checking and bleeding 21
Rear anti-roll bar – removal and refitting 15
Rear hub and bearings – renewal 8
Rear hub carrier – removal and refitting 9
Rear subframe – removal and refitting 13

Section number

Rear suspension link arms – removal, overhaul and refitting 14
Rear suspension spring – removal and refitting 12
Rear suspension strut – overhaul 11
Rear suspension strut and spring – removal and refitting 10
Steering column – removal, inspection and refitting 17
Steering gear – adjustment 25
Steering gear assembly – removal, overhaul and refitting 19
Steering gear rubber bellows – renewal 20
Steering wheel – removal and refitting 16
Suspension and steering check . . . . See Chapter 1A or 1B
Track rod – removal and refitting 24
Track rod balljoint – removal and refitting 23
Wheel alignment and steering angles – general information 26
Wheel and tyre maintenance and tyre pressure
    checks . . . . See Weekly checks

Degrees of difficulty

Easy, suitable for novice with little experience	**Fairly easy,** suitable for beginner with some experience	**Fairly difficult,** suitable for competent DIY mechanic	**Difficult,** suitable for experienced DIY mechanic	**Very difficult,** suitable for expert DIY or professional

Specifications

Roadwheels

Type . . . .   Pressed-steel or aluminium alloy (depending on model)
Size:
  Normal roadwheels . . . .   6J x 15, 7J x 15 or 7J x 16 (depending on model)
  Spare wheel (space saver type) . . . .   4B x 15
Tyre pressures . . . .   Refer to the sticker attached to the base of the pillar in the driver's door aperture

Wheel alignment and steering angles

Front wheel alignment:
  Toe setting (per wheel) . . . .   +10' ± 2'
  Camber:
    Standard setting*:
      Standard suspension (code 1BA) . . . .   -30' ± 25'
      Sports suspension (code 1BE) . . . .   -47' ± 25'
      Heavy duty suspension (code 1BR) . . . .   -21' ± 25'
    Maximum difference between sides . . . .   ± 30'
Rear wheel alignment:
  Toe setting*:
    Standard suspension (code 1BA) . . . .   +20' +10' -5'
    Sports suspension (code 1BE) . . . .   +20' +10' -5'
    Heavy duty suspension (code 1BR) . . . .   +20' +10' -5'
  Camber:
    Standard setting . . . .   -1° 20' ± 30'
    Maximum difference between sides . . . .   30'
* The suspension type code is stamped on the vehicle identification (VIN) plate.

Torque wrench settings	Nm	lbf ft
Front suspension		
Anti-roll bar:		
Drop link:		
Lower joint-to-anti-roll bar bolt*:		
Stage 1	40	30
Stage 2	Angle-tighten a further 90°	
Upper joint-to-suspension arm bolt*:		
Stage 1	40	30
Stage 2	Angle-tighten a further 90°	
Mounting clamp nuts*	25	18
Diagonal strut bolts (Cabriolet models)	65	48
Hub bearing housing-to-hub carrier:		
Stage 1	80	59
Stage 2	Angle-tighten a further 90°	
Hub bolt*:		
M14 bolt:		
Stage 1	115	85
Stage 2	Angle-tighten a further 180°	
M16 bolt:		
Stage 1	200	148
Stage 2	Angle-tighten a further 180°	
Lower suspension arms:		
Front lower arm-to-hub carrier balljoint nut*	110	81
Front lower arm-to-subframe bolt/nut*:		
Stage 1	70	52
Stage 2	Angle-tighten a further 180°	
Rear lower arm-to-hub carrier balljoint nut*	110	81
Rear lower arm-to-subframe bolt/nut*:		
Stage 1	70	52
Stage 2	Angle-tighten a further 180°	
Subframe:		
Front mounting bracket bolts*	75	55
Main mounting bolts*:		
Stage 1	110	81
Stage 2	Angle-tighten a further 90°	
Rear mounting bracket bolts*	55	41
Suspension strut:		
Lower mounting nut to suspension arm*	90	66
Piston rod nut*	50	37
Upper mounting bolt	75	55
Upper suspension arms:		
Front upper arm-to-bracket nut*:		
Stage 1	50	37
Stage 2	Angle-tighten a further 90°	
Hub carrier-to-upper arm clamp bolt/nut*	40	30
Rear upper arm-to-bracket nut*:		
Stage 1	50	37
Stage 2	Angle-tighten a further 90°	
Rear suspension		
Anti-roll bar:		
Clamp bolts	25	18
Drop link:		
Upper bolt	45	33
Lower bolts	25	18
Hub carrier bolts:		
Lower mounting bolts/nuts*:		
Stage 1	85	63
Stage 2	Angle-tighten a further 90°	
Upper mounting nut*	95	70
Rear hub flange bolt*:		
Stage 1	200	148
Stage 2	Angle-tighten a further 180°	

Torque wrench settings (continued)

	Nm	lbf ft
Rear suspension (continued)		
Suspension strut:		
Lower mounting bolt/nut*:		
Stage 1	150	111
Stage 2	Angle-tighten a further 90°	
Shock absorber piston nut*	25	18
Upper mounting bolts.	36	27
Subframe mounting bolts*:		
Stage 1	110	81
Stage 2	Angle-tighten a further 90°	
Track rod mounting bolts*:		
Stage 1	85	63
Stage 2	Angle-tighten a further 90°	
Transverse link arm:		
Outer mounting bolt/nut*	95	70
Inner mounting bolt*:		
Stage 1	85	63
Stage 2	Angle-tighten a further 90°	
Trapezium link:		
Front inner mounting nut*	95	70
Rear inner mounting bolt/nut*:		
Stage 1	85	63
Stage 2	Angle-tighten a further 90°	
Stone guard bolts.	25	18
Steering		
Power steering pump hose banjo bolt	50	37
Power steering pump mounting bolts	20	15
Steering column:		
Mounting bolts	23	17
Universal joint pinch-bolt	30	22
Steering gear:		
Hydraulic pipe union bolts:		
Supply pipe.	40	30
Return pipe union	40	30
Return pipe banjo bolt	47	35
Expansion hose banjo bolt	35	26
Centring hole plug	22	16
Mounting bolts*:		
Stage 1	40	30
Stage 2	Angle-tighten a further 90°	
Steering wheel retaining bolt*	50	37
Track rod:		
Adjustment locknut.	40	30
Balljoint-to-hub carrier pinch-bolt/nut*	45	33
Toe curve adjustment/retaining bolt	7	5
Track rod to steering gear.	100	74
Roadwheels		
Wheel bolts.	120	89

* Use new fasteners.

1 General information

1 The front suspension is fully independent, utilising four transverse arms (two upper and two lower) and a solid upright (or hub carrier) in an unequal-length, double-wishbone configuration. Coil spring-over-telescopic shock absorber struts are connected between the front lower transverse arm and upper transverse arm mounting bracket. The hub carriers house the wheel bearings, brake calipers and the hub/disc assemblies, and are connected to the upper and lower transverse arms by means of balljoints. A front anti-roll bar is fitted to all models; the anti-roll bar is rubber-mounted onto the subframe, and is connected to the front lower transverse arms by a drop link. The subframe provides mountings for all the lower suspension components as well as the engine and transmission mountings.

2 The rear suspension is fully independent, with a lower trapezium link, an upper transverse link arm, and a lower track control rod, which are connected to the body by rubber bushes. A telescopic shock absorber and separate coil spring is fitted between the hub carrier and rear subframe each side. A rear anti-roll bar is incorporated into the rear axle design to reduce body roll.

3 The suspension type code is stamped on the vehicle identification (VIN) plate and on the identification label in the spare wheel well, or luggage compartment floor.

4 The steering column has a flexible coupling at its lower end and is secured to the steering gear pinion by means of a clamp bolt.

5 The steering gear is mounted onto the vehicle body and is connected by two track rods, with balljoints at their outer ends, to bosses projecting rearwards from the suspension hub carriers. The track rod ends

2.7 Undo the nut and pull the clamp bolt (arrowed) from the top of the hub carrier

are threaded, to facilitate adjustment. The hydraulic steering system is powered by a belt-driven pump, which is driven off the crankshaft pulley.

2 Front hub bearings and hub carrier – renewal

Note: *The bearing is a sealed, pre-adjusted and pre-lubricated, double-row roller type, and is intended to last the car's entire service life without maintenance or attention. Never overtighten the hub bolt in an attempt to adjust the bearing.*

Note: *A hydraulic press will be required to dismantle and rebuild the assembly; if such a tool is not available, a large bench vice and spacers (such as large sockets) may serve as an adequate substitute. The bearing's inner races are an interference fit on the hub; if the inner race remains on the hub when it is pressed out of the hub carrier, a knife-edged bearing puller may be required to remove it.*

Front hub bearings

1 Park the vehicle on a level surface, switch off the ignition, apply the handbrake firmly.
2 Remove the wheel trim/hub centre cap and then slacken the driveshaft bolt by a few turns, with reference to Chapter 8. If necessary, have an assistant depress the brake pedal at the same time.
3 Raise the front of the vehicle and rest it securely on axle stands (see *Jacking and*

2.9 Undo the 4 bolts and detach the hub from the carrier

vehicle support). Remove the appropriate front roadwheel.
4 On vehicles equipped with gas discharge headlamps, release the clip and disconnect the vehicle level sensor connecting rod from the front lower transverse arm; see Chapter 12 for details.
5 Refer to Chapter 9 and carry out the following:
   a) *Unbolt the brake caliper, together with its mounting bracket, from the hub carrier and suspend it from the coil spring.*
   b) *Remove the brake disc.*
   c) *Remove the ABS wheel speed sensor from the hub carrier. Release the ABS wheel sensor wiring from its retaining clips in the wheel arch. Pull the rubber grommet from the inner wheel arch to reveal the sensor connector. Disconnect the lead, and pull it through the hub carrier and away from the vehicle.*
6 Undo the screws and detach the brake disc shield from the hub carrier.
7 Undo the securing nut and extract the clamp bolt from the top of the hub carrier (see Section 5). Separate the front and rear upper transverse arm balljoints from the top of the hub carrier, but do not force the slots apart with a screwdriver or similar in an attempt to free the balljoint pins **(see illustration)**. Take care to avoid damaging the balljoint rubber gaiters. Discard the nut and bolt, new ones must be fitted.
8 Pull the hub carrier assembly outwards, and at the same time, pull the end of the driveshaft from the wheel hub. Tie the driveshaft to the vehicle body, etc; do not let it hang down or the driveshaft joints may be damaged.
9 Unscrew the 4 multi-splined bolts, and detach the hub from the carrier **(see illustration)**.
10 Press the hub from the bearing, If the bearing's inner race remains on the hub, remove it using a bearing puller. Note that new bearings are supplied integral with the bearing housing.
11 Press the new bearing assembly on to the hub, using a tubular spacer which bears only on the inner bearing race.
12 Fit the hub bearing assembly to the hub carrier, then insert the bolts and tighten them to the specified torque.
13 The remainder of refitting is a reversal of removal, noting the following points:
   a) *Tighten the driveshaft bolt to the Stage 1 torque setting with the vehicle on axle stands, but only carry out the Stage 2 angle-tightening setting once the vehicle is back on its wheels (see Chapter 8).*
   b) *Tighten all fasteners to their specified torque where given.*

Hub carrier

14 Proceed as described in paragraphs 1 to 7 of this Section.
15 Unbolt the track rod balljoint from the hub carrier, as described in Section 23.
16 Undo the securing nuts, then separate

the front and rear lower transverse arms from the base of the hub carrier, with the aid of a balljoint splitter (see Section 5). Avoid damaging the rubber gaiters.
17 Grasp the hub carrier and gradually draw it off the driveshaft. Use a hub puller if the driveshaft is a tight fit in the hub. Tie the driveshaft to the vehicle body, etc; do not let it hang down or the driveshaft joints may be damaged.
18 If required, undo the 4 countersunk bolts and detach the hub bearing housing from the hub carrier.
19 Refitting is a reversal of removal, noting the following points:
   a) *Tighten the driveshaft bolt to the Stage 1 torque setting with the vehicle on axle stands, but only carry out the Stage 2 angle-tightening setting once the vehicle is back on its wheels (see Chapter 8).*
   b) *Tighten all fasteners to their specified torque where given.*
   c) *Have the front wheel alignment checked at the earliest opportunity.*

3 Front suspension strut – removal and refitting

Removal

1 Remove the wheel trim/hub cap (as applicable) and slacken the wheel bolts by half a turn with the vehicle resting on its wheels.
2 Chock the rear wheels of the car, firmly apply the handbrake, then jack up the front of the car and support it securely on axle stands (see *Jacking and vehicle support*). Remove the appropriate front roadwheel.
3 On vehicles equipped with gas discharge headlamps, release the clip and disconnect the vehicle level sensor connecting rod from the front lower transverse arm; see Chapter 12 for details.
4 Unbolt the brake caliper, together with its mounting bracket, from the hub carrier and suspend it from the suspension.
5 Undo the securing nut and extract the clamp bolt from the top of the hub carrier (see Section 5). Separate the front and rear upper transverse arm balljoints from the top of the hub carrier, but do not force the slots apart with a screwdriver or similar in an attempt to free the balljoint pins **(see illustration 2.7)**. Take care to avoid damaging the balljoint rubber gaiters. Discard the nut and bolt, new ones must be fitted. If the balljoints are reluctant to detach, apply releasing fluid and a little heat from a hot air gun. Take care as the aluminium hub carrier is easily damaged.
6 Support the underside of the hub carrier on a trolley jack or an axle stand.
7 Undo the nut and remove the suspension strut lower mounting bolt from the transverse arm **(see illustration)**.
8 Undo the bolt and move the coolant expansion tank to one side.

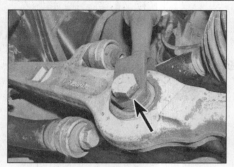

3.7 Undo the and remove the shock absorber lower mounting bolt (arrowed)

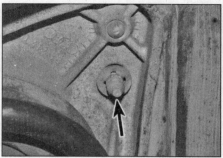

3.9 Prise off and discard the retaining clip (arrowed)

3.10a Pull up the rubber sealing strip (arrowed) . . .

3.10b . . . then pull forward the plenum chamber cover (arrowed)

3.10c Prise out the grommet and undo the 3 upper mounting bolts (arrowed)

9 Prise off the retaining clip from the upper mounting underside. Discard the clip, it need not be refitted **(see illustration)**
10 Remove the plenum chamber cover, then prise out the grommet, and remove the 3 upper mounting bolts **(see illustrations)**. Withdraw the strut, complete with upper mounting bracket, from the wheel arch, taking care not to damage the driveshaft or steering rack gaiters.

Refitting

11 Offer up the suspension strut to the wheel arch and refit the upper mounting bolt with their washers. Tighten the bolts to the specified torque, and refit the grommet.
12 Bolt the strut lower mounting to the lower transverse arm, fit a new securing nut but hand-tighten it only at this stage. Note the bolt is inserted from the front.
13 Reconnect the upper transverse arms to the top of the hub carrier as described in Section 5. Refit the new clamp bolt, together with a new self-locking nut and tighten it to the specified torque. Press down on both transverse arms as you tighten the nut, to ensure that the balljoints are properly seated in the hub carrier.
14 The remainder of refitting is a reversal of removal. Tighten the lower shock mounting bolt/nut once the vehicle is on the ground.

4 Front suspension strut
– overhaul

⚠ *Warning: Before attempting to dismantle the front suspension strut, a suitable tool to hold the coil spring in compression must be obtained. Adjustable coil spring compressors are readily available, and are recommended for this operation. Any attempt to dismantle the strut without such a tool is likely to result in damage or personal injury.*

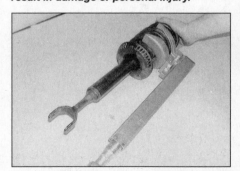

4.2 Compress the coil spring evenly and progressively until all tension is relieved from the spring seats

1 With the strut removed from the car, clean away all external dirt. If required, mount the strut upright in a vice to provide stability. Pad the vice jaws with wood or aluminium, to prevent damage to the strut lower mountings.
2 Fit the spring compressor and compress the coil spring evenly and progressively until tension is relieved from the spring seats **(see illustration)**.
3 Slacken the shock absorber piston nut whilst retaining the piston with a suitable Allen key. This can be achieved using either a spanner with an angled head, or by using a socket with a centre hole large enough to allow the Allen key to pass through and a hex fitting at the top; the socket can then be turned with an open-ended spanner. Alternatively, use a socket and hollow ratchet that allows an Allen key to pass through the centre of the ratchet **(see illustration)**.
4 Remove the nut, then lift off the rubber retaining cap, washer, and mounting plate complete with protective sleeve/bump stop **(see illustrations)**.
5 Lift off the coil spring (together with the compressors).
6 Remove the lower spring seat, then if required, remove the protective cap, mark the position of the lower spring support in relation to the shock absorber, and loosen the lower spring support from the shock absorber body

4.3 Use an Allen key to counterhold whilst slackening the piston nut

4.4a Lift off the rubber retaining cap . . .

4.4b . . . and washer . . .

4.4c . . . followed by the mounting plate complete with protective sleeve/bump stop

4.6a Remove the protective cap . . .

4.6b . . . then make alignment marks and remove the lower spring support

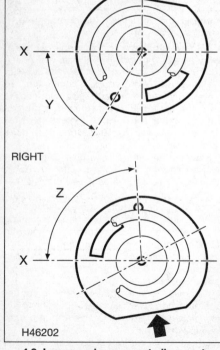

4.9 Lower spring support alignment

X = Centre line through the lower mounting bolt
$Y = 65° \pm 2°$ $Z = 87° \pm 2°$

The arrow indicates the cut-away for body clearance

by tapping it lightly with a soft-faced mallet **(see illustrations)**.

7 Examine the shock absorber for signs of fluid leakage. Check the piston rod for signs of pitting along its entire length, and check the shock absorber body for signs of damage or serious corrosion. While holding it in an upright position, test the operation of the shock absorber by moving the piston through a full stroke, and then through short strokes of 50 to 100 mm. In both cases, the resistance felt should be smooth and continuous. If the resistance is jerky, or uneven, or if there is any visible sign of wear or damage to the shock absorber, renewal will be necessary. **Note:** *Shock absorbers must be renewed in pairs, to preserve the handling characteristics of the vehicle.*

8 Inspect all other components for signs of damage or deterioration, and renew as required.

9 Refit the lower spring support to the shock absorber body, aligning the previously-made marks. If the support is being fitted to a new shock absorber, align the support as shown **(see illustration)**. Refit the protective cap.

10 Refit the lower spring seat, ensuring that it engages correctly with the recess in the lower spring support **(see illustration)**.

11 Refit the compressed coil spring to the strut base, ensuring that the end of the coil bears against the corresponding stop on the spring seat **(see illustration)**.

12 Ensure the rubber upper spring seat is correctly located, then (if removed) refit the protective cap and bump stop **(see illustration)**.

13 Refit the upper mounting plate to the top of the strut. Ensure the spring seat is correctly aligned, and the end of the spring fits up against the stop in the seat.

14 Refit the rubber retaining cap and washer.

4.10 Ensure the lower spring seat aligns correctly

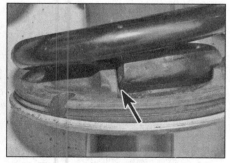

4.11 The end of the spring must abut the corresponding stop in the seat (arrowed)

15 Fit a new piston rod nut, then retain the shock absorber piston rod using the method employed during removal and tighten the nut to the specified torque.

16 With the strut clamped vertically in a bench vice, set the position of the upper spring mounting plate as shown **(see illustration)**.

17 Ensure all components are correctly seated and both spring ends are in contact with their stops then progressively release the spring compressor and remove it from the strut.

18 Refit the strut to the vehicle as described in Section 3.

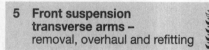

<table>
<tr><td>5</td><td>Front suspension transverse arms – removal, overhaul and refitting</td></tr>
</table>

Upper arms

Removal

1 Remove the suspension strut as described in Section 3.

2 Mount the lower end of the strut in a bench vice, then slacken and remove the nut and bolt securing the appropriate upper transverse arm to the mounting bracket **(see illustration)**.

Overhaul

3 Thoroughly clean the arm and the area around the arm mountings, removing all traces of dirt, thread locking compound and underseal if necessary, then check carefully for cracks, distortion or any other signs of wear or damage, paying particular attention to the inner pivot bush and balljoint. The balljoint is an integral part of the lower arm and cannot be renewed separately. If the arm or balljoint are damaged then the complete assembly must be renewed.

4 Renewal of the inner pivot bush will require the use of a hydraulic press and several spacers and is therefore best entrusted to an Audi dealer or garage with access to the necessary equipment. If such equipment is available, press out the old bush and install the new one using a spacer which bears only on the bush outer edge. Ensure the bush is correctly positioned so that the cavities are aligned with the centre axis of the arm **(see illustration)**.

Refitting

5 Offer up the transverse arms to the mounting bracket, insert a new securing bolt and screw on a new securing nut.

6 Position the transverse arms as shown **(see illustrations)**. Hold the arm in this position and tighten the securing nut to the specified Stage 1 and 2 torque settings. This ensures that the rubber bushes are not stressed when the vehicle is lowered onto its wheels.

7 Refit the suspension strut as described in Section 3.

4.12 Refit the protective sleeve/bump stop to the upper mounting plate

Rear lower arm (guide link)

Removal

8 Chock the rear wheels, firmly apply the handbrake, then jack up the front of the vehicle and support on axle stands (see *Jacking and vehicle support*). Remove the appropriate front roadwheel. Whilst the wheel is removed, refit at least one wheel bolt to ensure the brake disc remains correctly positioned on the hub.

9 Undo the mounting bolts and detach the brake caliper from the hub carrier. Suspend the caliper from the suspension coil using string or wire – do not allow the caliper to be suspended by the brake hose.

10 Undo the arm balljoint securing nut until it's flush with the end of the threads (use a 4 mm Allen key to counterhold the balljoint shank), then separate the arm from the base of the hub carrier, with the aid of a balljoint

5.2 Undo the nut and bolt, then detach the upper arm(s) from the mounting plate

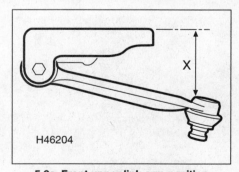

5.6a Front upper link arm position
$X = 81 \pm 2$ mm

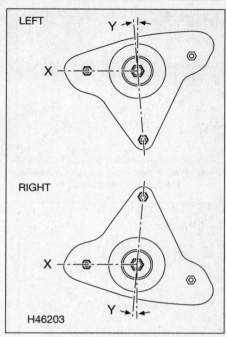

4.16 Upper spring seat alignment

X = Centre line through the lower mounting bolt
Y = 7°

splitter – avoid damaging the rubber gaiter **(see illustrations)**.

11 Slacken and remove the nut from the bolt at the inboard end of the guide link **(see illustration)**. To allow the bolt to be withdrawn,

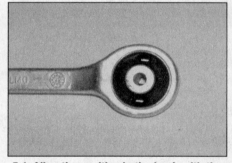

5.4 Align the cavities in the bush with the centre axis of the arm

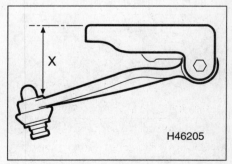

5.6b Rear upper link arm position
$X = 70 \pm 2$ mm

5.10a Use a 4 mm Allen key to counterhold the balljoint shank nut . . .

5.10b . . . then use a balljoint splitter to separate the balljoint

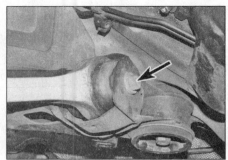

5.11 Undo the guide link inner bolt (arrowed)

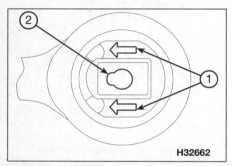

5.14 Ensure the arrows on the hydro-mounting (1) or the central groove (2) point towards the balljoint

the corner of the subframe must be lowered slightly. To do this, position a workshop trolley jack and block of wood under the subframe, unscrew and remove the two support plate bolts, then slacken and withdraw the subframe securing bolt.

12 Lower the subframe slightly, withdraw the guide link inboard securing bolt then remove the arm from the vehicle.

Overhaul

13 Thoroughly clean the arm and the area around the arm mountings, removing all traces of dirt, thread locking compound and underseal if necessary, then check carefully for cracks, distortion or any other signs of wear or damage, paying particular attention to the inner pivot bush and balljoint. Note that the inner bush has a hydraulic action; fluid leakage indicates that the bush has been damaged and must be renewed. The balljoint

5.19 Detach the front lower arm balljoint from the hub carrier

is an integral part of the lower arm and cannot be renewed separately. If the arm or balljoint are damaged then the complete assembly must be renewed.

14 Renewal of the inner pivot bush will require the use of a hydraulic press and several spacers and is therefore best entrusted to an Audi dealer or garage with access to the necessary equipment. If such equipment is available, press out the old bush and install the new one using a spacer which bears only on the bush outer edge. Ensure the bush is correctly positioned so that the arrows or central groove points towards the balljoint **(see illustration)**.

Refitting

15 Refitting is a reversal of removal noting the following points:
 a) *Use new transverse arm and subframe securing nuts and bolts.*
 b) *Delay tightening the transverse arm inboard securing bolt until the vehicle is resting on its roadwheels.*
 c) *Tighten all fixings to the correct torque, where specified.*

Front lower arm (track control link)

Removal

16 Chock the rear wheels, firmly apply the handbrake, then jack up the front of the vehicle and support on axle stands. Remove the appropriate front roadwheel. Whilst the wheel is removed, refit at least one wheel bolt to ensure the brake disc remains correctly positioned on the hub.

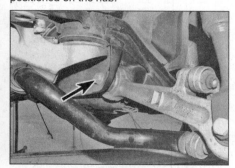

5.23 Front lower arm inboard bolt (arrowed)

17 Release the fasteners and remove the engine undershield.

18 On vehicles equipped with gas discharge headlamps, release the clip and disconnect the vehicle level sensor connecting rod from the front lower transverse arm; see Chapter 12 for details.

19 Undo the securing nut until it's flush with the end of the balljoint shank threads, then separate the front lower transverse arm from the base of the hub carrier, with the aid of a balljoint splitter (avoid damaging the rubber gaiter). If necessary, use a 4 mm Allen key to counterhold the nut **(see illustration)**.

20 Position a trolley jack under the hub carrier to prevent the suspension extending too far and damaging the upper link arms.

21 Undo the nut and remove the suspension strut lower mounting bolt from the front transverse arm.

22 Remove the securing nut and detach the anti-roll bar drop link from the transverse arm as described in Section 6.

23 Unscrew the nut and withdraw the transverse arm inboard securing bolt, then remove the transverse arm from the vehicle **(see illustration)**.

Overhaul

24 Thoroughly clean the arm and the area around the arm mountings, removing all traces of dirt, thread locking compound and underseal if necessary, then check carefully for cracks, distortion or any other signs of wear or damage, paying particular attention to the inner and strut pivot bushes and balljoint. The balljoint is an integral part of the lower arm and cannot be renewed separately. If the arm or balljoint are damaged then the complete assembly must be renewed.

25 Renewal of the inner and strut pivot bushes will require the use of a hydraulic press and several spacers and is therefore best entrusted to an Audi dealer or garage with access to the necessary equipment.

Refitting

26 Refitting is a reversal of removal noting the following points:
 a) *Use new transverse arm and strut securing nuts and bolts.*
 b) *To avoid damaging the bushes, delay tightening the transverse arm inboard*

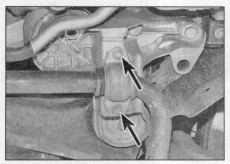

6.3 Undo the nuts securing the anti-roll bar clamps each side (arrowed)

6.4 Undo the bolt and detach the drop links from the lower track control links

6.7 The anti-roll bar bushes are fitted with the slot at the top (arrowed)

securing nut, the strut securing nut and the anti-roll bar drop link securing nut to their final torque settings until the vehicle is resting on its roadwheels.
c) Tighten all fixings to the correct torque, where specified

6 Front suspension anti-roll bar – removal and refitting

Removal

1 The anti-roll bar must be removed/refitted with the vehicle resting on its wheels. For this reason the following operation will be much easier if the vehicle can be positioned over an inspection pit. Alternatively drive the vehicle onto ramps to increase the clearance between the front of the vehicle and the ground.
2 Release the fasteners and remove the undershield from beneath the engine to gain access to the anti-roll bar mounting clamps.
3 Slacken and remove the nuts securing both the anti-roll bar mounting clamps to the subframe. Remove the clamps and discard the nuts; new ones should be used on refitting **(see illustration)**.
4 Unscrew the securing bolts and detach the drop links from the lower track control links each side. Discard the bolts, new ones must be fitted **(see illustration)**.
5 Unscrew the bolts securing the anti-roll bar ends to the drop links and discard them; new bolts should be used on refitting.
6 Lower the anti-roll bar, and remove it from under the vehicle.
7 Renew the anti-roll bar if it is damaged or distorted. Renew the mounting bushes if they are perished or worn **(see illustration)**.

Refitting

8 Mount the drop links onto the lower arms, then fit the bolts – hand tighten them only at this stage. Ensure that the concave side of the drop link faces the front of the vehicle.
9 Manoeuvre the anti-roll bar into position and engage it with the ends of the drop links. Insert the new securing bolts, tightening them lightly only at this stage.
10 Refit the mounting clamps to the anti-roll bar mounting bushes. Ensure both clamps are

correctly located on the bushes then fit the new retaining nuts. Tighten the retaining nuts lightly only at this stage.
11 Rock the vehicle from side-to-side, to settle the anti-roll bar in position. Tighten all four anti-roll bar drop link bolts to the specified torque settings. Also tighten the anti-roll bar mounting clamp nuts to the specified torque.
12 Refit the undershield and tighten the fixings securely.

7 Front suspension subframe – removal and refitting

Note: All subframe mounting nuts and bolts must be renewed.

Removal

1 Chock the rear wheels, firmly apply the handbrake, then jack up the front of the vehicle and support on axle stands (see Jacking and vehicle support).
2 Remove both front roadwheels. Whilst the wheel is removed, refit at least one wheel bolt to ensure the brake discs remain correctly positioned on the hub.
3 Remove the fasteners and retaining clips and remove the undershield from beneath the engine/transmission unit.
4 Attach a lifting bracket to the rear of the engine and support the weight of the engine/transmission unit, using either a lifting beam or an engine hoist.
5 On vehicles equipped with gas discharge headlamps, release the clip and disconnect the ride height sensor connecting rod from the front lower transverse arm; see Chapter 12 for details.

Cabriolet models

6 Release the fasteners and remove the front outer underbody trims.
7 Make alignment marks between the diagonal struts and the vehicle body using paint or felt tip pen, then undo the Torx bolts and remove the diagonal strut each side **(see illustration)**.

All models

8 Undo the retaining screws, then carefully prise the ABS wheel speed sensor wiring from the hub carrier.

9 Undo the mounting bolts and slide the caliper mounting from the hub carrier each side. Suspend the calipers from the coil springs using string or wire to prevent any strain on the brake hose.
10 Unbolt the anti-roll bar drop links from both lower suspension arms, with reference to Section 6.
11 Unbolt the inboard ends of both rear lower guide links from the subframe with reference to Section 5. Note that this will entail unbolting the rear corners of the subframe from the underside of the vehicle and lowering it slightly to allow the guide links bolts to be withdrawn.
12 Unbolt the lower ends of both suspension struts from the front lower track control links with reference to Section 3.
13 Unbolt the inboard ends of both front lower track control links from the subframe with reference to Section 5.
14 Suspend the hub carrier, suspension strut and track control links from the inside of the wheel arch using lengths of wire to avoid straining the suspension bushes and balljoints.
15 Ensure that the engine and transmission are securely suspended by the lifting equipment, then unbolt the transmission mountings from the subframe.
16 Slacken and withdraw the two subframe securing bolts, located to the rear of the anti-roll bar clamp brackets.
17 Slacken the four subframe securing bolts located forward of the anti-roll bar clamps brackets, until the subframe can be released from its mountings. Do not remove the bolts completely.

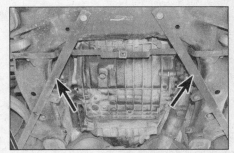

7.7 Make alignment marks then undo the Torx bolts and remove the front diagonal struts (arrowed)

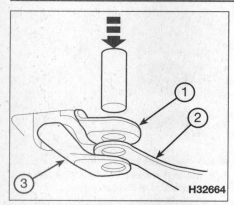

7.24 Pass a wooden dowel (arrowed) through each of the alignment holes in the front corners of the subframe

1 Bracket (upper) 3 Bracket (lower)
2 Subframe

18 Carefully lower the subframe and withdraw it from the underside of the vehicle.

Overhaul

19 Renewal of the bonded subframe bushes requires access to a hydraulic press and a number of specially-shaped extraction/fitment tools. Fabrication of alternative tools is not recommended due to the risk of damage to the subframe bush mountings. For this reason, it's best to entrust bush renewal work to an Audi dealer or suitably-equipped specialist.

Refitting

20 Offer the subframe up to the underside of the engine compartment and engage the front mountings with their respective brackets. Fit the new subframe front mounting bolts, but do not fully tighten them at this stage.
21 Reconnect the transmission mountings to the subframe.
22 Reconnect the lower end of the suspension strut to the front lower transverse arm with reference to Section 3, then reconnect the front and rear lower transverse arms to the subframe with reference to Section 5. Do not fully tighten the securing nuts and bolts at this stage.
23 Refit the gas discharge headlamp ride height sensor pushrod to the front lower transverse arm with reference to Chapter 12 (where applicable).
24 Obtain two lengths of wooden dowel, each roughly 15 mm in diameter and 150 mm in length. Working through the wheel arches, pass a dowel through each of the alignment holes in the front corners of the subframe. Adjust the position of the subframe until both dowels pass through all three alignment holes on each side **(see illustration)**.
25 Refit the mounting brackets at the rear corners of the subframe, insert the new brackets securing bolts and tighten them lightly. With the brackets in place, fit new subframe rear mounting bolts and tighten them lightly.

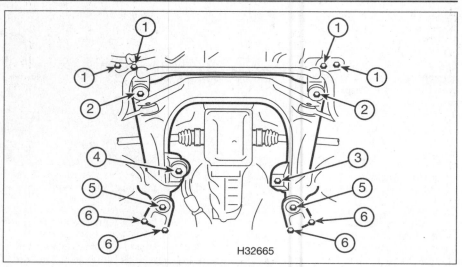

H32665

7.27 Subframe mounting bolt details

1 Rear mounting bracket bolts
2 Main mounting bolts
3 Transmission mounting bolts (typical)
4 Transmission mounting bolts (typical)
5 Main mounting bolts
6 Front bracket mounting bolts

26 Remove the engine hoist/support bar (as applicable) then tighten the subframe and suspension mounting bolts in the order given in the following paragraphs.
27 Tighten the four main subframe securing bolts to their specified first and second Stage torques **(see illustration)**.
28 Tighten the four subframe front mounting bolts to their specified torque.
29 Tighten the four subframe rear mounting bracket bolts to their specified torques.
30 Tighten the transmission mounting bolts to their specified torques, with reference to Chapter 7A, 7B or 7C as applicable.
31 Tighten the front and rear lower arms inboard securing bolts to their specified torques, with reference to Section 5.
32 Refit the anti-roll bar drop link with reference to Section 6. Use new securing bolts and tighten them to the specified torques.
33 Tighten the strut-to-front lower arm securing nut to the specified torque (see Section 4).
34 Refit the ABS wheel speed sensor and tighten the retaining screws to their specified torque (see Chapter 9).

8.3 Use a chisel to prise off the grease cap

Cabriolet models

35 Refit the diagonal struts, using the alignment marks previously-made, Fit the new mounting bolts, but do not tighten them yet.

All models

36 Refit the roadwheels and lower the vehicle to the ground. Now tighten the lower arms mounting bolts, and on Cabriolet models, tighten the diagonal strut bolts to the specified torque.
37 Securely refit the undershield. Tighten the wheel bolts to the specified torque.
38 On completion, have the front wheel alignment and steering angles checked and if necessary adjusted at the earliest possible opportunity.

8 Rear hub and bearings – renewal

1 The rear wheel hub bearings are housed in the rear brake disc/hub. The bearings are an integral assembly with the hub, and are maintenance-free. If defective, the bearings must be renewed with the hub as a complete unit.
2 Chock the front wheels, then jack up the rear of the vehicle and support it securely on axle stands (see Jacking and vehicle support).
3 Prise off the grease cap from the hub **(see illustration)**.
4 Refit the wheel and lower the vehicle to the ground.
5 Slacken the hub flange bolt 90° (a quarter of a turn) **(see illustration)**.
6 Raise the vehicle, remove the road wheel again, then remove the brake disc as described in Chapter 9.
7 Undo the retaining bolt, and pull the ABS

wheel sensor from the hub carrier **(see illustration)**.

8 Completely unscrew the flange bolt and pull the hub and bearing from the hub carrier. If the bearing is reluctant to move, attach a slide hammer to the hub and pull it from position **(see illustration)**. Discard the flange bolt, a new one must be fitted.

9 Ensure the stub axle is clean, then fit the new hub/bearing assembly into position. Fit the new flange bolt, bolt only tighten it to the specified Stage 1 torque at this stage.

10 Refit the roadwheel, lower the vehicle to the ground, and tighten the flange bolt through the Stage 2 angle-tightening setting.

11 Raise the vehicle and remove the road-wheel again, then drive in the new grease cap.

12 The remainder of refitting is a reversal of removal.

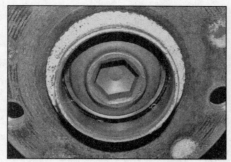

8.5 Use a 17 mm Allen bit to slacken the hub bolt

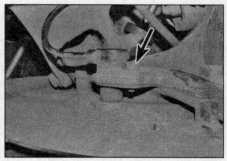

8.7 ABS wheel speed sensor retaining bolt (arrowed)

9 Rear hub carrier – removal and refitting

Removal

1 If the bearing and hub are to be removed from the hub carrier, proceed as described in paragraphs 1 to 6 of Section 8.

2 If the bearing is to remain on the hub carrier, begin by jacking up the rear of the vehicle, and supporting it securely on axle stands (see *Jacking and vehicle support*).

3 Remove the brake disc as described in Chapter 9.

4 Remove the coil spring as described in Section 12.

5 Undo the 3 bolts securing the brake back plate to the hub carrier.

6 Undo the retaining bolt, and pull the ABS wheel speed sensor from the hub carrier **(see illustration 8.7)**.

7 Using a felt-tip pen or paint, mark the position of the upper transverse link eccentric bolt in relation to the hub carrier, then undo and remove the bolts securing the hub carrier in the following sequence:

a) *Shock absorber lower mounting bolt.*

b) *Hub carrier lower mounting bolts.*

c) *Hub carrier upper mounting bolt.*

8 Detach the hub carrier from the vehicle.

Overhaul

9 Renewal of the bonded hub carrier bush requires access to a hydraulic press and a number of specially-shaped extraction/fitment tools. Fabrication of alternative tools is not recommended due to the risk of damage to the bush mountings. For this reason, it's best to entrust bush renewal work to an Audi dealer or suitably-equipped specialist.

Refitting

10 Refitting is a reversal of removal, noting the following points:

a) *Set the hub carrier upper transverse link*

eccentric bolt to its original position using the alignment marks made during removal.

b) *Tighten the hub carrier mounting bolts when the vehicle is back on the ground.*

c) *Tighten all fasteners to their specified torque where given.*

d) *Have the wheel alignment checked at the earliest opportunity.*

10 Rear suspension strut – removal and refitting

Removal

1 Chock the front wheels, then jack up the rear of the car and support it on axle stands (see *Jacking and vehicle support*). Remove the relevant rear roadwheel.

2 Position a trolley jack underneath the rear hub carrier and raise it until the shock absorber starts to compress.

3 Slacken and remove the nut, then withdraw the lower mounting bolt which secures the strut to the axle **(see illustration)**. Discard the nut and bolt; new items should be used on refitting.

4 Undo and remove the two upper strut mounting bolts from under the wheel arch **(see illustration)**.

5 Compress the strut and manoeuvre the strut from the vehicle.

Refitting

6 Position the strut with the longer side of the lower mounting bush against the bracket on

10.4 Strut upper mounting bolts

8.8 If necessary, use a slide hammer to pull the hub from position

the hub carrier **(see illustration)**, then refit the upper mounting bolts, and tighten them to the specified torque.

7 Fit the new lower mounting bolt and nut. Only finger tighten them at this stage.

10.3 Undo the nut and remove the lower shock absorber mounting bolt

10.6 The longer side of the bush must fit against the hub carrier (arrowed)

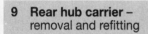

11.2 Hold the damper rod, and slacken the nut

8 Remove the trolley jack, refit the road wheels and lower the vehicle to the ground.
9 Tighten the strut lower mounting bolt/nut to the specified torque.
10 Tighten the wheel bolts to the specified torque.

11 Rear suspension strut – overhaul

1 With the strut removed from the car, clean away all external dirt, then mount it upright in a vice.
2 Slacken the damper rod nut whilst retaining the damper rod with a suitable spanner **(see illustration)**. Discard the nut, a new one must be fitted.
3 Lift off the upper mounting, bump stop and protective tube **(see illustration)**.
4 Examine the shock absorber for signs of fluid leakage. Check the piston for signs of pitting along its entire length, and check the shock body for signs of damage. While holding it in an upright position, test the operation of the shock absorber by moving the piston through a full stroke, and then through short strokes of 50 to 100 mm. In both cases, the resistance felt should be smooth and continuous. If the resistance is jerky, or uneven, or if there is any visible sign of wear or damage to the shock absorber, renewal will be necessary.
Caution: Shock absorbers must be renewed in pairs. Different versions of shock absorbers are fitted to different models

12.2 Compress the coil spring

11.3 Lift off the mounting, bump stop and protective tube

– ensure that you have the correct version for your vehicle.
5 Inspect all other components for signs of damage or deterioration, and renew any that are suspect.
6 Slide the protective tube over the damper rod then refit the bump stop, followed by the upper mounting.
7 Fully extend the piston rod and screw on the new nut. Counterhold the damper rod to prevent it from rotating and tighten the nut to the specified torque.
8 Refit the strut to the vehicle as described in Section 10.

12 Rear suspension spring – removal and refitting

⚠ *Warning: Before attempting to remove the coil spring, a suitable tool to hold the coil spring in compression must be obtained. Adjustable coil spring compressors are readily available, and are essential for this operation. Any attempt to dismantle the strut without such a tool is likely to result in damage or personal injury.*

Removal

1 Chock the front wheels, jack up the rear of the vehicle and support it securely on axle stands (see *Jacking and vehicle support*).
2 Fit the spring compressor, and compress the coil spring evenly and progressively until tension is relieved from the spring seats **(see**

12.4 The pin on the base of the spring seat engages with a hole in the trapezium link (arrowed)

illustration). Take care not to damage the trapezium link.
3 Manoeuvre the compressed spring from the vehicle. Remove the upper and lower spring seats.

Refitting

4 Refit the lower spring seat to the trapezium link. Note that the seat has a locating pin, which engages in a corresponding hole in the link **(see illustration)**.
5 Fit the compressed spring into position, with the tapered end with the colour-coding at the bottom. Ensure the end of the spring contacts the limit stop in the lower seat.
6 Refit the upper spring seat to the spring, and slowly decompress the spring. Guide the upper seat into place as the coil is released.
7 Refit the roadwheel, lower the vehicle to the ground, and tighten the wheel bolts to the specified torque.

13 Rear subframe – removal and refitting

Note: *The following procedure details removal of the subframe complete with link arms, hub carriers, and trapezium links. If required, remove these components as described elsewhere in this Chapter, then unbolt and remove the subframe using the relevant information from this Section.*

Removal

1 Chock the front wheels, engage 1st gear (or P), then slacken the rear roadwheel bolts. Raise and support the vehicle at the rear on axle stands (see *Jacking and vehicle support*). Remove the rear roadwheels.
2 Release the fasteners and remove the rear and side underbody covers.

Cabriolet models

3 Using paint or a felt tip pen, mark the position of the rear diagonal struts in relation to the vehicle body, then undo the bolts and remove the struts **(see illustration 7.7)**. Discard the bolts, new ones must be fitted.

All models

4 Remove the rear section of the exhaust system as described in Chapter 4D.
5 Remove the coil spring as described in Section 12.
6 Unscrew and remove the shock absorber upper mounting bolts.
7 Undo the bolts and remove the trapezium link stone guards (where fitted).
8 Undo the bolts and detach the handbrake cable bracket from the underside of the trapezium links **(see illustration)**.
9 Undo the bolts and slide the brake caliper and mounting bracket from the hub carrier. Suspend the caliper from the vehicle body using string or wire, to prevent the brake hose from any strain.
10 Undo the retaining bolt, then pull the ABS

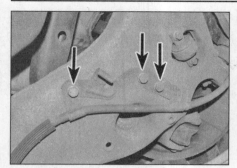

13.8 Undo the bolts (arrowed) and detach the handbrake cable brackets from the trapezium link

14.2 Make alignment marks between the bolt eccentric washer and the hub carrier

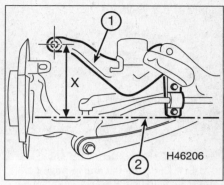

14.6 Transverse link arm position

1 = Transverse link arm   *2 = Straight-edge*
                    X = 142 ± 1 mm

wheel speed sensor from the hub carrier, along with the harness guide.

11 On models fitted with gas discharge headlamps, disconnect the ride height sensor pushrod from the trapezium link; refer to Chapter 12 for details.

12 Position a suitable workshop trolley jack with the necessary wooden blocks under the subframe, and take its weight.

13 Unscrew and remove the subframe mounting bolts, then with the help of an assistant, carefully lower the subframe, guiding the caliper and handbrake cable over the upper transverse links. Take care not to stretch the brake hoses. Discard the subframe bolts, new ones must be fitted.

14 Manoeuvre the assembly from under the vehicle.

15 If the subframe hydro-bushes are worn, they must be renewed. This task can only be performed with the help of special Audi tools. For this reason, we recommend the task be entrusted to an Audi dealer or suitably-equipped specialist.

Refitting

16 Refitting is a reversal of the removal procedure, noting the following point:
 a) *Renew the subframe mounting bolts.*
 b) *Renew all self-locking nuts.*
 c) *Tighten all fasteners to their specified torque where given.*
 d) *The bonded rubber bushes fitted to the suspension link arms can only rotate so far – consequently their mounting bolts must only be tightened once the vehicle is back on the ground.*
 e) *On completion, the rear wheel alignment may need to be checked.*

14 Rear suspension link arms – removal, overhaul and refitting

Upper arm (transverse link)

Removal

1 In order to remove the transverse link inner mounting bolt, the subframe must be removed as described in Section 13.

2 Use paint or a felt-tip pen to mark the position of the link outer eccentric mounting bolt in relation to the hub carrier **(see illustration)**, then unscrew and remove the bolt.

3 Unscrew and remove the inner mounting bolt, and remove the link arm.

Overhaul

4 Renewal of the bonded hub carrier bush requires access to a hydraulic press and a number of specially-shaped extraction/fitment tools. Fabrication of alternative tools is not recommended due to the risk of damage to the bush mountings. For this reason, it's best to entrust bush renewal work to an Audi dealer or suitably-equipped specialist.

Refitting

5 Note that the link arms are marked R or L to indicate which side of the vehicle they are fitted to.

6 Bolt the link arm loosely to the subframe using a new bolt, then place a straight-edge flat on the mounting bracket of the anti-roll bar. Position the link arm as shown and tighten the bolt to the specified torque **(see illustration)**.

7 Reconnect the link arm to the hub carrier, aligning the eccentric bolt using the previously-made marks, and tighten the nut to 20 Nm (15 lbf ft) only.

8 Refit the subframe as described in Section 13.

9 With the vehicle back on the ground, slacken the transverse link arm-to-hub carrier bolt, then tighten it to the specified torque.

Trapezium link removal

Note: *The right-hand trapezium link mounting bolts can only be removed once the subframe has been lowered slightly as described in Section 13.*

10 Release the fasteners and remove the underbody trim in front of the trapezium link.

Cabriolet models

11 Using paint or a felt tip pen, mark the position of the rear diagonal struts in relation to the vehicle body, then undo the bolts and remove the struts **(see illustration 7.7)**. Discard the bolts, new ones must be fitted.

All models

12 Remove the rear suspension coil spring as described in Section 12.

13 Undo the bolts and remove the stone guard from the underside of the trapezium link (where fitted).

14 On models fitted with gas discharge headlamps, disconnect the ride height sensor pushrod from the trapezium link; refer to Chapter 12 for details.

15 Undo the centre bracket bolt, then release the clips and detach the ABS wheel speed sensor wiring harness guide from the trapezium link **(see illustration)**.

16 Undo the nut securing the drop link to the anti-roll bar, and separate the two. Use an open-ended spanner to counterhold the nut.

17 Mark the position of the eccentric bolt at the front inner mounting of the trapezium link

14.15 Undo the centre bolt (arrowed) then unclip the ABS sensor wiring harness guide

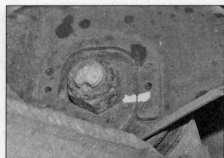

14.16 Make alignment marks between the eccentric washer and the subframe

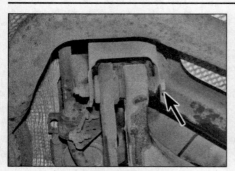

14.17 Undo the nut and remove the trapezium link inner rear bolt (arrowed)

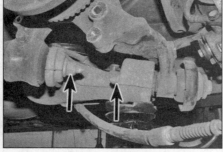

14.19 Undo the nuts (arrowed) and remove the hub carrier-to-trapezium link bolts

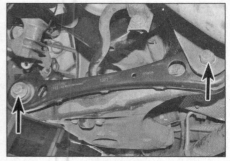

14.22 Rear lower link arm mounting bolts (arrowed)

in relation to the subframe, then undo the nut and remove the bolt **(see illustration)**. Note that if removing the right-hand trapezium link, the subframe will need to be lowered slightly (see Section 13), to remove the bolt.
18 Undo the nut and bolt securing the trapezium link at the rear innermost mounting **(see illustration)**.
19 Undo and remove the bolts securing the trapezium link to the hub carrier, and manoeuvre the link from under the vehicle **(see illustration)**.

Trapezium link refitting

20 Refitting is a reversal of removal, noting the following points:
 a) *Renew all self-locking nuts.*
 b) *Ensure the eccentric bolt at the front inner mounting of the link is refitted to its original position using the marks made on removal.*
 c) *Renew the hub carrier-to-trapezium link bolts/nuts, and the rear innermost link mounting bolt.*
 d) *The bonded rubber bushes fitted to the suspension link arms can only rotate so far – consequently their mounting bolts must only be tightened once the vehicle is back on the ground.*
 e) *On completion, the rear wheel alignment may need to be checked*

Rear lower link arm (track rod)

Removal

21 Remove the suspension coil spring as described in Section 12.

22 Undo the inner and outer track rod mounting bolts/nuts and detach the rod from the vehicle **(see illustration)**. Discard the nuts and bolts, new ones must be fitted.

Refitting

23 Position the Track rod, and fit the new nuts and bolts. Only tighten them to 20 Nm (15 lbf ft) at this stage.
24 Refit the coil spring with reference to Section 12.
25 When the vehicle is back on the ground, tighten the track rod mounting nuts/bolts to the specified torque.
26 On completion, the rear wheel alignment may need to be checked.

15 Rear anti-roll bar – removal and refitting

Removal

1 Chock the front wheels, then jack up the rear of the vehicle and support it securely on axle stands (see *Jacking and vehicle support*).
2 Release the fasteners and remove the rear underbody trim.

Cabriolet models

3 Using paint or a felt tip pen, mark the position of the rear diagonal struts in relation to the vehicle body, then undo the bolts and remove the struts **(see illustration 7.7)**. Discard the bolts, new ones must be fitted.

All models

4 On vehicles with heavy duty suspension, undo the bolts and remove the stone guard from the underside of the trapezium link.
5 Undo the 2 bolts each side securing the lower end of the anti-roll bar drop links to the trapezium links **(see illustration)**.
6 Undo the bolt securing each drop link to the anti-roll bar. Use an open-ended spanner to counterhold the bolt **(see illustration)**.
7 Undo the 2 bolts each side securing the anti-roll bar clamps to the subframe, and manoeuvre the anti-roll bar from under the vehicle **(see illustration)**.
8 Remove the clamps and the rubber bushes. Examine the condition of the bushes. If they show signs of wear or damage, renew them.

Refitting

9 Fit the rubber bushes to the anti-roll bar, ensuring they make contact with the collar on the bar.
10 Manoeuvre the bar into position, and refit the clamps and retaining bolts. Only finger-tighten these bolts at this stage.
11 Attach the drop links to the anti-roll bar, fit the upper and lower mounting bolts and tighten them to the specified torque.
12 Lower the vehicle to the ground and 'bounce' on the rear of the vehicle several times. Now tighten the anti-roll bar clamp bolts to the specified torque.
13 The remainder of refitting is a reversal of removal.

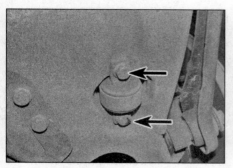

15.5 Undo the two bolts (arrowed) securing the anti-roll bar links

15.6 Use a second spanner to counterhold the link balljoint nut

15.7 Undo the bolts and detach the anti-roll bar clamps

16 Steering wheel –
removal and refitting

Warning: Refer to the precautions given in Chapter 12 before handling airbag system components.

Removal

1 Remove the airbag unit as described in Chapter 12.
2 Position the front wheels in the straight-ahead position and engage the steering lock.
3 Slacken and remove the steering wheel securing bolt, then mark the steering wheel and steering column shaft in relation to each other **(see illustrations)**. Discard the securing bolt, a new one must be fitted.
4 Disconnect the wiring plug, and lift the steering wheel off the column splines, taking care not to damage the contact unit wiring. **Do not** rotate the contact unit whilst the wheel is removed.

Refitting

5 Refitting is a reversal of removal, noting the following points:
a) Use the markings made during removal to ensure that the alignment between the steering wheel and column is correct.
b) Fit a new steering wheel securing bolt and tighten it to the correct torque.
c) On completion, refit the airbag unit as described in Chapter 12.

17 Steering column –
removal, inspection and refitting

Warning: Refer to the precautions given in Chapter 12, regarding the safe handling of airbag system components, before proceeding.

Removal

1 Fully extend the steering column and place the steering wheel in its lowest position. Remove the steering wheel from the steering column, as described in Section 16.
2 Undo the 3 retaining screws and remove the

16.3a Undo the steering wheel retaining bolt

upper and lower column shrouds. The shrouds are retained by 2 Torx bolts and 1 Allen screw inserted from the underside of the column, and two screws securing the upper shroud gaiter trim to the facia **(see illustrations)**. Note that it will be necessary to undo the 2.5 mm Allen screw and remove the steering column height adjustment lever.
3 Undo the steering column switch module retaining screw on the underside of the assembly **(see illustration)**.
4 Note their fitted positions, then disconnect the wiring plugs from the column switch module, and carefully pull the entire switch module over the end of the steering column **(see illustration)**.
5 Note their fitted positions, then disconnect the ignition switch/immobiliser reader coil wiring connectors.
6 On models with automatic/Multitronic

17.2a Undo the column shroud retaining screws (arrowed) . . .

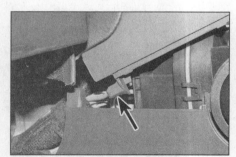

17.2c Note how the rear edge of the upper shroud hooks into the lower shroud (arrowed)

17.3 Switch module retaining Allen screw (arrowed)

16.3b Make alignment marks between the wheel and the shaft (arrowed)

transmission, disconnect the locking cable from the ignition switch, as described in Chapter 7B or 7C as applicable.
7 Detach and remove the lower facia trim/storage tray and insulation panels on the driver's side – see Chapter 11.
8 Note the harness routing, then undo the cable ties and release the wiring harness from the steering column.
9 In order to prevent the top and bottom sections of the steering column extending or compressing too far, it is now necessary to use cable ties, or length of wire, from the adjustment spring to the lower universal joint to stop the column extending too far. We also attached a length of metal rod to the lower section to prevent the column being compressed too far **(see illustrations)**.
Caution: Do not allow the upper and lower sections of the steering column to become

17.2b . . . then undo the 2.5 mm Allen screw securing the adjustment lever

17.4 Pull the switch module over the end of the steering column

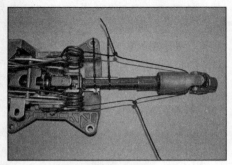

17.9a Use cable ties to prevent the column extending . . .

17.9b . . . and a length of rod to prevent it from compressing (shown with the column removed for clarity)

17.10 Unscrew the universal joint pinch-bolt (arrowed)

17.11 Steering column retaining bolts (arrowed)

separated or excessively compressed whilst the steering column is detached from the steering gear, as this can cause the internal components to become detached and misaligned.

10 Unscrew the pinch-bolt securing the universal joint at the base of the steering column to the steering gear (see illustration).

11 Remove the four steering column mounting bolts and withdraw the column assembly from the vehicle, pulling the steering column universal joint off the steering gear pinion as the assembly is withdrawn (see illustration).

12 Check the various components for excessive wear. If the column has been damaged in any way, it must be renewed as a unit.

13 If required, remove the ignition switch/steering column lock, as described in Section 18.

Refitting

14 Refitting is a reversal of the removal procedure, noting the following points:

a) Ensure that the protective plastic cap is still in place on the pivot bolt that protrudes from the left-hand side of the steering column. If the cap has been lost, cover the end of the bolt with thick adhesive tape to prevent the wiring harness from chafing.

b) Where applicable, refit the ignition switch/column lock as described in Section 18.

c) Fit the four steering column upper securing bolts, but do not tighten them yet.

d) Insert the pinch-bolt that secures the universal joint at the base of the steering column to the steering gear, and tighten it to the specified torque.

e) Now tighten the four upper steering column securing bolts to the specified torque.

f) Remove the wire that was used to secure the upper and lower sections of the steering column together.

g) Reconnect the locking cable on models with automatic or Multitronic transmission as described in Chapter 7B or 7C.

h) Refit the driver's airbag as described in Chapter 12.

i) On completion, ensure that the steering action, and the operation of the column switches, is satisfactory.

j) New columns are supplied with a transport lock, which must be removed once the column is fitted.

18 Ignition switch/ steering column lock – removal and refitting

Lock cylinder

Note: Removal of the lock cylinder requires the use of the vehicle's spare ignition key, which is fitted with a narrow-profile, moulded plastic grip. The grip fitted to the standard key, fitted with a built-in immobiliser transmitter and/or lock illumination torch is too bulky to be used in the removal procedure.

Note: The immobiliser reader coil is integral with the lock cylinder. If a new lock cylinder/reader coil is to be fitted, the reader coil specifications must be noted for reprogramming, using VAS 5051 specialist equipment. Entrust this task to an Audi dealer or suitably equipped-specialist.

Removal

1 Remove the steering wheel (Section 16).

2 Remove the steering column combination switch module as described in Chapter 12.

3 Carefully unplug the wiring connector from immobiliser reader coil on the ignition lock housing (see illustration).

4 On models with automatic or Multitronic transmission, turn the ignition switch to the 'on' position, lift the interlock lever slightly, and pull the locking cable from the switch housing – see Chapter 7B or 7C.

5 On all models, insert the spare key (see note at the beginning of this sub-Section) into the ignition switch and turn it to the 'on' position. In this position, a small hole which allows access to the lock cylinder retaining tang hole is exposed.

6 Insert a thin screwdriver or a length of 1.5 mm diameter welding rod (chamfered at the end) into the access hole until it is felt to contact the retaining tang (see illustration).

7 Hold the screwdriver/rod in position, then grasp the key and withdraw the lock cylinder and reader coil from the housing (see illustration).

⚠ **Warning: Do not attempt to operate the steering lock with the cylinder removed, otherwise irreparable damage to the mechanism will occur.**

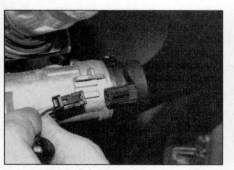

18.3 Disconnect the reader coil wiring plug

18.6 Insert a thin (1.5 mm) diameter wire into the hole (arrowed) . . .

Refitting

8 Fit the key to the new lock cylinder and turn it to the 'on' position.

9 Re-insert the thin screwdriver/welding rod into the access hole in the lock.

10 Slide the new lock cylinder into position, then pull out the screwdriver/welding rod, and push the cylinder into the housing until the retaining tang can be heard to engage with a click.

11 Pull lightly on the key to check that the cylinder is securely held in position.

12 Reconnect the wiring to the sensor ring, checking that the connector is pushed fully home.

13 On automatic or Multitronic models, reconnect the locking cable as described in Chapter 7B or 7C.

14 Refit the steering column combination switches as described in Chapter 12.

15 Refit the steering wheel as described in Section 16.

16 If a new lock cylinder/reader coil has been fitted, have the coil specifications reprogrammed – see the note at the start of this Section.

Ignition switch

Note: *The lock cylinder does not have to be removed to complete this procedure.*

Removal

17 Remove the steering wheel, as described in Section 16.

18 Remove the steering column combination switch module as described in Chapter 12.

19 Unplug the multiway wiring connector from the rear of the ignition switch (**see illustration**).

20 Carefully scoop the locking compound from the two bolt holes on the left-hand side of the lock cylinder housing, to expose the heads of the ignition switch securing screws.

21 Undo the ignition switch securing screws and withdraw the switch from the lock cylinder housing (**see illustration**).

Refitting

22 Ensure the switch is correctly positioned (rotated as far anti-clockwise as possible) then refit it to the rear of the lock cylinder housing. Ensure the switch is correctly engaged with the lock and slide it fully into position.

23 Clean the threads of the retaining screws then apply a drop of locking compound to each screw. Refit the screws to the lock assembly and tighten them securely. Apply a drop of locking compound to the heads of both screws after they have been tightened.

24 Refit the wiring connector to the rear of the ignition switch.

25 Refit the steering column combination switch module as described in Chapter 12.

26 Refit the steering wheel as described in Section 16.

Steering lock

Removal

27 Remove the steering column as described in Section 17.

18.7 . . . then pull the lock cylinder from place

28 Clamp the steering column in a bench vice, then use a chisel to remove the 2 shear bolts securing the lock to the column (**see illustration**).

Refitting

29 Position the lock housing, and insert the new shear bolts. Tighten the bolts until their heads shear off.

30 The remainder of refitting is a reversal of removal.

19 Steering gear assembly – removal, overhaul and refitting

Removal

1 Remove the battery as described in Chapter 5A.

2 Set the wheels in the straight-ahead position, then remove the ignition key and engage the steering lock.

3 Remove the driver's side storage compartment as described in Chapter 11.

4 In order to prevent the top and bottom sections of the steering column extending or compressing too far, it is now necessary to insert a cable tie, or length of wire, through the hole in the lower section and secure it to the spring on the upper section (**see illustrations 17.9a and 17.9b**).

Caution: Do not allow the upper and lower sections of the steering column to become separated whilst the steering column is

18.21 Undo the retaining screws (arrowed)

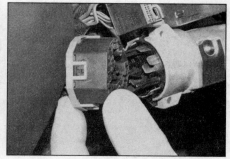

18.19 Disconnect the ignition switch wiring plug

detached from the steering gear, as this can cause the internal components to become detached and misaligned.

5 Unscrew the pinch-bolt securing the universal joint at the base of the steering column to the steering gear (**see illustration 17.10**).

6 Pull the steering column universal joint off the steering gear pinion and move it to one side.

7 Remove the bulkhead seal from around the steering gear pinion.

8 Using brake hose clamps, clamp both the supply and return hoses near the power steering fluid reservoir. This will minimise fluid loss during subsequent operations.

9 Firmly apply the handbrake then jack up the from of the vehicle and support it on axle stands. Remove both front roadwheels. Whilst the wheels are removed secure the discs to the hubs with a least one roadwheel bolt each.

10 Remove the right-hand hub carrier assembly as described in Section 2, paragraphs 1 to 8.

11 Remove the left-hand track rod balljoint pinch-bolt and retaining bolt, and separate the balljoint from the hub carrier. Take care to avoid damaging the track rod bellows as you do this.

12 Unbolt the bottom of the right-hand suspension strut from the suspension lower arm as described in Section 3, but do not slacken or remove the strut upper mounting nuts.

13 Undo the plastic nut, prise out the clips

18.28 Use a chisel to remove the shear bolts (arrowed)

19.20a Right-hand mounting bolts: one accessible from below, and one above (arrowed)

19.20b On the left-hand side, one accessible once the battery has been removed (arrowed) . . .

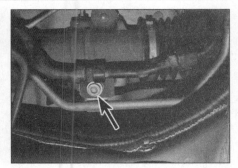

19.20c . . . and one from underneath (arrowed)

and remove the section of the inner wheel arch liner that shrouds the point where the track rod ends enters the engine compartment.

14 Unbolt and remove the heat shield from the front of the steering gear.

15 Make a note of the correct routing of all wiring and hoses around the steering gear to ensure they are correctly positioned on refitting.

16 Undo the bolt and detach the hose bracket from the steering gear.

17 Mark the unions to ensure that they are correctly positioned on reassembly, then unscrew the feed and return pipe union bolts from the steering gear assembly; be prepared for fluid spillage, and position a suitable container beneath the pipes whilst unscrewing the union bolts. Disconnect both pipes and recover the sealing rings; discard the rings – new ones must be used on refitting. Plug the pipe ends and steering gear orifices, to prevent fluid leakage and to keep dirt out of the hydraulic system.

18 Free the power steering pipes from the retaining clips on the underside of the steering gear housing and position them clear of the underside of the steering gear.

19 On models with air conditioning, disconnect the wiring connector in the plenum chamber.

20 Slacken and remove the bolts securing the steering gear in position. There are four bolts in total; two either side of the pinion housing at the right-hand side of the steering gear (one accessible from above the housing and one accessible from below), and two at the left-hand end of the steering gear (one accessible from above, and one from below). Remove the battery (see Chapter 5A) to access the bolt from above **(see illustrations)**.

21 With the aid of an assistant, free the steering gear pinion from the bulkhead then manoeuvre the steering gear out of position via the right-hand wheel arch aperture. Take great care not to damage any wiring/hoses or the rubber gaiter as the steering gear is removed.

22 With the steering gear removed, check the pinion housing gaiter for signs of damage or deterioration and renew if necessary.

Overhaul

23 Examine the steering gear assembly for signs of wear or damage, and check that the rack moves freely throughout the full length of its travel, with no signs of roughness or excessive free play between the steering gear pinion and rack. Inspect all the steering gear fluid unions for signs of leakage, and check that all union bolts are securely tightened.

24 It is possible to overhaul the steering gear assembly housing components, but this task should be entrusted to an Audi dealer or specialist. The only components which can be renewed easily by the home mechanic are the steering gear gaiters (rubber bellows) and the track rod balljoints. Track rod balljoint and steering gear rubber bellows renewal procedures are covered elsewhere in this Chapter.

Refitting

25 Before the steering gear can be refitted, it must be centred as follows. Remove the socket-head bolt from the tapped inspection hole at the side of the pinion gear housing. Move the right-hand track rod by hand until the alignment hole – drilled into the surface of the steering rack – is visible through the inspection hole. Obtain a bolt of the same thread as that removed from the inspection hole and file the end of it to a conical point. Thread the bolt into the inspection hole and turn it until the pointed end engages with the drilled alignment hole in the steering rack; check that the rack is immobilised by trying to move the right-hand track rod end. The steering gear is now locked in the centre position **(see illustration)**.

26 With the aid of an assistant, carefully manoeuvre the steering gear into position, ensuring that the wiring/hoses are all correctly routed around the steering gear.

27 Fit the two steering gear securing bolts that are accessed from above, but only hand-tighten them at this stage.

28 Position the rigid hydraulic pipes in their retaining clips on the underside of the steering gear, then reconnect the feed and return pipes to the steering gear, positioning a new sealing ring on each side of each end fitting, then screw in the union bolts. Ensure the pipes are correctly routed, then tighten both union bolts to their respective specified torque settings. Tighten the hydraulic pipe retaining clip bolt(s) securely. Refit the hose bracket to the steering gear, then remove the clamps from the fluid reservoir hoses.

29 Fit the remaining steering gear securing bolt from below and tighten it to its specified torque. On completion, tighten the two upper securing bolts to their specified torque settings.

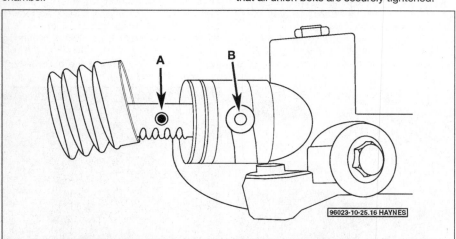

96023-10-25.16 HAYNES

19.25 Align the hole in the rack (A) with the inspection hole (B) and thread the specially fabricated bolt into the hole

30 Working inside the vehicle, from the driver's footwell, press the bulkhead seal over the steering gear pinion and into position on the bulkhead.

31 Reconnect the universal joint at the base of the steering column to the steering gear pinion. Insert the pinch-bolt and tighten it to the specified torque.

32 Remove the wire that was used to secure the upper and lower sections of the steering column together.

33 Remove the home-made locking bolt from the inspection hole on the side of the steering gear, then refit the original socket-head bolt to seal the inspection hole and tighten to the specified torque.

34 Refit the trim panels to the underside of the driver's side of the facia.

35 Refit the plastic cover to the inside of the wheel arch, over the track rod end, and secure it with the press stud clips and the plastic nut(s). Reconnect the left-hand track rod balljoint and tighten the bolts to the specified torque.

36 Refit the bottom of the right-hand suspension strut to the suspension lower arm as described in Section 3. Tighten the securing nut and bolt to the specified torque.

37 Refit the right-hand hub carrier assembly as described in Section 2. Take care to avoid damaging the track rod bellows as you do this.

38 Refit the heat shield panel to the front of the steering gear.

39 On models with air conditioning, reconnect the wiring plug in the plenum chamber.

40 Refit the roadwheels then lower the vehicle to the ground and tighten the wheel bolts to the specified torque.

41 Tighten the driveshaft bolt to the specified torque, as described in Chapter 8, then refit the hub cap/wheel trim.

42 Refit the battery with reference to Chapter 5A. Refit the cover panel over the plenum chamber.

43 Top-up the power steering fluid and bleed the hydraulic system with reference to Section 21.

44 On completion, have the front wheel alignment checked by an Audi dealer or specialist.

20 Steering gear rubber bellows – renewal

1 The steering gear bellows can be removed and refitted with the steering gear unit *in situ* or removed from the vehicle.

2 Measure the exposed amount of adjustment thread showing on the inboard side of the track rod end balljoint locknut. This will act as a guide to the adjustment position when refitting the balljoint to the rod. Loosen off the locknut, and detach the track rod end from the track rod as described in Section 23.

3 Unscrew and remove the locking nut from the track rod.

20.4a Prise/cut off the inner gaiter clip

4 Release the retaining clips and withdraw the bellows from the steering gear and track rod **(see illustrations)**.

5 Refit in the reverse order of removal. Smear the inner bore of the bellows with lubricant prior to fitting to ease its assembly. Renew the balljoint locknuts. Use new clips to retain the bellows and ensure that the end of the bellows locates correctly in the groove machined into the track rod, without twisting.

6 On completion, have the front wheel alignment checked and if necessary adjusted (see Section 26).

21 Power steering system – level checking and bleeding

Level checking

1 Position the vehicle on level ground with the front wheels straight-ahead and the engine stopped. The level check may be made with the hydraulic fluid cold or hot.

2 The power steering fluid reservoir is located on the left-hand side of the engine compartment. Slowly unscrew and remove the filler cap, which incorporates a fluid level dipstick **(see illustration)**.

3 Wipe clean the dipstick with a clean cloth, then screw it onto the reservoir and unscrew it again.

4 If the fluid is cold (ambient temperature about 20°C), the level should be close to the MAX mark. If the fluid is at operating

21.2 Power steering fluid reservoir cap

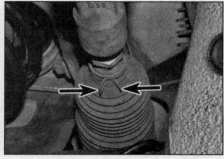

20.4b Use a pair of pliers to squeeze together the ends of the outer gaiter clip (arrowed)

temperature (above 80°C), the level should be 10 mm above the MAX mark **(see illustration)**.

5 Where topping-up is required, add the specified type of fluid as necessary. On completion refit and tighten the cap.

Bleeding

6 The bleeding procedure varies depending on the extent of the work carried out to the steering hydraulic system.

If the steering gear has been removed or renewed

7 Check and if necessary top-up with the specified fluid with reference to the previous sub-Section.

8 Jack up the front of the vehicle and support it on axle stands to remove the weight from the front wheels.

9 Start the engine and allow it to idle for 2 seconds, then switch it off. Wait 30 seconds, then check the fluid level and top-up if necessary.

10 Repeat the procedure in paragraph 9 until the fluid level remains constant.

11 With the engine switched off, turn the steering wheel from lock-to-lock 10 times, then check the fluid level and top-up if necessary.

12 Start the engine and allow it to idle, then turn the steering wheel from lock-to-lock 10 times, then switch off the engine.

13 Check the fluid level, and if necessary top-up.

14 Any remaining air in the system will dissipate after the vehicle has been driven 7 to 15 miles, so check the fluid level again after this distance.

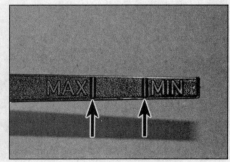

21.4 Power steering fluid dipstick maximum and minimum marks (arrowed)

22.7 Power steering pump supply and pressure pipes

If any other component has been removed or renewed

15 Check and if necessary top-up with the specified fluid with reference to the previous sub-Section.

16 Start the engine and allow it to idle for 2 seconds, then switch it off. Wait 30 seconds, then check the fluid level and top-up if necessary.

17 Repeat the procedure in paragraph 16, until the fluid level remains constant.

18 Start the engine and leave it running for 2 to 3 minutes, without turning the steering wheel.

19 Check the fluid level, and if necessary top-up.

20 Any remaining air in the system will dissipate after the vehicle has been driven 7 to 15 miles, so check the fluid level again after this distance.

22 Power steering pump – removal and refitting

Removal

1 Firmly apply the handbrake then jack up the front of the vehicle and support it on axle stands (see *Jacking and vehicle support*).

2 Undo the retaining fasteners and remove the undershield from beneath the engine.

3 Move the lock carrier at the front of the engine compartment to the Service position; refer to Chapter 11 for details.

4 Refer to the relevant part of Chapter 2 and remove the auxiliary drivebelt.

5 Using brake hose clamps, clamp both the supply and return hoses near the power steering fluid reservoir. This will minimise fluid loss during subsequent operations.

6 Wipe clean the area around the power steering pump fluid pipe unions and hose connections.

7 Unscrew the union bolt and disconnect fluid pressure pipe from the pump; be prepared for fluid spillage, and position a suitable container beneath the pipe whilst unscrewing the union bolt **(see illustration)**. Disconnect the pipe and recover the sealing rings; discard the rings new ones must be used on refitting. Plug the pipe end and steering pump orifice, to minimise fluid leakage and to keep dirt out of the hydraulic system.

8 Slacken the clip and disconnect the fluid supply hose from the rear of the power steering pump. Plug the end of the hose and cover the pump fluid port to prevent contamination.

9 Using a strap wrench to prevent the pulley from rotating, undo the retaining bolts and remove the power steering pump pulley (where applicable). Note that on some models, the pulley has access holes to removal of the mounting bolts, rendering removal of the pulley unnecessary.

10 Slacken and remove the pump mounting bolts and withdraw the pump from its bracket **(see illustrations)**.

11 If the power steering pump is faulty it must be renewed; it is a sealed unit and cannot be overhauled.

Refitting

12 If a new pump is to be fitted, it must be primed with fluid prior to fitting, to ensure adequate lubrication during its initial stages of operation. Failure to do this could cause noisy operation and may lead to early pump failure. To prime the pump, pour the specified grade of hydraulic fluid (see *Lubricants and fluids*) into the fluid supply port on the pump, and simultaneously rotate the pump pulley. When the fluid exits from the fluid delivery union, it is primed and ready for use.

13 Manoeuvre the pump into position, then refit its mounting bolts and tighten them to the specified torque. Refit the pump pulley.

14 Fit a new sealing ring to each side of the hydraulic fluid pressure pipe end fitting then reconnect the pipe to the pump and screw in the union bolt. Ensure the pipe is correctly routed then tighten the union bolt to the specified torque.

15 Reconnect the supply hose to the pump and secure it in position with the retaining clip. Remove the hose clamps used to minimise fluid loss.

16 Refit and tension the auxiliary drivebelt(s) as described in the relevant part of Chapter 2.

17 Refit the lock carrier crossmember to the front of the engine compartment, as described in Chapter 11.

18 Refit the engine compartment undershield, ensuring it is securely held by all its retaining screws and fasteners.

19 On completion, top-up the hydraulic fluid and bleed the system as described in Section 21.

23 Track rod balljoint – removal and refitting

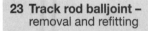

Removal

1 Apply the handbrake, then jack up the front of the vehicle and support it on axle stands (see *Jacking and vehicle support*). Remove the appropriate front roadwheel. Whilst the wheel is removed, secure the brake disc to the hub with a roadwheel bolt.

22.10a On some models, the pump mounting bolts are accessible through the pump pulley (arrowed) . . .

22.10b . . . and have a mounting bolt at the rear of the pump (arrowed)

2 Slacken and withdraw the retaining bolt, followed by the pinch-bolt and nut then push down on the track rod to detach it from the rear of the hub carrier **(see illustrations)**.

3 To give greater clearance, unscrew the plastic nuts and extract the press-fit clips then detach the plastic track rod cover from the wheel arch.

4 If the balljoint is to be re-used, use a straight-edge and a scriber, or similar, to mark its relationship to the track rod adjustment nut.

5 Hold the track rod adjustment flats, and unscrew the balljoint locknut by a quarter of a turn. Do not move the locknut from this position, as it will serve as a handy reference mark on refitting.

6 Counting the **exact** number of turns necessary to do so, unscrew the balljoint assembly from the track rod.

7 Carefully clean the balljoint and the threads. Renew the balljoint if its movement is sloppy or too stiff, if excessively worn, or if damaged in any way; carefully check the stud taper and threads. If the balljoint gaiter is damaged, the complete balljoint assembly must be renewed; it is not possible to obtain the gaiter separately.

Refitting

8 Screw the balljoint onto the track rod by the number of turns noted on removal. This should bring the balljoint locknut to within a quarter of a turn from the track rod, with the alignment marks that were made on removal (if applicable) lined up. Counterhold the track rod adjustment flats and tighten the locknut to the specified torque.

9 Locate the balljoint shank in the rear of the hub carrier, push the shank into the hub carrier as far as possible using hand pressure along, then fit the pinch-bolt with a new nut and tighten them to the specified torque. Ensure the cut-out in the shank aligns with the pinch bolt.

10 Refit the top retaining bolt and tighten it to the specified torque.

11 Refit the roadwheel, then lower the vehicle to the ground and tighten the roadwheel bolts to the specified torque.

12 Check and, if necessary, have the wheel alignment checked by an Audi dealer or suitabl-equipped specialist.

24 Track rod –
removal and refitting

Removal

1 Apply the handbrake, then jack up the front of the vehicle and support it on axle stands (see *Jacking and vehicle support*). Remove the appropriate front roadwheel. Whilst the wheel is removed, secure the brake disc to the hub with a roadwheel bolt.

2 Slacken and withdraw the adjustment bolt,

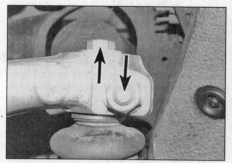

23.2a Undo the bolt at the top, then undo the pinch-bolt and nut (arrowed)

followed by the pinch-bolt and nut then push down on the track rod balljoint to detach it from the rear of the hub carrier (see previous Section).

3 Unscrew the plastic nuts and extract the press-fit clips, then detach the plastic track rod cover from the wheel arch.

4 Release the retaining clips and slide the rubber bellows towards the outboard end of the track rod; this will expose the large integral hex nut at the inner end of the track rod.

5 Hold the track rod hex nut securing using a large open-ended spanner, and unscrew the track rod from the end of the steering gear.

6 If the balljoint is to be re-used, use a straight-edge and a scriber, or similar, to mark its relationship to the track rod adjustment nut. Remove the balljoint from the track rod with reference to Section 23. **Note:** *If both track rods are to be removed, and the L and R markings on the track rod balljoints are no longer visible, mark the rods to avoid confusion on refitting.*

Refitting

7 Refitting is a reversal of removal noting the following points:
a) *Tighten the track rod to the specified torque, using a suitable 'crow's foot' adapter.*
b) *Ensure that the rubber bellows is securely refitted, using new clips where necessary.*
c) *On completion have the front wheel alignment checked and if necessary adjusted.*

25 Steering gear –
adjustment

1 With the vehicle stationary and the engine switched off, turn the steering wheel from side-to-side. If there is any undue slackness in the steering gear, resulting in noise or rattles the steering gear can be adjusted as follows.

2 Apply the handbrake and chock the rear wheels. Raise and support the front of the vehicle on axle stands (see *Jacking and vehicle support*).

3 Have an assistant turn the steering wheel back-and-forth by half a turn in each direction.

23.2b Note the cut-out in the balljoint shank for the pinch-bolt (arrowed)

Tighten the self-locking adjustment screw by approximately one eighth of a turn at a time until the rattling or looseness is eradicated **(see illustration)**.

4 Lower the vehicle to the ground, then road test the car. If the steering fails to self-centre after cornering, loosen the adjustment screw a fraction at a time until it does.

5 If, when the correct self-centring point is reached, there is still excessive play in the steering, retighten the adjuster nut a fraction to take up the play.

6 If the adjustment procedures listed above do not provide satisfactory steering adjustment, it is probable that the steering gear is worn beyond an acceptable level, and it must be removed and overhauled.

26 Wheel alignment
and steering angles –
general information

Definitions

1 A car's steering and suspension geometry is defined in four basic settings – all angles are expressed in degrees; the steering axis is defined as an imaginary line drawn through the axis of the suspension strut, extended where necessary to contact the ground **(see illustration overleaf)**.

2 Camber is the angle between each roadwheel and a vertical line drawn through its centre and tyre contact patch, when viewed from the front or rear of the car. Positive

25.3 Tighten the adjustment screw one eighth of a turn at a time (arrowed)

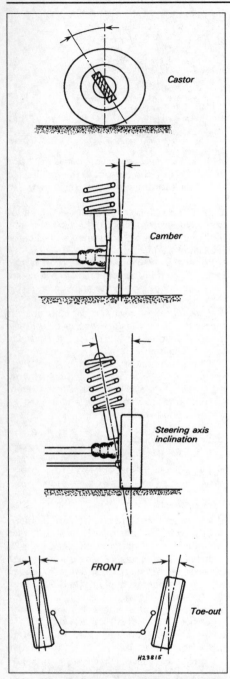

26.1 Wheel alignment and steering angle measurements

camber is when the roadwheels are tilted outwards from the vertical at the top; negative camber is when they are tilted inwards. The individual front wheel camber angles cannot be adjusted, but the overall camber angle between both front wheels can be balanced out by repositioning the suspension subframe. The rear wheel camber angle is also specified but no adjustment is possible.

3 Castor is the angle between the steering axis and a vertical line drawn through each roadwheel's centre and tyre contact patch, when viewed from the side of the car. Positive castor is when the steering axis is tilted so that it contacts the ground ahead of the vertical; negative castor is when it contacts the ground behind the vertical. The castor angle is not adjustable.

4 Toe is the difference, viewed from above, between lines drawn through the roadwheel centres and the car's centre-line. Toe-in is when the roadwheels point inwards, towards each other at the front, while toe-out is when they splay outwards from each other at the front.

5 The front wheel toe setting is adjusted by screwing the track rod adjusters in or out of its balljoints, to alter the effective length of the track rod assembly. The rear wheel alignment can be altered by repositioning the eccentric bolts at the top of the hub carrier, and the front mounting of the trapezium link.

Checking and adjustment

6 Due to the fact that Audi insist that the alignment of all four wheels is checked at the same time, the special measuring equipment necessary to check the wheel alignment and steering angles, and the skill required to use it properly, the checking and adjustment of these settings is best left to an Audi dealer or similar expert. Note that most tyre-fitting shops now possess sophisticated checking equipment.

Chapter 11
Bodywork and fittings

Contents

Section number

Bonnet and strut – removal, refitting and adjustment 7
Bonnet lock and release cable – removal and refitting 8
Boot lid – removal and refitting 12
Boot lid lock components – removal and refitting 13
Boot lid/tailgate support strut(s) – removal and refitting 15
Bumpers – removal and refitting 9
Central locking system – general 18
Centre console – removal and refitting. 28
Door handles and lock cylinder – removal and refitting 20
Door lock – removal and refitting 19
Door mirror components – removal and refitting 27
Door rattles – tracing and rectification 6
Door trim panel – removal and refitting 17
Door window glass, frame and regulator – removal and refitting. . . . 21
Doors – removal and refitting. 24
Facia, associated panels and crossmember – removal and refitting 29
General description 1
Glovebox – removal and refitting 30
Grab handles – removal and refitting 37

Section number

Interior mirror – removal and refitting. 31
Interior trim – removal and refitting 33
Hood – removal and refitting 22
Hood hydraulic unit – general information, removal and refitting. . . . 23
Lock carrier – removal, refitting and Service position 10
Maintenance – bodywork and underframe. 2
Maintenance – upholstery and carpets 3
Major body damage – repair 5
Minor body damage – repair 4
Seat belt tensioning mechanism – general information 34
Seat belts – general, removal and refitting. 35
Seats – removal and refitting 32
Sunroof – general 26
Sunvisors – removal and refitting. 36
Tailgate – removal and refitting. 14
Tailgate lock, cylinder and handle – removal and refitting 16
Wheel arch liners – removal and refitting. 11
Windscreen, rear window glass and rear side window glass –
  general information. 25

Degrees of difficulty

Easy, suitable for novice with little experience	**Fairly easy,** suitable for beginner with some experience	**Fairly difficult,** suitable for competent DIY mechanic	**Difficult,** suitable for experienced DIY mechanic	**Very difficult,** suitable for expert DIY or professional

Specifications

Torque wrench settings	Nm	lbf ft
Bonnet hinge bolts	23	17
Bonnet lock bolts	15	11
Boot lid (Saloon) mounting bolts	22	16
Door hinge bolts	32	24
Door lock screws	20	15
Door mirror bolt	12	9
Front bumper centre mounting bolts	26	19
Front bumper mounting tube-to-bodywork bolts	40	30
Hood compartment lid hinge bolts	21	15
Hood main bracket bolts	36	27
Rear bumper bar mounting bolts	18	13
Seat belt anchor bolts	55	41
Seat belt front stalk mounting bolt:		
Hexagon head bolt	24	18
Socket head bolt	34	25
Seat belt inertia reel bolt	55	41
Seat retaining bolts	50	37
Tailgate (Avant) mounting bolts/nuts	22	16
Window frame to door:		
M8	32	24
M6	10	7
Window motor to regulator	4	3

1 General description

Three body types are produced – the four-door Saloon, the five-door Avant and the two-door Cabriolet. The body is of all-steel construction, and incorporates calculated impact crumple zones at the front and rear, with a central safety cell passenger compartment.

During manufacture, the underbody is treated with underseal and, as a further anti-rust aid, some of the more exposed body panels are galvanised. The bumpers and wheel arch liners are plastic mouldings, for durability and strength.

2 Maintenance – bodywork and underframe

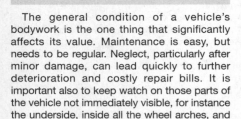

The general condition of a vehicle's bodywork is the one thing that significantly affects its value. Maintenance is easy, but needs to be regular. Neglect, particularly after minor damage, can lead quickly to further deterioration and costly repair bills. It is important also to keep watch on those parts of the vehicle not immediately visible, for instance the underside, inside all the wheel arches, and the lower part of the engine compartment.

The basic maintenance routine for the bodywork is washing – preferably with a lot of water, from a hose. This will remove all the loose solids which may have stuck to the vehicle. It is important to flush these off in such a way as to prevent grit from scratching the finish. The wheel arches and underframe need washing in the same way, to remove any accumulated mud which will retain moisture and tend to encourage rust. Paradoxically enough, the best time to clean the underframe and wheel arches is in wet weather, when the mud is thoroughly wet and soft. In very wet weather, the underframe is usually cleaned of large accumulations automatically, and this is a good time for inspection.

Periodically, except on vehicles with a wax-based underbody protective coating, it is a good idea to have the whole of the underframe of the vehicle steam-cleaned, engine compartment included, so that a thorough inspection can be carried out to see what minor repairs and renovations are necessary. Steam cleaning is available at many garages, and is necessary for the removal of the accumulation of oily grime, which sometimes is allowed to become thick in certain areas. If steam-cleaning facilities are not available, there are some excellent grease solvents available which can be brush-applied; the dirt can then be simply hosed off. Note that these methods should not be used on vehicles with wax-based underbody protective coating, or the coating will be removed. Such vehicles should be inspected annually, preferably just

before Winter, when the underbody should be washed down, and any damage to the wax coating repaired. Ideally, a completely fresh coat should be applied. It would also be worth considering the use of wax-based protection for injection into door panels, sills, box sections, etc, as an additional safeguard against rust damage, where such protection is not provided by the vehicle manufacturer.

After washing paintwork, wipe off with a chamois leather to give an unspotted clear finish. A coat of clear protective wax polish will give added protection against chemical pollutants in the air. If the paintwork sheen has dulled or oxidised, use a cleaner/polisher combination to restore the brilliance of the shine. This requires a little effort, but such dulling is usually caused because regular washing has been neglected. Care needs to be taken with metallic paintwork, as special non-abrasive cleaner/polisher is required to avoid damage to the finish. Always check that the door and ventilator opening drain holes and pipes are completely clear, so that water can be drained out. Brightwork should be treated in the same way as paintwork. Windscreens and windows can be kept clear of the smeary film which often appears, by proprietary glass cleaner. Never use any form of wax or other body or chromium polish on glass.

3 Maintenance – upholstery and carpets

Mats and carpets should be brushed or vacuum-cleaned regularly, to keep them free of grit. If they are badly stained, remove them from the vehicle for scrubbing or sponging, and make quite sure they are dry before refitting. Seats and interior trim panels can be kept clean by wiping with a damp cloth. If they do become stained (which can be more apparent on light-coloured upholstery), use a little liquid detergent and a soft nail brush to scour the grime out of the grain of the material. Do not forget to keep the headlining clean in the same way as the upholstery. When using liquid cleaners inside the vehicle, do not over-wet the surfaces being cleaned. Excessive damp could get into the seams and padded interior, causing stains, offensive odours or even rot. If the inside of the vehicle gets wet accidentally, it is worthwhile taking some trouble to dry it out properly, particularly where carpets are involved. *Do not leave oil or electric heaters inside the vehicle for this purpose.*

4 Minor body damage – repair

Minor scratches

If the scratch is very superficial, and does not penetrate to the metal of the bodywork,

repair is very simple. Lightly rub the area of the scratch with a paintwork renovator or a very fine cutting paste to remove loose paint from the scratch, and to clear the surrounding bodywork of wax polish. Rinse the area with clean water.

Apply touch-up paint to the scratch using a fine paint brush; continue to apply fine layers of paint until the surface of the paint in the scratch is level with the surrounding paintwork. Allow the new paint at least two weeks to harden, then blend it into the surrounding paintwork by rubbing the scratch area with a paintwork renovator or a very fine cutting paste. Finally, apply wax polish.

Where the scratch has penetrated right through to the metal of the bodywork, causing the metal to rust, a different repair technique is required. Remove any loose rust from the bottom of the scratch with a penknife, then apply rust-inhibiting paint to prevent the formation of rust in the future. Using a rubber or nylon applicator, fill the scratch with bodystopper paste. If required, this paste can be mixed with cellulose thinners to provide a very thin paste which is ideal for filling narrow scratches. Before the stopper-paste in the scratch hardens, wrap a piece of smooth cotton rag around the top of a finger. Dip the finger in cellulose thinners, and quickly sweep it across the surface of the stopper-paste in the scratch; this will ensure that the surface of the stopper-paste is slightly hollowed. The scratch can now be painted over as described earlier in this Section.

Dents

When deep denting of the vehicle's bodywork has taken place, the first task is to pull the dent out, until the affected bodywork almost attains its original shape. There is little point in trying to restore the original shape completely, as the metal in the damaged area will have stretched on impact, and cannot be reshaped fully to its original contour. It is better to bring the level of the dent up to a point which is about 3 mm below the level of the surrounding bodywork. In cases where the dent is very shallow anyway, it is not worth trying to pull it out at all. If the underside of the dent is accessible, it can be hammered out gently from behind, using a mallet with a wooden or plastic head. Whilst doing this, hold a suitable block of wood firmly against the outside of the panel, to absorb the impact from the hammer blows and thus prevent a large area of the bodywork from being 'belled-out'.

Should the dent be in a section of the bodywork which has a double skin, or some other factor making it inaccessible from behind, a different technique is called for. Drill several small holes through the metal inside the area – particularly in the deeper section. Then screw long self-tapping screws into the holes, just sufficiently for them to gain a good purchase in the metal. Now the dent can be pulled out by pulling on the protruding heads of the screws with a pair of pliers.

The next stage of the repair is the removal of the paint from the damaged area, and from an inch or so of the surrounding 'sound' bodywork. This is accomplished most easily by using a wire brush or abrasive pad on a power drill, although it can be done just as effectively by hand, using sheets of abrasive paper. To complete the preparation for filling, score the surface of the bare metal with a screwdriver or the tang of a file, or alternatively, drill small holes in the affected area. This will provide a good 'key' for the filler paste.

To complete the repair, see the Section on filling and respraying.

Rust holes or gashes

Remove all paint from the affected area, and from an inch or so of the surrounding 'sound' bodywork, using an abrasive pad or a wire brush on a power drill. If these are not available, a few sheets of abrasive paper will do the job most effectively. With the paint removed, you will be able to judge the severity of the corrosion, and therefore decide whether to renew the whole panel (if this is possible) or to repair the affected area. New body panels are not as expensive as most people think, and it is often quicker and more satisfactory to fit a new panel than to attempt to repair large areas of corrosion.

Remove all fittings from the affected area, except those which will act as a guide to the original shape of the damaged bodywork (eg headlight shells etc). Then, using tin snips or a hacksaw blade, remove all loose metal and any other metal badly affected by corrosion. Hammer the edges of the hole inwards, to create a slight depression for the filler paste.

Wire-brush the affected area to remove the powdery rust from the surface of the remaining metal. Paint the affected area with rust-inhibiting paint; if the back of the rusted area is accessible, treat this also.

Before filling can take place, it will be necessary to block the hole in some way. This can be achieved with aluminium or plastic mesh, or aluminium tape.

Aluminium or plastic mesh, or glass-fibre matting, is probably the best material to use for a large hole. Cut a piece to the approximate size and shape of the hole to be filled, then position it in the hole so that its edges are below the level of the surrounding bodywork. It can be retained in position by several blobs of filler paste around its periphery.

Aluminium tape should be used for small or very narrow holes. Pull a piece off the roll, trim it to the approximate size and shape required, then pull off the backing paper (if used) and stick the tape over the hole; it can be overlapped if the thickness of one piece is insufficient. Burnish down the edges of the tape with the handle of a screwdriver or similar, to ensure that the tape is securely attached to the metal underneath.

Filling and respraying

Before using this Section, see the Sections on dent, deep scratch, rust holes and gash repairs.

Many types of bodyfiller are available, but generally speaking, those proprietary kits which contain a tin of filler paste and a tube of resin hardener are best for this type of repair which can be used directly from the tube. A wide, flexible plastic or nylon applicator will be found invaluable for imparting a smooth and well-contoured finish to the surface of the filler.

Mix up a little filler on a clean piece of card or board – measure the hardener carefully (follow the maker's instructions on the pack), otherwise the filler will set too rapidly or too slowly. Using the applicator, apply the filler paste to the prepared area; draw the applicator across the surface of the filler to achieve the correct contour and to level the surface. When a contour that approximates to the correct one is achieved, stop working the paste – if you carry on too long, the paste will become sticky and begin to 'pick-up' on the applicator. Continue to add thin layers of filler paste at 20-minute intervals, until the level of the filler is just proud of the surrounding bodywork.

Once the filler has hardened, the excess can be removed using a metal plane or file. From then on, progressively-finer grades of abrasive paper should be used, starting with a 40-grade production paper, and finishing with a 400-grade wet-and-dry paper. Always wrap the abrasive paper around a flat rubber, cork, or wooden block – otherwise the surface of the filler will not be completely flat. During the smoothing of the filler surface, the wet-and-dry paper should be periodically rinsed in water. This will ensure that a very smooth finish is imparted to the filler at the final stage.

At this stage, the 'dent' should be surrounded by a ring of bare metal, which in turn should be encircled by the finely 'feathered' edge of the good paintwork. Rinse the repair area with clean water, until all the dust produced by the rubbing-down operation has gone.

Spray the whole area with a light coat of primer – this will show up any imperfections in the surface of the filler. Repair these imperfections with fresh filler paste or bodystopper, and again smooth the surface with abrasive paper. If bodystopper is used, it can be mixed with cellulose thinners, to form a thin paste which is ideal for filling small holes. Repeat this spray-and-repair procedure until you are satisfied that the surface of the filler, and the feathered edge of the paintwork, are perfect. Clean the repair area with clean water, and allow to dry fully.

The repair area is now ready for final spraying. Paint spraying must be carried out in a warm, dry, windless and dust-free atmosphere. This condition can be created artificially if you have access to a large indoor working area, but if you are forced to work in the open, you will have to pick your day very carefully. If you are working indoors, dousing the floor in the work area with water will help to settle the dust which would otherwise be in the atmosphere. If the repair area is confined to one body panel, mask off the surrounding panels; this will help to minimise the effects of a slight mismatch in paint colours. Bodywork fittings (e.g. chrome strips, door handles etc) will also need to be masked off. Use genuine masking tape, and several thickness of newspaper, for the masking operations.

Before starting to spray, agitate the aerosol can thoroughly, then spray a test area (an old tin, or similar) until the technique is mastered. Cover the repair area with a thick coat of primer; the thickness should be built up using several thin layers of paint, rather than one thick one. Using 400 grade wet-and-dry paper, rub down the surface of the primer until it is smooth. While doing this, the work area should be thoroughly doused with water, and the wet-and-dry paper periodically rinsed in water. Allow to dry before spraying on more paint.

Spray on the top coat, again building up the thickness by using several thin layers of paint. Start spraying at the top of the repair area, and then, using a side-to-side motion, work until the whole repair area and about 2 inches of the surrounding original paintwork is covered. Remove all masking material 10 to 15 minutes after spraying on the final coat of paint.

Allow the new paint at least two weeks to harden, then, using a paintwork renovator or a very fine cutting paste, blend the edges of the paint into the existing paintwork. Finally, apply wax polish.

Plastic components

With the use of more and more plastic body components by the vehicle manufacturers (e.g. bumpers, spoilers, and in some cases major body panels), rectification of more serious damage to such items has become a matter of either entrusting repair work to a specialist in this field, or renewing complete components. Repair of such damage by the DIY owner is not feasible, owing to the cost of the equipment and materials required for effecting such repairs. The basic technique involves making a groove along the line of the crack in the plastic, using a rotary burr in a power drill. The damaged part is then welded back together, using a hot air gun to heat up and fuse a plastic filler rod into the groove. Any excess plastic is then removed, and the area rubbed down to a smooth finish. It is important that a filler rod of the correct plastic is used, as body components can be made of a variety of different types (e.g. polycarbonate, ABS, polypropylene).

Damage of a less serious nature (abrasions, minor cracks etc) can be repaired by the DIY owner using a two-part epoxy filler repair material which can be used directly from the tube. Once mixed in equal proportions, this is used in similar fashion to the bodywork filler used on metal panels. The filler is usually cured in twenty to thirty minutes, ready for sanding and painting.

If the owner is renewing a complete component himself, or if he has repaired it with epoxy filler, he will be left with the problem of finding a suitable paint for finishing which is compatible with the type of plastic used. At one time, the use of a universal paint was not possible, owing to the complex range of plastics met with in body component applications. Standard paints, generally speaking, will not bond to plastic or rubber satisfactorily, but professional matched paints, to match any plastic or rubber finish, can be obtained from some dealers. However, it is now possible to obtain a plastic body parts finishing kit which consists of a pre-primer treatment, a primer and coloured top coat. Full instructions are normally supplied with a kit, but basically the method of use is to first apply the pre-primer to the component concerned, and allow it to dry for up to 30 minutes. Then the primer is applied, and left to dry for about an hour before finally applying the special-coloured top coat. The result is a correctly coloured component, where the paint will flex with the plastic or rubber, a property that standard paint does not normally possess.

5 Major body damage – repair

Where serious damage has occurred, or large areas need renewal due to neglect, it means that complete new panels will need welding-in, and this is best left to professionals. If the damage is due to impact, it will also be necessary to check completely the alignment of the bodyshell, and this can only be carried out accurately by a Audi dealer using special jigs. If the body is left misaligned, it is primarily dangerous, as the car will not handle properly, and secondly, uneven stresses will be imposed on the steering, suspension and possibly transmission, causing abnormal wear, or complete failure, particularly to such items as the tyres.

6 Door rattles – tracing and rectification

1 Check first that the door is not loose at the hinges, and that the latch is holding the door firmly in position. Check also that the door lines up with the aperture in the body. If the door is out of alignment, adjust it with reference to Section 24.
2 If the latch is holding the door in the correct position, but the latch still rattles, the lock mechanism is worn and should be renewed.
3 Other rattles from the door could be caused by wear in the window operating mechanism, interior lock mechanism, loose glass channels or loose wiring.

7 Bonnet and strut – removal, refitting and adjustment

Bonnet
Removal

1 Fully open the bonnet, then place some

7.2a Prise the washer jet grommet from the bonnet underside . . .

7.5 Undo the bonnet retaining nuts each side

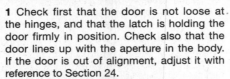

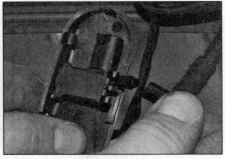

7.2b . . . and disconnect the washer tubes

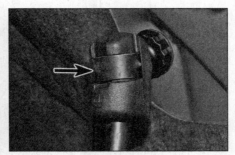

7.10 Lift the retaining springs (arrowed) and pull the end of the strut from the pivot pin

cardboard or rags beneath the corners by the hinges to protect the bodywork.
2 Prise the grommets from the bonnet under-side, and disconnect the windscreen washer tubes from the jets. Unplug the heated jet wiring connectors (where applicable) and pull hose/loom from the bonnet (see illustrations).
3 Prop the bonnet open using two stout lengths of wood, one positioned at each corner. Alternatively, enlist the help of an assistant to support the bonnet.
4 Disconnect the gas strut from the bonnet, with reference to the information given later in this Section.
5 Mark the location of the hinges with a pencil, then slacken the four hinge-to-bonnet retaining nuts (two each side) (see illustration).
6 Support the bonnet as the securing bolts are unscrewed, then withdraw the bonnet from the car.

Refitting and adjustment

7 Refitting is a reversal of removal. Ensure that the hinges are adjusted to their original positions. Close the bonnet very carefully initially; misalignment may cause the edges of the bonnet to damage the bodywork. If necessary, adjust the hinges to their original positions and check that the bonnet is level with the surrounding bodywork. If necessary, adjust the height of the bonnet front edge by screwing the rubber buffers in or out.
8 Check that the bonnet lock operates in a satisfactory manner. In particular, check that the safety catch holds the bonnet after the bonnet release cable has been pulled.

Strut
Removal

9 Prop the bonnet open using two stout lengths of wood, one positioned at each corner. Alternatively, enlist the help of an assistant to support the bonnet.
10 Slightly lift the retaining springs in the mountings at each end of the strut, using a suitable screwdriver (see illustration).
11 Pull the strut mounting from the pivot pin.
Refitting
12 Refitting is a reversal of removal.

8 Bonnet lock and release cable – removal and refitting

Bonnet lock
Removal

1 Open the bonnet and locate the bonnet lock mechanism, mounted underneath the bonnet slam panel at the front of the engine compartment. Disconnect the cable from the lock mechanism as described in later in this Section.
2 Using a felt-tip pen or paint, make alignment marks around the bonnet lock to aid refitting.

3 Slacken and withdraw the 4 securing bolts and move the lock mechanism away from the slam panel **(see illustrations)**. Disconnect the wiring plug as the assembly is withdrawn.

Refitting

4 Position the lock mechanism on the slam panel, aligning the previously-made marks, and tighten the retaining bolts to the specified torque.

5 Reconnect the lock wiring plug.

6 Reconnect the cable as described in this Section. Check the action of the release cable/lock before closing the bonnet.

Cable

Removal

7 Jack up the front of the vehicle, and support it securely on axle stands (see *Jacking and vehicle support*).

8 Remove the right-hand front roadwheel, then release the fasteners and remove the wheel arch liner.

9 Remove the driver's side storage compartment as described in Chapter 11.

10 Undo the bolt and detach the release handle, then disconnect the cable from the handle **(see illustration)**.

11 Release the retaining clips, release the outer cable from the bracket, then prise out the end fitting from the lock and disconnect the inner cable **(see illustration)**.

12 Free the release cable from all its retaining clips in the engine compartment and wheel arch.

13 Attach a suitable length of strong cord to the end of the release cable at the release handle end, then carefully draw the cable through into the engine compartment.

14 Undo the cord from the cable, and leave the cord ends exposed in the engine compartment and footwell.

Refitting

15 Refit in the reverse order of removal. Tie the inner end of the cable to the exposed cord in the engine compartment, carefully pull the cable through to the release handle, then untie the cord.

16 When positioning the cable in the engine compartment and wheel arch, ensure that it is re-routed correctly to avoid kinks, sharp bends and chafing. Check for satisfactory operation

8.3a The bonnet lock is secured by 2 bolts at front (arrowed) . . .

8.10 Bonnet release handle bolt (arrowed)

of the cable and the lock before closing the bonnet. Ensure that the bonnet locks properly when closed, and also that the safety catch operates correctly when the bonnet release cable is actuated.

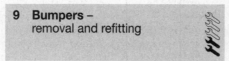

9 Bumpers – removal and refitting

Front bumper

Removal

1 Jack up the front of the vehicle and support it securely on axle stands (see *Jacking and vehicle support*). Remove the front roadwheels.

2 Depress the retaining clips, and prise out the intake grilles surrounding the front foglights **(see illustration)**.

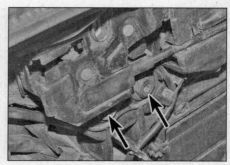

8.3b . . . and two bolts at the rear (arrowed)

8.11 Depress the retaining clip and slide the release cable end fitting from the catch assembly

3 Rotate the fasteners 90° and detach the front edge of the engine undershield from the bumper.

4 Undo the fasteners and fold back the front section of the wheel arch liners.

5 Undo the 3 nuts and one Torx screw each side securing the bumper outer edges to the front wings **(see illustrations)**.

6 Slacken the Allen screw each side accessible through the foglight apertures **(see illustration)**.

7 With the help of an assistant, pull the ends of the front bumper outwards from the guides on each side, and withdraw it from the front of the car.

8 Disconnect the wiring from the foglights as the bumper is withdrawn.

Refitting

9 Refitting is a reversal of removal. On completion, check for satisfactory operation of the accessory components as applicable.

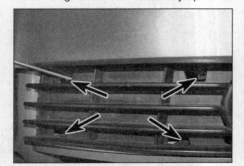

9.2 Release the retaining clips (arrowed) and pull out the foglight grille surround

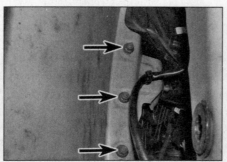

9.5a Undo the bumper retaining nuts (arrowed) . . .

9.5b . . . and the single screw securing the bumper (arrowed)

9.6 Slacken the bumper bolt in the foglight apertures (arrowed)

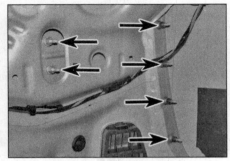

9.11a Bumper retaining nuts (arrowed) – Saloon models

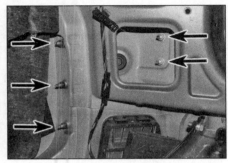

9.11b Bumper retaining nuts (arrowed) – Avant models

9.12 Retaining screws on the underside of the bumper (arrowed)

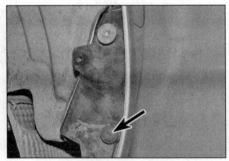

9.14 Undo the Torx bolt (arrowed) securing the front edge of the rear bumper

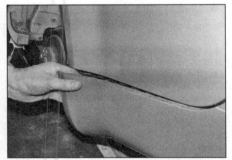

9.15 Pull the ends of the bumper from the guides

Rear bumper

Removal

10 Remove the luggage compartment side trims as described in Section 33, then disconnect the parking sensors wiring plugs at the control unit (where fitted).

11 Working inside the luggage compartment, undo the nuts each side **(see illustrations)**. Note that on Avant models, undo the bolts/nuts and move the speaker/amplifier/resonator assembly (where fitted) to one side to access the driver's side nuts.

12 From under the bumper, undo the two central securing screws **(see illustration)**.

13 Undo the fasteners and pull back the wheel arch liners where they contact the edges of the bumper.

14 Undo the bolt each side securing the bumper edge **(see illustration)**.

15 With the help of an assistant, release the

ends of the rear bumper from the guides on each side, and withdraw it from the rear of the car **(see illustration)**.

16 If required, the bumper bar can be removed by unscrewing the mounting bolts **(see illustration)**.

Refitting

17 Refit in the reverse order of removal. Loosely fit all retaining bolts and screws before fully tightening them. Tighten the bumper bar retaining bolts to the specified torque.

10 Lock carrier – removal, refitting and Service position

General information

1 The lock carrier is the name given to the section of bodywork that is mounted across the front of the engine compartment. A number of major components, including the bonnet lock mechanism, front bumper, radiator, automatic transmission fluid cooler and front light clusters are mounted on the lock carrier. The construction of the Audi A4 bodywork is such that the lock carrier and its associated components can be removed without being extensively dismantled. In addition, the lock carrier can be moved forward several centimetres to a 'service' position without having to disconnect the various hoses, pipes and wiring harnesses that serve the components mounted on it. In this position, access to components at the front of the engine compartment is greatly improved.

Removal

2 Disconnect the battery negative lead (see Chapter 5A). **Note:** *If the vehicle has a security-coded radio, check that you have a copy of the code number before disconnecting the battery. Refer to your Audi dealer if in doubt.*

3 Refer to Section 9 and remove the front bumper.

4 Undo the screws and remove the engine undershield **(see illustrations)**.

5 With reference to Section 8, disconnect the bonnet release cable from the bonnet lock mechanism.

6 Remove the securing screw(s) and detach the air inlet grille and ducting from the lock carrier **(see illustration 10.20)**. Where applicable, loosen the clips and disconnect the air pipes from the intercooler.

7 Disconnect the wiring plugs from the rear of the headlight units, and the 2 connectors behind the left-hand headlight **(see illustration)**.

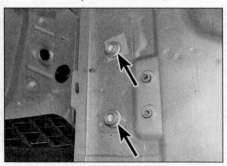

9.16 The bumper bar is retained by 2 bolts (arrowed) each side

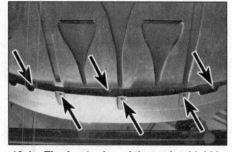

10.4a The front edge of the undershield is secured by 3 screws to the front bumper, and 3 screws to the lock carrier (arrowed)

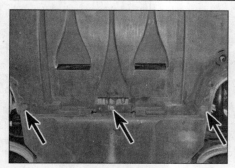

10.4b Engine undershield-to-transmission undershield fasteners (arrowed)

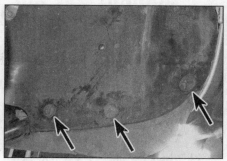

10.4c Engine undershield-to-wheel arch liner fasteners (arrowed)

10.7 Disconnect the wiring plugs behind the left-hand headlight

10.10 The rubber shroud each side is secured by a single screw (arrowed)

10.11a Release the hydraulic fluid hose clips (arrowed)

10.11b Hydraulic fluid cooler retaining bolts (arrowed)

Release the looms from their retaining clips.

8 Disconnect the wiring from the crash sensors, either side of the radiator, and release the wiring harness from its retaining clips.

9 Drain the coolant as described in Chapter 1A or 1B, then disconnect the coolant hoses from the radiator as described in Chapter 3.

10 Undo the retaining screws and remove the rubber shrouds either side of the condenser (see illustration).

11 Use pipe clamps to minimise fluid loss, then release the clips and disconnect the hydraulic fluid cooler from the rubber hoses – be prepared for fluid spillage. Unbolt the hydraulic fluid cooler from the lock carrier and radiator (see illustrations).

12 The air conditioning condenser must now be removed from the lock carrier and secured to a suitable point at the front of the engine compartment using cable ties or wire. To release the condenser, disconnect the pressure switch wiring plug, then undo the 4 Torx screws and detach the condenser from the lock carrier (see illustrations). Lower the condenser from position.

⚠ **Warning: Do not disconnect the refrigerant pipes from the condenser (refer to the precautions in Chapter 3 regarding the dangers of air conditioning system refrigerant).**
Caution: Do not allow the condenser to hang by its refrigerant pipes, as the strain may cause them to fracture.

13 Release the ends of the lock carrier rubber sealing strip from each front wing; there is no need to remove the strip from the lock carrier completely.

14 Unscrew and remove the bolts securing the lock carrier to the top of the front wing on each side of the vehicle (see illustration).

15 Unscrew and remove the bolt beneath each headlight at the side (see illustration).

16 Enlist the help of an assistant to support

10.12a Disconnect the pressure switch wiring plug . . .

10.14 Remove the 2 screws each side (arrowed)

the lock carrier during this final stage. Unscrew and remove the front impact absorber Torx bolts (three on the right-hand side, three on the left-hand side) then withdraw the lock carrier from the front of the vehicle (see illustration 10.24).

10.12b . . . then remove the condenser bolts (arrowed)

10.15 Remove the bolt under each headlight (arrowed)

10.21 Undo the screws (arrowed) securing the air intake ducting to the lock carrier

Refitting

17 Refit in the reverse order of removal. Check the operation of the front lights, and the bonnet lock and safety catch, on completion. Refill and bleed the cooling system as described in Chapter 1A or 1B, and have the headlights checked for correct beam alignment.

Service position

Note: *To carry out this procedure, it will necessary to fabricate two service tools, using two 8 mm diameter 300 mm lengths of threaded rod and a selection of hex nuts.*

18 Disconnect the battery negative lead (see Chapter 5A). Note: *If the vehicle has a security-coded radio, check that you have a copy of the code number before disconnecting the battery. Refer to your Audi dealer if in doubt.*

19 Refer to Section 9 and remove the front bumper.

11.3 The bolt (arrowed) secures the fuel filler neck as well as the wheel arch liner

12.3a Undo the screw in the handle recess . . .

10.24 We used a length of 8 mm threaded rod, with a tube slid over it (arrowed) to allow the lock carrier to slide forward

20 Unclip and remove the plastic cover each side of the engine compartment (where fitted).

21 Remove the securing screw(s) and detach the air inlet grille/ducting from the lock carrier (see illustration).

22 Unscrew and remove the screws securing the lock carrier to the top of the front wing on each side of the vehicle (see illustration 10.14). Peel off the rubber seal at the top of the lock carrier.

23 Unscrew and remove bolt beneath each headlight at the side (see illustration 10.15).

24 Insert a length of 8 mm threaded rod into the threaded hole each side/above the impact absorbers (see illustration). At the other end of the rods position a locknut and washer to limit the forward movement of the lock carrier.

25 Undo the 3 Torx bolts each side securing the impact absorbers (see illustration).

26 With the help of an assistant, carefully draw the lock carrier forwards until the rear

12.2 Undo the screw, then release the warning triangle holder retaining clips (arrowed)

12.3b . . . remove the latch cover . . .

10.25 Impact absorber Torx bolts (arrowed)

lock carrier-to-wing hole aligns with the front hole on the wing. Refit a bolt to secure the lock carrier in this position.

27 The lock carrier can be refitted by following the removal procedure in reverse. Ensure that all fixings are tightened to the correct torque wrench setting, where specified. On completion, have the headlights checked for correct beam alignment.

11 Wheel arch liners – removal and refitting

Removal

1 Loosen the relevant wheel bolts, then raise the front or rear of the car and support on axle stands (see *Jacking and vehicle support*). Remove the relevant roadwheel.

2 The liner is secured by quick-release screws and normal screws. The quick-release screws are removed by twisting them 90° anti-clockwise.

3 Undo and remove the liner securing screws. Note the right-hand rear liner is also retained by a hexagon-headed bolt which also secures the filler neck to the body (see illustration).

4 Lower the liner out of position, and manoeuvre it out from under the wing.

Refitting

5 Refitting is a reversal of removal. Renew any fasteners which were broken on removal.

12 Boot lid – removal and refitting

Removal

1 Raise the boot lid, then remove warning triangle from its holder.

2 Remove the securing screw and detach the warning triangle holder from the boot lid (see illustration).

3 Undo the trim retaining screw from the hand grip recess, then carefully pull away the trim (see illustrations). If necessary, use a wide-blade screwdriver to prise the clips from the boot lid. Recover the boot lid latch cover.

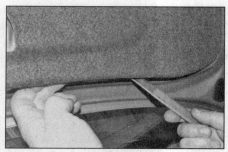

12.3c ... and pull the trim from the boot lid using a flat tool to release the retaining clips

12.4 Prise out the grommet and pull the wiring harness from the boot lid

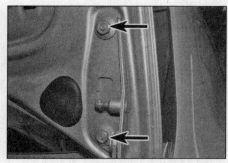

12.5 Prise out the clip a little, and pull the strut from the pivot

4 Unplug the wiring connectors from the lock switch and number plate light units, then release the grommet and withdraw the wiring harness from the boot lid (see illustration).

5 Prise up the spring clips from the upper and lower balljoints using a small screwdriver, then release the gas struts from the boot lid hinges (see illustration). Have an assistant support the boot lid.

6 Mark the relationship between the boot lid and the hinges by drawing around the outside of each hinge with a marker pen (see illustration).

7 Place cloths or pieces of cardboard over the surfaces of the rear wings to prevent damage during removal.

8 Enlist the aid of an assistant to support the boot lid, then unscrew and remove the hinge-to-boot lid retaining nuts (see illustration), and lift the lid clear.

Refitting

9 Refit in the reverse order of removal. Check the lid for correct alignment, and if necessary loosen off the hinge bolts to adjust, then retighten them; there should be an even gap between the outside edge of the boot lid and the surrounding bodywork.

12.6 Make alignment marks between the hinge and lid

Lock unit

Removal

6 Release the retaining clip and disconnect the operating rod from the lock motor, and the

13.3 Disconnect the cable from the lock cylinder

13.4b ... then twist the cylinder assembly 90° and withdraw it

13 Boot lid lock components
– removal and refitting

1 Remove the trim from inside the boot lid, as described in Section 12.

Lock cylinder

Removal

2 Disconnect the wiring from the lock cylinder assembly.

3 Detach the cable from the lock cylinder assembly (see illustration).

4 Unscrew the Torx screw, turn the cylinder through 90° then withdraw the lock cylinder from the boot lid handle mechanism (see illustrations).

Refitting

5 Refitting is a reversal of removal.

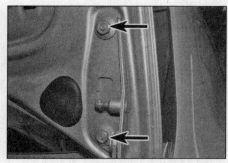

12.8 Hinge retaining nuts (arrowed)

cable from the lock cylinder assembly (see illustration).

7 Mark the fitted position of the lock with a marker pen, then unscrew the retaining nuts and withdraw the lock unit from the boot lid

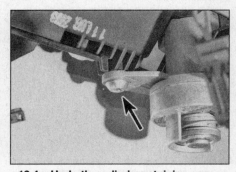

13.4a Undo the cylinder retaining screw (arrowed) ...

13.6 Disconnect the lock operating rod

13.7 Undo the lock retaining nuts (arrowed)

(see illustration). Disconnect the wiring plug as the lock is withdrawn.

Refitting

8 Refit in the reverse order of removal.

Handle

Removal

9 Remove the lock cylinder as previously described in this Section.
10 Undo the 4 retaining nuts, then depress the clips and pull the handle/number plate light units from the boot lid **(see illustration)**. Disconnect the wiring plug as the unit is withdrawn.

Refitting

11 Refitting is a reversal of removal.

Lock motor

12 Remove the boot lid trim panel as described in Section 12.

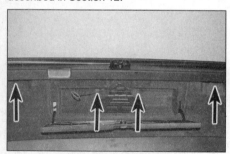

14.2 The tailgate trim screws are located in the handle recesses, and in the warning triangle recess (arrowed)

14.3c . . . and disengage it in the direction of the arrow from the locating hole in the window surround trim

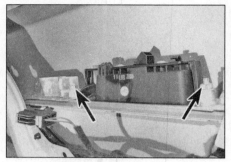

13.10 Undo the handle retaining nuts (2 right-hand nuts arrowed)

13 Release the clip and disconnect the operating rod from the lock **(see illustration 13.6)**.
14 Slacken the 2 Torx bolts, and manoeuvre the motor from place **(see illustration)**. Disconnect the wiring plug as the motor is withdrawn.
15 Refitting is a reversal of removal.

14 Tailgate –
removal and refitting

Removal

1 Open the tailgate and remove the warning triangle.
2 Unscrew the four lower trim panel securing screws. Two are located in the grab handle recesses, and two at the centre, lower edge of the trim **(see illustration)**.
3 Carefully prise the lower section of the

14.3a Pull the lower part of the trim panel from the tailgate to release the 'push-in' clips (arrowed) . . .

14.4a Undo the screw each side (arrowed) . . .

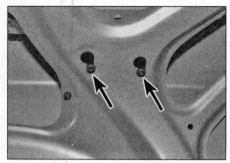

13.14 Boot lid lock motor retaining Torx bolts (arrowed)

trim panel from the tailgate using just enough force to overcome the spring clips **(see illustrations)**. Disconnect the light wiring plug as the panel is withdrawn.
4 Undo the screws, then unclip the upper section of the trim panel from the tailgate rear window aperture **(see illustrations)**. The trim panel is held by two clips each side, and three clips along its top edge.
5 Disconnect the wiring from the tailgate components (lock switch, wiper motor, number plate light units and demister element) at the connectors. Note the routing and attachment locations of the wires.
6 Disconnect the hose for the rear screen washer jet.
7 Mark the relationship between the tailgate and its hinges using a felt tip pen.
8 Enlist the aid of an assistant to help support the tailgate, then detach the tailgate struts with reference to Section 15.

14.3b . . . then use a flat-bladed tool with a hook at the end to pull the trim down . . .

14.4b . . . and pull the trim from the tailgate to release the retaining clips (arrowed)

9 Prise off the plastic covers, then unscrew and remove the tailgate-to-hinge securing bolts, and lift the tailgate clear of the vehicle.

Refitting

10 Refit in the reverse order of removal. Check that the tailgate is correctly aligned before fully tightening the tailgate hinge bolts.
11 The fit and closing tension of the tailgate can be adjusted by altering the positions of the rubber buffers at the upper and lower edges of the tailgate.

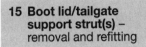

15 Boot lid/tailgate support strut(s) – removal and refitting

Removal

1 Open the boot lid or tailgate and support it in its open position, or have an assistant hold it open.
2 Disconnect the strut(s) at the upper and lower balljoints by lifting (not removing) the spring clips, and prising the joint free **(see illustration)**.
3 If a strut is defective in operation, it must be renewed. Do not attempt to dismantle and repair the strut. Note that the struts are filled with pressurised gas, and so should not be punctured or disposed of by incineration.

Refitting

4 Refit in the reverse order of removal. Ensure that the strut is securely engaged with the balljoints.

16 Tailgate lock, cylinder and handle – removal and refitting

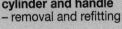

1 Remove the trim from inside the tailgate, as described in Section 14.

Lock cylinder housing and carrier

Note: *A lock cylinder is not fitted to all models.*

Removal

2 Disconnect the wiring plug from the lock cylinder.
3 Detach the cable from the lock.
4 Unscrew the mounting bolt, then rotate the cylinder 90° and pull it from position.

Refitting

5 Refitting is a reversal of removal.

Lock unit

Removal

6 Prise out the retaining clip and detach the cable (where fitted) from the lock unit.
7 Release the clip and disconnect the operating rod from the lock unit.

15.2 Prise up the strut balljoint spring clip

8 Mark the fitted position of the lock with a marker pen, then unscrew the retaining nuts and withdraw the lock unit from the tailgate **(see illustration)**.

Refitting

9 Refit in the reverse order of removal.

Handle

Removal

10 Remove the lock cylinder assembly as described previously in this Section.
11 Disconnect the wiring plug from the handle.
12 Undo the 4 retaining nuts, depress the clips and remove the handle.

Refitting

13 Refitting is a reversal of removal.

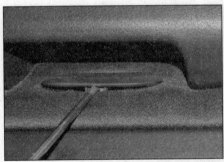

17.1 Prise up and remove the panel at the base of the armrest on the driver's door

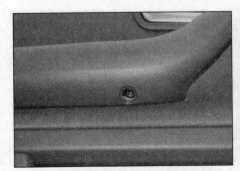

17.2b . . . or single screw (passenger's side trim)

16.8 Lock retaining nuts (arrowed)

17 Door trim panel – removal and refitting

Front door

Removal

1 On the driver's door, open the door and prise out the trim panel at the base of the armrest with a blunt flat-bladed tool **(see illustration)**.
2 Undo the 2 screws in the armrest aperture (driver's door) or single screw accessible through the armrest **(see illustrations)**.
3 Undo the screw at the base of the door trim in the centre **(see illustration)**.
4 Starting at the front edge, carefully pull the trim panel above the interior release handle

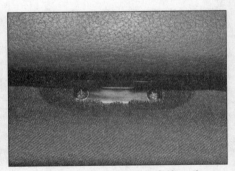

17.2a Undo the 2 screws below the armrest (driver's side trim) . . .

17.3 Remove the screw (arrowed) in the centre of the panel at its lower edge

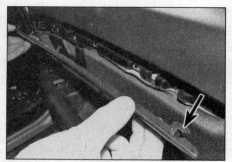

17.4 Pull the trim away, then slide it forwards to unhook the rear edge (arrowed)

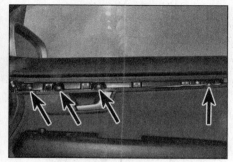

17.5 Undo the 4 screws in the panel recess (arrowed)

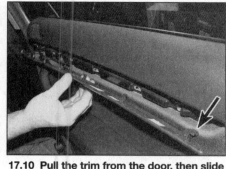

17.10 Pull the trim from the door, then slide it forwards to disengage the hook (arrowed)

away from the door to release the clips, then slide it to the front to unhook the rear edge of the trim panel **(see illustration)**.

5 Undo the 4 screws in the trim panel recess **(see illustration)**.

6 Pull the trim away from the door frame, releasing the retaining clips, then lift the trim panel up squarely. Be prepared for some of the clips to break as the trim is removed.

7 Unhook the operating cable from the rear of the interior handle as it becomes accessible **(see illustration 17.15)**.

8 Note their fitted positions, and disconnect the wiring plugs from the top of the speaker and the window motor control unit as the panel is withdrawn.

Refitting

9 Refit in the reverse order of removal, noting the following point:

a) *Ensure that the wiring and connections*

are secure and correctly routed, clear of the window regulator and latch/lock components.

b) *Renew any damage retaining clips.*

c) *When reconnecting the interior handle release cable, ensure the hook on the end of the cable is facing upwards.*

Rear door

Removal

10 Starting at the front edge, unclip the trim panel above the interior release handle, then slide it to the front to remove it **(see illustration)**.

11 Undo the 3 screws in the trim panel recess **(see illustration)**.

12 On models with manual windows, insert a small screwdriver behind the handle knob to release the clip, and slide off the handle

trim. Undo the retaining screw, and pull the handle from the shaft **(see illustrations)**. Note the fitted position of the handle for refitting.

13 On all models, undo the cross-head screw at the lower edge of the armrest **(see illustration)**.

14 Carefully pull the trim away from the door frame, releasing the retaining clips. Lift the trim panel up squarely. Be prepared for some clips to break as they are released **(see illustration)**.

15 Unhook the operating cable from the rear of the interior handle as it becomes accessible **(see illustration)**.

16 Note their fitted positions, and disconnect the various wiring plugs as the panel is withdrawn. Release the wiring from its retaining clips on the rear of the door trim panel.

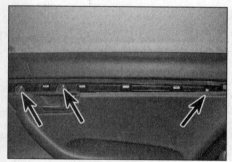

17.11 Undo the 3 screws (arrowed) in the trim panel recess

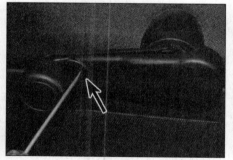

17.12a Depress the clip (arrowed) and slide the handle trim from place

17.12b Handle retaining screw (arrowed)

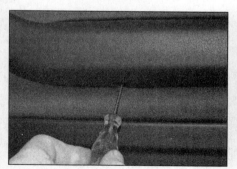

17.13 Undo the screw at the base of the armrest

17.14 Pull the door trim from the door to release the clips

17.15 Disconnect the cable from the interior handle as the panel is removed

Refitting

17 Check the door trim for any missing or broken clips, and renew where necessary.

18 Refit in the reverse order of removal, noting the following point:

   a) *Ensure that the wiring and connections are secure and correctly routed, clear of the window regulator and latch/lock components.*

   b) *When reconnecting the interior handle release cable, ensure the hook on the end of the cable is facing upwards.*

   c) *The window winder handle (where fitted) should be positioned at approximately 5° to the vertical pointing downwards.*

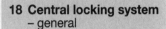

18 Central locking system
   – general

Refer to the information given in Chapter 12.

19 Door lock –
   removal and refitting

Removal

1 Refer to Section 21 and remove the window glass, frame and regulator assembly.

2 Slide the clip to one side, and detach the lock operating rod from the exterior handle **(see illustration)**.

3 Pull the plastic cover from the lock assembly (where fitted) **(see illustration)**.

4 Undo the 2 retaining screws at the edge of the door, and manoeuvre the lock from position. Disconnect the lock wiring plug(s) as it's withdrawn **(see illustrations)**.

5 If required, the interior handle cable can be detached by prising up the outer cable fitting, rotating the inner cable fitting 90°, and lifting it from place **(see illustrations)**.

Refitting

6 Refitting is a reversal of the removal procedure. Check that the door striker enters the lock centrally when the door is closed, and if necessary adjust the position of the striker **(see illustrations)**.

20 Door handles
   and lock cylinder –
   removal and refitting

Exterior handles

Removal

1 Refer to Section 21 and remove the window glass, frame and regulator assembly. If removing the driver's side handle, first remove the lock cylinder as described in this Section.

19.2 Slide out the clip, then pull the end of the rod from the exterior handle

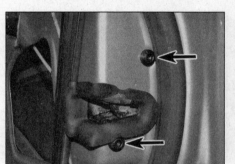

19.4a Undo the 2 multispline screws securing the lock to the door (arrowed) . . .

2 Slide the clip to one side, and detach the lock operating rod from the exterior handle **(see illustration 19.2)**.

3 Insert a screwdriver into the door handle mounting, and slide the mounting retaining

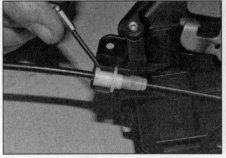

19.5a Prise out the outer cable . . .

19.6a When refitting the driver's door lock, ensure the lock cylinder rod (arrowed) enters the slot in the lock

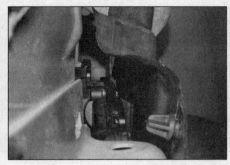

19.3 Pull the plastic cover from the lock

19.4b . . . and manoeuvre the lock from the door

clip forwards (front doors) or rearwards (rear doors). If the clip is reluctant to move, use tool to carefully prise out the clip tab as shown **(see illustrations)**. Remove the handle and mounting from the door.

19.5b . . . then rotate the end fitting 90° and disengage it

19.6b Slacken the screws and adjust the position of the striker

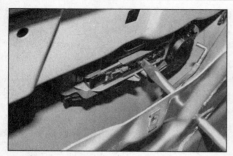

20.3a Insert a screwdriver through the door, and slide the retaining clip forwards (front door) or rearwards (rear door)

20.3b Lift the tab to allow the clip to slide – front door (arrowed) . . .

20.3c . . . or rear door (arrowed) . . .

20.3d . . . and remove the outer handle from the door

4 If required, use a small screwdriver to slide the retaining clip and remove the outer cover from the handle (see illustrations).

Refitting

5 Refitting is a reversal of removal.

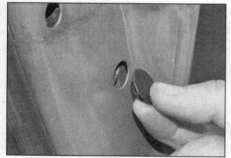

20.6 Prise out the plastic cap . . .

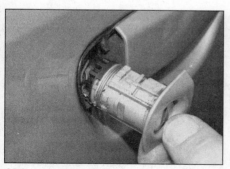

20.8 . . . the lock cylinder will emerge from the door

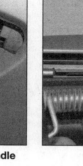

20.4a Slide the catch . . .

Lock cylinder

Removal

6 Remove the cap from the Torx bolt nearest the external door handle on the rear end face of the door (see illustration).

20.7 . . . as the Torx bolt is rotated anti-clockwise (arrowed) . . .

20.12a Release the retaining clips . . .

20.4b . . . and remove the outer cover

7 Rotate the Torx bolt as far as it will go anti-clockwise (see illustration).
8 Withdraw the lock cylinder housing from the door (see illustration).

Refitting

9 Refitting is a reversal of removal.

Interior handles

Removal

10 With reference to Section 17 remove the door trim panel.
11 Disconnect the wiring from the central locking switch (where fitted).
12 Undo the retaining bolt, depress the retaining clips and remove the interior door handle to the front (see illustrations).

Refitting

13 Refitting is a reversal of removal.

20.12b . . . undo the bolt (arrowed) and slide the interior door handle to the front

21.2 Undo the 3 Torx bolts securing the regulator to the door (arrowed)

21.4 Pull the sealing strip (arrowed) from the frame around the window

21.5 Pull the plastic trim from behind the mirror

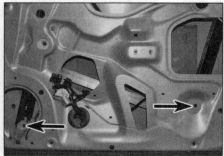

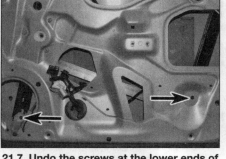

21.7 Undo the screws at the lower ends of the regulator rails (arrowed)

21.8a Prise out the grommet and undo the screw at the rear edge of the door

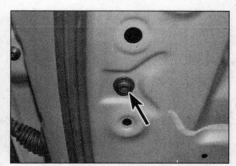

21.8b Undo the Torx bolt half-way down the front edge of the door (arrowed) . . .

21 Door window glass, frame and regulator – removal and refitting

Note: *Removal and refitting of the door windows on Cabriolet models, and subsequent resetting of the windows' position, is an involved process, considered to be beyond the scope of the DIY owner. We recommend this task be entrusted to an Audi dealer or specialist.*

Front door

Removal

1 Position the door window half-way down, then remove the door trim as described in Section 17.

2 Undo the 3 Torx bolts and pull the window motor from the regulator shaft **(see illustration)**

3 Undo the 3 bolts and remove the main speaker from the door frame (see Chapter 12), then carefully peel the door sealing sheet from the door frame.

4 Carefully pull the rubber sealing strip from the frame around the window **(see illustration)**.

5 Prise away the triangular plastic trim behind the mirror from the front of the door **(see illustration)**.

6 The window frame and regulator are secured to the door panel by several bolts, as described in this Section. Before unscrewing the bolts, mark their position relative to the door panel using a felt-tip pen or paint.

7 Undo the 2 screws at the base of the regulator guide rails **(see illustration)**.

8 Prise out the grommet at the door rear edge, then undo the window frame retaining bolt at the rear of the door, and the 2 bolts at the front of the door **(see illustrations)**.

9 Pull the rubber outer sealing strip from the rear edge of the door frame **(see illustration)**.

10 Unclip the mirror wiring loom from the door, and feed the wiring plug through the rubber grommet.

11 Squeeze together the sides of the regulator retaining clips and push them through the door frame **(see illustrations)**.

21.8c . . . and the one at the top of the front edge (arrowed)

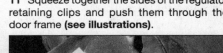

21.9 Pull the sealing strip from the rear edge of the door

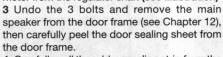
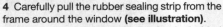

21.11a Squeeze together the sides of the 3 regulator retaining clips and push them through the door panel (arrowed)

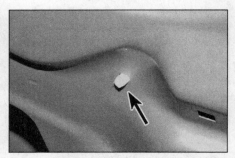

21.11b Squeeze together the sides of the regulator cable retaining clip (arrowed) and push it through the door panel

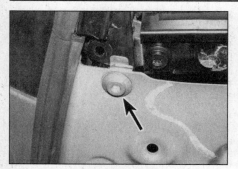

21.12a Undo the Torx bolt at the front of the door (arrowed) . . .

21.12b . . . and the bolt at the rear of the door (arrowed)

21.12c Recover the shims . . .

21.12d . . . then lift the window, regulator and frame from the door

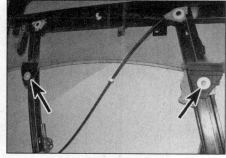

21.13a Undo the regulator clamp Torx bolts (arrowed) . . .

21.13b . . . lift off the clamp inner covers, and make alignment marks before lifting out the window glass

12 Undo the 2 bolts at the top edge of the door panel, recover the shims, then lift the window glass, frame and regulator from the door panel **(see illustrations)**.

13 Undo the 2 Torx bolts, mark the positions of the clamps on the regulator, and detach the window from the regulator **(see illustrations)**.

14 Undo the 2 countersunk bolts, release the cable from the retaining clip, and detach the regulator assembly from the window frame **(see illustration)**.

Refitting

15 Refitting is a reversal of removal, noting the following points:

a) *Ensure the regulator guide rails are fitted parallel to the front edge of the frame.*

b) *Slide the glass into position, but only finger-tighten the retaining bolts. Then pull the glass rearwards into the guide, then securely tighten the bolts.*

c) *Insert the frame into position, then fit the two bolts at the top of the door panel, but only finger-tighten them. Then press the top of the frame inwards slightly, and tighten the bolt at the rear edge of the door, and the one at the base of the door frame at the front to the specified torque. Then tighten the remaining bolts to the specified torque, aligning the previously-made marks.*

d) *Check the fit of the window frame in the door aperture, and if necessary adjust the angle of the frame by slackening the retaining bolts, and repositioning the frame.*

e) *After refitting the door trim, switch the ignition on then off. Now raise the window as far as it will go, and hold the button in this position for approximately 2 seconds. This resets the basic position of the window for the control system.*

Rear door

16 Position the door window half-way down, then remove the door trim as described in Section 17.

17 Undo the 3 Torx bolts and pull the window motor or manual winder mechanism (as applicable) from the regulator shaft **(see illustrations)**

18 Carefully peel the weatherproof sheet from the door frame, and the rubber weatherstrip from the window frame **(see illustrations)**.

19 Pull the upper trim ends from the front and rear of the door, and the triangular trim from the rear corner of the window **(see illustrations)**.

20 The window frame and regulator is secured to the door panel by several bolts, as described in this Section. Before unscrewing the bolts, mark their position relative to the door panel using a felt-tip pen or paint.

21.14 Undo the 2 bolts (arrowed), release the cable clip and remove the regulator

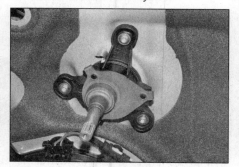

21.17a Undo the 3 Torx bolts securing the handle assembly

21.17b On models with electric rear windows, undo the 3 Torx bolts (arrowed)

21.18a Carefully peel away the weatherproof sheet . . .

21.18b . . . and the rubber seal from the window frame

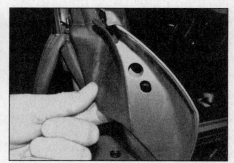

21.19a Pull the trim ends from the front and rear of the door . . .

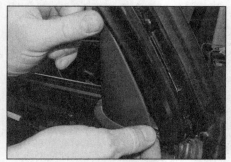

21.19b . . . and the triangular trim from the rear corner of the window

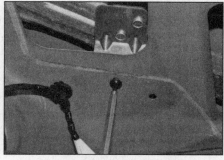

21.21 Undo the Torx bolt at the lower end of the regulator assembly

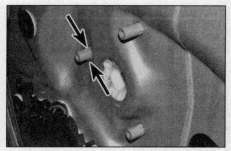

21.22 Squeeze together the sides of the 3 retaining clips (arrowed) and push them through the door panel

21 Undo the bolt at the base of the regulator assembly (see illustration).
22 Using a pair of pliers, squeeze together the sides of the retaining clips and push the regulator into the door cavity (see illustration).

Release the regulator cable retaining clip in the same manner.
23 Prise out the grommets at the door rear and front edges, then undo the bolts under the grommets (see illustrations).

24 The window frame and regulator is now secured by 3 bolts at the top edge of the door panel, and 1 bolt at the rear edge of the door. Undo the bolts, and lift the frame and regulator from the door panel (see illustrations).

21.23a Prise out the grommets at the rear edge of the door (arrowed) . . .

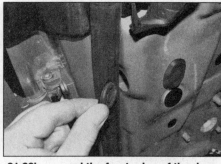

21.23b . . . and the front edge of the door. Undo the bolts hidden by the grommets

21.24a Undo the bolt at the front of the door (arrowed) . . .

21.24b . . . the rear of the door (arrowed) . . .

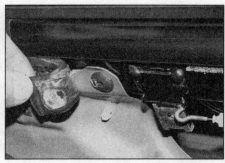

21.24c . . . under the rubber strip at the top of the door . . .

21.24d . . . and the rear edge of the door (arrowed) . . .

21.24e . . . then lift the window, frame, and regulator from the door

25 Undo the 2 bolts, and detach the window from the regulator **(see illustration)**.
26 Undo the 1 countersunk bolt, release the retaining clip, and detach the regulator assembly from the window frame **(see illustration)**.

Refitting

27 Refitting is a reversal of removal, noting the following points:
a) Slide the glass upwards into position, but only finger-tighten the retaining bolts. Then pull the glass rearwards into the guide, then securely tighten the bolts.
b) Insert the frame into position, then fit the retaining bolts, but only finger-tighten them. Then press the top of the frame inwards slightly, and tighten the bolts at the rear and front edges of the door to the specified torque. Then tighten the remaining bolts to the specified torque, aligning the previously-made marks.

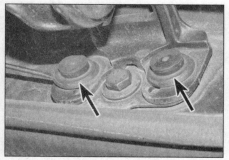

22.3 Prise up the plastic caps and undo the hinge bolts (arrowed)

22.5a Prise out the top cylinder clip . . .

21.25 Undo the 2 Torx bolts securing the window to the regulator

c) Check the fit of the window frame in the door aperture, and if necessary adjust the angle of the frame by slackening the retaining bolts, and repositioning the frame.
d) After refitting the door trim, switch the ignition on then off. Now raise the window as far as it will go, and hold the button in this position for approximately 2 seconds. This resets the basic position of the window for the control system.

22 Hood – removal and refitting

Removal

1 Remove the rear side trim panels, as described in Section 33.
2 Move the hood to the half-open position.

22.4 Swivel the retaining clips out, then pull them downwards from the ball end of the strut

22.5b . . . and the lower cylinder clip (arrowed)

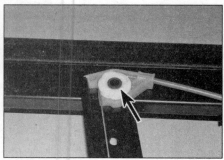

21.26 Undo the bolt (arrowed) and detach the regulator assembly from the frame

Note: With the ignition switched on, the hood hydraulic system remains pressurised for 10 minutes after it was last used. After this time the hood will begin to fall. Briefly touching the operating button will pressurise the system for a further 10 minutes. If necessary, take steps to prop the hood in position.

3 Prise up the plastic caps, and undo the 2 outer bolts securing the hood compartment lid hinge, leaving the 3rd central bolt in place **(see illustration)**.
4 Prise out the retaining spring clips and pull the tops of the operating cylinders from the mountings on the compartment lid **(see illustration)**. Have an assistant support the lid. Lay the cylinder down in the hood compartment, fold the compartment lid hinges forward and lift the compartment lid from position.
5 Prise out the retaining clips and disconnect the hood hydraulic cylinders from the ball-end mountings **(see illustrations)**.
6 Release the hydraulic pipes and wiring from the retaining clips and cable ties, then manoeuvre the cylinders from the hood assembly and lay them in the hood compartment. Note that there is no need to disconnect the hydraulic pipes **(see illustration)**.
7 Working inside the vehicle, undo the nuts and move the electrical box to one side, then disconnect the wiring plugs on the right-hand side, then note their routing and release the cables from the guides and cable ties **(see illustrations)**.
8 Working on the right-hand side of the hood, undo the 2 cross-head screws and remove the top switch unit **(see illustration)**. Release

22.6 Manoeuvre the cylinders from the hood without disconnecting the hydraulic pipes

22.7a Undo the nuts (arrowed) and remove the electrical box to one side . . .

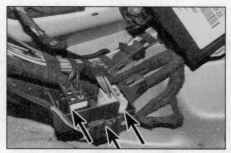

22.7b . . . then disconnect the wiring plugs (arrowed) and release the cable harnesses from the clips and guides

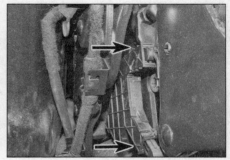

22.8a Top switch unit retaining screws (arrowed)

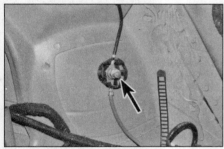

22.9 Undo the nut (arrowed) and disconnect the heated rear screws earth connection

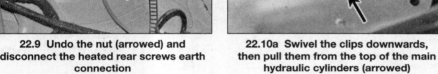
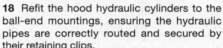
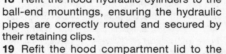

22.10a Swivel the clips downwards, then pull them from the top of the main hydraulic cylinders (arrowed)

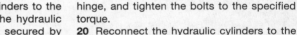

22.10b Slacken the bracket retaining bolts (arrowed)

the cable ties and the connector, note the harness routing and remove the switch from the vehicle.

9 Disconnect the heated rear window earth lead **(see illustration)**.

10 Prise out the locking pins at the top of the main hydraulic cylinders, slacken the retaining bracket nuts, manoeuvre the cylinders from their pivot points, and lay them down in the vehicle **(see illustrations)**. Recover the plastic washers either side of the cylinder pivot points.

11 Carefully peel back the foam on the vehicle body brackets, then slacken the main hood support brackets' retaining Allen screws by 2 complete turns **(see illustrations)**.

12 Enlist assistance to support the hood each side, then completely undo the support bracket bolts each side as shown **(see illustration)**.

13 Lift the hood upwards, pull the cables upwards from the vehicle, and manoeuvre the hood backwards and away from the vehicle.

Refitting

14 Manoeuvre the hood into position, insert the main bracket retaining bolts, and tighten them to the specified torque.

15 Position the main hydraulic cylinders, ensure the plastic washers are in place at the pivot points, then fasten the retaining bracket nuts, and refit the locking pins **(see illustration)**.

16 Refit the top switch unit and tighten the retaining screws securely.

17 Reconnect all wiring plugs, and ensure all the cable harnesses are routed in their original positions.

18 Refit the hood hydraulic cylinders to the ball-end mountings, ensuring the hydraulic pipes are correctly routed and secured by their retaining clips.

19 Refit the hood compartment lid to the

hinge, and tighten the bolts to the specified torque.

20 Reconnect the hydraulic cylinders to the ball-end mountings on the compartment lid and refit the retaining clips.

22.11a Carefully peel back the foam . . .

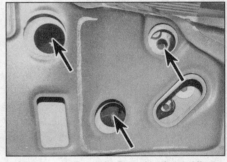

22.11b . . . then slacken the three Allen screws securing the hood (arrowed)

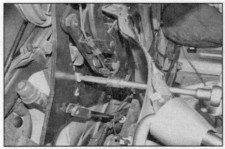

22.12 Use an extension and hexagonal bit working through the holes in the bodywork to undo the hood retaining bolts

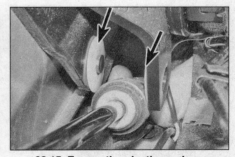

22.15 Ensure the plastic washers (arrowed) are fitted each side of the main hydraulic cylinders

22.21a Side window lateral position adjustment screws and locknuts (arrowed)

21 Before refitting the side panel trims, lower the door and side windows at least 50 mm, then close the hood. Now raise the windows and check they move correctly into the rubber seals. If they don't, the positions of the windows can be adjusted as follows:

a) *To adjust the lateral position, remove the loudspeaker, slacken the position adjusting screw locknuts, then turn the screw until the horizontal position of the window is correct. Tighten the locknuts* **(see illustration).**

b) *To adjust the vertical angle and closing height, slacken the 3 window positioning bolts* **(see illustration),** *and adjust the window position. Tighten the bolts securely.*

c) *If necessary, this procedure also applies to the door windows.*

22 With the windows correctly positioned, refit the rear side trim panels.

23.3 Hood hydraulic unit retaining nuts (arrowed)

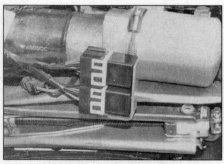

23.7 The hood relays are attached to the hydraulic unit

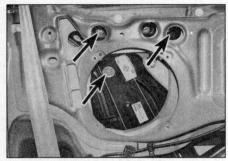

22.21b Side window vertical angle and closing height positioning bolts (arrowed)

23 Hood (Cabriolet) hydraulic unit – general information, removal and refitting

General information

1 The hood on Cabriolet models, is operated by an electro-hydraulic system, consisting of an electrically-driven hydraulic pump, 3 sets of hydraulic cylinders, and an actuator unit made up of solenoids and hydraulic valves. The system requires no maintenance, and should only require topping-up or bleeding following component renewal. Due to the complexity of the system, DIY procedures are limited to removal and refitting of the main hydraulic unit as a whole, whilst cylinder removal is described within Section 22. **Note:** *Before attempting any repair, consult an Audi dealer or parts specialist with regard to the availability of parts.*

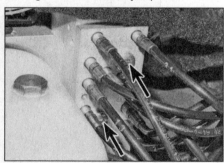

23.6 Undo the two screws (arrowed) and pull the plate away with the pipes

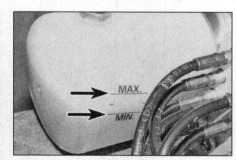

23.8 The fluid MAX and MIN levels are marked on the side of the reservoir (arrowed)

Caution: *When working on any part of the hydraulic system, absolute cleanliness must be observed. Any ingress of dirt could cause extensive damage to the system.*

Removal

2 Remove the luggage compartment right-hand side panel trim as described in Section 33.

3 Undo the unit retaining nuts **(see illustration)**. Note that to improve access, undo the 2 nuts and move the audio amplifier/bracket to one side.

4 Release the hydraulic pipes/cables from the retaining clips/cable ties.

5 Note their fitted positions, then disconnect the wiring plugs, and lift the hydraulic unit from position to access the hydraulic pipes.

6 Undo the connector plate retaining screws, then pull the plate away with the pipes. Each pipe is retained by a circlip. Prise out the circlip and pull the pipe from the plate. Note that absolute cleanliness must be observed **(see illustration)**. Plug/cover the openings to prevent contamination, and be prepared for fluid spillage. **Note:** *The pipe seal is pressed into the hydraulic unit and cannot be renewed separately.*

7 Withdraw the unit from the vehicle. Note the relays attached to the unit **(see illustration)**.

Refitting

8 Refitting is a reversal of removal, but prior to refitting the luggage compartment side trim panel, top-up and bleed the system as follows:

a) *The fluid level must be checked with the hood stowed in its compartment.*

b) *The fluid level can be seen through the reservoir. If necessary, unscrew the cap and fill the system to the MAX level* **(see illustration)**.

c) *Start the engine, open and close the hood 4 or 5 times, then stow it in its compartment.*

d) *Recheck the fluid level and top-up if necessary.*

e) *Refit the luggage compartment side panel trim.*

24 Doors – removal and refitting

Removal

1 Remove the door trim as described in Section 17.

2 Unclip the trim panel from the lower A-pillar. Disconnect the door wiring harness at the multiway connector, pull the bellows between the pillar and door away from the A-pillar, and feed the door wiring loom through the aperture.

3 Mark the relationship between the hinges and the door, using a marker pen.

4 Get an assistant to support the weight of the door, or support it with blocks. If blocks are used, make sure the door will be securely supported (it is a heavy and awkward component), and pad the blocks with some rag to prevent damage to the underside of the door.

5 On the upper hinge, undo the bolt securing the hinge to the door frame **(see illustration)**.
6 Unscrew and remove the bolts that secure the lower hinge to the door.
7 Remove the door.
8 Clean the bolt threads with a wire brush, and the nut threads with a tap, and treat them with thread-locking fluid when refitting the door.

Refitting

9 Refitting is a reversal of the removal procedure. Use the markings made during removal to ensure that the hinges are positioned correctly on the door. Note that the hinges have elongated mounting holes to allow the position of the door to be adjusted.
10 On completion, shut the door and check it for closure and alignment. Check the depth at which the striker enters the lock. If adjustment is required, slacken the securing bolts and reposition the striker plate **(see illustration 19.6b)**.

25 Windscreen, rear window glass and rear side window glass – general information

The windscreen, rear window glass, and rear side window glass are directly bonded to the metalwork. Their removal and refitting requires the use of special tools not readily available to the home mechanic. This work should therefore be left to an Audi dealer, or a glass specialist.

26 Sunroof – general

1 A sliding/tilting sunroof is fitted to some models. When fitted correctly, the roof panel in the fully closed position should be level with, or no more than 1.0 mm lower than, the roof panel at the leading edge. The rear edge

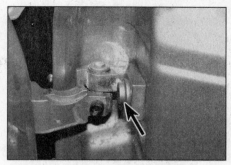

24.5 Undo the upper hinge bolt (arrowed)

must be level with, or no more than 1.0 mm higher than, the roof panel at the rear.
2 Removal and refitting, and adjustments to the roof panel, are best entrusted to an Audi garage, as specialised tools are required.
3 The sunroof panel motor can be removed and refitted as described in Chapter 12. If the motor malfunctions when the roof panel is in the open position, it can be wound shut manually; refer to Chapter 12.
4 If the sunroof water drain hoses become blocked, they may be cleared by probing them with a length of suitable cable (an old speedometer drive cable is ideal). The front drain tubes terminate just below the A-pillars, between the pillar and the door – cleaning is carried out from the sunroof end. The rear drain tubes terminate behind the rear wheel arch, behind the bumper cover. Cleaning is carried out from the bottom end of the hose (remove the bumper as described in this Chapter).

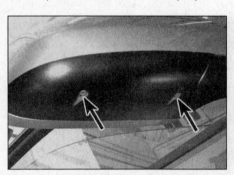

27.2a Undo the two screws on the base of the mirror housing (arrowed) . . .

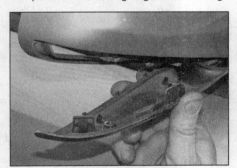

27.2c . . . and pull down the front edge of the panel

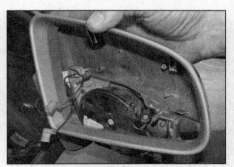

27.3 Prise the mirror housing upwards

27 Door mirror components – removal and refitting

Mirror housing

Renewal

1 Remove the mirror as described in this Section.
2 Working underneath the housing, undo the 2 screws, and pull the lower panel downwards **(see illustrations)**.
3 Carefully prise the mirror housing upwards to release the retaining clips, and remove it **(see illustration)**. Take great care not to damage the paintwork.
4 Refitting is a reversal of removal, ensuring the retaining clips fully engine with the mirror adjustment unit.

Mirror

 Warning: Wear gloves and eye protection when carrying out this operation, particularly if the mirror glass is broken.

Renewal

5 Press in the top of the mirror, then insert a flat-bladed blunt tool behind the base of the mirror, and carefully prise the lower part of the mirror from the retaining clips. Use the tool to carefully prise the top part of the mirror from the clips **(see illustration)**.
6 Disconnect the heater element wiring plugs as the mirror is withdrawn.

27.2b . . . then release the clips (outer clip arrowed) . . .

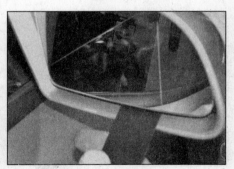

27.5 Insert a flat tool behind the lower edge of the mirror, and lever it from the clips

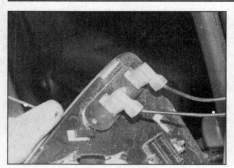

27.7a Reconnect the mirror heater wiring plugs

27.7b Ensure the friction pin on the back of the mirror engages in the slot (arrowed)

27.9 Mirror assembly retaining Torx bolt (arrowed)

7 To refit, reconnect the wiring plugs, and insert the friction pin into the slot in the mirror adjustment unit **(see illustrations)**. Press firmly at the centre of the mirror glass to engage the retaining clip. On completion, check the operation of the mirror adjustment

mechanism using the adjustment knob/ buttons.

Complete assembly

Note: *The following procedure is the one recommended by Audi. However, should you have sufficient wiring skills, it is possible to renew the assembly without window and frame removal, by removing the mirror housing (see above), and cutting the plugs from the mirror motor/glass wiring loom. Undo the mirror retaining bolt (see paragraph 9), remove the assembly, then rejoin the wires to the plugs on the new mirror assembly.*

Removal

8 Remove the window and frame as described in Section 21.
9 Undo the retaining bolt and withdraw the mirror from the door **(see illustration)**. Release the wiring loom from the window frame.
10 To remove the mirror adjustment

mechanism, first remove the mirror glass as described earlier in this Section. Undo the securing screws and remove the mechanism from the mirror body.

Refitting

11 Refitting the mirror is a reversal of the removal procedure. Check the operation of the mirror adjustment on completion.

28 Centre console – removal and refitting

Removal

1 Lift up the cover trim and pull the rear ashtray upwards from position (where fitted) **(see illustration)**.
2 Working in the rear ashtray aperture, press the retaining clips outwards and swivel the mounting plate for the rear seat heating switches (where fitted) rearwards **(see illustration)**. Disconnect the switch wiring plugs as the unit is withdrawn.
3 On models with a centre arm rest, slacken the nut in the rear ashtray aperture, and manoeuvre the centre armrest from the centre console **(see illustration)**.
4 Carefully prise up the gear lever/selector surround trim and unclip it from the gaiter (where fitted) **(see illustrations)**.
5 Remove the audio unit as described in Chapter 12.
6 Remove the heater/air conditioning control panel as described in Chapter 3.

28.1 Lift up the cover and remove the ashtray

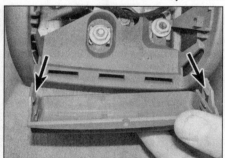

28.2 Pres the retaining clips (arrowed) outwards

28.3 Undo the centre armrest retaining nut (arrowed)

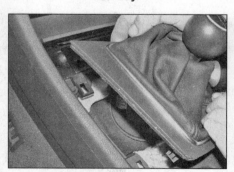

28.4a Prise up the gear lever/selector lever surround trim

28.4b On manual transmission models, unclip it from the gaiter

28.7 Prise the trim panel rearwards

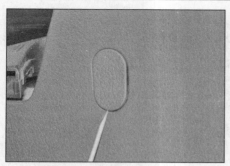

28.9a Prise out the plastic caps each side of the console at the front . . .

28.9b . . . then undo the screw each side

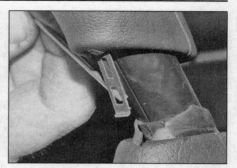

28.10 Release the clip on the underside of the lever grip

7 Carefully prise the switch trim panel beneath the dash centre vents rearwards and remove it **(see illustration)**.

8 Ensure the handbrake is fully applied, then on automatic transmission models, move the selector lever to the rearmost position.

9 Prise out the plastic caps at the front of the console on each side, and undo the retaining screws **(see illustrations)**.

10 Use a small screwdriver to release the clip on its underside, then pull the handbrake lever grip forwards from the lever **(see illustration)**.

11 Prise out the rubber element, then use a small screwdriver to spread apart the retaining clips and pull the handbrake lever trim forwards and detach it from the lever **(see illustrations)**

12 Carefully prise the plastic trim panel under the handbrake lever from position, then undo the 2 screws beneath it, and lift out the connecting piece **(see illustrations)**.

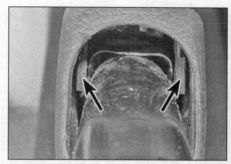

28.11a Use a screwdriver to spread apart the handbrake lever trim clips (arrowed)

13 Prise up and remove the panel above the front ashtray, then undo the two screws and remove the ashtray from place **(see illustrations)**. Disconnect any wiring plugs as the unit is withdrawn.

14 The centre console is now secured by 8

28.11b Note how the rear of the lever trim locates in the centre console

screws in the audio unit/transmission lever apertures, and 2 nuts at the rear. Undo the screws/nuts and pull the console firmly to the rear and upwards, manoeuvre it over the transmission lever and handbrake lever, and remove it from the vehicle **(see illustrations)**.

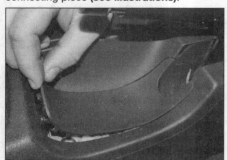

28.12a Prise up the trim panel . . .

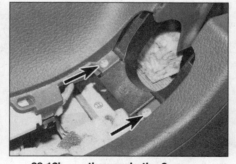

28.12b . . . then undo the 2 screws (arrowed) . . .

28.12c . . . and lift out the connecting piece

28.13a Prise up and remove the panel above the ashtray . . .

28.13b . . . then undo the 2 screws (arrowed) and lift out the ashtray

28.14a Undo the 2 screws at the rear of the gear/selector lever aperture (arrowed) . . .

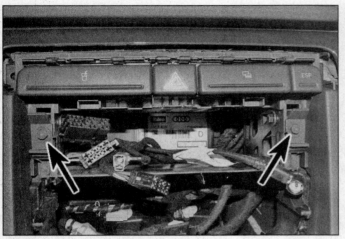

28.14b . . . 2 screws at the top of the console (arrowed) . . .

28.14c . . . 2 screws at the front of the gear/selector lever aperture (arrowed) . . .

Disconnect any wiring plugs as the console is withdrawn.

Refitting

15 Refitting is a reversal of the removal procedure.

29 Facia, associated panels and crossmember – removal and refitting

Facia

Removal

1 Disconnect the battery negative lead (refer to Chapter 5A). **Note:** *If the vehicle has a security-coded radio, check that you have a copy of the code number before disconnecting the battery. Refer to your Audi dealer if in doubt.*

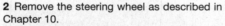

28.14d . . . 2 screws below the heater/ air conditioning control panel aperture (arrowed) . . .

2 Remove the steering wheel as described in Chapter 10.
3 Remove the driver's side storage compartment as described in Section 33.
4 Remove the instrument cluster, ESP and

28.14e . . . and 2 nuts (arrowed) at the rear of the console

hazard warning switches as described in Chapter 12.
5 Remove the passenger's side glovebox as described in Section 30.
6 Remove the passenger's side airbag as described in Chapter 12.
7 Remove the centre console as described in Section 28.
8 The centre section of the facia panel is secured by 4 screws. 2 in the audio unit aperture facing sideways, and one in each upper corner of the section. Undo the screws and remove the centre section **(see illustration)**.
9 Remove the main light switch and headlight range control switch as described in Chapter 12.
10 Fully extend the steering column, and set it in its lowest position. Undo the 3 screws and remove the upper and lower column shrouds. Note that to remove the lower shroud, undo the 2.5 mm Allen screw and remove the column adjustment handle **(see illustrations)**.
11 Prise up the cover in the facia centre demister vent, undo the retaining screw, and remove the sunlight sensor **(see illustrations)**. Disconnect the sensor wiring plugs as it is withdrawn.
12 Undo the screw in the sunlight sensor aperture, and carefully prise up the facia centre demister vent **(see illustrations)**.
13 Undo the 2 bolts in the centre demister

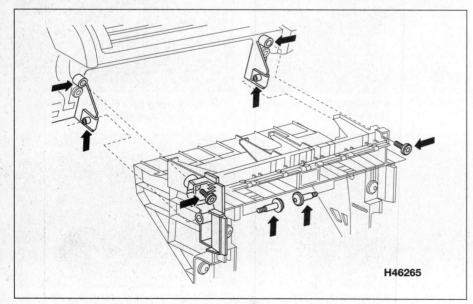

29.8 Undo the screws (arrowed) and remove the facia centre section

H46265

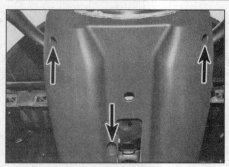

29.10a Undo the column shroud retaining screws (arrowed) . . .

29.10b . . . then undo the 2.5 mm Allen screw securing the adjustment lever

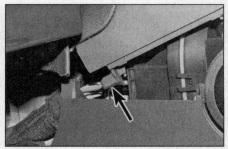

29.10c Note how the rear edge of the upper shroud hooks into the lower shroud (arrowed)

29.11a Prise up the cover . . .

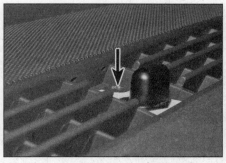

29.11b . . . undo the screw (arrowed), and remove the sunlight sensor

29.12a Undo the screw . . .

vent aperture, and manoeuvre the loudspeaker from the facia (see illustration). Disconnect the speaker wiring plug as it is withdrawn.
14 Disconnect the wiring plugs from the left-

and right-hand side vent temperature sensors, and the centre vent (see illustrations).
15 Carefully prise off the trim panels from each end of the facia (see illustration).

16 Undo the 2 bolts at each end of the facia (see illustration).
17 Remove the 2 bolts in the instrument cluster aperture (see illustration).

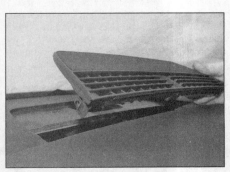

29.12b . . . and remove the centre demister vent

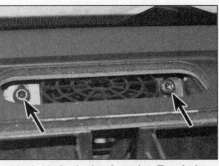

29.13 Undo the loudspeaker Torx bolts (arrowed)

29.14a Disconnect the left- and right-hand vent temperature sensors wiring plugs (left-hand vent plug arrowed) . . .

29.14b . . . and the centre vent sensor plug

29.15 Prise the panel from the each end of the facia

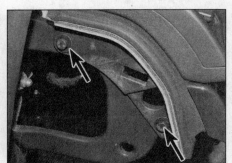

29.16 Undo the 2 bolts (arrowed) at each end of the facia

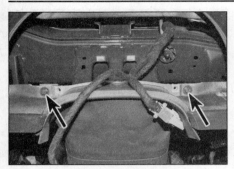

29.17 The facia is retained by 2 bolts in the instrument cluster aperture (arrowed) . . .

29.18 . . . 4 bolts in the centre of the facia (arrowed) . . .

29.19 . . . and one bolt in the right-hand rear corner (arrowed)

29.23 Undo the fusebox retaining screws (arrowed)

29.24 Undo the relay carrier plate nuts (arrowed)

29.25 Unscrew the Allen screw securing the pedal bracket to the crossmember (arrowed)

18 Undo the 4 bolts in the centre of the facia **(see illustration)**.
19 Undo the bolt at the right-hand rear corner of the facia **(see illustration)**.
20 Make a final check to ensure that all wiring looms are released from their retaining clips and carefully withdraw the facia.

Refitting

21 Refitting is a reversal of the removal process. Ensure that the heater control cables and all wiring harnesses are correctly routed and clipped in position.

Facia crossmember

Removal

22 Remove the facia as described above.
23 Undo the 2 retaining screws, and detach the fusebox at the driver's end of the facia **(see illustration)**. Release the wiring harness from the crossmember, and move the fusebox to one side.
24 Undo the nuts securing the relay carriers plate(s), then release the wiring harness retaining clips and lay the relay carrier plates to one side **(see illustration)**.
25 Unscrew the single Allen screw securing

the brake/clutch pedal support bracket to the crossmember **(see illustration)**.
26 Mark the relationship of the steering column to the crossmember, slacken and remove the four retaining bolts, and lower the steering column from the crossmember. Support the column on an axle stand. Do not allow it to hang down unsupported, or the steering universal joint may be damaged **(see illustration)**.
27 Undo the 6 bolts securing the right-hand support bracket **(see illustration)**. Note that it is sufficient to slacken the upper, foremost bolt, and allow the support to swivel.

29.26 Steering column mounting bolts (arrowed)

29.27 Facia crossmember right-hand support bracket

29.30 Undo the bolts and remove the bracket at the passenger's end of the facia (arrowed)

29.32a Move the ECM to one side, and undo the wiring connector plate screws (arrowed) . . .

29.32b . . . then undo the Allen screw (arrowed) in the plenum chamber

29.34a The crossmember is secured by 2 nuts at the driver's end . . .

29.34b . . . and one at the passenger's end

29.35 Prise out the pin and remove the centre vent

28 Unclip the centre-top air duct from the heater/air conditioning housing.

29 Undo the bolts and remove the left-hand support bracket. Release any wiring loom retaining clips.

30 Undo the heater/air conditioning support bracket bolts at the passenger's end of the crossmember **(see illustration)**.

31 Working in the engine compartment, remove the ECM from the plenum chamber as described in the relevant part of Chapter 4. There is no need to disconnect the ECM wiring plugs.

32 Working through the aperture exposed by the ECM removal, undo the two screws securing the wiring connector plate to the crossmember, and the screw securing the crossmember to the plenum chamber **(see illustrations)**.

33 Undo the nuts and detach the electrical earth connections from each end, and the centre of the crossmember.

34 The crossmember is secured by 1 nut at the passenger's end, 2 at the driver's end, and 1 bolt on the driver's side securing it to the bulkhead. Undo the nuts/bolt and pull the crossmember rearwards a few millimetres **(see illustrations)**.

35 The centre vent is pinned to the crossmember, but the pins can only be accessed once the crossmember has been partly withdrawn. Prise out the pins and withdraw the vent **(see illustration)**.

36 Prise out the clips and detach the wiring loom from the front edge of the crossmember. Make a final check to ensure all wiring connectors/loom retaining clips are released, and remove the crossmember.

Refitting

37 Refitting is the reversal of removal, bearing in mind the following points:
  a) *Ensure all wiring looms are routed correctly, and secured properly.*
  b) *Tighten all fasteners securely.*

30 Glovebox –
removal and refitting

Removal

1 Open the glovebox lid and undo the 3 bolts at the top edge, and the 2 bolts at the lower edge **(see illustrations)**.

2 Pull the glovebox downwards, note their fitted positions and disconnect the wiring plugs as the glovebox is withdrawn.

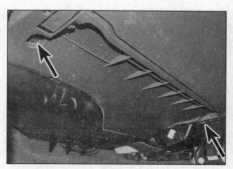

30.1a Undo the 2 bolts at the lower edge of the glovebox (arrowed) . . .

Refitting

3 Refit in the reverse order of removal.

31 Interior mirror –
removal and refitting

⚠ *Warning: Use extreme care whilst attempting this procedure; the windscreen is easily cracked.*

Basic mirror with rigid base

Removal

1 Twist the mirror 90° anti-clockwise, and remove it from the mounting plate.

Refitting

2 To refit, position the support arm at 90° to the vertical, then carefully turn it clockwise to the point where the lock spring is felt to engage.

30.1b . . . and the 3 at the top edge (arrowed)

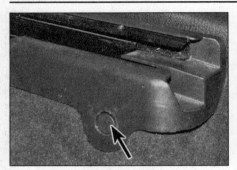

32.3 Prise out the seal rail cover retaining clip (arrowed)

Mirror with automatic anti-dazzle and/or compass

Removal

3 Carefully unclip the cable duct cover, and unplug the wiring connector.

4 Twist the mirror 90° anti-clockwise, and remove it from the mounting plate. Do not apply pressure to the cable duct, as it's easily damaged.

Refitting

5 Refitting is a reversal of removal.

Mirror mounting plate

6 If the mirror mounting plate becomes detached, clean away the old glue, then apply a suitable glass-to-metal glue in accordance with the glue manufacturer's instructions, and refit the mounting plate into position. Ensure that the plate is correctly orientated, so that when the mirror is fully fitted to it, the mirror support arm is vertical.

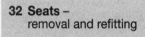

32 Seats – removal and refitting

Front seat

⚠️ **Warning: Both front seats are equipped with side airbags. Prior to disconnecting the airbag wiring plug, it is essential you are electrostatically discharged by touching a door lock or vehicle body briefly.**

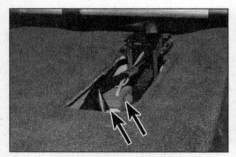

32.8a Lift up the cover under the front seat, and disconnect the wiring plugs (arrowed)

32.6 Prise out the clip, undo the Torx bolt, and remove the cover from the rear of the seat rail (arrowed)

1 Disconnect the battery negative cable (see Chapter 5A).

2 Move the seat rearwards to the extent of its travel.

3 At the inner side of the outer seat rail, prise out the securing clip, and prise up the seat rail cover and pull it forwards from the rail (see illustration).

4 Undo the multipoint bolt at the front of each seat rail securing the seat to the vehicle body.

5 Move the seat fully forwards.

6 Prise out the clip, and undo the Torx bolt on each rail, and remove the covers (see illustration).

7 Undo the bolt at the rear of the each seat rail.

8 Lift up the cover in the floor then unplug the airbag wiring plug (see warning above), and where fitted, disconnect the wiring plugs for the seat heating and motor systems, and remove the seat from the vehicle. If required, prise up the seat belt anchor plastic cover, lever out the retaining clip, and push the seat belt anchor downwards to disconnect it from the seat (see illustrations). Due to the risk of injury or component failure, no further dismantling of the seats is recommended.

Note: *Whilst the seat is removed from the vehicle, Audi insist that the side airbag should still be earthed. This can be achieved with an Audi adapter/loom (VAS 6036) plugged into the connector on the seat and the connector to the airbag module. In the absence of the Audi adapter/loom, connect a cable from the yellow connector under the seat to a good chassis earth point.*

32.8b Prise up the plastic cover, lever out the clip (arrowed) and push the seat belt anchor downwards to disconnect it

9 Refit the seat in the reverse order of removal. **Note:** *After refitting the seat(s), the airbag warning light on the dash may signal a fault. Take the vehicle to an Audi dealer or suitably-equipped specialist to have the self diagnosis system interrogated and the fault code erased.*

Rear seat bench

Saloon and Cabriolet models

10 On models with rear seat side airbags, disconnect the battery negative cable (see Chapter 5A).

11 Grasp the front lower edge of the seat and pull it upwards to release the retaining pins from their plastic sockets. Note that the plastic sockets should be removed from the floor during seat removal and discarded – fit new ones before installing the seat bench (see illustration).

12 Slide the seat bench forward and remove it from the vehicle. Disconnect the airbag wiring plug as the seat is removed (where applicable).

13 Refit the seat bench in the reverse order of removal, using new seat plastic sockets.

Avant models

14 On models with rear seat side airbags, disconnect the battery negative cable (see Chapter 5A).

15 Grasp the front lower edge of the seat and pull it upwards to release the retaining pins from their plastic sockets. Note that the plastic sockets should be removed from the floor during seat removal and discarded – fit new ones before installing the seat bench.

16 Slide the seat bench forward and remove it from the vehicle. Disconnect the airbag wiring plug as the seat is removed (where applicable).

17 Refit the seat bench in the reverse order of removal, using new seat plastic sockets.

One-piece rear seat backrest

18 Remove the rear seat bench as described above.

19 Remove the head restraints, by pressing the release button (where fitted) and pulling the head restraints from the seat backs, then on models with guides that incorporate a 'slide-in locking mechanism' insert a thin

32.11 Renew the plastic sockets

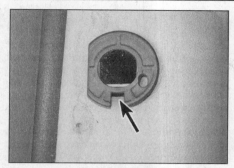

32.19a Insert thin screwdriver into the slot alongside the headrest guide (arrowed) . . .

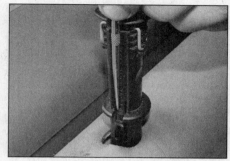

32.19b . . . then lever in the retaining clip (shown with the guide removed for clarity)

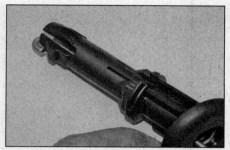

32.19c Use a length of welding rod with a hook on the end to lever in the retaining clip at the base of the headrest guide

32.19d Then pull the guide from the seat back

32.21 When refitting the seat back, ensure the lugs at the lower edge of the seat back engage with the slots in the vehicle body

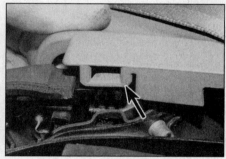

32.22a Prise out the clip (arrowed) . . .

bladed screwdriver (2 mm max) alongside the head restraint guide, and lever in the retaining clip. On models without the 'slide-in locking mechanism', insert a tool with a hook fashioned on the end to the base of the guide (stiff welding rod will suffice), and lever in the retaining clip located at the front edge **(see illustrations)**. Pull the guides from the seat backrest.

Saloon models

20 Fold down the centre armrest, push the locking tabs outwards, and remove the ski hatch frame (where applicable). Pull the top edge of the backrest forwards to release it from the plastic retaining sockets, then lift it up to release it from the lower clips. Audi insist that the plastic retaining sockets must be renewed.
21 Refit the seat backrest in the reverse order of removal **(see illustration)**.

Cabriolet models

22 Open the convertible top compartment by operating the hood opening button, then prise out the clip at the outer edge, pull up the front edge and disengage the seat belt webbing guide from the top of the seat back **(see illustrations)**.
23 Pull the seat back central hatch forwards at the top and lift it from place **(see illustration)**.
24 Undo the bolts at the lower edge of the backrest and lift the seat back from place **(see illustration)**.
25 Refit the seat backrest in the reverse order of removal.

Split rear seat backrest

26 Fold down both backrests, then prise up the trim from the centre hinge **(see illustration)**.

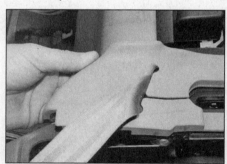

32.22b . . . and manoeuvre the seat belt webbing guide from the seat back

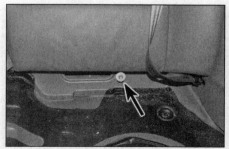

32.24 Undo the bolts (left-hand bolt arrowed) at the base of the seat back each side

27 Undo the retaining bolt, lift out the clip and remove the backrest, disengaging the backrest from the locating pin on the vehicle body **(see illustration)**. To completely remove

32.23 Open the central hatch, and lift it from place

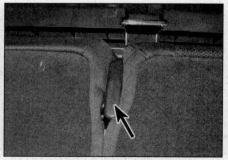

32.26 Prise up the trim from the centre hinge (arrowed) . . .

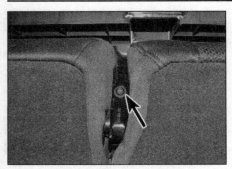

32.27 . . . then undo the bolt and lift out the backrest (arrowed)

the backrest, undo the centre seat belt anchorage bolt.

28 Refit the seat backrest in the reverse order of removal.

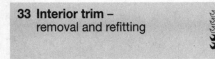

33 Interior trim – removal and refitting

Interior trim panels

Removal

1 The interior trim panels are secured using either screws or various types of trim fasteners, usually studs or clips.

2 Check that there are no other panels overlapping the one to be removed; usually there is a sequence that has to be followed, and this will only become obvious on close inspection.

3 Remove all obvious fasteners, such as screws. If the panel will not come free, it is held by hidden clips or fasteners. These are usually situated around the edge of the panel and can be prised up to release them; note, however that they can break quite easily so new ones should be available. The best way of releasing such clips without the correct type of tool is to use a large flat-bladed screwdriver. Note in many cases that the adjacent sealing strip must be prised back to release a panel.

4 When removing a panel, **never** use excessive force or the panel may be damaged; always check carefully that all fasteners or other relevant components have been removed or released before attempting to withdraw a panel.

Refitting

5 Refitting is the reverse of the removal procedure; secure the fasteners by pressing them firmly into place and ensure that all disturbed components are correctly secured to prevent rattles.

Carpets

6 The passenger compartment floor carpet is in one piece and is secured at its edges by screws or clips, usually the same fasteners used to secure the various adjoining trim panels.

7 Carpet removal and refitting is reasonably straightforward but very time-consuming because all adjoining trim panels must be removed first, as must components such as the seats, the centre console and seat belt lower anchorages.

Headlining

8 The headlining is clipped to the roof and can be withdrawn only once all fittings such as the grab handles, sunvisors, sunroof (if fitted), windscreen and rear quarter windows' and related trim panels have been removed, and the door, tailgate and sunroof aperture sealing strips (as applicable) have been prised clear.

9 Note that headlining removal requires considerable skill and experience if it is to be carried out without damage and is therefore best entrusted to an expert.

Parcel shelf (Saloon models)

10 Remove the rear seat backrest (models with a one-piece backrest), or fold the rear seat backrests forwards (as applicable) – see Section 32, then remove the D-pillar trim panels as described in this Section.

11 Prise up the loudspeaker panel from the shelf, undo the bolts securing the speakers to the parcel shelf, and the bolts securing the sunblind (where applicable). Disconnect the sunblind wiring plug as it's withdrawn.

12 Pull the parcel shelf forwards to release the clips at its front edge, and manoeuvre it from the cabin **(see illustration)**. Disconnect the high-level brake light wiring plug as the shelf is withdrawn.

13 Refitting is a reversal of removal.

A-pillar trim

Upper section

14 Remove the sunvisor as described in Section 36.

15 Fold down the roof grab handle, prise down the flaps, and undo the 2 bolts **(see illustrations)**.

16 Prise out the airbag label at the rear of the pillar trim, then undo the bolt in the label aperture **(see illustration)**.

17 Starting at the rear, pull the A-pillar trim from place, releasing the 3 push-on clips, then pull it to the rear to release it from the facia panel. Manoeuvre the trim from the cabin.

18 Refitting is a reversal of removal, ensuring the lug at the front edge of the trim engages correctly **(see illustration)**.

Lower section/sill trim

19 Unclip the trim panel from the end of the

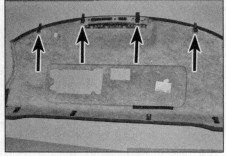

33.12 Note the locating lugs at the rear edge of the parcel shelf (arrowed)

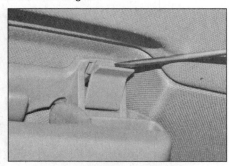

33.15a Fold down the flaps . . .

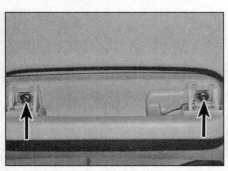

33.15b . . . then undo the Torx bolts (arrowed)

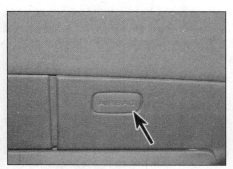

33.16 Prise out the airbag label (arrowed), and remove the bolt beneath

33.18 Note how the lug engages with the pin (arrowed)

33.19 Pull the pillar intermediate trim from place (arrowed)

33.20 Pull the sill trim upwards to release the clips

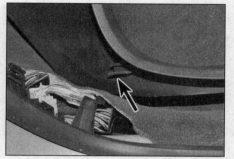

33.21 Note how the hook (arrowed) on the sill trim engages with the bracket

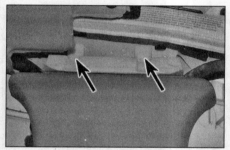

33.26 Pull the pillar trim downwards to disengage the hooks at the top edge (arrowed)

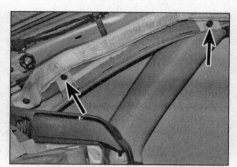

33.33a Undo the screws at the top and rear edges of the C-pillar trim (arrowed) . . .

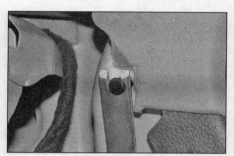

33.33b . . . then prise out the centre pin and lever out the plastic rivet at the lower front edge

facia, then carefully pull the pillar intermediate trim from place (see illustration).

20 Unclip the trim at the upper edge, then pull up the rear of the trim to release it from the 2 clips on the sill (see illustration).

21 Pull the trim rearwards to release it from the hooked bracket on the vehicle body (see illustration).

22 Refitting is a reversal of removal, ensuring the hooked bracket is correctly engaged.

B-pillar trim

Upper section

23 Prise up the plastic cover over the seat belt lower anchorage point on the front seat, then lever out the clip, push the belt anchorage downwards and detach it from the seat (see illustration 32.8b).

24 Release the rear of the A-pillar trim as previously described in this Section.

25 On Saloon models, release the front edge of the D-pillar trim as described in this Section. On Avant models, remove the trim above the rear doors as described in paragraphs 42 to 44 of this Section.

26 Pull the lower edge of the B-pillar upper trim inwards to release the retaining clips, then pull the trim downwards to release it from the hooks at the top edge (see illustration). Feed the seat belt through the trim as it is withdrawn.

27 Refitting is a reversal of removal, ensuring the seatbelt height adjuster mechanism aligns correctly with the inside of the trim.

Lower section

28 Remove the upper section of the B-pillar trim as previously described.

29 Unclip the rear end of the lower A-pillar trim, as previously described in this Section.

30 Pull the lower section of the B-pillar trim upwards to release it from the clip at the rear lower edge of the pillar and the clip at the upper edge.

31 Refitting is a reversal of removal, ensuring the guide pin at the rear of the trim engages correctly with the sill.

C-pillar trim

Saloon models

32 Remove the rear parcel shelf as described in this Section.

33 Undo the bolt at the top of the C-pillar trim panel, and the bolt at the rear edge, then prise out the centre pin and lever out the plastic expanding rivet at the front lower edge of the trim (see illustrations).

34 Reach under the seat belt guide, push up the retaining clip, then push the guide

rearwards (see illustration).

35 Pull the pillar trim inwards to release the retaining clip, then remove it along with the seat belt guide.

36 Refit the C-pillar trim and clip it into place.

37 Refit the seat belt guide, and thread the seat belt into place.

38 The remainder of refitting is a reversal of removal.

Avant models

39 Remove the rear seat backrest as described in Section 32.

40 Remove the rear seat side padding. The padding is secured by 1 bolt at its base, then slacken the locknut and unscrew the bolt at the top (see illustration 33.73a and 33.73b).

41 Remove the luggage compartment side trim panel, as described in this Section.

42 Remove the A-pillar trim and D-pillar trim as described in this Section.

43 Fold down the roof grab handle, fold

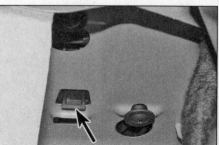

33.34 Push up the retaining clip, and slide the seat belt guide rearwards (arrowed – viewed from beneath the guide)

33.43 Pull down the handle, fold down the flaps and undo the bolts (arrowed)

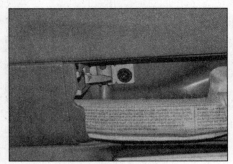

33.44a Undo the Torx bolt at the rear of the C-pillar trim . . .

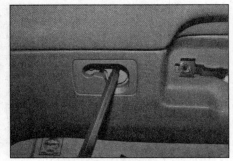

33.44b . . . then press in the cover and undo the Torx bolt

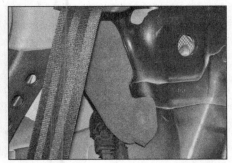

33.45a Pull out the foam packing . . .

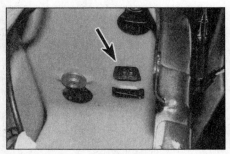

33.45b . . . then working underneath, depress the clip (arrowed) and slide the seat belt guide rearwards

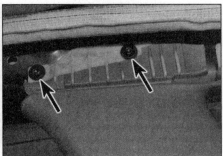

33.46a Undo the Torx bolts at the top of the C-pillar trim (arrowed) . . .

33.46b . . . then pull the trim inwards to release the clip. Note the locating pin (arrowed)

down the flaps, and unscrew the 2 bolts **(see illustration)**.

44 Undo the Torx bolt at the rear of the trim above the rear passenger's door, then press in the cover and undo the Torx bolt just in front

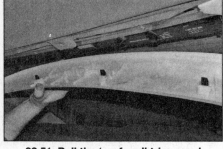

33.51 Pull the 'roof end' trim panel downwards to release the clips

of the grab handle aperture **(see illustrations)**. Remove the trim.

45 Pull out the foam, then working underneath the seat belt guide, depress the clip and slide the guide rearwards to remove it **(see illustrations)**.

46 Slacken the head airbag rear mounting bolts above the C-pillar, then undo the 2 bolts at the top of the C-pillar trim, and pull the trim inwards to release it from the vehicle body **(see illustrations)**.

47 Refitting is a reversal of removal.

D-pillar trim

Saloon models

48 Release the rear edge of the A-pillar trim as previously described in this Section.

49 Fold down the roof grab handle, prise down the flaps and remove the 2 mounting bolts **(see illustration 33.15a and 33.15b)**.

50 Pull the front edge of the D-pillar trim from the B-pillar.

51 Carefully pull down the 'roof end' trim to release it from the 4 retaining clips **(see illustration)**.

52 Undo the screw in the top corner, then pull the trim from the D-pillar to release the 3 retaining clips, and pull the trim up from the parcel shelf **(see illustrations)**.

53 Refitting is a reversal of removal.

Avant models

54 Pull the roof end trim downwards to release it from the 4 retaining clips **(see illustration)**.

55 Press-in the cover plate in the load guard securing lug (above the rear side window), and undo the Torx screw in the aperture **(see illustration)**.

56 Unclip/unscrew the rear edge of the luggage compartment side trim as described in this Section.

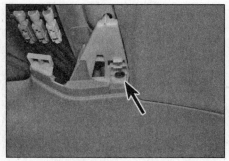

33.52a Undo the screw at the top of the D-pillar trim (arrowed)

33.52b Pull the D-pillar trim upwards from the parcel shelf

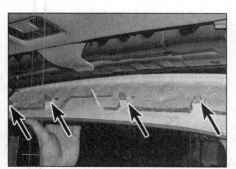

33.54 Pull the roof end trim downwards to release the clips (arrowed)

33.55 Press in the cover, and undo the screw

33.57 Release the push-in clips, then pull the trim rearwards to release the front clip (arrowed)

33.60 Undo the two bolts at the lower edge of the driver's storage compartment/ panel, and the one at the end (arrowed)

33.61 Unclip the diagnostic socket as the panel is withdrawn

33.66 Undo the nuts (arrowed) and pull the rear sill trim upwards

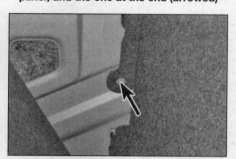

33.68 Unscrew the fasteners at the centre, outer edges of the rear seat backrest trim (arrowed)

57 Starting at the top, pull the D-pillar trim inwards to release the retaining clips, then pull it rearwards to release it from the clip at the front edge **(see illustration)**.

58 Refitting is a reversal of removal.

Driver's storage compartment

59 Carefully pull the trim panel from the end of the facia **(see illustration 29.15)**.

60 Undo the bolt at the end of the storage compartment, and the 2 bolts at its lower edge **(see illustration)**.

61 Starting at the top, pull the compartment from the facia panel, unclipping the diagnostic socket, and any wiring plugs as the compartment is withdrawn **(see illustration)**.

62 Refitting is a reversal of removal.

Anti-soiling tray

63 Release the tray from the fastener under the parcel shelf.

64 Release the lower retaining clips, and lift out the tray.

65 Refitting is a reversal of removal.

Luggage compartment side trim

Saloon models

66 Take out the luggage compartment floor covering, then undo the 2 nuts behind the spare wheel, and pull the rear sill trim upwards from its retaining clips **(see illustration)**. Disconnect the luggage compartment light as the trim is withdrawn.

67 Where fitted, lift the load securing ring, and undo the 2 bolts in the ring recess.

68 Unscrew and remove the fasteners at the centre, outer edges of the rear seat backrest trim **(see illustration)**.

69 Lift the outer edge of the storage box in the left-hand side trim panel, and disengage the clips at the inner edge **(see illustration)**.

70 Pull the rubber weatherstrip from the boot

lid aperture, then carefully release the clips at the top rear edges of the trim panel using a flat-bladed tool **(see illustration)**. Release the clips at the top, centre and rear lower edge of the luggage compartment trim, then pull the trim inwards and manoeuvre the trim from the cabin.

71 Refitting is a reversal of removal.

Avant models

72 Remove the luggage compartment floor covering, then undo the 4 Torx bolts and pull the tailgate sill trim upwards to release its retaining clips **(see illustration)**.

73 Remove the rear seat bench as described in Section 32, then remove the rear seat side padding. The padding is secured by 1 bolt at its base, then slacken the locknut and unscrew the bolt at the top **(see illustrations)**.

74 Lift the load securing ring, and undo the 2 Torx bolts in the ring recesses **(see illustration)**.

33.69 Remove the storage box

33.70 Prise out the centre pins, then lever out the clips around the edge of the luggage compartment side trim

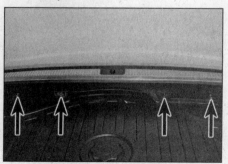

33.72 Undo the 4 Torx bolts (arrowed) and pull the sill trim upwards

33.73a Undo the bolt (arrowed) at the base of the rear seat side padding . . .

33.73b . . . then slacken the locknut and undo the bolt

33.74 Lift the load securing rings, and undo the Torx bolts

33.75 Undo the bolt (arrowed) at the rear, upper edge of the trim

33.76 Pull the trim panel inwards to release the clips

33.79 Note the push-in clips on the underside of the rear cross panel (arrowed)

33.80a Prise out the covers (arrowed) and undo the two horizontal screws . . .

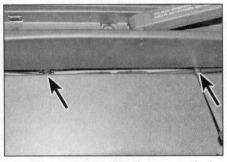

33.80b . . . followed by the two vertical screws (arrowed)

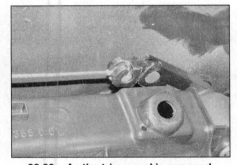

33.80c As the trim panel is removed, disengage the Bowden cable

75 Undo the bolt at the upper rear corner of the luggage compartment side trim (see illustration).

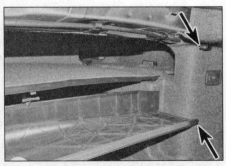

33.81 Bent the hood storage flap slightly to disengage the end of the flap from the hinge pin (arrowed), then slide the flap forwards to disengage the central hooks

76 Pull the luggage compartment side trim inwards to release the 4 retaining clips (see illustration). Manoeuvre the trim from the cabin. Disconnect the power socket wiring plug as the trim is withdrawn (where applicable).

77 Refitting is a reversal of removal.

Cabriolet models

78 Ensure the hood is closed. Take out the luggage compartment floor covering, then prise out the luggage compartment light from the rear cross-panel and disconnect the wiring plug.

79 Remove the rear cross-panel by pulling it upwards from the retaining clips (see illustration).

80 Pull open the storage box release lever, prise out the 2 covers and undo the 2 horizontal and 2 vertical retaining screws securing the hood storage box handle mount trim. Pull the

trim from the retaining clips and disengage the Bowden cable (see illustrations).

81 Bend the hood top compartment flap slightly and disengage it from the hinges. Slide the flap forwards to release it from the central hooks underneath (see illustration).

82 Prise out the luggage compartment light from the side panel, and disconnect the wiring plug.

83 Release the clip at the top of the luggage compartment side trim, then pull the rear edge of the trim forwards to release the retaining clip, and manoeuvre the trim from the vehicle. Disconnect the power socket wiring plug as the trim is removed.

84 Refitting is a reversal of removal.

Rear side trim – Cabriolet models only

85 Remove the rear seat bench and backrest as described in Section 32.

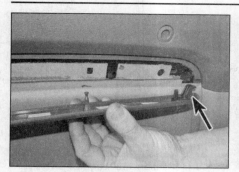

33.86 Note the hook at the front edge of the trim panel (arrowed)

86 Pull out the trim panel from the centre section of the rear side trim, starting at the rear edge, then slide it rearwards **(see illustration)**.
87 Lift out the centre section of the trim panel **(see illustration)**.
88 Undo the bolt at the rear upper corner of the trim, then pull the trim inwards to release the retaining clips **(see illustrations)**. If required, prise off the plastic cover, and undo the lower seat belt anchorage bolt. Free the seat belt from the lower anchorage rail and feed it through the side trim. Manoeuvre the trim from the cabin.
89 Refitting is a reversal of removal, ensuring the side trim retaining clips are in place before refitting the trim, and the top of the trim engages properly with the rubber guide as the trim is lowered into place.

34 Seat belt tensioning mechanism – general information

All models are fitted with seat belt pretensioners that are integrated into the airbag control system. The system is designed to instantaneously take up any slack in the seat belt in the case of a direct or oblique frontal impact, therefore reducing the possibility of injury to the occupants. Each front seat inertia reel is fitted with its own tensioner, which is triggered by a frontal impact above a predetermined force. Lesser impacts and impacts to the rear of the vehicle will not trigger the system.

When the system is triggered, the explosive gas in the tensioner mechanism retracts and locks the seat belt. This prevents the seat belt moving and keeps the occupant firmly in position in the seat. Once the tensioner has been triggered, the seat belt will be permanently locked and the assembly must be renewed, together with the impact sensors.

Always disconnect the battery negative lead (see Chapter 5A) before working on the pretensioners.

Note the following warnings before contemplating any work on the front seat belts.

 Warning:
• *Do not expose the tensioner mechanism to temperatures in excess of 100°C.*

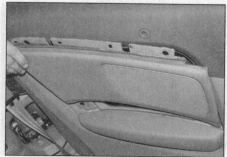

33.87 Lift out the centre section of the side trim

• *If the tensioner mechanism is dropped, it must be renewed, even it has suffered no apparent damage.*
• *Do not allow any solvents to come into contact with the tensioner mechanism.*
• *Do not attempt to open the tensioner mechanism as it contains explosive gas.*
• *Tensioners must be discharged before they are disposed of, but this task should be entrusted to an Audi dealer.*

35 Seat belts – general, removal and refitting

Note: R*efer to the warnings in Section 34 before working on the front seat belts.*

General

1 Periodically check the belts for fraying or other damage. If evident, renew the belt.
2 If the belts become dirty, wipe them with a damp cloth, using a little liquid detergent only.
3 Check the tightness of the anchor bolts, and if they are ever disconnected, make quite sure that the original sequence of fitting of washers, bushes, and anchor plate is retained.
4 Access to the front belt height adjuster and inertia reel units can be made by removing the trim from the B-pillar on the side concerned.
5 The rear seat belt anchorages can be checked by removing the rear seat bench. Access to the rear seat inertia reel units is made by removing the rear seat backrest, parcel shelf and luggage area side trim.
6 The torque wrench settings for the seat belt

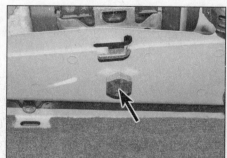

35.11a Undo the inertia reel mounting bolt (arrowed)

33.88a Undo the Torx bolt at the rear, upper corner of the trim panel (arrowed)

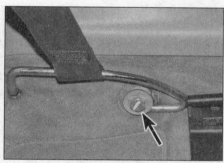

33.88b Seat belt lower anchorage bolt (arrowed)

anchor bolts and other attachments are given in the Specifications at the start of this Chapter.
7 Never modify the seat belts, or alter the attachments to the body, in any way.

Removal

Front seat belt

8 Disconnect the battery negative lead as described in Chapter 5A.
9 Remove the upper and lower B-pillar trims as described in Section 33.
10 Detach the outer seat belt anchorage point, and release the belt from the guide on the side of the seat **(see illustration 32.8b)**.
11 Undo the inertia reel mounting bolt and manoeuvre the reel from the pillar. Disconnect the pretensioners wiring plug by prising up the locking element, and disconnecting the plug **(see illustrations)**.
12 Undo the bolt at the upper seat belt anchorage point **(see illustration)**.

35.11b Prise out the locking element and disconnect the pretensioner wiring plug

35.12 Undo the seat belt upper anchorage bolt

35.13 Seat belt stalk mounting bolt (arrowed)

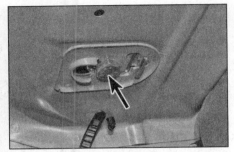

35.15 Slacken the rear side seat belt inertia reel mounting bolt (arrowed) from the luggage compartment

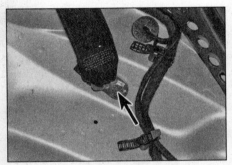

35.16 Rear side seat belt lower anchorage point bolt (arrowed)

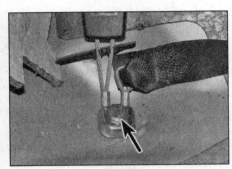

35.19 Centre seat belt lower anchorage point (arrowed)

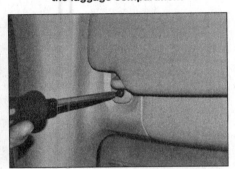

36.1 Undo the Torx screw securing the sunvisor hinge

13 To remove the front seat belt stalk, first remove the front seat as described in Section 32. Unscrew the bolt, remove the washer, and withdraw the stalk from the seat. On models with a buckle sensor, disconnect the wiring plug and release the cable from the retaining clip **(see illustration)**.

Rear side seat belt

14 On Saloon models, remove the C-pillar trim and luggage compartment side trim as described in Section 33, on Avant models, only remove the luggage compartment side trim.
15 Working in the luggage compartment, undo the bolt on the underside of the inertia reel **(see illustration)**.
16 Undo the lower seat belt anchorage point bolt and remove the belt **(see illustration)**.

Rear centre seat belt

Note: *Removal of the backrest-mounted rear centre seat belt inertia reel requires removal of the backrest upholstery and is best left to a specialist.*

17 Remove the rear bench seat and backrest as described in Section 32.
18 Remove the parcel shelf (where applicable) as described in Section 33.
19 Note the orientation of any spacers/ washers, then undo the lower anchorage point bolt **(see illustration)**.
20 Working in the luggage compartment, undo the bolt on the underside of the inertia reel.
21 Remove the seat belt from the vehicle.

Refitting

22 Refitting is a reversal of removal, ensuring all bolts are tighten to their specified torque where given.

36 Sunvisors –
removal and refitting

Removal

1 Swing the sunvisor out of its retaining clip.

Prise off the plastic cover to expose the clip retaining screw. Undo the screw and remove the retaining clip **(see illustration)**.
2 To remove the sunvisor/hinge, prise out the plastic cap, undo the retaining screw and remove the hinge/visor.

Refitting

3 Refitting is a reversal of removal.

37 Grab handles –
removal and refitting

Removal

1 Hold down the grab handle, and prise out the plastic caps. Undo the retaining screws and remove the handles **(see illustrations 33.15a and 33.15b)**.

Refitting

2 Refitting is a reversal of removal.

Chapter 12
Body electrical system

Contents

Aerial and audio amplifiers – removal and refitting 20
Airbag system – general information and precautions........... 22
Airbag system components – removal and refitting............. 23
Anti-theft alarm system – general information 24
Central locking system – general information 17
Convenience system electronic control unit – removal and refitting . 25
Electrical fault finding – general information 2
Exterior light bulbs – renewal 7
Exterior light units – removal, refitting and beam adjustment 9
Fuel filler flap locking motor – removal and refitting.............. 26
Fuses and relays – general information 3
Gas discharge headlight system – component removal, refitting and adjustment 10
General information and precautions........................ 1
Horns – removal and refitting.............................. 15
Ignition switch/steering column lock – removal and refitting 4
Instrument panel – removal and refitting 11
Interior light bulbs – renewal 8
On-board power supply control unit – removal and refitting 27
Parking aid components – general, removal and refitting 18
Radio/CD player/Autochanger – removal and refitting........... 19
Speakers – removal and refitting 21
Steering column combination switch – removal and refitting 5
Sunroof motor – removal and refitting 16
Switches – removal and refitting 6
Tailgate wiper motor – removal and refitting 14
Washer system – general 13
Windscreen wiper components – removal and refitting........... 12

Degrees of difficulty

Easy, suitable for novice with little experience	Fairly easy, suitable for beginner with some experience	Fairly difficult, suitable for competent DIY mechanic	Difficult, suitable for experienced DIY mechanic	Very difficult, suitable for expert DIY or professional

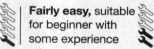

Specifications

System type .... 12 volt, negative earth

Bulbs — Power rating (watts)

	Power rating (watts)
Direction indicators	21
Direction indicator side repeaters	5
Foglamp:	
Front	55 H11
Rear	21
Headlight:	
Dipped:	
Halogen headlights	55 H7
Gas discharge headlights	35 D1S
Main	55 H7
High-level brake light	LEDs
Number plate light	5
Luggage compartment light	5 capless
Reversing light	21
Sidelights	5
Stop and tail lights	21/5
Stop-light (separate)	21
Tail light (separate)	5

Torque wrench settings

	Nm	lbf ft
Airbag control unit nuts	7	5
Crash sensor bolts	9	7
Driver's airbag-to-steering wheel screws	7	5
Head airbag retaining bolts	4	3
Passenger airbag unit nuts/screws	9	7
Rear combination light bolt	6	4
Rear window wiper arm nut	15	11
Windscreen wiper arm nuts	16	12
Windscreen wiper linkage bolts	8	6

1 General information and precautions

⚠️ **Warning: Before carrying out any work on the electrical system, read through the precautions given in 'Safety first!' at the beginning of this manual, and in Chapter 5A.**

1 The electrical system is of 12 volt negative earth type. Power for the lights and all electrical accessories is supplied by a lead-acid type battery which is charged by the alternator.

2 This Chapter covers repair and service procedures for the various electrical components not associated with the engine. Information on the battery, alternator and starter motor can be found in Chapter 5A.

3 It should be noted that prior to working on any component in the electrical system, the battery negative terminal should first be disconnected to prevent the possibility of electrical short-circuits and/or fires. **Note:** *If the vehicle has a security-coded radio, check that you have a copy of the code number before disconnecting the battery. Refer to your Audi dealer if in doubt.*

2 Electrical fault finding – general information

Note: *Refer to the precautions given in 'Safety first!' and in Chapter 5A before starting work. The following tests relate to testing of the main electrical circuits, and should not be used to test delicate electronic circuits (such as anti-lock braking systems), particularly where an electronic control module is used.*

Caution: The Audi A4 electrical system is extremely complex. Many of the ECMs are connected via a 'Databus' system, where they are able to share information from the various sensors, and communicate with each other. For instance, as the automatic gearbox approaches a gear ratio shift point, it signals the engine management ECM via the Databus. As the gearchange is made by the transmission ECM, the engine management ECM retards the ignition timing, momentarily reducing engine output, to ensure a smoother transition from one gear ratio to the next. Due to the design of the Databus system, it is not advisable to backprobe the ECMs with a multimeter in the traditional manner. Instead, the electrical systems are equipped with a sophisticated self-diagnosis system, which can interrogate the various ECMs to reveal stored fault codes, and help pinpoint faults. In order to access the self-diagnosis system, specialist test equipment (a fault code reader/scanner) is required.

General

1 Typically, electrical circuit consists of an electrical component, any switches, relays, motors, fuses, fusible links or circuit breakers related to that component, and the wiring and connectors which link the component to both the battery and the chassis. To help to pinpoint a problem in an electrical circuit, wiring diagrams are included at the end of this Chapter.

2 Have a good look at the appropriate wiring diagram, before attempting to diagnose an electrical fault, to obtain a complete understanding of the components included in the particular circuit concerned. The possible sources of a fault can be narrowed down by noting if other components related to the circuit are operating properly. If several components or circuits fail at one time, the problem is likely to be related to a shared fuse or earth connection.

3 An electrical problem will usually stem from simple cause, such as loose or corroded connections, a faulty earth connection, a blown fuse, a melted fusible link, or a faulty relay (refer to Section 3 for details of testing relays). Visually inspect the condition of all fuses, wires and connections in a problem circuit before testing the components. Use the wiring diagrams to determine which terminal connections will need to be checked in order to pinpoint the trouble-spot.

4 The basic tools required for electrical fault finding include a circuit tester or voltmeter (a 12 volt bulb with a set of test leads can also be used for certain tests); a self-powered test light (sometimes known as a continuity tester); an ohmmeter (to measure resistance); a battery and set of test leads; and a jumper wire, preferably with a circuit breaker or fuse incorporated, which can be used to bypass suspect wires or electrical components. Before attempting to locate a problem with test instruments, use the wiring diagram to determine where to make the connections.

5 Sometimes, an intermittent wiring fault (usually caused to a poor or dirty connection, or damaged wiring insulation) can be pinpointed by performing a wiggle test on the wiring. This involves wiggling the wiring by hand to see if the fault occurs as the wiring is moved. It should be possible to narrow down the source of the fault to a particular section of wiring. This method of testing can be used in conjunction with any of the tests described in the following sub-Sections.

6 Apart from problems due to poor connections, two basic types of fault can occur in an electrical circuit: open-circuit, or short-circuit.

7 Largely, open-circuit faults are caused by a break somewhere in the circuit, which prevents current from flowing. An open-circuit fault will prevent a component from working, but will not cause the relevant circuit fuse to blow.

8 Low resistance or short-circuit faults are caused by a 'short'; a failure point which allows the current flowing in the circuit to 'escape' along an alternative route, somewhere in the circuit. This typically occurs when a positive supply wire touches either an earth wire, or an earthed component such as the bodyshell. Such faults are normally caused by a breakdown in wiring insulation, A short circuit fault will normally cause the relevant circuit fuse to blow.

9 Fuses are designed to protect a circuit from being overloaded. A blown fuse indicates that there may be problem in that particular circuit and it is important to identify and rectify the problem before renewing the fuse. Always renew a blown fuse with one of the correct current rating; fitting a fuse of a different rating may cause an overloaded circuit to overheat and even catch fire.

Finding an open-circuit

10 One of the most straightforward ways of finding an open-circuit fault is by using a circuit test meter or voltmeter. Connect one lead of the meter to either the negative battery terminal or a known good earth. Connect the other lead to a connector in the circuit being tested, preferably nearest to the battery or fuse. Switch on the circuit, bearing in mind that some circuits are live only when the ignition switch is moved to a particular position. If voltage is present (indicated either by the tester bulb lighting or a voltmeter reading, as applicable), this means that the section of the circuit between the relevant connector and the battery is problem-free. Continue to check the remainder of the circuit in the same fashion. When a point is reached at which no voltage is present, the problem must lie between that point and the previous test point with voltage. Most problems can be traced to a broken, corroded or loose connection.

⚠️ **Warning: Under no circumstances may live measuring instruments such as ohmmeters, voltmeters or a bulb and test leads be used to test any of the airbag circuitry. Any testing of these components must be left to an Audi dealer or specialist, as there is a danger of activating the system if the correct procedures are not followed.**

Finding a short-circuit

11 Loading the circuit during testing will produce false results and may damage your test equipment, so all electrical loads must be disconnected from the circuit before it can be checked for short circuits. Loads are the components which draw current from a circuit, such as bulbs, motors, heating elements, etc.

12 Keep both the ignition and the circuit under test switched off, then remove the relevant fuse from the circuit, and connect a circuit test meter or voltmeter to the fuse connections.

13 Switch on the circuit, bearing in mind that some circuits are live only when the ignition switch is moved to a particular position. If voltage is present (indicated either by the tester bulb lighting or a voltmeter reading, as applicable), this means that there is a short-

circuit. If no voltage is present, but the fuse still blows with the load(s) connected, this indicates an internal fault in the load(s).

Finding an earth fault

14 The battery negative terminal is connected to 'earth': the metal of the engine/transmission and the car body – and most systems are wired so that they only receive a positive feed, the current returning through the metal of the car body. This means that the component mounting and the body form part of that circuit. Loose or corroded mountings can therefore cause a range of electrical faults, ranging from total failure of a circuit, to a puzzling partial fault. In particular, lights may shine dimly (especially when another circuit sharing the same earth point is in operation), motors (eg, wiper motors or the radiator auxiliary cooling fan motor) may run slowly, and the operation of one circuit may have an apparently unrelated effect on another. Note that on many vehicles, earth straps are used between certain components, such as the engine/transmission and the body, usually where there is no metal-to-metal contact between components due to flexible rubber mountings, etc **(see illustrations)**.

15 To check whether a component is properly earthed, disconnect the battery and connect one lead of an ohmmeter to a known good earth point. Connect the other lead to the wire or earth connection being tested. The resistance reading should be zero; if not, check the connection as follows.

16 If an earth connection is thought to be faulty, dismantle the connection and clean back to bare metal both the bodyshell and the wire terminal or the component earth connection mating surface. Be careful to remove all traces of dirt and corrosion, then use a knife to trim away any paint, so that a clean metal-to-metal joint is made. On reassembly, tighten the joint fasteners securely; if a wire terminal is being refitted, use serrated washers between the terminal and the bodyshell to ensure a clean and secure connection. When the connection is remade, prevent the onset of corrosion in the future by applying a coat of petroleum jelly or silicone-based grease or by spraying on (at regular intervals) a proprietary ignition sealer or a water dispersant lubricant.

2.14a Earth strap between the right-hand engine mounting and the chassis

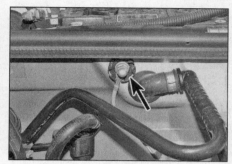

2.14b Earth connection on the engine compartment partition panel (arrowed)

2.14c Earth connection on the inner wing, left-hand side of the plenum chamber (arrowed)

2.14d There are several earth connections on the facia crossmember

3 Fuses and relays –
general information

Main fuses

1 The fuses are located on a single panel at the right-hand end of the facia on RHD models, and at the left-hand end on LHD models.

2 Access to the fuses is gained by pulling open the cover panel **(see illustrations)**.

3 Each fuse is numbered; the fuses' ratings and circuits they protect are listed on the rear

face of the cover panel. A list of fuses is given with the wiring diagrams.

4 On some models (depending on specification), some additional fuses are located in separate holders next to the relays.

5 To remove a fuse, first switch off the circuit concerned (or the ignition), then pull the fuse out of its terminals. The wire within the fuse should be visible; if the fuse is blown the wire will have a break in it, which will be visible through the plastic casing.

6 Always renew a fuse with one of an identical rating; never use a fuse with a different rating from the original or substitute anything else. Never renew a fuse more than once without tracing the source of the trouble. The fuse rating is stamped on top of the fuse; note that the fuses are also colour-coded for easy recognition.

7 If a new fuse blows immediately, find the cause before renewing it again; a short to earth as a result of faulty insulation is most likely. Where a fuse protects more than one circuit, try to isolate the defect by switching on each circuit in turn (if possible) until the fuse blows again. Always carry a supply of spare fuses of each relevant rating on the vehicle, a spare of each rating should be clipped into the base of the fusebox.

Fusible links

8 On all models, a fusible link is located adjacent to the battery in the plenum chamber **(see illustration)**. A melted link indicates a serious wiring fault – renewing the link should **not** be attempted without first diagnosing the cause of the problem.

9 Prior to renewing the link, first disconnect

3.2a Prise open the cover at the driver's end of the facia . . .

3.2b . . . to gain access to the fusebox

3.8 A fusible link (arrowed) is located alongside the battery

the battery negative cable (see Chapter 5A). Unclip the cover to gain access to the metal link. Slacken the retaining screws/nuts, then slide the link out of position.

10 Fit the new link (noting the information given in paragraphs 6 and 7) then tighten its retaining screws securely and clip the cover into position.

Relays

11 The main relays are located behind a panel on the driver's side of the facia, whilst others are located in the plenum chamber at the back of the engine compartment. The facia relays are mounted on common base, which is accessed by removing the driver's side storage compartment **(see illustrations)**. The plenum chamber relays are removed by removing the engine management ECM as described in the relevant part of Chapter 4.

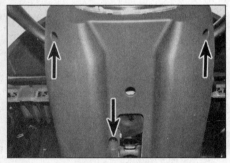

5.3a Undo the column shroud retaining screws (arrowed) . . .

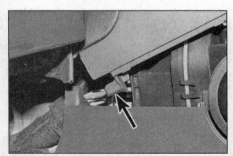

5.3c Note how the rear edge of the upper shroud hooks into the lower shroud (arrowed)

3.11a The main relay carrier is located behind the lower facia panel on the driver's side

12 The relays are of sealed construction, and cannot be repaired if faulty. The relays are of the plug-in type, and may be removed by pulling directly from their terminals. In some cases, it will be necessary to prise the two plastic clips outwards before removing the relay.

13 If a circuit or system controlled by a relay develops a fault and the relay is suspect, operate the system; if the relay is functioning, it should be possible to hear it click as it is energised. If this is the case, the fault lies with the components or wiring of the system. If the relay is not being energised, then either the relay is not receiving a main supply or a switching voltage, or the relay itself is faulty. Testing is by the substitution of a known good unit, but be careful; while some relays are identical in appearance and in operation, others look similar but perform different functions.

5.3b . . . then undo the 2.5 mm Allen screw securing the adjustment lever

5.4a Switch module retaining Allen screw (arrowed)

3.11b The auxiliary relay carrier is located under the ECM in the plenum chamber

14 To renew a relay, first ensure that the ignition switch is off. The relay can then simply be pulled out from the socket and the new relay pressed in.

4 Ignition switch/ steering column lock – removal and refitting

Refer to the information given in Chapter 10.

5 Steering column combination switch – removal and refitting

Removal

1 Disconnect the battery negative lead (refer to Section 1 and Chapter 5A).

2 Refer to Chapter 10 and remove the steering wheel.

3 Undo the retaining screws and remove the upper and lower column shrouds. The shrouds are retained by two cross-head screws and a hexagon socket-head bolt. It will be necessary to undo the 2.5 mm Allen screw and remove the column adjustment lever to completely remove the lower shroud **(see illustrations)**.

4 Slacken the retaining screw and remove the combination switch assembly from the steering column, disconnecting the wiring plugs as the switch is withdrawn **(see illustrations)**.

5 Undo the 2 Torx bolts and detach the wiper switch from the assembly **(see illustration)**.
Note: *Do not turn the spring contact assembly*

5.4b Pull the switch module over the end of the steering column

5.5 Undo the 2 Torx bolts (arrowed) and remove the wiper switch

5.6a Undo the remaining Torx bolts (arrowed) . . .

5.6b . . . and remove the control unit

whilst the steering wheel is removed. On models equipped with ESP, the steering angle sensor can be detached from the combination switch, but after re-installation, specialist equipment is required to perform a 'zero comparison'. Therefore we recommend that removal and refitting of the angle sensor is entrusted to an Audi dealer or specialist.

6 If required, undo the remaining 2 Torx bolts and detach the steering column electronics control unit (see illustrations). No further dismantling is recommended.

Refitting

7 Refit the switch over the steering column, reconnecting the wiring plugs and tighten the retaining screw. The remainder of refitting is a reversal of removal, noting that the upper column shroud engages with locating lugs at the front edge. Ensure that the wiring connections are securely made. Check for satisfactory operation on completion.

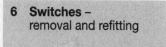

6 Switches – removal and refitting

Facia-mounted light switch

1 With the light switch in position O, press the switch centre inwards and turn it slightly to the right. Hold this position and pull the switch from the facia (see illustrations).
2 As the switch is withdrawn from the facia, disconnect the wiring plug.
3 To refit, reconnect the wiring plug.

4 Hold the switch and press the rotary part inwards and slightly to the right.
5 Insert the switch into the dash, turn the rotary part to position O and release. Check the switch for correct operation.

Glovebox light switch

6 Carefully prise the end panel from the passenger's end of the facia.
7 Working through the end of the facia, disconnect the switch wiring plug, and pull out the switch pivot pin (see illustration).
8 Swivel the switch in an anti-clockwise direction, and remove it from position.
9 Refitting is a reversal of removal.

Door mirror adjuster

10 Remove the door inner trim panel, as described in Chapter 11.
11 Detach the wiring connector, then carefully release the retaining clips and pull the switch

6.1a Turn the light switch to position O . . .

downwards and out of the door trim (see illustration).
12 Refit in the reverse order of removal.

Sunroof control

13 Carefully prise the interior/reading light lens from place, then undo the 2 screws and detach the light unit from the headlining.
14 Disconnect the sunroof switch wiring plug, then undo the 3 screws and remove the switch.
15 Refit in the reverse order of removal.

Central locking switch

Front

16 Remove the door trim panel as described in Chapter 11.
17 Disconnect the wiring plug from the switch, then press the switch from the panel (see illustration).
18 Refitting is a reversal of removal.

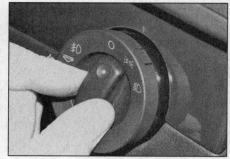

6.1b . . . and pull it from the facia

6.7 Glovebox light switch wiring plug (arrowed)

6.11 Release the clips (arrowed) and pull the switch downwards from the panel

6.17 Release the clip and press the central locking switch from the door trim panel

6.24 Release the clips (arrowed) and press the switch from the panel

6.28 Squeeze together the side of the clip securing the handbrake warning switch (arrowed)

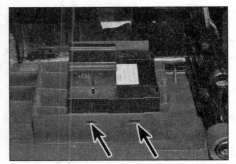

6.32 Release the clips (arrowed) and pull the switch from the panel

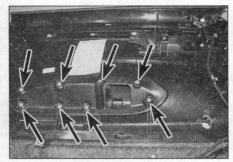

6.36 Undo the screws (arrowed) securing the armrest to the panel

6.37 Release the clips each side and pull the switch from the panel

6.42 Reach through the light switch aperture, and push the range control switch from position

Rear

19 Remove the ashtray from the rear of the centre console.
20 Press the retaining clips outwards, and swivel the switch panel to the rear.
21 Disconnect the switch wiring plug, and unclip the switch from the panel.
22 Refitting is a reversal of removal.

Luggage compartment release/ interior monitoring switches

23 Remove the door trim panel as described in Chapter 11.
24 Disconnect the switch wiring plugs, then release the retaining clips, and press the switch from the trim panel **(see illustration)**.
25 Refitting is a reversal of removal.

Courtesy light switches

26 The courtesy light are controlled by microswitches incorporated into the door

locks. The switches are not available separately. If defective, the door lock assembly must be renewed (see Chapter 11).

Handbrake warning switch

27 Remove the rear section of the centre console as described in Chapter 11.
28 The switch is simply clipped in place on the handbrake lever mounting bracket **(see illustration)**.
29 Detach the wiring connector from the switch.
30 Refit in the reverse order of removal.

Window switches

Front door switch panel

31 Remove the door trim panel as described in Chapter 11.
32 Carefully release the retaining clips **(see illustration)**.
33 Pull the switch from the panel, and

disconnect the wiring plug.
34 Refitting is a reversal of removal.

Rear door switch

35 Remove the door trim panel as described in Chapter 11.
36 Working on the inside of the door trim panel, undo the retaining Torx screws and detach the armrest from the panel **(see illustration)**. Disconnect the wiring plugs as the armrest is removed.
37 Release the retaining clips and pull the switch downwards from the panel **(see illustration)**.
38 Refitting is a reversal of removal.

Stop-light switch

39 Refer to Chapter 9.

Steering column switch

40 Refer to Section 5.

Headlight control

41 Remove the light switch as described in paragraphs 1 and 2 of this Section.
42 Reach through the light switch aperture and push the headlight range control switch from the facia. Disconnect the wiring plug as the switch is withdrawn **(see illustration)**.
43 Refit in the reverse order of removal.

Hazard warning/ESP/parking aid

44 Open the passenger's side glovebox, then using a screwdriver, carefully prise the trim from above the switch **(see illustration)**. Take great care not to damage the surrounding area.
45 Carefully prise the switch from position **(see illustration)**.

6.44 Carefully prise the trim from place . . .

6.45 . . . then prise out the switch

7.3 Unclip the wiring connectors from behind the left-hand headlight

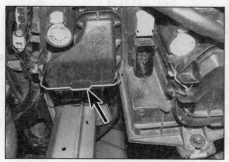

7.5 Push the clip downwards (arrowed)

7.6 Release the bulb retaining clip (arrowed)

46 Disconnect the wiring plug(s) from the switch.

47 To refit, reconnect the wiring plug(s), push the switch into the appropriate hole in the facia, then refit the trim.

Seat heating switches

48 The front seat heating switches are integral with the heating/air conditioning control panel, and cannot be renewed separately. Removal of the panel is described in Chapter 3.

49 To remove the rear seat switches, first remove the rear ashtray.

50 Press the switch panel retaining clips to the outside, and swivel the panel rearwards.

51 Disconnect the switch wiring plugs, then unclip the relevant switch from the panel.

52 Refitting is a reversal of removal.

Function select switch

53 Open the flap for the cigarette lighter in the centre console, and press the select switch from position.

54 Disconnect the switch wiring plug as it's withdrawn.

55 Refitting is a reversal of removal.

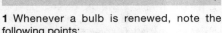

7 Exterior light bulbs – renewal

1 Whenever a bulb is renewed, note the following points:

a) *Remember that if the light has just been in use, the bulb may be extremely hot.*

b) **Do not** *touch the bulb glass with the fingers, as the small deposits can cause the bulb to cloud over.*

c) *Always check the bulb contacts and holder, ensuring that there is clean metal-to-metal contact. Clean off any corrosion or dirt before fitting a new bulb.*

d) *Wherever bayonet-type bulbs are fitted, ensure that the live contacts bear firmly against the bulb contact.*

e) *Always ensure that the new bulb is of the correct rating and that it is completely clean before fitting it.*

Headlight main beam

Note: *This section does not cover bulb*

renewal on models fitted with gas discharge headlights; refer to Section 10 for renewal details.

Left-hand side

2 Remove the plastic cover (where fitted) from the left-hand side of the engine compartment.

3 Unclip the wiring connectors behind the headlight and move them to one side **(see illustration)**.

Right-hand side

4 Remove the air cleaner housing as described in the relevant part of Chapter 4.

Both sides

5 Push the retaining clip downwards and remove the plastic cover from the rear of the headlight **(see illustration)**.

6 Disconnect the wiring plug from the rear of the bulb, then release the retaining clip and remove the bulb from the headlight, noting which way around it's fitted **(see illustration)**. If the bulb is to be refitted, do not touch the glass with the fingers. If the glass is accidentally touched, clean it with methylated spirit.

7 Fit the new bulb using a reversal of the removal procedure.

Headlight dipped beam

Left-hand side

8 Remove the headlight as described in Section 9.

Right-hand side

9 Remove the air cleaner housing as described in the relevant part of Chapter 4.

7.10 Push the retaining clip (arrowed) to one side

Both sides

10 Release the clip and detach the plastic cover from the rear of the headlight **(see illustration)**.

11 Disconnect the wiring plug from the rear of the bulb, then release the retaining clip and remove the bulb from the headlight, noting which way around it's fitted **(see illustration)**. If the bulb is to be refitted, do not touch the glass with the fingers. If the glass is accidentally touched, clean it with methylated spirit.

12 Fit the new bulb using a reversal of the removal procedure.

Sidelight

Note: *This section does not cover sidelight bulb renewal on models fitted with gas discharge headlights; refer to Section 10 for renewal details.*

Left-hand side

13 Remove the plastic cover (where fitted) from the left-hand side of the engine compartment **(see illustration 7.2)**.

14 Unclip the wiring connector from behind the headlight and move them to one side **(see illustration 7.3)**.

15 Push the retaining clip downwards and remove the plastic cover from the rear of the headlight **(see illustration 7.5)**.

16 Rotate the headlight range control motor clockwise to expose the sidelight bulbholder **(see illustration)**.

Right-hand side

17 Remove the air cleaner housing as described in the relevant part of Chapter 4.

7.11 Release the dipped beam bulb retaining clip (arrowed)

7.16 Rotate the headlight range control motor clockwise to expose the sidelight bulb (arrowed)

7.20 Squeeze together the retaining tabs each side, and pull the bulbholder from the headlight

7.21 Pull the sidelight capless (wedge-type) bulb from the holder

7.24 Disconnect the foglamp wiring plug

7.25 Rotate the bulb and holder anti-clockwise

7.28 Rotate the indicator bulbholder anti-clockwise

18 Push the retaining clip downwards and remove the plastic cover from the rear of the headlight (see illustration 7.5).
19 Rotate the headlight range control motor anti-clockwise to expose the bulbholder.

Both sides

20 Release the 2 retaining tabs and pull the bulbholder from the headlight (see illustration).
21 Pull the wedge-type bulb directly from the bulbholder (see illustration).
22 Fit the new bulb using a reversal of the removal procedure.

Front foglamp

23 Remove the front foglamp as described in Section 9.
24 Disconnect the wiring from the bulbholder (see illustration).
25 Rotate the bulbholder anti-clockwise and

pull it from the foglamp (see illustration). Note that the bulb is integral with the bulbholder.
26 Fit the new bulb using a reversal of the removal procedure.

Direction indicator

27 Remove the headlight as described in Section 9.
28 Rotate the bulbholder anti-clockwise and pull it from the headlight (see illustration).
29 Depress and twist the bulb to remove it from the bulbholder (see illustration).
30 Fit the new bulb using a reversal of the removal procedure.

Direction indicator side repeater

31 Push the lens towards the front of the vehicle, then tilt it out at the rear to release the lens from the bodywork (see illustration). Note: *The side repeater can be fitted either way round, and it is impossible to determine*

how it is fitted. If difficulty is experienced, push the lens in the opposite direction.
32 Hold the side repeater in one hand then pull out the rubber bulbholder (see illustration).
33 Pull the wedge-type bulb from the bulbholder.
34 Fit the new bulb using a reversal of the removal procedure.

Rear combination light

Saloon models

35 Fold the precut section of the luggage compartment trim to one side to access the retaining nut, then undo the nut and swivel the rear light unit outwards. Disengage the locating pins from the body as the light unit is withdrawn (see illustrations 9.16 and 9.17).
36 Disconnect the wiring plug from the bulbholder assembly.

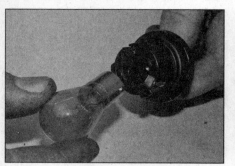

7.29 The indicator bulb is a bayonet-fit in the holder

7.31 Push the lens forwards and pull out the rear edge

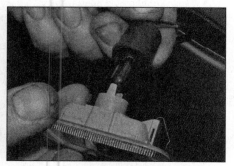

7.32 Pull the bulbholder from the lens

7.37 Squeeze together the retaining tabs and remove the bulbholder

7.38 Press and twist the bulb anti-clockwise

7.40 Prise out the plastic cap (arrowed) . . .

7.41a . . . then remove the retaining screw . . .

7.41b . . . and pull the light sideways from position. Note the locating pins (arrowed)

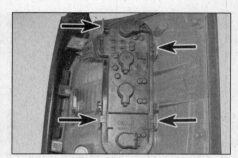

7.42 Push apart the retaining clips (arrowed), and pull the bulbholder assembly from the light

37 Squeeze the plastic tabs and withdraw the bulbholder from the rear light unit **(see illustration)**.
38 Press and twist the relevant bulb anti-clockwise, and withdraw it from the bulbholder **(see illustration)**.
39 Fit the new bulb using a reversal of the removal procedure.

Avant models

40 Prise out the plastic cap from the luggage compartment trim panel rear edge **(see illustration)**.
41 Remove the rear light retaining bolt in the cap aperture, and swivel the rear light unit outwards, disengaging the locating pins as the unit is withdrawn **(see illustrations)**.
42 Disconnect the bulbholder assembly wiring plug, then press apart the retaining clips and detach the bulbholder from the light unit **(see illustration)**.

43 To remove the bulbs, depress and twist the relevant bulb anti-clockwise.
44 Fit the new bulb using a reversal of the removal procedure.

Number plate light

45 The number plate lights are located in the boot lid or tailgate, just above the number plate. For better access to the retaining screws, open the boot lid or tailgate. Undo the retaining screw and prise out the relevant lens/bulbholder **(see illustration)**.
46 Remove the festoon-type bulb from its holder **(see illustration)**.
47 Fit the new bulb using a reversal of the removal procedure.

High-level stop-light

Saloon models

48 With the boot lid open, disconnect the

high-level stop-light wiring plug, then use a screwdriver to release the retaining clips and remove the light unit **(see illustration)**. Note that LEDs are soldered to a printed circuit board and it is not possible to renew a single LED. Where an LED is not functioning, the complete stop-light unit must be renewed.
49 Press the new stop-light unit into position until retained by the clips.

Avant models

50 Remove the tailgate trim panels as described in Chapter 11.
51 Insert a screwdriver through the wiring hole in the tailgate, and slide the retaining rail to the right **(see illustration)**. Note that this will cause the four retaining clips and the retaining rail to detach from the rear of the light unit.
52 Starting on the right-hand side, carefully prise the light unit from the outside of the

7.45 Undo the number plate lens screw

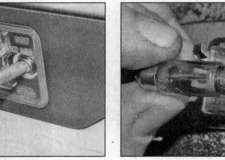

7.46 Pull the festoon bulb from the contacts

7.48 Release the high-level stop-light retaining clips (arrowed)

7.51 Working through the wiring aperture, slide the retaining rail to the right

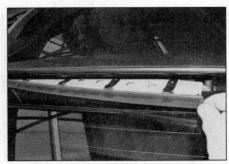

7.52 Prise the right-hand side of the high-level stop-light from the tailgate

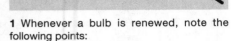

1 Whenever a bulb is renewed, note the following points:

a) *Remember that if the light has just been in use, the bulb may be extremely hot.*

b) *Always check the bulb contacts and holder, ensuring that there is clean metal-to-metal contact between the bulb and its live and earth. Clean off any corrosion or dirt before fitting a new bulb.*

c) *Wherever bayonet-type bulbs are fitted, ensure that the live contact(s) bear firmly against the bulb contact.*

d) *Always ensure that the new bulb is of the correct rating and that it is completely clean before fitting it.*

Interior/reading lights

Front reading lights

2 Unclip the cover from the light unit **(see illustrations)**.

3 Twist the bulb and remove it from the holder.

Front interior lights

4 Unclip the lens, and pull the festoon bulb from the spring contacts **(see illustrations)**.

Rear light

5 Prise free the light unit, then twist and withdraw the bulb from the holder **(see illustrations)**.

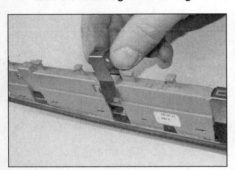

7.54a Refit the clips to the rear of the high-level stop-light . . .

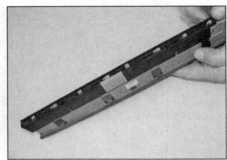

7.54b . . . then refit the retaining rail to hold the clips

tailgate, disconnecting the wiring plug as it's withdrawn **(see illustration)**.

53 The LEDs are soldered to a printed circuit board and it is not possible to renew a single LED. Where an LED is not functioning, the complete stop-light unit must be renewed.

54 Recover the retaining clips and rail, and reset them on the rear of the light unit **(see illustrations)**. Reconnect the wiring plug, and refit the light unit into the tailgate. It should engage with an audible click.

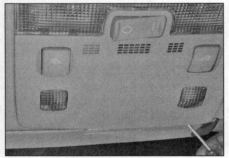

8.2a Prise out the front edge . . .

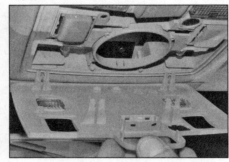

8.2b . . . and remove the reading light cover

8.4a Unclip the interior light lens . . .

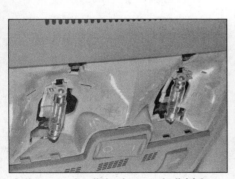

8.4b . . . and pull the festoon bulb(s) from the contacts

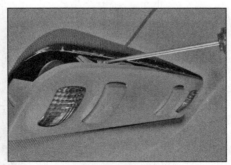

8.5a Carefully prise the light unit from the headlining

8.5b Twist the bulb anti-clockwise to remove it

All lights

6 Fit the new bulb using a reversal of the removal procedure.

Glovebox light

7 Insert a flat-bladed screwdriver behind the end of the lens, depress the retaining clip and prise free the light lens/unit **(see illustration)**.
8 Pull the capless bulb from its holder.
9 Fit the new bulb using a reversal of the removal procedure.

Sunvisor/vanity mirror light

10 Working at the outer end, prise free the lens from the headlining above the sunvisor. The festoon bulbs can be extracted from their holders.
11 Fit the new bulb using a reversal of the removal procedure.

Instrument panel bulbs

12 On all models covered by this Manual, it is not possible to renew the instrument panel bulbs individually as they are of LED design and soldered to a printed circuit board. Where an LED is not functioning, the complete instrument panel must be renewed.

Luggage compartment light

Saloon models

13 Insert a flat-bladed screwdriver behind the end of the lens, depress the retaining clip and prise free the light lens/unit **(see illustration)**.
14 Prise the reflector from place and extract the capless bulb from its holder **(see illustration)**.
15 Fit the new bulb using a reversal of the removal procedure.

Avant models

16 Insert a screwdriver into the recess and carefully prise off the lens.
17 Extract the festoon bulb from the holder.
18 Fit the new bulb using a reversal of the removal procedure.
19 To remove the tailgate-mounted bulb, carefully prise away the lens as shown **(see illustration)**.
20 Lift away the reflector (where fitted) and pull the bulb from the contacts.
21 Fit the new bulb using a reversal of the removal procedure.

Ashtray illumination

22 Remove the heater/air conditioning control panel as described in Chapter 3.
23 Remove the ashtray insert, then prise up the gear lever/selector lever surround trim.
24 Undo the 2 bolts, and lift the ashtray upwards.
25 Release the retaining clip and swivel the ashtray light from the retainer.
26 Fit the new bulb using a reversal of the removal procedure.

Switch illumination

27 Switch illumination bulbs are usually built into the switch itself, and cannot be renewed

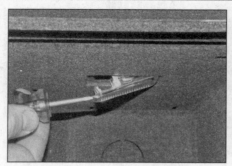

8.7 Prise out the end of the glovebox light lens

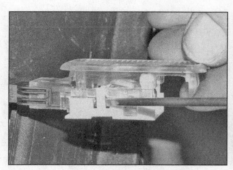

8.14 ... and prise free the reflector

separately. Refer to Section 6 and remove the switch – bulb renewal should then be self-evident, if it is possible; otherwise, renew the switch.

Heater/air conditioning control panel illumination

28 The control panel is illuminated by non-renewable LEDs. If defective, the control panel may need to be renewed.

Door handle illumination

29 Remove the door trim panel as described in Chapter 11.
30 Pull the bulb from the holder.
31 Refitting is a reversal of removal.

Door courtesy light

32 Use a screwdriver to depress the retaining clip at the end of the lens, and prise the unit from the door.

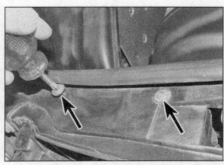

9.2 Undo the air intake duct screws (arrowed)

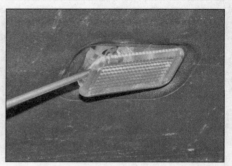

8.13 Prise the luggage compartment light from the panel . . .

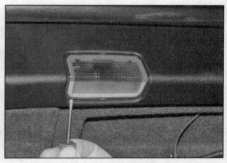

8.19 Carefully prise the lens from the tailgate trim panel

33 Disconnect the wiring and remove the courtesy light unit.
34 Prise off the cover (where fitted) and pull the bulb from the contacts.
35 Fit the new bulb using a reversal of the removal procedure.

| 9 | Exterior light units – removal, refitting and beam adjustment | |

Headlight unit removal

Caution: On models equipped with gas discharge headlights, disconnect the battery negative lead as described in Chapter 5A, prior to working on the headlights.
1 Unclip the plastic panel from the relevant side of the engine compartment (where fitted).

Right-hand headlight

2 Undo the 2 bolts and remove the air intake duct from the lock carrier panel **(see illustration)**.

Both sides

3 Remove the 2 bolts at the top of the headlight, and slacken the bolts at the rear of the headlight a few turns – there's no need to remove them **(see illustrations)**.
4 Slide the headlight unit forwards, prise the wiring loom clip from the headlight casing, then disconnect the wiring plug and withdraw it from the front of the car **(see illustration)**. Take care not to damage the vehicle paintwork as the headlight is removed.

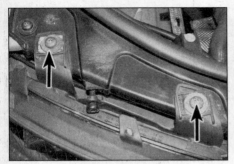

9.3a Undo the two bolts on the top of the headlight (arrowed) . . .

9.3b . . . then slacken the ones at the rear (arrowed)

9.4 Prise the wiring loom clip from the headlight casing

9.5 Use the stop-screw (arrowed) to adjust the gap between the headlight and the surrounding bodywork

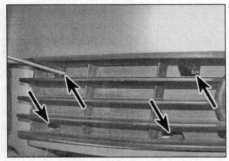

9.6 Release the 4 retaining clips (arrowed)

9.7 Front foglamp retaining Torx bolts (arrowed)

Headlight unit refitting

5 Refitting is a reversal of the removal procedure. If a new unit is being fitted, using the stop-screw, align it so that the gap between the headlight and surrounding bodywork is even **(see illustration)**. On completion check for satisfactory operation, and have the headlight beam adjustment checked as soon as possible.

Front foglamp

Removal

6 Using a screwdriver, release the 4 retaining clips and pull the air intake grille from the lower section of the bumper **(see illustration)**.
7 Undo the 2 mounting bolts, withdraw the foglamp from the front bumper, and disconnect the wiring **(see illustration)**.

Refitting

8 Refitting is a reversal of removal, but

have the foglamp beam setting checked at the earliest opportunity. An approximate adjustment can be made by positioning the car 10 metres in front of a wall marked with the centre point of the foglamp lens. Turn the adjustment screw as required. Note that only height adjustment is possible – there is no lateral adjustment.

Direction indicator side repeater

Removal and refitting

9 The procedure is as described for bulb renewal in Section 7.

Range control motor

Removal

10 Remove the headlight unit as previously described in this Section.
11 Release the clip and remove the plastic

cover from the rear of the headlight behind the main beam.
12 Rotate the motor unit (clockwise for the left-hand headlight, anti-clockwise for right-hand headlight) until it is felt to disengage from the rear of the headlight unit.
13 Disconnect the wiring from the range control motor.
14 Tilt the unit upwards so that the balljoint at the end of the adjustment shaft disengages downwards from the socket at the rear of the lens, then withdraw the motor from the headlight unit **(see illustration)**.

Refitting

15 Refitting is a reversal of removal. It may be necessary to lift the reflector to allow the adjustment shaft balljoint to engage with its socket. On completion, check for satisfactory operation, and have the headlight beam adjustment checked as soon as possible.

Rear combination light (Saloon)

Removal

16 With the boot lid open, fold forward the access flap and undo the light unit retaining bolt **(see illustration)**.
17 Swivel the light unit outwards, and disengage the locating pins from the body **(see illustration)**. Disconnect the wiring plug.

Refitting

18 Refitting is a reversal of removal, but tighten the mounting bolt to the specified torque, and ensure that the seal is correctly positioned.

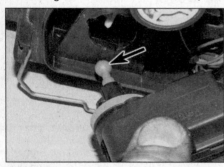

9.14 Disengage the balljoint (arrowed) from the socket

9.16 Lift the flap and remove the light retaining bolt

Rear combination light (Avant)

Removal

19 Prise out the cap from the luggage compartment trim panel rear edge (**see illustration 7.40**).

20 Remove the rear light retaining bolt in the cap aperture, and swivel the rear light unit outwards, disengaging the locating pins as the unit is withdrawn (**see illustrations 7.41a and 7.41b**).

21 Disconnect the bulbholder assembly wiring plug.

Refitting

22 Refitting is a reversal of removal, but tighten the mounting nuts to the specified torque, and ensure that the seal is correctly positioned.

Number plate light

23 The procedure is as described for bulb renewal in Section 7.

High-level stop-light

24 The procedure is as described for bulb renewal in Section 7.

Beam adjustment

Halogen headlights

25 Accurate adjustment of the headlight beam is only possible using optical beam setting equipment, and this work should therefore be carried out by an Audi dealer or suitably-equipped workshop. Tyre pressures must correct, the car must be loaded with the driver (or equivalent of 75 kg), and the fuel tank should be at least 90% full. If the fuel tank is only half full, an additional weight of 30 kg must be positioned in the luggage compartment.

26 For reference, the headlights can be adjusted using the adjuster screws, accessible via the top of each light unit (**see illustration**).

27 Some models are equipped with an electrically-operated headlight beam adjustment system which is controlled through the switch in the facia. On these models, ensure that the switch is set to the basic O position before adjusting the headlight aim.

---

10 Gas discharge headlight system – component removal, refitting and adjustment

General information

1 Gas discharge headlights were available as an optional extra on all models covered in this manual. The headlights are fitted with bulbs that produce light by means of an electric arc, rather than by heating a metal filament as in conventional halogen bulbs. The arc is generated by a control circuit which operates at voltages of above 28 000 volts. The intensity of the emitted

9.17 Note the locating pins (arrowed)

light means that the headlight beam has to be controlled dynamically to avoid dazzling other road users. An electronic control unit monitors the vehicle's pitch and overall ride height by sensors mounted on the front and rear suspension and adjusts the beam range accordingly, using the range control motors built into the headlight units.

 Warning: The discharge bulb starter circuitry operates at extremely high voltages. To avoid the risk of electric shock, ensure that the battery negative cable is disconnected before working on the headlight units (see Chapter 5A), then additionally switch the dipped beam on and off to discharge any residual voltage.

Bulb renewal

Headlight main beam

2 Remove the headlight as described in Section 9.

3 Push the retaining clip downwards, and remove the plastic cover from the rear of the headlight (**see illustration 7.5**).

4 Disconnect the wiring plug from the rear of the bulb, then release the retaining clip and pull the bulb from the reflector (**see illustration 7.6**). Note how the lugs on the bulb engage with the slots in the reflector. If the bulb is to be refitted, do not touch the glass with the fingers. If the glass is accidentally touched, clean it with methylated spirit.

5 Fit the new bulb using a reversal of the removal procedure.

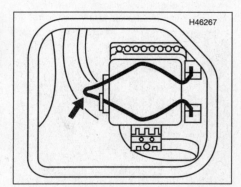

10.8 Release the clip and withdrawn the bulb

9.26 Headlight aim adjustment screws (arrowed)

Headlight dipped beam

Caution: The dipped beam bulb is under gas pressure of at least 10 bars, therefore it is recommended that protective glasses are worn during this procedure.

6 Remove the headlight as described in Section 9.

7 Release the retaining clip and detach the plastic cover from the rear of the light unit.

8 Release the retaining clip and pull the gas discharge lamp from the reflector (**see illustration**). Disconnect the wiring plug as the lamp is withdrawn. If the lamp is to be re-used, do not touch the lamp glass with bare fingers. If the glass is accidentally touched, clean it with methylated spirit.

9 Fit the new bulb using a reversal of removal procedure, ensuring the lug at the top of the lamp engages correctly with the corresponding slot in the reflector.

Sidelight

10 Remove the headlight as described in Section 9.

11 Push the retaining clip downwards and remove the plastic cover from behind the main beam bulb location (**see illustration 7.5**).

12 Release the retaining clips and pull the bulbholder from the reflector (**see illustration 7.20**).

13 Pull the wedge-type bulb directly from the bulbholder.

14 Fit the new bulb using a reversal of the removal procedure.

Direction indicator

15 Remove the headlight as described in Section 9.

16 Rotate the bulbholder anti-clockwise and pull it from the headlight (**see illustration 7.28**).

17 Depress and twist the bulb to remove it from the bulbholder (**see illustration 7.29**).

18 Fit the new bulb using a reversal of the removal procedure.

Bulb control unit

Removal

19 Remove the headlight dipped beam as described in this Section.

20 Undo the 6 bolts and detach the control unit from the base of the headlight housing (**see illustration**). Disconnect the wiring plugs as the unit is withdrawn.

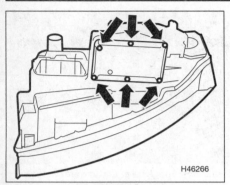

10.20 Undo the screws (arrowed) on the base of the headlight unit

Refitting

21 Refitting is a reversal of removal.

Front ride height sensor

Removal

22 The sensor is mounted on the track control link of the left-hand wheel. Apply the handbrake, then jack up the front of the vehicle and support it on axle stands (see *Jacking and vehicle support*).
23 Unplug the wiring connector from the sensor.
24 Unscrew the link retaining nut while counterholding the flats on the ball-head pin with a further spanner.
25 Unscrew the 2 mounting bolts and remove the front ride height sensor.

Refitting

26 Refitting is a reversal of removal. Note that if a new sensor has been fitted, then the headlight basic setting procedure must be carried out. This requires access to Audi diagnostic equipment – entrust this task to an Audi dealer or suitably-equipped specialist.

Rear ride height sensor

Removal

27 The sensor is secured to the left-hand trapezium link and the rear subframe. Chock the front wheels, then jack up the rear of the vehicle and support it on axle stands (*see Jacking and vehicle support*). Remove the left-hand rear roadwheel.
28 Undo the bolt securing the sensor arm bracket to the trapezium link.

29 Undo the 2 bolts securing the sensor to the mounting bracket. Disconnect the wiring plug as the sensor is withdrawn.

Refitting

30 Refitting is a reversal of removal. Note that if a new sensor has been fitted, then the headlight basic setting procedure must be carried out. This requires access to Audi diagnostic equipment – entrust this task to an Audi dealer or suitably-equipped specialist.

Setting-up for left- or right-hand drive

31 On models equipped with gas discharge headlights, the 'dipping' characteristics of the unit can be set-up for countries who drive on the left or right. Remove the headlight as described in Section 9.
32 Release the clip and remove the plastic cover from the rear of the headlight behind the dipped beam location.
33 Press the lever upwards for driving on the right, and down for driving on the left.

Beam adjustment

34 The headlight range is controlled dynamically by an electronic control unit which monitors the ride height of the vehicle by sensors fitted to the front and rear suspension. Beam adjustment can only be carried out using Audi test equipment.

Range control electronic control unit

Removal

35 The electronic control unit is located behind the passenger's glovebox. Remove the glovebox as described in Chapter 11.
36 Disconnect the unit wiring plug, then undo the 2 bolts and remove the control unit.

Refitting

37 Refitting is a reversal of removal.

Range control positioning motor

Removal

38 Remove the relevant headlight as described in Section 9.
39 Push the retaining clip downwards, and remove the plastic cover from the rear of the headlight, behind the main beam location.

40 Rotate the motor unit (clockwise for the left-hand headlight, anti-clockwise for right-hand headlight) until it is felt to disengage from the rear of the headlight unit.
41 Disconnect the wiring from the range control motor.
42 Tilt the unit upwards so that the balljoint at the end of the adjustment shaft disengages downwards from the socket at the rear of the lens, then withdraw the motor from the headlight unit.

Refitting

43 Refitting is a reversal of removal. It may be necessary to lift the reflector to allow the adjustment shaft balljoint to engage with its socket. On completion, check for satisfactory operation, and have the headlight beam adjustment checked as soon as possible.

11 Instrument panel – removal and refitting

Note: *The instrument panel includes the immobiliser control unit and its function is included in the vehicle's self-diagnosis program. If the instrument panel has a fault, it would be prudent to have the vehicle's fault code memory interrogated by an Audi dealer or specialist, prior to removing the panel.*
Note: *If the instrument panel is being substituted with a new or exchange unit, the assistance of an Audi dealer or specialist is required to initialise/adapt the various instrument panel functions.*

Removal

1 Fully extend the steering column, and move it to its lowest position.
2 Carefully prise the instrument trim panel above the steering column rearwards from place **(see illustration)**.
3 Undo the 2 Torx bolts securing the instrument panel at its lower edge **(see illustration)**.
4 Unclip the trim panel from the driver's side end of the facia.
5 Reach through the end of the facia and push the instrument panel from place.
6 As the panel is withdrawn, release the locking catches and disconnect the wiring plugs **(see illustration)**.

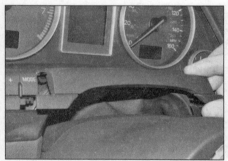

11.2 Prise away the trim panel below the instrument panel

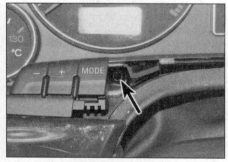

11.3 Undo the 2 Torx bolts at the lower edge of the panel (left-hand screw arrowed)

11.6 Release the locking catch and disconnect the wiring plugs

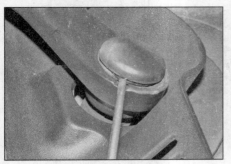

12.3a Prise off the plastic cover . . .

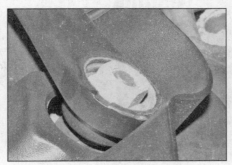

12.3b . . . and undo the spindle nut

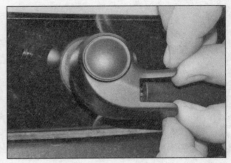

12.3c Pull the 2 sides apart, and remove the cover

12.3d Prise the washer jet hose from the wiper spindle

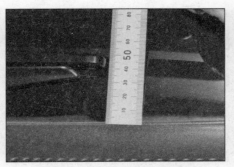

12.4 Set the end of the driver's blade 44 mm above the edge of the windscreen

12.6a Pull up the rubber seal (arrowed) . . .

Refitting

7 Refitting is a reversal of removal, but see the note at the beginning of this section.

---

12 Windscreen wiper components – removal and refitting

Wiper blades

1 Refer to *Weekly checks*.

Wiper arms

2 If the wipers are not in their parked position, switch on the ignition, and allow the motor to automatically park.

3 Before removing an arm, mark its parked position on the glass with a strip of adhesive tape. Open the bonnet, prise off the cover and unscrew the spindle nut **(see illustrations)**. Note that on Avant models, prise apart the two cover sides slightly and pull the cover from place. Pull out the washer jet and undo the spindle nut **(see illustrations)**. Remove the washer and ease the arm from the spindle by rocking it slowly from side-to-side.

4 Refitting is a reversal of removal, but before tightening the spindle nuts, position the wiper blades as marked before removal. If the position of the blades has been lost, or the windscreen renewed, position the blades so that the end of the driver's side blade is 44 mm above the bottom edge of the windscreen, and the end of the passenger's blade is 24 mm **(see illustration)**.

Wiper motor

Removal

5 Remove the wiper arms as described in the previous sub-Section.

6 Pull up the rubber seal at the front edge of the plenum chamber cover, then pull the cover forwards **(see illustrations)**.

7 Release the retaining clips and remove the windscreen panel grille **(see illustration)**.

8 Unscrew the five self-tapping screws securing the control module housing cover.

9 Using a screwdriver, carefully prise both linkage arms from the balljoint stud **(see illustration)**.

10 Undo the nut and detach the crank arm from the wiper motor **(see illustration)**.

11 Unclip any hoses/pipes/wires from the

12.6b . . . then pull the plenum chamber cover forwards (arrowed)

12.7 Release 3 clips (one in the centre, one at each end) and pull the windscreen panel grille upwards to release it (arrowed)

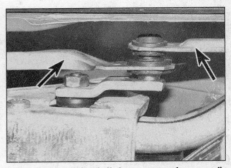

12.9 Prise up both linkage arms (arrowed) from the balljoint stud

12.10 Hold the motor crank to prevent it from turning whilst slackening the nut

12.11 Wiper motor linkage retaining bolts (arrowed)

12.12 Wiper motor Torx bolts

12.13 Set the motor crank arm to 2° from the centre line of the linkage

wiper linkage, then undo the 3 mounting bolts and manoeuvre the assembly from position **(see illustration)**. Disconnect the wiring plug as the assembly is withdrawn.

12 To separate the motor from the linkage,

undo the three retaining bolts and remove the motor **(see illustration)**.

Refitting

13 When refitting, with the motor/linkage back in place, reconnect the wiring plug then

operate the touch-wipe button to set the motor in the rest position. Refit the crank arm and position it so the arm is 2° from the centre line of the linkage, and tighten the retaining nut securely **(see illustration)**. The remainder of refitting is a reversal of removal.

13 Washer system – general

1 All models are fitted with a windscreen washer system. Avant models also have a tailgate washer, and some models are fitted with headlight washers.

2 The fluid reservoir for the windscreen/ headlight washer is located behind the left-hand side of the front bumper. The windscreen washer fluid pump is attached to the side of the reservoir body, as is the level sensor **(see illustrations)** and where headlight washers are fitted, a lift cylinder/accumulator is located in the supply tube, behind the front bumper. Access to the reservoir, pump and lift cylinder is achieved by removing either the left-hand front wheel arch liner or front bumper.

3 The tailgate washer is fed by the same reservoir and pump, operating in the reverse direction.

4 The reservoir fluid level must be regularly topped-up with windscreen washer fluid containing an antifreeze agent, but not cooling system antifreeze – see *Weekly checks*.

5 The supply hoses are attached by rubber couplings to their various connections, and if required, can be detached by simply pulling them free from the appropriate connector.

6 The windscreen washer jets can be adjusted by inserting a pin into the jet and altering the aim as required. To remove a washer jet, open the bonnet, and pull down the rear edge of the plastic cover under the jet **(see illustration)**.

7 Pull off the hose, disconnect the wiring plug, and remove the jet.

8 The headlight washer jets are best adjusted using the Audi tool, and should therefore be entrusted to an Audi garage to set.

13.2a Washer fluid reservoir retaining screws (arrowed – viewed from the wheel arch)

13.2b Washer fluid pump

14 Tailgate wiper motor – removal and refitting

Removal

1 Make sure the tailgate wiper is switched off and in its rest position, then remove the tailgate trim panel as described in Chapter 11.

2 Remove the wiper arm and blade as described in Section 12.

3 Detach the wiring connector from the wiper motor, then disconnect the washer jet hose.

4 Undo the 3 wiper motor mounting nuts and remove the wiper motor from the tailgate **(see illustration)**. Check the condition of the spindle rubber grommet in the tailgate, and if necessary, renew it.

13.6 Pull down the rear edge of the plastic cover under the jet

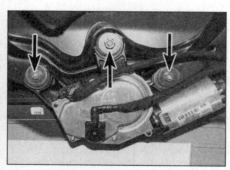

14.4 Tailgate motor retaining nuts (arrowed)

Refitting

5 Refit in the reverse order of removal. Refit the wiper arm and blade so that the arm is parked correctly.

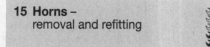

15 Horns – removal and refitting

Removal

1 The horns are located at the front end of the vehicle, on the right- and left-hand corners between the front bumper and the inner wing. Access to the horns is achieved by removing the relevant front headlight (see Section 9).
2 Pull the parking aid sensor (where fitted) from the bumper, then unplug the horn wiring plug, undo the mounting nut and remove the horn from the vehicle (see illustration).

Refitting

3 Refit in the reverse order of removal. Check for satisfactory operation on completion.

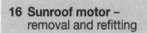

16 Sunroof motor – removal and refitting

Closing sunroof manually

1 If the motor malfunctions when the roof panel is in the open position, it can be wound shut manually. To do this, unclip the lens from the overhead interior light by inserting a screwdriver into the lens' recesses (see illustration 8.4a).
2 Release the crank tool from the inside of the fusebox cover, then insert it into the hexagonal socket adjacent to the interior light bulb. The tool can then be turned to close the sunroof as required.

Motor

3 At the time of writing, no information was available concerning removal and refitting of the motor.

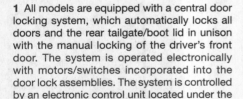

17 Central locking system – general information

1 All models are equipped with a central door locking system, which automatically locks all doors and the rear tailgate/boot lid in unison with the manual locking of the driver's front door. The system is operated electronically with motors/switches incorporated into the door lock assemblies. The system is controlled by an electronic control unit located under the carpet in front of the left-hand front seat (see Section 25).
2 The control unit is equipped with a self-diagnosis capability. Should the system develop a fault, have the control unit

interrogated by an Audi dealer or suitably-equipped specialist. Once the fault has been established, refer to the relevant Section of Chapter 11 to renew a door lock or tailgate/boot lid lock as applicable.

18 Parking aid components – general, removal and refitting

General information

1 The parking aid system is available on all models. Four ultrasound sensors located in the bumpers measure the distance to the closest object behind or in front the car, and inform the driver using acoustic signals from a buzzer located under the rear luggage compartment trim. The nearer the object, the more frequent the acoustic signals.
2 The system includes a control unit and self-diagnosis program, and therefore, in the event of a fault, the vehicle should be taken to an Audi dealer or suitably-equipped specialist.

Control unit

3 The control unit is located behind the left-hand trim in the rear luggage compartment. Remove the luggage compartment side panel trim as described in Chapter 11.
4 On Saloon models, undo the 4 screws and remove the base retainer. As the unit is removed, disconnect the wiring plugs.
5 On Avant models, undo the 3 screws and remove the base retainer.
6 On all models, disconnect the control unit wiring plugs, then undo the 2 screws and remove the control unit (see illustration).
7 Refitting is a reversal of removal.

Range/distance sensor

Front sensors

8 To remove the outer sensors, remove the appropriate headlight as described in Section 9.
9 To remove the inner sensors, remove the bumper as described in Chapter 11.
10 Disconnect the sensor wiring plug, then push the retaining clips apart, and pull the sensor from position.
11 Refitting is a reversal of removal. Press the sensor firmly into position until the retaining clips engage.

Rear sensors

12 It is not necessary to remove the rear bumper. Undo the 2 bolts at the centre, underneath the bumper, then reach under the bumper and press the retaining clips outwards. Now press out the sensor inwards from the outside of the bumper.
13 Disconnect the wiring and remove the sensor.

Refitting

14 Refitting is a reversal of removal. Press the sensor firmly into position until the retaining clips engage.

15.2 Horn mounting nut (arrowed)

Warning buzzer

Rear buzzer

15 On Saloon models, the rear warning buzzer is located beneath the rear shelf. Remove the parcel shelf as described in Chapter 11. Undo the retaining screw, lift the buzzer from position, and disconnect the wiring plug.
16 On Avant models, the warning buzzer is located behind the left-hand rear luggage compartment trim. Remove the trim as described in Chapter 11, then undo the retaining screw and lift the buzzer from position. Disconnect the wiring plug.
17 Refitting is a reversal of removal.

Front buzzer

18 Remove the driver's side storage compartment as described in Chapter 11.
19 Disconnect the wiring plug, then undo the Torx screw and remove the buzzer.
20 Refitting is a reversal of removal.

19 Radio/CD player/ autochanger – removal and refitting

Note: This Section applies only to standard-fit audio equipment.

Removal

Radio/CD player

1 The radio/CD player is fitted with special mounting clips, requiring the use of special removal tools (tool T10057), which should be supplied with the vehicle, or may be obtained from an in-car entertainment specialist.

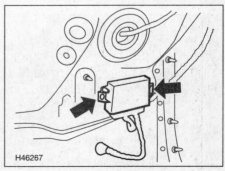

18.6 Parking aid control unit screws (arrowed)

19.1 Audio unit removal tool

Alternatively, it may be possible to make up some removal tools **(see illustration)**.

2 Disconnect the battery negative lead (refer to Chapter 5A).

3 Insert the removal rods in the holes provided on the lower, or upper and lower edges of the radio/CD player unit (depending on model).

4 Slide the removal tools fully into the slots until they locate.

5 Withdraw the radio/CD player from the mounting case **(see illustration)**, then disconnect the loudspeaker, supply and aerial plugs. Note that some radio units also have a fuse fitted on the rear face.

Autochanger

6 Open the passenger's glovebox, and insert the special Audi tools into the slots in the front face of the autochanger.

7 Pull the autochanger from position, then disconnect the wiring plugs.

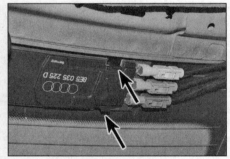

20.3 Release the clips and detach the aerial amplifier (left-hand end clips arrowed)

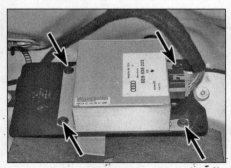

20.9 Audio amplifier mounting screws (arrowed)

19.5 Fully insert the tools and pull the unit from the facia

Refitting

Radio/CD player

8 Refitting is a reversal of removal, but push the radio fully into its case until the spring clips are engaged. If the radio is of the security code type, it will be necessary to enter the code number before using the radio.

Autochanger

9 Reconnect the wiring plugs, and push the unit fully into position, until the retaining clips engage.

20 Aerial and audio amplifiers – removal and refitting

Aerial amplifier

Saloon models

1 Carefully remove the headlining end trim panel.

2 Note their fitted positions, then disconnect the various wiring plugs from the amplifier.

3 Release the 6 retaining clips and remove the amplifier **(see illustration)**.

4 Refitting is a reversal of removal.

Avant models

5 Remove the left-hand side luggage compartment side trim panel as described in Chapter 11.

6 Note their fitted positions, then disconnect the various wiring plugs from the amplifier. Undo the 3 screws, and remove the amplifier.

7 Refitting is a reversal of removal.

21.3 Low frequency door speaker screws (arrowed)

Audio amplifier

8 On both the Saloon and Avant models, the audio amplifier is located behind the right-hand side luggage compartment side trim panel. Remove the panel as described in Chapter 11.

9 Disconnect the wiring plug, then undo the 4 screws and remove the amplifier **(see illustration)**.

10 Refitting is a reversal of removal.

21 Speakers – removal and refitting

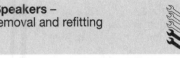

1 The audio system speakers are fitted in the front and rear door trim panels, the facia panel, under the rear parcel shelf (Saloon models), and behind the luggage compartment side trim panel (Avant models). Separate mid-range and high frequency tweeters are fitted in the front and rear door trim panels.

Door speakers

Low frequency speaker

2 To remove a door-mounted speaker, remove the appropriate door trim as described in Chapter 11.

3 Disconnect the speaker wiring plugs, then undo the retaining screws and remove the speaker **(see illustration)**.

4 Refit in the reverse order of removal.

High frequency front speaker

5 Remove the door inner trim panel as described in Chapter 11.

6 Disconnect the wiring plug to the speaker, then release the 3 retaining clips and detach the speaker and grille from the trim panel **(see illustration)**.

7 If required, release the clips and detach the speaker from the grille.

8 Refit in the reverse order of removal.

High frequency rear speaker

9 Remove the door inner trim panel as described in Chapter 11.

10 Disconnect the wiring plug, then release the 3 retaining clips and detach the speaker from the door trim **(see illustration)**.

11 Refit in the reverse order of removal.

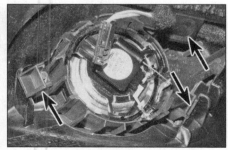

21.6 Release the clips (arrowed) and detach the speaker and grille panel from the door trim

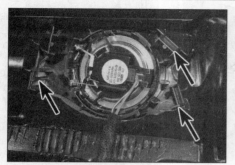

21.10 Rear door speaker retaining clips (arrowed)

21.12 Prise up the sunlight sensor surround

21.14a Undo the screw in the sunlight sensor aperture . . .

Facia speaker

12 Carefully prise up the trim from the sunlight sensor in the centre of the facia **(see illustration)**.

13 Undo the retaining bolt, and pull the sensor from the facia. Disconnect the wiring plug as the sensor is removed, and tape the wires to one side to prevent them disappearing into the facia recess.

14 Undo the screw in the sensor recess and remove the demister vent from the facia **(see illustrations)**.

15 Undo the 2 retaining screws, and manoeuvre the speaker from the facia **(see illustration)**. Disconnect the speaker wiring plug as it's withdrawn.

16 Refitting is a reversal of removal.

Parcel shelf speaker

17 Remove the parcel shelf as described in Chapter 11.

18 The speaker is secured by 2 bolts above the parcel shelf bracket, and 1 below. Undo the bolts, disconnect the wiring plug and remove the speaker **(see illustration)**.

19 Refitting is a reversal of removal.

Luggage compartment speaker

20 Remove the right-hand side luggage compartment side panel trim as described in Chapter 11.

21 Disconnect the wiring plugs, then undo the 4 bolts and remove the speaker complete with the resonator box.

22 Undo the 4 bolts and detach the speaker from the resonator **(see illustration)**.

23 Refitting is a reversal of removal.

21.14b . . . the lift out the centre vent

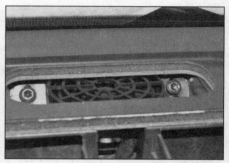

21.15 Undo the Torx screws and manoeuvre the speaker from the facia

90°C. When the airbag is removed, ensure that it is stored the correct way up to prevent possible inflation.

• *Do not allow any solvents or cleaning agents to contact the airbag assemblies. They must be cleaned using only a damp cloth.*

• *The airbags and control unit are both sensitive to impact. If either is dropped or damaged they should be renewed.*

• *Disconnect the airbag control unit wiring plug prior to using arc-welding equipment on the vehicle.*

Both a driver's and passenger's airbag were fitted as standard equipment to models in the Audi 4 range. The driver's airbag is fitted to the centre of the steering wheel. The passenger's airbag is fitted to the upper surface of the facia, above the glovebox. The airbag system consists of the airbag units (complete with

gas generators), an impact sensor, the control unit and a warning light in the instrument panel. Seat-mounted side airbags and overhead curtain airbags are also fitted on certain models, and seat belt tensioners are incorporated in the front seat belt reels.

The airbag system is triggered in the event of a direct or offset frontal impact above a predetermined force. The airbag is inflated within milliseconds, and forms a safety cushion between the driver and the steering wheel or the passenger and the facia. This prevents contact between the upper body and the steering wheel, column and facia, and therefore greatly reduces the risk of injury. The airbag then deflates almost immediately through vents in the side of the airbag.

Every time the ignition is switched on, the airbag control unit performs a self-test. The self-test takes approximately 3 seconds, and

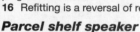

22 Airbag system –
general information
and precautions

⚠ **Warning: Before carrying out any operations on the airbag system, disconnect the battery negative terminal (see Chapter 5A). When operations are complete, make sure no one is inside the vehicle when the battery is reconnected.**

• *Note that the airbag(s) must not be subjected to temperatures in excess of*

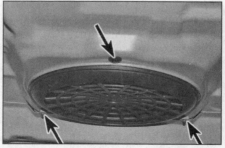

21.18 The parcel shelf speaker is retained by 1 bolt from below, and 2 from above (arrowed)

21.22 Undo the 4 bolts and remove the speaker

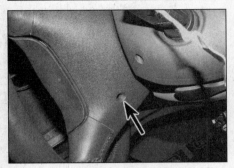

23.3a Turn the wheel to access the hole (arrowed) . . .

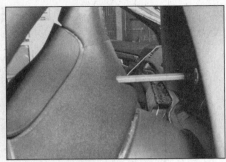

23.3b . . . then use a long Torx bit to slacken the airbag retaining screws

during this time the airbag warning light on the facia is illuminated. After the self-test has been completed, the warning light should go out. If the warning light fails to come on, remains illuminated after the initial 3-second period, or comes on at any time when the vehicle is being driven, there is a fault in the airbag system. The vehicle should then be taken to an Audi dealer or specialist for examination at the earliest possible opportunity.

23 Airbag system components – removal and refitting

Note: *Refer to the warnings in Section 22 before carrying out the following operations.*
1 Disconnect the battery negative terminal (see Chapter 5A).

Driver's airbag

2 Set the steering wheel to straight-ahead, then turn it 90° to the left or right. Release the steering column adjustment lever, and pull the wheel out and down as far as possible.
3 Locate the access hole in the reverse side of the steering wheel, and slacken the Torx screw securing the airbag to the steering wheel (see illustrations). Turn the airbag 180° and slacken the second Torx screw on the opposite side.
4 Temporarily touch the striker plate of the front door to discharge any electrostatic electricity. Return the steering wheel to the straight-ahead position, then carefully lift the airbag assembly away from the steering wheel and disconnect the wiring connector from the rear of the unit along with the horn button wiring plug (see illustrations). Note that the airbag must not be knocked or dropped, and

should be stored with its padded surface uppermost.
5 On refitting, reconnect the wiring connectors and locate the airbag unit in the steering wheel, making sure the wire does not become trapped, and tighten the Torx screws to the specified torque. Switch on the ignition, **then** reconnect the battery negative lead (see Chapter 5A). Ensure no-one is in the vehicle when the battery is reconnected.

Passenger airbag

6 Remove the passenger's glovebox as described in Chapter 11.
7 Depress the locking catch, then disconnect the airbag wiring plug **(see illustration)**.
8 Remove the brace under the airbag unit **(see illustration)**.
9 Undo the 4 retaining nuts **(see illustration)**.
10 Undo the bolts and remove the support brackets securing the airbag to the facia crossmember, then lower the airbag from position. Note that the airbag must not be knocked or dropped, and should be stored with its hinged surface uppermost.
11 Refitting is a reversal of removal. Ensure that the wiring connector is securely reconnected. Ensure that no-one is inside the vehicle. Switch on the ignition, then reconnect the battery negative lead.

Airbag wiring contact unit

12 Set the front wheels in the straight-ahead position, then remove the steering wheel as described in Chapter 10.
13 Undo the 3 retaining screws located underneath the lower steering column shroud, and separate the two upper and lower shrouds. Note that it is necessary to undo the 2.5 mm Allen screw and remove the steering column adjustment lever if the lower shroud is to be completely removed **(see illustrations 5.3a, 5.3b and 5.3c)**.
14 Disconnect the wiring plug on the top of the contact unit, and release the three locking clips. If the contact unit is to be re-used, use self-adhesive tape to secure the contact unit in the straight-ahead position. Remove the contact unit from the steering column switch **(see illustrations)**.

23.4a Lift the airbag from position . . .

23.4b . . . then lift the locking catch and unplug the connector

23.7 Prise out the locking catch on the connector (arrowed)

23.8 Undo the bolts and remove the brace (arrowed)

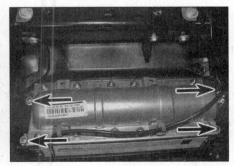

23.9 Airbag retaining nuts (arrowed)

23.14a Release the contact unit retaining clips (left-hand one arrowed)

23.14b Disconnect the contact unit wiring plug

23.17 The arrow on the airbag control unit must point to the front of the vehicle

15 Refitting is a reversal or removal, bearing in mind the following points:
a) *Ensure that the front wheels are in the straight-ahead position.*
b) *Ensure that the wiring plug is securely reconnected.*
c) *On models with ESP, if a new contact unit/steering angle sensor has been fitted, it must be initialised/adapted. Access to specialised diagnostic equipment is required. Consult your Audi dealer or specialist.*
d) *Ensure that no-one is inside the vehicle, switch on the ignition, then reconnect the battery negative lead.*

Airbag control unit

16 Refer to Chapter 11 and remove the centre console.
17 The control unit is located beneath the handbrake lever **(see illustration)**. Release the locking device and disconnect the wiring plug for the control unit.
18 Undo the retaining nuts and remove the control unit.
19 Refitting is a reversal of removal.

Side airbags

20 The side airbags are incorporated into the side of the front and rear seats. Removal of the units requires the seat upholstery to be removed. This is a specialist task, which we recommend should be entrusted to an Audi dealer or specialist.

Head airbags

21 Remove the sunvisor, A-pillar trim, B-pillar trim, and D-pillar trim as described in Chapter 11. On Avant models, also undo the bolts and remove the trim panel above the rear side door.
22 Pull the roof end trim downwards from its position above the rear windscreen.

Version 1

23 Depress the locking catch and disconnect the airbag wiring connector.
24 Undo the Torx bolts, then remove the head airbag assembly. Discard the bolts, new one must be fitted.
25 Begin refitting by installing the centre airbag bracket into the roof frame.

26 Insert the 2 remaining brackets into the roof frame.
27 Insert and tighten the 2 new bolts either side of the wiring connector on the air bag gas generator.
28 Working from the rear, insert and tighten the new retaining bolts to the specified torque.

Version 2

29 Prise out the locking element and disconnect the airbag wiring plug.
30 Undo the nut adjacent to the airbag gas generator.
31 Undo the retaining bolts, and unclip the retainers from the roof frame. Remove the airbag. Discard the bolts, new ones must be fitted.
32 Begin refitting by clipping the retainers into the roof frame.
33 Refit the airbag over the mounting stud at the D-pillar, and finger-tighten the nut.
34 Fit the new retaining bolts, and tighten them to the specified torque.
35 Tighten the nut on the D-pillar to the specified torque.

Both versions

36 The remainder of refitting is a reversal of removal, noting the following:
a) *Turn the ignition on, ensure no-one is in the vehicle, then reconnect the battery negative lead (see Chapter 5A).*
b) *It is possible that when the battery is reconnected, the airbag warning light may indicate that a fault has been stored. Have the fault erased, and see if*

23.39 The front crash sensors are located inboard of the headlights on the rear of the lock carrier (arrowed)

it re-occurs – consult an Audi dealer or specialist.

Crash/lateral acceleration sensors removal

Front sensors

37 The front sensors are located either side of the radiator fan assembly on the lock carrier/crossmember. If removing the right-hand sensor, undo the 2 bolts and remove the air intake duct from the lock carrier (where applicable).
38 Release the retaining tab and disconnect the sensor wiring plug.
39 Undo the 2 bolts and remove the sensor **(see illustration)**.

Front side sensors

40 Remove the lower B-pillar trim as described in Chapter 11.
41 Undo the seat belt inertia reel bolt and move the reel to one side (see Chapter 11).
42 Take out the foam section from the lower B-pillar, and remove the crash sensor retaining bolts **(see illustration)**.
43 Release the locking tab and disconnect the sensor wiring plug **(see illustration)**. Note that the sensor must be handled carefully. Do not refit a sensor that has been dropped or knocked.

Rear side sensors

44 Remove the rear seat as described in Chapter 11.
45 Carefully unclip the rear side cushion.

23.42 Undo the 2 Allen screws securing the front side crash sensors (arrowed)

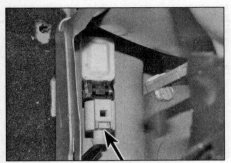

23.43 Release the wiring plug locking tab (arrowed)

46 Release the locking tab and disconnect the sensor wiring plug **(see illustration)**.

47 Undo the 2 bolts and remove the sensor. Note that the sensor must be handled carefully. Do not refit a sensor that has been dropped or knocked.

Crash/lateral acceleration sensors refitting

48 Refitting is a reversal of removal, noting the following points:

a) Turn the ignition on, ensure no-one is in the vehicle, **then** reconnect the battery negative lead (see Chapter 5A).

b) It is possible that when the battery is reconnected, the airbag warning light may indicate that a fault has been stored. Have the fault erased, and see if it re-occurs – consult an Audi dealer or specialist.

25.4 Open the box lid

25.5b Disconnect the wiring plugs from the control unit

23.46 The arrow on the front side sensors must face outwards

24 Anti-theft alarm system – general information

An anti-theft alarm and immobiliser system is fitted as standard equipment. Should the system become faulty, the vehicle should be taken to as Audi dealer or specialist for examination. They will have access to a special diagnostic tester which will quickly trace any fault present in the system.

25 Convenience system electronic control unit – removal and refitting

Removal

1 The convenience system electronic control

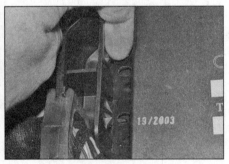

25.5a Release the clip securing the control unit

26.2 Undo the fuel filler flap release motor mounting bolts

unit (ECU) is responsible for the operation of the central locking, mirror adjustment, interior lighting, electric windows, heated exterior mirror, fuel filler flap release, reversing light, sunroof, anti-theft alarm, and interior lights. The ECU is located in front of the floor crossmember, under the carpet on the passenger's side.

2 Remove the passenger's seat and lower A-pillar trim as described in Chapter 11.

3 Fold back the carpet to access the control unit protective box.

4 Release the retaining clips and open the box lid **(see illustration)**.

5 Note their fitted positions, disconnect the wiring plugs, and release the ECU from the retaining clips **(see illustrations)**.

Refitting

6 Refitting is a reversal of removal. If a new ECU is being fitted, it will be necessary for the unit to be initialised prior to use by means of dedicated test equipment. Consult your local Audi dealer or suitably-equipped specialist.

26 Fuel filler flap locking motor – removal and refitting

Removal

1 Remove the right-hand side luggage compartment side trim panel, as described in Chapter 11.

2 Slacken the retaining bolts, slide the motor to the front and manoeuvre it from position **(see illustration)**. Note that the bolt heads are behind the motor, so the bolts have to be rotated clockwise to undo them.

3 Disconnect the wiring plug as the motor is withdrawn.

Refitting

4 Before refitting the motor, ensure the emergency release is fitted over the locking rod.

5 Manoeuvre the motor into position, ensuring the locking rod slides smoothly into the closed filler flap.

6 Reconnect the wiring plug and tighten the retaining bolts securely.

7 Refit the luggage compartment side trim panel.

27 On-board power supply control unit – removal and refitting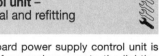

1 The on-board power supply control unit is responsible for supply power to the lighting system, washer/wiper system, horns and accessory circuits. The control unit receives signals via a Databus network from the lighting switch, hazard warning switch, steering column switch module, and the instrument panel module. The control unit is located behind the driver's side storage compartment.

Remove the compartment as described in Chapter 11.

2 Ensure the ignition is switched off, then undo the 2 nuts and detach the control unit **(see illustration)**.

3 Note their fitted positions, then unclip the 3 fuse carriers, and disconnect the unit's wiring plugs **(see illustration)**.

4 Refitting is a reversal of removal, noting that if a new unit is fitted, it may need to be adapted/initialised using Audi diagnostic equipment. Entrust this task to an Audi dealer or suitably-equipped specialist.

27.2 On-board power supply control unit mounting nuts (arrowed)

27.3 Unclip the fuse holders, and disconnect the wiring plugs

AUDI A4 wiring diagrams

Diagram 1

Key to symbols

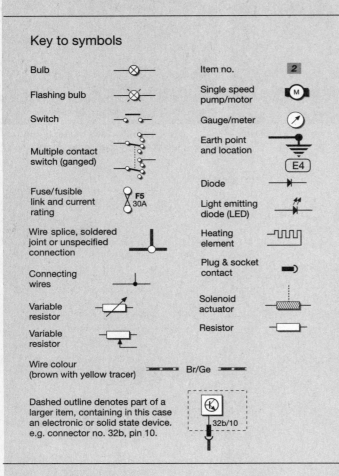

Bulb	
Flashing bulb	
Switch	
Multiple contact switch (ganged)	
Fuse/fusible link and current rating	F5 30A
Wire splice, soldered joint or unspecified connection	
Connecting wires	
Variable resistor	
Variable resistor	
Wire colour (brown with yellow tracer)	Br/Ge

Item no.   2

Single speed pump/motor   M

Gauge/meter

Earth point and location   E4

Diode

Light emitting diode (LED)

Heating element

Plug & socket contact

Solenoid actuator

Resistor

Dashed outline denotes part of a larger item, containing in this case an electronic or solid state device. e.g. connector no. 32b, pin 10.

32b/10

Passenger fusebox 6

Fuse	Rating	Circuit protected
F1	10A	Air conditioning
F2	5A	Footwell illumination
F3	5A	Heated washer jets
F4	5A	Engine cooling fan
F5	10A	Telephone, oil level sensor, multifunction switch, rear heated seats, rear window sun blind, automatic transmission
F6	5A	Air conditioning, pressure sensor
F7	10A	Electronic stability program (ESP), stop light switch, clutch pedal switch, steering angle sensor
F8	5A	Telephone
F9	15A	Brake servo (vacuum pump)
F10	10A	Headlight levelling
F11	-	Not used
F12	10A	Diagnostic connector
F13	10A	Steering column control unit
F14	10A	Stop lights
F15	10A	Instrument cluster, navigation system
F16	5A	Garage door opener
F17	10A	Parking distance sensor, self levelling suspension, tyre pressure monitor
F18	-	Not used
F19	15A	Front & rear foglights
F20	15A	RH dipped beam headlight, headlight levelling
F21	15A	LH dipped beam headlight, headlight levelling
F22	15A	Driver's & passenger's door control units
F23	15A	Driver's & passenger's door control units
F24	20A	Convenience system control unit
F25	30A	Heater blower
F26	30A	Heated rear window
F27	30A	Trailer socket control unit
F28	20A	Fuel pump, auxiliary pump for Diesel
F29	20A	Engine management
F30	20A	Sun roof
F31	15A	Reversing lights, automatic transmission, diagnostic connector, automatic ant-dazzle interior mirror
F32	20A	Engine management
F33	15A	Cigar lighter
F34	15A	Engine management
F35	30A	Accessory socket
F36	30A	Wiper system
F37	25A	Front washer/headlight washer pump
F38	15A	Convenience system control unit, boot lid release
F39	20A	Radio
F40	25A	Horn
F41	-	Not used
F42	25A	Electronic Stability Program (ESP)
F43	15A	Engine management
F44	30A	Heated seats

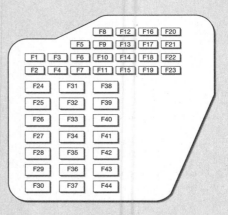

Earth locations

E1	In battery box
E2	On front apron
E3	Lower RH 'B' pillar
E4	Behind RH dash panel
E5	Lower RH 'A' pillar
E6	LH luggage compartment
E7	Lower LH 'A' pillar
E8	Lower LH 'B' pillar
E9	Near convenience system control unit
E10	LH engine compartment
E11	Under centre console
E12	RH 'D' pillar
E13	LH 'D' pillar

Key to circuits

Diagram 1	Information for wiring diagrams
Diagram 2	Typical starting, charging, horn, cigar lighter, accessory socket, engine cooling fan, supply to steering column & power supply control units
Diagram 3	Typical head, side, tail & no. plate lights, stop & reversing lights
Diagram 4	Typical direction indicators & hazard warning lights, front & rear foglights, headlight levelling & sunroof
Diagram 5	Typical interior lighting, wash/wipe & heated washer jets
Diagram 6	Typical instrument cluster, audio system & diagnostic connector
Diagram 7	Typical heated front/rear screen, heater blower & electric mirrors
Diagram 8	Typical central locking
Diagram 9	Typical electric windows

H33604

Wire colours

Ws White   **Or** Orange
Bl Blue   **Ro** Red
Gr Grey   **Rs** Pink
Ge Yellow   **Gn** Green
Br Brown   **Li** Purple
Sw Black

Key to items

1 Battery
2 Starter motor
3 Alternator
4 Ignition switch
5 Fusebox/relay plate
6 Horn relay
7 Low tone horn
8 Hi tone horn
9 Power supply control unit
10 Cigar lighter
11 Accessory socket
12 Horn switch
13 Steering column control unit
14 Engine cooling fan/control unit
15 Terminal 30 supply relay
16 Engine cooling fan fuse
17 'X' contact relay

Diagram 2

H33605

Typical starting & charging system
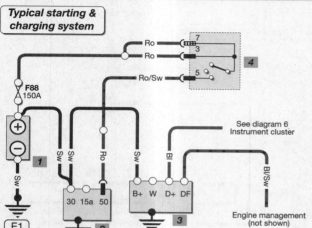

Typical engine cooling fan
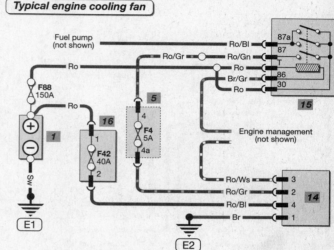

Typical horn
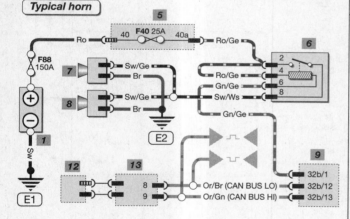

Typical supply to steering column & power supply control units
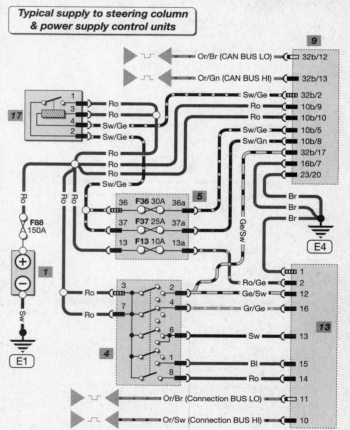

Typical cigar lighter & accessory socket
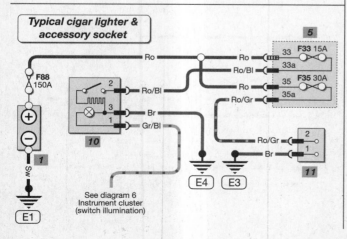

Wire colours

Ws White   **Or** Orange
Bl Blue   **Ro** Red
Gr Grey   **Rs** Pink
Ge Yellow   **Gn** Green
Br Brown   **Li** Purple
Sw Black

Key to items

1 Battery
4 Ignition switch
5 Fusebox/relay plate
9 Power supply control unit
13 Steering column control unit
17 'X' contact relay
20 Direction indicators/dip switch
21 Fog/lighting switch
   a = side/headlights
22 Number plate light
23 Convenience system control unit

24 LH front light unit
   a = side light
   b = dip beam
   c = main beam
25 RH front light unit
   (as above)
26 LH rear light unit
   a = tail light
   b = stop light
   c = reversing light

27 RH rear light unit
   (as above)
28 High level stop light
29 Stop light switch
30 Reversing light switch

Diagram 3

H33606

Typical headlights, side, tail & number plate lights

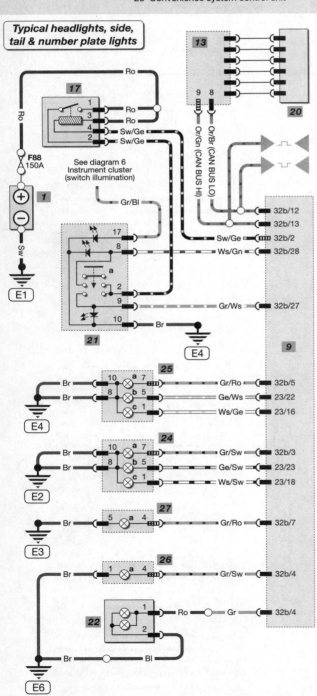

Typical stop & reversing lights

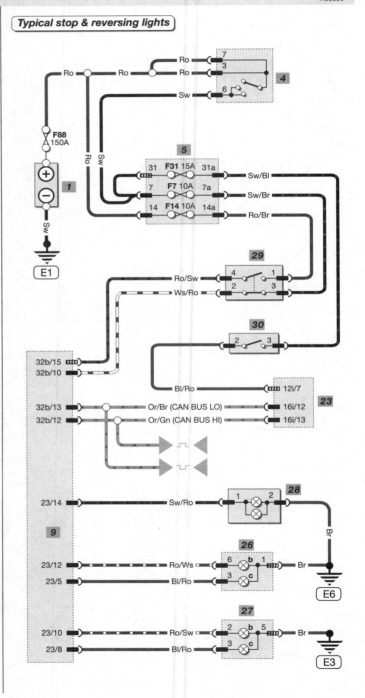

Wire colours

Ws White **Or** Orange
Bl Blue **Ro** Red
Gr Grey **Rs** Pink
Ge Yellow **Gn** Green
Br Brown **Li** Purple
Sw Black

Key to items

1 Battery
4 Ignition switch
5 Fusebox/relay plate
9 Power supply control unit
13 Steering column control unit
20 Direction indicators/dip switch
21 Fog/lighting switch
  b = front/rear foglight
23 Convenience system control unit
24 LH front light unit
  d = direction indicator
  e = headlight levelling

25 RH front light unit
  (as above)
26 LH rear light unit
  d = direction indicator
  e = foglight
27 RH rear light unit
  (as above)
35 LH indicator side repeater
36 RH indicator side repeater
37 Hazard warning switch
38 Headlight levelling switch
39 LH front foglight

40 RH front foglight
41 Front interior light assembly
42 Sunroof control unit/motor
43 Sunroof control switch

Diagram 4

H33607

Typical direction indicators & hazard warning lights

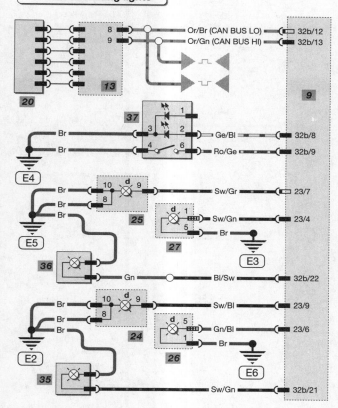

Typical headlight levelling

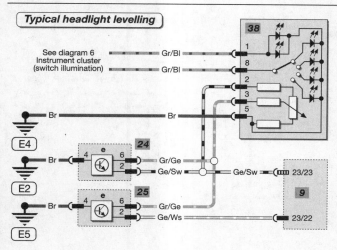

Typical front & rear foglights

Typical sunroof

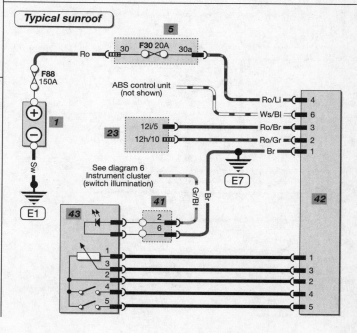

Wire colours

Ws White **Or** Orange
Bl Blue **Ro** Red
Gr Grey **Rs** Pink
Ge Yellow **Gn** Green
Br Brown **Li** Purple
Sw Black

Key to items

1 Battery
4 Ignition switch
5 Fusebox/relay plate
9 Power supply control unit
13 Steering column control unit
23 Convenience system control unit
48 Front interior light
49 Rear interior light
50 Luggage compartment light

51 Glove box light
52 Glove box light switch
53 LH front footwell light
54 LH rear footwell light
55 RH front footwell light
56 RH rear footwell light
57 LH vanity mirror light
58 LH vanity mirror light switch
59 RH vanity mirror light

60 RH vanity mirror light switch
61 Wiper switch
62 Headlight washer pump
63 Rear wiper motor (estate)
64 Windscreen washer pump
65 LH headlight washer jet heater
66 RH headlight washer jet heater
67 Windscreen wiper motor

Diagram 5

H33608

Typical interior lighting

Typical wash/wipe & heated washer jets

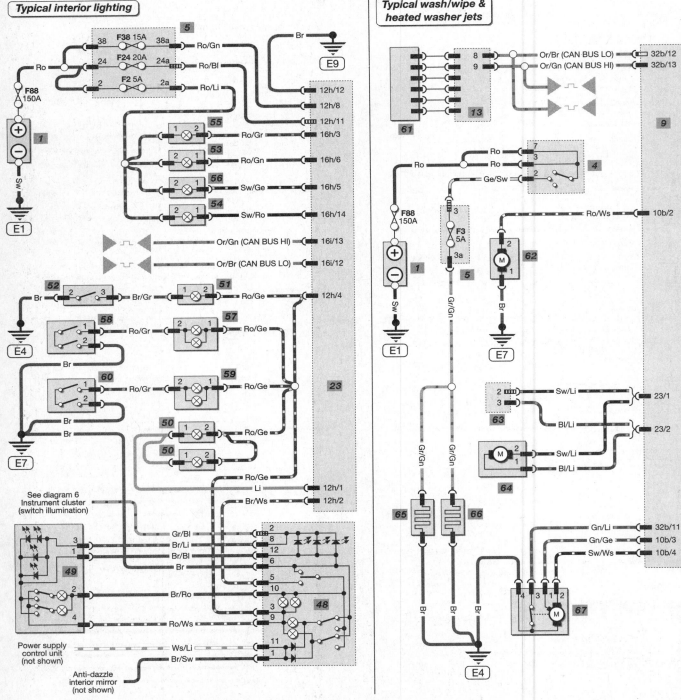

Wire colours

Ws	White	**Or**	Orange
Bl	Blue	**Ro**	Red
Gr	Grey	**Rs**	Pink
Ge	Yellow	**Gn**	Green
Br	Brown	**Li**	Purple
Sw	Black		

Key to items

1 = Battery
4 = Ignition switch
5 = Fusebox/relay plate
70 = Radio controlled clock receiver
71 = Immobiliser coil
72 = Brake fluid level switch
73 = Oil pressure switch
74 = Oil level/temperature sensor
75 = Ambient air temperature sensor
76 = Fuel gauge
77 = Coolant temperature sensor
78 = Low coolant temperature sensor
79 = Washer fluid level switch
80 = LH front pad wear sensor
81 = RH front pad wear sensor
82 = Instrument cluster
  a = coolant temperature gauge
  b = fuel gauge

c = tachometer
d = speedometer
e = alternator warning light
f = airbag warning light
g = main beam warning light
h = side light warning light
i = glow plug warning light
j = ESP warning light
k = brake system/handbrake warning light
l = engine management warning light
m = trailer warning light
n = ABS warning light
o = cruise control warning light
p = immobiliser warning light
q = seatbelt warning light
r = LH direction indicator
s = RH direction indicator
t = display/control unit

83 = Audio unit
84 = LH front bass speaker
85 = LH front mid range/tweeter speaker
86 = LH rear bass speaker
87 = LH rear mid range/tweeter speaker
88 = RH front bass speaker
89 = RH front mid range/tweeter speaker
90 = RH rear bass speaker
91 = RH rear mid range/tweeter speaker
92 = Diagnostic connector

Diagram 6

H33609

Typical instrument cluster

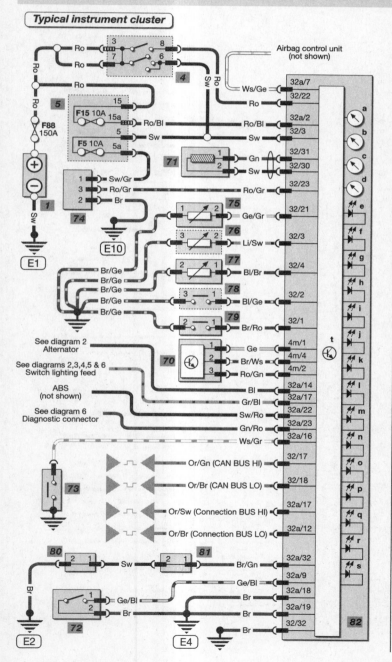

Typical audio system

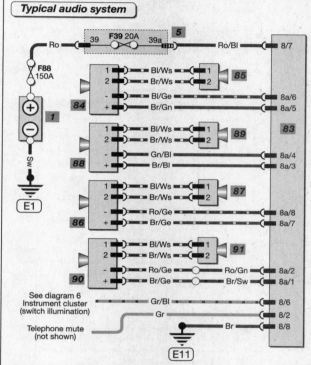

Diagnostic connector

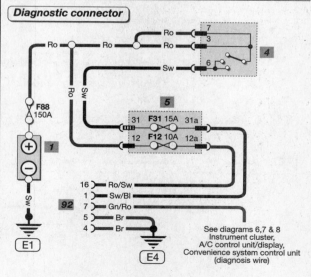

Wire colours

Ws White   **Or** Orange
Bl Blue   **Ro** Red
Gr Grey   **Rs** Pink
Ge Yellow   **Gn** Green
Br Brown   **Li** Purple
Sw Black

Key to items

1   Battery
4   Ignition switch
5   Fusebox/relay plate
23   Convenience system control unit
95   Air conditioning control unit/display
96   Heater blower motor/control unit
97   Solar cells (models with solar roof only)
98   Heated front screen voltage transformer
99   Heated front screen

100   Heated rear window
101   Suppressor
102   Single fuse
103   Driver's door control unit
104   Driver's mirror assembly
105   Mirror adjustment switch
106   Passenger's door control unit
107   Passenger's mirror assembly

Diagram 7

H33610

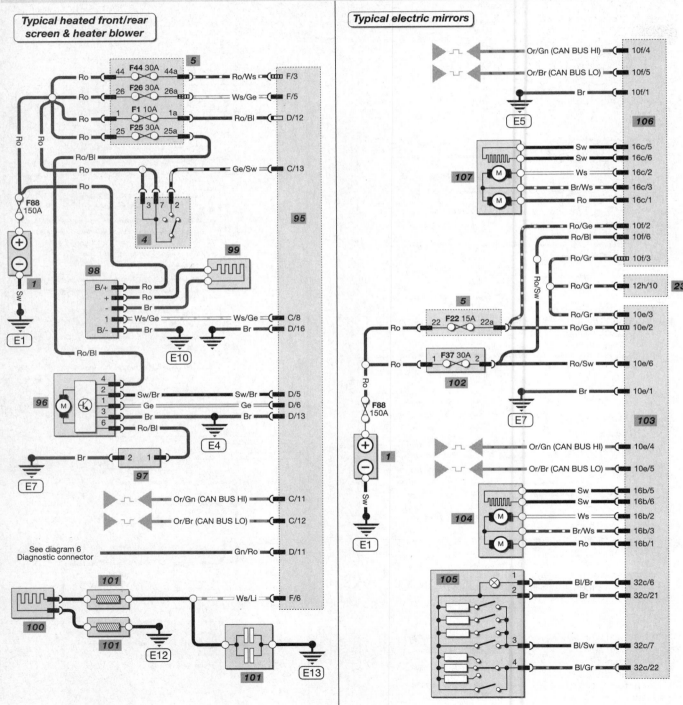

Typical heated front/rear screen & heater blower

Typical electric mirrors

Wire colours

Ws	White	**Or**	Orange
Bl	Blue	**Ro**	Red
Gr	Grey	**Rs**	Pink
Ge	Yellow	**Gn**	Green
Br	Brown	**Li**	Purple
Sw	Black		

Key to items

1	Battery
5	Fusebox/relay plate
23	Convenience system control unit
102	Single fuse
103	Driver's door control unit
106	Passenger's door control unit
110	Driver's door lock assembly
111	Passenger's door lock assembly
112	LH rear door lock assembly

113	RH rear door lock assembly
114	Filler flap motor
115	Boot lid/tailgate release motor
116	Boot lid/tailgate release switch
117	Central interior locking switch
118	Driver's interior locking switch
119	Passenger's interior locking switch
120	Central locking 'safe' indicator
121	Driver's door warning light

122	Driver's door entry light
123	Driver's door opening illumination
124	Passenger's door warning light
125	Passenger's door entry light
126	Passenger's door opening illumination
127	Release switch for boot lid/tailgate lock cylinder
128	Antenna

Diagram 8

H33611

Typical central locking

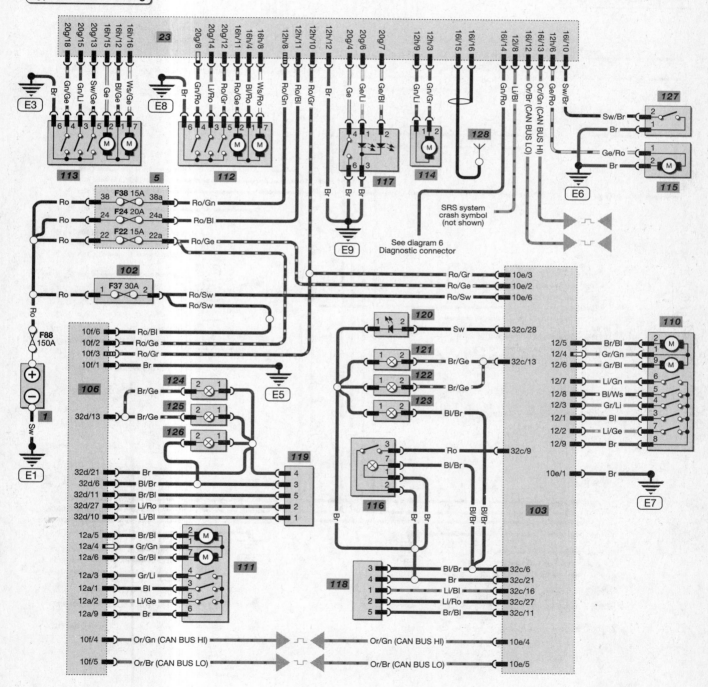

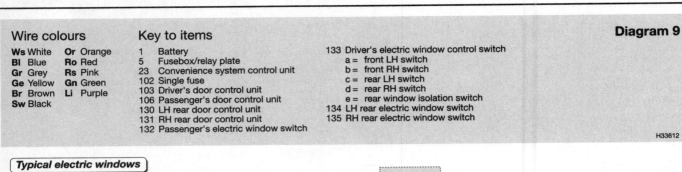

Diagram 9

Wire colours

Ws	White	**Or**	Orange
Bl	Blue	**Ro**	Red
Gr	Grey	**Rs**	Pink
Ge	Yellow	**Gn**	Green
Br	Brown	**Li**	Purple
Sw	Black		

Key to items

1   Battery
5   Fusebox/relay plate
23   Convenience system control unit
102   Single fuse
103   Driver's door control unit
106   Passenger's door control unit
130   LH rear door control unit
131   RH rear door control unit
132   Passenger's electric window switch

133   Driver's electric window control switch
  a =   front LH switch
  b =   front RH switch
  c =   rear LH switch
  d =   rear RH switch
  e =   rear window isolation switch
134   LH rear electric window switch
135   RH rear electric window switch

H33612

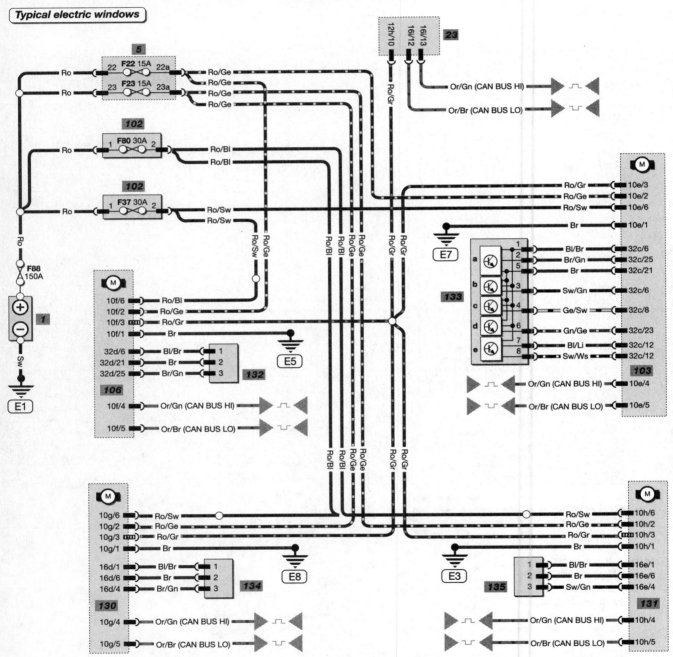

Typical electric windows

Dimensions and weights . . . . **REF•1**
Conversion factors . . . . **REF•2**
Jacking and vehicle support . . . . **REF•3**
Radio/CD/cassette unit anti-theft system –
  precaution . . . . **REF•3**
General repair procedures . . . . **REF•4**
Buying spare parts . . . . **REF•5**

Vehicle identification. . . . . **REF•5**
Tools and working facilities . . . . **REF•6**
MOT test checks . . . . **REF•8**
Fault finding . . . . **REF•12**
Glossary of technical terms . . . . **REF•20**
Index. . . . . **REF•24**

Dimensions and weights

Note: *All figures are approximate, and may vary according to model. Refer to manufacturer's data for exact figures.*

Dimensions
Overall length	4544 mm
Overall width (including mirrors).	1937 mm
Overall height (unladen, including roof rails)	1454 mm
Turning circle	11.1 m

Weights
Kerb weight	1505 kg (manual) or 1550 kg (automatic)
Maximum towing weight:	
Trailer without brakes	720 to 750 kg
Trailer with brakes.	1300 to 1700 kg
Maximum roof rack load	100 kg

Conversion factors

Length (distance)

Inches (in)	x 25.4	= Millimetres (mm)	x 0.0394	=	Inches (in)
Feet (ft)	x 0.305	= Metres (m)	x 3.281	=	Feet (ft)
Miles	x 1.609	= Kilometres (km)	x 0.621	=	Miles

Volume (capacity)

Cubic inches (cu in; in³)	x 16.387	= Cubic centimetres (cc; cm³)	x 0.061	=	Cubic inches (cu in; in³)
Imperial pints (Imp pt)	x 0.568	= Litres (l)	x 1.76	=	Imperial pints (Imp pt)
Imperial quarts (Imp qt)	x 1.137	= Litres (l)	x 0.88	=	Imperial quarts (Imp qt)
Imperial quarts (Imp qt)	x 1.201	= US quarts (US qt)	x 0.833	=	Imperial quarts (Imp qt)
US quarts (US qt)	x 0.946	= Litres (l)	x 1.057	=	US quarts (US qt)
Imperial gallons (Imp gal)	x 4.546	= Litres (l)	x 0.22	=	Imperial gallons (Imp gal)
Imperial gallons (Imp gal)	x 1.201	= US gallons (US gal)	x 0.833	=	Imperial gallons (Imp gal)
US gallons (US gal)	x 3.785	= Litres (l)	x 0.264	=	US gallons (US gal)

Mass (weight)

Ounces (oz)	x 28.35	= Grams (g)	x 0.035	=	Ounces (oz)
Pounds (lb)	x 0.454	= Kilograms (kg)	x 2.205	=	Pounds (lb)

Force

Ounces-force (ozf; oz)	x 0.278	= Newtons (N)	x 3.6	=	Ounces-force (ozf; oz)
Pounds-force (lbf; lb)	x 4.448	= Newtons (N)	x 0.225	=	Pounds-force (lbf; lb)
Newtons (N)	x 0.1	= Kilograms-force (kgf; kg)	x 9.81	=	Newtons (N)

Pressure

Pounds-force per square inch (psi; lbf/in²; lb/in²)	x 0.070	= Kilograms-force per square centimetre (kgf/cm²; kg/cm²)	x 14.223	=	Pounds-force per square inch (psi; lbf/in²; lb/in²)
Pounds-force per square inch (psi; lbf/in²; lb/in²)	x 0.068	= Atmospheres (atm)	x 14.696	=	Pounds-force per square inch (psi; lbf/in²; lb/in²)
Pounds-force per square inch (psi; lbf/in²; lb/in²)	x 0.069	= Bars	x 14.5	=	Pounds-force per square inch (psi; lbf/in²; lb/in²)
Pounds-force per square inch (psi; lbf/in²; lb/in²)	x 6.895	= Kilopascals (kPa)	x 0.145	=	Pounds-force per square inch (psi; lbf/in²; lb/in²)
Kilopascals (kPa)	x 0.01	= Kilograms-force per square centimetre (kgf/cm²; kg/cm²)	x 98.1	=	Kilopascals (kPa)
Millibar (mbar)	x 100	= Pascals (Pa)	x 0.01	=	Millibar (mbar)
Millibar (mbar)	x 0.0145	= Pounds-force per square inch (psi; lbf/in²; lb/in²)	x 68.947	=	Millibar (mbar)
Millibar (mbar)	x 0.75	= Millimetres of mercury (mmHg)	x 1.333	=	Millibar (mbar)
Millibar (mbar)	x 0.401	= Inches of water (inH₂O)	x 2.491	=	Millibar (mbar)
Millimetres of mercury (mmHg)	x 0.535	= Inches of water (inH₂O)	x 1.868	=	Millimetres of mercury (mmHg)
Inches of water (inH₂O)	x 0.036	= Pounds-force per square inch (psi; lbf/in²; lb/in²)	x 27.68	=	Inches of water (inH₂O)

Torque (moment of force)

Pounds-force inches (lbf in; lb in)	x 1.152	= Kilograms-force centimetre (kgf cm; kg cm)	x 0.868	=	Pounds-force inches (lbf in; lb in)
Pounds-force inches (lbf in; lb in)	x 0.113	= Newton metres (Nm)	x 8.85	=	Pounds-force inches (lbf in; lb in)
Pounds-force inches (lbf in; lb in)	x 0.083	= Pounds-force feet (lbf ft; lb ft)	x 12	=	Pounds-force inches (lbf in; lb in)
Pounds-force feet (lbf ft; lb ft)	x 0.138	= Kilograms-force metres (kgf m; kg m)	x 7.233	=	Pounds-force feet (lbf ft; lb ft)
Pounds-force feet (lbf ft; lb ft)	x 1.356	= Newton metres (Nm)	x 0.738	=	Pounds-force feet (lbf ft; lb ft)
Newton metres (Nm)	x 0.102	= Kilograms-force metres (kgf m; kg m)	x 9.804	=	Newton metres (Nm)

Power

Horsepower (hp)	x 745.7	= Watts (W)	x 0.0013	=	Horsepower (hp)

Velocity (speed)

Miles per hour (miles/hr; mph)	x 1.609	= Kilometres per hour (km/hr; kph)	x 0.621	=	Miles per hour (miles/hr; mph)

Fuel consumption*

Miles per gallon, Imperial (mpg)	x 0.354	= Kilometres per litre (km/l)	x 2.825	=	Miles per gallon, Imperial (mpg)
Miles per gallon, US (mpg)	x 0.425	= Kilometres per litre (km/l)	x 2.352	=	Miles per gallon, US (mpg)

Temperature

Degrees Fahrenheit = (°C x 1.8) + 32   Degrees Celsius (Degrees Centigrade; °C) = (°F - 32) x 0.56

It is common practice to convert from miles per gallon (mpg) to litres/100 kilometres (l/100km), where mpg x l/100 km = 282

The jack supplied with the vehicle tool kit should only be used for changing the roadwheels – see *Wheel changing* at the front of this manual. When carrying out any other kind of work, raise the vehicle using a hydraulic trolley jack, and always supplement the jack with axle stands positioned under the vehicle jacking points.

When using a trolley jack or axle stands, always position the jack head or axle stand head under, or adjacent to one of the relevant wheel changing jacking points under the sills **(see illustration)**. Use a block of wood between the jack or axle stand and the sill.

Do not attempt to jack the vehicle under the front crossmember, the sump, or any of the suspension components.

The jack supplied with the vehicle locates in the jacking points on the underside of the sills – see *Wheel changing* at the front of this manual. Ensure that the jack head is correctly engaged before attempting to raise the vehicle.

Never work under, around, or near a raised vehicle, unless it is adequately supported in at least two places.

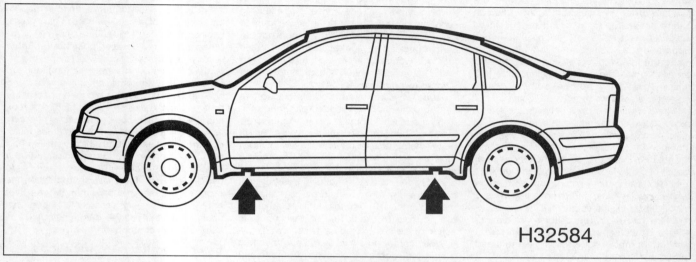

H32584

Vehicle jacking points under the sills

Radio/CD/cassette unit anti-theft system – precaution

The radio/CD/cassette unit fitted as standard equipment by Audi is equipped with a built-in security code to deter thieves. If the power source to the unit is cut, the anti-theft system will activate. Even if the power source is immediately reconnected, the unit will not function until the correct security code has been entered. Therefore, if you do not know the correct security code for the unit, do not disconnect the battery negative lead, or remove the unit from the vehicle.

Whenever servicing, repair or overhaul work is carried out on the car or its components, observe the following procedures and instructions. This will assist in carrying out the operation efficiently and to a professional standard of workmanship.

Joint mating faces and gaskets

When separating components at their mating faces, never insert screwdrivers or similar implements into the joint between the faces in order to prise them apart. This can cause severe damage which results in oil leaks, coolant leaks, etc upon reassembly. Separation is usually achieved by tapping along the joint with a soft-faced hammer in order to break the seal. However, note that this method may not be suitable where dowels are used for component location.

Where a gasket is used between the mating faces of two components, a new one must be fitted on reassembly; fit it dry unless otherwise stated in the repair procedure. Make sure that the mating faces are clean and dry, with all traces of old gasket removed. When cleaning a joint face, use a tool which is unlikely to score or damage the face, and remove any burrs or nicks with an oilstone or fine file.

Make sure that tapped holes are cleaned with a pipe cleaner, and keep them free of jointing compound, if this is being used, unless specifically instructed otherwise.

Ensure that all orifices, channels or pipes are clear, and blow through them, preferably using compressed air.

Oil seals

Oil seals can be removed by levering them out with a wide flat-bladed screwdriver or similar implement. Alternatively, a number of self-tapping screws may be screwed into the seal, and these used as a purchase for pliers or some similar device in order to pull the seal free.

Whenever an oil seal is removed from its working location, either individually or as part of an assembly, it should be renewed.

The very fine sealing lip of the seal is easily damaged, and will not seal if the surface it contacts is not completely clean and free from scratches, nicks or grooves. If the original sealing surface of the component cannot be restored, and the manufacturer has not made provision for slight relocation of the seal relative to the sealing surface, the component should be renewed.

Protect the lips of the seal from any surface which may damage them in the course of fitting. Use tape or a conical sleeve where possible. Lubricate the seal lips with oil before fitting and, on dual-lipped seals, fill the space between the lips with grease.

Unless otherwise stated, oil seals must be fitted with their sealing lips toward the lubricant to be sealed.

Use a tubular drift or block of wood of the appropriate size to install the seal and, if the seal housing is shouldered, drive the seal down to the shoulder. If the seal housing is unshouldered, the seal should be fitted with its face flush with the housing top face (unless otherwise instructed).

Screw threads and fastenings

Seized nuts, bolts and screws are quite a common occurrence where corrosion has set in, and the use of penetrating oil or releasing fluid will often overcome this problem if the offending item is soaked for a while before attempting to release it. The use of an impact driver may also provide a means of releasing such stubborn fastening devices, when used in conjunction with the appropriate screwdriver bit or socket. If none of these methods works, it may be necessary to resort to the careful application of heat, or the use of a hacksaw or nut splitter device.

Studs are usually removed by locking two nuts together on the threaded part, and then using a spanner on the lower nut to unscrew the stud. Studs or bolts which have broken off below the surface of the component in which they are mounted can sometimes be removed using a stud extractor. Always ensure that a blind tapped hole is completely free from oil, grease, water or other fluid before installing the bolt or stud. Failure to do this could cause the housing to crack due to the hydraulic action of the bolt or stud as it is screwed in.

When tightening a castellated nut to accept a split pin, tighten the nut to the specified torque, where applicable, and then tighten further to the next split pin hole. Never slacken the nut to align the split pin hole, unless stated in the repair procedure.

When checking or retightening a nut or bolt to a specified torque setting, slacken the nut or bolt by a quarter of a turn, and then retighten to the specified setting. However, this should not be attempted where angular tightening has been used.

For some screw fastenings, notably cylinder head bolts or nuts, torque wrench settings are no longer specified for the latter stages of tightening, "angle-tightening" being called up instead. Typically, a fairly low torque wrench setting will be applied to the bolts/nuts in the correct sequence, followed by one or more stages of tightening through specified angles.

Locknuts, locktabs and washers

Any fastening which will rotate against a component or housing during tightening should always have a washer between it and the relevant component or housing.

Spring or split washers should always be renewed when they are used to lock a critical component such as a big-end bearing retaining bolt or nut. Locktabs which are folded over to retain a nut or bolt should always be renewed.

Self-locking nuts can be re-used in non-critical areas, providing resistance can be felt when the locking portion passes over the bolt or stud thread. However, it should be noted that self-locking stiffnuts tend to lose their effectiveness after long periods of use, and should then be renewed as a matter of course.

Split pins must always be replaced with new ones of the correct size for the hole.

When thread-locking compound is found on the threads of a fastener which is to be re-used, it should be cleaned off with a wire brush and solvent, and fresh compound applied on reassembly.

Special tools

Some repair procedures in this manual entail the use of special tools such as a press, two or three-legged pullers, spring compressors, etc. Wherever possible, suitable readily-available alternatives to the manufacturer's special tools are described, and are shown in use. In some instances, where no alternative is possible, it has been necessary to resort to the use of a manufacturer's tool, and this has been done for reasons of safety as well as the efficient completion of the repair operation. Unless you are highly-skilled and have a thorough understanding of the procedures described, never attempt to bypass the use of any special tool when the procedure described specifies its use. Not only is there a very great risk of personal injury, but expensive damage could be caused to the components involved.

Environmental considerations

When disposing of used engine oil, brake fluid, antifreeze, etc, give due consideration to any detrimental environmental effects. Do not, for instance, pour any of the above liquids down drains into the general sewage system, or onto the ground to soak away. Many local council refuse tips provide a facility for waste oil disposal, as do some garages. If none of these facilities are available, consult your local Environmental Health Department, or the National Rivers Authority, for further advice.

With the universal tightening-up of legislation regarding the emission of environmentally-harmful substances from motor vehicles, most vehicles have tamperproof devices fitted to the main adjustment points of the fuel system. These devices are primarily designed to prevent unqualified persons from adjusting the fuel/air mixture, with the chance of a consequent increase in toxic emissions. If such devices are found during servicing or overhaul, they should, wherever possible, be renewed or refitted in accordance with the manufacturer's requirements or current legislation.

OIL CARE

FOLLOW THE CODE

OIL BANK LINE
0800 66 33 66
www.oilbankline.org.uk

Note: It is antisocial and illegal to dump oil down the drain. To find the location of your local oil recycling bank, call this number free.

Spare parts are available from many sources, including maker's appointed garages, accessory shops, and motor factors. To be sure of obtaining the correct parts, it will sometimes be necessary to quote the vehicle identification number. If possible, it can also be useful to take the old parts along for positive identification. Items such as starter motors and alternators may be available under a service exchange scheme – any parts returned should be clean.

Our advice regarding spare parts is as follows.

Officially appointed garages

This is the best source of parts which are peculiar to your car, and which are not otherwise generally available (eg, badges, interior trim, certain body panels, etc). It is also the only place at which you should buy parts if the vehicle is still under warranty.

Accessory shops

These are very good places to buy materials and components needed for the maintenance of your car (oil, air and fuel filters, light bulbs, drivebelts, greases, brake pads, touch-up paint, etc). Components of this nature sold by a reputable shop are usually of the same standard as those used by the car manufacturer.

Besides components, these shops also sell tools and general accessories, usually have convenient opening hours, charge lower prices, and can often be found close to home. Some accessory shops have parts counters where components needed for almost any repair job can be purchased or ordered.

Motor factors

Good factors will stock all the more important components which wear out comparatively quickly, and can sometimes supply individual components needed for the overhaul of a larger assembly (eg, brake seals and hydraulic parts, bearing shells, pistons, valves). They may also handle work such as cylinder block reboring, crankshaft regrinding, etc.

Tyre and exhaust specialists

These outlets may be independent, or members of a local or national chain. They frequently offer competitive prices when compared with a main dealer or local garage, but it will pay to obtain several quotes before making a decision. When researching prices, also ask what extras may be added – for instance fitting a new valve and balancing the wheel are both commonly charged on top of the price of a new tyre.

Other sources

Beware of parts or materials obtained from market stalls, car boot sales or similar outlets. Such items are not invariably sub-standard, but there is little chance of compensation if they do prove unsatisfactory. in the case of safety-critical components such as brake pads, there is the risk not only of financial loss, but also of an accident causing injury or death.

Second-hand components or assemblies obtained from a car breaker can be a good buy in some circumstances, but this sort of purchase is best made by the experienced DIY mechanic.

Vehicle identification

Modifications are a continuing and unpublicised process in vehicle manufacture, quite apart from major model changes. Spare parts manuals and lists are compiled upon a numerical basis, the individual vehicle identification numbers being essential to correct identification of the component concerned.

When ordering spare parts, always give as much information as possible. Quote the car model, year of manufacture, body and engine numbers as appropriate.

The *vehicle identification plate* and *vehicle data plate* is situated at the rear of the engine compartment **(see illustrations)**. The *vehicle identification number* is also repeated in the form of plate visible through the windscreen on the passenger's side **(see illustration)**.

The *engine number* is stamped on the left-hand side of the cylinder block. The *engine code* can also be found on the vehicle data stickers in the luggage compartment and at the rear of the engine compartment, and on a sticker on the toothed belt or valve cover.

Other identification numbers or codes are stamped on major items such as the gearbox, etc. These numbers are also printed on the Vehicle data sticker located in the luggage compartment adjacent to the spare wheel **(see illustration)**.

Vehicle identification number on the engine compartment partition panel

Vehicle identification sticker on the right-hand front inner wing

Vehicle identification number visible through the windscreen

Vehicle identification sticker in the luggage compartment (Engine code arrowed)

Introduction

A selection of good tools is a fundamental requirement for anyone contemplating the maintenance and repair of a motor vehicle. For the owner who does not possess any, their purchase will prove a considerable expense, offsetting some of the savings made by doing-it-yourself. However, provided that the tools purchased meet the relevant national safety standards and are of good quality, they will last for many years and prove an extremely worthwhile investment.

To help the average owner to decide which tools are needed to carry out the various tasks detailed in this manual, we have compiled three lists of tools under the following headings: *Maintenance and minor repair, Repair and overhaul*, and *Special*. Newcomers to practical mechanics should start off with the *Maintenance and minor repair* tool kit, and confine themselves to the simpler jobs around the vehicle. Then, as confidence and experience grow, more difficult tasks can be undertaken, with extra tools being purchased as, and when, they are needed. In this way, a *Maintenance and minor repair* tool kit can be built up into a *Repair and overhaul* tool kit over a considerable period of time, without any major cash outlays. The experienced do-it-yourselfer will have a tool kit good enough for most repair and overhaul procedures, and will add tools from the *Special* category when it is felt that the expense is justified by the amount of use to which these tools will be put.

Maintenance and minor repair tool kit

The tools given in this list should be considered as a minimum requirement if routine maintenance, servicing and minor repair operations are to be undertaken. We recommend the purchase of combination spanners (ring one end, open-ended the other); although more expensive than open-ended ones, they do give the advantages of both types of spanner.

☐ *Combination spanners:*
   Metric - 8 to 19 mm inclusive
☐ *Adjustable spanner - 35 mm jaw (approx.)*
☐ *Spark plug spanner (with rubber insert) - petrol models*
☐ *Spark plug gap adjustment tool - petrol models*
☐ *Set of feeler gauges*
☐ *Brake bleed nipple spanner*
☐ *Screwdrivers:*
   Flat blade - 100 mm long x 6 mm dia
   Cross blade - 100 mm long x 6 mm dia
   Torx - various sizes (not all vehicles)
☐ *Combination pliers*
☐ *Hacksaw (junior)*
☐ *Tyre pump*
☐ *Tyre pressure gauge*
☐ *Oil can*
☐ *Oil filter removal tool*
☐ *Fine emery cloth*
☐ *Wire brush (small)*
☐ *Funnel (medium size)*
☐ *Sump drain plug key (not all vehicles)*

Repair and overhaul tool kit

These tools are virtually essential for anyone undertaking any major repairs to a motor vehicle, and are additional to those given in the *Maintenance and minor repair* list. Included in this list is a comprehensive set of sockets. Although these are expensive, they will be found invaluable as they are so versatile - particularly if various drives are included in the set. We recommend the half-inch square-drive type, as this can be used with most proprietary torque wrenches.

The tools in this list will sometimes need to be supplemented by tools from the *Special* list:

☐ *Sockets (or box spanners) to cover range in previous list (including Torx sockets)*
☐ *Reversible ratchet drive (for use with sockets)*
☐ *Extension piece, 250 mm (for use with sockets)*
☐ *Universal joint (for use with sockets)*
☐ *Flexible handle or sliding T "breaker bar" (for use with sockets)*
☐ *Torque wrench (for use with sockets)*
☐ *Self-locking grips*
☐ *Ball pein hammer*
☐ *Soft-faced mallet (plastic or rubber)*
☐ *Screwdrivers:*
   Flat blade - long & sturdy, short (chubby), and narrow (electrician's) types
   Cross blade – long & sturdy, and short (chubby) types
☐ *Pliers:*
   Long-nosed
   Side cutters (electrician's)
   Circlip (internal and external)
☐ *Cold chisel - 25 mm*
☐ *Scriber*
☐ *Scraper*
☐ *Centre-punch*
☐ *Pin punch*
☐ *Hacksaw*
☐ *Brake hose clamp*
☐ *Brake/clutch bleeding kit*
☐ *Selection of twist drills*
☐ *Steel rule/straight-edge*
☐ *Allen keys (inc. splined/Torx type)*
☐ *Selection of files*
☐ *Wire brush*
☐ *Axle stands*
☐ *Jack (strong trolley or hydraulic type)*
☐ *Light with extension lead*
☐ *Universal electrical multi-meter*

Sockets and reversible ratchet drive

Brake bleeding kit

Torx key, socket and bit

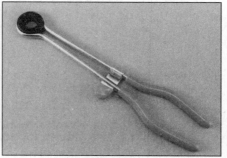

Hose clamp

Angular-tightening gauge

Special tools

The tools in this list are those which are not used regularly, are expensive to buy, or which need to be used in accordance with their manufacturers' instructions. Unless relatively difficult mechanical jobs are undertaken frequently, it will not be economic to buy many of these tools. Where this is the case, you could consider clubbing together with friends (or joining a motorists' club) to make a joint purchase, or borrowing the tools against a deposit from a local garage or tool hire specialist. It is worth noting that many of the larger DIY superstores now carry a large range of special tools for hire at modest rates.

The following list contains only those tools and instruments freely available to the public, and not those special tools produced by the vehicle manufacturer specifically for its dealer network. You will find occasional references to these manufacturers' special tools in the text of this manual. Generally, an alternative method of doing the job without the vehicle manufacturers' special tool is given. However, sometimes there is no alternative to using them. Where this is the case and the relevant tool cannot be bought or borrowed, you will have to entrust the work to a dealer.

- ☐ Angular-tightening gauge
- ☐ Valve spring compressor
- ☐ Valve grinding tool
- ☐ Piston ring compressor
- ☐ Piston ring removal/installation tool
- ☐ Cylinder bore hone
- ☐ Balljoint separator
- ☐ Coil spring compressors (where applicable)
- ☐ Two/three-legged hub and bearing puller
- ☐ Impact screwdriver
- ☐ Micrometer and/or vernier calipers
- ☐ Dial gauge
- ☐ Stroboscopic timing light
- ☐ Dwell angle meter/tachometer
- ☐ Fault code reader
- ☐ Cylinder compression gauge
- ☐ Hand-operated vacuum pump and gauge
- ☐ Clutch plate alignment set
- ☐ Brake shoe steady spring cup removal tool
- ☐ Bush and bearing removal/installation set
- ☐ Stud extractors
- ☐ Tap and die set
- ☐ Lifting tackle
- ☐ Trolley jack

Buying tools

Reputable motor accessory shops and superstores often offer excellent quality tools at discount prices, so it pays to shop around.

Remember, you don't have to buy the most expensive items on the shelf, but it is always advisable to steer clear of the very cheap tools. Beware of 'bargains' offered on market stalls or at car boot sales. There are plenty of good tools around at reasonable prices, but always aim to purchase items which meet the relevant national safety standards. If in doubt, ask the proprietor or manager of the shop for advice before making a purchase.

Care and maintenance of tools

Having purchased a reasonable tool kit, it is necessary to keep the tools in a clean and serviceable condition. After use, always wipe off any dirt, grease and metal particles using a clean, dry cloth, before putting the tools away. Never leave them lying around after they have been used. A simple tool rack on the garage or workshop wall for items such as screwdrivers and pliers is a good idea. Store all normal spanners and sockets in a metal box. Any measuring instruments, gauges, meters, etc, must be carefully stored where they cannot be damaged or become rusty.

Take a little care when tools are used. Hammer heads inevitably become marked, and screwdrivers lose the keen edge on their blades from time to time. A little timely attention with emery cloth or a file will soon restore items like this to a good finish.

Working facilities

Not to be forgotten when discussing tools is the workshop itself. If anything more than routine maintenance is to be carried out, a suitable working area becomes essential.

It is appreciated that many an owner-mechanic is forced by circumstances to remove an engine or similar item without the benefit of a garage or workshop. Having done this, any repairs should always be done under the cover of a roof.

Wherever possible, any dismantling should be done on a clean, flat workbench or table at a suitable working height.

Any workbench needs a vice; one with a jaw opening of 100 mm is suitable for most jobs. As mentioned previously, some clean dry storage space is also required for tools, as well as for any lubricants, cleaning fluids, touch-up paints etc, which become necessary.

Another item which may be required, and which has a much more general usage, is an electric drill with a chuck capacity of at least 8 mm. This, together with a good range of twist drills, is virtually essential for fitting accessories.

Last, but not least, always keep a supply of old newspapers and clean, lint-free rags available, and try to keep any working area as clean as possible.

Micrometers

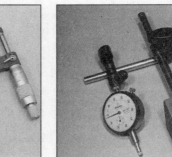

Dial test indicator ("dial gauge")

Strap wrench

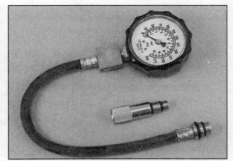

Compression tester

Fault code reader

This is a guide to getting your vehicle through the MOT test. Obviously it will not be possible to examine the vehicle to the same standard as the professional MOT tester. However, working through the following checks will enable you to identify any problem areas before submitting the vehicle for the test.

Where a testable component is in borderline condition, the tester has discretion in deciding whether to pass or fail it. The basis of such discretion is whether the tester would be happy for a close relative or friend to use the vehicle with the component in that condition. If the vehicle presented is clean and evidently well cared for, the tester may be more inclined to pass a borderline component than if the vehicle is scruffy and apparently neglected.

It has only been possible to summarise the test requirements here, based on the regulations in force at the time of printing. Test standards are becoming increasingly stringent, although there are some exemptions for older vehicles.

An assistant will be needed to help carry out some of these checks.

The checks have been sub-divided into four categories, as follows:

1 Checks carried out **FROM THE DRIVER'S SEAT**

2 Checks carried out **WITH THE VEHICLE ON THE GROUND**

3 Checks carried out **WITH THE VEHICLE RAISED AND THE WHEELS FREE TO TURN**

4 Checks carried out on **YOUR VEHICLE'S EXHAUST EMISSION SYSTEM**

---

1 Checks carried out **FROM THE DRIVER'S SEAT**

Handbrake

☐ Test the operation of the handbrake. Excessive travel (too many clicks) indicates incorrect brake or cable adjustment.
☐ Check that the handbrake cannot be released by tapping the lever sideways. Check the security of the lever mountings.

Footbrake

☐ Depress the brake pedal and check that it does not creep down to the floor, indicating a master cylinder fault. Release the pedal, wait a few seconds, then depress it again. If the pedal travels nearly to the floor before firm resistance is felt, brake adjustment or repair is necessary. If the pedal feels spongy, there is air in the hydraulic system which must be removed by bleeding.

☐ Check that the brake pedal is secure and in good condition. Check also for signs of fluid leaks on the pedal, floor or carpets, which would indicate failed seals in the brake master cylinder.
☐ Check the servo unit (when applicable) by operating the brake pedal several times, then keeping the pedal depressed and starting the engine. As the engine starts, the pedal will move down slightly. If not, the vacuum hose or the servo itself may be faulty.

Steering wheel and column

☐ Examine the steering wheel for fractures or looseness of the hub, spokes or rim.
☐ Move the steering wheel from side to side and then up and down. Check that the steering wheel is not loose on the column, indicating wear or a loose retaining nut. Continue moving the steering wheel as before, but also turn it slightly from left to right.
☐ Check that the steering wheel is not loose on the column, and that there is no abnormal

movement of the steering wheel, indicating wear in the column support bearings or couplings.

Windscreen, mirrors and sunvisor

☐ The windscreen must be free of cracks or other significant damage within the driver's field of view. (Small stone chips are acceptable.) Rear view mirrors must be secure, intact, and capable of being adjusted.

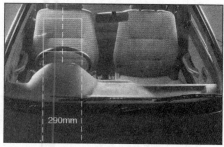

☐ The driver's sunvisor must be capable of being stored in the "up" position.

Seat belts and seats

Note: *The following checks are applicable to all seat belts, front and rear.*

☐ Examine the webbing of all the belts (including rear belts if fitted) for cuts, serious fraying or deterioration. Fasten and unfasten each belt to check the buckles. If applicable, check the retracting mechanism. Check the security of all seat belt mountings accessible from inside the vehicle.

☐ Seat belts with pre-tensioners, once activated, have a "flag" or similar showing on the seat belt stalk. This, in itself, is not a reason for test failure.

☐ The front seats themselves must be securely attached and the backrests must lock in the upright position.

Doors

☐ Both front doors must be able to be opened and closed from outside and inside, and must latch securely when closed.

2 Checks carried out WITH THE VEHICLE ON THE GROUND

Vehicle identification

☐ Number plates must be in good condition, secure and legible, with letters and numbers correctly spaced – spacing at (A) should be at least twice that at (B).

☐ The VIN plate and/or homologation plate must be legible.

Electrical equipment

☐ Switch on the ignition and check the operation of the horn.

☐ Check the windscreen washers and wipers, examining the wiper blades; renew damaged or perished blades. Also check the operation of the stop-lights.

☐ Check the operation of the sidelights and number plate lights. The lenses and reflectors must be secure, clean and undamaged.

☐ Check the operation and alignment of the headlights. The headlight reflectors must not be tarnished and the lenses must be undamaged.

☐ Switch on the ignition and check the operation of the direction indicators (including the instrument panel tell-tale) and the hazard warning lights. Operation of the sidelights and stop-lights must not affect the indicators - if it does, the cause is usually a bad earth at the rear light cluster.

☐ Check the operation of the rear foglight(s), including the warning light on the instrument panel or in the switch.

☐ The ABS warning light must illuminate in accordance with the manufacturers' design. For most vehicles, the ABS warning light should illuminate when the ignition is switched on, and (if the system is operating properly) extinguish after a few seconds. Refer to the owner's handbook.

Footbrake

☐ Examine the master cylinder, brake pipes and servo unit for leaks, loose mountings, corrosion or other damage.

☐ The fluid reservoir must be secure and the fluid level must be between the upper (**A**) and lower (**B**) markings.

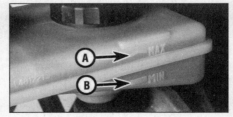

☐ Inspect both front brake flexible hoses for cracks or deterioration of the rubber. Turn the steering from lock to lock, and ensure that the hoses do not contact the wheel, tyre, or any part of the steering or suspension mechanism. With the brake pedal firmly depressed, check the hoses for bulges or leaks under pressure.

Steering and suspension

☐ Have your assistant turn the steering wheel from side to side slightly, up to the point where the steering gear just begins to transmit this movement to the roadwheels. Check for excessive free play between the steering wheel and the steering gear, indicating wear or insecurity of the steering column joints, the column-to-steering gear coupling, or the steering gear itself.

☐ Have your assistant turn the steering wheel more vigorously in each direction, so that the roadwheels just begin to turn. As this is done, examine all the steering joints, linkages, fittings and attachments. Renew any component that shows signs of wear or damage. On vehicles with power steering, check the security and condition of the steering pump, drivebelt and hoses.

☐ Check that the vehicle is standing level, and at approximately the correct ride height.

Shock absorbers

☐ Depress each corner of the vehicle in turn, then release it. The vehicle should rise and then settle in its normal position. If the vehicle continues to rise and fall, the shock absorber is defective. A shock absorber which has seized will also cause the vehicle to fail.

Exhaust system

☐ Start the engine. With your assistant holding a rag over the tailpipe, check the entire system for leaks. Repair or renew leaking sections.

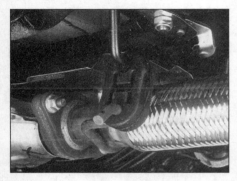

3 Checks carried out
WITH THE VEHICLE RAISED AND THE WHEELS FREE TO TURN

Jack up the front and rear of the vehicle, and securely support it on axle stands. Position the stands clear of the suspension assemblies. Ensure that the wheels are clear of the ground and that the steering can be turned from lock to lock.

Steering mechanism

☐ Have your assistant turn the steering from lock to lock. Check that the steering turns smoothly, and that no part of the steering mechanism, including a wheel or tyre, fouls any brake hose or pipe or any part of the body structure.
☐ Examine the steering rack rubber gaiters for damage or insecurity of the retaining clips. If power steering is fitted, check for signs of damage or leakage of the fluid hoses, pipes or connections. Also check for excessive stiffness or binding of the steering, a missing split pin or locking device, or severe corrosion of the body structure within 30 cm of any steering component attachment point.

Front and rear suspension and wheel bearings

☐ Starting at the front right-hand side, grasp the roadwheel at the 3 o'clock and 9 o'clock positions and rock gently but firmly. Check for free play or insecurity at the wheel bearings, suspension balljoints, or suspension mountings, pivots and attachments.
☐ Now grasp the wheel at the 12 o'clock and 6 o'clock positions and repeat the previous inspection. Spin the wheel, and check for roughness or tightness of the front wheel bearing.

☐ If excess free play is suspected at a component pivot point, this can be confirmed by using a large screwdriver or similar tool and levering between the mounting and the component attachment. This will confirm whether the wear is in the pivot bush, its retaining bolt, or in the mounting itself (the bolt holes can often become elongated).

☐ Carry out all the above checks at the other front wheel, and then at both rear wheels.

Springs and shock absorbers

☐ Examine the suspension struts (when applicable) for serious fluid leakage, corrosion, or damage to the casing. Also check the security of the mounting points.
☐ If coil springs are fitted, check that the spring ends locate in their seats, and that the spring is not corroded, cracked or broken.
☐ If leaf springs are fitted, check that all leaves are intact, that the axle is securely attached to each spring, and that there is no deterioration of the spring eye mountings, bushes, and shackles.

☐ The same general checks apply to vehicles fitted with other suspension types, such as torsion bars, hydraulic displacer units, etc. Ensure that all mountings and attachments are secure, that there are no signs of excessive wear, corrosion or damage, and (on hydraulic types) that there are no fluid leaks or damaged pipes.
☐ Inspect the shock absorbers for signs of serious fluid leakage. Check for wear of the mounting bushes or attachments, or damage to the body of the unit.

Driveshafts
(fwd vehicles only)

☐ Rotate each front wheel in turn and inspect the constant velocity joint gaiters for splits or damage. Also check that each driveshaft is straight and undamaged.

Braking system

☐ If possible without dismantling, check brake pad wear and disc condition. Ensure that the friction lining material has not worn excessively, (A) and that the discs are not fractured, pitted, scored or badly worn (B).

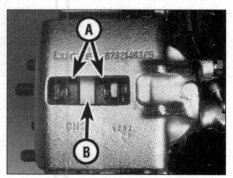

☐ Examine all the rigid brake pipes underneath the vehicle, and the flexible hose(s) at the rear. Look for corrosion, chafing or insecurity of the pipes, and for signs of bulging under pressure, chafing, splits or deterioration of the flexible hoses.
☐ Look for signs of fluid leaks at the brake calipers or on the brake backplates. Repair or renew leaking components.
☐ Slowly spin each wheel, while your assistant depresses and releases the footbrake. Ensure that each brake is operating and does not bind when the pedal is released.

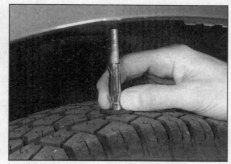

□ Examine the handbrake mechanism, checking for frayed or broken cables, excessive corrosion, or wear or insecurity of the linkage. Check that the mechanism works on each relevant wheel, and releases fully, without binding.

□ It is not possible to test brake efficiency without special equipment, but a road test can be carried out later to check that the vehicle pulls up in a straight line.

Fuel and exhaust systems

□ Inspect the fuel tank (including the filler cap), fuel pipes, hoses and unions. All components must be secure and free from leaks.

□ Examine the exhaust system over its entire length, checking for any damaged, broken or missing mountings, security of the retaining clamps and rust or corrosion.

Wheels and tyres

□ Examine the sidewalls and tread area of each tyre in turn. Check for cuts, tears, lumps, bulges, separation of the tread, and exposure of the ply or cord due to wear or damage. Check that the tyre bead is correctly seated on the wheel rim, that the valve is sound and properly seated, and that the wheel is not distorted or damaged.

□ Check that the tyres are of the correct size for the vehicle, that they are of the same size

and type on each axle, and that the pressures are correct.

□ Check the tyre tread depth. The legal minimum at the time of writing is 1.6 mm over at least three-quarters of the tread width. Abnormal tread wear may indicate incorrect front wheel alignment.

Body corrosion

□ Check the condition of the entire vehicle structure for signs of corrosion in load-bearing areas. (These include chassis box sections, side sills, cross-members, pillars, and all suspension, steering, braking system and seat belt mountings and anchorages.) Any corrosion which has seriously reduced the thickness of a load-bearing area is likely to cause the vehicle to fail. In this case professional repairs are likely to be needed.

□ Damage or corrosion which causes sharp or otherwise dangerous edges to be exposed will also cause the vehicle to fail.

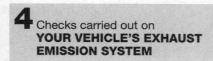

4 Checks carried out on YOUR VEHICLE'S EXHAUST EMISSION SYSTEM

Petrol models

□ The engine should be warmed up, and running well (ignition system in good order, air filter element clean, etc).

□ Before testing, run the engine at around 2500 rpm for 20 seconds. Let the engine drop to idle, and watch for smoke from the exhaust. If the idle speed is too high, or if dense blue or black smoke emerges for more than 5 seconds, the vehicle will fail. Typically, blue smoke signifies oil burning (engine wear); black smoke means unburnt fuel (dirty air cleaner element, or other fuel system fault).

□ An exhaust gas analyser for measuring carbon monoxide (CO) and hydrocarbons (HC) is now needed. If one cannot be hired or borrowed, have a local garage perform the check.

CO emissions (mixture)

□ The MOT tester has access to the CO limits for all vehicles. The CO level is measured at idle speed, and at 'fast idle' (2500 to 3000 rpm). The following limits are given as a general guide:

At idle speed – Less than 0.5% CO
At 'fast idle' – Less than 0.3% CO
Lambda reading – 0.97 to 1.03

□ If the CO level is too high, this may point to poor maintenance, a fuel injection system problem, faulty lambda (oxygen) sensor or catalytic converter. Try an injector cleaning treatment, and check the vehicle's ECU for fault codes.

HC emissions

□ The MOT tester has access to HC limits for all vehicles. The HC level is measured at 'fast idle' (2500 to 3000 rpm). The following limits are given as a general guide:

At 'fast idle' – Less than 200 ppm

□ Excessive HC emissions are typically caused by oil being burnt (worn engine), or by a blocked crankcase ventilation system ('breather'). If the engine oil is old and thin, an oil change may help. If the engine is running badly, check the vehicle's ECU for fault codes.

Diesel models

□ The only emission test for diesel engines is measuring exhaust smoke density, using a calibrated smoke meter. The test involves accelerating the engine at least 3 times to its maximum unloaded speed.

Note: *On engines with a timing belt, it is VITAL that the belt is in good condition before the test is carried out.*

□ With the engine warmed up, it is first purged by running at around 2500 rpm for 20 seconds. A governor check is then carried out, by slowly accelerating the engine to its maximum speed. After this, the smoke meter is connected, and the engine is accelerated quickly to maximum speed three times. If the smoke density is less than the limits given below, the vehicle will pass:

Non-turbo vehicles: 2.5m-1
Turbocharged vehicles: 3.0m-1

□ If excess smoke is produced, try fitting a new air cleaner element, or using an injector cleaning treatment. If the engine is running badly, where applicable, check the vehicle's ECU for fault codes. Also check the vehicle's EGR system, where applicable. At high mileages, the injectors may require professional attention.

Engine

- ☐ Engine fails to rotate when attempting to start
- ☐ Engine rotates, but will not start
- ☐ Engine difficult to start when cold
- ☐ Engine difficult to start when hot
- ☐ Starter motor noisy or excessively-rough in engagement
- ☐ Engine starts, but stops immediately
- ☐ Engine idles erratically
- ☐ Engine misfires at idle speed
- ☐ Engine misfires throughout the driving speed range
- ☐ Engine hesitates on acceleration
- ☐ Engine stalls
- ☐ Engine lacks power
- ☐ Engine backfires
- ☐ Oil pressure warning light illuminated with engine running
- ☐ Engine runs-on after switching off
- ☐ Engine noises

Cooling system

- ☐ Overheating
- ☐ Overcooling
- ☐ External coolant leakage
- ☐ Internal coolant leakage
- ☐ Corrosion

Fuel and exhaust systems

- ☐ Excessive fuel consumption
- ☐ Fuel leakage and/or fuel odour
- ☐ Excessive noise or fumes from exhaust system

Clutch

- ☐ Pedal travels to floor – no pressure or very little resistance
- ☐ Clutch fails to disengage (unable to select gears)
- ☐ Clutch slips (engine speed increases, with no increase in vehicle speed)
- ☐ Judder as clutch is engaged
- ☐ Noise when depressing or releasing clutch pedal

Manual transmission

- ☐ Noisy in neutral with engine running
- ☐ Noisy in one particular gear
- ☐ Difficulty engaging gears
- ☐ Jumps out of gear
- ☐ Vibration
- ☐ Lubricant leaks

Automatic/Multitronic transmission

- ☐ Fluid leakage
- ☐ General gear selection problems
- ☐ Transmission will not downshift (kickdown) with accelerator pedal fully depressed
- ☐ Engine will not start in any gear, or starts in gears other than Park or Neutral
- ☐ Transmission slips, shifts roughly, is noisy, or has no drive in forward or reverse gears

Driveshafts

- ☐ Vibration when accelerating or decelerating
- ☐ Clicking or knocking noise on turns (at slow speed on full-lock)

Braking system

- ☐ Vehicle pulls to one side under braking
- ☐ Noise (grinding or high-pitched squeal) when brakes applied
- ☐ Excessive brake pedal travel
- ☐ Brake pedal feels spongy when depressed
- ☐ Excessive brake pedal effort required to stop vehicle
- ☐ Judder felt through brake pedal or steering wheel when braking
- ☐ Pedal pulsates when braking hard
- ☐ Brakes binding
- ☐ Rear wheels locking under normal braking

Steering and suspension

- ☐ Vehicle pulls to one side
- ☐ Wheel wobble and vibration
- ☐ Excessive pitching and/or rolling around corners, or during braking
- ☐ Wandering or general instability
- ☐ Excessively-stiff steering
- ☐ Excessive play in steering
- ☐ Lack of power assistance
- ☐ Tyre wear excessive

Electrical system

- ☐ Battery will not hold a charge for more than a few days
- ☐ Ignition/no-charge warning light remains illuminated with engine running
- ☐ Ignition/no-charge warning light fails to come on
- ☐ Lights inoperative
- ☐ Instrument readings inaccurate or erratic
- ☐ Horn inoperative, or unsatisfactory in operation
- ☐ Windscreen/tailgate wipers inoperative, or unsatisfactory in operation
- ☐ Windscreen washers inoperative, or unsatisfactory in operation
- ☐ Electric windows inoperative, or unsatisfactory in operation

Introduction

The vehicle owner who does his or her own maintenance according to the recommended service schedules should not have to use this section of the manual very often. Modern component reliability is such that, provided those items subject to wear or deterioration are inspected or renewed at the specified intervals, sudden failure is comparatively rare. Faults do not usually just happen as a result of sudden failure, but develop over a period of time. Major mechanical failures in particular are usually preceded by characteristic symptoms over hundreds or even thousands of miles. Those components which do occasionally fail without warning are often small and easily carried in the vehicle.

With any fault-finding, the first step is to decide where to begin investigations. Sometimes this is obvious, but on other occasions, a little detective work will be necessary. The owner who makes half a dozen haphazard adjustments or replacements may be successful in curing a fault (or its symptoms), but will be none the wiser if the fault recurs, and ultimately may have spent more time and money than was necessary. A calm and logical approach will be found to be more satisfactory in the long run. Always take into account any warning signs or abnormalities that may have been noticed in the period preceding the fault – power loss, high or low gauge readings, unusual smells, etc – and remember that failure of components such as fuses or spark plugs may only be pointers to some underlying fault.

The pages which follow provide an easy-reference guide to the more common problems which may occur during the operation of the vehicle. These problems and their possible causes are grouped under headings denoting various components or systems, such as Engine, Cooling system, etc. The general

Chapter which deals with the problem is also shown in brackets; refer to the relevant part of that Chapter for system-specific information. Whatever the fault, certain basic principles apply. These are as follows:

Verify the fault. This is simply a matter of being sure that you know what the symptoms are before starting work. This is particularly important if you are investigating a fault for someone else, who may not have described it very accurately.

Don't overlook the obvious. For example, if the vehicle won't start, is there fuel in the tank? (Don't take anyone else's word on this particular point, and don't trust the fuel gauge either!) If an electrical fault is indicated, look for loose or broken wires before digging out the test gear.

Cure the disease, not the symptom. Substituting a flat battery with a fully-charged one will get you off the hard shoulder, but if the underlying cause is not attended to, the new battery will go the same way. Similarly, changing oil-fouled spark plugs for a new set will get you moving again, but remember that the reason for the fouling (if it wasn't simply an incorrect grade of plug) will have to be established and corrected.

Don't take anything for granted. Particularly, don't forget that a new component may itself be defective (especially if its been rattling around in the boot for months), and don't leave components out of a fault diagnosis sequence just because they are new or recently-fitted. When you do finally diagnose a difficult fault, you'll probably realise that all the evidence was there from the start.

Diesel fault diagnosis

The majority of starting problems on small diesel engines are electrical in origin. The mechanic who is familiar with petrol engines but less so with diesel may be inclined to view the diesel's injectors and pump in the same light as the spark plugs and distributor, but this is generally a mistake.

When investigating complaints of difficult starting for someone else, make sure that the correct starting procedure is understood and is being followed. Some drivers are unaware of the significance of the preheating warning light – many modern engines are sufficiently forgiving for this not to matter in mild weather, but with the onset of winter, problems begin.

As a rule of thumb, if the engine is difficult to start but runs well when it has finally got going, the problem is electrical (battery, starter motor or preheating system). If poor performance is combined with difficult starting, the problem is likely to be in the fuel system. The low-pressure (supply) side of the fuel system should be checked before suspecting the injectors and high-pressure pump. The most common fuel supply problem is air getting into the system, and any pipe from the fuel tank forwards must be scrutinised if air leakage is suspected. Normally the pump is the last item to suspect, since unless it has been tampered with, there is no reason for it to be at fault.

Engine

Engine fails to rotate when attempting to start

- [ ] Battery terminal connections loose or corroded (see *Weekly checks*).
- [ ] Battery discharged or faulty (Chapter 5A).
- [ ] Broken, loose or disconnected wiring in the starting circuit (Chapter 5A).
- [ ] Defective starter solenoid or switch (Chapter 5A).
- [ ] Defective starter motor (Chapter 5A).
- [ ] Starter pinion or flywheel/driveplate ring gear teeth loose or broken (Chapter 2 and 5A).
- [ ] Engine earth strap broken or disconnected (Chapter 5A or 12).

Engine rotates, but will not start

- [ ] Fuel tank empty.
- [ ] Battery discharged (engine rotates slowly) (Chapter 5A).
- [ ] Battery terminal connections loose or corroded (see *Weekly checks*).
- [ ] Ignition components damp or damaged – petrol models (Chapters 1A and 5B).
- [ ] Broken, loose or disconnected wiring in the ignition circuit – petrol models (Chapters 1A and 5B).
- [ ] Worn, faulty or incorrectly-gapped spark plugs – petrol models (Chapter 1A).
- [ ] Preheating system faulty – diesel models (Chapter 5D).
- [ ] Fuel injection system fault – petrol models (Chapter 4A or 4B).
- [ ] Air in fuel system – diesel models (Chapter 4C).
- [ ] Major mechanical failure (e.g. timing belt) (Chapter 2).

Engine difficult to start when cold

- [ ] Battery discharged (Chapter 5A).
- [ ] Battery terminal connections loose or corroded (see *Weekly checks*).
- [ ] Worn, faulty or incorrectly-gapped spark plugs – petrol models (Chapter 1A).
- [ ] Preheating system faulty – diesel models (Chapter 5D).
- [ ] Fuel injection system fault – petrol models (Chapter 4A or 4B).
- [ ] Other ignition system fault – petrol models (Chapters 1A and 5B).
- [ ] Low cylinder compressions (Chapter 2).

Engine difficult to start when hot

- [ ] Air filter element dirty or clogged (Chapter 1).
- [ ] Fuel injection system fault – petrol models (Chapter 4A or 4B).
- [ ] Low cylinder compressions (Chapter 2).

Starter motor noisy or excessively-rough in engagement

- [ ] Starter pinion or flywheel ring gear teeth loose or broken (Chapter 2 and 5A).
- [ ] Starter motor mounting bolts loose or missing (Chapter 5A).
- [ ] Starter motor internal components worn or damaged (Chapter 5A).

Engine starts, but stops immediately

- [ ] Loose or faulty electrical connections in the ignition circuit – petrol models (Chapters 1A and 5B).
- [ ] Vacuum leak at the throttle body or inlet manifold – petrol models (Chapter 4A or 4B).
- [ ] Blocked injector/fuel injection system fault – petrol models (Chapter 4A or 4B).

Engine (continued)

Engine idles erratically

- [ ] Air filter element clogged (Chapter 1).
- [ ] Vacuum leak at the throttle body, inlet manifold or associated hoses – petrol models (Chapter 4A or 4B).
- [ ] Worn, faulty or incorrectly-gapped spark plugs – petrol models (Chapter 1A).
- [ ] Uneven or low cylinder compressions (Chapter 2).
- [ ] Camshaft lobes worn (Chapter 2).
- [ ] Timing belt incorrectly fitted (Chapter 2).
- [ ] Blocked injector/fuel injection system fault – petrol models (Chapter 4A or 4B).
- [ ] Faulty injector(s) – diesel models (Chapter 4C).

Engine misfires at idle speed

- [ ] Worn, faulty or incorrectly-gapped spark plugs – petrol models (Chapter 1A).
- [ ] Vacuum leak at the throttle body, inlet manifold or associated hoses – petrol models (Chapter 4A or 4B).
- [ ] Blocked injector/fuel injection system fault – petrol models (Chapter 4A or 4B).
- [ ] Faulty injector(s) – diesel models (Chapter 4C).
- [ ] Uneven or low cylinder compressions (Chapter 2).
- [ ] Disconnected, leaking, or perished crankcase ventilation hoses (Chapter 4D).

Engine misfires throughout the driving speed range

- [ ] Fuel filter choked (Chapter 1).
- [ ] Fuel pump faulty, or delivery pressure low – petrol models (Chapter 4A or 4B).
- [ ] Fuel tank vent blocked, or fuel pipes restricted (Chapter 4).
- [ ] Vacuum leak at the throttle body, inlet manifold or associated hoses – petrol models (Chapter 4A or 4B).
- [ ] Worn, faulty or incorrectly-gapped spark plugs – petrol models (Chapter 1A).
- [ ] Faulty injector(s) – diesel models (Chapter 4C).
- [ ] Faulty ignition coil – petrol models (Chapter 5B).
- [ ] Uneven or low cylinder compressions (Chapter 2).
- [ ] Blocked injector/fuel injection system fault – petrol models (Chapter 4A or 4B).

Engine hesitates on acceleration

- [ ] Worn, faulty or incorrectly-gapped spark plugs – petrol models (Chapter 1A).
- [ ] Vacuum leak at the throttle body, inlet manifold or associated hoses – petrol models (Chapter 4A or 4B).
- [ ] Blocked injector/fuel injection system fault – petrol models (Chapter 4A or 4B).
- [ ] Faulty injector(s) – diesel models (Chapter 4C).

Engine stalls

- [ ] Vacuum leak at the throttle body, inlet manifold or associated hoses – petrol models (Chapter 4A or 4B).
- [ ] Fuel filter choked (Chapter 1).
- [ ] Fuel pump faulty, or delivery pressure low – petrol models (Chapter 4A or 4B).
- [ ] Fuel tank vent blocked, or fuel pipes restricted (Chapter 4).
- [ ] Blocked injector/fuel injection system fault – petrol models (Chapter 4A or 4B).
- [ ] Faulty injector(s) – diesel models (Chapter 4C).

Engine lacks power

- [ ] Timing belt incorrectly fitted or tensioned (Chapter 2).
- [ ] Fuel filter choked (Chapter 1).
- [ ] Fuel pump faulty, or delivery pressure low – petrol models (Chapter 4A or 4B).

- [ ] Uneven or low cylinder compressions (Chapter 2).
- [ ] Worn, faulty or incorrectly-gapped spark plugs – petrol models (Chapter 1A).
- [ ] Vacuum leak at the throttle body, inlet manifold or associated hoses – petrol models (Chapter 4A or 4B).
- [ ] Blocked injector/fuel injection system fault – petrol models (Chapter 4A or 4B).
- [ ] Faulty injector(s) – diesel models (Chapter 4C).
- [ ] Brakes binding (Chapters 1 and 9).
- [ ] Clutch slipping (Chapter 6).
- [ ] Air filter element clogged (Chapter 1).

Engine backfires

- [ ] Timing belt incorrectly fitted or tensioned (Chapter 2).
- [ ] Vacuum leak at the throttle body, inlet manifold or associated hoses – petrol models (Chapter 4A or 4B).
- [ ] Blocked injector/fuel injection system fault – petrol models (Chapter 4A or 4B).

Oil pressure warning light illuminated with engine running

- [ ] Low oil level, or incorrect oil grade (*Weekly checks*).
- [ ] Faulty oil pressure switch (Chapter 5A).
- [ ] Worn engine bearings and/or oil pump (Chapter 2).
- [ ] High engine operating temperature (Chapter 3).
- [ ] Oil pressure relief valve defective (Chapter 2).
- [ ] Oil pick-up strainer clogged (Chapter 2).

Engine runs-on after switching off

- [ ] Excessive carbon build-up in engine (Chapter 2).
- [ ] High engine operating temperature (Chapter 3).
- [ ] Fuel injection system fault – petrol models (Chapter 4A or 4B).
- [ ] Faulty stop solenoid – diesel models (Chapter 4C).

Engine noises

Pre-ignition (pinking) or knocking during acceleration or under load

- [ ] Ignition system fault – petrol models (Chapters 1A and 5B).
- [ ] Incorrect grade of spark plug – petrol models (Chapter 1A).
- [ ] Vacuum leak at the throttle body, inlet manifold or associated hoses – petrol models (Chapter 4A or 4B).
- [ ] Excessive carbon build-up in engine (Chapter 2).
- [ ] Blocked injector/fuel injection system fault – petrol models (Chapter 4A or 4B).

Whistling or wheezing noises

- [ ] Leaking inlet manifold or throttle body gasket – petrol models (Chapter 4A or 4B).
- [ ] Leaking exhaust manifold gasket or pipe-to-manifold joint (Chapter 4).
- [ ] Leaking vacuum hose (Chapters 4 and 9).
- [ ] Blowing cylinder head gasket (Chapter 2).

Tapping or rattling noises

- [ ] Worn valve gear or camshaft (Chapter 2).
- [ ] Ancillary component fault (coolant pump, alternator, etc) (Chapters 3, 5, etc).

Knocking or thumping noises

- [ ] Worn big-end bearings (regular heavy knocking, perhaps less under load) (Chapter 2).
- [ ] Worn main bearings (rumbling and knocking, perhaps worsening under load) (Chapter 2).
- [ ] Piston slap (most noticeable when cold) (Chapter 2).
- [ ] Ancillary component fault (coolant pump, alternator, etc) (Chapters 3, 5, etc).

Cooling system

Overheating

- ☐ Insufficient coolant in system (*Weekly checks*).
- ☐ Thermostat faulty (Chapter 3).
- ☐ Radiator core blocked, or grille restricted (Chapter 3).
- ☐ Electric cooling fan or thermostatic switch faulty (Chapter 3).
- ☐ Inaccurate temperature gauge sender unit (Chapter 3).
- ☐ Airlock in cooling system.
- ☐ Expansion tank pressure cap faulty (Chapter 3).

Overcooling

- ☐ Thermostat faulty (Chapter 3).
- ☐ Inaccurate temperature gauge sender unit (Chapter 3).

External coolant leakage

- ☐ Deteriorated or damaged hoses or hose clips (Chapter 1).

- ☐ Radiator core or heater matrix leaking (Chapter 3).
- ☐ Pressure cap faulty (Chapter 3).
- ☐ Coolant pump internal seal leaking (Chapter 3).
- ☐ Coolant pump-to-housing seal leaking (Chapter 3).
- ☐ Boiling due to overheating (Chapter 3).
- ☐ Core plug leaking (Chapter 2).

Internal coolant leakage

- ☐ Leaking cylinder head gasket (Chapter 2).
- ☐ Cracked cylinder head or cylinder block (Chapter 2).

Corrosion

- ☐ Infrequent draining and flushing (Chapter 1).
- ☐ Incorrect coolant mixture or inappropriate coolant type (see *Weekly checks*).

Fuel and exhaust systems

Excessive fuel consumption

- ☐ Air filter element dirty or clogged (Chapter 1).
- ☐ Fuel injection system fault – petrol models (Chapter 4A or 4B).
- ☐ Faulty injector(s) – diesel models (Chapter 4C).
- ☐ Ignition system fault – petrol models (Chapters 1A and 5B).
- ☐ Tyres under-inflated (see *Weekly checks*).

Fuel leakage and/or fuel odour

- ☐ Damaged fuel tank, pipes or connections (Chapter 4).

Excessive noise or fumes from exhaust system

- ☐ Leaking exhaust system or manifold joints (Chapters 1 and 4).
- ☐ Leaking, corroded or damaged silencers or pipe (Chapters 1 and 4).
- ☐ Broken mountings causing body or suspension contact (Chapter 1).

Clutch

Pedal travels to floor – no pressure or very little resistance

- ☐ Faulty master or slave cylinder (Chapter 6).
- ☐ Faulty hydraulic release system (Chapter 6).
- ☐ Broken clutch release bearing or arm (Chapter 6).
- ☐ Broken diaphragm spring in clutch pressure plate (Chapter 6).

Clutch fails to disengage (unable to select gears)

- ☐ Faulty master or slave cylinder (Chapter 6).
- ☐ Faulty hydraulic release system (Chapter 6).
- ☐ Clutch disc sticking on gearbox input shaft splines (Chapter 6).
- ☐ Clutch disc sticking to flywheel or pressure plate (Chapter 6).
- ☐ Faulty pressure plate assembly (Chapter 6).
- ☐ Clutch release mechanism worn or incorrectly assembled (Chapter 6).

Clutch slips (engine speed increases, with no increase in vehicle speed)

- ☐ Faulty hydraulic release system (Chapter 6).
- ☐ Clutch disc linings excessively worn (Chapter 6).
- ☐ Clutch disc linings contaminated with oil or grease (Chapter 6).
- ☐ Faulty pressure plate or weak diaphragm spring (Chapter 6).

Judder as clutch is engaged

- ☐ Clutch disc linings contaminated with oil or grease (Chapter 6).
- ☐ Clutch disc linings excessively worn (Chapter 6).
- ☐ Faulty or distorted pressure plate or diaphragm spring (Chapter 6).
- ☐ Worn or loose engine or gearbox mountings (Chapter 2).
- ☐ Clutch disc hub or gearbox input shaft splines worn (Chapter 6).

Noise when depressing or releasing clutch pedal

- ☐ Worn clutch release bearing (Chapter 6).
- ☐ Worn or dry clutch pedal pivot (Chapter 6).
- ☐ Faulty pressure plate assembly (Chapter 6).
- ☐ Pressure plate diaphragm spring broken (Chapter 6).
- ☐ Broken clutch friction plate cushioning springs (Chapter 6).

Manual transmission

Noisy in neutral with engine running

☐ Input shaft bearings worn (noise apparent with clutch pedal released, but not when depressed) (Chapter 7A).*
☐ Clutch release bearing worn (noise apparent with clutch pedal depressed, possibly less when released) (Chapter 6).

Noisy in one particular gear

☐ Worn, damaged or chipped gear teeth (Chapter 7A).*

Difficulty engaging gears

☐ Clutch fault (Chapter 6).
☐ Worn or damaged gear linkage (Chapter 7A).
☐ Worn synchroniser units (Chapter 7A).*

Jumps out of gear

☐ Worn or damaged gear linkage (Chapter 7A).

☐ Worn synchroniser units (Chapter 7A).*
☐ Worn selector forks (Chapter 7A).*

Vibration

☐ Lack of oil (Chapter 1).
☐ Worn bearings (Chapter 7A).*

Lubricant leaks

☐ Leaking oil seal (Chapter 7A).
☐ Leaking housing joint (Chapter 7A).*
☐ Leaking input shaft oil seal (Chapter 7A).

Although the corrective action necessary to remedy the symptoms described is beyond the scope of the home mechanic, the above information should be helpful in isolating the cause of the condition, so that the owner can communicate clearly with a professional mechanic.

Automatic/Multitronic transmission

Note: *Due to the complexity of the automatic/Multitronic transmission, it is difficult for the home mechanic to properly diagnose and service this unit. For problems other than the following, the vehicle should be taken to a dealer service department or automatic transmission specialist. Do not be too hasty in removing the transmission if a fault is suspected, as most of the testing is carried out with the unit still fitted.*

Fluid leakage

☐ Automatic transmission fluid is usually dark in colour. Fluid leaks should not be confused with engine oil, which can easily be blown onto the transmission by airflow.
☐ To determine the source of a leak, first remove all built-up dirt and grime from the transmission housing and surrounding areas using a degreasing agent, or by steam-cleaning. Drive the vehicle at low speed, so airflow will not blow the leak far from its source. Raise and support the vehicle, and determine where the leak is coming from.

General gear selection problems

☐ Chapter 7 deals with checking and adjusting the selector mechanism on automatic transmissions. The following are common problems which may be caused by a poorly-adjusted mechanism:
a) Engine starting in gears other than Park or Neutral.

b) Indicator panel indicating a gear other than the one actually being used.
c) Vehicle moves when in Park or Neutral.
d) Poor gear shift quality or erratic gear changes.
☐ Refer to Chapter 7B or 7C for the selector mechanism adjustment procedure.

Transmission will not downshift (kickdown) with accelerator pedal fully depressed

☐ Low transmission fluid level (Chapter 1).
☐ Incorrect selector mechanism adjustment (Chapter 7B).

Engine will not start in any gear, or starts in gears other than Park or Neutral

☐ Incorrect selector mechanism adjustment (Chapter 7B or 7C).

Transmission slips, shifts roughly, is noisy, or has no drive in forward or reverse gears

☐ There are many probable causes for the above problems, but unless there is a very obvious reason (such as a loose or corroded wiring plug connection on or near the transmission), the car should be taken to a franchise dealer or specialist for the fault to be diagnosed. The transmission control unit incorporates a self-diagnosis facility, and any fault codes can quickly be read and interpreted by a dealer with the proper diagnostic equipment.

Driveshafts

Vibration when accelerating or decelerating

☐ Worn inner constant velocity joint (Chapter 8).
☐ Bent or distorted driveshaft (Chapter 8).

Clicking or knocking noise on turns (at slow speed on full-lock)

☐ Worn outer constant velocity joint (Chapter 8).
☐ Lack of constant velocity joint lubricant, possibly due to damaged gaiter (Chapter 8).

Braking system

Note: *Before assuming that a brake problem exists, make sure that the tyres are in good condition and correctly inflated, that the front wheel alignment is correct, and that the vehicle is not loaded with weight in an unequal manner. Apart from checking the condition of all pipe and hose connections, any faults occurring on the anti-lock braking system should be referred to a Audi dealer for diagnosis.*

Vehicle pulls to one side under braking

- [ ] Worn, defective, damaged or contaminated front or rear brake pads on one side (Chapters 1 and 9).
- [ ] Seized or partially-seized front or rear brake caliper (Chapter 9).
- [ ] A mixture of brake pad lining materials fitted between sides (Chapter 9).
- [ ] Brake caliper mounting bolts loose (Chapter 9).
- [ ] Worn or damaged steering or suspension components (Chapters 1 and 10).

Noise (grinding or high-pitched squeal) when brakes applied

- [ ] Brake pad friction lining material worn down to metal backing (Chapters 1 and 9).
- [ ] Excessive corrosion of brake disc – may be apparent after the vehicle has been standing for some time (Chapters 1 and 9).
- [ ] Foreign object (stone chipping, etc) trapped between brake disc and shield (Chapters 1 and 9).

Excessive brake pedal travel

- [ ] Faulty master cylinder (Chapter 9).
- [ ] Air in hydraulic system (Chapter 9).
- [ ] Faulty vacuum servo unit (Chapter 9).
- [ ] Faulty vacuum pump, where fitted (Chapter 9).

Brake pedal feels spongy when depressed

- [ ] Air in hydraulic system (Chapter 9).
- [ ] Deteriorated flexible rubber brake hoses (Chapters 1 and 9).
- [ ] Master cylinder mountings loose (Chapter 9).
- [ ] Faulty master cylinder (Chapter 9).

Excessive brake pedal effort required to stop vehicle

- [ ] Faulty vacuum servo unit (Chapter 9).
- [ ] Disconnected, damaged or insecure brake servo vacuum hose (Chapters 1 and 9).
- [ ] Faulty vacuum pump, where fitted (Chapter 9).
- [ ] Primary or secondary hydraulic circuit failure (Chapter 9).
- [ ] Seized brake caliper (Chapter 9).
- [ ] Brake pads incorrectly fitted (Chapter 9).
- [ ] Incorrect grade of brake pads fitted (Chapter 9).
- [ ] Brake pads contaminated (Chapter 9).

Judder felt through brake pedal or steering wheel when braking

- [ ] Excessive run-out or distortion of brake disc(s) (Chapter 9).
- [ ] Brake pad linings worn (Chapters 1 and 9).
- [ ] Brake caliper mounting bolts loose (Chapter 9).
- [ ] Wear in suspension or steering components or mountings (Chapters 1 and 10).

Pedal pulsates when braking hard

- [ ] Normal feature of ABS – no fault

Brakes binding

- [ ] Seized brake caliper piston(s) (Chapter 9).
- [ ] Incorrectly-adjusted handbrake mechanism (Chapter 9).
- [ ] Faulty master cylinder (Chapter 9).

Rear wheels locking under normal braking

- [ ] Rear brake pad linings contaminated (Chapters 1 and 9).
- [ ] Rear brake discs warped (Chapters 1 and 9).

Steering and suspension

Note: *Before diagnosing suspension or steering faults, be sure that the trouble is not due to incorrect tyre pressures, mixtures of tyre types, or binding brakes.*

Vehicle pulls to one side

- [ ] Defective tyre (see *Weekly checks*).
- [ ] Excessive wear in suspension or steering components (Chapters 1 and 10).
- [ ] Incorrect front wheel alignment (Chapter 10).
- [ ] Accident damage to steering or suspension components (Chapters 1 and 10).

Wheel wobble and vibration

- [ ] Front roadwheels out of balance (vibration felt mainly through the steering wheel) (Chapter 10).
- [ ] Rear roadwheels out of balance (vibration felt throughout the vehicle) (Chapter 10).
- [ ] Roadwheels damaged or distorted (Chapter 10).
- [ ] Faulty or damaged tyre (*Weekly checks*).
- [ ] Worn steering or suspension joints, bushes or components (Chapters 1 and 10).
- [ ] Wheel bolts loose (Chapter 1 and 10).

Excessive pitching and/or rolling around corners, or during braking

- [ ] Defective shock absorbers (Chapters 1 and 10).

- [ ] Broken or weak coil spring and/or suspension component (Chapters 1 and 10).
- [ ] Worn or damaged anti-roll bar or mountings (Chapter 10).

Wandering or general instability

- [ ] Incorrect front wheel alignment (Chapter 10).
- [ ] Worn steering or suspension joints, bushes or components (Chapters 1 and 10).
- [ ] Roadwheels out of balance (Chapter 10).
- [ ] Faulty or damaged tyre (*Weekly checks*).
- [ ] Wheel bolts loose (Chapter 10).
- [ ] Defective shock absorbers (Chapters 1 and 10).

Excessively-stiff steering

- [ ] Seized track rod end balljoint or suspension balljoint (Chapters 1 and 10).
- [ ] Broken or incorrectly adjusted auxiliary drivebelt (Chapter 1).
- [ ] Incorrect front wheel alignment (Chapter 10).
- [ ] Steering gear damaged (Chapter 10).

Excessive play in steering

- [ ] Worn steering column universal joint(s) (Chapter 10).
- [ ] Worn steering track rod end balljoints (Chapters 1 and 10).
- [ ] Worn steering gear (Chapter 10).
- [ ] Worn steering or suspension joints, bushes or components (Chapters 1 and 10).

Steering and suspension (continued)

Lack of power assistance

- ☐ Broken or incorrectly-adjusted auxiliary drivebelt (Chapter 1).
- ☐ Incorrect power steering fluid level (*Weekly checks*).
- ☐ Restriction in power steering fluid hoses (Chapter 10).
- ☐ Faulty power steering pump (Chapter 10).
- ☐ Faulty steering gear (Chapter 10).

Tyre wear excessive

Tyres worn on inside or outside edges

- ☐ Incorrect camber or castor angles (Chapter 10).
- ☐ Worn steering or suspension joints, bushes or components (Chapters 1 and 10).
- ☐ Excessively-hard cornering.
- ☐ Accident damage.

Tyre treads exhibit feathered edges

- ☐ Incorrect toe setting (Chapter 10).

Tyres worn in centre of tread

- ☐ Tyres over-inflated (*Weekly checks*).

Tyres worn on inside and outside edges

- ☐ Tyres under-inflated (*Weekly checks*).
- ☐ Worn shock absorbers (Chapter 10).

Tyres worn unevenly

- ☐ Tyres/wheels out of balance (*Weekly checks*).
- ☐ Excessive wheel or tyre run-out (Chapter 10).
- ☐ Worn shock absorbers (Chapters 1 and 10).
- ☐ Faulty tyre (*Weekly checks*).

Electrical system

Note: *For problems associated with the starting system, refer to the faults listed under Engine earlier in this Section.*

Battery will not hold a charge more than a few days

- ☐ Battery defective internally (Chapter 5A).
- ☐ Battery electrolyte level low – where applicable (*Weekly checks*).
- ☐ Battery terminal connections loose or corroded (*Weekly checks*).
- ☐ Auxiliary drivebelt worn – or incorrectly adjusted, where applicable (Chapter 1).
- ☐ Alternator not charging at correct output (Chapter 5A).
- ☐ Alternator or voltage regulator faulty (Chapter 5A).
- ☐ Short-circuit causing continual battery drain (Chapters 5 and 12).

Ignition/no-charge warning light remains illuminated with engine running

- ☐ Auxiliary drivebelt broken, worn, or incorrectly adjusted (Chapter 1).
- ☐ Internal fault in alternator or voltage regulator (Chapter 5A).
- ☐ Broken, disconnected, or loose wiring in charging circuit (Chapter 5A).

Ignition/no-charge warning light fails to come on

- ☐ Broken, disconnected, or loose wiring in warning light circuit (Chapter 12).
- ☐ Alternator faulty (Chapter 5A).

Lights inoperative

- ☐ Bulb blown (Chapter 12).
- ☐ Corrosion of bulb or bulbholder contacts (Chapter 12).
- ☐ Blown fuse (Chapter 12).
- ☐ Faulty relay (Chapter 12).
- ☐ Broken, loose, or disconnected wiring (Chapter 12).
- ☐ Faulty switch (Chapter 12).

Instrument readings inaccurate or erratic

Fuel or temperature gauges give no reading

- ☐ Faulty gauge sender unit (Chapters 3 and 4).
- ☐ Wiring open-circuit (Chapter 12).
- ☐ Faulty gauge (Chapter 12).

Fuel or temperature gauges give continuous maximum reading

- ☐ Faulty gauge sender unit (Chapters 3 and 4).
- ☐ Wiring short-circuit (Chapter 12).
- ☐ Faulty gauge (Chapter 12).

Horn inoperative, or unsatisfactory in operation

Horn operates all the time

- ☐ Horn contacts permanently bridged or horn push stuck down (Chapter 12).

Horn fails to operate

- ☐ Blown fuse (Chapter 12).
- ☐ Cable or cable connections loose, broken or disconnected (Chapter 12).
- ☐ Faulty horn (Chapter 12).

Horn emits intermittent or unsatisfactory sound

- ☐ Cable connections loose (Chapter 12).
- ☐ Horn mountings loose (Chapter 12).
- ☐ Faulty horn (Chapter 12).

Windscreen/tailgate wipers inoperative, or unsatisfactory in operation

Wipers fail to operate, or operate very slowly

- ☐ Wiper blades stuck to screen, or linkage seized or binding (*Weekly checks* and Chapter 12).
- ☐ Blown fuse (Chapter 12).
- ☐ Cable or cable connections loose, broken or disconnected (Chapter 12).
- ☐ Faulty relay (Chapter 12).
- ☐ Faulty wiper motor (Chapter 12).

Wiper blades sweep over too large or too small an area of the glass

- ☐ Wiper arms incorrectly positioned on spindles (Chapter 12).
- ☐ Excessive wear of wiper linkage (Chapter 12).
- ☐ Wiper motor or linkage mountings loose or insecure (Chapter 12).

Wiper blades fail to clean the glass effectively

- ☐ Wiper blade rubbers worn or perished (*Weekly checks*).
- ☐ Wiper arm tension springs broken, or arm pivots seized (Chapter 12).
- ☐ Insufficient windscreen washer additive to adequately remove road film (*Weekly checks*).

Electrical system (continued)

Windscreen washers inoperative, or unsatisfactory in operation

One or more washer jets inoperative

☐ Blocked washer jet (Chapter 12).
☐ Disconnected, kinked or restricted fluid hose (Chapter 12).
☐ Insufficient fluid in washer reservoir (*Weekly checks*).

Washer pump fails to operate

☐ Broken or disconnected wiring or connections (Chapter 12).
☐ Blown fuse (Chapter 12).
☐ Faulty washer switch (Chapter 12).
☐ Faulty washer pump (Chapter 12).

Electric windows inoperative, or unsatisfactory in operation

Window glass will only move in one direction

☐ Faulty switch (Chapter 12).

Window glass slow to move

☐ Regulator seized or damaged, or in need of lubrication (Chapter 11).
☐ Door internal components or trim fouling regulator (Chapter 11).
☐ Faulty motor (Chapter 11).

Window glass fails to move

☐ Blown fuse (Chapter 12).
☐ Faulty relay (Chapter 12).
☐ Broken or disconnected wiring or connections (Chapter 12).
☐ Faulty motor (Chapter 12).

Central locking system inoperative, or unsatisfactory in operation

Complete system failure

☐ Blown fuse (Chapter 12).
☐ Faulty relay (Chapter 12).
☐ Broken or disconnected wiring or connections (Chapter 12).

Latch locks but will not unlock, or unlocks but will not lock

☐ Faulty switch (Chapter 12).
☐ Broken or disconnected latch operating rods or levers (Chapter 11).
☐ Faulty relay (Chapter 12).

One lock fails to operate

☐ Broken or disconnected wiring or connections (Chapter 12).
☐ Faulty motor (Chapter 11).
☐ Broken, binding or disconnected lock operating rods or levers (Chapter 11).
☐ Fault in door lock (Chapter 11).

A

ABS (Anti-lock brake system) A system, usually electronically controlled, that senses incipient wheel lockup during braking and relieves hydraulic pressure at wheels that are about to skid.

Air bag An inflatable bag hidden in the steering wheel (driver's side) or the dash or glovebox (passenger side). In a head-on collision, the bags inflate, preventing the driver and front passenger from being thrown forward into the steering wheel or windscreen.

Air cleaner A metal or plastic housing, containing a filter element, which removes dust and dirt from the air being drawn into the engine.

Air filter element The actual filter in an air cleaner system, usually manufactured from pleated paper and requiring renewal at regular intervals.

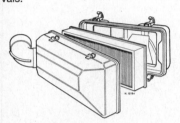
Air filter

Allen key A hexagonal wrench which fits into a recessed hexagonal hole.

Alligator clip A long-nosed spring-loaded metal clip with meshing teeth. Used to make temporary electrical connections.

Alternator A component in the electrical system which converts mechanical energy from a drivebelt into electrical energy to charge the battery and to operate the starting system, ignition system and electrical accessories.

Ampere (amp) A unit of measurement for the flow of electric current. One amp is the amount of current produced by one volt acting through a resistance of one ohm.

Anaerobic sealer A substance used to prevent bolts and screws from loosening. Anaerobic means that it does not require oxygen for activation. The Loctite brand is widely used.

Antifreeze A substance (usually ethylene glycol) mixed with water, and added to a vehicle's cooling system, to prevent freezing of the coolant in winter. Antifreeze also contains chemicals to inhibit corrosion and the formation of rust and other deposits that would tend to clog the radiator and coolant passages and reduce cooling efficiency.

Anti-seize compound A coating that reduces the risk of seizing on fasteners that are subjected to high temperatures, such as exhaust manifold bolts and nuts.

Asbestos A natural fibrous mineral with great heat resistance, commonly used in the composition of brake friction materials. Asbestos is a health hazard and the dust created by brake systems should never be inhaled or ingested.

Axle A shaft on which a wheel revolves, or which revolves with a wheel. Also, a solid beam that connects the two wheels at one end of the vehicle. An axle which also transmits power to the wheels is known as a live axle.

Axleshaft A single rotating shaft, on either side of the differential, which delivers power from the final drive assembly to the drive wheels. Also called a driveshaft or a halfshaft.

B

Ball bearing An anti-friction bearing consisting of a hardened inner and outer race with hardened steel balls between two races.

Bearing The curved surface on a shaft or in a bore, or the part assembled into either, that permits relative motion between them with minimum wear and friction.

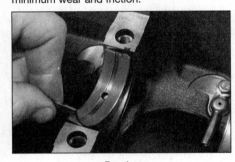
Bearing

Big-end bearing The bearing in the end of the connecting rod that's attached to the crankshaft.

Bleed nipple A valve on a brake wheel cylinder, caliper or other hydraulic component that is opened to purge the hydraulic system of air. Also called a bleed screw.

Brake bleeding Procedure for removing air from lines of a hydraulic brake system.

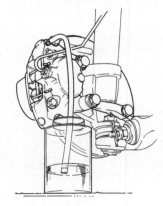
Brake bleeding

Brake disc The component of a disc brake that rotates with the wheels.

Brake drum The component of a drum brake that rotates with the wheels.

Brake linings The friction material which contacts the brake disc or drum to retard the vehicle's speed. The linings are bonded or riveted to the brake pads or shoes.

Brake pads The replaceable friction pads that pinch the brake disc when the brakes are applied. Brake pads consist of a friction material bonded or riveted to a rigid backing plate.

Brake shoe The crescent-shaped carrier to which the brake linings are mounted and which forces the lining against the rotating drum during braking.

Braking systems For more information on braking systems, consult the *Haynes Automotive Brake Manual*.

Breaker bar A long socket wrench handle providing greater leverage.

Bulkhead The insulated partition between the engine and the passenger compartment.

C

Caliper The non-rotating part of a disc-brake assembly that straddles the disc and carries the brake pads. The caliper also contains the hydraulic components that cause the pads to pinch the disc when the brakes are applied. A caliper is also a measuring tool that can be set to measure inside or outside dimensions of an object.

Camshaft A rotating shaft on which a series of cam lobes operate the valve mechanisms. The camshaft may be driven by gears, by sprockets and chain or by sprockets and a belt.

Canister A container in an evaporative emission control system; contains activated charcoal granules to trap vapours from the fuel system.

Canister

Carburettor A device which mixes fuel with air in the proper proportions to provide a desired power output from a spark ignition internal combustion engine.

Castellated Resembling the parapets along the top of a castle wall. For example, a castellated balljoint stud nut.

Castor In wheel alignment, the backward or forward tilt of the steering axis. Castor is positive when the steering axis is inclined rearward at the top.

Catalytic converter A silencer-like device in the exhaust system which converts certain pollutants in the exhaust gases into less harmful substances.

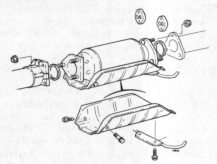

Catalytic converter

Circlip A ring-shaped clip used to prevent endwise movement of cylindrical parts and shafts. An internal circlip is installed in a groove in a housing; an external circlip fits into a groove on the outside of a cylindrical piece such as a shaft.

Clearance The amount of space between two parts. For example, between a piston and a cylinder, between a bearing and a journal, etc.

Coil spring A spiral of elastic steel found in various sizes throughout a vehicle, for example as a springing medium in the suspension and in the valve train.

Compression Reduction in volume, and increase in pressure and temperature, of a gas, caused by squeezing it into a smaller space.

Compression ratio The relationship between cylinder volume when the piston is at top dead centre and cylinder volume when the piston is at bottom dead centre.

Constant velocity (CV) joint A type of universal joint that cancels out vibrations caused by driving power being transmitted through an angle.

Core plug A disc or cup-shaped metal device inserted in a hole in a casting through which core was removed when the casting was formed. Also known as a freeze plug or expansion plug.

Crankcase The lower part of the engine block in which the crankshaft rotates.

Crankshaft The main rotating member, or shaft, running the length of the crankcase, with offset "throws" to which the connecting rods are attached.

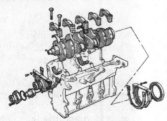

Crankshaft assembly

Crocodile clip See Alligator clip

D

Diagnostic code Code numbers obtained by accessing the diagnostic mode of an engine management computer. This code can be used to determine the area in the system where a malfunction may be located.

Disc brake A brake design incorporating a rotating disc onto which brake pads are squeezed. The resulting friction converts the energy of a moving vehicle into heat.

Double-overhead cam (DOHC) An engine that uses two overhead camshafts, usually one for the intake valves and one for the exhaust valves.

Drivebelt(s) The belt(s) used to drive accessories such as the alternator, water pump, power steering pump, air conditioning compressor, etc. off the crankshaft pulley.

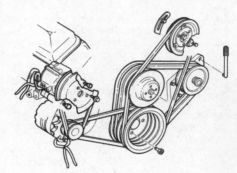

Accessory drivebelts

Driveshaft Any shaft used to transmit motion. Commonly used when referring to the axleshafts on a front wheel drive vehicle.

Drum brake A type of brake using a drum-shaped metal cylinder attached to the inner surface of the wheel. When the brake pedal is pressed, curved brake shoes with friction linings press against the inside of the drum to slow or stop the vehicle.

E

EGR valve A valve used to introduce exhaust gases into the intake air stream.

Electronic control unit (ECU) A computer which controls (for instance) ignition and fuel injection systems, or an anti-lock braking system. For more information refer to the *Haynes Automotive Electrical and Electronic Systems Manual.*

Electronic Fuel Injection (EFI) A computer controlled fuel system that distributes fuel through an injector located in each intake port of the engine.

Emergency brake A braking system, independent of the main hydraulic system, that can be used to slow or stop the vehicle if the primary brakes fail, or to hold the vehicle stationary even though the brake pedal isn't depressed. It usually consists of a hand lever that actuates either front or rear brakes mechanically through a series of cables and linkages. Also known as a handbrake or parking brake.

Endfloat The amount of lengthwise movement between two parts. As applied to a crankshaft, the distance that the crankshaft can move forward and back in the cylinder block.

Engine management system (EMS) A computer controlled system which manages the fuel injection and the ignition systems in an integrated fashion.

Exhaust manifold A part with several passages through which exhaust gases leave the engine combustion chambers and enter the exhaust pipe.

F

Fan clutch A viscous (fluid) drive coupling device which permits variable engine fan speeds in relation to engine speeds.

Feeler blade A thin strip or blade of hardened steel, ground to an exact thickness, used to check or measure clearances between parts.

Feeler blade

Firing order The order in which the engine cylinders fire, or deliver their power strokes, beginning with the number one cylinder.

Flywheel A heavy spinning wheel in which energy is absorbed and stored by means of momentum. On cars, the flywheel is attached to the crankshaft to smooth out firing impulses.

Free play The amount of travel before any action takes place. The "looseness" in a linkage, or an assembly of parts, between the initial application of force and actual movement. For example, the distance the brake pedal moves before the pistons in the master cylinder are actuated.

Fuse An electrical device which protects a circuit against accidental overload. The typical fuse contains a soft piece of metal which is calibrated to melt at a predetermined current flow (expressed as amps) and break the circuit.

Fusible link A circuit protection device consisting of a conductor surrounded by heat-resistant insulation. The conductor is smaller than the wire it protects, so it acts as the weakest link in the circuit. Unlike a blown fuse, a failed fusible link must frequently be cut from the wire for replacement.

G

Gap The distance the spark must travel in jumping from the centre electrode to the side electrode in a spark plug. Also refers to the spacing between the points in a contact breaker assembly in a conventional points-type ignition, or to the distance between the reluctor or rotor and the pickup coil in an electronic ignition.

Adjusting spark plug gap

Gasket Any thin, soft material - usually cork, cardboard, asbestos or soft metal - installed between two metal surfaces to ensure a good seal. For instance, the cylinder head gasket seals the joint between the block and the cylinder head.

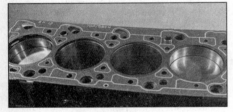

Gasket

Gauge An instrument panel display used to monitor engine conditions. A gauge with a movable pointer on a dial or a fixed scale is an analogue gauge. A gauge with a numerical readout is called a digital gauge.

H

Halfshaft A rotating shaft that transmits power from the final drive unit to a drive wheel, usually when referring to a live rear axle.

Harmonic balancer A device designed to reduce torsion or twisting vibration in the crankshaft. May be incorporated in the crankshaft pulley. Also known as a vibration damper.

Hone An abrasive tool for correcting small irregularities or differences in diameter in an engine cylinder, brake cylinder, etc.

Hydraulic tappet A tappet that utilises hydraulic pressure from the engine's lubrication system to maintain zero clearance (constant contact with both camshaft and valve stem). Automatically adjusts to variation in valve stem length. Hydraulic tappets also reduce valve noise.

I

Ignition timing The moment at which the spark plug fires, usually expressed in the number of crankshaft degrees before the piston reaches the top of its stroke.

Inlet manifold A tube or housing with passages through which flows the air-fuel mixture (carburettor vehicles and vehicles with throttle body injection) or air only (port fuel-injected vehicles) to the port openings in the cylinder head.

J

Jump start Starting the engine of a vehicle with a discharged or weak battery by attaching jump leads from the weak battery to a charged or helper battery.

L

Load Sensing Proportioning Valve (LSPV) A brake hydraulic system control valve that works like a proportioning valve, but also takes into consideration the amount of weight carried by the rear axle.

Locknut A nut used to lock an adjustment nut, or other threaded component, in place. For example, a locknut is employed to keep the adjusting nut on the rocker arm in position.

Lockwasher A form of washer designed to prevent an attaching nut from working loose.

M

MacPherson strut A type of front suspension system devised by Earle MacPherson at Ford of England. In its original form, a simple lateral link with the anti-roll bar creates the lower control arm. A long strut - an integral coil spring and shock absorber - is mounted between the body and the steering knuckle. Many modern so-called MacPherson strut systems use a conventional lower A-arm and don't rely on the anti-roll bar for location.

Multimeter An electrical test instrument with the capability to measure voltage, current and resistance.

N

NOx Oxides of Nitrogen. A common toxic pollutant emitted by petrol and diesel engines at higher temperatures.

O

Ohm The unit of electrical resistance. One volt applied to a resistance of one ohm will produce a current of one amp.

Ohmmeter An instrument for measuring electrical resistance.

O-ring A type of sealing ring made of a special rubber-like material; in use, the O-ring is compressed into a groove to provide the sealing action.

Overhead cam (ohc) engine An engine with the camshaft(s) located on top of the cylinder head(s).

Overhead valve (ohv) engine An engine with the valves located in the cylinder head, but with the camshaft located in the engine block.

Oxygen sensor A device installed in the engine exhaust manifold, which senses the oxygen content in the exhaust and converts this information into an electric current. Also called a Lambda sensor.

P

Phillips screw A type of screw head having a cross instead of a slot for a corresponding type of screwdriver.

Plastigage A thin strip of plastic thread, available in different sizes, used for measuring clearances. For example, a strip of Plastigage is laid across a bearing journal. The parts are assembled and dismantled; the width of the crushed strip indicates the clearance between journal and bearing.

Plastigage

Propeller shaft The long hollow tube with universal joints at both ends that carries power from the transmission to the differential on front-engined rear wheel drive vehicles.

Proportioning valve A hydraulic control valve which limits the amount of pressure to the rear brakes during panic stops to prevent wheel lock-up.

R

Rack-and-pinion steering A steering system with a pinion gear on the end of the steering shaft that mates with a rack (think of a geared wheel opened up and laid flat). When the steering wheel is turned, the pinion turns, moving the rack to the left or right. This movement is transmitted through the track rods to the steering arms at the wheels.

Radiator A liquid-to-air heat transfer device designed to reduce the temperature of the coolant in an internal combustion engine cooling system.

Refrigerant Any substance used as a heat transfer agent in an air-conditioning system. R-12 has been the principle refrigerant for many years; recently, however, manufacturers have begun using R-134a, a non-CFC substance that is considered less harmful to the ozone in the upper atmosphere.

Rocker arm A lever arm that rocks on a shaft or pivots on a stud. In an overhead valve engine, the rocker arm converts the upward movement of the pushrod into a downward movement to open a valve.

Rotor In a distributor, the rotating device inside the cap that connects the centre electrode and the outer terminals as it turns, distributing the high voltage from the coil secondary winding to the proper spark plug. Also, that part of an alternator which rotates inside the stator. Also, the rotating assembly of a turbocharger, including the compressor wheel, shaft and turbine wheel.

Runout The amount of wobble (in-and-out movement) of a gear or wheel as it's rotated. The amount a shaft rotates "out-of-true." The out-of-round condition of a rotating part.

S

Sealant A liquid or paste used to prevent leakage at a joint. Sometimes used in conjunction with a gasket.

Sealed beam lamp An older headlight design which integrates the reflector, lens and filaments into a hermetically-sealed one-piece unit. When a filament burns out or the lens cracks, the entire unit is simply replaced.

Serpentine drivebelt A single, long, wide accessory drivebelt that's used on some newer vehicles to drive all the accessories, instead of a series of smaller, shorter belts. Serpentine drivebelts are usually tensioned by an automatic tensioner.

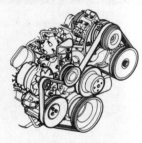

Serpentine drivebelt

Shim Thin spacer, commonly used to adjust the clearance or relative positions between two parts. For example, shims inserted into or under bucket tappets control valve clearances. Clearance is adjusted by changing the thickness of the shim.

Slide hammer A special puller that screws into or hooks onto a component such as a shaft or bearing; a heavy sliding handle on the shaft bottoms against the end of the shaft to knock the component free.

Sprocket A tooth or projection on the periphery of a wheel, shaped to engage with a chain or drivebelt. Commonly used to refer to the sprocket wheel itself.

Starter inhibitor switch On vehicles with an automatic transmission, a switch that prevents starting if the vehicle is not in Neutral or Park.

Strut See MacPherson strut.

T

Tappet A cylindrical component which transmits motion from the cam to the valve stem, either directly or via a pushrod and rocker arm. Also called a cam follower.

Thermostat A heat-controlled valve that regulates the flow of coolant between the cylinder block and the radiator, so maintaining optimum engine operating temperature. A thermostat is also used in some air cleaners in which the temperature is regulated.

Thrust bearing The bearing in the clutch assembly that is moved in to the release levers by clutch pedal action to disengage the clutch. Also referred to as a release bearing.

Timing belt A toothed belt which drives the camshaft. Serious engine damage may result if it breaks in service.

Timing chain A chain which drives the camshaft.

Toe-in The amount the front wheels are closer together at the front than at the rear. On rear wheel drive vehicles, a slight amount of toe-in is usually specified to keep the front wheels running parallel on the road by offsetting other forces that tend to spread the wheels apart.

Toe-out The amount the front wheels are closer together at the rear than at the front. On front wheel drive vehicles, a slight amount of toe-out is usually specified.

Tools For full information on choosing and using tools, refer to the *Haynes Automotive Tools Manual.*

Tracer A stripe of a second colour applied to a wire insulator to distinguish that wire from another one with the same colour insulator.

Tune-up A process of accurate and careful adjustments and parts replacement to obtain the best possible engine performance.

Turbocharger A centrifugal device, driven by exhaust gases, that pressurises the intake air. Normally used to increase the power output from a given engine displacement, but can also be used primarily to reduce exhaust emissions (as on VW's "Umwelt" Diesel engine).

U

Universal joint or U-joint A double-pivoted connection for transmitting power from a driving to a driven shaft through an angle. A U-joint consists of two Y-shaped yokes and a cross-shaped member called the spider.

V

Valve A device through which the flow of liquid, gas, vacuum, or loose material in bulk may be started, stopped, or regulated by a movable part that opens, shuts, or partially obstructs one or more ports or passageways. A valve is also the movable part of such a device.

Valve clearance The clearance between the valve tip (the end of the valve stem) and the rocker arm or tappet. The valve clearance is measured when the valve is closed.

Vernier caliper A precision measuring instrument that measures inside and outside dimensions. Not quite as accurate as a micrometer, but more convenient.

Viscosity The thickness of a liquid or its resistance to flow.

Volt A unit for expressing electrical "pressure" in a circuit. One volt that will produce a current of one ampere through a resistance of one ohm.

W

Welding Various processes used to join metal items by heating the areas to be joined to a molten state and fusing them together. For more information refer to the *Haynes Automotive Welding Manual.*

Wiring diagram A drawing portraying the components and wires in a vehicle's electrical system, using standardised symbols. For more information refer to the *Haynes Automotive Electrical and Electronic Systems Manual.*

*Note: References throughout this index are in the form "**Chapter number**" • "**Page number**". So, for example, 2C•15 refers to page 15 of Chapter 2C.*

A

A-pillar trim – 11•30
Accelerator pedal position sensor – 4A•8, 4B•8, 4C•3
Accessory shops – REF•5
Acknowledgements – 0•6
Aerial amplifier – 12•18
Air conditioning system – 3•10, 3•11
   control panel – 3•8
   control panel illumination – 12•11
Air filter – 1A•12, 1B•12, 4A•3, 4B•3, 4C•3
Air injection system – 4D•7
Air intake charge pressure/temperature sensor – 4C•9
Air temperature sensor – 4A•4, 4B•8
Air vent temperature sensors – 3•10
Airbags – 0•5, 1A•11, 1B•11, 12•19, 12•20
Airflow meter – 4A•4, 4B•3, 4C•9
Alarm system – 12•22, REF•3
Alternator – 5A•4, 5A•5
Altitude sensor – 4B•8
Amplifier – 12•18
Antifreeze – 0•12, 0•17, 1A•9, 1A•16, 1B•9, 1B•16
Anti-lock braking system (ABS) – 9•14, 9•15
Anti-roll bar – 10•9, 10•14
Anti-soiling tray – 11•33
Anti-theft alarm system – 12•22
   precaution – REF•3
Asbestos – 0•5
Ashtray illumination – 12•11
Audi A4 manual – 0•6
Audio amplifier – 12•18
Autochanger – 12•17
Automatic transmission – 7B•1 *et seq*
   automatic transmission fluid – 0•17, 1A•14, 1B•13
   fault finding – REF•16
   final drive oil – 1A•15, 1B•14
Auxiliary drivebelt – 1A•9, 1B•9, 2A•7, 2B•8, 2C•9
Auxiliary heater element – 3•10

B

B-pillar trim – 11•31
Balancer shaft housing – 2B•16
Battery – 0•5, 0•15, 1A•11, 1B•11, 5A•2
   disconnection – 5A•3
Big-end bearings – 2D•20
Bleeding
   brakes – 9•2
   clutch – 6•2
   fuel system – 4A•9
   power steering – 10•19
Blower motor/control unit – 3•8
Body corrosion – REF•11
Body electrical system – 12•1 *et seq*

Bodywork and fittings – 11•1 *et seq*
Bonnet and strut – 11•4
   lock and release cable – 11•4
Boot lid – 11•8, 11•9
   strut – 11•11
Brake fluid – 0•13, 0•17, 1A•15, 1B•14
Brake hydraulic circuit – 1A•9, 1B•9
Brake pads – 1A•7, 1B•7, 9•4, 9•6
Brake pedal – 9•11
   switches – 4C•10, 9•14
Brake pressure sensor – 9•17
Braking system – 1A•12, 1B•12, 9•1 *et seq*, REF•8, REF•9, REF•10
   fault finding – REF•17
Bulb control unit – 12•13
Bulbs – 12•7, 12•10
Bumpers – 11•5
Burning – 0•5
Buying spare parts – REF•5

C

C-pillar trim – 11•31
Cables
   bonnet lock – 11•4
   handbrake – 9•14
   locking – 7B•5, 7C•5
   selector – 7B•3, 7C•3
Cabriolet hood system fluid – 0•17
Calipers – 9•8, 9•9
Camshaft – 2D•12
   cover – 2A•8, 2B•8, 2C•11
   oil seals – 2A•9, 2B•9, 2C•11
   position sender – 4A•6, 4B•7, 4C•10
   sprocket – 2A•7, 2B•7, 2C•8
Carpets – 11•2, 11•30
Cassette unit anti-theft system –
   precaution – REF•3
Catalytic converter – 4D•6, 4D•7
CD player – 12•17
   anti-theft system – precaution – REF•3
Central flap control motor – 3•9
Central locking system – 12•17
   switch – 12•5
Centre console – 11•22
Charcoal canister – 4D•3
Charge pressure control valve – 4C•9
Charging – 5A•3, 5A•4
Clutch – 6•1 *et seq*
   fault finding – REF•15
   fluid – 0•13, 0•17, 1A•15, 1B•14
   pedal – 6•3, 6•8
   pedal switches – 4C•10
Coils – 5B•2
Compression test – 2A•4, 2B•4, 2C•5
Compressor – 3•11
Connecting rods – 2D•17, 2D•23
Console – 11•22
Convenience system electronic control
   unit – 12•22

Conversion factors – REF•2
Coolant – 0•12, 0•17, 1A•15, 1B•15
   pump – 3•7
   temperature sensor – 3•6, 4A•5, 4B•3, 4C•8
Cooling fan(s) – 3•5
Cooling, heating and ventilation systems – 3•1 *et seq*
   fault finding – REF•15
Courtesy light – 12•11
   switches – 12•6
Crankcase – 2D•20
Crankcase emission control – 4D•2, 4D•3
Crankshaft – 2D•19, 2D•21
   oil seals – 2A•10, 2B•9, 2C•11
   spigot bearing – 2B•17
   sprocket – 2A•7, 2B•7, 2C•9
Crash sensors – 12•21, 12•22
Crushing – 0•5
Cylinder block – 2D•20
Cylinder head – 2A•11, 2B•11, 2C•12, 2D•7

D

D-pillar trim – 11•32
Damper unit – 7C•2
Defrost flap control motor – 3•9
Dents – 11•2
Depressurisation fuel injection system – 4A•11, 4B•12
Diesel engine in-car repair procedures – 2C•1 *et seq*
   fault diagnosis – REF•13
Diesel injection equipment – 0•5
Dimensions – REF•1
Direction indicator – 12•8, 12•12, 12•13
Discs – 9•7, 9•8
Distance sensor – 12•17
Doors – 11•20, REF•9
   courtesy light – 12•11
   handle illumination – 12•11
   handles – 11•13
   locks – 11•13
   mirror adjuster – 12•5
   rattles – 11•4
   trim panel – 11•11
   window glass, frame and regulator – 11•15
Drier – 3•13
Drivebelt – 1A•9, 1B•9, 2A•7, 2B•8, 2C•9
Driveplate – 2A•13, 2B•13, 2C•16
Driver's storage compartment – 11•33
Driveshafts – 8•1 *et seq*, REF•10
   fault finding – REF•16
   flange oil seals – 7A•7
   gaiter – 1A•11, 1B•10
Drivetrain – 1A•12, 1B•12

E

Earth fault – 12•3
Electric cooling fan – 3•5, 3•6

*Note: References throughout this index are in the form "**Chapter number**" • "**Page number**". So, for example, 2C•15 refers to page 15 of Chapter 2C.*

Electric shock – 0•5
Electrical equipment – 1A•12, 1B•12, REF•9
Electrical systems – 0•16
  fault finding – 12•2, REF•19, REF•20
Electronic control module/unit
  fuel system – 4A•7, 4B•7, 4C•9
  convenience system – 12•22
  range control – 12•14
Emission control and exhaust systems –
  4D•1 *et seq*, REF•11
Engine fault finding – REF•13, REF•14
Engine management components – 4A•4,
  4B•3, 4C•8
Engine management self-diagnosis
  memory fault check – 1A•12, 1B•12
Engine oil – 0•12, 0•17, 1A•6, 1B•6
Engine removal and overhaul procedures –
  2D•1 *et seq*
Engine speed sensor – 4A•5, 4B•4, 4C•8
Environmental considerations – REF•4
ESP system – 9•16
  switch – 12•6
Evaporative emission control – 4D•2
Evaporator – 3•12, 3•13
Exhaust emissions – 1A•12, 1B•12, 4D•2
Exhaust Gas Recirculation (EGR) system –
  4D•3, 4D•4
Exhaust manifold – 4D•5
Exhaust specialists – REF•5
Exhaust system – 1A•8, 1B•8, 4D•2, 4D•6,
  REF•10, REF•11

F

Facia – 11•24
Facia-mounted light switch – 12•5
Fault finding – REF•12 *et seq*
  automatic transmission – REF•16
  braking system – REF•17
  clutch – REF•15
  cooling system – REF•15
  driveshafts – REF•16
  electrical system – 12•2, REF•19, REF•20
  engine – REF•13, REF•14
  fuel and exhaust systems – REF•15
  manual transmission – REF•16
  Multitronic transmission – REF•16
  steering and suspension – REF•17, REF•18
Filling and respraying – 11•3
Filter
  air – 1A•12, 1B•12, 4A•3, 4B•3, 4C•3
  fuel – 1B•12, 4A•8, 4B•8
  oil – 1A•6, 1B•6
  particulate – 4D•7
  pollen – 1A•10, 1B•9
Final drive oil – 0•17, 1A•15, 1B•14
Fire – 0•5
Fluids – 0•17, 1A•8, 1B•8
Flywheel – 2A•13, 2B•13, 2C•16
Foglamp – 12•8, 12•12

Footwell vent sensors – 3•10
Fresh air intake duct sensor – 3•10
Fresh air/recirculating airflaps motor – 3•9
Friction disc – 6•5
Fuel and exhaust systems fault finding –
  REF•15
Fuel cooler – 4C•13
Fuel filler flap locking motor – 12•22
Fuel filter – 1B•12, 4A•8, 4B•8
Fuel gauge sender unit – 4A•9, 4B•9, 4C•4
Fuel injection system – 4A•12, 4B•13
Fuel injectors – 4A•5, 4B•5, 4C•6
Fuel pressure regulator – 4A•8
Fuel pump – 4A•9, 4B•9, 4C•12
Fuel rail – 4A•5, 4B•4
Fuel system – REF•11
  bleeding – 4A•9
  diesel models – 4C•1 *et seq*
  direct petrol injection (FSI) models –
    4B•1 *et seq*
  indirect petrol injection models –
    4A•1 *et seq*
Fuel tank – 4A•10, 4B•11, 4C•5
Fuel temperature sensor – 4C•4
Fume or gas intoxication – 0•5
Function select switch – 12•7
Fusebox – 4C•10
Fuses – 12•3
Fusible links – 12•3

G

Gaiters
  driveshaft – 1A•11, 1B•10
  steering gear – 10•19
Garages – REF•5
Gas discharge headlight system – 12•13
Gashes – 11•3
Gaskets – REF•4
Gearchange linkage – 7A•2
General repair procedures – REF•4
Glossary of technical terms – REF•21 *et seq*
Glovebox – 11•27
  light – 12•11
  light switch – 12•5
Glow plugs – 5C•1
  fusebox – 4C•10
Grab handles – 11•36
Guide link – 10•7

H

Hall sender – 4A•6, 4B•7
Handbrake – 9•13, 9•14, REF•8
  warning switch – 12•6
Handles
  boot lid – 11•10
  doors – 11•13, 12•11
  grab – 11•36
  tailgate – 11•11

Hazard warning switch – 12•6
Head airbags – 12•21
Headlight – 1A•9, 1B•9, 12•11, 12•12, 12•13
  beam adjustment – 12•13, 12•14
  bulbs – 12•13
  control – 12•6
  dipped beam – 12•7, 12•13
  main beam – 12•7, 12•13
  washer system – 1A•12, 1B•11
Headlining – 11•30
Heating system – 3•8
  control panel – 3•8
  control panel illumination – 12•11
  heater element – 3•10
  matrix – 3•8, 3•12
High-level stop-light – 12•9, 12•13
High-pressure pump – 4B•9
Hinge lubrication – 1A•11, 1B•11
Hood – 11•18
  hood system fluid – 0•17
  hydraulic unit – 11•20
Horns – 12•17
Hoses – 1A•8, 1B•8, 3•2, 9•3
HT coils – 5B•2
Hub bearings and hub carrier – 10•4,
  10•10, 10•11
Hydraulic pipes and hoses – 9•3
Hydraulic tappets – 2A•13, 2B•13, 2C•16
Hydraulic unit (ABS) – 9•15
Hydrofluoric acid – 0•5

I

Identifying leaks – 0•10
Ignition switch – 10•16
Ignition system – petrol engines – 5B•1 *et seq*
  timing – 5B•3
Indicator – 12•8, 12•12, 12•13
Injector rocker shaft assembly – 2C•11
Injectors – 4A•5, 4B•5, 4C•6
Input shaft oil seal – 7A•7
Instruments – 1A•12, 1B•12, 12•14
  bulbs – 12•11
Intake air temperature sensor – 4A•4, 4B•8
Intake charge pressure/temperature
  sensor – 4C•9
Intake ducts – 4A•3, 4B•3, 4C•3
Intake manifold – 4A•11, 4B•12, 4C•12
  flap and valve – 4C•13
  pressure sensor – 4B•8
Intercooler – 4A•15, 4C•11
Interior lights – 12•10
Interior monitoring switch – 12•6

J

Jacking and vehicle support – REF•3
Joint mating faces – REF•4
Jump starting – 0•8

*Note: References throughout this index are in the form "**Chapter number**" • "**Page number**". So, for example, 2C•15 refers to page 15 of Chapter 2C.*

K

Knock sensors – 5B•3

L

Lateral acceleration sensors – 9•16, 12•21, 12•22
Leakdown test – 2C•6
Leaks – 0•10, 1A•8, 1B•8
Left- or right-hand drive – 12•14
Light switch – 12•5
Light units – 12•11
Link arms – 10•13, 10•14
Lock carrier – 11•6
Locking cable – 7B•5, 7C•5
Locknuts, locktabs and washers – REF•4
Locks
    bonnet – 11•4
    boot lid – 11•9
    central locking – 12•5
    doors – 11•13
    fuel filler flap – 12•22
    lubrication – 1A•11, 1B•11
    steering column – 10•16
    tailgate – 11•11
Lower arm – 10•7, 10•8
Lower link arm – 10•14
Lubricants and fluids – 0•17
Luggage compartment
    light – 12•11
    release switch – 12•6
    side trim – 11•33

M

Main bearings – 2D•20
Manifold flange/fuel rail – 4B•4
Manifold pressure sensor – 4B•8
Manifolds – 2C•14
    exhaust – 4D•5
    intake – 4A•11, 4B•12, 4C•12, 4C•13
Manual transmission – 7A•1 *et seq*
    fault finding – REF•16
    oil – 0•17, 1A•10, 1B•10
    switches – 7A•6
Master cylinder
    brake – 9•11
    clutch – 6•3
Matrix – 3•8, 3•12
Mirrors – 11•21, 11•27, REF•8
    adjuster – 12•5
MOT test checks – REF•8 *et seq*

Motor factors – REF•5
Mountings – 2A•15, 2B•14, 2C•17
Multifunction switch – 7A•6
Multitronic transmission – 7C•1 *et seq*
    damper unit – 7C•2
    fault finding – REF•16
    final drive oil – 1A•15, 1B•14
    fluid – 0•17, 1A•14, 1B•13

N

NOx storage catalyst – 4D•6
Number plate light – 12•9, 12•13

O

Oil
    engine – 0•12, 0•17, 1A•6, 1B•6
    final drive – 0•17, 1A•15, 1B•14
    manual gearbox – 0•17, 1A•10, 1B•10
Oil filter – 1A•6, 1B•6
Oil level/temperature sensor – 5A•6
Oil pressure warning light switch – 5A•6
Oil pump and pickup – 2A•16, 2B•16, 2C•19
Oil seals – REF•4
    camshaft – 2A•9, 2B•9, 2C•11
    crankshaft – 2A•10, 2B•9, 2C•11
    driveshaft flange – 7A•7
    input shaft – 7A•7
    selector shaft – 7A•8
On-board power supply control unit – 12•22
Open-circuit – 12•2
Oxygen sensors – 4A•6, 4B•7

P

Pads – 1A•7, 1B•7, 9•4, 9•6
Parcel shelf – 11•30
Parking aid components – 12•17
    switch – 12•6
Particulate filter – 4D•7
Pedals
    accelerator – 4A•8, 4B•8, 4C•3
    brake – 4C•10, 9•14
    clutch – 4C•10, 6•3, 6•8
Petrol engine in-car repair procedures
    1.8 and 2.0 litre indirect injection –
        2A•1 *et seq*
    2.0 litre direct injection – 2B•1 *et seq*
Photo-sensor – 3•13
Pipes – 9•3
Piston rings – 2D•23
Pistons – 2D•17, 2D•23

Plastic components – 11•3
Poisonous or irritant substances – 0•5
Pollen filter – 1A•10, 1B•9
Power steering fluid – 0•17, 10•19
Power steering pump – 10•20
Pre/post-heating systems – diesel
    models – 5C•1 *et seq*
Pressure plate – 6•5
Project vehicles – 0•6
Pump injector rocker shaft assembly –
    2C•11
Puncture repair – 0•9
Purge valve – 4D•2

R

Radiator – 1A•16, 1B•15, 3•3
Radio – 12•17
    anti-theft system – precaution – REF•3
Range control – 12•14
    motor – 12•12
Range/distance sensor – 12•17
Reading lights – 12•10
Rear combination light – 12•9, 12•12, 12•13
Rear side trim – 11•34
Rear window glass – 11•21
Receiver/drier – 3•13
Recirculating airflaps motor – 3•9
Regulator
    door window glass – 11•15
    voltage – 5A•5
Relays – 12•3
    diesel engine – 4C•10
Release bearing and lever – 6•7
Respraying – 11•3
Reversing light switch – 7A•6
Ride height sensor – 12•14, 12•14
Road test – 1A•12, 1B•12
Roadside repairs – 0•7 *et seq*
Roadspeed sensor – 7A•6
Rocker shaft assembly – 2C•11
Routine maintenance – bodywork and
    underframe – 11•2
Routine maintenance – upholstery and
    carpets – 11•2
Routine maintenance and servicing –
    diesel models – 1B•1 *et seq*
Routine maintenance and servicing –
    petrol models – 1A•1 *et seq*
Rust holes or gashes – 11•3

S

Safety first! – 0•5, 0•13

*Note: References throughout this index are in the form "**Chapter number**" • "**Page number**". So, for example, 2C•15 refers to page 15 of Chapter 2C.*

Scalding – 0•5
Scratches – 11•2
Screen washer fluid – 0•13
Screw threads and fastenings – REF•4
Seat belts – 11•35
Seats – 11•28
  heating switches – 12•7
Secondary air injection system – 4D•7
Selector cable – 7B•3, 7C•3
Selector shaft oil seal – 7A•8
Service interval display – 1A•8, 1B•8
Service position – 11•8
Servo unit – 9•11, 9•12
Shock absorbers – REF•9, REF•10
Short-circuit – 12•2
Side airbags – 12•21
Side trim – 11•33, 11•34
Side window glass – 11•21
Sidelight – 12•7, 12•13
Silencer – 4D•7
Slave cylinder – 6•4
Spark plugs – 1A•13
Speakers – 12•18
Spigot bearing – 2B•17
Springs – 10•12, REF•10
Sprockets – 2A•6, 2B•7, 2C•8
Starter motor – 5A•5, 5A•6
Starting and charging systems – 5A•1 *et seq*
Start-up after overhaul and reassembly –
  2D•25
Steering – 1A•11, 1A•12, 1B•11, 1B•12,
  REF•9, REF•10
  angle sensor – 9•17
  angles – 10•21
  column – 10•15, REF•8
  column switch – 12•4, 12•6
  gear – 10•17, 10•19, 10•21
  lock – 10•17
  wheel – 10•15, REF•8
Stop-light – 12•9, 12•13
  switch – 9•14, 12•6
Struts
  bonnet – 11•4
  boot lid – 11•11
  suspension – 10•4, 10•5, 10•11, 10•12
  tailgate – 11•11
Subframe – 10•9, 10•12
Sump – 2A•15, 2B•15, 2C•17
Sunlight photo-sensor – 3•13
Sunroof – 12•5, 11•21, 12•17
Sunroof lubrication – 1A•12, 1B•12
Sunvisors – 11•36
  light – 12•11

Suspension and steering – 1A•11, 1A•12,
  1B•11, 1B•12, 10•1 *et seq*, REF•9, REF•10
  fault finding – REF•17, REF•18
Switches – 12•5
  brake pedal – 4C•10, 9•14
  clutch pedal – 4C•10, 6•8
  ignition – 10•16
  illumination – 12•11
  multifunction – 7A•6
  oil pressure warning light – 5A•6
  reversing light – 7A•6
  steering column combination – 12•4
  stop-light – 9•14

T

Tailgate – 11•10, 11•11
  washer system – 1A•12, 1B•11
  wiper motor – 12•16
Tandem fuel pump – 4C•12
Tappets – 2A•13, 2B•13, 2C•16
TDC on No 1 cylinder – 2A•4, 2B•3, 2C•4
Technical terms – REF•21 *et seq*
Temperature flap control motors – 3•9
Temperature sensors – 3•6, 3•10, 3•13,
  4A•4, 4A•5, 4B•3, 4B•8, 4C•8, 4C•9,
  4C•10, 5A•6
Thermostat – 3•4
Throttle body/control unit – 4A•5, 4B•4
Throttle valve positioner – 4A•5, 4B•3
Throttle valve potentiometer – 4A•4, 4B•3
Timing – 5B•3
Timing belt – 1A•15, 2A•4, 2B•4,– 2C•6
  tensioner and sprockets – 2A•6, 2B•7, 2C•8
Timing marks – 2A•3
Tools and working facilities – REF•4,
  REF•6 *et seq*
Torque arm – 2C•17
Torque bracket – 2A•15, 2B•14
Towing – 0•10
Track control link – 10•8
Track rod – 10•14, 10•20, 10•21
Transverse arms – 10•7
Transverse link – 10•13
Trapezium link – 10•13, 10•14
Trim panels – 11•11, 11•30
Turbocharger – 4A•13, 4C•10
  boost pressure – 4A•8
Tyres – REF•11
  condition and pressure – 0•14
  pressures – 0•17
  specialists – REF•5

U

Underbody protection – 1A•10, 1B•10
Underbonnet check points – 0•11
Underframe – 11•2
Upholstery – 11•2
Upper arm – 10•13

V

Vacuum pump – 9•16, 9•17
Vacuum sensor – 9•17
Vacuum servo unit – 9•11, 9•12
Valve timing marks – 2A•3, 2B•3, 2C•4
Valves – 2D•12
Vanity mirror light – 12•11
Vehicle identification – REF•5, REF•9
Vehicle speed sensor – 4A•5
Vehicle support – REF•3
Ventilation control panel – 3•8
Ventilation system – 3•8
Viscous-coupled cooling fan – 3•6
Voltage regulator module – 5A•5

W

Washer system – 1A•12, 1B•11, 12•16
Water pump – 3•7
Weekly checks – 0•11 *et seq*
Weights – REF•1
Wheels – REF•11
  alignment – 10•21
  bearings – 10•4, 10•10, REF•10
  changing – 0•9
  sensor (ABS) – 9•15, 9•16
Wheel arch liners – 11•8
Windows – 11•21
  doors – 11•15
  switches – 12•6
Windscreen – 11•21, REF•8
  washer system – 1A•12, 1B•11
  wiper components – 12•15
Wiper arms – 12•15
Wiper blades – 0•15
Wiper motor – 12•15, 12•16
Wiring diagrams – 12•24 *et seq*
Working facilities – REF•6 *et seq*

Y

Yaw rate sensor – 9•16

Haynes Manuals – The Complete UK Car List

Title	Book No.
ALFA ROMEO Alfasud/Sprint (74 - 88) up to F *	0292
Alfa Romeo Alfetta (73 – 87) up to E *	0531
AUDI 80, 90 & Coupe Petrol (79 – Nov 88) up to F	0605
Audi 80, 90 & Coupe Petrol (Oct 86 – 90) D to H	1491
Audi 100 & A6 Petrol & Diesel (May 91 – May 97) H to P	3504
Audi A3 Petrol & Diesel (96 – May 03) P to 03	4253
Audi A3 Petrol & Diesel (June 03 – Mar 08) 03 to 08	4884
Audi A4 Petrol & Diesel (95 – 00) M to X	3575
Audi A4 Petrol & Diesel (01 – 04) X to 54	4609
Audi A4 Petrol & Diesel (Jan 05 – Feb 08) 54 to 57	4885
AUSTIN A35 & A40 (56 – 67) up to F *	0118
Mini (59 – 69) up to H *	0527
Mini (69 – 01) up to X	0646
Austin Healey 100/6 & 3000 (56 – 68) up to G *	0049
BEDFORD/Vauxhall Rascal & Suzuki Supercarry (86 – Oct 94) C to M	3015
BMW 1-Series 4-cyl Petrol & Diesel (04 – Aug 11) 54 to 11	4918
BMW 316, 320 & 320i (4-cyl)(75 – Feb 83) up to Y *	0276
BMW 3- & 5- Series Petrol (81 – 91) up to J	1948
BMW 3-Series Petrol (Apr 91 – 99) H to V	3210
BMW 3-Series Petrol (Sept 98 – 06) S to 56	4067
BMW 3-Series Petrol & Diesel (05 – Sept 08) 54 to 58	4782
BMW 5-Series 6-cyl Petrol (April 96 – Aug 03) N to 03	4151
BMW 5-Series Diesel (Sept 03 – 10) 53 to 10	4901
BMW 1500, 1502, 1600, 1602, 2000 & 2002 (59 – 77) up to S *	0240
CHRYSLER PT Cruiser Petrol (00-09) W to 09	4058
CITROEN 2CV, Ami & Dyane (67 – 90) up to H	0196
Citroen AX Petrol & Diesel (87- 97) D to P	3014
Citroen Berlingo & Peugeot Partner Petrol & Diesel (96 – 10) P to 60	4281
Citroen C1 Petrol (05 – 11) 05 to 11	4922
Citroen C3 Petrol & Diesel (02 – 09) 51 to 59	4890
Citroen C4 Petrol & Diesel (04 – 10) 54 to 60	5576
Citroen C5 Petrol & Diesel (01 – 08) Y to 08	4745
Citroen C15 Van Petrol & Diesel (89 – Oct 98) F to S	3509
Citroen CX Petrol (75 – 88) up to F	0528
Citroen Saxo Petrol & Diesel (96 – 04) N to 54	3506
Citroen Visa Petrol (79 – 88) up to F	0620
Citroen Xantia Petrol & Diesel (93 – 01) K to Y	3082
Citroen XM Petrol & Diesel (89 – 00) G to X	3451
Citroen Xsara Petrol & Diesel (97 – Sept 00) R to W	3751
Citroen Xsara Picasso Petrol & Diesel (00 – 02) W to 52	3944
Citroen Xsara Picasso (Mar 04 – 08) 04 to 58	4784
Citroen ZX Diesel (91 – 98) J to S	1922
Citroen ZX Petrol (91 – 98) H to S	1881
FIAT 126 (73 – 87) up to E *	0305
Fiat 500 (57 – 73) up to M *	0090
Fiat 500 & Panda (04 – 12) 53 to 61	5558
Fiat Bravo & Brava Petrol (95 – 00) N to W	3572
Fiat Cinquecento (93 – 98) K to R	3501
Fiat Panda (81 – 95) up to M	0793
Fiat Punto Petrol & Diesel (94 – Oct 99) L to V	3251
Fiat Punto Petrol (Oct 99 – July 03) V to 03	4066
Fiat Punto Petrol (03 – 07) 03 to 07	4746

Title	Book No.
Fiat Punto Petrol (Oct 99 – 07) V to 07	5634
Fiat X1/9 (74 – 89) up to G *	0273
FORD Anglia (59 – 68) up to G *	0001
Ford Capri II (& III) 1.6 & 2.0 (74 – 87) up to E *	0283
Ford Capri II (& III) 2.8 & 3.0 V6 (74 – 87) up to E	1309
Ford C-Max Petrol & Diesel (03 – 10) 53 to 60	4900
Ford Escort Mk I 1100 & 1300 (68 – 74) up to N *	0171
Ford Escort Mk I Mexico, RS 1600 & RS 2000 (70 – 74) up to N *	0139
Ford Escort Mk II Mexico, RS 1800 & RS 2000 (75 – 80) up to W *	0735
Ford Escort (75 – Aug 80) up to V *	0280
Ford Escort Petrol (Sept 80 – Sept 90) up to H	0686
Ford Escort & Orion Petrol (Sept 90 – 00) H to X	1737
Ford Escort & Orion Diesel (Sept 90 – 00) H to X	4081
Ford Fiesta Petrol (Feb 89 – Oct 95) F to N	1595
Ford Fiesta Petrol & Diesel (Oct 95 – Mar 02) N to 02	3397
Ford Fiesta Petrol & Diesel (Apr 02 – 08) 02 to 58	4170
Ford Fiesta Petrol & Diesel (08 – 11) 58 to 11	4907
Ford Focus Petrol & Diesel (98 – 01) S to Y	3759
Ford Focus Petrol & Diesel (Oct 01 – 05) 51 to 05	4167
Ford Focus Petrol (05 – 09) 54 to 09	4785
Ford Focus Diesel (05 – 09) 54 to 09	4807
Ford Fusion Petrol & Diesel (02 – 11) 02 to 61	5566
Ford Galaxy Petrol & Diesel (95 – Aug 00) M to W	3984
Ford Galaxy Petrol & Diesel (00 – 06) X to 06	5556
Ford Granada Petrol (Sept 77 – Feb 85) up to B *	0481
Ford Ka (96 – 08) P to 58	5567
Ford Mondeo Petrol (93 – Sept 00) K to X	1923
Ford Mondeo Petrol (Oct 00 – Jul 03) X to 03	3990
Ford Mondeo Petrol & Diesel (July 03 – 07) 03 to 56	4619
Ford Mondeo Petrol & Diesel (Apr 07 – 12) 07 to 61	5548
Ford Mondeo Diesel (93 – Sept 00) L to X	3465
Ford Sierra V6 Petrol (82 – 91) up to J	0904
Ford Transit Connect Diesel (02 – 11) 02 to 11	4903
Ford Transit Diesel (Feb 86 – 99) C to T	3019
Ford Transit Diesel (00 – Oct 06) X to 56	4775
Ford 1.6 & 1.8 litre Diesel Engine (84 – 96) A to N	1172
HILLMAN Imp (63 – 76) up to R *	0022
HONDA Civic (Feb 84 – Oct 87) A to E	1226
Honda Civic (Nov 91 – 96) J to N	3199
Honda Civic Petrol (Mar 95 – 00) M to X	4050
Honda Civic Petrol & Diesel (01 – 05) X to 55	4611
Honda CR-V Petrol & Diesel (02 – 06) 51 to 56	4747
Honda Jazz (02 to 08) 51 to 58	4735
JAGUAR E-Type (61 – 72) up to L *	0140
Jaguar Mk I & II, 240 & 340 (55 – 69) up to H *	0098
Jaguar XJ6, XJ & Sovereign, Daimler Sovereign (68 – Oct 86) up to D	0242
Jaguar XJ6 & Sovereign (Oct 86 – Sept 94) D to M	3261
Jaguar XJ12, XJS & Sovereign, Daimler Double Six (72 – 88) up to F	0478
JEEP Cherokee Petrol (93 – 96) K to N	1943
LAND ROVER 90, 110 & Defender Diesel (83 – 07) up to 56	3017
Land Rover Discovery Petrol & Diesel (89 – 98) G to S	3016

Title	Book No.
Land Rover Discovery Diesel (Nov 98 – Jul 04) S to 04	4606
Land Rover Discovery Diesel (Aug 04 – Apr 09) 04 to 09	5562
Land Rover Freelander Petrol & Diesel (97 – Sept 03) R to 53	3929
Land Rover Freelander (97 – Oct 06) R to 56	5571
Land Rover Series II, IIA & III 4-cyl Petrol (58 – 85) up to C	0314
Land Rover Series II, IIA & III Petrol & Diesel (58 – 85) up to C	5568
MAZDA 323 (Mar 81 – Oct 89) up to G	1608
Mazda 323 (Oct 89 – 98) G to R	3455
Mazda B1600, B1800 & B2000 Pick-up Petrol (72 – 88) up to F	0267
Mazda MX-5 (89 – 05) G to 05	5565
Mazda RX-7 (79 – 85) up to C *	0460
MERCEDES-BENZ 190, 190E & 190D Petrol & Diesel (83 – 93) A to L	3450
Mercedes-Benz 200D, 240D, 240TD, 300D & 300TD 123 Series Diesel (Oct 76 – 85) up to C	1114
Mercedes-Benz 250 & 280 (68 – 72) up to L *	0346
Mercedes-Benz 250 & 280 123 Series Petrol (Oct 76 – 84) up to B *	0677
Mercedes-Benz 124 Series Petrol & Diesel (85 – Aug 93) C to K	3253
Mercedes-Benz A-Class Petrol & Diesel (98 – 04) S to 54	4748
Mercedes-Benz C-Class Petrol & Diesel (93 – Aug 00) L to W	3511
Mercedes-Benz C-Class (00 – 07) X to 07	4780
Mercedes-Benz Sprinter Diesel (95 – Apr 06) M to 06	4902
MGA (55 – 62)	0475
MGB (62 – 80) up to W	0111
MGB 1962 to 1980 (special edition) *	4894
MG Midget & Austin-Healey Sprite (58 – 80) up to W *	0265
MINI Petrol (July 01 – 06) Y to 56	4273
MINI Petrol & Diesel (Nov 06 – 13) 56 to 13	4904
MITSUBISHI Shogun & L200 Pick-ups Petrol (83 – 94) up to M	1944
MORRIS Minor 1000 (56 – 71) up to K	0024
NISSAN Almera Petrol (95 – Feb 00) N to V	4053
Nissan Almera & Tino Petrol (Feb 00 – 07) V to 56	4612
Nissan Micra (83 – Jan 93) up to K	0931
Nissan Micra (93 – 02) K to 52	3254
Nissan Micra Petrol (03 – Oct 10) 52 to 60	4734
Nissan Primera Petrol (90 - Aug 99) H to T	1851
Nissan Qashqai Petrol & Diesel (07 – 12) 56 to 62	5610
OPEL Ascona & Manta (B-Series) (Sept 75 – 88) up to F *	0316
Opel Ascona Petrol (81 – 88)	3215
Opel Ascona Petrol (Oct 91 – Feb 98)	3156
Opel Corsa Petrol (83 – Mar 93)	3160
Opel Corsa Petrol (Mar 93 – 97)	3159
Opel Kadett Petrol (Oct 84 – Oct 91)	3196
Opel Omega & Senator Petrol (Nov 86 – 94)	3157
Opel Vectra Petrol (Oct 88 – Oct 95)	3158
PEUGEOT 106 Petrol & Diesel (91 – 04) J to 53)	1882
Peugeot 107 Petrol (05 – 11) 05 to 11	4923
Peugeot 205 Petrol (83 – 97) A to P	0932
Peugeot 206 Petrol & Diesel (98 – 01) S to X	3757

* Classic reprint

Title	Book No.
Peugeot 206 Petrol & Diesel (02 – 06) 51 to 06	4613
Peugeot 207 Petrol & Diesel (06 – July 09) 06 to 09	4787
Peugeot 306 Petrol & Diesel (93 – 02) K to 02	3073
Peugeot 307 Petrol & Diesel (01 – 08) Y to 58	4147
Peugeot 308 Petrol & Diesel (07 – 12) 07 to 12	5561
Peugeot 405 Diesel (88 – 97) E to P	3198
Peugeot 406 Petrol & Diesel (96 – Mar 99) N to T	3394
Peugeot 406 Petrol & Diesel (Mar 99 – 02) T to 52	3982
Peugeot 407 Diesel (04 -11) 53 to 11	5550
PORSCHE 911 (65 – 85) up to C	0264
Porsche 924 & 924 Turbo (76 – 85) up to C	0397
RANGE ROVER V8 Petrol (70 – Oct 92) up to K	0606
RELIANT Robin & Kitten (73 – 83) up to A *	0436
RENAULT 4 (61 – 86) up to D *	0072
Renault 5 Petrol (Feb 85 – 96) B to N	1219
Renault 19 Petrol (89 – 96) F to N	1646
Renault Clio Petrol (91 – May 98) H to R	1853
Renault Clio Petrol & Diesel (May 98 – May 01) R to Y	3906
Renault Clio Petrol & Diesel (June 01 – 05) Y to 55	4168
Renault Clio Petrol & Diesel (Oct 05 – May 09) 55 to 09	4788
Renault Espace Petrol & Diesel (85 – 96) C to N	3197
Renault Laguna Petrol & Diesel (94 – 00) L to W	3252
Renault Laguna Petrol & Diesel (Feb 01 – May 07) X to 07	4283
Renault Megane & Scenic Petrol & Diesel (96 – 99) N to T	3395
Renault Megane & Scenic Petrol & Diesel (Apr 99 – 02) T to 52	3916
Renault Megane Petrol & Diesel (Oct 02 – 08) 52 to 58	4284
Renault Scenic Petrol & Diesel (Sept 03 – 06) 53 to 06	4297
Renault Trafic Diesel (01 – 11) Y to 11	5551
ROVER 216 & 416 Petrol (89 – 96) G to N	1830
Rover 211, 214, 216, 218 & 220 Petrol & Diesel (Dec 95 – 99) N to V	3399
Rover 25 & MG ZR Petrol & Diesel (Oct 99 – 06) V to 06	4145
Rover 414, 416 & 420 Petrol & Diesel (May 95 – 99) M to V	3453
Rover 45 / MG ZS Petrol & Diesel (99 – 05) V to 55	4384
Rover 618, 620 & 623 Petrol (93 – 97) K to P	3257
Rover 75 / MG ZT Petrol & Diesel (99 – 06) S to 06	4292
Rover 820, 825 & 827 Petrol (86 – 95) D to N	1380
Rover 3500 (76 – 87) up to E *	0365
Rover Metro, 111 & 114 Petrol (May 90 – 98) G to S	1711
SAAB 95 & 96 (66 – 76) up to R *	0198
Saab 90, 99 & 900 (79 – Oct 93) up to L	0765
Saab 900 (Oct 93 – 98) L to R	3512
Saab 9000 4-cyl (85 – 98) C to S	1686
Saab 9-3 Petrol & Diesel (98 – Aug 02) R to 02	4614
Saab 9-3 Petrol & Diesel (92 – 07) 52 to 57	4749
Saab 9-3 Petrol & Diesel (07-on) 57 on	5569
Saab 9-5 4-cyl Petrol (97 – 05) R to 55	4156
Saab 9-5 (Sep 05 – Jun 10) 55 to 10	4891
SEAT Ibiza & Cordoba Petrol & Diesel (Oct 93 – Oct 99) L to V	3571
Seat Ibiza & Malaga Petrol (85 – 92) B to K	1609
Seat Ibiza Petrol & Diesel (May 02 – Apr 08) 02 to 08	4889

Title	Book No.
SKODA Fabia Petrol & Diesel (00 – 06) W to 06	4376
Skoda Felicia Petrol & Diesel (95 – 01) M to X	3505
Skoda Octavia Petrol (98 – April 04) R to 04	4285
Skoda Octavia Diesel (May 04 – 12) 04 to 61	5549
SUBARU 1600 & 1800 (Nov 79 – 90) up to H *	0995
SUNBEAM Alpine, Rapier & H120 (68 – 74) up to N *	0051
SUZUKI SJ Series, Samurai & Vitara 4-cyl Petrol (82 – 97) up to P	1942
Suzuki Supercarry & Bedford/Vauxhall Rascal (86 – Oct 94) C to M	3015
TOYOTA Avensis Petrol (98 – Jan 03) R to 52	4264
Toyota Aygo Petrol (05 – 11) 05 to 11	4921
Toyota Carina E Petrol (May 92 – 97) J to P	3256
Toyota Corolla (80 – 85) up to C	0683
Toyota Corolla (Sept 83 – Sept 87) A to E	1024
Toyota Corolla (Sept 87 – Aug 92) E to K	1683
Toyota Corolla Petrol (Aug 92 – 97) K to P	3259
Toyota Corolla Petrol (July 97 0 Feb 02) P to 51	4286
Toyota Corolla Petrol & Diesel (02 – Jan 07) 51 to 56	4791
Toyota Hi-Ace & Hi-Lux Petrol (69 – Oct 83) up to A	0304
Toyota RAV4 Petrol & Diesel (94 – 06) L to 55	4750
Toyota Yaris Petrol (99 – 05) T to 05	4265
TRIUMPH GT6 & Vitesse (62 0 74) up to N *	0112
Triumph Herald (59 – 71) up to K *	0010
Triumph Spitfire (62 – 81) up to X	0113
Triumph Stag (70 – 78) up to T *	0441
Triumph TR2, TR3, TR3A, TR4 & TR4A (52 – 67) up to F *	0028
Triumph TR5 & TR6 (67 – 75) up to P *	0031
Triumph TR7 (75 – 82) up to Y *	0322
VAUXHALL Astra Petrol (Oct 91 – Feb 98) J to R	1832
Vauxhall/Opel Astra & Zafira Petrol (Feb 98 – Apr 04) R to 04	3758
Vauxhall/Opel Astra & Zafira Diesel (Feb 98 – Apr 04) R to 04	3797
Vauxhall/Opel Astra Petrol (04 – 08)	4732
Vauxhall/Opel Astra Diesel (04 – 08)	4733
Vauxhall/Opel Astra Petrol & Diesel (Dec 09 – 13) 59 to 13	5578
Vauxhall/Opel Calibra (90 – 98) G to S	3502
Vauxhall Cavalier Petrol (Oct 88 0 95) F to N	1570
Vauxhall/Opel Corsa Diesel (Mar 93 – Oct 00) K to X	4087
Vauxhall Corsa Petrol (Mar 93 – 97) K to R	1985
Vauxhall/Opel Corsa Petrol (Apr 97 – Oct 00) P to X	3921
Vauxhall/Opel Corsa Petrol & Diesel (Oct 03 – Aug 06) 53 to 06	4617
Vauxhall/Opel Corsa Petrol & Diesel (Sept 06 – 10) 56 to 10	4886
Vauxhall/Opel Corsa Petrol & Diesel (00 – Aug 06) X to 06	5577
Vauxhall/Opel Frontera Petrol & Diesel (91 – Sept 98) J to S	3454
Vauxhall/Opel Insignia Petrol & Diesel (08 – 12) 08 to 61	5563
Vauxhall/Opel Meriva Petrol & Diesel (03 – May 10) 03 to 10	4893
Vauxhall/Opel Omega Petrol (94 – 99) L to T	3510
Vauxhall/Opel Vectra Petrol (95 – Feb 99) N to S	3396

Title	Book No.
Vauxhall/Opel Vectra Petrol & Diesel (Mar 99 – May 02) T to 02	3930
Vauxhall/Opel Vectra Petrol & Diesel (June 02 – Sept 05) 02 to 55	4618
Vauxhall/Opel Vectra Petrol & Diesel (Oct 05 – Oct 08) 55 to 58	4887
Vauxhall/Opel Vivaro Diesel (01 – 11) Y to 11	5552
Vauxhall/Opel Zafira Petrol & Diesel (05 -09) 05 to 09	4792
Vauxhall/Opel 1.5, 1.6 & 1.7 litre Diesel Engine (82 – 96) up to N	1222
VW Beetle 1200 (54 – 77) up to S	0036
VW Beetle 1300 & 1500 (65 – 75) up to P	0039
VW 1302 & 1302S (70 – 72) up to L *	0110
VW Beetle 1303, 1303S & GT (72 – 75) up to P	0159
VW Beetle Petrol & Diesel (Apr 99 – 07) T to 57	3798
VW Golf & Jetta Mk 1 Petrol 1.1 & 1.3 (74 – 84) up to A	0716
VW Golf, Jetta & Scirocco Mk 1 Petrol 1.5, 1.6 & 1.8 (74 – 84) up to A	0726
VW Golf & Jetta Mk 1 Diesel (78 – 84) up to A	0451
VW Golf & Jetta Mk 2 Petrol (Mar 84 – Feb 92) A to J	1081
VW Golf & Vento Petrol & Diesel (Feb 92 – Mar 98) J to R	3097
VW Golf & Bora Petrol & Diesel (Apr 98 – 00) R to X	3727
VW Golf & Bora 4-cyl Petrol & Diesel (01 – 03) X to 53	4169
VW Golf & Jetta Petrol & Diesel (04 – 09) 53 to 09	4610
VW LT Petrol Vans & Light Trucks (76 – 87) up to E	0637
VW Passat 4-cyl Petrol & Diesel (May 88 – 96) E to P	3498
VW Passat 4-cyl Petrol & Diesel (Dec 96 – Nov 00) P to X	3917
VW Passat Petrol & Diesel (Dec 00 – May 05) X to 05	4279
VW Passat Diesel (June 05 – 10) 05 to 60	4888
VW Polo Petrol (Nov 90 – Aug 94) H to L	3245
VW Polo Hatchback Petrol & Diesel (94 – 99) M to S	3500
VW Polo Hatchback Petrol (00 – Jan 02) V to 51	4150
VW Polo Petrol & Diesel (02 – May 05) 51 to 05	4608
VW Transporter 1600 (68 – 79) up to V	0082
VW Transporter 1700, 1800 & 2000 (72 – 79) up to V *	0226
VW Transporter (air cooled) Petrol (79 – 82) up to Y *	0638
VW Transporter (water cooled) Petrol (82 – 90) up to H	3452
VW Type 3 (63 – 73) up to M *	0084
VOLVO 120 & 130 Series (& P1800) (61 – 73) up to M *	0203
Volvo 142, 144 & 145 (66 – 74) up to N *	0129
Volvo 240 Series Petrol (74 – 93) up to K	0270
Volvo 440, 460 & 480 Petrol (87 – 97) D to P	1691
Volvo 740 & 760 Petrol (82 – 91) up to J	1258
Volvo 850 Petrol (92 – 96) J to P	3260
Volvo 940 Petrol (90 – 98) H to R	3249
Volvo S40 & V40 Petrol (96 – Mar 04) N to 04	3569
Volvo S40 & V50 Petrol & Diesel (Mar 04 – Jun 07) 04 to 07	4731
Volvo S60 Petrol & Diesel (01 – 08) X to 09	4793
Volvo S70, V70 & C70 Petrol (96 – 99) P to V	3573
Volvo V70 / S80 Petrol & Diesel (98 – 07) S to 07	4263
Volvo V70 Diesel (June 07 – 12) 07 to 61	5557
Volvo XV60 / 90 Diesel (03 – 12) 52 to 62	5630

* Classic reprint

CL 27.06.13

Preserving Our Motoring Heritage

< *The Model J Duesenberg Derham Tourster. Only eight of these magnificent cars were ever built – this is the only example to be found outside the United States of America*

Almost every car you've ever loved, loathed or desired is gathered under one roof at the Haynes Motor Museum. Over 300 immaculately presented cars and motorbikes represent every aspect of our motoring heritage, from elegant reminders of bygone days, such as the superb Model J Duesenberg to curiosities like the bug-eyed BMW Isetta. There are also many old friends and flames. Perhaps you remember the 1959 Ford Popular that you did your courting in? The magnificent 'Red Collection' is a spectacle of classic sports cars including AC, Alfa Romeo, Austin Healey, Ferrari, Lamborghini, Maserati, MG, Riley, Porsche and Triumph.

A Perfect Day Out

Each and every vehicle at the Haynes Motor Museum has played its part in the history and culture of Motoring. Today, they make a wonderful spectacle and a great day out for all the family. Bring the kids, bring Mum and Dad, but above all bring your camera to capture those golden memories for ever. You will also find an impressive array of motoring memorabilia, a comfortable 70 seat video cinema and one of the most extensive transport book shops in Britain. The Pit Stop Cafe serves everything from a cup of tea to wholesome, home-made meals or, if you prefer, you can enjoy the large picnic area nestled in the beautiful rural surroundings of Somerset.

John Haynes O.B.E., Founder and Chairman of the museum at the wheel of a Haynes Light 12.

< *Graham Hill's Lola Cosworth Formula 1 car next to a 1934 Riley Sports.*

The Museum is situated on the A359 Yeovil to Frome road at Sparkford, just off the A303 in Somerset. It is about 40 miles south of Bristol, and 25 minutes drive from the M5 intersection at Taunton.
Open 9.30am - 5.30pm (10.00am - 4.00pm Winter) 7 days a week, *except Christmas Day, Boxing Day and New Years Day*
Special rates available for schools, coach parties and outings Charitable Trust No. 292048